AF661142

Mathematical Techniques for Economic Analysis

Mathematical Techniques for Economic Analysis

(For Economics honours and Post-graduate students of Economics, Commerce, Management, BMS and students appearing for competitive examinations)

Dr. SARAT CHANDRA PATRA
M.A. (Eco) M.PHIL. NET (JRF), PH.D. (Eco)
Reader, Department of Economics,
Shri. M. D. Shah Mahila College,
(NAAC Acredited with 'A' grade)
Malad (West) Mumbai.

First Edition : 2010

Himalaya Publishing House

MUMBAI • NEW DELHI • NAGPUR • BENGALURU • HYDERABAD • CHENNAI • PUNE • LUCKNOW • AHMEDABAD • ERNAKULAM • INDORE • BHUBANESWAR

© Author

No part of this publication should be reproduced, stored in a retrieval system, or transmitted in any form or any means, electronic, mechanical, photocopying, recording and/or otherwise without the prior written permission of the publisher.

First Edition : 2010

Edition : 2017

Published by : Mrs. Meena Pandey for **Himalaya Publishing House Pvt. Ltd.,**
"Ramdoot", Dr. Bhalerao Marg, Girgaon, **Mumbai - 400 004.**
Phone: 2386 01 70/2386 38 63, Fax: 022-2387 71 78
Email: himpub@vsnl.com Website: www.himpub.com

Branch Offices

New Delhi : "Pooja Apartments", 4-B, Murari Lal Street, Ansari Road, Darya Ganj, **New Delhi - 110 002.** Phone:23270392, 23278631 Fax: 011-23256286

Nagpur : Kundanlal Chandak Industrial Estate, Ghat Road, **Nagpur - 440 018.** Phone: 2738731, 3296733 Telefax : 0712-2721215

Bengaluru : No. 16/1 (Old 12/1), 1st Floor, Next to Hotel Highlands, Madhava Nagar, Race Course Road, **Bengaluru - 560 001.** Phone : 22281541, 22385461, Telefax: 080-22286611

Hyderabad : No. 3-4-184, Lingampally, Besides Raghavendra Swamy Matham,Kachiguda, **Hyderabad - 500 027.** Phone: 040-27560041, 27550139, Mobile:- 09848130433

Chennai : No. 85/50, Bazullah Road, T. Nagar, **Chennai - 600 017.** Phone: 044-28144004/28144005

Pune : First Floor, "Laksha" Apartment, No. 527, Mehunpura, Shaniwarpeth (Near Prabhat Theatre), **Pune - 411 030.** Phone: 020-24496323/24496333

Lucknow : C-43, Sector - C, Ali Gunj, **Lucknow - 226 024.** Phone: 0522-2339329

Ahmedabad : 114, "SHAIL", 1st Floor, Opp. Madhu Sudan House, C.G.Road, Navrang Pura, **Ahmedabad– 380 009.** Phone: 079-26560126, Mobiles:- 09327324149,09314679413

Ernakulam : 39/104 A, Lakshmi Apartment, Karikkamuri Cross Rd., Ernakulam, **Cochin – 622011**, Kerala. Phone: 0484-2378012, 2378016, Mob.: 09344199799

Bhubaneswar : 5 Station Square, **Bhubaneswar (Orissa) - 751 001.** Mobile:- 9861046007, E-mail:- orissa@himpub.com

Indore : Kesardeep Avenue Extension, 73, Narayan Bagh, Flat No. 302, IIIrd Floor, Near Humpty Dumpty School, Narayan Bagh, **Indore 452 007(M.P.)** Mobile:- 09301386468

DTP by : Prerana Enterprises, Mumbai.

Printed by : Heramb Printers, Bhandup, Mumbai - 78.

Blessed from the great soul of
Mom "Satyabhama"
And
Owe a great debt to elder brother
Surya Narayan Patra (MBA, ICWA)

"Knowledge is the only source of power embodied in human being, delighted and enlightened from sincerity, dedication, honesty and hardwork bestowed. They constitute the pillars of triumphant, descent and complacent life. Effective and elucidating Textbooks can empower the minds of readers which is also an endless endeavor of the author."

Dr. S.C. Patra

Preface to the First Edition

This Textbook "Mathematical Techniques for Economic Analysis" is a basic and most essential textbook for Economics Honours and Post-graduate Economics Students of all Indian Universities. Students from Commerce faculty and all those appearing for competitive examinations can also find the book useful to them. The contents of the Book are made lucid and simple with numerous illustrations so that non-mathematical students can also derive immense benefit from it. It can serve the needs of the advanced learners who are intending to make application of mathematics in economic theory. Most of the time students opt for their specialization in Economics at B.A. and M.A. possess little background of mathematics. This textbook is designed to mitigate their problems and to transform them into experts in the subject of mathematical economics. The author carries this intension while producing this textbook.

The book can serve the requirements of students and teachers in faculties of Economics, Management, BMS and Commerce. It can be useful to all those who are also preparing for their competitive examinations like JRF, Entrance tests, Examinations like IES, IAS under UPSC and State Public Service Commissions. The Book incorporates chapter-wise solved questions of TYBA Economics papers of Mumbai University as sample paper solutions for the benefit of students of all Indian universities. The papers like "MATHEMATICS FOR ECONOMICS" or "QUANTITATIVE METHODS/TECHNIQUES FOR ECONOMIC ANALYSIS" or "APPLICATIONS OF MATHEMATICS IN ECONOMICS" seems to be a compulsory paper for Economics at B.A. and M.A. level. This book is a sincere effort to provide all necessary inputs facilitating students to face these challenges boldly at the time of studying and preparing their examinations.

The book contains the following topics in a nutshell:

(a) Differential calculus for one variable and several variable cases and their applications in economics. The techniques and applications of partial derivatives are provided with all simple and many exercises for students.

(b) Matrix algebra and determinants in detail and their applications to the Leontief's input-output analysis.

(c) Techniques of definite and indefinite integrals and their applications in economics as such obtaining consumer's and producer's surplus, Lorenz curve inequalities and other important applications.

(d) Solutions to the problems of constrained optimization of utility functions and output maximization/ cost minimization by the firm etc.

(e) Linear Programming technique to optimize the problems of minimization, maximization and duality of the linear programming. Both graphical solution to LPP and Simplex Method are presented and simplified. Numerous solved examples are incorporated making these concepts easy and exciting to our readers.

At the outset I am highly indebted to my parents. I owe a great debt to my beloved brother Surya Narayan for his selfless intentions in reshaping my career. I express thanks to my wife Sanjukta and children, Lipsa and Siddhant for being helpful and lovable all the time. I am grateful to my colleagues, friends and relatives for eagerly awaiting to see the book and become instrumental to learn mathematical applications in economics.

I would be extremely happy to receive comments, constructive suggestions, unbiased views and opinions from the readers, critics, teachers and colleagues and obviously student friends so that their views can be incorporated in the forthcoming editions.

I am extremely grateful to Mr. K.N. Pandey and Mr. Patil of Himalaya Publishing House for the privilege conferred on me to get an exposure to prepare the manuscript. I am also thankful to Mr. Amol and Rajendra, M/s. Prerana Enterprises.

Dr. S. C. Patra

CONTENTS

1 Introduction and Chapter Overview

Introduction:

1.1 An Introduction to Mathematical Economics

Mathematical techniques are increasingly applied to almost all branches of modern economics. Economist in the modern world finds it incomplete and inconceivable to remain aloof from basic mathematics, which is indispensable while applying economic principles into practice. Mathematical economic analysis is employed to derive theoretical results in micro and macroeconomics, international trade, public finance and other branches of economic literature.

The application of tools such as derivatives, partial derivatives, matrix algebra, differential and difference equations and integration have oversimplified economic theory. This has made economics a subject that is relatively applied in nature backed by logic and reasonings. Therefore, readers may discover the presence of mathematical tools in any branch of knowledge concerning economics that enables economists to derive concrete, analytical and applied results by using mathematics.

In this textbook of Mathematical Technique for Economic Analysis, all attempts are made by the author to introduce and familiarise the students with the most fundamental tools and methods from mathematics. These methods are extensively used in economic analysis. They also provide the means to simplify and verify economic principles while reaching the objective of scientific economic analysis.

1.2 An Approach to Economic Analysis

Mathematical economics is considered an approach to economic analysis. In that pursuit, it can be fundamentally different from the non-mathematical approach to economic analysis. The objective behind economic theory is to derive a set of theorems for a given set of postulates called *ceteris paribus*. But literary, economics being theoretical in nature can differ from mathematical economics. To differentiate them, it can be stated that while economic theory utilizes assumptions and conclusions in words, mathematical economics makes use of symbols. It employs equations rather than sentences as used in economic theory. Symbols and words are equivalents, in so far, symbols are also defined in words. Moreover by expressing in the symbolic form mathematical economics using deductive logic provides us with the economic principles in a more convincing and convenient way. Therefore, mathematical economics is more conducive to preciseness than economic theory is.

1.3 Geometrical and Mathematical Methods

Geometrical methods also provide a base to economic analysis, by the way, it forms a branch of mathematics itself. Through geometrical analysis, an economist can comprehend the relationship among economic variables which enables one to grasp and perceive economic theory better. Two-dimensional diagram is used to portray an indifference curve that represents an ordinal utility function. For example the utility function is given as $U = f(q_1, q_2)$, where q_1 and q_2 are some quantities of two goods. Despite its merits the geometrical method suffers from the serious dimensional problems. Therefore, the use of mathematical methods becomes obligatory when a consumer's utility function is to be defined in regard to three goods q_1, q_2 and q_3 with their per unit market prices p_1, p_2 and p_3 as given fixed. The optimum quantity purchases of these goods can be obtained by using a set of mathematically obtained equations and by applying derivatives. The limitations of the use of geometry has further widened the scope for the application of mathematical methods in economics.

1.4 Limitations of Mathematical Economics

Notwithstanding the advantages of using mathematical tools in economics, it is also an admitted fact that it is not everyone's cup of tea. The main drawback of mathematical economics is that the mathematical language may not be suitable to the vernacular economists. There exists the difficulties of communication between mathematical and non-mathematical economists. The economist having affluency of mathematical knowledge can limit himself to the problems that can be solved mathematically. There can be serious apprehension from this person for adopting inappropriate economic postulates just for the sake of mathematical convenience. He has been called upon not to be engulfed in mathematical methods while maintaining a safe distance from economic priciples.

1.5 Mathematical Approach is an Imperative for Economists

It is admitted that there should not be any misuse of mathematics in analysing economic principles. Mathematics shall retain a status of being a servant rather than becoming a master over the economist. However, the chief objective is to define economic principles in a scientific manner by enhancing its preciseness and applications to practical life. The economist while applying mathematical tools can seldom achieve the desired objective of complete preciseness since he is to be preoccupied with the economic, *a priori* concerning human behaviour.

A.C. Chiang in his book Mathematical Economics has aptly remarked "we might consider the mathematical approach as a mode of 'transportation', that can take us from a set of postulates (point of departure) to a set of conclusions (destination) at a good speed". "A theorist who wishes to get his conclusions more rapidly will find it convenient to drive the vehicle of mathematical techniques appropriate for his particular purpose". Highlighting importance of mathematics he says "For a serious 'driver'- to continue with the metaphor - some lessons in mathematics are imperative."[1]

Mathematical analysis prerequisites the social scientists in general and the economists in particular. An economist is required to be exposed to the mathematical tools like set theory, calculus, functions, probability, integration, martrix algebra, partial derivative, differential and difference equations, etc.

1. Chiang, A.C., *"Mathematical Economics"*.

1.6 An Analytical Overview of the Chapters

The textbook "Mathematical Techniques for Economic Analysis" contains eleven chapters in total. with an introduction forming itself a chapter.

Accordingly, we start with the second chapter of the textbook. This chapter deals with the basic concepts and mathematical tools. An attempt has been made in the chapter to briefly interpret basic mathematical tools like set theory and its operations, identity and equations, various types of functions and their graphs, the linear and non-linear functions used for economic analysis, concept of partial equilibrium and other elementary exercises of mathematics that serve as basic to an economist.

In an endeavour to expose the rules of differentiation of one variable case and its applications in economics, the concepts are presented with numerous illustrations in third and forth chapters. Derivative is the mathematics of marginal changes of a given variable. It has been indiscriminately used in economic theory concerning utility and demand analysis, behavior of the firm, elasticity of demand, revenue and cost analysis, market equilibrium and profit maximization by the firm. These applications are extensively incorporated in these two chapters providing thereby a complte exposure to our readers.

Fifth chapter deals with matrix algebra which differs widely from the ordinary algebraic operations. The use of matrices and determinants have oversimplified the system of equations in the real world system. The chapter includes methods for using determinants and matrix inversion for finding solution to the equilibrium level of outputs in different sectors of the economy in Leontief's input-output analysis. The model provides solution to internal consistency. Both matrix inverse method and Cramer's rule are presented and simplified in the chapter.

The sixth and seventh chapters of the book introduces our readers with the derivatives of functions of more than one variable cases. It deals with the techniques of partial differentiation and their applications in economics. These mathematical tools are extensively used to explain the cross elasticity of demand, joint cost functions, price discrimination and equilibrium output from the constrained optimizing behaviour of the firm, etc.,

Chapter eight incorporates the constrained optimizing behaviour of the consumers and firms by using the Lagrangian Multiplier method when these economic units intend to optimize their constrained objective functions subject to certain constraints. Readers are introduced with the concepts of Linear programming Problem in the ninth chapter and it forms a lengthy chapter for getting all detailed analysis as far practical to the author. Linear programming is an applied technique which has been increasingly used by all branches of sciences including the operation research and engineering. The programming technique is used when the user intends to optimize a given objective function subject to ceratin constraints called side conditions. This restricts the objective function due to the structural linear constraints limiting decision-making by the user. The graphical solution to the problems of maximisation and minimisation are provided. All necessary steps are made in an attempt to simplify the simplex method for finding solution to linear programming problems. Readers are also introduced with the use of Big-M method to solve minimization problems. The chapter also covers the concepts relating duality and its economic interpretations. The symmetry between the primal and its dual are also provided.

In the last two chapters tenth and eleventh, techniques of integral calculus and economic applications of definite and indefinite integrals are discussed in a lucid style with many illustrations. This is to make mathematics of integral calculus easy and exciting to our students and readers. Numerous illustrations are used to simplify the rules of integral calculus: definite and indefinite. An extensive applications of integral calculus concerning revenue, cost functions, Lorenz curve measurement of inequalities, Pareto income distribution, consumer's and producer's surplus are also provided with simplifications in the chapter.

❑❑❑

2 Basic Concepts

2.1 Variables, Constants and Parameters

A variable is defined to be something whose magnitude changes. An economist comes across many variables such as price, quantity, exports, imports, cost, revenue, income and output, etc. In economics, normally variables are expressed in symbolic forms like '*P*' for price, '*q*' for output, profit is denoted π, total cost is shown by '*C*' and total revenue by '*R*' and so on. The values of these variables are determined by solving equations in a given problem or the models formulated.

It is customary for an economist to define, formulate and use economic models to ensure integrating flexibility with realism to a certain degree. This facilitates him to derive solutions to the variables under interpretation. For example, given the linear demand and supply functions for a product in the goods market as $d_x = 10 - 5P$ and $S_x = -9 + 4P$, the job of the economist is to determine the market clearing level of price and quantity. This is obtained by equating demand and supply functions so as to reach equilibrium. Accordingly by setting $18 - 5P = -9 + 4P$ and solving this we get $P = 3$. This provides an equilibrium price at which quantity demanded is equal to quantity supplied. This amounts to 3 units. The solution values, price and quantity are obtained from this simple model of market equilibrium, so for equilibrium price, Demand = Supply.

Price and quantity in this simple model are referred to endogeneous variables. These variables are originating within the system of equations in the model. Against this there can be exogeneous variables also, which a model normally contains. These variables are assumed to be determined by forces outside the model and therefore their magnitudes are accepted as given or constant in the model. These variables are not determined within the system of equations of the model. However a variable regraded endogeneous to one specific model may be considerd exogeneous for another model. For example in the model of simple market equlibrium we have just cited above price of the goods is considered endogeneous. But a consumer while reaching equilibrium with the help of indifference curve analysis has to accept prices of goods he will be purchasing as given parameters for maximising his specified utility function subject to budget constraints.

When a constant is joined to a variable it is called coefficient of the variable. This coeffcient can be either symbolic or numerical. For example, in the demand function $q_x = a - bp$, the symbols 'a' and – 'b' are considered parameters or constants. It is indeed a difficult task to define and differentiate a cosntant from a parameter. Sometimes, a number taken is constant since it is fixed and serves the coeffcient of the variable while a parameter defined can be estimated by using some methods. But they can be interchangeably used in mathematical analysis and models.

The parametric constants are also represented by small alphabets and also by Greek letters α, β, γ, etc. For estimating the parameters in a model, empirically collected data can be used. Take for example, the empirical consumption function can be estimated by using data on national income and national consumption expenditure. A regession model is built on it. This can be a common subject for an economist. The simple and typical linear regression consumption function is $C = \alpha + \beta Y$, where the parameter 'α' refers to the intercept while the parameter β represents the slope of the regression equation of Consumption(C) on Income (Y).

Dependent and independent variables: One variable can assume different values depending on another variable, is regarded as dependent variable. For example in the linear consumption function $C = \alpha + \beta Y$, where 'C' is the dependent variable and Y is referred to the independent variable. This is because consumption exependiture (C) depends on the levels of national income (Y). The demand function can be explicitly stated as $D_x = f(P_x)$: the quantity demanded D_x is the dependent variable while (P_x) is the independent variable. Similarly the total cost function can be shown to be a dependent variable while firm's output is an independent variable. They can be functionally related as $C = f(q)$. The functional relationship between dependent and independent variables can be indicated by letters g, h, f, Ψ, φ, etc. As we will see later on the functional relationship between cost and output indicated by $C = f(q)$ is different from the relationship shown by $C = g(q)$.

2.2 Equations and Identities

The variables can form an exciting exercise only when they are expressed in relation to other variables. This relationship between variables can be established in the form of either an equation or an inequality. For example, $3X + 2Y = 18$ is an equation while an inequality can be shown by either $\leq$ types or $\geq$ types. $X - 3Y \leq 12$ is an inequality. It is different from the inequality $3X + 5Y \geq 18$. Both of them are different from the equations of $=$ types.

An equation can be defined to show equality of two expressions. An equation can be different from an identity. An equation satisfied by any value of the variable is said to be an identity. Its LHS (left hand side) is equal to the RHS (right hand side) for a specific value assigned to the variable. For example, $5(x - 2) = 5x - 10$ is an identity. By assigning value 1 to x, one can get –5 on either side of it. Similarly, when value 2 is assigned to x, 0 is obtained on either side.

Thus, for any given value of x, one can get the LHS and RHS that satisfy the same value for which it is referred to an identity. This equation satisfies all values of x. Thus $5(x - 2) = 5x - 10$ is an identity. This identity contains one variable x although there can also be more than one variable in an identity. Let us consider another equation $3x + 5 = 5x + 1$. For $x = 1$, LHS of the equation is 8 and RHS is 6. For $x = 2$, LHS is 11 and RHS is also 11. For any values of x, except $x = 2$, the LHS and RHS are not equal. Therefore it can not be an identity. We have many example from economic theory to consider it an identity. In the Keynesian theory, national income identity is comprised of national consumption and national investment expenditure, depicted by $Y = C + I$, where C = Consumption and I = Investment expenditure. An identity can be usually written and shown as $Y \equiv C + I$. The firm's profit function is the difference between revenue and cost. This is given by an identity, $\pi = R - C$. This forms a definitional equation that sets up an identity between two different expressions having the same meaning in its LHS and RHS.

Equations are of different types. The relation between the variables are shown in the form of equation can be called behavioural equation for one variable behaves in response to the changes taking place in the other variable. For example, the national consumption expenditure is to change with the national income. The equation representing the consumption function can be considered a behavioral equaion. Its functional relationship is expressed as $C = f(Y)$. An estimated consumption function can be shown to be $C = 85 - 0.8Y$. The total cost function of a firm can be shown to be comprised of the fixed and variable costs. We can have a linear cost function such as $C = 50 + 20q$, where 50 stands for the fixed cost.

The third type of equation can be referred to the equilibrium conditions such as $q_d = q_s$. The equations of this type forms a class in themselves. They are neither definitional nor behavioural equations. These equations are widely used in eonomics.

2.3 Number System

It is important to know the terms relating to number system. There are positive and negative integers, fractions, rational and irrational numbers. The whole positive numbers 1, 2, 3, 4, ..., 15, etc., are called positive integers and their counterparts –1, –2, –3, ..., –15 are the negative whole numbers, called negative integers. All these numbers form collectively a set of integers. There are also fractional values which can be positive or negative. They are not integers.

The positive fractions are $\frac{2}{3}, \frac{3}{8}, \frac{5}{7}$, etc., while negative fractions are $-\frac{2}{3}, -\frac{3}{8}, -\frac{5}{7}$, etc., together they make up the set of all fractions. These fractions have a common property that they are expressed as ratio of two integers. Fractions and integers together form the rational numbers. The numbers that cannot be expressed as a ratio of a pair of integers are called irrational numbers. For example $\sqrt{5}, \sqrt{2}, ...\sqrt{11}$ are irrational numbers, as they can't be put in the form of ratio of two integers.

A prime number is the one which is divisible either by 1 or by the number itself. These are 1, 3, 5, 7, 11, 13 and so on. Fig-2.1 depicts this number system.

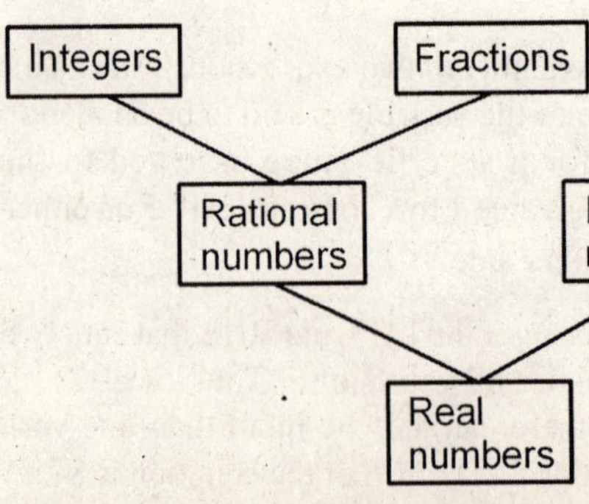

Fig. 2.1 : Number System.

2.4 Concept of Sets and their Operations

A set is a collection of objects. These objects are numbers, names, elements and any other expressions, like days, months, etc. A set will contain some elements in it.

Usually, a set is denoted by capital letters *A, B, X, Y, F*, etc., while elements of a set are represented by lower case letters. The elements of a set are put within some brackets like [ ], { }, ( ). Suppose a set denoted by *S* contains the numbers 4, 5 and 8, it can be written as $S = \{4, 5, 8\}$. When *R* denotes a set containing all positive integers, we need to describe these elements without enumerating them since this is not possible. This can be written as $R = \{x \mid x \text{ a positive integer}\}$. This is read as: *R* is a set of all numbers *x* such that *x* is a positive integer. A vertical bar | is inserted to describe this in the set by separating the general symbol for the elements. When we define a set named 'M' having all real numbers between 3 and 8, it can be expressed as $M = [x \mid 3 \leq x \leq 8]$.

Types of Sets:

(a) A set with finite numebr of elements is called a finite set. For example, a set containing all seven days can be written as

S = [*Sun, Mon, Tues, Wed, Thurs, Fri, Sat*]

When elements of a set are infinite, it is called an infinite set. For example, set *R* is shown as

$R = [x \mid 2^n$ where '*n*' is a positive integer. $\therefore = [1, 2, 4, 8, ...]$.

(b) A set containing no elements is called an empty set. It is denoted by ∅. It is also called a null set. A set of prime numbers having numbers more than 23 and less than 29 will be no element since no prime number is found between 23 and 29. Thus, it will form an empty set. This can be written as *S* where,

$S = [x \mid 23 \leq x \leq 29] = \varnothing$,

(c) A set containing only one element is called a singleton set and this can be given as $M = [5]$.

(d) One set containing many sets is called a set of sets. For example

$S = \{[5], [2, 3, 8], [-1, 3, 7, 9]\}$ is a set of sets.

(e) Equal sets: Two sets are said to be equal when they contain the same elements without any consideration to the order of the placement of elements in these sets. For example sets $A_l = A_2$ where $A_l = [3, 5, 7]$ and $A_2 = \{7, 3, 5\}$. To establish equality between two sets the order is immaterial.

(f) Two sets are equivalent: If both the sets conatin the same number of elements but they are different in numbers the sets are called equivalent sets. For example $S_l = [3, 5, 7]$ and $S_2 = \{8, 4, 1\}$ are equivalent sets.

(g) Set and subset: A kind of relationship exist between set and a subset. One set can be a subset of another set. For example, there are two sets *A* and *B*. It can be shown that set *B* is a subset of *A* when every element of *B* are also the elements of *A*. For example, $A = [1, 2, 3, 8, 7]$ and $B = \{8, 3\}$. In a formal way it can be shown that $x \in B \Rightarrow x \in A$. It means the element *x* included in set *B* implies that *x* is included in set *A*. The set inclusion symbol can also be used to show this. It can be written as $B \subset A$ meaning that set *B* is included in set *A*. The same is expressed by symbol $A \supset B$ meaning that set *A* includes set *B*.

When two sets A_1, A_2 are subsets of each other, it means $A_1 \supset A_2$ and $A_2 \supset A_2$. This is possible only when these two sets are equal sets, i.e., $A_1 = A_2$. When symbol ∈ is used, an element is shown to be included in a set whereas the symbol ⊂ is used to show that a subset is included in a set. Thus, ⊂ relates a subset to a set and the symbol $\in$ shows an element belongs to a set. All positive integers form a subset of the set of all rational numbers.

The question is how many sets can be formed from a set named say, 'A' containing 6 elements shown as $A = [a, b, c, d, e, f]$. Each element of A can be a subset of A. Then two elements can be shown to be subsets of set A and then the elements are to be shown in triples and so on.

In total we will have $2^n = 2^6 = 64$ subsets. The smallest possible subset of A is a subset with no element and it is called a null set.

Disjoint sets:

When two sets have no common element at all, two sets are said to be disjoint. For example, $A_1 = \{3,2,8,-4\}$ and $A_2 = \{-1,5,7,9\}$. These two sets have no common element. The elements they have are peculiar to each of them. In this case neither set is a subset of the other. In this case $A_1 \not\subset A_2$.

Illustration: Are the following statements correct? Justify

(a) If $A = \{2,3,5\}$, $2 \subset A$. This is not true because the element 2 belongs to set A, which can be written as $2 \in A$ and not $2 \subset A$.

(b) If $A_1 = \{8,9,7,3\}$ and $A_2 = \{9,7\}$, $A_2 \in A_1$. This statement is wrong. The correct way of expressing this is $A_2 \subset A_1$.

(c) If $B = \{5,8,3\}$, $2 \subset B$. This is a correct expression. But $3 \subset B$ is a wrong expression while $3 \in B$ is a proper way of expressing a set.

(d) $5 \in \{3,6,2,7\}$. This is a wrong statement since 5 does not belong to the given set. Therefore, the correct expression is $5 \notin \{3,6,2,7\}$.

(e) When $B = \{3,6,2,7\}$, $M = \{a, c, f\}$, $M \subset B$, the statement is wrongly expressed. The correct way of stating it is, $M \not\subset B$.This is because M does not form a subset of B.

(f) What is the difference of these expressions: $\varnothing$, $\{0\}$ and $\{\phi\}$?

$\varnothing$ is a null set or empty set. $\{0\}$ is a set with one element 0. $\{\phi\}$ is a set having one element ϕ.

Set operations: Following set operations are important to study:

Union and intersection of sets: Union of two sets A and B refers to the formation of a new set containing only those elements belonging to A or B or both A and B. Symbolically, it is expressed as $A \cup B$. For example, when we are given $A = \{4,6,5,7\}$, $B = \{2,3,8\}$, these two sets are neither equal nor equivalent nor disjoint nor either one is a subset of the other. The set operation is such that $A \cup B = \{2,3,4,6,5,7,8\}$, or $B \cup A$.

The intersection of two sets: The intersection of two sets A_1 and A_2 forms a new set, that will contain only those elements which belong to both the sets. Symbolically it can be written as $A_1 \cap A_2$ or $A_2 \cap A_1$. This can be read as A_1 intersection A_2 or A_2 intersection A_1.

Following example shows the intersection of two sets:

$A_1 = \{1,2,3,5,7\}$ $A_2 = \{2,8,5,3\}$, $A_1 \cap A_2$ or $A_2 \cap A_1 = \{2,3,5\}$

When there is no common element in two sets as given below, the intersection of two sets will be an empty set, shown as, ϕ.

For example, $A = \{3,5,7\}$ $B = \{2,8,9\}$, $A \cap B$ or $B \cap A \phi$. Sets A and B are called disjoint sets and their intersection will be an empty set. Formal definition of expressing union and intersection of two sets are shown as

$A \cap B = \{x/x \in A \text{ and } x \in B\}$,

$A \cup B = \{x/x \in A \text{ or } x \in B\}$,

When three different sets are given as $A = \{2,8,7\}$ $B = \{3,4,5\}$ and $C = \{1,5,4,8\}$,

$A \cup B \cup C = \{1,2,3,4,5,7,8\}$. The set operations will satisfy that $(A \cup B) \cup C = A \cup (B \cup C)$. Similarly for intersection of three sets it will also hold that $(A \cap B) \cap C = A \cap (B \cap C)$.

Universal and complement set:

The total number of elements or objects forming universe is referred to the universal set. All other subsets are derived from the universal set. Suppose, there are 30 students in a class then a universal set of all 30 students can be formed.

If the first eight positive integers form an universal set then it can be written as $U = \{1,2,3,4,5,6,7,8\}$.

We will have another set A as $A = \{1,2,3,7,8\}$. Now, we can define a set called complement of A and it is symbolically expressed as $\tilde{A}$. This complement set is the one that contains all the numbers of universal set U, which are not there in set A. Thus $\tilde{A} = \{4,5,6\}$. The complement of an universal set itself will be an empty set. Thus, $\tilde{U} = \phi$.

Set operations shown with the help of Venn diagram:

The Venn diagram is shown in Fig. 2.2 (*a,b* and *c*). Fig. 2.2 (a) represents the union of two sets A and B, $A \cup B$. All the points in the shaded area shows this union of A and B sets. Fig. 2.2 (b) shows the intersection of two sets A and B, and this is indicated by the shaded area. Thus it is $A \cap B$. Fig. 2.2 (c) shows complement of set A. It is shown by the shaded area representing $U - A$.

In fig. 2.3 (*a* and *b*) $A \cup B \cup C$ and $A \cap B \cap C$ are shown by the shaded area.

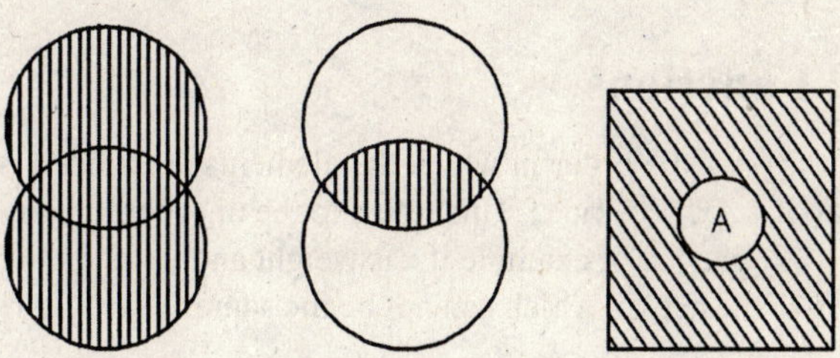

(*a*) $A \cup B$ (*b*) $A \cap B$ (*c*) $\tilde{A}$

***Fig. 2.2 :** (a, b, c)*

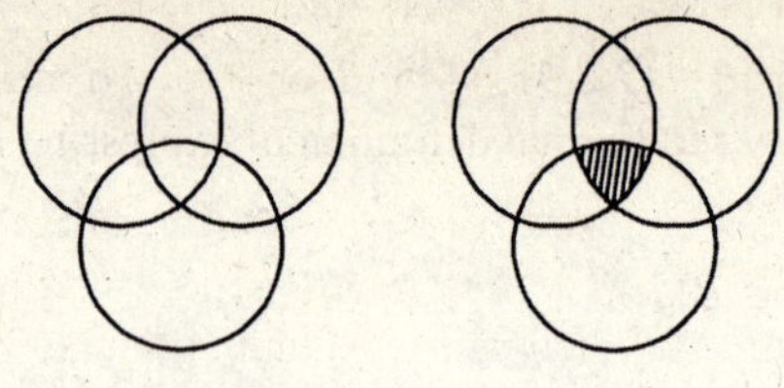

(*a*) $A \cup B \cup C$ (*b*) $A \cap B \cap C$

***Fig. 2.3 :** (a, b)*

Illustrations:

Given $A = \{3,5\}$, $B = \{4,6,7\}$, $C = \{2,4\}$

It can be verified that when unions and intersections are combined the distributive law holds true in set operation and therefore

$A \cup (B \cap C) = (A \cup B) \cap (A \cup C)$ and

$A \cap (B \cup C) = (A \cap B) \cup (A \cap C)$. From the above sets *A*, *B* and *C* we can obtain $B \cap C = \{4\}$, $A \cup (B \cap C) = \{3,4,5\}$.

Now $A \cup B = \{3,4,5,6,7\}$ and $A \cup C = \{2,3,4,5\}$

$(A \cup B) \cap (A \cup C) = \{3,4,5\}$. Thus it is verified that

$A \cap (B \cup C) = (A \cap B) \cup (A \cap C) = \{3,4,5\}$

Similarly it can be verified that $A \cap (B \cup C) = (A \cap B) \cup (A \cap C)$

$(B \cup C) = \{2,4,6,7\}$, $A \cap (B \cup C) = \{3,5\} \cap \{2,4,6,7\} \varnothing$

$A \cap B = \{3,5\} \cap \{4,6,7\} = \varnothing$ and $A \cap C = \{3,5\} \cap \{2,4\} = \varnothing$

$(A \cap B) \cup (A \cap C) = \varnothing \cap \varnothing = \varnothing$. $A \cap (B \cup C) = (A \cap B) \cup (A \cap C) = \varnothing$. The distributive law is verified.

2.5 Relations and Functions

In writing a set $A = \{x, y\}$ the order in which the elements are placed is immaterial. Therefore in set operations we can see that $A = \{x, y\} = \{y, x\}$. This refers to the unordered pair. When ordering of pairs does carry its significance $\{x, y\} \neq \{y, x\}$. For example if *x* is weight and *y* stands for age of students in a class, we can form the ordered pairs of these two, which can not be the same. Thus $\{x, y\} = \{45,15\} \neq \{15,45\}$, where $\{x = \text{weight}, y = \text{age}\}$.

The ordered pairs are important to study while explaining relations and functions. Take for example from two sets $A = \{2, 3\}$ and $B = \{4, 5\}$, we can generate all possible ordered pairs $\{2, 4\}$, $\{2, 5\}$, $\{3, 4\}$ and $\{3, 5\}$. This is called Cartesian product of sets *A* and *B* and read as $A \times B$, *A* cross *B*.

Any set of ordered pairs will establish relation of *y* value with *x* value when these values are shown on a two-dimensional graph. For given an *x* value, one or more *y* value will be determined by that relation. Suppose, we have a set given $A = [xy \mid y = 3x]$ the ordered pairs formed are for $x = 0, y = 0$:, $x = 1$, $y = 3$, $x = 2$, $y = 6$ and so on. This will form a relation between *x* and *y* values. By plotting these values on a graph we will obtain a straight line for $y = 3x$. This graph will represent all the points showing the ordered pairs of x and y values.

A relation between x and y is such that for each x value there exists a corresponding y value from the relation $y = 3x$. In that case, 'y' is said to be a function of 'x'. This functional relationship is shown by $y = f(x)$. This relationship is such that a given 'x' value will determine a unique 'y' value. This function shows a relation although all relations may not be called as functions.

A function is called mapping or transformation. When $y = f(x)$, 'f' indicates the functional notation. There can be different functional notations used to denote different functions. It is customary to use symbols of Greek letters ϕ, φ and also small letters, g, f, h and so on. The functional relations shown by $y = g(x)$ is diffeent from $y = f(x)$. The common expression in both the functional relation is that 'y' is dependent variable while 'x' is independent variable. In economic theory, total cost can be considered a dependent variable while output is an independent variable. The functional relation is $C = h(q)$. If the firm's total fixed cost is Rs. 500 and Variable Cost is $C = 10q$, the firm's total cost function can be shown to be $TC = 500 + 10q$. This forms the linear total cost function of the firm. If the firm decides to produce a maximum of 100 units per day, firm's total output can vary between 0 and 100 a day. Accordingly firm's total cost will vary between 500 and 1500.

Thus, the domain is the set of values $0 \leq q \leq 100$ or $D = [q / 0 \leq q \leq 100]$.

The range for total cost will be the cost for $q = 0$ ($TC = 500$) to $q = 100$ ($TC = 1500$)..

Accordingly the range for total cost is , Range = $\{C / 500 \leq C \leq 1500\}$.

2.6 Types of Functions

There are several types of functions and each one will represent a different rule of maping. The functional relation shown in $y = f(x)$ is a general statement indicating the possibility of mapping.

Following are the different types of functions:

(a) Constant functions:

This refers to a function whose range consist of one element For example $y = f(x) = 12$ means $y=12$ for all possible values of 'x' and $y=12$ remains fixed for all values that x can take. The coordinate plane will appear a horizontal line parallel to X-axis. In the cost functions we have the total fixed cost curve which is a constant quantity say 'K'. Graphically, it will represent a horizontal straight line. When we take differentiation of this constant function with respect to output, it will become zero. This function has got some importance of its own in economic theory.

(b) Explicit and implicit functions:

When x and y are related as $y = f(x)$, it is such that the LHS contains only one variable 'y' while RHS contains the only variable 'x', so that 'y' is said to be an explicit function of 'x'. This also means that *'y' is dependent variable and 'x' is the independent variable.* There can be another type of function exhibiting relationship between two variables, called implicit function. The implicit functions establish the functional relationship between two variables 'x' and 'y' in such a way that either variable can be considered an independent variable. For this function neither 'y' is expressed exclusively a function of 'x' nor 'x' is expressed exclusively a function of 'y'. This type of implicit function is symbolically expressed as $f(x, y) = 0$. We can have many examples of implicit functions. For example, $2xy - 2y + 3x = 0$ is an implict function. When we solve this equation for 'y' expressing 'y' in terms of 'x' , it can be shown in the form $y = f(x)$. It is obtained as follows:

$2xy - 2y - 3x = 0$ or $2y(x-1) = 3x$ and $y = \dfrac{3x}{2(x-1)}$.

For $y = f(x)$, 'y' is the dependent variable while 'x' is the independent variable. This implies that 'y' is an explicit function of 'x'. However we can get another explicit function from the same impilicit function. This function is derived by expressing 'x' in terms of 'y'. This is obtained as

$2xy - 2y - 3x = 0$ or $x(2y-3) = 2y$ and $x = \dfrac{2y}{(2y-3)}$,

We can write this as $x = g(y)$, where 'x' is the dependent variable and 'y' stands for independent variabe. In this way from this implicit function we have derived two explicit functions:

$$y = f(x) \text{ and } x = g(y).$$

However it is not always possible to derive an explicit function from an implicit function. For this, the variables are to be separated into dependent and independent variables.

***(c)* Inverse functions:**

It is exhibited that two explicit functions can be derived from an implicit function and neither variable is shown to be an explicit function of the other. In fact, these two functions are said to be the inverse functions of each other. In $y = f(x)$, 'y' is an explicit function of 'x' and for $x = g(y)$, 'x' is an explicit function of 'y'. These two functions are defined by one equation and they are shown to be related as inverse of one another. Take for example $y = x^2$ is an explicit function of 'y' expressed in terms of 'x'. From this function, we can also get $x = \sqrt{y}$ where 'x' is an explict function of 'y'. These two functions are inverse of ecah other.

For $y = f(x)$ we can also write $x = f^{-1}(y)$. This is read as inverse of $y = f(x)$.

Illustrations:

Given the following implicit functions find the explict functions if they can be derived from it:

(1) If $8x - 2y - 6 = 0$, From this function derive and obtain two explicit functions. These are shown as

$$x = \frac{6-2y}{8} \text{ and } y = \frac{8x-6}{2}$$

(2) For $x^2 + 2y^2 - 18 = 0$, two explicit functions derived from this implict function are

$x = \pm\sqrt{18-2y^2}$, which $x = +\sqrt{18-2y^2}$ and $x = -\sqrt{18-2y^2}$

In this way we get two dfferent values of 'x' for a given value of 'y'. Similarly for 'y' we can obtain

$y = \pm\sqrt{\dfrac{18-x^2}{2}}$. Two different values of 'y' for a given value of 'x' obtained are

$$y = +\sqrt{\frac{18-x^2}{2}}, \text{ and } y = -\sqrt{\frac{18-x^2}{2}}.$$

***(d)* Single-valued and multi-valued functions:**

A function stated either explicitly or implicitly by an equation when yields only one dependent variable corresponding to a given value of independent variable, it is called a single-valued function. For example, $y = 4 + 2x$ will give a single value of 'y' for a given value assigned to 'x'.

If $x = 0$, $y = 4$; for $x = 1$, $y = 6$, for $x = 2$, $y = 8$ and so on. Against this single-valued function, another function called multi-valued function can be derived when each independent variable will provide more than one dependent variable. We have already seen the implicit function $x^2 + 2y^2 - 18 = 0$, which gives us two dependent variables, when either 'x' or 'y' are taken as independent variable.

***(e)* Rational functions:**

A function such as $y = \dfrac{x^2 - 1}{2x^2 + 3x - 9}$ is a rational function. In this function, 'y' is expressed as a ratio of two polynomials in the variable 'x'. The rational function which is applied in economics can be given in the form of $y = \dfrac{a}{x}$, where 'a' is a constant. The best example is the firm's averge fixed cost functionn. This can be taken as 'y' while 'x' stands for output and 'x' for total fixed cost, so that $a = yx = TFC$. When we plot this function, $a = xy$ on a graph, the graph obtained for AFC (y) will form a rectangular hyperbola. It satisfies the property that every point on the curve will yield a given amount 'a', the TFC ($a = xy$).

***(f)* Polynomial functions:**

The general form of polynomial function is given by $y = \alpha_0 + \alpha_1 x + \alpha_2 x^2 + \alpha_3 x^3 + ... + \alpha_n x^n$. For this function, each term contains a coefficient with the first term $x^0 = 1$ so that $\alpha_0 x^3 = \alpha_0$. The second term is $\alpha_1 x$ while the third term is $\alpha_2 x^2$ and so on. In this way each term contains a coefficient and a non-negative integer power of the 'x' variable. When we put $n = 0$, $y = \alpha_0$. It provides a constant function. When it is plotted in the coordinate plane, we get the ordered pair $(0, \alpha_0)$ so that for $x = 0$ or any value it can have, $y = \alpha_0$. This is y-intercept. The graph for this will be a horizontal line parallel to X-axis, as shown in fig. 2.4.

For $n = 1$, the polynomial function becomes $y = \alpha_0 + \alpha_1 x$. This is a linear function with y-intercept α_0. The slope of the straight line is α_1. This indicates that a unit increase in 'x' will result in to an increase in 'y' by the amount equal to α_1. The given function takes a positive slope. ($\alpha_1 > 0$). In economic theory, we get the supply function for a good. It has a positive slope since quantity supplied of a good is an increasing function of its own price. This has been graphically shown in fig-2.5, where X-axis depicts price and Y-axis shows amount supplied of the good.

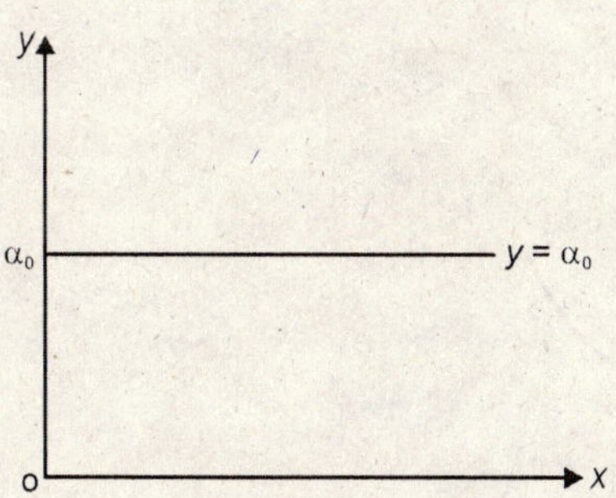

Fig. 2.4 : $y = \alpha_o$

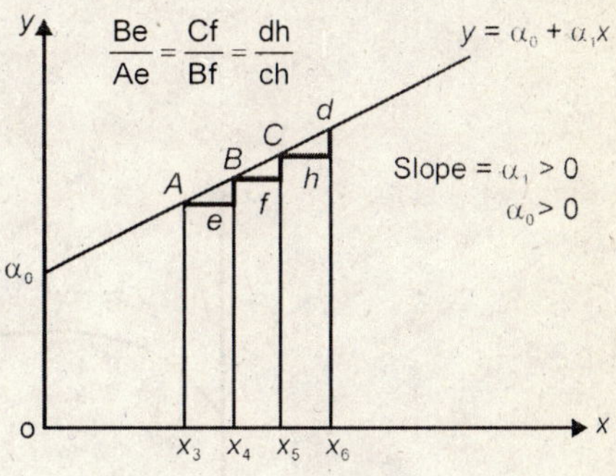

Fig. 2.5 : $y = \alpha_o + \alpha_1 x$

The linear demand function can be shown by equation, $y = \alpha_0 - \alpha_1 x$. By plotting this on a graph, we will geta straight linedemand curve, downward sloping from left to the right. The slope of this line is $-\alpha_1$ as shown in fig-2.6, where *X*-axis represents price and *Y*-axis shows quantity demanded for the good.

Now we will assign $n = 2$, for this we will get a polynomial function, $y = \alpha_0 + \alpha_1 x + \alpha_2 x^2$ > This forms a quadratic equation. This is a polynomial function of degree 2. Its graph is shown in Fig. 2.7. The quadratic function is normally written in the form, $ax^2 + bx + c = 0$, where *a, b* and *c* are constants. The solution to the quadratic equation can be done either by using factorial method or by solving the quadratic equationusing a formula. This function will provide two different values for the variable '*x*', shown below:

$x = \dfrac{-b \pm \sqrt{b^2 - 4ac}}{2a}$. This gives us with two values for '*x*' and these are

$$(1) \quad x_1 = \frac{-b + \sqrt{b^2 - 4ac}}{2a} \quad \text{and} \quad (2) \quad x_2 = \frac{-b - \sqrt{b^2 - 4ac}}{2a}$$

We will assign now 3 to '*n*'. For $n = 3$, we get the polynomial function $y = \alpha_0 + \alpha_1 x + \alpha_2 x^2 + \alpha_3 x^3$, which is a cubic function. It is a polynomial function of degree 3. Its graph is shown in Fig. 2.8. This function can be shown in a more usual form, $y = ax^3 + bx^2 + cx + d$, where *a, b, c* and *d* are constants.

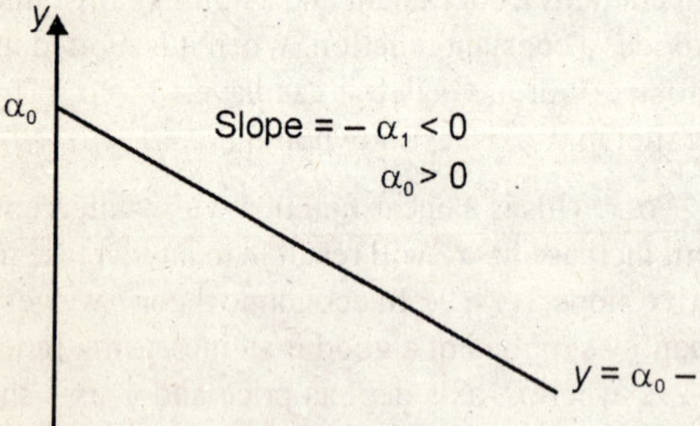

Fig. 2.6 : Linear demand curve

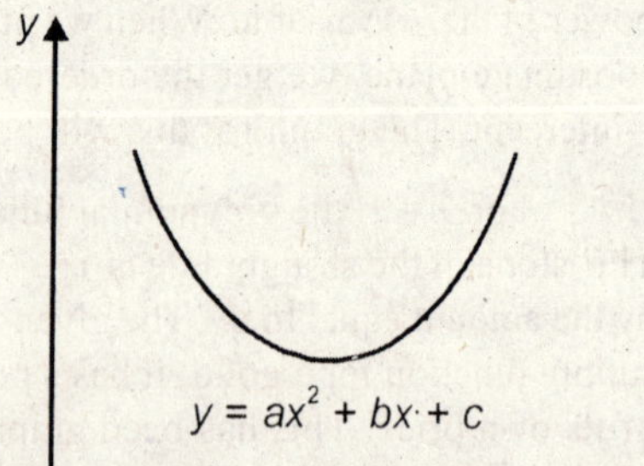

Fig. 2.7 : A quadratic function

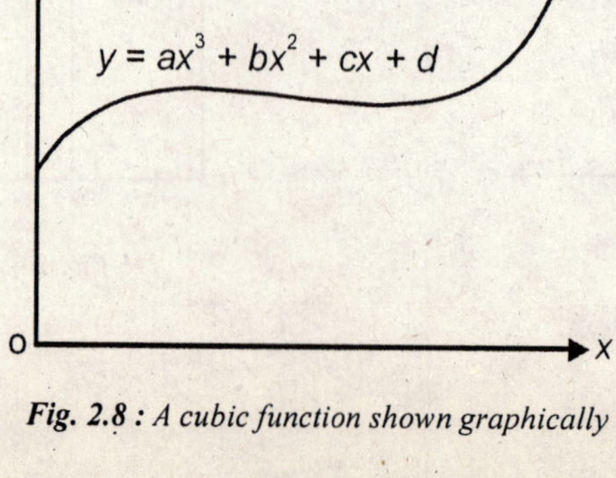

Fig. 2.8 : A cubic function shown graphically

***(g)* Algebraic and non-algebraic functions:**

A function expressed in terms of polynomials and roots of polynomials are called algebraic functions. A function like $y = \sqrt{x^2 + 7}$ is also an algebraic function although it is not rational. All algebraic functions are obtained with a finite number of algebraic opertaions involving addition, subtraction, multiplication and division etc. A function which is not algebraic is called non-algebraic or transcendental fucntions. The exponential function given by $y = a^x$ where the independnet variable x, appears in the exponent is non-algebraic. The logarithmic functions like $y = \log_a x$ is also non-algebraic.

***(h)* Monotonic functions:**

When 'y' is a single-valued function of 'x' variable, such as $y = 3x$, it can be shown that 'y' increases when 'x' will increase and 'y' decreases with decrease in 'x'. For this we can say that 'y' is an increasing fucntion of x. There can also be a decreasing fucntion of 'y' with respect to 'x'. For example, we are given the linear demand function as $y = 3 - 2x$. When this function is graphically represented we will get a downward sloping demand curve. The relation between 'x' and 'y' are such that as 'x' increases 'y' will decrease so that 'y' is said to be a decreasing function of 'x'. These decreasing and increasing fucntions are also called monotonic functions.

***(i)* Functions of two or more independent variables:**

The function $y = f(x)$, has a single independent variable 'x'. However the given function can be extended to have more than one independent variables. For example, the function, $Z = f(x, y)$, where 'x' and 'y' are two independent variables while 'Z' is the dependent variable. From Economic theory we can take an example that firm's output (q) is a function of two inputs, labour and capital. This can be expressed in the form of a production function as such, $q = g(K, L)$. This function depicts two independent variables 'K' and 'L', while the dependent variable shown is 'q'. Just like $y = f(x)$ maps a point in the domain into a point in the range so also the multi-variable function 'g' will do the same. The domain in this case will have a set of ordered pairs (K, L) for outpu (q) is determined by the specified values of both the variables K and L. The domain of the function will be some subset of the points K, L plane. Accordingly the value of the function (q) for a given point in the domain (K_1, L_1) is indicated by the height of the vertical line q_1. The association between three variables are shown by K_1, L_1, q_1 and K_2, L_2, q_2 and so on. While $y = f(x)$ is a set of ordered pairs, the function $q = g(K, L)$ is a set of ordered triples. This has been portrayed in Fig-2.9.

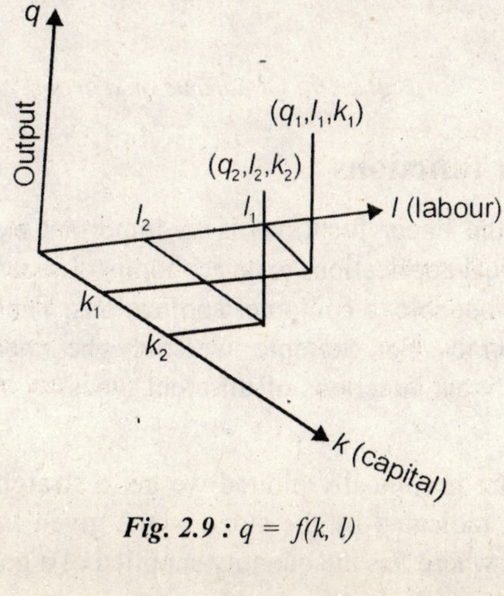

Fig. 2.9 : $q = f(k, l)$

2.7 Graphical Representation of Functions

Different functions can be graphically represented to fit into the coordinate system. We can introduce the Cartesian coordinate system first, to show the four different quadrants on a graph.

2.7.1. Cartesian coordinate system

Different quandrants of a graph are shown in Fig. 2.10:

Point 'M' with $x = 6$ and $y = 4$ is located in the first quadrant. This pair of 'x' and 'y' positive values can lie only in quadrant 1. This quadrant will represent all the positive values of 'x' and 'y'. The second quadrant will depict the pairs of 'x' and 'y' values when 'x' is negative and 'y' is positive. The third quadrant will have the pair of negative values assigned to 'x' and 'y'. The forth quadrant will portray the pairs of 'x' and 'y' when 'x' is positive while 'y' is negative. For example, point 'R' represents $x = -4$ and $y = 6$, and point 'L' represent $x = -2$ and $y = -6$. At point 'N', $x = 4$ and $y = -6$ are represented.

When the function is given by $y = f(x) = 3$, it is called y-intercept. This is indicated at point 'Q' in Fig-2.10. The function $x = f(y) = 5$, gives us the x-intercept 'A', depicting $x = 5$ and $y = 0$.

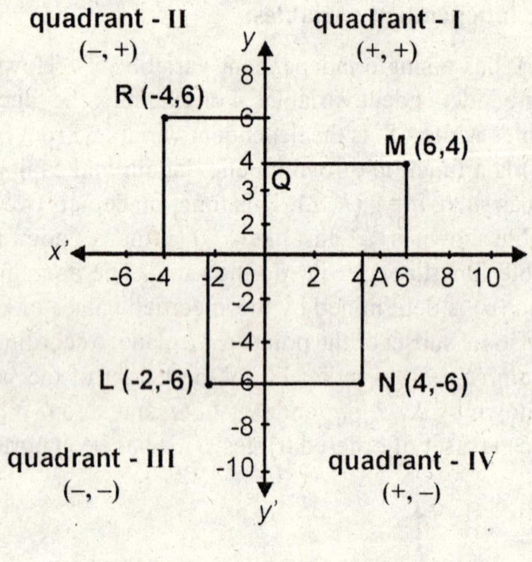

Fig. 2.10 : Quadrants on a graph

2.7.2. Graphing the linear functions

Graphically plotting of the linear fucntions is an important exercise in general and economics in particular. It has got many practical applications to an economist. Linear functions are simple as they possess some mathematical properties amenable to computer applications. These functions are also simple to use in business, commerce and economics. For example, we study the linear regression models in economics. Moreover many times the non-linear functions of different types are also converted in to linear functions because of its simplicity.

When linear functions are graphically plotted we get a straight line slopping either downward or upward, depending on the sign indicated by the slope of the given linear function. we will have a linear supply function as $S = -3 + 5P$, where S is the quantity supplied of a good while 'P' stands for its price. The graph of this function establishes a relation between quantity supplied at different price. To project the graph we need to have the ordered pairs of S and P. Here we take price as the independent variable. it is depicted along X-axis. The quantity supplied and demanded are always shown along the Y-axis for they constitute dependent variables. The ordered pairs of S and P for the function $S = -3 + 5P$, are represented in the following table. The same are also graphically portrayed in Fig-2.11.

Price :	0	1	2	3	4	5
Supply	– 3	2	7	12	17	22

We will now have a linear demand function, $D = 14 - 2P$. This function showing the relationship between price and demand are represenetd along the X-axis and Y-axis respectively in the same graph. Accordingly we get two staright lines, one for the deamnd function and the other one is for the supply function. These linear lines so obtained take opposite slopes and they intersect at point 'E' in Fig. 2.11. This corresponds to the equilibrium in goods market as it determines the price and quantity that clears the market. The equlibrium quantity damanded and supplied can also be determined by drawing a perpendicular from the intersection point 'E' to Y-axis. It gives us quantity of 9 units. Another perpendicular drawn to X-axis provides equilibrium price that ensure equality between demand and supply and thus clearing the market. The ordered pairs of price and quantity demanded are shown in the follwoing table:

Price :	0	1	2	3	4	5
Demand	14	12	10	8	6	4

The y-intersecpt of this demand curve is 14. This indicates that the quantity demanded will be 14 units corresponding to the price of the good is zero.

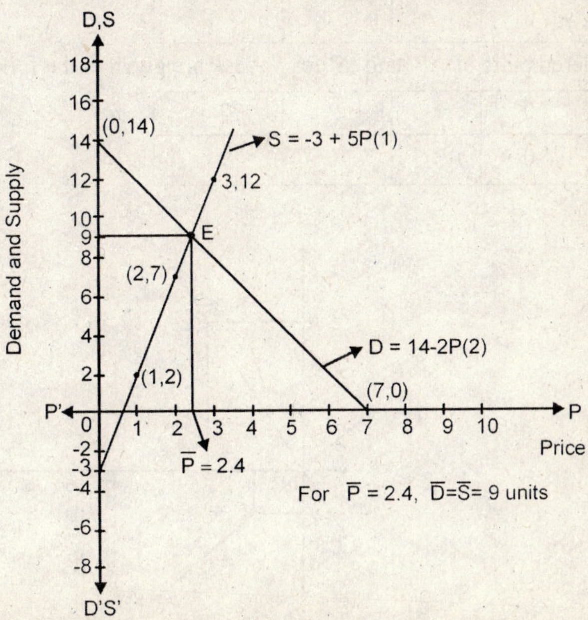

Fig. 2.11 : Linear Supply and Demand functions

Likewise we have the y-intercept for the supply curve which is –3, indicating that the quatity supplied will be negative for price is zero. A positive qunatity is supplied only for the price exceeding 0.6 is also clear from the diagram. The supply curve also shows that the quantity supplied will incraese with increase in its price for S > 0 if P > 0.6.

This supply function has an intercept –3 and slope 5. The demand fucntion is seen to have an intercept 14 and slope –2. This linear demand and supply functions are graphically represented in a more general form as $y = \alpha_0 \pm \alpha_1 x$ stating y-intercept α_0 and slope α_1.

2.7.3 Graph of a function without intercept

We will now see how to graph a function which do not have an intercept. For $y = \alpha_0 - \alpha_1 x$, '$y$' is shown to be a decreasing function of 'x' as 'y' decraeses for all values of 'x', and $x > 0$. The demand function depicted above shows this relationship between demand (y) and price (x). The supply function can be shown in a more general way as $y = -\alpha_0 + \alpha_1 x$. This is an increasing function of 'x' for 'y' increases for all positive values of 'x' or $x > 0$. The above supply function depicts this relationship. There are two important cases which need attention now are as follows: (1) The graphical representation of a function which has only an intercept and no slope. (2) The graphical representation of a function which has only slope and no intercept.

Let us have the typical demand function as $D = f(P) = 5$. Its graphical representation will provide us a horizontal line with Y-intercept 5. Assume that the demand and supply functions have no intercept but only their corresponding slope. How can we plot these functions on graph? Let us take the supply function as $S = f(P) = 3P$ and demand fucntion as $D = f(P) = -2P$. These functions represnt the general form of functions, $y = \alpha_0 \pm \alpha_1 x$ with $\alpha_0 = 0$ and slope $\pm \alpha_1 \neq 0$. For graphical representation of the demand function $D = -2P$, we need to find the ordered pairs of 'P' and 'D', which are shown in table below:

P	0	1	2	3
D	0	–2	–4	– 6

The ordered pairs of 'P' and 'S' for $S = 3P$ are given in the follwoing table

X	0	1	2	3
Y	0	3	6	9

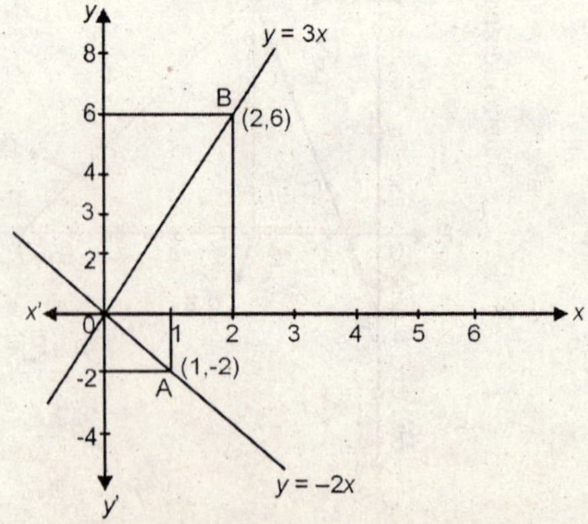

Fig. 2.12 : Graph of the functions with no intercept

By mapping these functions we get two straight lines: $S = 3P$ has a slope $2 > 0$. The line representing this starts from the origin ($y = 0, x = 0$) and slopes positive with a rate of change constant at 2. Similarly the function Dy $= -2P$ has a negative slope $-2 < 0$. The line representing this is also starting from the origin ($y = 0$ for $x = 0$) and it takes a negative slope with a rate of change constant at -2.

2.7.4 Graph of a function, given by $xy = b$ (constant)

This type of function is given by $xy = b$, where 'b' is a constant. This type of function is found in economics. The total fixed cost of a firm is constant quantity irrespective of the rate of output. If 'y' represents Average Fixed Cost (*AFC*) and 'x' stands for output, we can obtain $y = \frac{b}{x}$. The graph for this type of function will be a rectangular hyperbola. Therefore *AFC* curve is a rectangular hyperbola. The property of the curve is that for each value of 'x' we get the same amount of fixed cost, indicated by 'b'. Following data can be used to obatin *AFC* fucntion, where we have taken 'C' as total fixed cost and 'q' as output. Total Fixed Cost is taken 100. Accordingly we can get the curve $AFC = C = \frac{100}{q}$. The values of 'q' and *AFC* (*C*) are tabulated below and the same is graphically plotted in Fig. 2.13.

q	1	2	3	4
C (AFC)	100	50	33.33	25

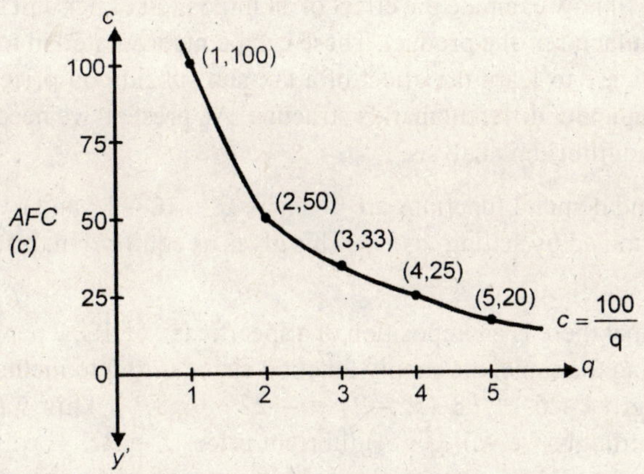

Fig. 2.13 : Rectangular hyperbola

2.8 Applications of Functions and Graphs in Economic Theory

It has been already presented how different functions are used in economic theory. In fact economists make a frequent use of these functions and graphs for explaining economic variables they deal with. The linear demand, supply and cost functions are widely used in break-even analysis and for determining profit function of the firm. The use of linear functions constitute an important topic in the linear programming technique, serves as a very important tool in economic anlaysis.

Some illustrations and exercises stating the application of functions and graphs in economic theory are attempted in the following texts:

2.8.1 Partial Market Equilibrium Analysis:

An equilibrium is characterized by the tendency of absence of any change. Equilibrium for a commodity in goods market is considerd to be a partial equilibrium analysis. For given the dmand and supply functions for a commodity 'q' as $q_d = \alpha - \beta P$ and $q_s = \alpha_1 - \gamma P$, we can determine the equilibrium price and quantity by equating demand and supply functions. This will bring equilibrium price as $P = \dfrac{\alpha + \alpha_1}{\beta + \gamma}$.

Equilibrium demand and supply corresponding to this price are $q_d = q_s$. These are given as

$$q_d = \alpha - \beta\left\{\frac{\alpha+\alpha_1}{\beta+\gamma}\right\} = \frac{\alpha\gamma - \alpha_1\beta}{\beta+\gamma} \text{ and } q_s = -\alpha_1 + \gamma\left\{\frac{\alpha+\alpha_1}{\beta+\gamma}\right\} = \frac{\alpha\gamma - \alpha_1\beta}{\beta+\gamma}$$

Illustration:

For given the linear demand and supply functions for a commodity in the goods market as $q_d = 18 - 2P$ and $q_s = -6 + 8P$, find equilibrium or market clearing price. This corresponds to the price at which $q_d = q_s$. By solving the equations we get the price 3 and at this price we get $q_d = q_s = 12$.

2.8.2 The Effect of Imposition of Tax and Granting of Subsidy on Market Equilibrium:

We have discussed how the equilibrium price and quantity demanded and supplied are determined in a simple market model. We will now examine the effect of an impositon of per unit tax on the commodity and grant of a subsidy to the manufacturer of a product. These can be incorporated in to the above simple market equilibrium models. Students are to learn the effect of a tax and subsidy on price, quantity demanded and supplied and profit of the firm under different market structure. At present we need to find these cases while studying the simple market equilibrium analysis.

Suppose the supply and demand functions are given as $q_d = 18 - 2P$ and $q_s = -6 + 8P$. Accordingly the equilibrium price is determined by setting $q_d = q_s$. This gives us equilibrium price, Rs. 2.40. At this price $q_d = q_s = 13.2$ units.

We will now assume that there is an imposition of a specific tax of Rs. 2 per unit of the product so that the demand function remaining the same, the supply function changes to q_s to include per unit tax. The new supply function becomes $q_s = -6 + 8(P - 2) = -22 + 8P$. This will be used to establish new equilibrium price. Accordingly we will get equilibrium price, P = Rs. 4, which means, the new price exceeds the pre-tax price as $4 > 2.4$. Corresponding to this price quantity demanded = quantity supplied $(18 - 2P) = (-22 + 8P) = 10$, $(10 < 13.2)$.

Thus the impact of impositioin of tax is the reduction in the quantity supplied and demanded following a rise in price of the taxed product, $10 < 13.2$. The result of the specific tax is a rise in the equilibrium price and decrease in equilibrium quantity.

Now we can examine the consequence of granting of a subsidy of Re. 1/- to the manufacturer of the product. This will alter the already established equilibrium price and quantity. When a subsidy is granted the equilibrium price can be seen to decrease and quantity demanded and supplied will rise. With the subsidy granted the supply function changes to $q_s = -6 + 8(P + 1) = 2 + 8P$. To restore equilibrium we need to equate, $q_d = q_s$ so that $2 + 8P = 18 - 2P$. This provides us with new price, P = Rs. 1.6 , [$1.6 < 2.4$]. at this price quantity demanded and supplied will be 14.8 units, $\{14.8 > 13.2\}$.

So it is established that equilibrium quantity demanded and supplied becomes larger while price is lower due to the grant of a subsidy on the product of the manufacturer.

2.8.3 Partial Market Equilibrium in case of Quadratic Functions:

If we are given the supply and demand functions as $q_s = -1 + 4P$ and $q_d = 4 - P^2$, we can find equilibrium price and quantity easily by setting $q_s = q_{d.}$ or $-1 + 4p = 4 - P^2$ or $5 - P^2 - 4P = 0$. This forms a quadratic equation, which ha to be solved to determine price. This equation can also be writen as $P^2 + 4P - 5 = 0$. Solving for P we get two values: $P = 1$ and $P = -5$. Since equilibrium price can not be negative, we have to accept the positive value of price, P = Re. 1, as the equilibrium price. At this price, deamnd = supply = 3.

2.8.4 Keynesian Income Approach

(1) From the simple Keynesian expenditure identity we get $E = Y = C + I$, which means aggregate expenditure(E) is comprised of aggregate Consumption and Investment expenditure. Let us suppose the consumption function is in the form $C = 80 + 0.8\ Y$ and $I = 100$ crores. with these information we can derive the equilibrium level of income. From this we can also derive the saving function for we know that $Y = C + S$. This simple derivation is shown below:

Since $Y = C + I$, where $C = 80 + 0.8\ Y$ and $I = 100$.

$Y = 80 + 0.8\ Y + 100$. Solving for Y we get Y = Rs. 900 crores.

Aggregate consumption is $C = 80 + 0.8\ Y$ = Rs. 800 crores.

The required saving function is obtained from $Y = C + S$ or $S = Y - C$.

Accordingly, $S = Y - 80 + 0.8\ Y = -80 + 0.2\ Y$. This is the required saving function. Total savings for the above equilibrium income is $S = -80 + 0.2\,(900) = 100$. This is found the same as the Investment expenditure. Thus $S = I$ = Rs. 100 crores is derived from the above analysis, forms saving and investment equality at the level of equilibrium income.

(2) In the simple Keynesian model of income, we can also incorporate the governmnet sector so that the income now becomes $Y = C + I + G$, where G denotes the government expenditure or purchases in the aggregate expenditure.

To have an illustration let us take an example. Suppose the full-employment income level for the economy or potential income of the country is Rs. 3500 crores. If the government expenditure is 80 crores while the consumption function is given by $C = 120 + 0.9Y$, what will be the investment expenditure that will enable the economy to produce its potential level of income Rs. 3500 crores? The solution is provided below:

For $Y = C + I + G$, we are given $G = 80$ and $C = 120 + 0.9\,Y$. The potential income is Y = Rs 3500 crores. Substituting these values we get the required levels of investment expenditure that will produce potential output as

$3500 = 120 + 0.9Y + 80 + I$ or $I = 3500 - 0.9\ (3500) - 120 - 80 = 150$ crores. An investment expenditure of Rs. 150 crores will enable the economy to reach its potential output level of Rs. 3500 crores.

EXERCISE – 2

(1) State the meaning of the following terms and differentiate them:

(a) Endogeneous and exogeneous variables.

(b) Parameter and constant.

(c) Equation and identity.

(d) General and partial equilibrium.

(e) Linear and non-linear functions.

(f) Rational and irrational numbers.

(g) Equal and equivalent sets.

(h) Union and intersection of sets.

(i) Set and subset.

(2) Express the meaning of the following terms briefly:

(a) Complement sets

(b) Venn diagram

(c) Disjoint sets

(d) Equilibrium

(e) Real number

(f) Prime number

(g) Integer

(h) Single valued function

(i) Multi-valued function

(j) Quadratic equations

(k) Polynomial functions

(3) Distinguish between the following:

(a) Implicit and explicit functions.

(b) Union and intersection of sets.

(c) Logarithmic and exponential functions.

(d) Parameter and variable.

(e) Single-valued and multi-valued functions.

(4) Graph the following functions :

(i) $y = 8 + 3x$

(ii) $S = -4 + 5P$

(iii) $D = -16 + 4P$

(iv) $Y = -\dfrac{X}{2}$

(5) Solve the following polynomial functions by either factoring and using quadratic equation:

(a) $x^2 + 4x - 5 = 0$

(b) $x^3 - 3x^2 - 4 = 0$

(c) $x^3 - 5x^2 + 4x = 0$

(6) Find equilibrium for given

(i) $q_d = q_s$, for $q_d = 5 - P^2$ and $q_s = 8P - 3$

(ii) $q_d = q_s$, for $q_d = 8 - P^2$ and $q_s = P^2 - 3$

(7) The following demand and supply functions are given as $q_d = 22 - 3P$ and $q_s = 5P - 18$, find

(a) Equilibrium price and quantity demanded and supplied.

(b) Equilibrium price and quantity when Rs. 3 of specific tax is imposed on the good.

(c) When producer is given Rs. 2 subsidy on the porduct what will be its effect on price and quantity supplied?

(8) When the potential level or full-employment is assumed to be Rs. 8000 crores, determine the government spending required if Investment is Rs. 200 crores while consumption function is $C = 150 + 0.85Y$, in the model

$Y - C + I + G.$

(9) If the savings function is $S = -88 + 0.15Y$, derive the consumption function and determine these variables for an equilibrium income of Rs. 500 crores.

(10) Given the following sets

$A_1 = \{2, 7, 6\}$, $A_2 = \{1, 2, 6\}$, $A_3 = \{4, 2, 6\}$ and $A_4 = \{2, 6\}$

Which of the following statements are true. Correct them if they are wrong.

(a) $A_1 = A_2$ *(b)* $3 \notin A_2$ *(c)* $A_1 \supset A_4$ *(d)* $A_1 = A_3$ *(e)* $A_4 \subset A_2$ *(f)* $A_2 \supset \{1,2\}$

(g) $A_1 \cup A_2 = \{1,2,4,6\}$ *(h)* $A_1 \cap A_2 = \varnothing$ *(i)* $A_3 \cap A_4 = \{4,2,6\}$

❑ ❑ ❑

3 DIFFERENTIATION : FUNCTIONS OF ONE VARIABLE CASE

3.1 What is Differentiation?

Calculus is the mathematics of change. The operation of calculus is called differentiation. It refers to finding the rate of change of a variable corresponding to a small change in the indepedent variable influencing it. When we study only one independent variable influencing the dependent variable, we obtain derivative of a function of one variable. When there is a study of several variables influencing the dependent variable, it refers to the derivative of a function of more than one variable.

In economics we study that total utility is a function of units of a good a consumer has. This can be written as $U = f(X)$, where U = utility and 'X' refers to the commodity. By finding differentiation of U with respect to X, we get the derivative of U with respect to *(w.r.t.)* X. This is $\frac{dU}{dX}$. This is also called marginal utility of X. This provides the rate of change in utility when there is a small change in quantity purchased of X. But when $U = f(X, Y)$, read as utility is the function of goods X and Y, we need to obtain differentiation of utility function either with respect to good X by keeping Y as constant or with respect to good Y by keeping X as constant. These are called partial derivatives. This refers to the differentiation of more than one independent variables.

In the present chapter, we will confine to the study of differentiations of one variable case only. We have many illustrations from economics literature, particularly microeconomics and macroeconomics that makes the study of derivative of functions of one variable quite relevant to economics. For example in Keynesian economics, aggregate consumption expenditure is a function of national income. This can be expressed in mathematical form, $C = f(Y)$ where C = Consumption expenditure while Y stands for national income.

By differentiating *C, w.r.t. Y,* we obtain $\frac{dC}{dY}$. This is called marginal propensity to consume or MPC.

It determines the slope of the consumption function. A linear consumption function is given by the equation, $C = \overline{C} + cY$, where $\overline{C}$ is the autonomous consumption expenditure, called an intercept and *'c'* stands for the slope of the consumption function or *MPC*.

Derivatives are useful in so far it furnishes a mathematical treatmnet to the microeconomic theory. For example, we can write the demand function in amathematical form, $D_x = \alpha - \beta P_x$, where D_x = demand for *'X'* commodity, while α and β are the parameters. By differentiating D_x with respect to price, P_x, we get $\frac{dD_x}{dP_x} = -\beta$. This indicates slope of this demand curve. Its negative sign dictates the slope of the demand curve to have a negative slope. This establishes an inverse relationship between price and demand. In this chapter we will anlyze differentiation of functions with one independent variable and its practical applications in economic theory.

3.2 Differentiation of a Single Variable

Differential calculus are used for finding the instantaneous rate of change of a given function. For example, when we write, $Y = f(X)$, read as *'Y'* is the function of *'X'*. When we differentiate *Y w.r.t. X*, we get $\frac{dY}{dx}$. Now we can insert change in X by ΔX (a small increment in X) so that Y will also change by ΔY and accordingly the function changes to

$$Y = f(X),$$

$$Y + \Delta Y = f(X + \Delta X), \quad \Delta Y = f(X + \Delta X) - Y \qquad [Y = f(X)]$$

or $\Delta Y = f(X + \Delta X) - f(X)$

Dividing ΔX on both sides we get

$$\frac{\Delta Y}{\Delta X} = \frac{f(X + \Delta X) - f(X)}{\Delta X}.$$ Applying limit to $\frac{\Delta Y}{\Delta X}$,

$$\lim_{\Delta X \to 0} \frac{\Delta Y}{\Delta X} = \lim_{\Delta X \to 0} \left[\frac{f(X + \Delta X) - f(X)}{\Delta X}\right] = \frac{dY}{dX} \qquad \left[\text{Since } \lim_{\Delta X \to 0} \frac{\Delta Y}{\Delta X} = \frac{dY}{dX}\right]$$

Following illustration is used to simplify this.

If $Y = 3x^2$, find $\frac{dy}{dx}$.

Since 'y' increases by Δy when x increases by Δx, we get

$y + \Delta y = 3\,(x + \Delta x)^2$

$\Delta y = 3\,(x + \Delta x)^2 - 3x^2$ as $(y = 3x^2)$

$\Delta y = 3\,[x^2 + 2x\,\Delta x + (\Delta x)^2] - 3x^2$

$\Delta y = 3x^2 + 6x\,\Delta x + 3\,(\Delta x)^2 - 3x^2 = 6x\,\Delta x + 3\,(\Delta x)^2$

$$\frac{dy}{dx} = \lim_{\Delta x \to 0} \frac{\Delta y}{\Delta x} = \frac{6x\Delta x}{\Delta x} + \frac{3(\Delta x)^2}{\Delta x} = 6x \quad [\Delta x = 0]$$

$$\therefore \text{ For } Y = 3x^2, \quad \frac{dy}{dx} = 6x$$

3.3 Rules of Differentiation

The functional relationship depicted between two variables in $y = f(x)$ is not always so simple as shown in the form $y = 3x^2$. On the contrary this relationship can take into any form. Therefore some rules of derivative or differentiation are provided to evaluate $\frac{dy}{dx}$ for different types of functions. Following important rules of differentiation are applied to evaluate $\frac{dy}{dx}$.

3.3.1 Differentiation of functions in power terms

(i) If $y = f(x) = x^5$, Find $\frac{dy}{dx}$

$$\frac{dy}{dx} = \frac{d}{dx}(x^5) = 5x^{5-1} = 5x^4$$

In general form the rule is shown as $y = x^n$

$$\frac{dy}{dx} = \frac{d}{dx}(x^n) = nx^{n-1}$$

(ii) For $y = \frac{1}{x}$, find $\frac{dy}{dx}$,

The given function is $y = \frac{1}{x} = x^{-1}$

$$\frac{dy}{dx} = \frac{d}{dx}(x^{-1}) = -1\,x^{-1-1} = -x^{-2} = -\frac{1}{x^2}$$

(iii) If $y = \sqrt{x}$, Find $\frac{dy}{dx}$.

$$y = \sqrt{x} = x^{\frac{1}{2}}, \quad \frac{dy}{dx} = \frac{d}{dx}(x^{\frac{1}{2}}) = \frac{1}{2}\,x^{\frac{1}{2}-1} = \frac{1}{2}\,x^{-\frac{1}{2}} = \frac{1}{2x^{\frac{1}{2}}} = \frac{1}{2\sqrt{x}}$$

(iv) If $y = \sqrt[3]{x^2}$, Find $\frac{dy}{dx}$.

$$y = \sqrt[3]{x^2} = x^{\frac{2}{3}},$$

$$\frac{dy}{dx} = \frac{d}{dx}(x^{\frac{2}{3}}) = \frac{2}{3}\,x^{\frac{2}{3}-1} = \frac{2}{3}\,x^{-\frac{1}{3}} = \frac{2}{3\sqrt[3]{x}}$$

3.3.2 Differentiation of a Constant

When the functional relationship is given in the form as $y = k$, where k is a constant. The rule states that derivative of a constant is zero.

Since $y = k$, it can be written as $y = k\,x^0$ (as $x^0 = 1$)

$$\therefore \frac{dy}{dx} = k\frac{d}{dx}(x^0) = k\,(0)\,x^{0-1} = 0 \therefore \text{ Derivative of a constant is zero}$$

We can apply this rule to a functions like $y = 5$.

This can be written as $y = 5x^0$,

$$\therefore \frac{dy}{dx} = 5\frac{d}{dx}(x^0) = 5\,(0)\,x^{0-1} = 0$$

However, when the variable *'x'* is multiplied by a constant, $\frac{dy}{dx}$ of the function is not zero. Here the derivative of *'y', w.r.t. 'x'* is to get multiplied by the constant. For example

(i) Given $y = 3\,x^2$, we get 3 a constant. Its derivative is evaluated as

$$\frac{dy}{dx} = 3\frac{d}{dx}(x^2) = 3\,(2x) = 6x\,.$$

(ii) For $y = a\,x^5$, Find $\frac{dy}{dx}$

$$\frac{dy}{dx} = a\frac{d}{dx}(x^5) = a\,(5)\,x^{5-1} = 5ax^4 \quad [\text{ '}a\text{' is to be taken as a constant}]$$

(iii) If $y = \frac{3}{x^2}$, Find $\frac{dy}{dx}$.

$$y = \frac{3}{x^2} = 3\,x^{-2},\quad \frac{dy}{dx} = 3\frac{d}{dx}(x^{-2}) = 3\,(-2)\,x^{-2-1} = -6\,x^{-3} = -\frac{6}{x^3}$$

(iv) or $y = \frac{2}{\sqrt[3]{x}}$, find $\frac{dy}{dx}$

$$y = \frac{2}{\sqrt[3]{x}} = \frac{2}{x^{\frac{1}{3}}} = 2x^{-\frac{1}{3}},$$

$$\frac{dy}{dx} = 2\frac{d}{dx}(x^{-\frac{1}{3}}) = 2\left(-\frac{1}{3}\right)x^{-\frac{1}{3}-1} = -\frac{2}{3}x^{-\frac{4}{3}} = -\frac{2}{3\sqrt[3]{x^4}}$$

3.3.3 Differentiation of sum or difference of a function

In general form, when $y = g(x) + f(x)$, $\frac{dy}{dx} = g'(x) + f'(x)$

where $g'(x) = \frac{d}{dx}[\,g(x)\,]$ and $f'(x) = \frac{d}{dx}[\,f'(x)\,]$

Similarly if $y = f(x) - g(x) + \phi(x)$

$$\frac{dy}{dx} = f'(x) - g'(x) + \phi'(x)$$

Illustrations:

(i) If $y = 2x^2 + 8x + 9$ find $\frac{dy}{dx}$

$$\frac{dy}{dx} = 2\frac{d}{dx}(x^2) + 8\frac{d}{dx}(x) + \frac{d}{dx}(9)$$

$$= 2(2x) + 8(1) + 0 = 4x + 8$$

(ii) If $y = \frac{1}{x^2} + 3x^5 + \sqrt{x} - 4x$, find $\frac{dy}{dx}$

$$\frac{dy}{dx} = \frac{d}{dx}\left(\frac{1}{x^2}\right) + 3\frac{d}{dx}(x^5) + \frac{d}{dx}(\sqrt{x}) - 4\frac{d}{dx}(x)$$

$$= \frac{d}{dx}(x^{-2}) + 3\frac{d}{dx}(x^5) + \frac{d}{dx}(x^{\frac{1}{2}}) - 4\frac{d}{dx}(x)$$

$$\frac{dy}{dx} = -2x^{-3} + 15x^4 + \frac{1}{2\sqrt{x}} - 4$$

(iii) If $y = u + v + w + r$, find $\frac{dy}{dx}$.

$$\frac{dy}{dx} = \frac{d}{dx}(u) + \frac{d}{dx}(v) + \frac{d}{dx}(w) + \frac{d}{dx}(r)$$

3.3.4 Differentiation of a Product (Multiplication Rule)

The general form is given by $y = g(x)\,\phi(x)$, then

$$\frac{dy}{dx} = g'(x)\,\phi(x) + \phi'(x)\,g(x)$$

Similarly if $y = g(x)\,f(x)\,\phi(x)$

$$\frac{dy}{dx} = g(x)\,f'(x)\,\phi(x) + g(x)\,f(x)\,\varphi'(x) + f(x)\,\varphi(x)\,g'(x)$$

To express the rule in a more simplified way, we can write it as

$y = uv$, so that $\frac{dy}{dx} = uv' + vu' = u\frac{dv}{dx} + v\frac{du}{dx}$

when $y = uvw$, $\frac{dy}{dx} = uv\frac{dw}{dx} + vw\frac{du}{dx} + uw\frac{dv}{dx}$

Illustrations:

(i) $y = (2x^2 + 3x)(x + z)$, find $\frac{dy}{dx}$.

Take $(2x^2 + 3x) = u$ and $(x + z) = v$

$$\frac{dy}{dx} = u\frac{dv}{dx} + v\frac{du}{dx}$$

$$= (2x^2 + 3x)\frac{d}{dx}(x+2) + (x+2)\frac{d}{dx}(2x^2 + 3x)$$

$$= (2x^2 + 3x)(1) + (x + 2)(4x + 3) = 2x^2 + 3x + 4x^2 + 3x + 8x + 6$$

$$\frac{dy}{dx} = 6x^2 + 14x + 6$$

(ii) For $y = (3x^3 + 8x^2)(x^5 + 4x^3)$ find $\frac{dy}{dx}$.

$$\frac{dy}{dx} = (3x^3 + 8x^2)\frac{d}{dx}(x^5 + 4x^3) + (x^5 + 4x^3)\frac{d}{dx}(3x^3 + 8x^2)$$

$$\frac{dy}{dx} = (3x^3 + 8x^2)(5x^4 + 12x^2) + (x^5 + 4x^3)(9x^2 + 16x)$$

(iii) If $y = (x + 2)(x^2 - 5)(x + 3x^2)$, find $\frac{dy}{dx}$

$$\frac{dy}{dx} = (x+2)(x^2-5)\frac{d}{dx}(x+3x^2) + (x+2)(x+3x^2)\frac{d}{dx}(x^2-5) + (x+3x^2)(x^2-5)\frac{d}{dx}(x+2)$$

$$= (x + 2)(x^2 - 5)(1 + 6x) + (x + 2)(x + 3x^2)(2x) + (x + 3x^2)(x^2 - 5)$$

3.3.5 Differentiation of a Quotient (division rule)

This rule is applied to evaluate derivative of y, *w.r.t.* x when y is expressed as a quotient of two functions such as:

Given $y = \frac{g(x)}{\phi(x)}$, evaluate $\frac{dy}{dx}$.

This function can be in the form $y = \frac{u}{v}$ so that $\frac{dy}{dx}$ is

$$\frac{dy}{dx} = \frac{\phi(x)\,g'(x) - g(x)\,\phi'(x)}{[\,\phi(x)\,]^2}.$$

The standard formula for $y = \frac{u}{v}$ is given as $\frac{dy}{dx} = \frac{v\frac{du}{dx} - u\frac{dv}{dx}}{v^2}$

Following illustrutions are used for simplification of this rule.

(i) For $y = \dfrac{3x^2 + 8x}{x^3 - 2x}$, Find $\dfrac{dy}{dx}$,

$$\frac{dy}{dx} = \frac{(x^3 - 2x)\frac{d}{dx}(3x^2 + 8x) - (3x^2 + 8x)\frac{d}{dx}(x^3 - 2x)}{(x^3 - 2x)^2}$$

$$\frac{dy}{dx} = \frac{(x^3 - 2x)(6x + 8) - (3x^2 + 8x)(3x^3 - 2)}{(x^3 - 2x)^2}$$

We have the freedom to apply either product rule or quotient rule for evaluating the differentiation of a given function.

For example when $y = \dfrac{1}{x\sqrt{x}}$, we can evaluate $\dfrac{dy}{dx}$ by using first product rule and then quotient rule, although same answer will be obtained from both the rules applied.

Taking, $\dfrac{1}{x} = u$, $\dfrac{1}{\sqrt{x}} = x^{-\frac{1}{2}} = v$, $\dfrac{dy}{dx} = u\dfrac{dv}{dx} + v\dfrac{du}{dx}$

$$\therefore \frac{dy}{dx} = \left(\frac{1}{x}\right)\frac{d}{dx}\left(x^{-\frac{1}{2}}\right) + \left(x^{-\frac{1}{2}}\right)\frac{d}{dx}\left(\frac{1}{x}\right) = \frac{1}{x}\left(-\frac{1}{2}x^{-\frac{3}{2}}\right) + \left(x^{-\frac{1}{2}}\right)\left(-1x^{-2}\right)$$

$$\frac{dy}{dx} = -\frac{1}{2x\,x^{\frac{3}{2}}} - \frac{1}{\sqrt{x}\,x^2} = -\frac{1}{2x^{\frac{5}{2}}} - \frac{1}{x^{\frac{5}{2}}} = \frac{-1-2}{2x^{\frac{5}{2}}} = -\frac{3}{2x^{\frac{5}{2}}}$$

Alternatively solving directly for $\dfrac{dy}{dx}$ we get

$$y = \frac{1}{x\sqrt{x}} = \frac{1}{x\,x^{\frac{1}{2}}} = \frac{1}{x^{\frac{3}{2}}} \therefore y = x^{-\frac{3}{2}}$$

$$\frac{dy}{dx} = -\frac{3}{2}x^{-\frac{3}{2}-1} = \frac{-3}{2}x^{-\frac{5}{2}} = -\frac{3}{2x^{\frac{5}{2}}}$$

By applying the first rule of derivative we got the same answer as above. Thus a given functional relationship of the type $y = f(x)$ can be solved by any rules of differentiation provided the rule is applicable to the problem.

Another illustration is given as $y = \dfrac{x^2 + 5}{x}$, find $\dfrac{dy}{dx}$

Applying quotient rule we obtain $\dfrac{dy}{dx}$ as

$$\frac{dy}{dx}=\frac{(x)\frac{d}{dx}(x^2+5)-(x^2+5)\frac{d}{dx}(x)}{x^2}$$

$$=\frac{x(2x)-(x^2+5)(1)}{x^2}=\frac{2x^2-x^2-5}{x^2}=\frac{x^2-5}{x^2}$$

The product rule is applied to the same function which is rewritten as

$y=(x^{-1})(x^2+5)$ so that

$$\frac{dy}{dx}=(x^{-1})\frac{d}{dx}(x^2+5)+(x^2+5)\frac{d}{dx}(x^{-1})$$

$$\frac{dy}{dx}=(x^{-1})(2x)+(x^2+5)(-x^{-2})=\frac{2x}{x}-\frac{(x^2+5)}{x^2}=\frac{x^2-5}{x^2}$$

3.3.6 Differentiation of roots of expression

When the function is expressed in roots, a different rule can be applied. This is named the substitution rule. This rule is applied in the following illustrations for evaluating $\frac{dy}{dx}$.

Illustrations:

(i) If $y=\sqrt{8x^2+3x+7}$

The given function can be rewritten as $y=\sqrt{u}=u^{\frac{1}{2}}$, when $8x^2+3x+7=u$.

Since $y=u^{\frac{1}{2}}$. $\therefore y=f(u)$ and $u=f(x)$ and

$$\frac{dy}{dx}=\left\{\frac{dy}{du}\right\}\left\{\frac{du}{dx}\right\}$$

$$\frac{dy}{du}=\frac{d}{du}(u^{\frac{1}{2}})=\frac{1}{2}u^{-\frac{1}{2}}=\frac{1}{2\sqrt{u}}$$, Diffentiating u we get $\frac{du}{dx}=16x+3$

$$\therefore \frac{dy}{dx}=\frac{1}{2\sqrt{8x^2+3x+7}}(16x+3)=\frac{16x+3}{2\sqrt{8x^2+3x+7}}$$

(ii) Find $\frac{dy}{dx}$, for $y=(x^3-5x^2+7)^{\frac{3}{2}}$

Take $x^3-5x^2+7=u$, so that $y=u^{\frac{3}{2}}$ and $\frac{dy}{dx}=\left\{\frac{dy}{du}\right\}\left\{\frac{du}{dx}\right\}$

$$\frac{dy}{du}=\frac{3}{2}u^{\frac{3}{2}-1}=\frac{3}{2}u^{\frac{1}{2}}=\frac{3}{2}\sqrt{u}=\frac{3}{2}\sqrt{x^3-5x^2+7}$$

$$\frac{du}{dx}=\frac{d}{dx}(x^3-5x^2+7)=3x^2-10x$$

$$\frac{dy}{dx}=\frac{dy}{du}\frac{du}{dx}=\frac{3\sqrt{x^3-5x^2+7}\;(3x^2-10x)}{2}$$

(iii) Find $\frac{dy}{dx}$, if $y=\frac{1}{\sqrt{x^3-8x+2}}$

By taking $x^3-8x+2=u$ we can write y = $u^{-\frac{1}{2}}$

$$\frac{dy}{du}=-\frac{1}{2}u^{-\frac{1}{2}-1}=-\frac{1}{2}u^{-\frac{3}{2}}=-\frac{1}{2\sqrt{u^3}} \text{ and } \frac{du}{dx}=\frac{d}{dx}(x^3-8x+2)=3x^2-8$$

$$\therefore \frac{dy}{dx}=\frac{dy}{du}\frac{du}{dx}=-\frac{1}{2\sqrt{(x^3-8x+2)^3}}(3x^2-8)=-\frac{(3x^2-8)}{2\sqrt{(x^3-8x+2)^3}}$$

(iv) Find $\frac{dy}{dx}$, for $y=\frac{x+3}{\sqrt{x+1}}$

$$y=\frac{x+3}{\sqrt{x+1}}=\frac{x+3}{(x+1)^{\frac{1}{2}}}.$$

We can apply the rule $y=\frac{u}{v}$ so that $\frac{dy}{dx}=\frac{v\frac{du}{dx}-u\frac{dv}{dx}}{v^2}$

$$\frac{dy}{dx}=\frac{(x+1)^{\frac{1}{2}}\frac{d}{dx}(x+3)-(x+3)\frac{d}{dx}(x+1)^{\frac{1}{2}}}{\left[(x+1)^{\frac{1}{2}}\right]^2}=\frac{(x+1)^{\frac{1}{2}}(1)-(x+3)\frac{1}{2}(x+1)^{-\frac{1}{2}}(1)}{(x+1)}$$

$$=\frac{\sqrt{x+1}-\frac{x+3}{2\sqrt{x+1}}}{(x+1)}=\frac{\frac{2(\sqrt{x+1})(\sqrt{x+1})-(x+3)}{2\sqrt{x+1}}}{x+1}=\frac{2(x+1)-(x+3)}{2(x+1)\;(x+1)^{\frac{1}{2}}}=\frac{2x+2-x-3}{2(x+1)^{1+\frac{1}{2}}}$$

$$\frac{dy}{dx} = \frac{x-1}{2(x+1)^{\frac{3}{2}}} = \frac{x-1}{2\sqrt{(x+1)^3}}$$

We will now evaluate the same problem using the product rule. We get the same answer when this rule is aplied.

$$y = \frac{x+3}{\sqrt{x+1}} = (x+1)^{-\frac{1}{2}}.(x+3)$$

$$\frac{dy}{dx} = (x+1)^{-\frac{1}{2}}\frac{d}{dx}(x+3) + (x+3)\frac{d}{dx}(x+1)^{-\frac{1}{2}} = (x+1)^{-\frac{1}{2}} + (x+3)\left(-\frac{1}{2}\right)(x+1)^{-\frac{1}{2}-1} \quad (1)$$

$$\frac{dy}{dx} = \frac{1}{\sqrt{x+1}} - \frac{(x+3)}{2(x+1)^{\frac{3}{2}}} = \frac{2(x+1)-(x+3)}{2\left(\sqrt{x+1}\right)^3(x+1)} = \frac{2x+2-x-3}{2(x+1)^{\frac{3}{2}}} = \frac{x-1}{2\sqrt{(x+1)^3}}$$

(v) Find $\frac{dy}{dx}$, for $y = (2x^2+8)^3(x^3+5x)^2$

$$\frac{dy}{dx} = (2x^2+8)^3\frac{d}{dx}(x^3+5x)^2 + (x^3+5x)^2\frac{d}{dx}(2x^2+8)^3$$

$$= (2x^2+8)^3\,2(x^3+5x)(3x^2+5) + (x^3+5x)^2\,3(2x^3+8)^2(4x)$$

$$\frac{dy}{dx} = 2(2x^2+8)^3(x^3+5x)(3x^2+5) + 12x(x^3+5x)^2(2x^2+8)^2$$

(vi) If $y = (x^2-1)^3(x^3+1)^2$, find $\frac{dy}{dx}$

$$\frac{dy}{dx} = (x^2-1)^3\frac{d}{dx}(x^3+1)^2 + (x^3+1)^2\frac{d}{dx}(x^2-1)^3$$

$$= (x^2-1)^3\,2(x^3+1)(3x^2) + (x^3+1)^2\,3(x^2-1)^2(2x)$$

$$\frac{dy}{dx} = 6x^2(x^2-1)^3(x^3+1) + 6x(x^3+1)^2(x^2-1)^2$$

(vii) If $y = \sqrt[3]{(5+x^2)^2}$, find $\frac{dy}{dx}$.

Take Take $y = \sqrt[3]{u^2}$, and $u = 5+x^2$, $\quad \therefore \frac{dy}{dx} = \frac{dy}{du}\cdot\frac{du}{dx}$.

For $y = u^{\frac{2}{3}}, \frac{dy}{du} = \frac{2}{3}u^{\frac{2}{3}-1} = \frac{2}{3}u^{-\frac{1}{3}} = \frac{2}{3}(5+x^2)^{-\frac{1}{3}} = \frac{2}{3\sqrt[3]{(5+x^2)}}$ and $\frac{du}{dx} = 2x$

$$\therefore \frac{dy}{dx} = \frac{2}{3\sqrt[3]{(5+x^2)}}(2x) = \frac{4x}{3\sqrt[3]{(5+x^2)}}$$

3.3.7 Derivative of a Function of a Function: Chain Rule

When variables *'y'* and *'x'* are not directly related, we need to apply the chain rule.

If $y = f(z)$ and $z = f(x)$, then, $\dfrac{dy}{dx} = \dfrac{dy}{dz} \cdot \dfrac{dz}{dx}$

Illustrations:

(i) If $y = z^3 + 3z^2$ and $z = x^2$,

$\dfrac{dy}{dx} = \dfrac{dy}{dz} \cdot \dfrac{dz}{dx} = (3z^2 + 6z)(2x)$. By substituting $z = x^2$ we get

$$\frac{dy}{dx} = \left[3(x^2)^2 + 6(x^2)\right]2x = (3x^4 + 6x^2)(2x) = 6x^5 + 12x^3$$

The general form of the chain rule is that for $y = f(u)$ and $u = g(x)$

$$\frac{dy}{dx} = \frac{dy}{du} \cdot \frac{du}{dx} = f'(u)\, g'(x) = \frac{d}{du}[\, f(u)\,] \frac{d}{dx}[\, g(x)\,]$$

(ii) If $y = x^3 + 3x$ and $z = y^2 + 5$, find $\dfrac{dz}{dx}$.

Applying chain rule we get $\dfrac{dz}{dx} = \dfrac{dz}{dy} \cdot \dfrac{dy}{dx}$

$\dfrac{dz}{dy} = \dfrac{d}{dy}(y^2 + 5) = 2y$ and $\dfrac{dy}{dx} = \dfrac{d}{dx}(x^3 + 3x) = 3x^2 + 3$

$$\frac{dz}{dx} = 2y\,(3x^2 + 3) = 2(x^3 + 3x)\,(3x^2 + 3) = 2\left[\, 3x^5 + 3x^3 + 9x^3 + 9x \,\right]$$

$$\therefore \frac{dz}{dx} = 6x^5 + 24x^3 + 18x$$

(iii) Find the differentiation of the function *'t', with respect to 'x'* for given $y = x^2 + 4x$ and $t = 3y^2 + 5$.

We are required to find $\dfrac{dt}{dx}$. For this the formula is $\dfrac{dt}{dx} = \dfrac{dt}{dy} \cdot \dfrac{dy}{dx}$

$\dfrac{dt}{dy} = \dfrac{d}{dy}(3y^2 + 5) = 6y = 6\,(x^2 + 4x)$ and $\dfrac{dy}{dx} = \dfrac{d}{dx}(x^2 + 4x) = 2x + 4$

$$\therefore \frac{dt}{dx} = 6\,(x^2 + 4x)\,(2x + 4) = 12x^3 + 72x^2 + 96x$$

3.3.8 For inverse relation we can apply the following rule to find $\frac{dy}{dx}$

We have evaluated $\frac{dy}{dx}$ when the expression of a function is given in the form $y = f(x)$. But when *we* are given $x = f(y)$, then we need to apply the inverse relation to find $\frac{dy}{dx}$, where $\frac{dy}{dx} = \frac{1}{dx/dy}$

Alternatively the given function need to be changed to get it in the form $y = f(x)$ to apply the rule $\frac{dy}{dx}$.

Following illustrations are used to simplify this evaluation.

(i) If $x = y^3$, find $\frac{dy}{dx}$

Differentiating both sides *w.r.t.* x obtain

$$\frac{dx}{dx} = \frac{d}{dx}(y^3) \text{ or } 1 = 3y^2\frac{dy}{dx} \text{ or } \frac{dy}{dx} = \frac{1}{3y^2}.$$

Otherwise by changing the function in the form $y = f(x)$ we get

$$x = y^3 \quad \therefore y = \sqrt[3]{x} = x^{\frac{1}{3}} \text{ and } y^2 = \left(x^{\frac{1}{3}}\right)^2 = x^{\frac{2}{3}}$$

$$\therefore \frac{dy}{dx} = \frac{1}{3y^2} = \frac{1}{3x^{\frac{2}{3}}} = \frac{1}{3\sqrt[3]{x^2}}, \text{ since } y^2 = x^{\frac{2}{3}}$$

(ii) If $x^2 + y^2 = 4$ find $\frac{dy}{dx}$.

Given $x^2 + y^2 = 4$, we get $y^2 = 4 - x^2$ and

$$y = \pm\sqrt{4 - x^2}$$

$$\frac{dy}{dx} = \pm\frac{d}{dx}(4 - x^2)^{\frac{1}{2}} = \pm\frac{1}{2}(4 - x^2)^{-\frac{1}{2}}(-2x)$$

$$\frac{dy}{dx} = \pm\frac{-2x}{2\sqrt{4 - x^2}} = \pm\frac{-x}{\sqrt{4 - x^2}}$$

(iii) If $xy = 8$ find $\frac{dy}{dx}$

For $xy = 8$, $y = \frac{8}{x}$, $\frac{dy}{dx} = 8\frac{d}{dx}\left(\frac{1}{x}\right) = 8(-1)x^{-2} = -\frac{8}{x^2}$

(iv) Find $\frac{dy}{dx}$ if $x = kt^3$ and $y = 3kt$

We need to evaluate it in the form $\frac{dy}{dx} = \frac{dy}{dt} \cdot \frac{dt}{dx}$

From $x = kt^3$ we will get $\frac{dx}{dt}$ and than $\frac{dt}{dx} = \frac{1}{dx/dt}$

$$\therefore \frac{dy}{dx} = \frac{dy}{dt} \cdot \frac{dt}{dx} = \frac{dy}{dt} \cdot \frac{1}{dx/dt}$$

$$\frac{dy}{dt} = \frac{d}{dt}(y) = \frac{d}{dt}(3kt) = 3k \text{ and } \frac{dx}{dt} = \frac{d}{dt}(x) = \frac{d}{dt}(kt^3) = 3kt^2$$

$$\therefore \frac{dy}{dx} = (3k)\frac{1}{3kt^2} = \frac{1}{t^2}$$

3.3.9 Differentiation of Logarithmic Functions

The natural logarithm is shown as $ln\, x$ for all positive x.

The derivative of $\log_e x$ is written as $ln\, x$. Its derivative is evaluated as

$$\frac{d}{dx}(\log_e x) = \frac{1}{x} \cdot \frac{dx}{dx} = \frac{1}{x}$$

The general form of logarithmic function is $y = \log_e u$ and

$$\frac{dy}{dx} = \frac{1}{u} \cdot \frac{du}{dx}, \text{ where } u = f(x)$$

Illustrations:

(i) If $y = \log_e(x^2 + 3x)$, find $\frac{dy}{dx}$

Taking $y = \log_e u$, where $u = (x^2 + 3x)$,

$$\frac{dy}{dx} = \frac{1}{u} \cdot \frac{d}{dx}(u)$$

$$\frac{dy}{dx} = \frac{1}{(x^2 + 3x)} \frac{d}{dx}(x^2 + 3x) = \frac{2x + 3}{(x^2 + 3x)}$$

(ii) If $y = \log_e x^2$ find $\frac{dy}{dx}$

$$\frac{dy}{dx} = \frac{1}{x^2}\frac{d}{dx}(x^2) = \frac{2x}{x^2} = \frac{2}{x}$$

(iii) *(a)* If $y = \log_e f(x) + \log_e g(x)$, find $\frac{dy}{dx}$

$$\frac{dy}{dx} = \frac{1}{f(x)}\frac{d}{dx}[\,f(x)\,] + \frac{1}{g(x)}\frac{d}{dx}[\,g(x)\,]$$

If $y = \log_e \frac{f(x)}{g(x)}$, find $\frac{dy}{dx}$.

The above function can be written as $y = \log_e f(x) - \log_e g(x)$

The rule is that $\log_e \frac{a}{b} = \log_e a - \log_e b$ and $\log_e ab = \log_e a + \log_e b$

(b) If $y = \log_e g(x)\ \phi(x)$, it can be written $y = \log_e g(x) + \log_e \phi(x)$

$$\frac{dy}{dx} = \frac{1}{g(x)}\frac{d}{dx}[\,g(x)\,] + \frac{1}{\phi(x)}\frac{d}{dx}[\,\phi(x)\,]$$

(c) If $y = [\log_e f(x)]^n$, we can also write as $y = n \log_e f(x)$

$$\frac{dy}{dx} = n\frac{1}{f(x)}\frac{d}{dx}[\,f(x)\,]$$

(d) If $y = \log_a u = \frac{\log_e u}{\log_e a} = \frac{1}{\log_e a}\log_e u$

$$\frac{dy}{dx} = \frac{1}{\log_e a}\frac{d}{dx}\log_e u = \frac{1}{\log_e a}\cdot\frac{1}{u}\cdot\frac{du}{dx}$$

Following illustrations are used to simplify the derivative of logarithmic functions:

(1) If $y = \log_e x^3$, find $\frac{dy}{dx}$

$$\frac{dy}{dx} = \frac{1}{x^3}\frac{d}{dx}(x^3) = \frac{3x^2}{x^3} = \frac{3}{x}$$

(2) If $y = 8 \log_e x^2$, find $\frac{dy}{dx}$

$$\frac{dy}{dx} = 8\frac{1}{x^2}\frac{d}{dx}(x^2) = \frac{(8)(2x)}{x^2} = \frac{16}{x}$$

(3) If $y = \log_a x^3$, find $\frac{dy}{dx}$.

We can also write $\log_a x^3 = \frac{\log_e x^3}{\log_e a} = \frac{1}{\log_e a}\log_e x^3$

$$\frac{dy}{dx} = \frac{1}{\log_e a}\frac{d}{dx}(\log_e x^3) = \frac{1}{\log_e a}\cdot\frac{1}{x^3}\frac{d}{dx}(x^3) = \frac{3x^2}{\log_e a\, x^3} = \frac{3}{x \log_e a}$$

(4) $y = \log_7 x^2$, find $\frac{dy}{dx}$

We can write $y = \log_7 x^2 = \frac{\log_e x^2}{\log_e 7}$

$$\therefore \frac{dy}{dx} = \frac{1}{\log_e 7}\frac{d}{dx}\left[\log_e x^2\right] = \frac{2x}{\log_e 7x^2} = \frac{2}{x \log_e 7}$$

(5) $y = (\log_e x)^3$, find $\frac{dy}{dx}$

$y = (\log_e x)^3 = 3 \log_e x$

$$\frac{dy}{dx} = 3\frac{1}{x}\frac{dx}{dx} = \frac{3}{x}$$

(6) For $y = a^x$, find $\frac{dy}{dx}$.

We can solve this $y = a^x$ by introducing log on both sides as:

$\log_e y = \log_e a^x = x \log_a a$

$$\frac{1}{y}\cdot\frac{dy}{dx} = x\frac{d}{dx}(\log_e a) + \log_e a\frac{d}{dx}(x)$$

$$= x\cdot\frac{1}{a}\cdot\frac{d}{dx}(a) + \log_e a\,(1) = 0 + \log_e a = \log_e a$$

$$\therefore \frac{1}{y}\frac{dy}{dx} = \log_e a \text{ and } \frac{dy}{dx} = y \log_e a = a^x \log_e a$$

(7) $y = x^x$ find $\frac{dy}{dx}$

Introducing log both sides we get, $\log_e y = x \log_e x$

$$\frac{1}{y}\frac{dy}{dx} = x\frac{d}{dx}(\log_e x) + \log_e x\frac{d}{dx}(x) = x\frac{1}{x} + \log_e x$$

$$\frac{1}{y}\frac{dy}{dx} = 1 + \log_e x, \quad \frac{dy}{dx} = x^x(1 + \log_e x)$$

(8) $y = 7^x$, find $\frac{dy}{dx}$

Introducing log both sides, $\log_e y = x \log_e 7$,

$$\frac{1}{y}\frac{dy}{dx} = x\frac{d}{dx}(\log_e 7) + \log_e 7\frac{d}{dx}(x) = x\frac{1}{7}\frac{d}{dx}(7) + \log_e 7$$

$$\frac{1}{y}\frac{dy}{dx} = 0 + \log_e 7 = \log_e 7 \quad \frac{dy}{dx} = y\log_e 7 = 7^x \log_e 7$$

(9) $y = \log_e(ax^2 + bx + c)$, find $\frac{dy}{dx}$

$$\frac{dy}{dx} = \frac{1}{(ax^2+bx+c)}\frac{d}{dx}(ax^2+bx+c) = \frac{2ax+b}{ax^2+bx+c}$$

(10) $y = \log_e(x + 5)(x - 2)$, find $\frac{dy}{dx}$

$y = \log_e(x + 5)(x - 2) = \log_e(x + 5) + \log_e(x - 2)$

$$\frac{dy}{dx} = \frac{1}{x+5}\frac{d}{dx}(x+5) + \frac{1}{x-2}\frac{d}{dx}(x-2)$$

$$\frac{dy}{dx} = \frac{1}{x+5} + \frac{1}{x-2}$$

(11) $y = (x^3+3)\log_e(x^2+1)$, find $\frac{dy}{dx}$

$$\frac{dy}{dx} = (x^3+3)\frac{d}{dx}\left[\log_e(x^2+1)\right] + \log_e(x^2+1)\frac{d}{dx}(x^3+3)$$

$$= \frac{(x^3+3)(2x)}{(x^2+1)} + \log_e(x^2+1)(3x^2)$$

$$\frac{dy}{dx} = \frac{2x^4+6x+3x^2(x^2+1)\log_e(x^2+1)}{(x^2+1)}$$

(12) $y = \log_e \sqrt{5-x^2}$, find $\frac{dy}{dx}$

$$y = \log_e \sqrt{5-x^2} = \log_e (5-x^2)^{\frac{1}{2}}$$

$$\frac{dy}{dx} = \frac{1}{\sqrt{5-x^2}} \frac{d}{dx}(5-x^2)^{\frac{1}{2}}$$

$$= \frac{\frac{1}{2}(5-x^2)^{\frac{-1}{2}}(-2x)}{\sqrt{5-x^2}} = \frac{-2x}{2\sqrt{5-x^2}\ \sqrt{5-x^2}}$$

$$\frac{dy}{dx} = -\frac{x}{(5-x^2)}$$

(13) For $y = e^x \log_e x$

$$\frac{dy}{dx} = e^x \frac{d}{dx} \log_e x + \log_e x \frac{d}{dx} e^x$$

$$\frac{dy}{dx} = \frac{e^x}{x} + e^x \log_e x = e^x \left[\frac{1}{x} + \log_e x \right]$$

3.3.10 Derivative of Exponential Functions

The exponential and logarithmic expression of a function have a definite relationship. The inverse of $y = \log_e x$ is the exponential. Therefore when $x = e^y$, $y = \log_e x$ The rules for exponential function are provided for evaluating $\frac{dy}{dx}$. When $y = e^x$ the formula for finding $\frac{dy}{dx}$ is provided.

We can solve this by using the first principle of differentiation as:

Given $y = e^x$, $y + \Delta y = e^{x+\Delta x}$

$$\Delta y = e^{x+\Delta x} - y = e^{x+\Delta x} - e^x$$

$$\Delta y = e^x e^{\Delta x} - e^x = e^x \left[e^{\Delta x} - 1 \right]$$

$$e^{\Delta x} - 1 = \left[1 + \Delta x + \frac{\Delta x^2}{2} + \cdots\cdots - 1 \right]$$

$$\frac{\Delta y}{\Delta x} = e^x \left[\frac{1}{\Delta x} + \frac{\Delta x}{\Delta x} + \frac{\Delta x^2}{2} + \cdots\cdots - \frac{1}{\Delta x} \right]$$

$$\lim_{\Delta x \to 0} \frac{\Delta y}{\Delta x} = \frac{dy}{dx} = e^x \left[0 + 1 + 0 \cdots\cdots + 0 \right]. \ \frac{dy}{dx} = e^x \ (1) = e^x$$

The standard formula used for finding $\frac{dy}{dx}$ in case of exponential functions is shown as:

If $y = e^{x^2}$, $\frac{dy}{dx} = e^{x^2} \frac{d}{dx}(x^2) = 2x\, e^{x^2}$

Illustrations:

(i) For $y = e^{x^2 + 3x + 4}$ find $\frac{dy}{dx}$

$$\frac{dy}{dx} = e^{x^2+3x+4} \frac{d}{dx}(x^2 + 3x + 4) = (2x+3)e^{x^2+3x+4}$$

(ii) For $y = x^{-2} e^{x2}$ find $\frac{dy}{dx}$

$$\frac{dy}{dx} = x^{-2} \frac{d}{dn}(e^{x^2}) + e^{x^2} \frac{d}{dx}(x^{-2}) = x^{-2} e^{x^2}(2x) + e^{x^2}(-2)\, x^{-3}$$

$$\frac{dy}{dx} = \frac{2x\, e^{x^2}}{x^2} - \frac{2\, e^{x^2}}{x^3} = \frac{2\, e^{x^2}}{x} - \frac{2\, e^{x^2}}{x^3}$$

(iii) For $y = e^{x}$ find $\frac{dy}{dx}$ and show that $\frac{dy}{dx} + y = 0$.

$$\frac{dy}{dx} = e^{-x} \frac{d}{dx}(-x) = e^{-x}(-1) = -e^{-x}$$

Since $\frac{dy}{dx} = -e^{-x}$, $y = e^{-x}$, $-y = -e^{-x}$

$$\frac{dy}{dx} + y = e^{-x} + e^{-x} = 0 \text{ or } \frac{dy}{dx} = e^{-x} = -y \text{ or } \frac{dy}{dx} + y = 0$$

(iv) For $y = e^{x^3+2x} \log_e (3x^3 + 5x)$

$$\frac{dy}{dx} = \log_e (3x^3 + 5x) \frac{d}{dx} e^{x^3+2x} + e^{x^3+2x} \frac{d}{dx} \log_e (3x^3 + 5x)$$

$$= \log_e (3x^3 + 5x)\, e^{x^3+2x} (3x^2 + 2) + e^{x^3+2x} \frac{1}{(3x^3 + 5x)} (9x^2 + 5)$$

$$\frac{dy}{dx} = (3x^2 + 2) \log_e (3x^3 + 5x)\, e^{x^3+2x} + \frac{(9x^2 + 5)\, e^{x^3+2x}}{(3x^3 + 5x)}$$

(v) $y=\sqrt{\frac{1-x}{1+x}}$ find $\frac{dy}{dx}$

Introducing log on both sides

$$\log_e y=\log_e\sqrt{\frac{1-x}{1+x}}=\log_e\left(\frac{1-x}{1+x}\right)^{\frac{1}{2}}$$

$$\frac{1}{y}\frac{dy}{dx}=\frac{1}{2}\frac{d}{dx}\log_e\left(\frac{1-x}{1+x}\right)$$

$$=\frac{1}{2}\left[\frac{d}{dx}\log_e(1-x)-\frac{d}{dx}\log_e(1+x)\right]$$

$$\frac{dy}{dx}=\frac{y}{2}\left[\frac{-1}{1-x}-\frac{1}{1+x}\right]=\frac{y}{2}\left[\frac{-(1+x)-(1-x)}{(1-x)(1+x)}\right]=-\frac{y}{(1-x^2)}$$

(vi) For $y=\left(1-\sqrt{x}\right)\left(1+\sqrt{x}\right)$, find $\frac{dy}{dx}$

Given $y=\left(1-\sqrt{x}\right)\left(1+\sqrt{x}\right)$, $y=1-x$ and

$\frac{dy}{dx}=-1$. Alternatively we can also solve this problem by using product rule.

For $y=\left(1-\sqrt{x}\right)\left(1+\sqrt{x}\right)$,

$$\frac{dy}{dx}=\left(1-\sqrt{x}\right)\frac{d}{dx}\left(1+\sqrt{x}\right)+\left(1-\sqrt{x}\right)\frac{d}{dx}\left(1-\sqrt{x}\right)$$

$$=\left(1-\sqrt{x}\right)\frac{1}{2}x^{-1/2}+\left(1+\sqrt{x}\right)\left(-\frac{1}{2}x^{-1/2}\right)$$

$$=\frac{1-\sqrt{x}}{2\sqrt{x}}+\frac{1+\sqrt{x}}{2\sqrt{x}}=\frac{1-\sqrt{x}-x-\sqrt{x}}{2\sqrt{x}}=\frac{2\sqrt{x}}{2\sqrt{x}}=-1$$

(vii) For $y=a^{x^3}$, find $\frac{dy}{dx}$.

Introducing log both sides we get, $\log_e y=x^3\log_e a$

$$\frac{1}{y}\frac{dy}{dx}=x^3\frac{d}{dx}\log_e a+\log_e a\frac{d}{dx}x^3$$

$$\frac{1}{y}\frac{dy}{dx}=3x^2\log_e a$$

$$\frac{dy}{dx} = y3x^2 \log_e a = 3x^2 a^{x^3} \log_e a$$

(viii) For $y = 5^{x^x}$, find $\frac{dy}{dx}$.

Given $y = 5^{x^x}$, $\log_e y = x^x \log_e 5$

$$\frac{1}{y}\frac{dy}{dx} = \frac{d}{dx}\left[x^x \log_e 5 \right]$$

$$\frac{dy}{dx} = y\frac{d}{dx}\left[x^x \log_e 5\right] = y\left[x^x \frac{d}{dx}\log_e 5 + \log_e 5 \frac{d}{dx} x^x \right]$$

$$= y\left[\log_e 5 \frac{d}{dx} x^x \right] = 5^{x^x} [\log_e 5(1+\log_e x)]$$

(ix) For $y = x^x$, find $\frac{dy}{dx}$.

Given $y = x^x$, $\log_e y = x \log_e x$

$$\frac{1}{y}\frac{dy}{dx} = \frac{d}{dx}[x \log_e x] = x\frac{d}{dx}\log_e x + \log_e x \frac{d}{dx} x$$

$$\frac{1}{y}\frac{dy}{dx} = \frac{x}{x} + \log_e x = 1 + \log_e x$$

$$\frac{dy}{dx} = y(1+\log_e x) = x^x(1+\log_e x)$$

(x) For $y = 7^x + x^7 + e^x$ find $\frac{dy}{dx}$.

$$\frac{dy}{dx} = 7^x \log_e 7 + 7x^6 + e^x$$

3.3.11 Derivative of Implicit Functions

Many times 'x' and 'y' variables are not related in the form $y = f(x)$ so that the right hand side contains only 'x' and the left hand side contains only 'y'. For this type of functions it is difficult to solve explicitly for 'y' in terms of 'x' while finding $\frac{dy}{dx}$. This function is called implicit function. This is in the form of $f(x, y) = 0$. The functional relationship between 'x' and 'y' are such that they are not independent of each other since either variable determines the other variable due to the existence of their mutual relationsip.

From this type of function two different explicit functions can be fromed. These are $y = f(x)$ and $x = \phi(y)$. However it is not always possible to derive an explicit function from a simple implicit function.The differentiation of an implicit function is different. Following illustrations can be used to explain the process of differentiating this type of functions. These functions are to be differentiated term by term for finding $\frac{dy}{dx}$.

For example, $xy^2 + xy - 5 = 0$, $x^2 + y^3 = 1$, $x^2 + xy + y + 7 = 0$ are all implicit functions.

Illustrations:

(i) Find $\frac{dy}{dx}$ for the function $x^3y + y^2 - 5x = 0$

Given the function $x^3y + y^2 + 5x = 0$, differntiating term by term we get

$$x^3\frac{dy}{dx} + y\frac{d}{dx}(x^3) + \frac{d}{dx}(y^2) - 5\frac{d}{dx}(x) = 0$$

or $x^3\frac{dy}{dx} + y(3x^2) + 2y\frac{dy}{dx} - 5(1) = 0$

or $x^3\frac{dy}{dx} + 3x^2y + 2y\frac{dy}{dx} - 5 = 0$

or $\frac{dy}{dx}(x^3 + 2y) = 5 - 3x^2y$ and $\frac{dy}{dx} = \frac{5 - 3x^2y}{x^3 + 2y}$

(ii) Given $x^2 + y^2 - 3x = 8y$, find $\frac{dy}{dx}$

For given $x^2 + y^2 - 3x = 8y$, differentiating each term we get

$\frac{d}{dx}(x^2) + \frac{d}{dx}(y^2) - 3\frac{d}{dx}(x) = 8\frac{d}{dx}(y)$ or $2x + 2y\frac{dy}{dx} - 3 = 8\frac{dy}{dx}$

or $2y\frac{dy}{dx} - 8\frac{dy}{dx} = 3 - 2x$ or $\frac{dy}{dx}(2y - 8) = 3 - 2x$

$$\frac{dy}{dx} = \frac{3 - 2x}{2y - 8}$$

(iii) Find $\frac{dy}{dx}$ for $x^2 + y^2 = K^2$,

Differentiating each term we get $\frac{d}{dx}(x^2) + \frac{d}{dx}(y^2) = \frac{d}{dx}(k^2)$

$2x + 2y\frac{dy}{dx} = 0$ or $2y\frac{dy}{dx} = -2x$

$$\therefore \frac{dy}{dx} = \frac{-2x}{2y} = -\frac{x}{y}$$

(iv) Find $\frac{dy}{dx}$ for $4x^3 + x^2y - 6xy^2 - 4y^3 = 8$

Differentiating each term,

$$4\frac{d}{dx}(x^3) + x^2\frac{dy}{dx} + y\frac{d}{dx}(x^2) - 6x\frac{d}{dx}(y^2) - 6y^2\frac{d}{dx}(x) - 4\frac{d}{dx}(y^3) = \frac{d}{dx}(8)$$

$$12x^2 + x^2\frac{dy}{dx} + 2xy - 12xy\frac{dy}{dx} - 6y^2 - 12y^2\frac{dy}{dx} = 0$$

$$\frac{dy}{dx}(x^2 - 12xy - 12y^2) = 6y^2 - 2xy - 12x^2$$

$$\frac{dy}{dx} = \frac{6y^2 - 2xy - 12x^2}{(x^2 - 12xy - 12y^2)}$$

(v) For $7x^2 = y^3$ find $\frac{dy}{dx}$

Differentiating term by term we get,

$$7\frac{d}{dx}(x^2) = \frac{d}{dx}(y^3) \text{ or } 14x = 3y^2\frac{dy}{dx},$$

$$\frac{dy}{dx} = \frac{14x}{3y^2}$$

(vi) Find $\frac{dy}{dx}$ for $\sqrt{x} + \sqrt{y} = \sqrt{k}$

For $\sqrt{x} + \sqrt{y} = \sqrt{k} = (x)^{\frac{1}{2}} + (y)^{\frac{1}{2}} = k^{\frac{1}{2}}$, Differentiating term by term we get,

$$\frac{d}{dx}\left(x^{\frac{1}{2}}\right) + \frac{d}{dx}\left(y^{\frac{1}{2}}\right) = \frac{d}{dx}\left(k^{\frac{1}{2}}\right)$$

$$\text{or } \frac{1}{2}x^{-\frac{1}{2}} + \frac{1}{2}y^{-\frac{1}{2}}\frac{dy}{dx} = 0 \text{ or } \frac{1}{2\sqrt{x}} + \frac{1}{2\sqrt{y}}\frac{dy}{dx} = 0$$

$$\text{or } \frac{1}{2\sqrt{y}}\frac{dy}{dx} = -\frac{1}{2\sqrt{x}} \text{ and}$$

$$\frac{dy}{dx} = -\frac{2\sqrt{y}}{2\sqrt{x}} = \frac{-\sqrt{y}}{\sqrt{x}} = -\sqrt{\frac{y}{x}}$$

(vii) For $7x^2 = y^3$. Find $\frac{dy}{dx}$ and $\frac{dx}{dy}$ and prove that $\frac{dy}{dx}\frac{dx}{dy} = 1$

$$7\frac{d}{dx}(x^2) = \frac{d}{dx}(y^3) \text{ or } 14x = 3y^2\frac{dy}{dx} \text{ or } \frac{dy}{dx} = \frac{14x}{3y^2}$$

From the same function $7x^2 = y^3$, we obtain $\frac{dx}{dy}$ as

$$7\frac{d}{dy}(x^2) = \frac{d}{dy}(y^3). \text{ or } 14x\frac{dx}{dy} = 3y^2 \text{ or } \frac{dx}{dy} = \frac{3y^2}{14x}$$

$$\therefore \left(\frac{dy}{dx}\right)\left(\frac{dx}{dy}\right) = \left(\frac{14x}{3y^2}\right)\left(\frac{3y^2}{14x}\right) = 1, \text{ proved}$$

(viii) If $(x-y)^2 = (2x+5)^2$ find $\frac{dy}{dx}$ and $\frac{dx}{dy}$. Prove that $\frac{dy}{dx}\frac{dx}{dy} = 1$

Given $(x-y)^2 = (2x+5)^2$. Differentiating term by term we get

$$2(x-y)\frac{d}{dx}(x) + 2(x-y)\frac{d}{dx}(-y) = 2(2x+5)\frac{d}{dx}(2x) + 2(2x+5)\frac{d}{dx}(5)$$

or $2(x-y) - 2(x-y)\frac{dy}{dx} = 4(2x+5) + 0$

or $-2(x-y)\frac{dy}{dx} = 4(2x+5) - 2(x-y) = 6x + 2y + 20$

$$\frac{dy}{dx} = \frac{6x+2y+20}{2(y-x)} = \frac{2(3x+y+10)}{2(y-x)} = \frac{3x+y+10}{(y-x)}$$

We will evaluate $\frac{dx}{dy}$ from this function $(x-y)^2 = (2x+5)^2$

$$2(x-y)\frac{dx}{dy} + 2(x-y)\frac{d}{dy}(-y) = 2(2x+5)\frac{d}{dy}(2x) + 0$$

or $2(x-y)\frac{dx}{dy} - 2(x-y) = 4(2x+5)\frac{dx}{dy}$

$$2(x-y)\frac{dx}{dy} - 4(2x+5)\frac{dx}{dy} = 2(x-y)$$

$$\frac{dx}{dy}\left[2(x-y) - 4(2x+5)\right] = 2(x-y)$$

$$\frac{dx}{dy}\left[2x - 2y - 8x - 20\right] = 2(x-y)$$

$$\frac{dx}{dy} = \frac{2(x-y)}{-6x-2y-20} = \frac{-2(y-x)}{-2(3x+y+10)} = \frac{y-x}{3x+y+10}$$

$$\left(\frac{dy}{dx}\right)\left(\frac{dx}{dy}\right) = \left[\frac{(3x+y+10)}{(y-x)}\right]\left[\frac{(y-x)}{(3x+y+10)}\right] = 1$$

So it is proved that for the given function $(x-y)^2 = (2x+5)^2$, $\frac{dy}{dx}\frac{dx}{dy} = 1$

3.4. Higher Order Derivatives and their Significance in Economics

The functional relationship between two variables '*x*' and '*y*' can be shown in any form. It's general expression is $y = f(x)$.

The expression $\frac{dy}{dx}$ is the derivative of 'y', with respect to 'x'. It measures the rate of charge in 'y' due to a small change in 'x' variable. But we can also evaluate the derivative of a derivative and this is referred to its higher order derivatives.

Thus if $y = 18x^3$, $\frac{dy}{dx} = 54x^2$ is the first order derivative of 'y', *w.r.t.* 'x'. This derivative measures the rate of change in 'y' variable *w.r.t.* 'x'.

The second order derivative is $\frac{d^2y}{dx^2} = \frac{d}{dx}\left\{\frac{dy}{dx}\right\}$. This measures the rate at which $\frac{dy}{dx}$ changes due to a small change in 'x' variable.

If we further differentiate 'y' *w.r.t.* 'x'., we get the third order derivative of 'y', *w.r.t.* 'x' and this is written as $\frac{d^3y}{dx^3} = \frac{d}{dx}\left(\frac{d^2y}{dx^2}\right)$.

For example if $y = g(x)$

$$\frac{dy}{dx} = \frac{d}{dx}[g(x)] = g'(x), \quad \frac{d^2y}{dx^2} = \frac{d}{dx}[g'(x)] = g''(x) \text{ and } \frac{d^3y}{dx^3} = \frac{d}{dx}[g''(x)] = g'''(x) \text{ and so on.}$$

Illustrations:

(1) Find all the higher order derivatives of $y = x^3 - 7x^2 + 3x$

$$\frac{dy}{dx} = 3x^2 - 14x + 3, \quad \frac{d^2y}{dx^2} = 6x - 14, \quad \frac{d^3y}{dx^3} = 6, \quad \frac{d^4y}{dx^4} = \frac{d}{dx}(6) = 0$$

(2) Find the second order derivative of $y = \frac{1}{\sqrt{x}}$

$$y = \frac{1}{\sqrt{x}} = x^{-\frac{1}{2}}, \quad \frac{dy}{dx} = -\frac{1}{2}x^{-\frac{1}{2}-1} = -\frac{1}{2}x^{-\frac{3}{2}}$$

$$\frac{d^2y}{dx^2} = -\frac{1}{2}\frac{d}{dx}\left[\frac{1}{x^{\frac{3}{2}}}\right] = -\frac{1}{2}\frac{d}{dx}\left[x^{-\frac{3}{2}}\right] = -\frac{1}{2}\left(-\frac{3}{2}\right)x^{-\frac{3}{2}-1} = \frac{3}{4}x^{-\frac{5}{4}} = \frac{3}{4x^{\frac{5}{4}}} = \frac{3}{4\sqrt[4]{x^5}}$$

(3) If $f(x) = x^3 - 4x^2 + 5$, find $f'(x)$, $f'(1)$ and $f''(2)$

Given $y = f(x) = x^3 - 4x^2 + 5$, $f'(x) = \frac{dy}{dx} = f'(x) = 3x^2 - 8x$

$f'(1)$ means $f'(x)$ at $x = 1$, $f'(1) = 3x^2 - 8x = 3(1)^2 - 8(1) = -5$

$$f''(2) = f''(x) = \frac{d^2y}{dx^2} = \frac{d}{dx}[f'(x)] = \frac{d}{dx}(3x^2 - 8x) = 6x - 8 = 4$$

We can also find the value of 'x' for which $f'(x)$ is zero as:

$f'(x) = 3x^2 - 8x = 0$ or $x(3x - 8) = 0$, which means either $x = 0$, or $3x - 8 = 0$ or $x = \frac{8}{3}$.

Thus $f'(x) = 0$ if $x = 0$ or $x = \frac{8}{3}$

(4) If $y = \log x$, prove that $x^2 \frac{d^2y}{dx^2} + 1 = 0$

Given $y = \log x$ or $\frac{dy}{dx} = \frac{1}{x}$

$$\frac{d^2y}{dx^2} = \frac{d}{dx}\left(\frac{1}{x}\right) = \frac{d}{dx}(x^{-1}) = -x^{-2} = -\frac{1}{x^2}, \quad \frac{d^2y}{dx^2} = -\frac{1}{x^2}$$

By cross multiplying , $x^2 \frac{d^2y}{dx^2} = -1$ or $x^2 \frac{d^2y}{dx^2} + 1 = 0$ proved.

(5) F i n d s e $y = \log_e e^{ax^2 + bx + m}$ n d o

$$\frac{dy}{dx} = \frac{1}{e^{ax^2+bx+m}} \frac{d}{dx} e^{ax^2+bx+m} = \frac{(2ax+b)\, e^{ax^2+bx+m}}{e^{ax^2+bx+m}} = 2ax + b$$

$$\frac{d^2y}{dx^2} = \frac{d}{dx}(2ax + b) = 2a$$

(6) If $y = x^2 \log_e x$, find $\frac{d^3y}{dx^3}$

$$\frac{dy}{dx} = \frac{d}{dx}\left[x^2 \log_e x\right] = x^2 \frac{d}{dx}(\log_e x) + \log_e x \frac{d}{dx} x^2 = \frac{x^2}{x} + 2x \log_e x$$

$$\frac{dy}{dx} = x + 2x \log_e x, \quad \frac{d^2y}{dx^2} = \frac{d}{dx}\left[x + 2x\log_e x\right] = 1 + 2\log_e x + \frac{2x}{x} = 3 + 2\log_e x$$

$$\frac{d^3y}{dx^3} = \frac{d}{dx}\left(\frac{d^2y}{dx^3}\right) = \frac{d}{dx}(3 + 2\log_e x) = \frac{2}{x}$$

(7) If $y = \sqrt{2 - x^2}$ find $\frac{d^2y}{dx^2}$

Given $y = \sqrt{2 - x^2} = (2 - x^2)^{\frac{1}{2}}$

$$\frac{dy}{dx} = \frac{1}{2}(2 - x^2)^{-\frac{1}{2}}(-2x) = \frac{-2x}{2\sqrt{2 - x^2}} = \frac{-x}{\sqrt{2 - x^2}}$$

$$\frac{d^2y}{dx^2} = \frac{d}{dx}\left(\frac{dy}{dx}\right) = \frac{d}{dx}\left[\frac{-x}{(2 - x^2)^{\frac{1}{2}}}\right]$$

$$= -\left[\frac{(2-x^2)^{\frac{1}{2}}(1) - x\frac{1}{2}(2-x^2)^{\frac{1}{2}-1}(-2x)}{(2-x^2)}\right] = -\left[\frac{\sqrt{2-x^2} + \frac{2x^2}{2\sqrt{2-x^2}}}{(2-x^2)}\right]$$

$$= \frac{-\left[(2-x^2)+x^2\right]}{(2-x^2)(2-x^2)^{\frac{1}{2}}} = \frac{-2+x^2-x^2}{(2-x^2)^{\frac{3}{2}}} = \frac{-2}{\sqrt{(2-x^2)^3}}$$

(8) If $y = x^3 - 8x^2 + 7x$, find all derivatives at $x = 1$, $x = 2$,

For $y = x^3 - 8x^2 + 7x$. $\frac{dy}{dx} = f'(x) = 3x^2 - 16x + 7$

at $x = 1$, $f'(1) = 3(1)^2 - 16(1) + 7 = -6$ and

at $x = 2$, $f'(2) = 3(2)^2 - 16(2) + 7 = -13$

$\frac{d^2y}{dx^2} = f''(x) = 6x - 16$, at $x = 1$, $f''(1) = 6 - 16 = -10$

at $x = 2$, $f''(2) = 12 - 16 = -4$

$$\therefore \quad \frac{d^3y}{dx^3} = 6, \quad \frac{d^4y}{dx^4} = 0$$

3.5 Relationship Between Sign of the Derivative and the Slope of the Curve : Their applications in Economics

Students of economics are familiar with various types of curves like indifference curve, average and marginal cost curves, revenue curves, marginal revenue product and value of marginal product curves and so on. They are interrelated in some definite way that are relevant to study in economics. These curves possess some mathematically derived properties. Derivative can be used to sudy and establish the nature of their relationship. The slope and shape of the curve can be ascertained through derivatives. The rising and falling nature of the curve is indicated by the derivative of a given function.

Derivative is a very useful mathematical tool to understand the slope, sign and nature of the functions expressed as $y = f(x)$ .For example the indifference curve is the locus of various alternative combinations of two goods say q_1, and q_2 and it slopes downward and convex to the origin. This is stated in a mathematical form through utility function defined as $U = f(q_1, q_2)$. we know from economic theory that while moving along the indifference curve there is no change in utility. this can be mathematically derived as $du = 0$ and

$$du = f_1\, dq_1 + f_2\, dq_2 = 0\,, \quad \frac{dq_2}{dq_1} = -\frac{f_1}{f_2} = -\frac{MU_{q1}}{MU_{q2}} \text{ or } MRS_{q1q2} = -\frac{dq_2}{dq_1} = \frac{MU_{q1}}{MU_{q2}}$$

This negative sign indicates downward slope of the indifference curve from left to the right. If $\frac{d^2q_2}{dq_1^2} > 0$ i.e., the second order derivative is found positive, the indifference curve is said to be convex to the origin.

In this way the first order and second order derivatives of a given function provide the information regarding the slope and the shape of the curve. This is an important topic in consumer behaviour.

Moreover the relationship between average and marginal cost can also be established using derivatives. Economic theory states that when *AC (*average cost*)* falls, *MC* (marginal cost) is less than *AC*. When *AC* rises *MC* is more than *AC* and when *AC* is minimum *AC* and *MC* are equal. This relationship can be verified through the derivatives as they provide us the marginal values in economics.

Therefore, from utility theory we can derive marginal utilities as shown below:

For $U = f(q_1, q_2)$, $\frac{dU}{dq_1}$ is MU of $q_1 = f_1$, $\frac{dU}{dq_2}$ is MU of $q_2 = f_2$

From the Keynesian consumption function of linear type as given $C = a + bY = 200 + 0.5Y$ we get,

$MPC = \frac{dC}{dY} = b$. For this function $MPC = b = 0.5$

Theoritically, $b = MPC = \frac{\Delta C}{\Delta Y} = \frac{dC}{dY}$

We can also study the cost function of the firm as given by

$C = 10Q^2 + 8Q + 20$, where C = Total Cost, $TFC = 20$, $TVC = 10Q^2 + 8Q$ and

$C = TC = TVC + TFC$

or $\underbrace{C}_{TC} = \underbrace{10Q^2 + 8Q}_{TVC} + \underbrace{20}_{TFC}$

We have learned from economic theory that *MC* is independent of fixed cost. *MC* refers to the change in total cost in relation to a change in output and this is nothing but the change in *TVC*.

Therefore $MC = \frac{\Delta C}{\Delta Q} = \frac{\Delta TVC}{\Delta Q}$

Applying derivative we need to differentiate total cost function with respect to output to get MC,

i.e. $\frac{dC}{dQ}$. While evaluating this the constant term, $TFC = 20$ vanishes so that $MC = \frac{dC}{dQ} = 20Q + 8$.

This also corresponds to the slope of *TVC* curve.

3.6 Sign of the Derivative and Nature of a given Function are Related

Derivative $\frac{dy}{dx}$ shows the rate of change in Y with respect to X. Its sign can be positive, negative or zero. There exists a relationship between $\frac{dy}{dx}$ and slope of the curve. To get it understood we will use the total cost function, $C = f(Q)$ where C = Total Cost and Q = Output. A numerical total cost function is given as $C = Q^2 - 8Q + 20$. From this we get $MC = \frac{dC}{dQ} = 2Q - 8$. If the sign of $\frac{dC}{dQ}$ is positive, MC is said to be rising, if it is negative MC is falling, and when it is zero, MC is either a maximum or a minimum. We can also determine the output (Q) corresponding to which $\frac{dC}{dQ} = 0$.

MC takes a stationary point when $\frac{dC}{dQ} = 0$. It meaans when $2Q - 8 = 0$, $Q = 4$. Thus at $Q = 4$, MC curve takes a stationary value and it is constant.

If $\frac{dC}{dQ} = 2Q - 8 < 0$, it means for all $Q < 4$, MC curve is falling. If we have, $Q = 2$,

$\frac{dC}{dQ} = 2(2) - (8) = 4 - 8 = -4 < 0$, which means MC is decreasing

This has been shown graphically in the following fig. 3.1.

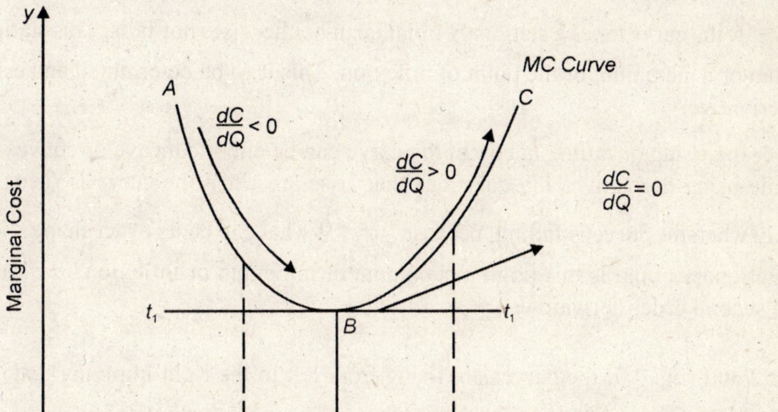

Fig. 3.1 : Shape of MC curve

It can be verified that for $Q > 4$, $MC = \frac{dC}{dQ} > 0$.

From the diagram we can see that MC is minimum (takes stationary value) at $Q = 4$.

In fig. 3.1, X-axis shows output and Y-axis represents MC.

We can see that $\frac{dC}{dQ} < 0$, between A & B. Thus MC decreases as Q increases inthis range of Q.

At $Q = 4$, $\frac{dC}{dQ} = 0$ and this is stationary point of the MC curve.

For $Q > 4$, $\frac{dC}{dQ} > 0$, MC curve rises for all output.

Point *'B'* is the stationary point which occurs when $Q = 4$ units. This also means the TC is not changing for a moment, but the very next moment it rises when *'Q'* exceeds 4 units, $Q > 4$. The MC curve changes its course from falling to rising after $Q = 4$. Therefore point *'B'* is the turning point of the curve.

From $\frac{dy}{dx}$ we get the information regarding the curve is rising or falling or stationary. However the exact shape of the curve still remains undetermined. What we have learned till now is

(i) When $\frac{dy}{dx} > 0$, the curve rises form left to the right

(ii) When $\frac{dy}{dx} < 0$, the curve falls form left to the right and when

(iii) $\frac{dy}{dx} = 0$, the curve takes a stationary point i.e. it neither rises nor falls. This stationary point can be either a minimum or a maximum or the point of inflexion. This is to be determined and established from the second order derivative.

Moreover the rising or falling nature of the curve can be either concave or convex. This is also to be established while using derivatives the questions that arise are when the curve is rising, what is its exact shape? Similarly when the curve is falling, because $\frac{dy}{dx} < 0$, what can be its exact shape? Likewise when the curve takes a stationary point, is this point a maximum or minimum or inflexion? We can get their answer from the use of second order derivatives.

In fig. 3.2 and fig. 3.3, the curves are rising from left to the right implying that $\frac{dy}{dx} > 0$ in both the cases. But in fig. 3.2, the curve is increasing at an increasing rate. Thus slope of the curve is positive and increasing when the value of *'x'* increases on x-axis. This curve is concave upward or convex downward. In terms of the first and second derivative of the function, we will get

$\frac{dy}{dx} = f'(x) > 0$ and $\frac{d^2y}{dx^2} = f''(x) > 0$. This is evident in fig. 3.2,where $\frac{dy}{dx} > 0$, $\frac{d^2y}{dx^2} > 0$.

This curve is increasing at an in creasing rate. The slopes corresponding to D, E and F are also obtained by drawing tangents to these points, t_4t_4, t_5t_5 and t_6t_6. They repreesnt increasing slope for every rise in X. This is also measured by θ : The curve is concave upward. since $\theta_3 > \theta_2 > \theta_1$ or $\theta_3 < \theta_2 < \theta_1$

Now switchover to the fig. 3.3, where $\frac{dy}{dx} > 0, \frac{d^2y}{dx^2} < 0.$

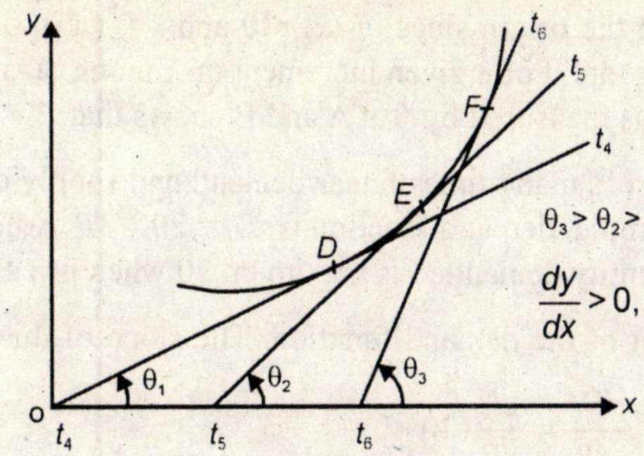

***Fig. 3.2** : Curve rises at an increasing rate*

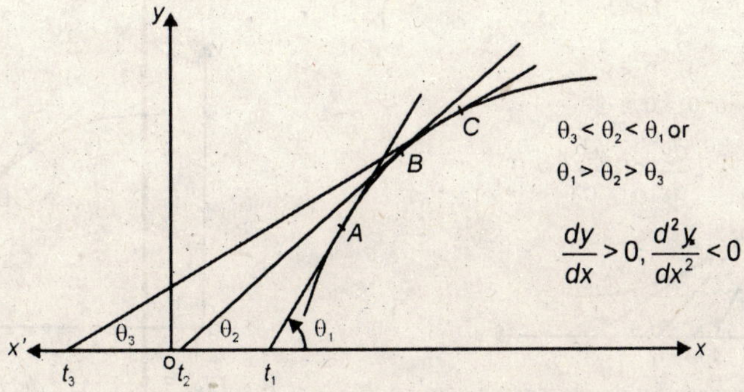

***Fig. 3.3** : Curve rises at a decreasing rate*

This curve is increasing at a decreasing rate. The slope of the curve is positive but decreasing as X increases along X-axis. The slopes corresponding to D, E and F are determined by drawing tangents to these points, t_1t_1, $t_2t_2$and t_3t_3. They repreesnt decreasing slopes as X increases. these slopes are measured by θ.

Since $\theta_3 < \theta_2 < \theta_1$ or $\theta_3 > \theta_2 > \theta_1$, curve is *convex upward.*

Now we will establish the shape of the curves which are decreasing: The curve can take the downward slope and it can be either concave or convex downward.

The curve will be convex downward if $\frac{dy}{dx} < 0$ and $\frac{d^2y}{dx^2} > 0$. This curve is relatively flater to the right hand side and steeper to the left hand side. The slopes corresponding to M and N are shown by drawing tangents tt and t_1t_1 to these points. They repreesnt decreasing slope for a rise in X, measured by θ. Since $\theta_2 > \theta_1$ for a given increase in X, $-\Delta y$ becomes smaller and smaller. Therefore the slope of the curve is negative but increases when value of X increases along X–axis. Symbolically $f'(x) < 0$ and $f''(x) > 0$. This curve is convex downward, shown in fig. 3.4.

In fig.3.5, the curve is taking a negative slope also as $\frac{dy}{dx} = f'(x) < 0$ but the slope of the curve is concave downward or concave to the origin since $f'(x) < 0$ and $f''(x) < 0$. This means the value of the function decreases at a decreasing rate. For a given increment in X along X-axis, $-\Delta y$ goes on increasing as one slides along the curve. Slope is measured by θ at A and B shows that $\theta_2 < \theta_1$ when X increases.

In economics we come across many times linear demand and supply curves which are straight lines with or without intercept. For example demand function is $D_x = 20 - 3P_x$ where P_x is the market price of 'x' commodity. It shows that the quantity demanded is maximum 20 when price of the product is zero.

This refers to the intercept of the demand function. The slope of this demand curve is -3. this is derived from the first derivative, $\frac{dD_x}{dP} = \frac{d}{dP}(20 - 3x) = -3$.

By plotting this function on a graph we will get a straight line downward sloping demand curve with an intercept on y-axis equal to 20 and slope -3. This is a linear demand curve.

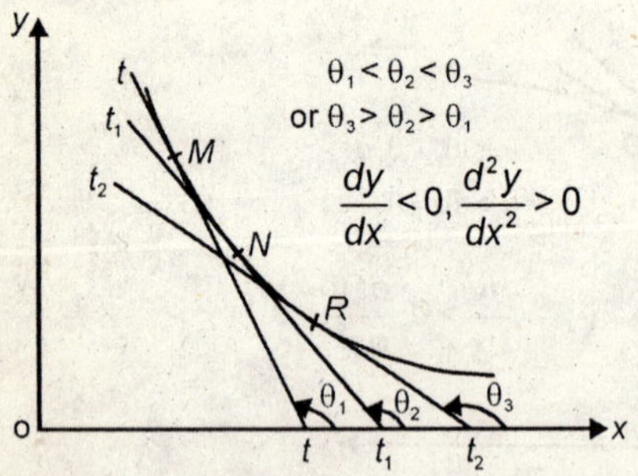

Fig. 3.4 : Curve decreases at an increasing rate

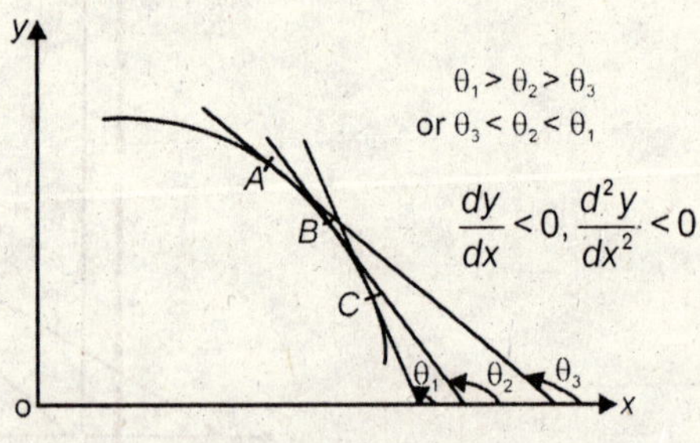

Fig. 3.5 : Curve decreases at a decreasing rate

3.7 Derivative Determines the Rising and Falling Nature of Curves

From $\frac{dy}{dx}$ we can determine whether the given function is rising or falling or stationary, corresponding to the independent variable (x), taking different values. This functional relationship is expressed by $y = f(x)$. In economics we come across different forms of fucntions for studying the relationship among variables. For example $Q = f(l)$, where l = labour and Q = output. Similarly we get $C = f(Q)$ and so on. We will have some illustrations showing the rising and falling nature of functions. These are as follows:

[1 $y = 2x^2 - 6x - 7$, find whether the curve is rising or falling at $x = 2$ and $x = 3$. Also find 'x' for which the curve reaches staionary point. Establish whether this stationary point is a maximum or a minimum.

For given $y = 2x^2 - 6x - 7$, $\frac{dy}{dx} = 4x - 6$

If $\frac{dy}{dx} > 0$, the curve is rising and if $\frac{dy}{dx} < 0$, the curve is falling.

If $\frac{dy}{dx} = 0$, the curve takes stationary point, which can be a maximum or a minimum or inflexion point.

Since $\frac{dy}{dx} = 4x - 6$, to know whether the function is rising or falling, we are provided with x values, which we need to substitute in the derivative

$\therefore$ $\frac{dy}{dx}$ at $x = 2$ and at $x = 3$ are to be evaluated.

$\frac{dy}{dx}$ at $x = 2$ is $\frac{dy}{dx} = 4x - 6 = 4(2) - 6 = 8 - 6 = 2 > 0.$

$\therefore$ The curve rises at $x = 2$, as $\frac{dy}{dx} = 2 > 0.$

At $x = 3, \frac{dy}{dx} = 4(3) - 6 = 12 - 6 = 6 > 0.$

Thus the curve is rising at $x = 2$ and $x = 3$.

For the curve to take stationary point, $\frac{dy}{dx} = 4x - 6 = 0$ and $x = 1.5$

$\therefore$ At $x = 1.5$, the curve has a minimum since $\frac{d^2y}{dx^2} = 4 > 0$.

So it is found that for all values of $x < 1.5$, the curve is falling, for $x = 1.5$ it ha a minimum and for $x > 1.5$ the curve rises.

(2) If $y = 2x^3 - 5x^2$, determine whether the curve is rising or falling at $x = 1$.

$\frac{dy}{dx} = 6x^2 - 10x,$

At $x = 1$, $\frac{dy}{dx} = 4(1)^2 - 10(1) = 6 - 10 = -4 < 0$. Thus the curve is falling at $x = 1$.

(3) If $Q = 3L^2 - 5L$, find whether MP of labour is rising or falling at $L = 1$ and 2

$MP_L = \frac{dQ}{dL} = 6L - 5$, at L = 1, $\frac{dQ}{dL} = 6 - 5 = 1 > 0$ $\therefore$ MP rises at L = 1.

At $L = 2$, $\frac{dQ}{dL} = 6L - 5 = 6(2) - 5 = 7$, MP rises at L = 2

$\therefore$ MP_l increases both at $L = 1$ and $L = 2$.

(4) If $Q = 15 + 10L - L^2$ find whether MP_L is rising or falling at L = 2 and 4. Also find the number of labour units used at which MP_L is zero.

We are given $Q = 15 + 10L - L^2$

$$\frac{dQ}{dL} = MP_L = 10 - 2L,$$

At $L = 2$, $MP_L = 10 - 2L = 10 - 4 = 6 > 0$, $\therefore$ MP_L are positive at L = 2.

Thus MP curve rises at $L = 2$.

For $MP_L = 0$, $\frac{dQ}{dL} = 10 - 2L = 0$ *or* $L = 5$.

$\therefore$ When 5 units of labour is employed, MP_L is zero.

At this point of employment of labour total product will be maximum.

3.8 Derivative is used to Determine Maximum, Minimum and Point of Inflexion

The maximum, minimum and inflexionary values of a given function can be obtained by applying the first and second order derivatives.

Let us consider a function $y = f(x)$ is $y = 2x^2 - 12x + 7$

To establish the given function to be increasing or decreasing we need to find the x value at which the function takes a stationary point. For this obtain the first order derivate and set it to zero as

$$\frac{dy}{dx} = 4x - 12 = 0 \text{ or } x = 3.$$

$\therefore$ at $x = 3$, 'y' will take its stationary value. This stationary point can be either a maximum or a minimum point. This can be detremined from the application of its second order derivative.

$$\frac{d^2y}{dx^2} = \frac{d}{dx}\left(\frac{dy}{dx}\right) = \frac{d}{dx}(4x - 12) = 4.$$

Since $\frac{dy}{dx} = 0$ and $\frac{d^2y}{dx^2} > 0$, the given function has a minimum at $x = 3$.

There are two conditions that must be satisfied for a given function to be called a minimum. These are *(a)* Necessary condition, *(b)* Sufficient condition. This rule is also applied to find the maximum. The necessary condition is also called the first order condition, while the second-order condition is called sufficient condition.

The first order condition is the same for both minimum and maximum and it is

$\frac{dy}{dx} = 0$, while the second order condition for minimum is $\frac{d^2y}{dx^2} > 0$.

For maximum the second order condition for maximum is $\frac{d^2y}{dx^2} < 0$

Thus a given function $y = f(x)$, is said to be minimum if *i)* $\frac{dy}{dx} = f'(x) = 0$. (ii) $\frac{d^2y}{dx^2} = f''(x) > 0$

Maximum if *i)* $\frac{dy}{dx} = f'(x) = 0$. (ii) $\frac{d^2y}{dx^2} = f''(x) < 0$

In our example $y = 2x^2 - 12x + 7$, $\frac{dy}{dx} = 4x - 12 = 0$ $\therefore$ $x = 3$

At $x = 3$, the given function has a minimum, since $\frac{d^2y}{dx^2} = 4 > 0$.

The minimum value of '*y*' is the *y* that corresponds to $x = 3$ and this is equal to

$y = 2(3)^2 - 12(3) + 7 = 2 \times 9 = 36 + 7 = -11$

This also implies that the given function decreases for $x < 3$, reaches a minimum at $x = 3$ and increases for $x > 3$. This can also be verified.

If $x < 3$ say $x = 2$, it can be seen that $\frac{dy}{dx} < 0$, At $x = 2$, $\frac{dy}{dx} = 4x - 12 = -4 < 0$.

For $x > 3$ say $x = 4$, it can be seen that $\frac{dy}{dx} > 0$, At $x = 4$, $\frac{dy}{dx} = 4x - 12 = 16 - 12 = 4 > 0$.

(ii) If the total cost function is $C = 3x^3 - 12x^2 + 15x$, find output (x) for which *MC* is minimum.

For *MC* to be minimum it needs to be satisfied that , $\frac{d}{dx}\left(\frac{dC}{dx}\right) = 0$ and $\frac{d^2}{dx^2}\left(\frac{dC}{dx}\right) > 0$

Given $C = 3x^3 - 12x^2 + 15x$, $\frac{dC}{dx} = 9x^2 - 24x + 15$ and

$\frac{d}{dx}\left(\frac{dC}{dx}\right) = 18x - 24 = 0$, and $x = \frac{4}{3}$, MC curve takes a stationary point at $x = \frac{4}{3}$,

To get MC to be minimum we need to apply the second order condition also. This is given by

$$\frac{d^2}{dx^2}\left(\frac{dC}{dx}\right) = \frac{d}{dx}(18x - 24) = 18 > 0.$$

Since $\frac{d}{dx}\left(\frac{dC}{dx}\right) = 0$ and $\frac{d^2}{dx^2}\left(\frac{dC}{dx}\right) > 0$, *MC* is minimum at $x = \frac{4}{3}$ is verified.

This also means for $x < \frac{4}{3}$, *MC* decreases and for $x > \frac{4}{3}$ *MC* increases.

The conditons for maximisation are given by the conditions as follows:

(i) Necessary condition is : $\frac{dy}{dx} = 0$

(ii) Sufficient condition is : $\frac{d^2y}{dx^2} < 0$

Let us consider a function, $y = 10 + 8x - x^2$. Find the maximum or minimum for this function.

From $y = 10 + 8x - x^2$, we get $\frac{dy}{dx} = \frac{d}{dx}(10 + 8x - x^2) = 8 - 2x = 0$

or $x = 4$. The given function 'y' has a stationary point at $x = 4$. The second order condition is

$$\frac{d^2y}{dx^2} = \frac{d}{dx}\left(\frac{dy}{dx}\right) = \frac{d}{dx}(8 - 2x) = -2 < 0$$

Since $\frac{d}{dx}\left(\frac{dy}{dx}\right) = 0$ and $\frac{d^2}{dx^2}\left(\frac{dy}{dx}\right) < 0$, 'y' is maximum at $x = 4$.

The given function $y = 10 + 8x - x^2$ has a maximum at $x = 4$. It also means that for $x < 4$, say $x = 3$, $\frac{dy}{dx} = 8 - 2x = 8 - 2(3) = 8 - 6 = 2 > 0$. Thus the curve is rising for $x < 4$.

Similarly we can see that for $x > 4$, say $x = 5$, $\frac{dy}{dx} = 8 - 2x = 8 - 2(5) = -2 < 0$.

It means the curve is falling for $x = 5$.

The example of $y = 2x^2 - 12x + 7$, has a minimum at $x = 3$ is graphically shown in Fig. 3.6.

From our example $y = 10 + 8x - x^2$, we have seen that 'y' reaches a maximum at $x = 4$ is graphically demonstrated in Fig. 3.7 below.

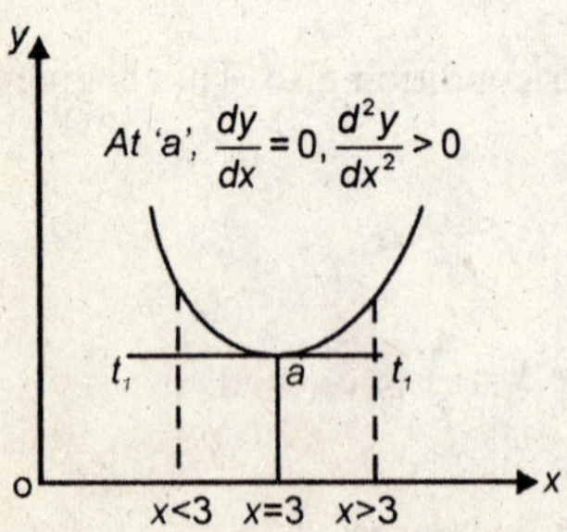

***Fig. 3.6 :** Minimum Point*

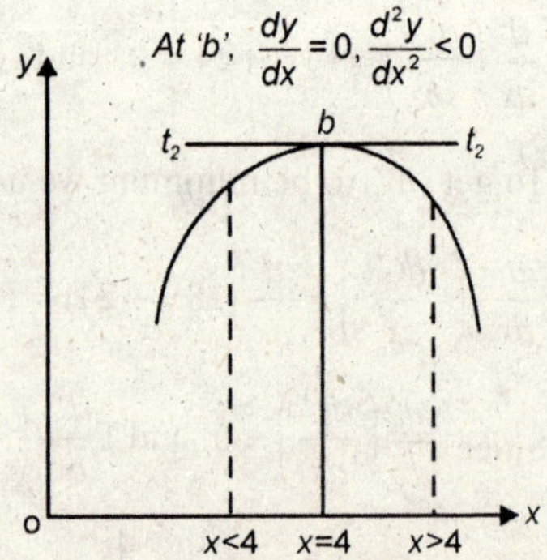

***Fig. 3.7 :** Maximum Point*

For $x < 3$, $\frac{dy}{dx} < 0$ at $x = 3$, $\frac{dy}{dx} = 0$ for $x > 3$, $\frac{dy}{dx} > 0$	For $x < 4$, $\frac{dy}{dx} > 0$ at $x = 4$, $\frac{dy}{dx} = 0$ for $x > 4$, $\frac{dy}{dx} < 0$
Order condition (For Minimum)	Order condition (For Maximum)
$\frac{dy}{dx} = f'(x) = 0$ $\frac{d^2y}{dx^2} = f''(x) > 0$	$\frac{dy}{dx} = f'(x) = 0$ $\frac{d^2y}{dx^2} = f''(x) < 0$

The necessary and sufficient conditions are applied to find the extreme values of a function. The second order derivative or simply second derivative $f''(x)$ is used to measure the rate of charge in $f'(x)$. It enables us to find whether $f'(x)$ increases or decreases, at an increasing rate or at a decreasing rate.

Point of inflexion

There is yet another possibility that can exist is that, a given function corresponding to the point wehre its $\frac{dy}{dx}$ is zerocan also be neither a maximum nor a minimum. This refers to the point of inflexion.

For example if $y = x^3 - 3x^2 = 3x + 8$, now to establish whether the function has a maximum or minimum at the stationary point, we need to evaluate $\frac{dy}{dx} = 0$.

For $y = x^3 - 3x^2 + 3x + 8$, $\frac{dy}{dx} = 3x^2 - 6x + 3 = 0$. This is a quadratic equation. Solving this we get

$3(x^2 - 2x + 1) = 0$, which means $(x^2 - 2x + 1) = 0$ as $3 \neq 0$

Thus $(x^2 - 2x + 1) = (x - 1)^2 = 0$, or $x - 1 = 0$ and $x = 1$

This function has a stationary point at $x = 1$. This can also be verified that for $x = 1$, $\frac{dy}{dx} = 0$.

But this stationary point can be a maximum or minimum. This can be established from $\frac{d^2y}{dx^2}$.

If $\frac{d^2y}{dx^2} = f''(x) > 0$, '$y$' has a minimum at $x = 1$

If $\frac{d^2y}{dx^2} = f''(x) < 0$, '$y$' has a maximum at $x = 1$

But in this case $\frac{d^2y}{dx^2} = \frac{d}{dx}(3x^2 - 6x + 3) = 6x - 6 = 0$, at $x = 1$

Since the second derivative obtained is neither positive nor negative but it is equal to zero at $x = 1$, this stationary point indicates the point of inflexion for the given function or the curve. Therefore at $x = 1$, the curve is neither a minimum nor a maximum. It also implies that for $x < 1$ and $x > 1$, the curve increases on either side. This can be verified as

Suppose $x = \frac{1}{2}$, which means $x < 1$, $\frac{dy}{dx} = 3x^2 - 6x + 3 = 3\left(\frac{1}{2}\right)^2 - 6\left(\frac{1}{2}\right) + 3 = \frac{3}{4} - 3 + 3 = \frac{3}{4} > 0$

Now take $x = 2$ means $x > 1$, $\frac{dy}{dx} = 3x^2 - 6x + 3 = 3(2)^2 - 6(2) + 3 = 3 > 0$

The point of inflexion is graphically shown in Fig. 3.8. The given function 'y' or the curve as such is seen to rise before point 'A' is reached. It raeches a stationary point at A (where it is neither increasing nor decreasing) and then again it rises after point 'A' is reached.

Point 'A' is therefore defined a point of inflexion. The tangent t_1t_1 is drawn to this point is seen to be parallel to x-axis. This is also obtained from the expression of $\frac{dy}{dx} = 0$ at point 'A'.

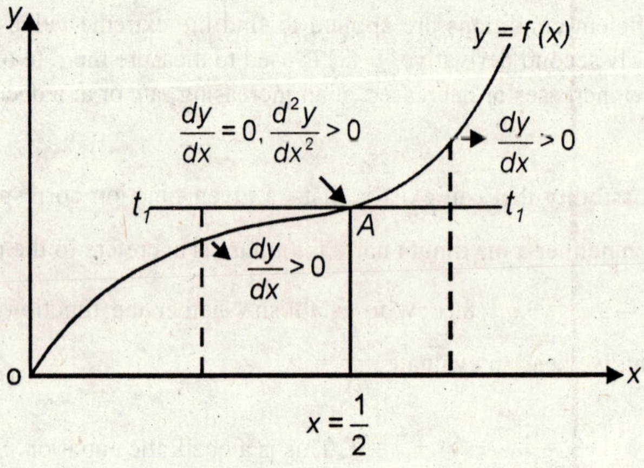

Fig. 3.8 : Point of in flexion at 'A'

Before point 'A', $\frac{dy}{dx} > 0$ and after point 'A' also $\frac{dy}{dx} > 0$.

Following illustrations are presented to obtain the maximum or minimum or point of inflexion of different functions. The value of 'x' for which the given function has a stationary point to be determined. The values corresponding to the maximum or minimum are obtained.

Find Maxima or Minima or inflexionary point as the case may be from the following functions:

(1) $y = 2x^2 - 8x + 2$

To determine the stationary point, we find $\frac{dy}{dx} = 0$

$$\frac{dy}{dx} = \frac{d}{dx}(2x^2 - 8x + 2) = 4x - 8 = 0 \text{ or } x = 2$$

Thus the given function 'y' has a stationary value at $x = 2$. This can provide either a maximum or minimum and for this we need to evaluate $\frac{d^2y}{dx^2}$. Accordingly we get

$$\frac{d^2y}{dx^2} = \frac{d}{dx}\left(\frac{dy}{dx}\right) = \frac{d}{dx}(4x - 8) = 4 > 0.$$

Since $\frac{d^2y}{dx^2} > 0$, the stationary value is said to be a minimum. Thus the curve has a minima at $x = 2$

(2) $y = x^3 - 3x^2 + 5$

From $y = x^3 - 3x^2 + 5$, $\frac{dy}{dx} = 3x^2 - 6x = 0$ or $3x(x - 2) = 0$. This means either $x = 0$ or $x = 2$.

$\therefore$ Stationary value occurs when either $x = 0$ or $x = 2$.

To know this maximum or minimum at the stationary point we need to evaluate $\frac{d^2y}{dx^2}$.

$$\frac{d^2y}{dx^2} = \frac{d}{dx}\left(\frac{dy}{dx}\right) = \frac{d}{dx}(3x^2 - 6x) = 6x - 6$$

If we take $x = 0$, $\frac{d^2y}{dx^2} = 6x - 6 = -6 < 0$.

It means the given function has a maximum at $x = 0$, since at $x = 0$, $\frac{dy}{dx} = 0$ and $\frac{d^2y}{dx^2} < 0$

Now at $x = 2$, $\frac{d^2y}{dx^2} = 6x - 6 = 12 - 6 = 6 > 0$,

This means the given function has a minimum at $x = 2$, since at $x = 2$, $\frac{dy}{dx} = 0$ and $\frac{d^2y}{dx^2} > 0$

(3) If $y = x + \frac{1}{x}$, show that the function has one minimum value and one maximum value.

For, $y = x + \frac{1}{x} = x + x^{-1}$, $\frac{dy}{dx} = 1 - x^{-2} = 1 - \frac{1}{x^2} = 0$ or $(x^2 - 1) = 0$. or $(x + 1)(x - 1) = 0$.

$\therefore$ Either $x + 1 = 0$ and $x = -1$ or $x - 1 = 0$ and $x = +1$

Therefore the curve has a stationary value at $x = +1$ or at $x = -1$

To k now whether the stationary point is maxima or minima, we need to apply second order condition

$$\frac{d^2y}{dx^2} = \frac{d}{dx}(1 - x^{-2}) = -(-2)x^{-3} = +2x^{-3} = \frac{2}{x^3}$$

Since $\frac{d^2y}{dx^2} = \frac{2}{x^3}$, for $x = -1$, $\frac{d^2y}{dx^2} = -2 < 0$, thus the curve has a maximum at $x = -1$

This maximum value is the value of 'y' that corresponds to $x = -1$. This is obtained as

$y = x + \frac{1}{x} = (-1) + \frac{1}{-1} = -1 - 1 = -2$. Thus $y = -2$ at $x = -1$

Now when $x = +1$, $\frac{d^2y}{dx^2} = \frac{2}{x^3} = \frac{2}{1^3} = 2 > 0$ $\therefore$ at $x = +1$, 'y' has a minimum and this minimum is

$y = x + \frac{1}{x}$ at $x = 1$. This is $y = 1 + \frac{1}{1} = 1 + 1 = 2$. $\therefore$ $y = 2$ at $x = 1$.

So it is proved that the function has one minimum value and one maximum value

(4) Find the maximum and minimum values of the function $y = x^3 - 3x + 5$

$\frac{dy}{dx} = f'(x) = 3x^2 - 3 = 0$ or $3(x^2 - 1) = 0$ or $3(x + 1)(x - 1) = 0$

Since $3 \neq 0$, either $x + 1 = 0$ or $x - 1 = 0$

If $x + 1 = 0$, $x = -1$ and If $x - 1 = 0$, $x = +1$

Thus at $x = \pm 1$ the given function has a stationary value, which can be either a maximum or a minimum depending on $\frac{d^2y}{dx^2} = f''(x)$.

$$\frac{d}{dx}\left(\frac{dy}{dx}\right) = \frac{d^2y}{dx^2} = \frac{d}{dx}(3x^2 - 3) = 6x$$

At $x = -1$, $\frac{d^2y}{dx^2} = -6 < 0$, which means the curve has a maximum at $x = -1$. This maximum value is given by, $y = x^3 - 3x + 5$ at $x = -1$. $y = (-1)^3 - 3(-1) + 5 = 7$.

At $x = +1$, $\frac{d^2y}{dx^2} = 6 < 0$. It implies that the function has a minimum at $x = 1$. This minimum value is the 'y' value corresponding to $x = 1$. Accordingly, $y = (1)^3 - 3(1) + 5 = 1 - 3 + 5 = 3$.

(5) Given $y = \frac{1}{3}x^3 - 2x^2 + 4x + 8$, show that the curve rises before and after the stationary point.

For given $y = \frac{1}{3}x^3 - 2x^2 + 4x + 8$, $\frac{dy}{dx} = f'(x) = \frac{3x^2}{3} - 4x + 4 = 0$

or $x^2 - 4x + 4 = 0$ or $(x - 2)^2 = 0$. It means $x - 2 = 0$ or $x = 2$.

Thus the given function 'y' has a stationary point at $x = 2$. At this point

$$\frac{d^2y}{dx^2} = \frac{d}{dx}(x^2 - 4x + 4) = 2x - 4 \text{. At } x = 2, \quad \frac{d^2y}{dx^2} = 2x - 4 = 0 .$$

Since both $f'(x) = 0$ and $f''(x) = 0$ at the stationary point $x = 2$, it means the given fucntion 'y' is neither a maximum nor a minimum at the stationary point. The curve therefore increases before and after this stationary value, $x = 2$.

It can be verified that the curve rises from left to the right for $x < 2$ and also for $x > 2$

$$\therefore \frac{dy}{dx} > 0 \text{ for } x < 2 \text{ and } \frac{dy}{dx} > 0 \text{ for } x > 2$$

For example if $x < 2$ say $x = 1$, $\frac{dy}{dx} = x^2 - 4x + 4$.

At $x = 1$, $y = (1)^2 - 4(1) + 4 = 1 - 4 + 4 = 1 > 0$.

Similarly we can see that $\frac{dy}{dx}$ at $x > 2$ say $x = 3$ is positive,

For $x = 3$, $y = (3)^2 - 4(3) + 4 = 9 - 12 + 4 = 1 > 0$.

Since the function rises both at $x > 2$ and $x < 2$, stationary point is the point of inflexion of the curve.

(6) For $y = -x^3 + \frac{9}{2}x^2 - 6x + 10$, find the maximum or minimum or point of inflexion.

For $y = -x^3 + \frac{9}{2}x^2 - 6x + 10$, $\frac{dy}{dx} = -3x^2 + 9x - 6 = 0$ or $-3(x^2 + 3x + 2) = 0$

or $3(x^2 - 3x + 2) = 0$, as $3 \neq 0$, $(x^2 - 3x + 2) = 0$.

$x^2 - 3x + 2$ is a quadratic equation. Solving this we can get 'x'. The formula to solve the equation is

$\frac{-b \pm \sqrt{b^2 - 4ac}}{2a}$ .Applying this formula we can obtain

$$x_{12} = \frac{3 \pm \sqrt{9 - 8}}{2} = \frac{3 \pm 1}{2} \quad \therefore x = 1 \text{ or } x = 2 \text{, It means } \frac{dy}{dx} = 0 \text{ when } x = 1 \text{ or } x = 2.$$

To know minima or maxima we have to evaluate $\frac{d^2y}{dx^2}$

$$\frac{d^2y}{dx^2} = \frac{d}{dy}(-3x^2 + 9x - 6) = -6x + 9$$

If $x = 1$, $\frac{d^2y}{dx^2} = -6 + 9 = 3 > 0$. It means at $x = 1$, the function or the curve has a minimum.

This minimum value is given by $y = -x^3 + \frac{9}{2}x^2 - 6x + 10$ at $x = 1$ is equal to

$$y = -(1)^3 + \frac{9}{2}(1)^2 - 6(1) + 10 = 3 + \frac{9}{2} = \frac{15}{12} = 7.5$$

Now at $x = 2$, $\frac{d^2y}{dx^2} = -6x + 9 = -6(2) + 9 = -3 < 0$.

Therefore, the function has a maximum at $x = 2$. The maximum value is obatined as

$$y = -x^3 + \frac{9}{2}x^2 - 6x + 10 \text{ at } x = 2$$

$$y = -(2)^3 + \frac{9}{2}(2)^2 - 6(2) + 10 = -8 + 18 - 12 + 10 = 8$$

(7) Find maxima or minima for $y = \frac{x}{1+x^2}$

$$y = \frac{x}{1+x^2} = (x)\ (1+x^2)^{-1}$$

$$\frac{dy}{dx} = \frac{d}{dx}\left[(x)(1+x^2)^{-1}\right] = (1+x^2)^{-1} + (x)(-1)(1+x^2)^{-2}(2x)$$

$$= \frac{1}{(1+x^2)} - \frac{2x^2}{(1+x^2)^2},\ \frac{dy}{dx} = \frac{1+x^2-2x^2}{(1+x^2)^2} = 0 \text{ or } \frac{dy}{dx} = 1 - x^2 = 0 \text{ or } (1-x)(1+x) = 0$$

$\therefore$ Either $(1 - x) = 0$ and $x = 1$ or $(1 + x) = 0$ and $x = -1$

To know maxima on minima at $x = \pm 1$, we need to evaluate $\frac{d^2y}{dx^2}$.

$$\frac{d^2y}{dx^2} = \frac{d}{dx}\left[\frac{dy}{dx}\right] = \frac{d}{dx}\left[(1+x^2)^{-1} - 2x^2(1+x^2)^{-2}\right]$$

$$= -(1+x^2)^{-2}(2x) - 4x(1+x^2)^{-2} - 2x^2(-2)(1+x^2)^{-3}(2x)$$

$$\frac{d^2y}{dx^2} = \frac{-2x}{(1+x^2)^2} - \frac{4x}{(1+x^2)^2} + \frac{8x^3}{(1+x^2)^3}$$

At $x = -1$, $\frac{d^2y}{dx^2} = \frac{-2(-1)}{[1+1]^2} - \frac{4(-1)}{[1+1]^2} + \frac{8(-1)^3}{[1+1]^3} = \frac{2}{4} + \frac{4}{4} - \frac{8}{8} = \frac{1}{2} > 0.$

Since $\frac{d^2y}{dx^2} > 0$ at $x = -1$, the given function 'y' or the curve has a minimum at $x = -1$.

This minimum value value of 'y' is, $y = \frac{x}{1+x^2} = \frac{(-1)}{1+(-1)^2} = -\frac{1}{2}$

Now for $x = +1$, $\frac{d^2y}{dx^2} = \frac{-2(1)}{4} - \frac{4(1)}{4} + \frac{8(1)}{8} = -\frac{2}{4} - 1 + 1 = -\frac{1}{2} < 0.$

Since $\frac{d^2y}{dx^2} < 0$ at $x = 1$, it implies that the given function or the curve has a maximum at $x = 1$.

This maximum value is, $y = \frac{x}{1+x^2}$ at $x = 1$. $y = \frac{(1)}{2} = \frac{1}{2}$

3.9. Solved Questions on Derivatives of TYBA (Economics) Papers of Mumbai University

(1) *(a)* $y = \frac{\log x}{x}$, find $\frac{dy}{dx}$ (May 1999)

$$\frac{dy}{dx} = \frac{(x)\frac{d}{dx}(\log x) - (\log x)\frac{d}{dx}(x)}{x^2} = \frac{x \cdot \frac{1}{x} - (\log x)}{x^2} = \frac{(1 - \log x)}{x^2}$$

(b) $y = (x^2 + 2x - 1)(3x + 5)^2$, find $\frac{dy}{dx}$ (May 1999)

$$\frac{dy}{dx} = (x^2 + 2x - 1)\frac{dy}{dx}(3x+5)^2 + (3x+5)^2\frac{d}{dx}(x^2 + 2x - 1)$$

$$= 2(x^2 + 2x - 1)\ (3x+5)(3) + (3x+5)^2(2x+2)$$

$$\frac{dy}{dx} = 6(x^2 + 2x - 1)(3x+5) + (3x+5)^2\ (2x+2)$$

(2) *(a)* Find $\frac{dy}{dx}$ for $y = \frac{3x-4}{x^2+3}$ (Oct. 1999)

$$\frac{dy}{dx} = \frac{(x^2+3)\frac{d}{dx}(3x-4) - (3x-4)\frac{d}{dx}(x^2+3)}{(x^2+3)^2}$$

$$\frac{dy}{dx} = \frac{(x^2+3)(3) - 2x(3x-4)}{(x^2+3)^2}$$

$$= \frac{3x^2 + 9 - 6x^2 + 8x}{(x^2+3)^2} = \frac{-3x^2 + 8x + 9}{(x^2+3)^2} = -\frac{(3x^2 - 8x - 9)}{(x^2+3)^2}$$

(b) Find $\frac{dy}{dx}$ for $y = \frac{x}{(x+1)\ (x+2)}$ (Oct., 1999)

$$y = \frac{x}{(x+1)\ (x+2)} = \frac{x}{(x^2 + 2x + x + 2)} = \frac{x}{(x^2 + 3x + 2)}$$

$$\frac{dy}{dx} = \frac{(x^2 + 3x + 2) - x(2x+3)}{(x^2 + 3x + 2)^2}$$

$$= \frac{x^2 + 3x + 2 - 2x^2 - 3x}{(x^2 + 3x + 2)^2} = \frac{-x^2 + 2}{(x^2 + 3x + 2)^2}$$

$$\frac{dy}{dx} = \frac{-(x^2 - 2)}{(x^2 + 3x + 2)^2}$$

(3) *(a)* If $y=(2x-3)^{\frac{5}{2}}$ find $\frac{dy}{dx}$ (May, 2000)

$$y=(2x-3)^{\frac{5}{2}}$$

$$\frac{dy}{dx}=\frac{5}{2}(2x-3)^{\frac{5}{2}-1}\frac{d}{dx}(2x-3)=\frac{5}{2}(2x-3)^{\frac{3}{2}}(2)==5\sqrt{(2x-3)^3}$$

(b) $y=2^{x^2+1}$ find $\frac{dy}{dx}$ (May, 2000)

$$y=2^{x^2+1},\ \frac{dy}{dx}=2^{x^2+1}\log 2\frac{d}{dx}(x^2+1)=2x\cdot 2^{x^2+1}\log 2=2x\log 2\cdot 2^{x^2+1}$$

(c) $y=\log_e(\log_e x)$ find $\frac{dy}{dx}$ (May, 2000)

$$\frac{dy}{dx}=\frac{d}{dx}\left[\log_e(\log_e x)\right]=\frac{1}{\log_e x}\frac{d}{dx}(\log_e x)=\frac{1}{x\log_e x}$$

(4) *(a)* $y=x^4+4\sqrt{x}-5e^x$, find $\frac{dy}{dx}$ (Oct., 2000)

$$y=x^4+4\sqrt{x}-5e^x$$

$$\frac{dy}{dx}=\frac{d}{dx}(x^4)+4\frac{d}{dx}(\sqrt{x})-5\frac{d}{dx}(e^x)=4x^3+4\frac{1}{2}x^{-\frac{1}{2}}-5e^x$$

$$=4x^3+\frac{2}{\sqrt{x}}-5e^x$$

(b) $y=(3x-5)\log_e x-4.2^x$ (Oct., 2000)

$$\frac{dy}{dx}=(3x-5)\frac{d}{dx}(\log_e x)+\log_e x\frac{d}{dx}(3x-5)-4\frac{d}{dx}(2^x)$$

$$=\frac{(3x-5)}{x}+3\log_e x-4.2^x\log_e 2$$

$$\frac{dy}{dx}=\frac{(3x-5)+3x\log_e x-4x\,2^x\log_e 2}{x}$$

(c) If $y=e^{x^2+1}$ find $\frac{dy}{dx}$ (Oct., 2000)

$$y=e^{x^2+1},\ \frac{dy}{dx}=e^{x^2+1}\frac{d}{dx}(x^2+1)=2x\ e^{x^2+1}$$

(d) If $y = x^x$ find $\frac{dy}{dx}$ (Oct., 2000)

$y = x^x$, $\log_e y = x \log_e x$

$$\frac{1}{y}\frac{dy}{dx} = x\frac{d}{dx}(\log_e x) + \log_e x\frac{d}{dx}(x) = \frac{x}{x} + \log_e x = 1 + \log_e x$$

$$\frac{1}{y}\frac{dy}{dx} = (1 + \log_e x), \frac{dy}{dx} = y(1 + \log_e x) = x^x(1 + \log_e x)$$

(5) (a) Find $\frac{dy}{dx}$ for the following (May, 2001)

$$y = \sqrt[3]{(3x^2 - 2x + 1)^2}$$

$$y = \sqrt[3]{(3x^2 - 2x + 1)^2} = (3x^2 - 2x + 1)^{\frac{2}{3}}$$

$$\frac{dy}{dx} = \frac{2}{3}(3x^2 - 2x + 1)^{\frac{2}{3}-1}\frac{d}{dx}(3x^2 - 2x + 1)$$

$$= \frac{2(6x - 2)}{3\sqrt[3]{(3x^2 - 2x + 1)}} = \frac{12x - 4}{3\sqrt[3]{(3x^2 - 2x + 1)}}$$

(b) $y = \log_e x + e^x + x^2$

$$\frac{dy}{dx} = \frac{1}{x} + e^x + 2x = \frac{1 + x\,e^x + 2x^2}{x}$$

(6) Find $\frac{dy}{dx}$ for the following (Oct., 2001)

(a) $$y = \frac{x^2 5^x}{x^2 + 1}, \frac{dy}{dx} = \frac{(x^2 + 1)\frac{d}{dx}(x^2 5^x) - x^2 5^x \frac{d}{dx}(x^2 + 1)}{(x^2 + 1)^2}$$

$$= \frac{(x^2 + 1)\left[x^2\frac{d}{dx}5^x + 5^x\frac{d}{dx}(x^2)\right] - x^2 5^x(2x)}{(x^2 + 1)^2}$$

$$= \frac{(x^2 + 1)(x^2 5^x \log 5 + 2x5^x) - 2x^3 5^x}{(x^2 + 1)^2}$$

(b) $y = 4x^3 \log_e x$

$$\frac{dy}{dx} = 4\left[x^3\frac{dy}{dx}\log_e x + \log_e x\frac{d}{dx}x^3\right] = \frac{4x^3}{x} + 4.3x^2 \log_e x$$

$$\frac{dy}{dx} = \frac{4x^3 + 12x^3 \log_e x}{x}$$

(c) $y = x^{e^x}$ Introducing log both sides we get $\log_e y = e^x \log_e x$

$$\frac{1}{y}\frac{dy}{dx} = e^x \frac{d}{dx}(\log_e x) + \log_e x \frac{d}{dx}(e^x) = \frac{e^x}{x} + e^x \log_e x$$

$$\frac{dy}{dx} = y\left[\frac{e^x}{x} + e^x \log_e x\right] = \frac{x^{e^x} e^x}{x} + e^x x^{e^x} \log_e x$$

$$= \frac{e^x\, x^{ex} + x^{ex} e^x x \log_e x}{x} = \frac{e^x x^{ex}[1 + x \log_e x]}{x}$$

(7) (a) Find $\frac{dy}{dx}$ for the following (April, 2002)

$$y = 2^{x^3-3x^2+2x-1}, \quad \frac{dy}{dx} = 2^{x^3-3x^2+2x-1} \log_e 2 \frac{d}{dx}(x^3 - 3x^2 + 2x - 1)$$

$$\frac{dy}{dx} = (3x^2 - 6x + 2)\ 2^{x^3-3x^2+2x-1} \log_e 2$$

(b) $y = x^4 - 3x^2 - 7x + 4\sqrt{x} - 5$

$$\frac{dy}{dx} = \frac{d}{dx}(x^4) - 3\frac{d}{dx}(x^2) - 7\frac{d}{dx}(x) + 4\frac{d}{dx}\sqrt{x} - \frac{d}{dx}(5)$$

$$= 4x^3 - 6x - 7 + \frac{4}{2\sqrt{x}} = 4x^4 - 6x - 7 + \frac{2}{\sqrt{x}}$$

(c) $y = (3 - 6x)^{\frac{2}{3}}$

$$\frac{dy}{dx} = \frac{2}{3}(3-6x)^{\frac{2}{3}-1} \frac{d}{dx}(3-6x) = \frac{2(-6)}{3\sqrt[3]{3-6x}} = \frac{-4}{\sqrt[3]{(3-6x)}}$$

(8) Find $\frac{dy}{dx}$ for the following (Oct., 2003)

(a) $y = (3 - 4x^2)^2$

$$\frac{dy}{dx} = 2\,(3-4x^2)\,(-8x) = -16x\,(3-4x^2)$$

$$= -48x + 64x^3 = 64x^3 - 48x$$

(b) $y = \dfrac{x}{\sqrt{5x^2 - 10x + 2}}$

$$\frac{dy}{dx} = \frac{\sqrt{5x^2 - 10x + 2}\ \frac{d}{dx}(x) - x\frac{d}{dx}(5x^2 - 10x + 2)^{\frac{1}{2}}}{(5x^2 - 10x + 2)}$$

$$\frac{dy}{dx}=\frac{\sqrt{5x^2-10x+2}-\dfrac{x(10x-10)}{2\sqrt{5x^2-10x+2}}}{(5x^2-10x+2)}$$

$$=\frac{2(5x^2-10x+2)-10x^2+10x}{(5x^2+10x+2)^{\frac{3}{2}}}=\frac{10x^2-20x+4-10x^2+10x}{2(5x^2+10x+2)^{\frac{3}{2}}}$$

$$=\frac{4-10x}{2(5x^2+10x+2)^{\frac{3}{2}}}=\frac{2(2-5x)}{2\sqrt{(5x^2+10x+2)^3}}=\frac{(2-5x)}{\sqrt{(5x^2+10x+2)^3}}$$

(9) *(a)* Find $\frac{dy}{dx}$ for the following (April, 2003)

$y=\sqrt{x^2+3x-2}$, $\frac{dy}{dx}=\frac{(2x+3)}{2\sqrt{x^2+3x-2}}$

(b) $y=\frac{\log_e(x+2)}{\log_e(x+1)}$

$y=\log_e(x+2)-\log_e(x+1)$, $\frac{dy}{dx}=\frac{1}{x+2}-\frac{1}{x+1}$

(c) $y=\frac{(2x+1)(3x+1)}{(4x+1)}$

$$y=\frac{(2x+1)(3x+1)}{(4x+1)}=\frac{(6x^2+2x+3x+1)}{4x+1}=\frac{(6x^2+5x+1)}{(4x+1)}$$

$$\frac{dy}{dx}=\frac{(4x+1)(12x+5)-(6x^2+5x+1)(4)}{(4x+1)^2}$$

$$\frac{dy}{dx}=\frac{48x^2+20x+12x+5-24x^2-20x-4}{(4x+1)^2}=\frac{24x^2+12x+1}{(4x+1)^2}$$

(10) *(a)* Find $\frac{dy}{dx}$ for the following (Oct., 2003)

$$y=x+\frac{4}{x}-\frac{2}{x^7}$$

$$\frac{dy}{dx}=\frac{d}{dx}(x)+4\frac{d}{dx}(x^{-1})-2\frac{d}{dx}(x^{-7})=1-4x^{-2}+14x^{-8}=1-\frac{4}{x^2}+\frac{14}{x^8}$$

(b) $y = \left[x - \frac{1}{x}\right]^3$

$$\frac{dy}{dx} = 3\left(x - \frac{1}{x}\right)^2 \frac{d}{dx}\left(x - \frac{1}{x}\right) = 3\left(x - \frac{1}{x}\right)^2 \left[\frac{d}{dx}(x) - \frac{d}{dx}(x^{-1})\right]$$

$$= 3\left(x - \frac{1}{x}\right)^2 (1 + x^{-2}) = 3\left(x - \frac{1}{x}\right)^2 \left(1 + \frac{1}{x^2}\right)$$

(c) $y = \log_e x + e^{5x} + \sqrt{x} + 3^x$

$$\frac{dy}{dx} = \frac{d}{dx}(\log_e x) + \frac{d}{dx}e^{5x} + \frac{d}{dx}\sqrt{x} + \frac{d}{dx}3^x$$

$$= \frac{1}{x} + 5\,e^{5x} + \frac{1}{2\sqrt{x}} + 3^x \log 3$$

(11) (a) Find $\frac{dy}{dx}$ for the following (April, 2004)

$$y = \frac{x\,e^x}{1 + x \log_e x}$$

$$\frac{dy}{dx} = \frac{(1 + x \log_e x)\frac{d}{dx}x\,e^x - x\,e^x \frac{d}{dx}(1 + x \log_e x)}{(1 + x \log_e x)^2}$$

$$\frac{dy}{dx} = \frac{(1 + x \log_e x)(e^x + x\,e^x) - x\,e^x(1 + \log_e x)}{(1 + x \log_e x)^2} = \frac{e^x + x\,e^x - x\,e^x}{1 + x \log_e x} = \frac{e^x}{1 + x \log_e x}$$

(b) $y = 4x^7 + 7 \log_e x + 10e^x + 5.3^x - 100$

$$\frac{dy}{dx} = 4\frac{d}{dx}(x^7) + 7\frac{d}{dx}(\log_e x) + 10\frac{d}{dx}(e^x) + 5\frac{d}{dx}3^x - \frac{d}{dx}(100)$$

$$= 28x^6 + \frac{7}{x} + 10e^x + 5.3^x \log_e 3$$

(c) $y = \sqrt{3x^2 - x + 2}$, $\frac{dy}{dx} = \frac{d}{dx}(3x^2 - x + 2)^{\frac{1}{2}} = \frac{(6x - 1)}{2\sqrt{3x^2 - x + 2}}$

3.10. Additional Solved Problems on Differentiation:

Find $\frac{dy}{dx}$ of the following functions:

(1) $y = x^3 - \log x + e^x + 3^x + 10$, $\frac{dy}{dx} = 3x^2 - \frac{1}{x} + e^x + 3^x \log 3$

(2) $y = 3x^5 - 7\log x - 3e^x + 5.2^x - 50$

$$\frac{dy}{dx} = 15x^2 - \frac{7}{x} - 3e^x + 5\,2^x \log 2$$

(3) $y = x^3 + 3^x + 3^3$

$$\frac{dy}{dx} = 3x^2 + 3^x \log 3 \qquad \left[as\ \frac{d}{dx}(3)^3 = 0\right]$$

(4) $y = x^{\frac{5}{2}} - 5x^{\frac{3}{2}} + 5\sqrt{x} - 3$

$$\frac{dy}{dx} = \frac{5}{2}x^{\frac{3}{2}} - \frac{15}{2}x^{\frac{1}{2}} + \frac{5}{2\sqrt{x}} = \frac{5\sqrt{x^3}}{2} + \frac{15\sqrt{x}}{2} + \frac{5}{2\sqrt{x}}$$

(5) $y = x^{-\frac{3}{2}} - 5x^{\frac{5}{2}} - 8\sqrt{x} + 7x - 10$

$$\frac{dy}{dx} = -\frac{3}{2}x^{-\frac{5}{2}} - \frac{25}{2}x^{\frac{3}{2}} - \frac{8}{2\sqrt{x}} + 7 = -\frac{3}{2\sqrt{x^5}} - \frac{25\sqrt{x^3}}{2} - \frac{8}{2\sqrt{x}} + 7$$

(6) $y = (x^2 - 3x + 6)(5e^x - 3\log x)$

$$\frac{dy}{dx} = (x^2 - 3x + 6)\left(5e^x - \frac{3}{x}\right) + (5e^x - 3\log x)(2x - 3)$$

$$= \frac{(x^2 - 3x + 6)(5x\,e^x - 3) + x(2x - 3)(5e^x - 3\log x)}{x}$$

(7) $y = (x^{\frac{5}{2}} + 4\sqrt{x} - 8)(3\log x - 5e^x + 8^x)$

$$\frac{dy}{dx} = (x^{\frac{5}{2}} + 4\sqrt{x} - 8)\frac{d}{dx}(3\log x - 5e^x + 8^x) + (3\log x - 5e^x + 8^x)\frac{d}{dx}(x^{\frac{5}{2}} + 4\sqrt{x} - 8)$$

$$= (x^{\frac{5}{2}} + 4\sqrt{x} - 8)\left(\frac{3}{x} - 5e^x + 8^x \log 8\right) + (3\log x - 5e^x + 8^x)\left(\frac{5}{2}x^{\frac{3}{2}} + \frac{2}{\sqrt{x}}\right)$$

(8) $y = x^{\frac{3}{2}}\, 8^x - 5\,e^x \log x$

$$\frac{dy}{dx} = x^{\frac{3}{2}}\frac{d}{dx}(8^x) + 8^x \frac{d}{dx}x^{\frac{3}{2}} - 5e^x \frac{d}{dx}\log x - 5\log x \frac{d}{dx}e^x$$

$$= x^{\frac{3}{2}} 8^x \log 8 + \frac{8^x 3\sqrt{x}}{2} - \frac{5e^x}{x} - 5e^x \log x$$

$$= 8^x \log 8\,\sqrt{x^3} + \frac{8^x\, 3\sqrt{x}}{2} - \frac{5e^x}{x} - 5e^x \log x$$

(9) $y = \dfrac{\log x}{3^x}, \quad \dfrac{dy}{dx} = \dfrac{3^x \dfrac{d}{dx}(\log x) - \log x \dfrac{d}{dx}(3^x)}{(3^x)^2}$

$$= \frac{\dfrac{3^x}{x} - \log x\, 3^x \log 3}{(3^x)^2} = \frac{3^x - 3^x x \log x \log 3}{x(3^x)^2}$$

(10) $y = \dfrac{x - \sqrt{x}}{\sqrt{x} + 5}, \quad \dfrac{dy}{dx} = \dfrac{(x+5)\dfrac{d}{dx}\left[x - \sqrt{x}\right] - (x - \sqrt{x})\dfrac{d}{dx}\left[\sqrt{x} + 5\right]}{(\sqrt{x} + 5)^2}$

$$= \frac{(\sqrt{x}+5)\left(1 - \dfrac{1}{2\sqrt{x}}\right) - \dfrac{(x - \sqrt{x})}{2\sqrt{x}}}{(\sqrt{x}+5)^2} = \frac{\dfrac{(\sqrt{x}+5)(2\sqrt{x}-1)}{2\sqrt{x}} - \dfrac{(x-\sqrt{x})}{2\sqrt{x}}}{(\sqrt{x}+5)^2}$$

$$= \frac{(\sqrt{x}+5)(2\sqrt{x}-1) - (x - \sqrt{x})}{2\sqrt{x}(\sqrt{x}+5)^2} = \frac{2x - \sqrt{x} + 10\sqrt{x} - 5 - x + \sqrt{x}}{2\sqrt{x}\left\{\sqrt{x}+5\right\}^2}$$

$$\frac{dy}{dx} = \frac{x + 10\sqrt{x} - 5}{2\sqrt{x}(\sqrt{x}+5)^2}$$

(11) $y = \dfrac{7\log x + x^3}{e^x},$

$$\frac{dy}{dx} = \frac{e^x \dfrac{d}{dx}\left[7\log x + x^3\right] - (7\log x + x^3)\dfrac{d}{dx}(e^x)}{(e^x)^2} = \frac{e^x\left[\dfrac{7}{x} + 3x^2\right] - (7\log x + x^3)(e^x)}{(e^x)^2}$$

$$= \frac{e^x\left[7 + 3x^3 - 7x\log x - x^4\right]}{x(e^x)^2} = \frac{7 + 3x^3 - 7x\log x - x^4}{x\, e^x}$$

(12) $y = \dfrac{e^x - x^2}{2x^2 + 3^x}, \quad \dfrac{dy}{dx} = \dfrac{(2x^2 + 3^x)(e^x - 2x) - (e^x - x^2(4x + 3^x \log 3)}{(2x^2 + 3^x)^2}$

(13) $y = \dfrac{x^2 \log x}{x^2 + 1}, \quad \dfrac{dy}{dx} = \dfrac{(x^2+1)(2x\log x + x) - (x^2 \log x)(2x)}{(x^2+1)^2}$

(14) $y = 2x^8 - 3\log x + 5^x + 8e^x - 27$

$$\frac{dy}{dx} = 16x^7 - \frac{3}{x} + 5^x \log 5 + 8e^x$$

(15) $y = (x^3 - 3x^2 + 5x - 8)(2e^x - 5\log x)$

$$\frac{dy}{dx} = (x^3 - 3x^2 + 5x - 8)\left(2e^x - \frac{5}{x}\right) + (2e^x - 5\log x)(3x^2 - 6x + 5)$$

(16) $y = (5x^2 - 3x)(7^x - 6e^{x^2})$

$$\frac{dy}{dx} = (5x^2 - 3x)(7^x \log 7 - 12xe^{x^2}) + (7^x - 6e^{x^2})(10x - 3)$$

(17) $y = x^{-2}3^x + e^x \log^x x$

$$\frac{dy}{dx} = -2x^{-3}3^x + x^{-2}3^x \log 3 + \frac{e^x}{x} + e^x \log x$$

$$\frac{dy}{dx} = -2x^{-3}3^x + x^{-2}3^x \log 3 + \frac{e^x}{x} + e^x \log x = -\frac{2.3^x}{x^3} + \frac{3^x \log 3}{x^2} + \frac{e^x}{x} + e^x \log x$$

(18) $y = 5^{x^3+x^2+x} + e^{x^3+x^2+x} - \log(x^3 + x^2 + x)$

$$\frac{dy}{dx} = 5^{x^3+x^2+x}\frac{d}{dx}(x^3 + x^2 + x)\log 5 + e^{x^3+x^2+x}\frac{d}{dx}(x^3 + x^2 + x) + \frac{\frac{d}{dx}(x^3 + x^2 + x)}{x^3 + x^2 + x}$$

$$\frac{dy}{dx} = (3x^2 + 2x + 1)\left[5^{x^3+x^2+x}\log 5 + e^{x^3+x^2+x} + \frac{1}{(x^3 + x^2 + x)}\right]$$

(19) $y = \dfrac{\log(x^2 + 3)}{5^{3x+2}}$

$$\frac{dy}{dx} = \frac{5^{3x+2}\dfrac{2x}{x^2+3} - \log(x^2 + 3)\, 3.5^{3x+2}\log 5}{(5^{3x+2})^2} = \frac{\dfrac{2x\, 5^{3x+2} - 3(x^2 + 3)\log(x^2 + 3)5^{3x+2}\log 5}{x^2 + 3}}{(5^{3x+2})^2}$$

$$= \frac{2x\, 5^{3x+2} - 3(x^2 + 3)\log(x^2 + 3)5^{3x+2}\log 5}{(x^2 + 3)(5^{3x+2})^2} = \frac{2x + 3(x^2 + 3)\log(x^2 + 3)\log 5}{(x^2 + 3)5^{3x+2}}$$

(20) $y = \log(\log x)$, $\dfrac{dy}{dx} = \dfrac{1}{\log x}\dfrac{d}{dx}(\log x) = \dfrac{1}{x \log x}$

(21) $y = \dfrac{\log(\log x)}{\sqrt{e^x + 5}}$, $\dfrac{dy}{dx} = \dfrac{\sqrt{e^x+5}\,\dfrac{d}{dx}\log(\log x) - \log(\log x)\dfrac{d}{dx}\sqrt{e^x+5}}{(e^x+5)}$

$$= \frac{\dfrac{\sqrt{e^x+5}}{x \log x} - \dfrac{\log(\log x)\frac{1}{2}(e^x+5)^{-\frac{1}{2}}e^x}{2\sqrt{e^n+5}}}{(e^x+5)} = \frac{\dfrac{\sqrt{e^x+5}}{x\log x} - \dfrac{\log(\log x)e^x}{2\sqrt{e^x+5}}}{(e^x+5)}$$

(22) $y = \sqrt{x^3+x^2+x+5}\;\; e^{x^2+1}$

$$\frac{dy}{dx} = e^{x^2+1}\frac{1}{2}(x^3+x^2+x+5)^{-\frac{1}{2}}(3x^2+2x+1) + 2xe^{x^2+1}\sqrt{x^3+x^2+x+5}$$

$$\frac{dy}{dx} = \frac{(3x^2+2x+1)e^{x^2+1}}{\sqrt{x^3+x^2+x+5}} + 2xe^{x^2+1}\sqrt{x^3+x^2+x+5}$$

(23) $y = \dfrac{1}{(x^2+1)^3}$, or $y = (x^2+1)^{-3}$,

$$\frac{dy}{dx} = -3(x^2+1)^{-4}\frac{d}{dx}(x^2+1) = -\frac{6x}{(x^2+1)^4}$$

(24) $y = \dfrac{3}{x^5+e^n}$, or $y = 3(x^5+e^x)^{-1}$

$$\frac{dy}{dx} = -3(x^5+e^x)^{-2}\frac{d}{dx}(x^5+e^x) = -3(x^5+e^x)^{-2}(5x^4+e^x) = -\frac{3(5x^4+e^x)}{(x^5+e^x)^2}$$

(25) $y = \sqrt{x^3-8} - \sqrt{x^2+4}$

$$\frac{dy}{dx} = \frac{1}{2}(x^3-8)^{-\frac{1}{2}}(3x^2) - \frac{1}{2}(x^2+4)^{-\frac{1}{2}}(2x) = \frac{3x^2}{2\sqrt{x^3-8}} - \frac{2x}{2\sqrt{x^2+4}}$$

(26) $y = 7^{x^2+5x+1}$

$$\frac{dy}{dx} = 7^{x^2+5x+1}\frac{d}{dx}(x^2+5x+1)\log 7 = (2x+5)7^{x^2+5x+1}\log 7$$

(27) $y = 8^{\log x - x^2}$

$$\frac{dy}{dx} = 8^{\log x - x^2} \frac{d}{dx}(\log x - x^2)\log 8 = \left\{\frac{1}{x} - 2x\right\} 8^{\log x - x^2} \log 8$$

$$= \frac{(1-2x^2)8^{\log x - x^2} \log 8}{x}$$

(28) $y = 5^{3^x - e^x + x^2}$

$$\frac{dy}{dx} = 5^{3^x - e^x + x^2} \frac{d}{dx}(3^x - e^x + x^2)\log 5 = (3^x \log 3 - e^x + 2x)\, 5^{3^x - e^x + x^2} \log 5$$

(29) $y = 5^{e^{x^2} + \log x - 5^x}$

$$\frac{dy}{dx} = 5^{e^{x^2} + \log x - 5^x} \frac{d}{dx}(e^{x^2} + \log x - 5^x)\log 5$$

$$= (2xe^{x^2} + \frac{1}{x} - 5^x \log 5)5^{e^{x^2} + \log x - 5^x} \log 5$$

(30) $y = \log(3e^x + x^2 + 4^x)$, $\dfrac{dy}{dx} = \dfrac{3e^x + 2x + 4^x \log 4}{3e^x + x^2 + 4^x}$

(31) $y = \log(x^5 + \sqrt{x} + 5^x)$, $\dfrac{dy}{dx} = \dfrac{5x^4 + \dfrac{1}{2\sqrt{x}} + 5^x \log 5}{(x^5 + \sqrt{x} + 5^x)}$

(32) $y = \sqrt{7x^3 - 3x^2 + 6} + e^{3x^2 + 8x - 2}$

$$\frac{dy}{dx} = \frac{21x^2 - 6x}{2\sqrt{7x^3 - 3x^2 + 6}} + (6x+8)\, e^{3x^2 + 8x - 2}$$

(33) $y = (x^4 - 3x^2 + 5)^3 + 8^{7x^2 + 4}$

$$\frac{dy}{dx} = 3\,(4x^3 - 6x)\,(x^4 - 3x^2 + 5)^2 + 14x\, 8^{7x^2 + 4} \log 8$$

(34) $y = (x^3 - x^2 + x)^3 e^{4x^2 - 9}$

$$\frac{dy}{dx} = 3(x^3 - x^2 + x)^2(3x^2 - 2x + 1)e^{4x^2 - 9} + 8x\, e^{4x^2 - 9}(x^3 - x^2 + x)^3$$

(35) $y = 8^{3x+5^x} \log(x^2+5)$

$$\frac{dy}{dx} = \frac{8^{3x+5^x}(2x)}{(x^2+5)} + \log(x^2+5)\, 8^{3x+5^x}(3+5^x \log 5)\log 8$$

$$= \frac{2x.8^{3x+5^x}}{(x^2+5)} + (3+5^x \log x)\log(x^2+5)8^{3x+5^x} \log 8$$

(36) $y = e^{x^2-x+2}\log(x+1)$

$$\frac{dy}{dx} = (2x-1)\log_e(x+1)e^{x^2-x+2} + \frac{e^{x^2-x+2}}{(x+1)}$$

(37) $y = \dfrac{x^2 \log(3x+5)}{e^{4x+8}}$

$$\frac{dy}{dx} = \frac{e^{4x+8}\frac{d}{dx}\left\{x^2\log(3x+5)\right\} - x^2\log(3x+5)\frac{d}{dx}(e^{4x+8})}{(e^{4x+8})^2}$$

$$= \frac{e^{4x+8}\left[\left\{\frac{3x^2}{3x+5} + 2x\log(3x+5)\right\} - 4x^2\log(3x+5)\right]}{(e^{4x+8})^2}$$

$$= \frac{3x^2 + 2x(3x+5)\log(3x+5) - 4x^2(3x+5)\log(3x+5)}{(3x+5)e^{4x+8}}$$

(38) $y = \log[\log(5x^2+5^x)]$

$$\frac{dy}{dx} = \frac{1}{\log(5x^2+5^x)}\frac{d}{dx}\log(5x^2+5^x) = \frac{10x+5^x\log 5}{\log(5x^2+5^x)(5x^2+5^x)}$$

(39) $y = \log[\log(e^x+3^x)]$

$$\frac{dy}{dx} = \frac{1}{\log(e^x+3^x)}\frac{d}{dx}\log(e^x+3^x) = \frac{e^x+3^x\log 3}{(e^x+3^x)\log(e^x+3^x)}$$

(40) $y = \log[\log(\log x^2)]$

$$\frac{dy}{dx} = \frac{1}{\log(\log x^2)}\frac{d}{dx}\log(\log x^2)$$

$$= \frac{1}{\log(\log x^2)} \times \frac{1}{(\log x^2)}\frac{d}{dx}(\log x^2) = \frac{2}{x(\log x^2)\log(\log x^2)}$$

EXERCISE – 3

(A) Solve the following for $\frac{dy}{dx}$

(1) $y = x^3$

(2) $y = \sqrt[3]{x^2+5}$

(3) $y = 7x^4 + 2x^3 - \sqrt{x} + \sqrt[5]{x^3}$

(4) $y = 8x^{-3/2}$

(5) $y = x^2 - 4x + \log x$

(6) $y = 3x^2(5x+2)$

(7) $y = (3x^2+2x)(x^2-3x)$

(8) $y = \frac{1}{x^2\sqrt{x}}$

(9) $y = (x+2)(x-3)(2x+5)$

(10) $y = \frac{3x^2+5}{x-2}$

(11) $y = (x^3-3)^2(3x^2+8)^3$

(12) $y = \sqrt{(x+1)}(3x^2+4x)$

(13) $y = \frac{x-1}{(x+1)^{1/3}}$

(14) $y = \frac{x+5}{\sqrt{x^3}}$

(15) $y = \frac{x-3}{\sqrt{x+3}}$

(16) $y = \sqrt{3x^2+5x+7}$

(17) $y = (x^2+7x-3)^{2/3}(x^2+6)^{2/3}$

(18) $x = at^2$ and $y = 3at$

$$\left[\frac{dy}{dx}=\frac{dy}{dt}.\frac{dt}{dx}=\frac{3}{2t}, \text{where } \frac{dt}{dx}=\frac{1}{dx/dt}\right]$$

(19) $Z = x^2 - 3x + 5$ and $y = 5\,Z^2 + 2$

$$\left[\frac{dy}{dx}=\frac{dy}{dz}.\frac{dz}{dx}.,\quad \frac{dy}{dx}=10(x^2-3x+5)\,(2x-3)\right]$$

(20) $x^2 + y^2 = t^2$

(21) $\sqrt{x}+\sqrt{y}=\sqrt{k}$

(22) $5x^2 = y^3$

(23) $y = \log.\log(3x^2 + 2x)$

(24) $y=\dfrac{1}{\log(x+1)}$

(25) $y = a^{x^2}$

(26) $y = x^{x^2}$

(27) $y = e^{x^3-3x^2+7}$

(28) $y=\dfrac{e^x-3}{e^x+3}$

(29) $y = 4^{e^{x^{2+3}}}$

(30) $y = e^{x^3-3x+8}\log(x^3-3x+8)$

(31) $y = (3-\sqrt{3})\,(3+\sqrt{x})$

(32) $y=\sqrt{\dfrac{2+\sqrt{x}}{2-\sqrt{x}}}$

(33) $y^2x + 5xy + x^2 = 8$

(34) $y = (2x^3 + 3^x)e^{-5x^2}$

(35) $y=\dfrac{(x-3)\,(2x+5)}{(x+5)\,(3-x)}$

(36) $y=\sqrt{\dfrac{(x-1)\,(x+2)}{(3x-4)\,(x-8)}}$

(37) $y = 10^x + \log(3x^2 - 1) + x^2 - 6x$

(38) $Z = 3x^2 - 9x, y = Z^2 + 2z$

(39) $y = e^{3x^2} + \sqrt[5]{(5x^2 - 1)} - 5$

(40) $x^2 y = 5$

(41) $x^2 - 2xy = 8$

(42) $2x^2 - y^2 = 3$

(43) $y = \log(x + \sqrt{t^2 + x^2})$

(B) Determine the nature of the following function. Find whether they are rising or falling or depict the point of inflexion at $x = 3$ and $x = 1$.

(1) $y = x^3 - 3x^2 + 2$

(2) $y = x^2 + 3x$

(3) $y = x^2 - 6x + 8$

(4) $y = \dfrac{2x + 5}{x - 2}$

(C) Find the value of 'x' which gives stationary point for y and determine whether the stationary point is a maximum or minimum or point of inflexion.

(1) $y = x^2 - 6x + 4$

(2) $y = x3 - 3x^2 + 15$

(3) $y = 2x + \dfrac{1}{x}$

(4) $y = \dfrac{3 - x^2}{3 + x^2}$

❑ ❑ ❑

4 APPLICATIONS OF DERIVATIVE IN ECONOMICS

4.1 Economic Theory and Applications of Derivatives

The first order derivative measures the rate of change in economic variables. It determines the marginal changes in variables. This has got much applications in economic theory. For example by differentiating total revenue (R) with respect to output (Q) we obtain $\frac{dR}{dQ}$. This is called marginal revenue of the firm. Similarly by differentiating total cost (C) with respect to output (Q), we arrive at the MC (marginal cost), $\frac{dC}{dQ}$. From the Keynesian theory of employment, consumption function is stated where $= MPC =$. It represents the slope of the consumption function.

Derivative can be a tool to explain various concepts like elasticity of demand, elasticity of substitution and cost elasticity etc.

4.2 Derivatives and Elasticity of Demand

Consumer's ordinary demand function for q_1 (Commodity Q_1) can be written as $q_1 = f[P_1, P_2, M°]$, where P_1 = price of commodity Q_1, P_2 = price of commodity Q_2 and $M°$ is the given money income. q_1 and q_2 are assumed to be related goods. The relatationship is either by the way of substitutes or by the way of complementarity. Accodingly cross elasticity of demand e_{12} and e_{21} can be evaluated.

e_{12} refers to the cross elasticity of demand for q_1 with respect to price of q_2 and e_{21} indicates the cross elasticity of demand for q_2 with respect to price of q_1. These are given as

$$e_{12} = \frac{d(\log_e q_1)}{d(\log_e p_2)} = \frac{dq_1}{dp_2} \times \frac{p_2}{q_1} \quad \text{and} \quad e_{21} = \frac{d(\log_e q_2)}{d(\log_e p_1)} = \frac{dq_2}{dp_1} \times \frac{p_1}{q_2}$$

The sign and the magnitude of these elasticities can dictate the nature of relationship between q_1 and q_2.

When we assume p_2 and M^p are given parameters so that by defining $q_1 = f(p_1)$, we will obtain price elasticity of demand for q_1 (e_{11}).

$$e_{11} = \frac{\text{Proportionate change in quantity demanded for } q_1}{\text{Proportionate change in } p_1}$$

$$e_{11} = \frac{d(\log_e q_1)}{d(\log_e p_1)} = \frac{dq_1}{dp_1} \times \frac{p_1}{q_1}$$

Numerically a large value of e_{11} implies that quantity is highly responsive to changes in its price. Commodities which have numerically high elasticities $(e_{11} < -1)$ are luxury goods while goods for which $e_{11} > -1$ are called necessaries. Normally e_{11} is negative as $\frac{dq_1}{dp_1}$ is negative, since demand (q_1) and price (p_1) are inversely related.

Following illustrations are used to show the process of evaluating price elasticity of demand (e_{11}) at different prices.

(1) Given the demand function for q_1 as $q_1 = 10 - 14p_1 + p^2{}_1$, find e_{11} at $p_1 = 8$.

Since $q_1 = 10 - 14p_1 + p^2{}_1$, $e_{11} = \frac{dq_1}{dp_1} \cdot \frac{p_1}{q_1}$

$$\frac{dq_1}{dp_1} = \frac{d}{dp_1}(10 - 14p_1 + p_1^2) = -14 + 2p_1$$

$$e_{11} = \frac{(-14 + 2p_1)\, p_1}{q_1} = \frac{(-14 + 2p_1)(p_1)}{10 - 14p_1 + p_1^2}$$

Now given that $p_1 = 8$, $e_{11} = \frac{[-14 + 2(8)]\, 8}{10 - 14(8) + (8)^2} = \frac{16}{-38}$, or $e_{11} = -0.42$ or $|e_{11}| = 0.42$

(2) Mr. Mahesh estimated his demand function for wheat $P = 10 - 2D$, where, P = price, D = demand, find elasticity of demand at $P = 2$ and 3.

Elasticity of demand is e_{11} where

$$e_{11} = \frac{dD}{dP} \times \frac{P}{D}$$

Since estimated demand function is given in the form $P = 10 - 2D$, we need to rearrange this to get

$$2D = 10 - P \quad \text{or} \quad D = 5 - \frac{P}{2}$$

$$\frac{dD}{dP} = -\frac{1}{2} \text{ and } \quad e_{11} = -\frac{1}{2} \times \frac{P}{D} = \frac{-P}{2\left\{5-\frac{P}{2}\right\}}$$

For $P = 2,\ e_{11} = \dfrac{-2}{2\left\{5-\frac{2}{2}\right\}} = \dfrac{-2}{2\,(5-1)} = \dfrac{-2}{8} = -0.25$ or $|e_{11}| = 0.25$

For $P = 3,\ e_{11} = \dfrac{-3}{2\left[5-\frac{3}{2}\right]} = \dfrac{-3}{2\times\left(\frac{7}{2}\right)} = -0.43$

$\therefore\ |e_{11}| = 0.43$ at $P = 3$ and $|e_{11}| = 0.25$ at $P = 2$

(3) If the demand law is given by $x_1 = \dfrac{10}{P_1+1}$ find elasticity of demand e_d at $P_1 = 2$

Demand function is $x_1 = \dfrac{10}{P_1+1} = 10(P_1+1)^{-1}$,

From this we get $e_d = \dfrac{dx_1}{dP_1} \times \dfrac{P_1}{x_1}$, where $\dfrac{dx_1}{dP_1} = -10(P_1+1)^{-2} = \dfrac{-10}{(P_1+1)^2}$

At $P_1 = 2,\ \dfrac{dx_1}{dP_1} = \dfrac{-10}{(2+1)^2} = -\dfrac{10}{9},\quad x_1 = \dfrac{10}{P_1+1} = \dfrac{10}{3}$

$\therefore\ e_d = \left(\dfrac{dx_1}{dP_1}\right)\left(\dfrac{P_1}{x_1}\right) = \left(\dfrac{-10}{9}\right)\left(\dfrac{2}{10/3}\right) = -\dfrac{60}{90} = -0.67$ or $|e_{11}| = 0.67$ at $P = 2$

(4) Given the demand function $p_1 = 50 - 3x_1$ findelasticity of demand $e_d$at $p_1 = 2$ and prove that $e_d = \dfrac{AR}{AR-MR}$ at this price.

(a) For $p_1 = 50 - 3x_1$, $e_d = \dfrac{dx_1}{dp_1} \times \dfrac{p_1}{x_1}$ and $\dfrac{dp_1}{dx_1} = -3 \quad \therefore \dfrac{1}{\frac{dp_1}{dx_{11}}} = -\dfrac{1}{3}$.

Now e_d at $p_1 = 2$ can be evaluated to be

$e_d = \dfrac{dx_1}{dp_1} \times \dfrac{p_1}{x_1} = -\dfrac{1}{3} \times \dfrac{(50-3x_1)}{x_1}$. Substituting $p_1 = 2$, we get, $2 = 50 - 3x_1 \quad \therefore x_1 = 16$.

$$\therefore e_d = -\frac{1}{3} \times \frac{2}{16} = -\frac{1}{24} \text{ or } |e_d| = \frac{1}{24} = 0.042.$$

We can get the same solution if apply the formula $e = \dfrac{AR}{AR - MR}$, where AR = Avenage revenue or Price and MR = Marginal revenue

Since = $p_1 = 50 - 3x_1$, $TR = p_1 x_1 = (50 - 3x_1)\, x_1 = 50x_1 - 3x_1^2$ and

$$MR = \frac{d}{dx_1}(TR) = \frac{d}{dx_1}(50x_1 - 3x_1^2) = 50 - 6x_1$$

For $p_1 = 2$, $x_1 = 16$, $\text{MR} = 50 - 6x_1 = 50 - 6 \times 16 = -46$

$$e = \frac{AR}{AR - MR} = \frac{2}{2 - (-46)} = \frac{1}{24}$$

So it is proved that $e_d = \dfrac{1}{24} = \dfrac{AR}{AR - MR} = 0.042$

(5) Given the supply function $q_s = 2p^2 + 5$, find the elasticity of supply at $p = 4$.

e_s = elasticity of supply and it is given as

$$e_s = \frac{\text{proportionate change in qty. supplied of a good}}{\text{proportionate change in price of the good}}$$

$$e_s = \frac{dq_s}{dp} \times \frac{p}{q_s}.$$

For given $q_s = 2p^2 + 5$, $\dfrac{dq_s}{dp} = 4p$

At $p = 4$, $q_s = 2p^2 + 5 = 2(4)^2 + 5 = 37$ and $\dfrac{dq_s}{dp} = 4p = 16$

$$\therefore e_s = (4p)\left(\frac{p}{q_s}\right) = \frac{16 \times 4}{37} = \frac{64}{37} = 1.73$$

(6) Compute the elasticity of supply for the following supply function at $p = 4$ and $p = 16$

$S = 18 + 0.08\text{p} + \sqrt{p}$.

For given $S = 18 + 0.08p + \sqrt{p}$, $e_S = \dfrac{dS}{dp} \times \dfrac{p}{S}$, and $\dfrac{dS}{dp} = 0.8 + \dfrac{1}{2\sqrt{p}}$

(a) at $p = 4$, $S = 18 + 0.08p + \sqrt{p} = 18 + 0.08\,(4) + \sqrt{4} = 20.32$

$$\frac{dS}{dp} = 0.8 + \frac{1}{2\sqrt{p}} = 0.8 + \frac{1}{4} = \frac{3.2 + 1}{4} = 1.05$$

$$\therefore e_s = \frac{dS}{dp} \times \frac{p}{S} = \frac{(1.05)\,(4)}{20.32} = \frac{4.2}{20.32} = 0.207$$

(b) At $p = 16$, $\frac{ds}{dp} = 0.8 + \frac{1}{2\sqrt{p}} = 0.8 + \frac{1}{8} = \frac{7.4}{8}$

$S = 18 + 0.08\,(16) + \sqrt{16} = 23.28$, and $e_s = \frac{7.4}{8} \times \frac{16}{23.28} = 0.636$

(7) If the demand for 'x' commodity is given by $20x = 10 + 5y$, where y = income and 'x' refers to the quantity demanded for the good.

(a) Obtain income elasticity of demand (e_y) at $y = 350$.

Income elasticity formula is given by $e_y = \frac{dx}{dy} \times \frac{y}{x}$, where x = Qty. demanded and y = Income

We are given $20x = 10 + 5y$, Rearranging this we get $x = \frac{10+5y}{20} = \frac{1}{2} + \frac{5}{20}y$,

$\frac{dx}{dy} = \frac{5}{20}$, At $y = 350$, $x = \frac{1}{2} + \frac{5}{20}y = \frac{1}{2} + \frac{5}{20} \times 350 = 88$

$$e_y = \frac{dx}{dy} \times \frac{y}{x} = \left(\frac{5}{20}\right)\left(\frac{350}{88}\right) = \frac{1750}{1760} = 0.99\,.$$

(b) The sign and value of e_y for commodity x stand for what?

The sign and numerical value of e_y is important to ascertain the nature of the commdity 'x'.

(i) If $e_y > 1$, the commdity 'x' seems to be a luxury good.

(ii) If e_y is positive but less than unity i.e. $0 < e_y < 1$, 'x' is said to be a necessary good.

(iii) If e_y takes a negative sign i.e. $e_y < 0$, the commodity 'x' in question is said to be an inferior good or a Giffen good.

(8) How can you compute MR from given the demand function for a commodity as, $q_d = 30 - 5p - p^2$? Evaluate elasticity of demand at $P = 2$, where P = Price.

(i) There is a definite mathematical relationship among MR, demand elasticity and price and this is provided in the following formula

$MR = AR\left(\frac{e-1}{e}\right) = p\left(\frac{e-1}{e}\right)$, where e = price elasticity of demand.

(ii) For the demand function $q_d = 30 - 5p - p^2$, we can find e_d at $p = 2$.

$e_d = \frac{dq_d}{dp} \times \frac{p}{q_d}$ and $\frac{dq_d}{dp} = -5 - 2p$

At $p = 2$, $q_d = 30 - 5p - p^2 = 30 - 10 - 2^2 = 16$ and

$$\frac{dq_d}{dp} = -5 - 2p = -9,\ e_d = \frac{dq_d}{dp} \times \frac{p}{q_d} = (-9)\left(\frac{2}{16}\right) = \frac{-18}{16} = -1.125$$

Substituting $e = 1.125$ and $p = 2$, we get MR

$MR = P\left(\frac{e-1}{e}\right) = 2\left(\frac{1.125-1}{1.125}\right) = 0.22 > 0$ Since $e > 1$, $MR > 0$.

4.3 Price, MR, TR and Demand Elasticity in Perfectly Competitive Commodity Market

Markets are classified into perfect competition and imperfect competition. The firm under perfectly competive commodity market faces a horizontal sloping demand curve. It is perfectly elastic ($e_d = \infty$). Therefore firm's *AR* is equal to *MR*. {AR = price =MR}

Firm's total revenue (R) = price × quantity = (p) (q)

$$MR = \frac{dR}{dq} = \frac{d}{dq}(pq) = P.\frac{dq}{dq} + q\frac{dp}{dq} = p, \quad \therefore MR = \text{Price.} \quad \left[\frac{dp}{dq} = 0\right]$$

The firm's supply function is roughly equal to its marginal cost curve. It can be defined with reference to following three situations :

(a) Supply for a very short period: It refers to the period for which output can ' t be adjusted.

(b) Short period: During this period output can be varied by employing variable units of variable factors combined with the fixed amounts of the fixed factors. Thus the plant size remains unaltered.

(c) Long-run period: During long-run, output is readily adjusted by varying quantities of all inputs employed.

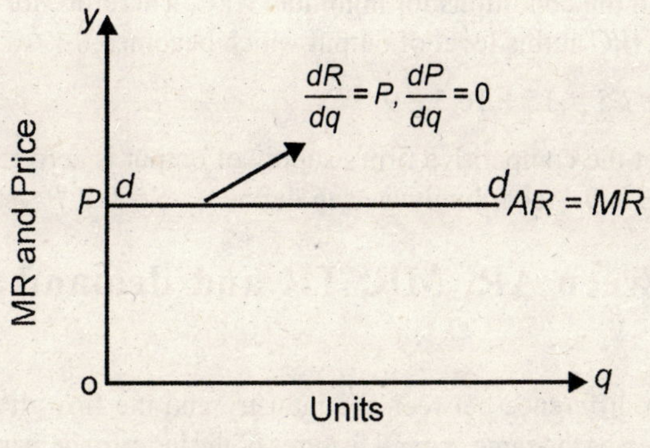

Fig. 4.1: Demand curve of competitive firm

The supply function of the competitive firm is obtained from the first order condition of profit maximisation;

$$MR = MC \quad \text{or} \quad \frac{dR}{dq} = \frac{dC}{dq}.$$

No difference exists between price and MR of a firm under perfect competition. In short-run the firm will supply output only when price exceeds the minimum average variable cost (AVC). Mathematically the supply function of *i*th firm is $S_i = S_i(P)$ for $P >$ minimum *AVC*. $S_i = 0$ if $P <$ mini *AVC*.

Suppose we are given the total cost functions of a firm as

$C_i = 0.3\, q_i^3 - 3\, q_i^2 + 16.5 q_i + 25$

From this we can get the $TVC = 0.3\, q_i^3 - 3\, q_i^2 + 16.5\, q_i$ whereas firm's $TFC = 25$.

Accordingly we get $TC = TVC + TFC$.

Firm's marginal cost (MC) is given by $MC = \frac{dC_j}{dq_j} = \frac{d(TVC)}{dq_j}$

It indicates that *MC* will depend on *TVC* only in so far *TFC* vanishes while computing *MC*, obtained by differentiating total cost *w.r.t.* output *q*. Accordingly we get

$TVC = 0.3\,q_j^3 - 3\,q_j^2 + 16.5q_j$, and $AVC = \frac{TVC}{q_j} = 0.3q_j^2 - 3q_j + 16.5$

AVC is said to be minimum when $\frac{d}{dq_j}(AVC) = 0$ and $\frac{d^2}{dq_j^2}(AVC) > 0$

From the given function we get, $\frac{d}{dq_j}(AVC) = \frac{d}{dq_j}(0.3q_j^2 - 3q_j + 16.5) = 0.6q_j - 3 = 0$

or $0.6q_j = 3$ and $q_j = \frac{3}{0.6} = 5$. Thus for $q_j = 5$, *AVC* is minimum. However this also requires to satisfy the second order condition, which is given by

$$\frac{d^2}{dq_j^2}(AVC) = \frac{d}{dq_j}(0.6q_j - 3) = 0.6 > 0.$$

Thus $q_j = 5$, satisfies both the conditions for minimum *AVC*. Therefore for $q_j = 5$, *AVC* is minimum. This minimum *AVC* is equal to *AVC* at this level of output which becomes,

$$0.3\,(5)^2 - 3\,(5) + 16.5 = 7.5 - 15 + 16.5 = 9$$

From this we can say that the competitive firm's supply of output is zero if price of the product falls short of Rs. 9 for minimum *AVC* is 9. Accordingly we can define $\therefore\ S = 0$ if $P < 9$ and $S > 0$ if $P \geq 9$

4.4 Relationship between AR, MR, TR and demand elasticity under monopoly

In monopoly there is no difference between the industry and the firm. It is one-firm industry. The monopolist's demand curve possesses the same general features of the industry demand curve of the competitive commodity market. The quantity demanded for monopolist's output is a single-valued function of the price. Thus $q_d = f(p)$. The demand curve slopes downward form left to the right. Monopolist's output sold increases by reducing price that he charges from consumers. The perfectly competitive firm in contrast accepts the price as a parameter and adjusts output produced to maximize profit. The firm's demand curve is pefectly elastic with *AR* = *MR*. It has the following implications:

(a) First, he can sell as much output as he produces at the ruling price.

(b) There is no need to reduce price to increase sales.

(c) The firm is a price taker and not a price maker.

The monopolist on the contrary is a price-maker and not a price-taker. However he can't fix both price and output. This is because his price (output) is determined by the demand curve he faces once he selects output (price). The price-quantity combination that maximizes profits of the monopoly firm is invariant with respect to his choice of the independent variable.

The firm's total revenue is given by $R = pq$ where p = price and q = output.

Firm's marginal revenue (MR) is $\frac{dR}{dq}$.

For $R = pq, MR = \frac{dR}{dq} = P\frac{dq}{dq} + q\frac{dp}{dq} = p + q\frac{dp}{dq} < P$ as $\frac{dp}{dq} < 0$

For competitive firm $\frac{dp}{dq} = 0$, while for the monoplist $\frac{dp}{dq} \neq 0$

The sign of $\frac{dp}{dq}$ is negative for $q > 0$ $\therefore MR < P$ or $P > MR$

When a competitive firm expands output by one unit, his total revenue increases by the amount equal to the market price of the product. It is for this reason MR = Price. But the monopolist has to reduce price in order to increase sale of an extra unit of product for the demand curve he faces is monotonically decreasing. Thus MR is less than price for any positive output. If the demand curve is a linear one, the rate of decline in MR will be twice the rate of decline in price. If the demand and MR curves are extended to touch X-axis, MR will cut X-axis half the distance AR cuts the x-axis measured from point of origin.

For example if $P = \alpha - \beta q$, $TR = q(\alpha - \beta q) = \alpha q - \beta q^2$ and

$MR = \frac{d}{dq}(pq) = \alpha - 2\beta q$, the slope of the demand curve is found constant and it is $\frac{dp}{dq} = -\beta$.

The distance between price and MR is given by βq. The relationship between AR, MR and 'e' [price elasticity of demand] is diagramatically shown in fig. 4.2.

'e' at point 'A' is $\frac{Ad}{Ap} = \frac{AQ}{PM}$.

Since $\Delta\, PMC = \Delta\, CAB$, their corresponding sides are also equal. $\therefore PM = AB$.

It can be easily proved that $\angle PCM = \angle ACB$ as they are vertically opposite.

$\angle PMC = \angle CAB$, 90° each $\therefore \angle CPM = \angle ABC$.

Now $e = \frac{AQ}{PC} = \frac{AQ}{AB} = \frac{AQ}{AQ - BQ} = \frac{AR}{AR - MR}$ and rearranging we get

$e\,AR - e\,MR = AR$ or $e\,AR - AR = e\,MR$ or $AR\,(e-1) = e\,MR$

or $MR = AR\left(\frac{e-1}{e}\right)$, $AR = MR\left(\frac{e}{e-1}\right)$ and $e = \frac{AR}{AR - MR}$

Mathematically the relationship between MR, elasticity and price are derived as

Since $MR = P + q\frac{dp}{dq}$ and $e = -\frac{dq}{dp} \times \frac{p}{q}$, we get

$-\frac{1}{e} = \frac{dp}{dq} \times \frac{q}{p}$ and $-\frac{p}{e} = q\frac{dp}{dq}$,

$$MR = p + \left(\frac{-p}{e}\right) = p - \frac{p}{e} = \frac{ep - p}{e} = p\left(\frac{e-1}{e}\right), \therefore\ MR = p\left(\frac{e-1}{e}\right)$$

For $e = 1$, $MR = 0$. For $e > 1$, $MR > 0$ and For $e < 1$, $MR < 0$.

The implication of this is that the monopolist can reach equilibrium only at a point in the range of *AR* curve where $e > 1$. This is because *MR* must be positive since *MC* is assumed a positive quantity.

This is essential for the firm to reach equilibrium, which requires equality of *MR* and *MC* or $\frac{dR}{dq} = \frac{dC}{dq}$.

From figure 4.3 it can be noticed that *TR* curve increases upto output $0q_1$ for $MR = \frac{dR}{dq} > 0$. TR reaches a maximum at point *M* where $\frac{dR}{dq} = 0$. For output $q > 0q_1$, *MR* is negative for which *TR* decreases.

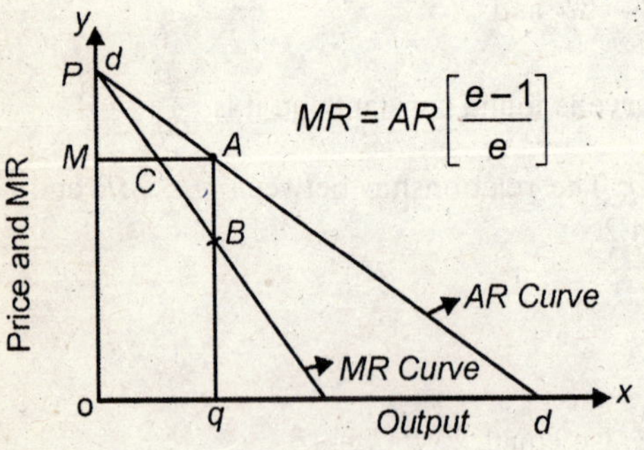

Fig. 4.2: Relationship between AR and MR

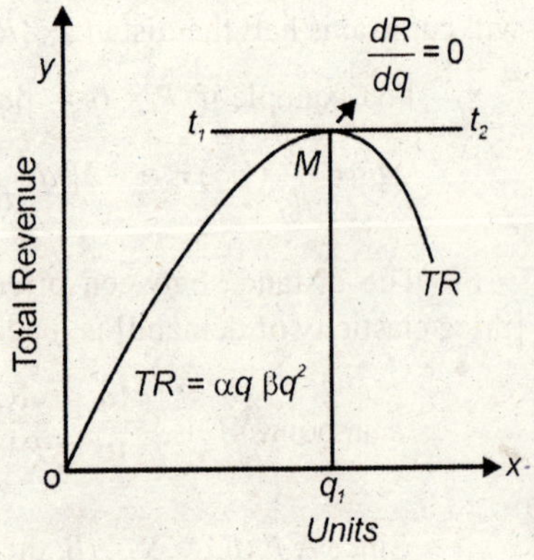

Fig. 4.3: TR curve

The relationship between *AR, MR, e* and *TR* are also shown in fig. 4.4. *TR* increases for output in between *O* and *Q* since *MR* > 0. TR is maximum at *M* where *MR* = 0. This occurs at OQ level of output. Corresponding to this OQ output $e = 1$,

(a) $\therefore$ when $e = 1$, $MR = 0$, TR = maximum.

(b) For $e > 1$, $MR > 0$, *TR* increases. This happens for $Q < OQ$.

(c) For $e < 1$, $MR < 0$, *TR* decreases. This is witnessed for $Q > OQ$.

Illustrations

(1) If the demand curve for *x* commodity is given by $P = 10 - 4x$.

Find *(a)* Total revenue and marginal revenue *(b)* *x* for which *MR* is zero. *(c)* *MR* at $x = 1$ and $x = 2$.

(a) For given $P = 10 - 4x$, where P = Price, x = Qty. demanded,

Total revenue $(R) = Px = (10 - 4x)\,x = 10x - 4x^2$

$$MR = \frac{dR}{dx} = 10 - 8x\text{, For } MR = 0,\ 10 - 8x = 0.\text{ or } x = \frac{10}{8} = 1.25$$

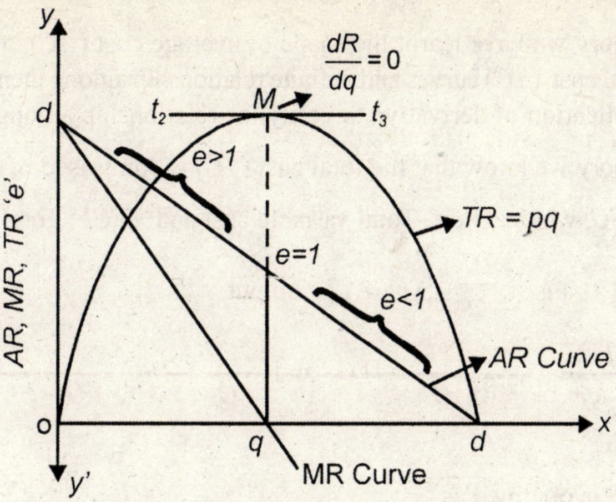

Fig. 4.4: Relationship between AR, MR, TR and 'e'

(b) when $x = 1.25$, $MR = 0$ and TR = maximum

This maximum $TR = 10x - 4x^2 = 10\,(1.25) - 4\,(1.25)^2 = 6.25$

(c) At $x = 1$, $MR = 10 - 8x = 10 - 8\,(1) = 2$.

At $x = 2$, $MR = 10 - 8\,(2) = -6$ (*MR* is negative).

This is obvious for when $x = 1.25$, $MR = 0$. Thus for $x > 1.25$, MR < 0

(2) If $P = 15 - \frac{x^2}{3}$, wher P = price and x = demand, Find,

(a) TR and MR functions *(b)* MR for $x = 1$ and $x = 3$

(c) x for which MR = 0. *(d)* Maximum *TR*.

(a) Given $P = 15 - \frac{x^2}{3}$, Total revenue is $TR = (P)\,(x) = 15x - \frac{x^3}{3}$

Marginal revenue function is $MR = \frac{d(TR)}{dx} = 15 - x^2$

(b) *MR* when $x = 1$ is $15 - x^2 = 15 - (1)^2 = 14$.

MR for $x = 3$ is $15 - x^2 = 15 - (3)^2 = 6$,

$\therefore$ $MR = 14$ for $x = 1$ and $MR = 6$ at $x = 3$.

(c) x for which $MR = 0$ is obtained. Thus $MR = 15 - x^2 = 0$ or $15 = x^2$ and

$x = \pm\sqrt{15} = \pm 3.873$ or $x = 3.873$, for x can not be negative.

(d) At $x = 3.873$, $MR = 0$ and therefore *TR* is maximum at this output.

This maximum *TR* is equal to *TR* corresponding to $x = 3.873$. This is equal to

$$TR = 15(3.873) - \frac{(3.873)^3}{3} = 58.075 - 19.365 = 38.73$$

4.5 Derivatives used for Evaluating MC, AC and AVC

From economic theory we have learnt the shape of average cost (*AC*), average variable cost (*AVC*), marginal cost (*MC*) and total cost (*TC*) curves and definite relationship among them. This theoritical knowledge can enable us to make application of derivative to verify the relationship among these cost curves.

From economic theory we know that the total cost (*TC*) is comprised of TVC and TFC.

$\therefore$ $TC = TVC + TFC$, where TVC = Total variable cost and TFC = Total fixed cost.

The averange cost (*AC*) is = $\frac{TC}{Q}$, where Q = output.

$$AC=\frac{TC}{Q}=\frac{TVC}{Q}+\frac{TFC}{Q} \text{ where } \frac{TVC}{Q}=AVC, \text{ and } \frac{TFC}{Q}=AFC$$

$\therefore AC = AVC + AFC$.

Marginal cost (*MC*) is obatined as

$$MC=\frac{\Delta TC}{\Delta Q}=\frac{d}{dQ}(TC)=\frac{d}{dQ}(TVC).$$

From the *TC* function (*C*) we can evaluate *AC, AVC, MC* and verify their relationships.

From economic theory we have learnt that:

(a) *AVC* and *AC* curves are *U*-shaped. These curves first decrease, reach minimum points and then increase.

(b) *MC* curve is also *U*-shaped. It first decreases, reaches a minimum and then increases.

(c) It is the *MC* curve that reaches its minimum first at the smaller level of output than the level of output at which *AVC* and *AC* attain their respective minimum points. After reaching minimum, the MC curve increases. The rising portion of MC intersects the minimum points of first *AVC* and then *AC* curves.

$\therefore$ In the range of output where *AVC* decreases, $MC < AVC$. In the range of output where *AVC* is increasing MC > AVC and when AVC is minimum $MC = AVC$. The same type of relationship is established between *AC* and *MC*.

Mathematically: If C = total cost, $AC=\frac{C}{Q}$, $MC=\frac{dC}{dQ}$.

The above theoritically stated relationships need to be verified mathematically using derivatives. this is attempted here.

When *AC* decreases, $MC < AC$. This is proved below:

AC decreases means $\frac{d}{dQ}\left(\frac{C}{Q}\right)<0$

$$\frac{d}{dQ}\left(\frac{C}{Q}\right)=\frac{Q.\frac{dC}{dQ}-C.\frac{dQ}{dQ}}{Q^2}=\frac{Q.\partial C/\partial Q}{Q^2}-\frac{C}{Q^2}=\frac{1}{Q}\left[\frac{\partial C}{\partial Q}-\frac{C}{Q}\right]<0$$

$$or \left[\frac{\partial C}{\partial Q}-\frac{C}{Q}\right]<0 \text{ or } \frac{\partial C}{\partial Q}<\frac{C}{Q} \text{ or } MC < AC$$

So it is proved that when AC is decreasing $MC < AC$.

Similarly it can be verified that when AC is increasing $MC > AC$. AC is increasing means

$$\frac{1}{Q}\left[\frac{\partial C}{\partial Q}-\frac{C}{Q}\right]>0 \text{ or } \left[\frac{\partial C}{\partial Q}-\frac{C}{Q}\right]>0 \text{ or } \frac{\partial C}{\partial Q}>\frac{C}{Q} \text{ or } MC < AC$$

It can be shown that when AC is constant and minimum, AC and MC are equal AC is said to be minimum when

$\frac{d}{dQ}(AC)=0.$ and $\frac{d^2}{dQ^2}(AC)>0$. Accordingly we get

$$\frac{d}{dQ}\left(\frac{C}{Q}\right)=0 \text{ or } \left[\frac{\partial C}{\partial Q}-\frac{C}{Q}\right]=0 \text{ or } \frac{\partial C}{\partial Q}=\frac{C}{Q} \text{ or } MC=AC.$$

The short-run and long-run cost functions

The short-run and long-run cost functions are different in the sense that in short-run, TC is comprised of TVC and TFC, where $TVC = f(q)$ and $TFC = k$ (constant).

$\therefore TC = C = f(q) + k,$

But the long-run cost function has no fixed costs. For this we can write $C = f(q)$.

Marginal, average cost functions areaccordingly,

$$\frac{dC}{dq}=MC=\frac{d}{dq}f(q)=f'(q) \text{ and } AC=\frac{C}{q}=\frac{f(q)}{q}+\frac{k}{q},$$

$$AVC=\frac{f(q)}{q} \text{ and } AFC=\frac{k}{q}$$

Illustrations

(1) Given the total cost function $C = q^3 - 3q^2 + 15q + 25$, Find AC and MC at $q = 5$

For given, $C = q^3 - 3q^2 + 15q + 25$, $AC=\frac{C}{q}=q^2-3q+15+\frac{25}{q}$

At $q=5, AC=(5)^2-3(5)+15+\frac{25}{5}=30$

$$MC=\frac{dC}{dq}=\frac{d}{dq}(q^3-3q^2+15q+25)=3q^2-6q+15$$

At $q = 5$, $MC = 3(5)^2 - 6(5) + 15 = 60$

(2) Given the total cost function $C = aq^3 - bq^2 + cq$, Find,

(a) The output (q) for which AC is minimum.

(b) Prove that corresponding to this output, $AC = MC$.

Given $C = aq^3 - bq^2 + cq$, AC and MC are obtained as

$$AC = \frac{C}{q} = aq^2 - bq + c\,,\quad MC = \frac{dC}{dq} = 3aq^2 - 2bq + c$$

For AC to be minimum, $\frac{d}{dq}(AC) = 0$, and $\frac{d^2}{dq^2}(AC) > 0$

$$\frac{d}{dq}(AC) = \frac{d}{dq}(aq^2 - bq + c) = 2aq - b = 0 \text{ and } q = \frac{b}{2a}.$$

$\therefore$ at $q = \frac{b}{2a}$, AC is minimum. This must also satisfy the second order condition given by:

$$\frac{d^2}{dq^2}(AC) = \frac{d}{dq}(2aq - b) = 2a > 0 \text{ as } a > 0$$

The minimum AC is AC at $q = \frac{b}{2a}$. This is obtained by substituting $q = \frac{b}{2a}$.

Minimum Ac is , $AC = a\left(\frac{b}{2a}\right)^2 - b\left(\frac{b}{2a}\right) + c = \frac{b^2}{4a} - \frac{b^2}{2a} + c = \frac{-b^2 + 4ac}{4a}$

It can be verified that when AC is minimum, $AC = MC = \frac{-b^2 + 4ac}{4a}$

For this we need to substitute $q = \frac{b}{2a}$ in MC function. This gives

$$MC = 3a\left(\frac{b}{2a}\right)^2 - 2b\left(\frac{b}{2a}\right) + c = \frac{3ab^2}{4a^2} - \frac{2b^2}{2a} + c = \frac{-b^2 + 4ac}{4a}$$

$\therefore$ it is proved that $AC = MC$ when AC is minimum.

(3) If the total cost function is $C = Q^3 - 2Q^2 + 2Q$. Find,

(a) Average cost function. *(b)*Marginal cost function.

(c) Output (Q) for which AC is minimum.

(d) What is this minimum AC?

(e) At what level of output MC gets its minimum?

(f) Verify that the level of output at which AC is minimum, $AC = MC$.

Solution:

(a) Given $C = Q^3 - 2Q^2 + 2Q$, .AC function is $AC = \frac{C}{Q} = Q^2 - 2Q + 2$

(b) MC function.is, $MC = \frac{dC}{dQ} = 3Q^2 - 4Q + 2$

(c) For AC to be minimum, $\frac{d}{dQ}(AC) = 0$, and $\frac{d^2}{dQ^2}(AC) > 0$

$$\frac{d}{dQ}(AC) = \frac{d}{dQ}(Q^2 - 2Q + 2) = 2Q - 2 = 0 \text{ or } Q = 1,$$

$$\frac{d^2}{dQ^2}(AC) = \frac{d}{dQ}(2Q - 2) = 2 > 0, \therefore \text{ At } Q = 1, \ AC \text{ is minimum.}$$

(*d*) The minimum AC is AC at $Q = 1$. Accordingly we get $AC = Q^2 - 2Q + 2 = (1)^2 - 2(1) + 2 = 1$.

Thus minimum AC is 1.

(*e*) MC is minimum when $\frac{d}{dQ}(MC) = 0, \quad \frac{d^2}{dQ^2}(MC) > 0.$

$$\frac{d}{dQ}(MC) = \frac{d}{dQ}(3Q^2 - 4Q + 2) = 6Q - 4 = 0. \text{ or } Q = \frac{4}{6} = \frac{2}{3}$$

$\therefore$ At $Q = \frac{2}{3}$, MC is minimum. This needs to fulfill the second order condition given as

$$\frac{d^2}{dQ^2}(MC) = \frac{d}{dQ}(6Q - 4) = 6 > 0. \therefore MC \text{ is minimum when } Q = \frac{2}{3}.$$

The minimum MC is, MC at $Q = \frac{2}{3}$.

$$\text{at } Q = \frac{2}{3}, MC = 3Q^2 - 4Q + 2 = 3\left(\frac{2}{3}\right)^2 - 4\left(\frac{2}{3}\right) + 2 = 0.67$$

$\therefore$ AC is minimum at $Q = 1$ and this minimum $AC = 1$ and

MC is minimum at $Q = 0.67$ and this minimum $MC = 0.67$

(*e*) When AC is minimum, $MC = AC$. It means for $Q = 1$, $AC = MC$.

At $Q = 1$ we have already got $AC = 1$.

At $Q = 1$, $MC = MC(1) = 3Q^2 - 4Q + 2 = 3(1)^2 - 4(1) + 2 = 1$.

$\therefore$ it is verified that at $Q = 1$, $AC = MC = 1$.

(4) Given the total cost function $C = Q^3 - 6Q^2 + 15Q$. Find,

(*a*) Average cost function. (*b*) Marginal cost function.

(*c*) Output (Q) for which AC is minimum. What is thia minimum AC?

(*d*) Output (Q) for which MC is minimum. What is thia minimum MC?

(*e*) Prove that when AC is minimum, $AC = MC$.

Solution:

(*a*) For Given $C = Q^3 - 6Q^2 + 15Q$, $AC = \frac{C}{Q} = Q^2 - 6Q + 15$

(*b*) $MC = \frac{dC}{dQ} = 3Q^2 - 12Q + 15$

(c) For AC to be minimum, $\frac{d}{dQ}(AC)=0$ and $\frac{d^2}{dQ^2}(AC)>0$.

$$\frac{d}{dQ}(AC) = \frac{d}{dQ}(Q^2 - 6Q + 15) = 2Q - 6 = 0 \text{ or } Q = 3.$$

$\therefore$ at $Q = 3$, AC is minimum. It can also be verified that $\frac{d^2}{dQ^2}(AC) > 0$

$$\frac{d^2}{dQ^2}(AC) = \frac{d}{dQ}(2Q - 6) = 2 > 0$$

This AC is minimum at $Q = 3$. The minimum AC is given by

$AC(3) = (3)^2 - 6(3) + 15 = 6.$

(d) MC is minimum when $\frac{d}{dQ}(MC) = 0$ and $\frac{d^2}{dQ^2}(MC) > 0$

$$\frac{d}{dQ}(3Q^2 - 12Q + 15) = 6Q - 12 = 0, Q = 2.$$

$$\frac{d^2}{dQ^2}(MC) = \frac{d}{dQ}(6Q - 12) = 6 > 0.$$

$\therefore$ MC is Minimum corresponding to $Q = 2$. Minimum MC is MC at = 2,

$MC(2) = 3Q^2 - 12Q + 15 = 3(2)^2 - 12(2) + 15 = 3$

(e) When AC is minimum it can be seen that $AC = MC$.

AC is minimum at $Q = 3$. $\therefore$ when $Q = 3$, $AC = MC$.

For $Q = 3$, $AC = 6$, $\therefore$ at $Q = 3$, MC is also 6. This is to be verified.

At $Q = 3$, $MC = 3Q^2 - 12Q + 15 = 3(3)^2 - 12(3) + 15 = 6$.

$\therefore$ It is proved that when AC is minimum, $AC = MC = 6$.

4.6 Elasticity of Total and Average Cost

Given the total cost function $C = f(Q) = aQ^2 + bQ$, Find,

(a) elasticity of total cost function and

(b) elasticity of average cost function

Solution:

(a) For $C = aQ^2 + bQ$, elasticity of total cost is given by (e_C).

It is given by $e_c = \frac{Q}{C} \cdot \frac{dC}{dQ}$, where $\frac{dC}{dQ} = MC$, $\frac{C}{Q} = AC$, and $\frac{Q}{C} = \frac{1}{AC}$

$$\therefore\ e_c = \frac{Q}{C} \cdot \frac{dC}{dQ} = \frac{dC/dQ}{C/Q} = \frac{MC}{AC}$$

For given $C = aQ^2 + bQ$, we get $MC = \dfrac{dC}{dQ} = 2aQ + b$ and $AC = \dfrac{C}{Q} = aQ + b.$

$$\therefore\ e_c = \frac{MC}{AC} = \frac{2aQ+b}{aQ+b}$$

(b) Eleasticity of average cost (e_{AC}) is equal to $e_C - 1$ or $e_{AC} = e_C - 1$.

The formula of elasticity of average cost is

$$e_{AC} = \frac{Q}{C/Q}\cdot\frac{d}{dQ}\left(\frac{C}{Q}\right) = \frac{Q^2}{C}\frac{d}{dQ}\left(\frac{C}{Q}=\right) = \frac{Q^2}{C}\left[\frac{Q\dfrac{dC}{dQ} - C\cdot\dfrac{dQ}{dQ}}{Q^2}\right]$$

$$= \frac{Q^2}{C}\left[\frac{Q\dfrac{dC}{dQ} - C}{Q^2}\right] = \frac{Q^2}{C}\cdot\frac{1}{Q^2}\left[Q\frac{dC}{dQ} - C\right]$$

$$= \frac{1}{C}\left[Q\frac{dC}{dQ} - C\right] = \frac{Q}{C}\cdot\frac{dC}{dQ} - 1 = \frac{dC/dQ}{C/Q} - 1 = \frac{MC}{AC} - 1 = e_c - 1$$

From $C = aQ^2 + bQ$, $AC = \dfrac{C}{Q} = aQ + b$ and

$$e_{AC} = \frac{Q}{C/Q}\frac{d}{dQ}\left(\frac{C}{Q}\right) = \frac{Q}{AC}\cdot\frac{d}{dQ}(AC) = \frac{Q}{aQ+b}[a] = \frac{aQ}{aQ+b}$$

We will also get the same by using the formula

$$\frac{MC}{AC} - 1 = \frac{2aQ+b}{aQ+b} - 1 = \frac{2aQ+b-aQ-b}{aQ+b} = \frac{aQ}{aQ+b}.$$

4.7 Firm's Equilibrium Under Perfect Competition

A firm under perfect competition is said to be in equilibrium when it produces profit maximizing output. π) is given by the difference between total revenue (R) and total cost (C).

$\pi = R - C.$

Total revenue and total cost functions are $R = \phi(q)$ and $C = f(q)$ and $\pi = R - C = \phi(q) - f(q)$,

For a competitive firm, $P = MR$ or $P = \dfrac{dR}{dq}$. This can be derived from $R = Pq$ so that

$$MR = \frac{dR}{dq} = P + q\frac{dP}{dq} = P \text{ for } \frac{dP}{dq} = 0.$$

$\therefore$ For $R = \phi(q)$, $MR = R' = \phi'(q) = P$. (P = Price) $\therefore$ MR = Price

The conditions for profit maximization of competitive firm is similar to any other firm.

The necessary and sufficient conditions are given by

(a) Necessary or First-order condition is , $\frac{d\pi}{dq}=0$, where π (Profit) = $\phi(q) - f(q) = R - C$.

$$\frac{d\pi}{dq}=\phi'(q)-f'(q)=0 \quad \text{or } \phi'(q)=f'(q) \text{ or } MR = MC.$$

(b) The sufficient or second order condition for profit maximization is $\frac{d^2\pi}{dq^2}<0$.

$$\frac{d^2\pi}{dq^2}=\frac{d}{dq}\left(\frac{d\pi}{dq}\right)=\frac{d}{dq}[\phi'(q)-f'(q)]<0$$

$$\text{or } \phi''(q)-f''(q)<0 \text{ or } \phi''(q)<f''(q).$$

In terms of economic theory this condition implies that *MC* curve must be rising at the equilibrium point so that it cuts the horizontal *MR* curve from below. This is shown in the fig.4.5 at point '*E*' where $MR = MC$ or $\phi'(q) = f'(q)$. This will also fulfill the condition $\phi''(q) < f''(q)$. The equality between *MR* and *MC* is also taking place at point *'R'* in fig. 4.5. But this is the point of minimum profit and not maximum profit since at this point $\phi''(q) > f''(q)$.

At point 'R', $\frac{d\pi}{dq}=0$ or $\varphi'(q)-f'(q)$ or $MR=MC$ and $\frac{d^2\pi}{dq^2}>0$, $\phi''(q)>f''(q)$.

Therefore at OQ_1 output or at point '*R*', the firm fails to reach equilibrium despite that

$\frac{d\pi}{dq}=0$ or $MR = MC$.

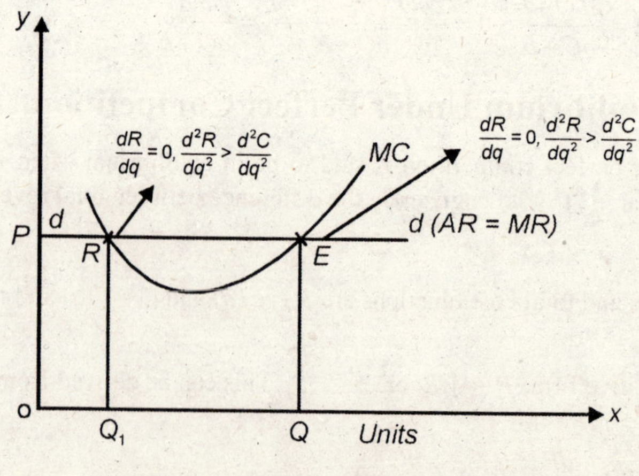

Fig. 4.5: *Equilibrium of the firm*

This is due to the fact that at this point of equality, the second order condition is not flfilled. Therefore the firm's profit can increase by expanding output beyond OQ_1 since $MC < MR$,, which means the firm adds more to revenue than to the total cost from every additional unit produced and sold.. But after OQ output is attained, firm must stop production at OQ level of output, since for output beyond OQ level, $MC > MR$.. This implies that further porduction after OQ, will add more to total cost than to total revenue, causing thereby loss to the firm, what the firm does not like. Thus mere equality between MR and MC is a necessary but not a sufficient condition for profit maximization or firm's equilibrium. It requires both the conditions to get fulfilled at the equilibrium point.

Illustrations on the Competitive Firm's Equilibrium.

(1) A competitive firm's price (P) and cost function (C) are given as $P = 15$ and $C = \frac{1}{3}Q^3 - 5Q^2 + 28Q + 25$ where Q = Output. Determine:

(a) The profit maximizing level of output and the amount of profit of the firm.

(b) What should be the minimum acceptable price to the firm so that it can offer any positive quantity for sale in the market?

(c) Suppose the competitive price falls to Rs. 10 per unit, what would be the profit maximizing output? Find the level of profit also at this price.

(d) Can the firm continue to produce output when it makes a loss at equilibrium ? why?

Solution:

(a) For $C = \frac{1}{3}Q^3 - 5Q^2 + 28Q + 25$, the competitive firm's total revenue and profit functions are formed as, Total Revenue (R) = $PQ = 15Q$. Profit = $R - C$.

Firm's profit maximizing output refers to the output corresponding to which profit is maximum. The conditions for maximizing (π) profit function are given as

$$\frac{d\pi}{dQ} = 0 \text{ and } \frac{d^2\pi}{dQ^2} = \frac{d}{dQ}\left(\frac{d\pi}{dQ}\right) < 0.$$

For $\pi = R - C$, $\frac{d\pi}{dQ} = R' - C' = 0$. or $\frac{dR}{dQ} = \frac{dC}{dQ}$.

For $P = 15$, $R = 15Q$, $R' = \frac{dR}{dQ} = 15 = MR$

From $C = \frac{1}{3}Q^3 - 5Q^2 + 28Q + 25$, $MC = \frac{dC}{dQ} = Q^2 - 10Q + 28$

At equilibrium $MR = MC$ or $\frac{dR}{dQ} = \frac{dC}{dQ}$

or $15 = Q^2 - 10Q + 28$ or $Q^2 - 10Q + 28 - 15 = 0$

or $Q^2 - 10Q + 13 = 0$. Solving this quadratic equation we can obtain output, Q.

The formula for solving quadratic equation is given as

$$\frac{-b \pm \sqrt{b^2 - 4ac}}{2a}.$$

For our Problem, we will substitute $b = -10$, $a = 1$, $c = 13$ and Q is the variable to be solved.

$$\therefore\ Q = \frac{-(-10) \pm \sqrt{(-10)^2 - 4(1)(13)}}{2(1)} = \frac{10 \pm \sqrt{100 - 52}}{2}$$

$$= \frac{10 \pm \sqrt{48}}{2} = \frac{10 \pm 6.93}{2}.$$ This means Q = 8.456 or Q = 1.53

To determine profit maximizing output (Q) we need to evaluate and see that $\frac{d^2\pi}{dQ^2} < 0.$ or $\frac{d^2R}{dQ^2} < \frac{d^2C}{dQ^2}$

$$\frac{d^2\pi}{dQ^2} = \frac{d^2R}{dQ^2} - \frac{d^2C}{dQ^2} < 0 \text{ or } \frac{d^2R}{dQ^2} < \frac{d^2C}{dQ^2}$$

$$\frac{d^2R}{dQ^2} = \frac{d}{dQ}\left(\frac{dR}{dQ}\right) = \frac{d}{dQ}(15) = 0 \text{ and } \frac{d^2C}{dQ^2} = \frac{d}{dQ}\left(\frac{dC}{dQ}\right) = \frac{d}{dQ}(Q^2 - 10Q + 28) = 2Q - 10$$

For $Q = 1.535,\ \frac{d^2C}{dQ^2} = 2\,(1.531) - 10 = -\ 6.93\ \therefore \frac{d^2R}{dQ^2} > \frac{d^2C}{dQ^2}$ (as $0 > -\ 6.93$)

$\therefore$ Q can not be 1.535.

For $Q = 8.465$, $\frac{d^2C}{dQ^2} = 2Q - 10 = 2\,(8.465) - 10 = 6.93$, This means $\therefore \frac{d^2R}{dQ^2} < \frac{d^2C}{dQ^2}$ ($0 < 6.93$)

$\therefore$ $Q = 8.465$ is the equilibrium output that will maximise profit of the firm. At $Q = 8.465$,

$TR = PQ = (15)\,(8.465) = 126.\ 975$ and TC $= \frac{1}{3}(8.465)^3 - 5\,(8.465)^2 + 28\,(8.465) + 25 = 105.\ 93$,

$\pi = R - C = 126.975\ - 105.93 = 21.045$

$\therefore\ \pi = 21.045$ and $Q = 8.465$

(b) The competitive firm can sell any positive output at equilibrium point only if the competitive price exceeds to or equal to the minimum AVC. Symbolically, $p \geq \min.\ AVC$.

From $TC = C = \frac{1}{3}Q^3 - 5Q^2 + 28Q + 25$ we can obtain TVC anad AVC as

$$TVC = \frac{1}{3}Q^3 - 5Q^2 + 28Q,\quad TFC = 25\ \therefore\ AVC = \frac{TVC}{Q} = \frac{1}{3}Q^2 - 5Q + 28$$

For AVC to be minimum, $\frac{d}{dQ}(AVC) = 0,\quad \frac{d^2}{dQ^2}(AVC) > 0.$

$$\frac{d}{dQ}(AVC) = \frac{d}{dQ}\left(\frac{1}{3}Q^2 - 5Q + 28\right) = \frac{2}{3}Q - 5 = 0 \text{ or } Q = \frac{15}{2} = 7.5$$

$$\frac{d^2}{dQ^2}(AVC) = \frac{d}{dQ}\left(\frac{2}{3}Q - 5\right) = \frac{2}{3} > 0.$$

$\therefore$ At $Q = 7.5$, AVC is minimum. This minimum AVC is AVC at $Q = 7.5$.

$\therefore$ Minimum $AVC = \frac{1}{3}Q^2 - 5Q + 28 = \frac{1}{3}(7.5)^2 - 5(7.5) + 28 = 9.25$

This implies that the competitive firm will sell output at equilibrium only if the prevailing competitive price is equal to or more than 9.25. If $p < 9.25$, the profit maximizing firm or the loss minimising firm will shut down production.

When $p = 9.25$, $TVC = AVC \times Q = 9.25 \times 7.5 = 69.375$ and $TR = 9.25 \times 7.5 = 69.375$

$\therefore$ For $p = 9.25$, $TR = TVC$. But $TR < TC$, When $p = 9.25$ or $Q = 7.5$.

Since $TR = TVC$, Firm's Loss = $TFC = 25$. It makes no difference to the firm whether he shuts down productioin or continues to porduce at equilibrium point as $TR = TVC$. This is due to the fact that the firm will continue to bear TFC even if he shuts down production.

However when $p < 9.25$, firm's $TR < TVC$, it is wise for the firm to shut down, since in this case the loss will be minimum and restricted to the amount of TFC only.

(c) If the competitive price falls to Rs. 10 per unit, both the profit maximzing output and amount of profit will change at the equilibrium point. This can be derived as:

$R = PQ = 10Q$. $C = \frac{1}{3}Q^3 - 5Q^2 + 28Q + 25$ and $\pi = R - C$,

For Profit maximisation, $\frac{d\pi}{dQ} = \frac{dR}{dQ} - \frac{dC}{dQ} = 0$ or $\frac{dR}{dQ} = \frac{dC}{dQ}$

$\frac{dR}{dQ} = \frac{d}{dQ}(10Q) = 10$ and $\frac{dC}{dQ} = \frac{d}{dQ}\left(\frac{1}{3}Q^3 - 5Q^2 + 28Q + 25\right) = Q^2 - 10Q + 28$

$\therefore$ at equilibrium, $10 = Q^2 - 10Q + 28$ *or* $Q^2 - 10Q + 18 = 0$.

Solving this quadratic equation for Q, we get $Q = \frac{10 \pm \sqrt{100 - 72}}{2} = \frac{10 \pm 5.29}{2}$.

From this we obtain Q = 7. 645 or Q = 2.355

If $Q = 7.645$, $\frac{d^2C}{dQ^2} = 2Q - 10 = 5.29$ $\therefore$ $\frac{d^2R}{dQ^2} < \frac{d^2C}{dQ^2}$ as $0 < 5.29$

$\therefore$ $Q = 7.645$ is the profit maximizing output.

Alternatively we can see that when $Q = 2.355$, $\frac{d^2R}{dQ} > \frac{d^2C}{dQ^2}$ as $0 > -5.29$.

$\therefore$ Q can not be 2.355 and the equilibrium level of output is $Q = 7.645$.

Firm's profit = $R - C$, where $R = PQ = 10 \times 7.645 = 76.45$ and

$$C = \frac{1}{3}Q^3 - 5Q^2 + 28Q + 25 = \frac{1}{3}(7.645)^3 - 5(7.645)^2 + 28(7.645) + 25 = 95.27$$

$\pi = 76.45 - 95.77 = -19.32$ = Loss. Negative profit implies loss to the firm.

(d) Despite that the firm makes a loss, it is prudent to continue production at the equilibrium point in order to minimise the loss. Suppose the firm produces $[Q = 7.645]$ output at $P = 10$, his loss = Rs. 19.32. But when the firm does not produce, its total loss is equal to the extent of TFC = Rs. 25. It means the firm's position is relatively better when it continues production and makes a loss of Rs. 19.32 and not Rs. 25, otherwise. So what we find is that when $TR > TVC$ although $TR < TC$, the firm will remain in producing output.

In our exaample $\boxed{TR = 76.45,}$ $\boxed{TC = 95.77,}$ $\boxed{TFC = 25\,,}$ $\boxed{TVC = 70.77}$

4.8 Firm's Equilibrium under Monopoly

The monopoly is the market that makes no difference between the firm and the industry. Firm's demand curve is negatively sloped with $MR < AR$ (price).

Firm's total revenue function is $R = Pq$ and

$$MR = \frac{dR}{dq} = P + q\frac{dP}{dq} < \text{Price,} \quad \left[\frac{dP}{dq} < 0\right]$$

Let us suppose that the monopolist is facing a linear demand curve, given $P = \alpha - \beta q$, so that its total revenue and marginal revenue are defined as

$$R = \alpha q - \beta q^2 \text{ and } MR = \frac{dR}{dq} = \alpha - 2\beta q,$$

The demand curve is monotonically decreasing with $MR < P$ if $q > 0$. The rate of decline in MR is twice the rate of decline of average revenue (price). MR cuts the X- axis exactly half the distance AR will cut the X- axis measured from the point of origin.

Price elasticty of demand for the monopolist's product is given by:

$$e = \left\{\frac{-P}{q}\right\}\left\{\frac{dq}{dp}\right\} \text{ and } MR = P\left(\frac{e-1}{e}\right)$$

The conditions of profit maximization under monopoly are shown below. Thse are similar to that of the competetive firm. π is the difference between R and C. Thus $\pi = R - C$.

Profit maximization requires the firm to fulfill the following conditions:

The necessary condition is $\frac{d\pi}{dq} = 0,\ \frac{d^2\pi}{dq^2} < 0.$ for $R = R(q).,\ C = C(q)$ and $\pi = R(q) - C(q)$

From $\frac{d\pi}{dq} = 0$, we get $\frac{dR}{dq} - \frac{dC}{dq} = 0$, or $R'(q) - C'(q) = 0$, or $R'(q) = C'(q)$ or $MR = MC$

The sufficient condition is given by $\frac{d^2\pi}{dq^2} < 0$ or $R''(q) - C''(q) < 0$ or $R''(q) < C''(q)$.

This implies that the rate of increase in MR is to be less than the rate of increase in MC at equilibrium point. This condition can be fulfilled when an extra output produced adds less to TR and more to TC. This is shown in fig. 4. 6 where both the conditions are satisfied at equilibrium while in fig. 4.7, the second-order condition for profit maximization gets violated.

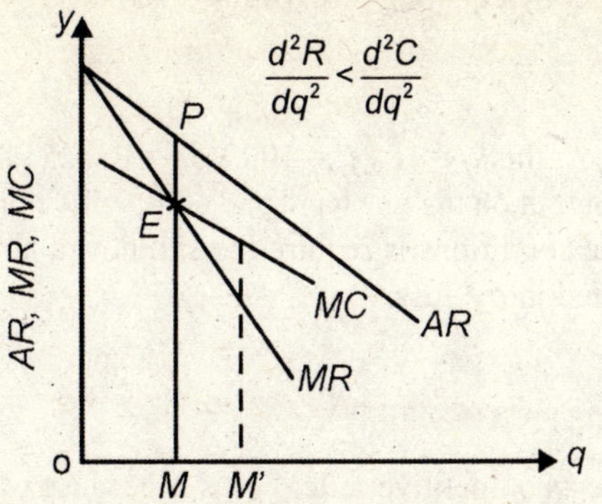

***Fig. 4.6:** MC cuts MR from below*

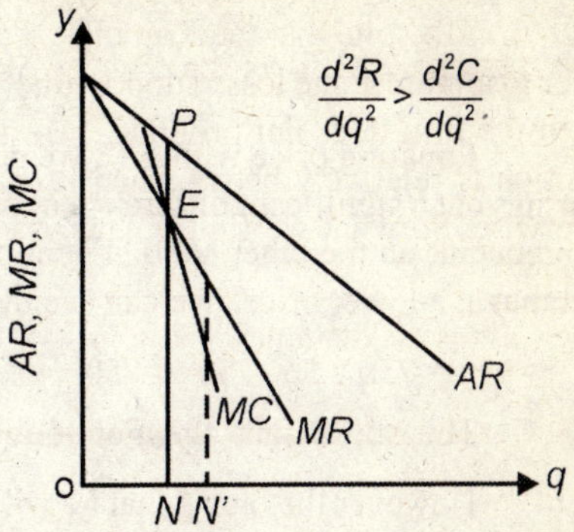

***Fig. 4.7:** MC cuts MR from above*

Illustrations:

(1) Consider the monopolist who faces a linear demand curve given by $P = 100 - 5q$. If the monopolist produces at a constant MC of Rs. 25 and incurs Rs 50 as total fixed cost, determine the profit maximizing output, monopoly profit and price.

We are given $MC = 25$ and $P = 100 - 5q$

From this we get, $TC = \int_0^q 25\,dq = 25q + K$, where $K = TFC$ $\therefore$ $TC = 50 + 25q$

For $P = 100 - 5q$, $R = Pq = 100q - 5q^2$ and $\pi = R - C = 100q - 5q^2 - 50 - 25q = 75q - 5q^2 - 50$

$$\frac{d\pi}{dq} = 75 - 10q = 0, \; or \; q = 7.5, \; \frac{d^2\pi}{dq^2} = 10 < 0$$

Thus equilibrium output is $q = 7.5$. Alternatively we can also establish this by equating MR and MC

For, $R = 100q - 5q^2$, $MR = \frac{dR}{dq} = R'(q) = 100 - 10q$ and $MC = \frac{dC}{dq} = C'(q) = 25$

At equilibrium, $R'(q) = C'(q)$ or $100 - 10q = 25$, $\therefore q = 7.5$

$$\frac{d^2R}{dq^2} = R''(q) = \frac{d}{dq}(100 - 10q) = -10 \text{ and } \frac{d^2C}{dq^2} = 0$$

This also fulfills the second order condition for $-10 < 0$ or $R''(q) < C''(q)$.

Thus π maximizing output is $q = 7.5$. Monopoly Price = $100 - 5q = 100 - 5(7.5)$ = Rs. 62.50.

Firm's profit is, $\pi = R - C = 75q - 5q^2 - 50 = 75(7.5) - 5(7.5)^2 - 50$ = Rs. 231.25

We have a question that can the monopolist behave like a competitive seller to sell its output by equating price with MC. If it is possible then what will happen to his porfit and price.

Let us suppose the monopoly firm sets price of its product by equating MR with MC so that

$$MC = \frac{dC}{dq} = 25, \frac{d^2C}{dq^2} = C''(q) = \frac{d}{dC}(25) = 0.$$

Equating price with MC, we get $100 - 5q = 25$ or $q = 15$. At this $q = 15$, $P = 100 - 5q =$ Rs. 25. This brings out a significant difference between monopoly price and output on the one hand and competitive price and output on the other hand. The monopolist under competitive conditions is required to sell now a larger output at a lower price. We can see that his profit is now converted into a loss.

$$\pi = 75q - 5q^2 - 50 = -50.$$

This shows that the monopolist incurs a loss when he equates MC with Price.

However the fact is that he will never do so to behave like a competitive seller. This is because when he faces a linear downward sloping demand curve, it can never pay him to set price equal to the MC. He will rather fix the price at the point of profit maximization only by equating MR with MC and never price with marginal cost.

For profit maximization the monopolist can fix either price or output

The monopoly firm attains its profit maximization point by fixing either price or output although he can never fix both the price and the output. When the monopolist fixes the output, his profit maximization is determined with respect to monopoly product by equating marginal revenue and marginal cost. In this case revenue and cost functions are to be differentiated with respect to output. But when the firm fixes the price his profit maximization is to be determined with respect to that price. In this case firm's revenue and cost functions are differentiated with respect to price. However in both these cases the firm achieves the same result despite that the conditions stated for profit maximization are slightly different under these alternative situations.

Solved Illustrations

(1) If the demand function of the firm is $P = 50 - \frac{1}{2}D$, where $P =$ price and $D =$ demand.

(a) Find the level of output which maximizes firm's total revenue. What will be the corresponding price for this output?

(b) If $TVC = 2D^2 - 15D$ and $TFC = 10$. Find Firm's Total Cost (C) and MC functions.

(c) What is the equilibrium level of output corresponding to the above demand and cost functions?

(d) Does the firm a monopolist or a competitive seller?

(e) What happens to the firm's price, output and profit if he behaves like a competitive firm by equating MC with price ?

(a) From fFirm's demand function is $P = 50 - \frac{1}{2}D$, we get total Revenue $(R) = PD = 50D - \frac{1}{2}D^2$

The output that corresponds to firm's maximum total revenue refers to the level of output at which MR is zero. This is obtained by

$$MR = \frac{dR}{dD} = 50 - D = 0 \text{ or } D = 50 \text{ and } P = 50 - \frac{1}{2}D = 25$$

$\therefore$ Firm's TR is maximum, when $D = 50$ and $P = 25$.

(*b*) From $TVC = 2D^2 - 15D$ and $TFC = 10$, we get $TC = C = TVC + TFC = 2D^2 - 15D + 10$.

Firm's *MC* function is $\frac{dC}{dD} = 4D - 15$.

(*c*) Firm's equilibrium level of output refers to the profit maximizing output. This is the output at which profit (π) is maximum. This can be derived as

$$\pi = R - C = 50D - \frac{1}{2}D^2 - 2D^2 + 15D - 10 = 65D - \frac{1}{2}D^2 - 2D^2 - 10$$

The conditions for π maximization are $\frac{d\pi}{dD} = 0$, $\frac{d^2\pi}{dD^2} < 0$, where

$$\frac{d\pi}{dD} = \frac{d}{dD}\left(65D - \frac{1}{2}D^2 - 2D^2 - 10\right) = 65 - D - 4D = 0 \text{ or } 65 = 5D \text{ or } D = 13.$$

$\therefore$ Profit is maximum when $D = 13$. But this also reqiors $\frac{d^2\pi}{dD^2} < 0$ to be fulfilled.

$$\frac{d^2\pi}{dD^2} = \frac{d}{dD}(65 - 5D) = -5 < 0.$$

$\therefore$ Firm maximizes π when $D = 13$. From this we geet equilibrium price $P = 43.5$ and firm's maximum profit is $\pi = R - C = 65D - \frac{1}{2}D^2 - 2D^2 - 10 = 65\,(13) - \frac{1}{2}(13)^2 - 2\,(13)^2 - 10 = 412.5$.

Thus at equilibrium $\boxed{P = \text{Rs. } 43.5}$ $\boxed{D = 13}$ $\boxed{\pi = 412.5}$

(*d*) The concerned firm is a monopolist since $P = 50 - \frac{1}{2}D$ and $\frac{dP}{dD} = -\frac{1}{2}$

This shows that price decreases for an increase in demand. ($P \neq MR$, and $P > MR$ for $D > 0$)

(*e*) If the above monopolist will behave like a firm under perfect competition by setting price and quantity at the point where price = *MC*, then

$$50 - \frac{1}{2}D = 4D - 15 \text{ or } \frac{9D}{2} = 65, \quad D = \frac{130}{9} = 14.44$$

Under this condition the firm will sell a larger quantity of output, D = 14.44, at a lower price. The price corresponding to this outpt is given by

$$P = 50 - \frac{1}{2}(14.44) = \text{Rs. } 42.78.$$

These price and output will also reduces firm's level of profit toan amount equal to

$$\pi = 65D - \frac{1}{2}D^2 - 2D^2 - 10 = 65\,(14.44) - \frac{1}{2}(14.44)^2 - 2\,(14.44)^2 - 10$$

$= 938.6 - 104.26 - 417.03 - 10 = 407.31$. Accordingly we get

$\boxed{P = 42.78,}$ $\boxed{D = 14.44}$ and $\boxed{\pi = 407.31}$

However the monopolist will not behave like a competitive firm since it reduces monopoly profit.

(2) For the monopolist the cost and the demand functions are given as $C = 0.004q^3 + 20q + 2000$ and $q = 112.5 - 0.25P$. Find profit maximizing output and the amount of profit of the firm.

Given $C = 0.004q^3 + 20q + 2000$ and $q = 112.5 - 0.25\ P$.

We have to first convert the demand function so as to express it in a different form. Rearranging it we get $0.25\ P = 112.5 - q$ or $P = \dfrac{112.5 - q}{0.25} = 450 - 4q$

For $P = 450 - 4q$ and $C = 0.004q^3 + 20q + 2000$, Revenue $(R) = Pq = 450q - 4q^2$ and profit is $\pi = R - C = 450q - 4q^2 - 0.004q^3 - 20q - 2000$. For equilibrium,

$$\frac{d\pi}{dq} = 0, \text{where } \frac{d\pi}{dq} = 450 - 8q - 0.012q^2 - 20 = 0 \text{ or } -\ 0.012q^2 - 8q + 430 = 0$$

or $0.012q^2 + 8q - 430 = 0$. Solving this equation we get

$$q = \frac{-8 \pm \sqrt{64 - 4\,(0.012)\,(-430)}}{2\,(0.012)} = \frac{-8 \pm 9.2}{0.024} = \frac{1.2}{0.024} = 50$$

$q = -\dfrac{17.2}{0.024}$ is impossible as output cannot be negative.

Thus equilibrium output is 50. At this level of output, $q = 50$, $P = 450 - 4q = 250$.

$\therefore$ Equilibrium price and quantity are $P = 250$ and $q = 50$. However this reqires to fulfill,

$$\frac{d^2\pi}{dq^2} = -0.024q - 8 = -0.024\,(50) - 8 = -\ 1.2 - 8 = -\ 9.2 < 0.$$

The maximum π corresponding to this 'q' is given by $\pi = 450q - 4q^2 - 0.004q^3 - 20q - 2000$

$= 430\,(50) - 4\,(50)^2 - 0.004\,(50)^3 - 2000 =$ Rs. 9000.

Thus euilibrium price, quantity and profit are : $\boxed{P = 250,}$ $\boxed{q = 50}$ and $\boxed{\pi = 9000}$

(3) Find the output that will maximize firm's net revenue and also the level of maximum profit.

For this the firm's demand and cost functions are given as $P = 21 - q$, $C = 30 + 5q$

Given $P = 21 - q$, Total revenue is $R = Pq = 21q - q^2$. Total cost $= C = 30 + 5q$.

Substituting these we obtain firm's π function, $\pi = R - C$.

The output which maximizes firm's net revenue refers to the profit maximizing output. This requires to maximize π with respect to (*w.r.t.*) output (q). This needs to fulfill the cnditions

$$\frac{d\pi}{dq} = 0 \text{ and } \frac{d^2\pi}{dq^2} < 0, \text{ While } \pi = R - C = 21q - q^2 - 5q - 30.$$

$$\frac{d\pi}{dq} = 21 - 2q - 5 = 0 \text{ or } 16 - 2q = 0. \text{ or } q = 8.$$

The second order condition given by $\frac{d^2\pi}{dq^2} = -2 < 0$.

$\therefore q = 8$ is the profit maximizing output. Maximum profit is π at $q = 8$.

Accordingly $\pi = 21(8) - (8)^2 - 5(8) - 30 = 34$ and $P = 21 - q = 21 - 8 = 13$.

Thus equilibrium price, output and profit are $\boxed{P = 13,}$ $\boxed{q = 8}$ and $\boxed{\pi = \text{Rs. } 34}$

(4) The firm faces a downward sloping demand curve. If its corresponding MR is Rs. 15, find pricewhen the demand elasticity with respect to this price is 3.

The relationship between AR (price), MR and elasticity of demand (e) are given by the formula

$$MR = P\left(\frac{e-1}{e}\right), P = MR\left(\frac{e}{e-1}\right),$$

For $MR = 15$, $e = 3$, $P = MR\left(\frac{e}{e-1}\right)$ or $P = 15\left(\frac{3}{3-1}\right) = \frac{45}{2} = \text{Rs. } 22.5$

4.9. Effects of Subsidy, Excise Duty on Monopoly Price, Output and Profit

Once the monopolist reaches equilibrium, there can be changes in the equlibrium quantity and price following imposition of tax on monopoly product and profits. It is imperative to analyse the effects of tax and subsidy on monopoly price, cost and profits. When subsidy per unit of monopoly product is granted the effects are seen to be favourable wheras imposition of a tax can raise price and cost of the monopoly product. We will analyze these effects in the market by considering first the effets under the model of a simple market equilibrium.

Simple Market Equilibrium Model and Effects of Tax and Subsidy

As usual the demand and supply equilibrium is established through the price mechanism so that at equilibrium point demand is equal to supply. When prevailing price is more than or less than equilibrium price, the result corresponds to either excess supply or excess demand respectively.

For illustration the demand and supply functions are given as $q_d = 20 - 2P$ and $q_s = P - 1$, where P = price. At equlibrium $q_d = q_s$. This gives equilibrium price and quantity $\bar{P} = 7$ and $q_d = q_s = 6$. If $P = 6 < \bar{P}$, $q_d = 8$ and $q_s = 5$, $q_d > q_s$. This is the case of excess demand. Similarly when $P = 8 > \bar{P}$, $q_d = 4$ and $q_s = 7$, $q_s > q_d$. This refers to excess supply.

Important is that when a tax is imposed on this product or a subsidy is granted to the product , the equilibrium price and quantities are getting distorted. Under these situations new equlibrium price and quantity are to be determined.

Suppose a specific tax or per unit tax of Rs.'t is imposed on the product, the seller will raise price of the product to cover this tax amount. The supply function accordingly changes from $S = f(P)$ to $S = f(P - t)$, although the demand function remains the same. Similarly when a subsidy (s) is granted to the product, the supply function accordingly changes from $S = f(P)$ to $S = f(P + s)$, while the demand function remain the same.

An illustration on Effects of Taxation and Subsidy on Monopoly Price and Quantity

To illustrate the effects of a tax or subsidy we will take above example , $q_d = 20 - 2P$ and $q_s = P - 1$. Let us assume that government imposes a per unit tax of Rs. 3 so that supply function changes to $q_s = P - 1 - 3 = P - 4$. The new equilibrium price and quantity are obtained by equating $20 - 2P = P - 4$, Accordingly we get $\bar{P} = 8$ and $q_s = q_d = 4$.

This implies that when a specific tax is imposed on product, price is increased from Rs. 7 to to Rs. 8 and $q_d = q_s$ is reduced from 6 to 4 units. Total tax revenue collected by the government is Rs. 3×4 = Rs. 12. We can study the effect of granting of a subsidy on this product of the firm on price and quantity. Suppose government provides a subsidy of Rs.3 on the product so that the supply function becomes $q_s = P - 1 + 3 = P + 2$. New equilibrium price and quantity will become $q_d = 20 - 2P$ and $q_s = P + 2$. Equating these demand and supply we get the equilibrium price Rs.6 and equilibrium quantity demanded and supplied will be $q_s = q_d = 8$

Monopolist's Equilibrium under the situation of imposition of a Specific Tax

The monopolist is said to be in equilibrium when it produces profit maximizing output. His equilibrium price and quantity alters with an imposition of specific tax on his product. To illustrate this pre-tax and post-tax equilibrium price and quantity let us take the demand and cost functions as

$P = \alpha - \beta q,\ C = aq^2 + bq + K.$

Revenue $= R = Pq = \alpha q - \beta q^2$. Firm's profit function is to be defined and maximized. Profit function is $\Pi = R - C = \alpha q - \beta q^2 - aq^2 - bq - K$. For maximum profit the conditions to be fulfilled are

$$\frac{d\pi}{dq} = 0, \quad \frac{d^2\pi}{dq^2} < 0, \text{ For given } \Pi = \alpha q - \beta q^2 - aq^2 - bq - K.$$

$$\frac{d\pi}{dq} = \alpha - 2\beta q - 2aq - b = 0. \text{ From this we get } q = \frac{\alpha - b}{2(\beta + a)}, \text{ and } P = \alpha - \beta\left\{\frac{\alpha - b}{2(\beta + a)}\right\}$$

These are pre-tax price and quanity at profit maximization point.

These equilibrium price and quanity will undergo a change in the post-tax situation when tax per unit of product 't' is imposed . This can be derived as follows:

With this demand function will remain the same and the cost function changes to

$C = aq^2 + bq + K + tq$. But $P = \alpha - \beta q$ and Revenue (R) is the same $= Pq = \alpha q - \beta q^2$.

The profit function changes accordingly to $\Pi = R - C = \alpha q - \beta q^2 - aq^2 - bq - K - tq$.

Maximizing this profit function we need to satify the conditions

$$\frac{d\pi}{dq} = 0, \quad \frac{d^2\pi}{dq^2} < 0, \text{ For now } \Pi = \alpha q - \beta q^2 - aq^2 - bq - K - tq.$$

$$\frac{d\pi}{dq} = \alpha - 2\beta q - 2aq - b - t = 0$$

From this we get $q = \dfrac{\alpha - b - t}{2(\beta + a)}$, and $P = \alpha - \beta\left\{\dfrac{\alpha - b - t}{2(\beta + a)}\right\}$

Thus equilibrium price and quantity are now different after tax is imposed.

Optimum tax rate

The above analysis shows that after imposition of specific tax, equilibrium price is increased and quantity supplied is decreased. The tax revenue collected will be equal to $R = \{t \times q\}$. The optimum tax rate is the tax rate which maximizes tax revenue of the government. This requires us to maximize R *w.r.t.* tax amount 't' and this is derived below:

$R = tq$, where, $q = \dfrac{\alpha - b - t}{2(\beta + a)}$, we get $R = qt = \dfrac{\alpha t - bt - t^2}{2(\beta + a)}$.

To maximize tax rate the conditions are

$\dfrac{dR}{dt} = 0$, $\dfrac{d^2R}{dt^2} < 0$, and $\dfrac{dR}{dt} = \dfrac{d}{dt}\left\{\dfrac{\alpha t - bt - t^2}{2(\beta + a)}\right\} = \dfrac{\alpha - b - 2t}{2(\beta + a)} = 0$. Rearranging this we get

$2t = \alpha - b$, and $t = \dfrac{\alpha - b}{2}$. This is the is optimium tax rate. This also satisfies the condition

$\dfrac{d^2R}{dt^2} = \dfrac{d}{dt}\left\{\dfrac{\alpha - b - 2t}{2(\beta + a)}\right\} = \dfrac{-1}{(\beta + a)} < 0$ for $\beta > 0$ and $a > 0$

Effect of Subsidy on Equilibrium Price and Quantity

The demand and cost functions remaining the same we can introduce the effect of subsidy granted to the monopoly product. This will alter the already established equilibrium price and quantity set by the monopolist. We can examine this by using the above demand and cost functions to derive new equilibrium price and quantity. For we are given $C = aq^2 + bq + K$ and $P = \alpha - \beta q$.

The price and quantity before subsidy is granted are already obtained as

$q = \dfrac{\alpha - b}{2(\beta + a)}$, and $P = \alpha - \left\{\dfrac{\alpha - b}{2(\beta + a)}\right\}$

Now with subsidy of amount 's' per unit is granted, the demand function remaining the same $P = \alpha - \beta q$, the cost function chnages to $C = aq^2 + bq + K - sq$. Accordingly the profit function becomes

$\Pi = R - C = \alpha q - \beta q^2 - aq^2 - bq - K + sq$. For Maximum profit the conditions are the same. These are

$\dfrac{d\pi}{dq} = 0$, $\dfrac{d^2\pi}{dq^2} < 0$, From $\Pi = \alpha q - \beta q^2 - aq^2 - bq - K + sq$, $\dfrac{d\pi}{dq} = \alpha - 2\beta q - 2aq - b + s = 0$

Rearranging this we get the equilibrium quantity and price as

$q = \dfrac{\alpha - b + s}{2(\beta + a)}$, and $P = \alpha - \beta\left\{\dfrac{\alpha - b + s}{2(\beta + a)}\right\}$

Total subsidy the manufacturer will receive is equal to '$s \times q$' $= \dfrac{\alpha s - bs + s^2}{2(\beta + a)}$,

The effect of a subsidy granted is seen to reduce price and increase quantity supplied by the firm. we have the following illustrations depicting these situations.

Illustrations 1:

The cost and demand functions of the monopolist are given as $C = 6q$ and $P = 30 - 2q$, find

(a) The equilibrium price, quantity and level of profit of the monopolist at equilibrium.

(b) What will be the effect of the imposition of a specific tax of Rs. 4 on price, quantity and profit ?

(c) Do they differ from the original equilibrium price, quantity and profits ?

(d) What is the rate of tax that will maximize the tax revenue of the government?

Solution:

We are given $C = 6q$ and $P = 30 - 2q$. From this we can get revenue and profit functions.

Revenue *(R)* = $pq = 30q - 2q^2$ and $\Pi = 30q - 2q^2 - 6q$.

The profit maximizing firm will apply the order conditons shown below. They provide profit maximizing output, price and level of profit:

For $\pi = R - C = 30q - 2q^2 - 6q$, setting $\dfrac{d\pi}{dq} = 0, \quad \dfrac{d^2\pi}{dq^2} < 0$, we get

$\dfrac{d\pi}{dq} = 30 - 4q - 6 = 0, \quad \dfrac{d^2\pi}{dq^2} = -4 < 0$. From $30 - 4q - 6 = 0$, we get, $q = 6$, and $P = 30 - 2q = 18$

$\pi = 24q - 2q^2 =$ Rs. 72.

Thus equilibrium quantity, price and profit are $\boxed{q = 6}$ $\boxed{P = 18}$ $\boxed{\pi = \text{Rs. } 72}$

After imposition of specific tax of Rs.4 per unit of the product, the cost function becomes $C = 6q + 4q$ although price remains the same , $P = 30 - 2q$. The profit function becomes

$\pi = R - C = 30q - 2q^2 - 6q - 4q$, setting $\dfrac{d\pi}{dq} = 0, \quad \dfrac{d^2\pi}{dq^2} < 0$, we get

$$\frac{d\pi}{dq} = 30 - 4q - 6 - 4 = 0, \quad \frac{d^2\pi}{dq^2} = -4 < 0, \therefore q = 5, \text{ and } P = 30 - 2q = 20$$

$\pi = 20q - 2q^2 =$ Rs. 50.

The new equilibrium quantity, price and profit are $\boxed{q = 5,}$ $\boxed{P = 20}$ and $\boxed{\pi = \text{Rs. } 50}$

Thus the effect of specific tax on monopoly price and quantity is seen to raise the price of the product from Rs. 18 to Rs. 20, while quantity sold is reduced from 6 to 5 units. The post-tax monopoly profit is reduced from Rs. 75 to Rs. 50.

For finding the rate of tax that wil maximize the tax revenue of the government, we need to use the same demand and cost functions $C = 6q + tq$ and $P = 30 - 2q$. Accordingly the profit function

$\pi = R - C = 30q - 2q^2 - 6q - tq$, setting $\frac{d\pi}{dq} = 0$, $\frac{d^2\pi}{dq^2} < 0$, we get $\frac{d\pi}{dq} = 30 - 4q - 6 - t = 0$,

From $24 - 4q - t = 0$, $q = 6 - \frac{t}{4}$, We also get $\frac{d^2\pi}{dq^2} = -4 < 0$. Substituting $q = 6 - \frac{t}{4}$

we can obtain price, $P = 30 - 2\left\{6 - \frac{t}{4}\right\} = 18 + \frac{t}{2}$

Thus equilibrium quantity and price are $q = 6 - \frac{t}{4}$, price $P = 18 + \frac{t}{2}$

To determine the tax rate that maximize the tax revenue we are required to maximize tax revenue $R = tq$ with respect to tax rate 't and for this the conditions to be fulfilled are given by

$\frac{dR}{dt} = 0$, $\frac{d^2R}{dt^2} < 0$, where $R = tq = t\left\{6 - \frac{t}{4}\right\} = 6t - \frac{t^2}{4}$. Setting the derivative to zero we get

$\frac{dR}{dt} = 6 - \frac{t}{2} = 0$, or $t =$ Rs. 12. This also requires to fulfill the condition $\frac{d^2R}{dt^2} < 0$,

We get that $\frac{d^2R}{dt^2} = -\frac{1}{2} < 0$,

Thus the optimum tax rate is $t = Rs.12$. This will maximize tax revenue of the government.

Maximum tax revenue is $R = tq = t\left\{6 - \frac{t}{4}\right\} = 12\left\{6 - \frac{12}{4}\right\} =$ Rs. 36

Equilibrium quantity sold is $q = \left\{6 - \frac{t}{4}\right\} = 3$ and price $= 18 + \frac{t}{2} =$ Rs. 24

Firm's profit for this tax rate is $\pi = 24q - 2q^2 - tq = 72 - 18 - 36 =$ Rs. 18

If the government will impose the tax rate Rs.12 per unit of product, the monopolist will produce only 3 units and get a maximum profit of Rs.18.

Illustrations 2:

Given the following cost and demand functions the monopolist is facing in the market $P = 100 - 0.5q^2$ and $C = \frac{1}{3}q^3 - 6q^2 + 108q$, Find equilibrium price,quantity and the level of profit. Determine the changes in price, quantity and profit if the tax rate of Rs.1.5 per unit is imposed on the monopoly product

For given $P = 100 - 0.5q^2$ and $C = \frac{1}{3}q^3 - 6q^2 + 108q$, firm's revenue function is $R = 100q - 0.5q^3$

firm's profit function is $\pi = R - C = -8q - 0.5q^3 - \frac{1}{3}q^3 + 6q^2$,

Setting $\frac{d\pi}{dq} = 0$, $\frac{d^2\pi}{dq^2} < 0$, we get $\frac{d\pi}{dq} = -8 - 2.5q^2 + 12q = 0$ or $2.5q^2 - 12q + 8 = 0$.

Solving this quadratic equation we get

$q = \frac{12 \pm \sqrt{144-4(2.5)(8)}}{5} = \frac{12 \pm 8}{5}$, which gives us $q = 4$ or $q = 0.8$. This can be known from $\frac{d^2\pi}{dq^2} < 0$

$\frac{d^2\pi}{dq^2} = -5q + 12$. When $q = 4$, $\frac{d^2\pi}{dq^2} = -5q + 12 = -8 < 0$

Thus equilibrium output corresponds to $q = 4$. It can be verified that for $q = 0.8$., the second order condition is not satisfied. Substituting the equilibrium output we get price is, $P = 100 - 0.5q^2 = 92$ and $\pi =$ Rs. 10.67. After imposition of tax of Rs.1.5 per unit of output q, profit, price and equilibrium output will alter as derived below:

$\pi = R - C = -8q - 0.5q^3 - \frac{1}{3}q^3 + 6q^2 - 1.5q$, Setting $\frac{d\pi}{dq} = 0$, $\frac{d^2\pi}{dq^2} < 0$,

$\frac{d\pi}{dq} = -9.5 - 2.5q^2 + 12q = 0$ or $2.5q^2 - 12q + 9.5 = 0$

Solving this quadratic equation we get $q = \frac{12 \pm \sqrt{144-4(2.5)(9.5)}}{5} = \frac{12 \pm 7}{5}$

Thus $q = 3.8$ or $q = 1$. This is to be decided from $\frac{d^2\pi}{dq^2} < 0$, and $\frac{d^2\pi}{dq^2} = -5q + 12$

For $q = 3.8$, $\frac{d^2\pi}{dq^2} = -5q + 12 = -7 < 0$. This has satisfied $\frac{d^2\pi}{dq^2} < 0$,

It can be seen that for $q = 1$, $\frac{d^2\pi}{dq^2} > 0$. Thus the post-tax output, price and profit are

$q = 3.8$, At this output $P = 100 - 0.5q^2 = 92.78$ and $\pi =$ Rs. 352.564 – 347.75 = Rs. 4.81

4.10 Derivatives to Evaluate Average and Marginal Products of Inputs

(1) If total output varies with the employment of factor (F), for given the production function $Q = 20 + 12F - F^2$. Find,

(a) Average product of the factor (AP_F)

(b) Marginal product of the factor (MP_F)

(c) The units of factor 'F' that will maximizes total output *(Q)*. Find, total output, AP_F & MP_F at that point.

Solution:

(a) For given $Q = f(F) = Q = 20 + 12F - F^2$, $AP_F = \frac{Q}{F} = \frac{20}{F} + 12 - F$ and

(b) $MP_F = \frac{dQ}{dF} = 12 - 2F$

(c) The employment of the input that maximize total product *(Q)* is the level of input where marginal product is zero.

For $MP_F = 0$, $MP_F = \frac{dQ}{dF} = 12 - 2F = 0$ or $F = 6$

Thus when 6 units of the factor is employed total product Q is maximum. This maximum output is Q at $F = 6$, Substituting this we get maximum output $Q = 20 + 12F - F^2 = 20 + 12(6) - (6)^2 = 56$

AP_F at $F = 6$ is $\frac{20}{6} + 12 - 6 = 9.333$. We have got MP_F at $F = 6$ to be zero.

(2) The production function is given as $Q = f(\overline{K}, l)$ where capital (K) is the fixed factor and labour (l) is a variable factor so that $Q = f(l)$ and this functional relation is given by

$Q = 16l + 3l^2 - \frac{l^3}{3}$. Find,

(a) The labour units reqired to produce maximum output. What is this level of output ?

(b) The value of maximum marginal product.

(c) The units of labour which maximizes AP_L. What is this maximum AP_L?

(d) Show that when AP_L is maximum, $MP_L = AP_L$

Solution:

(a) For $Q = 16l + 3l^2 - \frac{l^3}{3}$, the employment of units of labour that will maximize output *(Q)* refers to the point where $MP_L = 0$,

$Q = 16l + 3l^2 - \frac{l^3}{3}$, $MP_l = \frac{dQ}{dl} = 16 + 6l - l^2 = 0$ or $l^2 - 6l - 16 = 0$.

Solving the equation for l we get $l = \frac{6 \pm \sqrt{36 + 64}}{2} = \frac{6 \pm 10}{2}$,

$l = \frac{6+10}{2} = \frac{16}{2} = 8$ or $l = \frac{6-10}{2} = -2$, Thus $l = 8$ or $l = -2$.

Since employment of labour can't be negative, MP_l is said to be zero when $l = 8$. This also mean total product *(Q)* is maximum when 8 units of labour are employed. The conditions used to maximize output Q, *w.r.t.* labour(l) are given by

$\frac{dQ}{dl} = 0$, $\frac{d^2l}{dl^2} < 0$, $\frac{dQ}{dl} = 16 + 6l - l^2 = 0$. $\therefore l = 8$

$\frac{d^2Q}{dl^2} = 6 - 2l = 6 - 2(8) = -10 < 0$. $\therefore$ 'Q' is maximum when $l = 8$.

Q at $l = 8$ is $Q = 16l + 3l^2 \frac{-l^3}{3} = 16(8) + 3(8)^2 - \frac{8^2}{3} = 149.333$

(b) To find maximum value of MP of labour, we need to maximize MP_l, w.r.t. labour. This requires to fulfil the conditions

$$\frac{d}{dl}(MP_l)=0,\quad \frac{d^2}{dl^2}(MP_l)<0,\quad \frac{d}{dl}\left(\frac{dQ}{dl}\right)=\frac{d}{dl}(16+6l-l^2)=0 \;\therefore\; l=3$$

It means when 3 units of labour are employed MP_l is maximum. This should also satisfy the second order condition and this is given by

$$\frac{d^2}{dl^2}\left(\frac{dQ}{dl}\right)=\frac{d}{dl}(6-2l)=-2<0 \;\therefore\; MP_l \text{ is maximum at } l=3.$$

The maximum value of MP_l is MP_l at $l = 3$. This gives us $16 + 6l - l^2 = 16 + 6(3) - 3^2 = 25$.

(c) The units of labour that maximizes AP_l is obtained by maximizing AP_l w.r.t. labour (l).

For this the conditions are $\frac{d}{dl}(AP_l)=0$ and $\frac{d^2}{dl^2}(AP_l)<0$

$$AP_l=16+3l-\frac{l^2}{3},\text{ and } \frac{d}{dl}(AP_l)=\frac{d}{dl}\left[16+3l-\frac{l^2}{3}\right]=0$$

or $3-\frac{2}{3}l=0$ or $\frac{2}{3}l=3,\ l=4.5$

$\therefore$ AP_l is maximum when 4.5 units of labour are employed.

This also satisfies $\frac{d^2}{dl^2}(AP_l)<0$, for $\frac{d^2}{dl^2}(AP_l)=\frac{d}{dl}\left(3-\frac{2}{3}l\right)=-\frac{2}{3}<0$

The maximum AP_l is equal to AP_l at $l = 4.5$.

This is $16+3l-\frac{l^2}{3}=16+3(4.5)-\frac{(4.5)^2}{3}=29.5-6.75=22.75$

We can see that for AP_l is maximum, $AP_l = MP_l$. This means for $l = 4.5$, AP_l and MP_l are equal.

Since AP_l at $l = 4.5$ is 22.75, it means MP_l corresponding to $l = 4.5$ must be 22.75.

$MP_l = 16 + 6l - l^2$. For $l = 4.5$, MP is $16 + 6(4.5) - (4.5)^2 = 22.75$. Thus $AP = MP = 22.75$

4.11 Solved Questions of Examination Papers of TYBA (Economics) of Mumbai University

(i) Total revenue function is given by $R = 2x^3 - 63x^2 + 648x$, find x, for which the total revenue is maximum (x = output). (April/2004)

Total revenue (R) = $2x^3 - 63x^2 + 648x$.

The output corresponding to which R is maximum requires maximizing R, with respect to x.

For this the necessury and sufficient conditions to be fulfilled are given as:

$$\frac{dR}{dx}=0 \text{ and } \frac{d^2R}{dx^2}<0$$

$$\frac{dR}{dx} = \frac{d}{dx}(2x^3 - 63x^2 + 648x) = 6x^2 - 126x + 648 = 0 \text{ or } x^2 - 21x + 108 = 0.$$

Solving this quadratic equation we get x as

$$\frac{-(-21) \pm \sqrt{(-21)^2 - 4(1)(108)}}{2(1)} = \frac{21 \pm \sqrt{441 - 432}}{2} = \frac{21 \pm 3}{2}, x = 12 \text{ or } 9$$

To decide whether $x = 12$ or 9 we have to go for second order condition $\frac{d^2R}{dx^2}$, which must be negative,

$$\frac{d^2R}{dx^2} = \frac{d}{dx}\left(\frac{dR}{dx}\right) = \frac{d}{dx}(6x^2 - 126x + 648) = 12x - 126.$$

At $x = 12$, $\frac{d^2R}{dx^2} = 144 - 126 = 18 > 0$, For $x = 9$, $\frac{d^2R}{dx^2} = 108 - 126 = -18 < 0$

$\therefore$ the output (x) that maxizes revenue is equal to x = 9. Total revenue will be 2187.

(ii) The demand function is given by $D = \frac{2P+5}{P-2}$, where D = demand, P = price. Find , elasticity of demand when $P = 10$.

Given $D = \frac{2P+5}{P-2}$, Price elasticity of demand is $e = \frac{dD}{dP} \times \frac{P}{D}$

For $D = \frac{2\text{P}+5}{\text{P-2}}, \frac{dD}{dP} = \frac{d}{dP}\left[\frac{2P+5}{P-2}\right]$,

$$= \frac{(P-2)\frac{d}{dP}(2P+5) - (2P+5)\frac{d}{dP}(P-2)}{(P-2)^2}$$

$$= \frac{(P-2)(2) - (2P+5)(1)}{(P-2)^2} = \frac{2P - 4 - 2P - 5}{(P-2)^2} = -\frac{9}{(P-2)^2}$$

$e = \frac{-9}{(P-2)^2} \times \frac{P}{D}$. Since $P = 10$ is given at $P = 10$, $D = \frac{2P+5}{P-2} = \frac{2(10)+5}{10-2} = \frac{25}{8}$ and

$$\therefore e = \frac{-9}{(10-2)^2} \times \frac{10}{25/8} = \frac{-9}{64} \times \frac{10}{25} \times 8 = \frac{-720}{1600} \text{ or } e = -0.45$$

For finding the numerical value of 'e', we can write $|e| = 0.45$.

(iii) Examine the following function for maxima or minima. (Oct./2003)

$f(x) = 2x^3 - 9x^2 + 12x + 5$

For given $f(x) = 2x^3 - 9x^2 + 12x + 5$, the function has a minima if $f'(x) = 0$ and $f''(x) > 0$ and the function satisfies for a maxima if $f'(x) = 0$ and $f''(x) < 0$.

For $f(x) = 2x^3 - 9x^2 + 12x + 5$, $f'(x) = \frac{d}{dx}[f(x)] = 6x^3 - 18x + 12 = 0$

or $x^3 - 3x + 2 = 0$. Solving this quadratic equation we get output x as

$x = \frac{3 \pm \sqrt{(-3)^2 - 4(1)(2)}}{2(1)} = \frac{3 \pm 1}{2}$. This gives us $x = 2$ and $x = 1$

To know maxima or minima we need to evaluate $f''(x) = \frac{d}{dx}[f'(x)]$

$$f''(x) = \frac{d}{dx}(6x^2 - 18x + 12) = 12x - 18$$

$f''(x) = 24 - 18 = 6 > 0$ if $x = 2$, Thus the above function has a minima at $x = 2$ since at $x = 2$, $f'(x) = 0$ and $f''(x) = 6 > 0$,

If $x = 1$, the function has a maxima as at $x = 1$, $f'(x) = 0$, $f''(x) = -6 < 0$

Thus the function has a maximum at $x = 1$ and minima at $x = 2$.

(iv) Find elasticity of demand with respect to price '*p*' for the demand function $D = 50 - 5P - P^2$ at $P = 2$,

For given $D = 50 - 5P - P^2$, $e = \frac{dD}{dP} \times \frac{P}{D}$.

D at $P = 2$ is $D = 50 - 5(2) - (2)^2 = 36$ and $\frac{dD}{dP} = \frac{d}{dP}(50 - 5P - P^2) = -5 - 2P = -9$

$\therefore e = \frac{dD}{dP} \times \frac{P}{D} = (-9)\left(\frac{2}{36}\right) = -0.5$ or $|e| = 0.5$.

(v) Let the cost function of a firm is $C_x = 300x - 10x^2 + \frac{1}{3}x^3$, where $C(x)$ stands for cost function for output. Compute, *(a)* Output at which *MC* is minimum *(b)* Output at which *AC* is minimum *(c)* Output at which *AC* = *MC*.

Given, $C_x = 300x - 10x^2 + \frac{1}{3}x^3, AC = \frac{C}{x} = 300 - 10x + \frac{1}{3}x^2$

$$MC = \frac{dC}{dx} = \frac{d}{dx}\left(300x - 10x^2 + \frac{1}{3}x^3\right) = 300 - 20x + x^2$$

(a) Output at which *MC* is minimum requires to minimize *MC*, *w.r.t.* output.

The conditions for minimization of *MC* is given as

$$\frac{d}{dx}(MC)=0 \text{ and } \frac{d^2}{dx^2}(MC)>0,$$

$$\frac{dC}{dx}=300-20x+x^2,\ \frac{d}{dx}\left(\frac{dC}{dx}\right)=\frac{d}{dx}(300-20x+x^2)=-20+2x=0, x=10.$$

W $x = 10$, *MC* is minimum. $\frac{d^2}{dx^2}(MC)=2>0$ is also satisfied. Thus *MC* is minimum at $x = 10$.

(b) For *AC* to be minimum, the conditions are

$$\frac{d}{dx}\left(\frac{C}{x}\right)=0\quad \frac{d^2}{dx^2}\left(\frac{C}{x}\right)>0$$

$$\frac{d}{dx}\left(\frac{C}{x}\right)=\frac{d}{dx}\left(300-10x+\frac{x^2}{3}\right)=-10+\frac{2}{3}x=0 \text{ or } x=\frac{30}{2}=15$$

At $x = 15$, *AC* is minimum. For this $\frac{d^2}{dx^2}\left(\frac{C}{x}\right)=\frac{2}{3}>0$ is to be fulfilled

$\therefore$ At $x = 15$, *AC* is minimum.

(c) Now the minimum *AC* can be evaluated as *AC* at $x = 15$. This gives us

$$AC=300-10x+\frac{x^2}{3}=300-10(15)+\frac{(15)^2}{3}=150+75=225$$

We need to verify that when *AC* is minimum, *AC* = *MC*.

Since for output $x = 15$, *AC* is minimum and this minimum AC is 225, thus for this level of output, $x = 15$, *MC* is also to be equal to 225.

By substituting $x = 15$ in *MC* function, we can obtain MC = 225

$$MC=\frac{dC}{dx}=300-20x+x^2,\text{ at } x=15,\ \frac{dC}{dx}=300-20(15)+(15)^2=225$$

$\therefore$ At $x = 15$, $AC = MC = 225$

(vi) Examine the following for maxima or minima. $f(x) = x^3 - 3x^2$

For maxima or minima $f'(x)=0$ and if $f''(x)>0$, the function has a minima and if $f''(x)<0$, it has a maxima.

$$f'(x)=\frac{d}{dx}[f(x)]=3x^2+6x=0 \text{ or } 3x^2=-6x \text{ or } x=\frac{-6}{3}=-2$$

$f''(x) = 6x + 6 < 0$ if $x = -2$ Thus $f(x) = x^3 + 3x^2$ has a maxima at $x = -2$.

(viii) For a certain commodity the cost function is given by $C = x^2 - 3x + 10$ find (*a*) *AC*, (*b*) *MC*, (*c*) output *x*, when *AC* = *MC*.

Given $C = x^2 - 3x + 10$ *(a)* $AC = \frac{C}{x} = x - 3 + \frac{10}{x}$ *(b)* $MC = \frac{dC}{dx} = 2x - 3$ *(c)* Output for which *AC* is minimum means $\frac{d}{dx}(AC) = 0, \frac{d^2}{dx^2}(AC) > 0$

$$\frac{d}{dx}(AC) = \frac{d}{dx}\left[x - 3 + \frac{1}{x}10\right] = \frac{d}{dx}(x - 3 + 10x^{-1}) = 1 - 10x^{-2} = 0.$$

$$\text{or } 1 - \frac{10}{x^2} = 0 \text{ or } \frac{x^2 - 10}{x^2} = 0 \text{ or } x^2 - 10 = 0,\ x = \sqrt{10} = 3.162$$

AC is minimum when $x = 3.162$. For this the sufficient condition to be fulfilled is

$$\frac{d^2}{dx^2}(AC) = \frac{d}{dx}\left(1 - \frac{10}{x^2}\right) = \frac{20}{x^3} > 0 \text{ as } x = 3.162 > 0$$

$\therefore$ *AC* is minimum at $x = 3.162$ is verified.

Minimum *AC* is equal to *AC* at $x = 3.162$. This given us

$$AC = x - 3 + \frac{10}{x} = 3.162 - 3 + \frac{10}{3.162} = 3.325$$

$$MC = 2x - 3 = 2\,(3.162) - 3 = 3.325$$

$\therefore$ At $x = 3.162$, $AC = MC = 3.325$.

(viii) If, for a good, the demand function is given by $D = 510 - 25P$ where P = price, compute elasticity of demand *w.r.t.* price when P = Rs. 3.

For given $D = 510 - 25P$, $e = \frac{dD}{dP} \times \frac{P}{D}$ at P = 3, $D = 510 - 25P = 435$,

$$\frac{dD}{dP} = -25 \therefore e = (-25)\left(\frac{3}{435}\right) = \frac{-75}{435} = -0.172\ e = -0.172 \text{ or } |e| = 0.172.$$

EXERCISE – 4

(1) Given total cost function $C = 5q - 2q^2 + q^3$ evaluate *(a)* Average and marginal cost functions *(b)* Find output that minimize *AC* and *MC*.

(2) If marginal revenue is Rs. 25 and elasticity of demand *(e)* is 3 find price.

(3) For the following demand and cost functions calculate profit maximizing price, quantity and profits. *(a)* $P = 18 - 4x$ and $C = 10x - x^2$ *(b)* $x = 80 - 5P$ and $C = 75 + 3x$ *(c)* $P = \alpha - \beta x$ and $C = ax^2 + bx + c$

(4) A monopolist faces the cost function $C = \frac{1}{3}q^3 - q^2 + 400q + 80$ and the fixed market price is Rs. 350 per unit of q. Find profit maximizing output and profit.

(5) State the conditions for profit maximization of a monopolist in pre-tax and post-tax situation.

(6) The firm has estimated its cost function $C = 100 + 0.15x^2$ and $R = 5x$. Find profit maximizing output *(x)*.

(7) If $P = 20 - 4q$ is the demand function and $C = 6q$, find equilibrium price and output and determine the changes when a specific tax of Rs. 5 is levied on quantity produced by the monopolist.

(8) If the production function is given as $Q = f(x)$ is $Q = 30F + 5F^2 - \frac{F^3}{3}$

Find *(a)* average and marginal products *(b)* prove that when AP is maximum, $AP = MP$.

(9) If $P = 90 - \frac{1}{3}q$, find the output which maximizes total revenue.

(10) If the total output *(q)* is given in the production function $q = 20 + 12l - l^2$ where l = labour units, evaluate *(a) AP* and *MP* of labour at $l = 3$, $l = 4$, *(b)* find labour units that maximizes AP_l and MP_l

(11) If demand function is given $P = 15 - 5q$ and average cost = 5

Find *(a)* Total cost, marginal cost, *(b)* Total revenue, marginal revenue, *(c)* Find profit maximizing output.

(12) Determine the elasticity of total cost and average cost.

(13) If the demand function of the monopolist is $q = 30 - \frac{1}{3}P$.

(a) Find the level of output that maximizes total revenue *(b)* what would be the total revenue and price corresponding to this output *(q)*.

(14) If price = 25, elasticity of demand (e) is 2, find marginal revenue.

(15) If the demand function $P = 50 - 0.2q$ and cost function $C = 10q + 100$, find profit maximizing output and the amount of profit.

(16) Find maxima, minima and point of inflexion for the given function $f(x) = x^3 - 3x^3 + 3x + 8$

(17) Find the values of x for the function $f(x) = 10x^5 - 30x^4 + 10x^3$ that corresponds to maxima and minima.

(18) A competitive firm faces the following cost function $C = 20 + 15q + 5q^2 + \frac{1}{6}x^3$ and the sells the produce at a fixed price of Rs. 10 per unit. Find the quantity to be produced for maximizing profit.

(19) A manufacturer of calculater produces q units for which he faces the demand and cost functions as $q = 50 - 5P$ and $C = \frac{q^2}{25} + 2x + 55$. Find the number of calculater *(q)* he has to produce for maximizing profit.

(20) A monopolist has been given the following average cost and revenue functions $AC = 12 - 0.5q$ and $R = 30q - 2q^2$. Determine

(a) Profit maximizing output, Price and level of profit of the monopolistr.

(b) What will happen to the above equilibrium price, quantity and profit when there is an imposition of Rs. 3 tax on per unit of monopoly product?

(c) What will be the equilibrium price, quantity and profit when the monopolist receives a subsidy of Rs. 2 per unit of its product?

❑ ❑ ❑

5 MATRIX ALGEBRA: APPLICATIONS TO INPUT-OUTPUT ANALYSIS

5.1 Concept of a Matrix

The operation of matrix algebra is difterent from the ordinary algebra. Matrix algebra forms an important tool in so far it gives a suitable porcess of handling and dealing with a large system of equations. Through matrix operation and determinants, one can get an easy solution to the linear equations.

A matrix is defined as a rectangular array of numbers, parameters, variable, etc., enclosed by a pair of brackets. These elements are arranged in rows and columns. Matrices are generally denoted by capital letters *A, B, C..., X, Y, Z*, etc., while the numbers called elements are denoted by small letters *a, b, c, d....*, etc. The elements of a matrix are enclosed by square or rectangular brackets [ ] or parantheses ( ) or pair of bars || ||. A matrix with 'm' number of rows and 'n' number of columns is '$m \times n$' and has '*mn*' number of elements. The elements as such $a_{11}, a_{12}, a_{13}, ..., a_{mn}$ are arranged in a rectangular array of '*m*' number rows and '*n*' number of columns. When the matrix has '*p*' number of rows and '*q*' number of columns, it is of the order $p \times q$, read as '*p*' by '*q*' matrix.

Rows are shown along the horizontal line while columns are arranged vertically. The matrix has i^{th} rows and j^{th} columns where $i = 1, 2, ..., m$, and $j = 1, 2, ..., n$. The total number of elements of this matrix are $m \times n = mn$. This matrix of ith row and j^{th} column has the order '*m*' by '*n*'.

5.1.1. The general form of a matrix is shown in matrix [*A*] below, where

$$[A] = \begin{matrix} a_{11} & a_{12} \cdots\cdots a_{1n} \\ a_{21} & a_{22} \cdots\cdots a_{2n} \\ \vdots & \vdots \qquad \vdots \\ a_{m1} & a_{m2} \cdots\cdots a_{mn} \end{matrix} = [A$$

Any element in the matrix [*A*] is a_{ij} , implies i^{th} row and j^{th} column.

When $i = 5$ and $j = 6$, $a_{ij} = a_{56,}$ The element is located in 5th row and 6th column. Like wise the element a_{34} represesnts the element corresponding to 3rd row and 4th column.

5.1.2. In the matrix [*A*], each element has its definite position in a particular row and column

For example if we have two matrices [*X*] and [*Y*], they are not the same even though they have contained the same numbers or elements as shown below,

$$[X] = \begin{bmatrix} 2 & 3 \\ 1 & 5 \end{bmatrix}, \ [Y] = \begin{bmatrix} 2 & 1 \\ 3 & 5 \end{bmatrix}$$

Matrix [*X*] has two rows, [2, 3] and [1, 5] and matrix [*Y*] also has two rows are [2, 1] and [3, 5]. The numbers are the same in both the matrices [*X*] and [*Y*]. But these matrices are different. This is because the placement of each element in the row and column has its importance in a matrix.

Therefore two matrices [*X*] and [*Y*] are the same if and only if $x_{11} = y_{11}$, $x_{12} = y_{12}$, $x_{21} = y_{21}$ and $x_{22} = y_{22}$ as shown below.

$$X = \begin{bmatrix} x_{11} & x_{12} \\ x_{21} & x_{22} \end{bmatrix} \quad Y = \begin{bmatrix} y_{11} & y_{12} \\ y_{21} & y_{22} \end{bmatrix}$$

5.1.3. When the number of rows of a matrix is equal to number of its columns *i.e.* $i = j$, then it is called a square matrix

5.1.4. When a matrix has only one column it is called a column matrix or a column vector. For example matrix [*A*] shown below is a column matrix

$$A = \begin{bmatrix} a_{11} \\ a_{21} \\ a_{31} \end{bmatrix}$$. This matrix is of order 3×1 It has 3 rows and one column.

5.1.5. When a matrix has only one row, it is called a row matrix or a row vector

Matrix [*B*] shown below is a row matrix. It has one row and 3 columns..

$[B] = [b_{11} \ b_{12} \ b_{13}]$. It is of the order 1×3.

5.1.6. A matrix is called a null matrix or zero matrix when each of its element is zero.

For example [*A*] is a null matrix,

$$[A] = \begin{bmatrix} 0 & 0 \\ 0 & 0 \end{bmatrix}$$

5.1.7. The linear system of equations can be represented in a matrix form. Two simultaneous equations are given as

$x + 3y = 12$ and $5x + 2y = 15$. The coefficients of *X* and *Y* variables can be written in a matrix form as shown below:

$$\begin{bmatrix} 1 & 3 \\ 5 & 2 \end{bmatrix} \begin{bmatrix} x \\ y \end{bmatrix} = \begin{bmatrix} 12 \\ 15 \end{bmatrix} \quad \text{or } [A] \ [B] = [M]$$

Where $[A]=\begin{bmatrix}1 & 3\\ 5 & 2\end{bmatrix}$, $B=\begin{bmatrix}x\\ y\end{bmatrix}$, $M=\begin{bmatrix}12\\ 15\end{bmatrix}$ and $[AB]=[M]$

The following three simultaneous equations can be represented in matrix form:

$2A+3B+C=10$, $A+B+C=8$ and $A+B+5C=15$,

These equations are written in matrix form as

$$\begin{bmatrix}2 & 3 & 1\\ 1 & 1 & 1\\ 1 & 1 & 5\end{bmatrix}\begin{bmatrix}A\\ B\\ C\end{bmatrix}=\begin{bmatrix}10\\ 8\\ 15\end{bmatrix} \text{ or } [A]\,[M]=[R]$$

5.2. Types of Matrices

Matrices are of different types. These are as follows:

5.2.1. Row Matrix: A matrix having only one row is called a row vector or row matrix.

For example : $[A]=[1 \quad 2 \quad 0 \quad 5]$ is a row matrix of order 1×4.

$[B]=[5]$ is a row matrix of order $1\times 1=1$.

5.2.2. Column Matrix: A matrix having only one column is called a column matrix or a column vector.

For example : $A=\begin{bmatrix}3\\ 2\\ 0\end{bmatrix}$ is a column matrix of order $3\times 1=3$ and

$B=[3]$ is a column matrix of order $1\times 1=1$

5.2.3. Square Matrix: A matrix of order $p\times q$ is called a square matrix when $p=q$, *i.e.*, the number of rows are equal to the number of columns.

For example : $A=\begin{bmatrix}3 & 2\\ 1 & 0\end{bmatrix}$ is a square matrix of order 2. It has 2 rows and 2 columns.

$B=[5]$ is a square matrix of order 1. It has one row and one column.

$C=\begin{bmatrix}3 & 5 & 1\\ 2 & 6 & 4\\ 1 & 3 & 0\end{bmatrix}$ is a square matrix of order 3. It has 3 rows and 3 columns.

5.2.4. Null Matrix or Zero Matrix: When each of the elements of a matrix are zero it is a null matrix.

For example: $A=\begin{bmatrix}0 & 0\\ 0 & 0\end{bmatrix}$ and $B=\begin{bmatrix}0 & 0 & 0\\ 0 & 0 & 0\\ 0 & 0 & 0\end{bmatrix}$ are null matrices of order 2×2 and 3×3 respectively.

5.2.5. Diagonal Matrix: A square matrix $[A] = [a_{ij}]$ is said to be a diagonal matrix if all the elements except main diagonal elements are zero. It means in this matrix the main diagonal elements are non-zero while off-diagonal elements are zero.

For example: $A = \begin{bmatrix} 1 & 0 \\ 0 & 5 \end{bmatrix}$, $B = \begin{bmatrix} 5 & 0 & 0 \\ 0 & 7 & 0 \\ 0 & 0 & 11 \end{bmatrix}$ are diagonal matrices of order 2×2 and 3×3 respectively.

5.2.6. Scalar Matrix: A square matrix [A] whose the main diagonal elements are the same and off diagonal elements are zero is called a scalar matrix.

For example: $A = \begin{bmatrix} 6 & 0 & 0 \\ 0 & 6 & 0 \\ 0 & 0 & 6 \end{bmatrix}$ is a scalar matrix.

5.2.7. Identity Matrix: An identity matrix is also called a unit matrix. It is a square matrix whose main diagonal elements are one and off diagonal elements are zero.

Thus $a_{ij} = 0$ for $i \# j$ and $a_{ij} = 1$ for $i = j$.

The identity matrix of 2×2 and 3×3 order are shown below:

$I = \begin{bmatrix} 1 & 0 \\ 0 & 1 \end{bmatrix}$ and $I = \begin{bmatrix} 1 & 0 & 0 \\ 0 & 1 & 0 \\ 0 & 0 & 1 \end{bmatrix}$

This identity matrix 'I' has some important properties, such as:

(a) $AI = IA = A$, when AI and IA are conformable for multiplication.

(b) $I = I'$ (transpose of identity matrix is same as the original one)

5.2.8. Upper Triangular Matrix: A square matrix [A] whose elements $a_{ij} = 0$ for $i > j$ is an upper triangular matrix. Thus for this matrix all elements to the left of main diagonal are zero.

For example: $A = \begin{bmatrix} 3 & 2 & 6 \\ 0 & 5 & 4 \\ 0 & 0 & 8 \end{bmatrix}$ is an upper triangular matrix.

5.2.9. Lower Triangular Matrix: A square matrix [A] whose elements $a_{ij} = 0$ for $j > i$ or $i < j$ is called a lower triangular matrix. For this matrix, all elements to the right of the main diagonal are zero.

For example: $A = \begin{bmatrix} 8 & 0 & 0 \\ 3 & 5 & 0 \\ 7 & 2 & 3 \end{bmatrix}$

5.2.10. Symmetric Matrix: A symmetric matrix is a square matrix in which the elements are arranged in such a way that both sides of the main diagonal has the same elements. Thus $a_{ij} = a_{ji}$ for $i \# j$. This means $a_{12} = a_{21}$, $a_{13} = a_{31}$ and $a_{23} = a_{32}$ for a 3×3 matrix.

For example: $A = \begin{bmatrix} 3 & 2 & 0 \\ 2 & 5 & 1 \\ 0 & 1 & 7 \end{bmatrix}$ is a symmatric matrix.

It has an important property that the transpose of this matrix is the original matrix itself.

$\therefore A' = A$. When $A' = A$, A is said to be a symmetric matrix. However for identity matrix also we find $I' = I$. However these are different in many respects.

5.2.11. Singular Matrix: A square matrix $A = [a_{ij}]$ is said to be a singular matrix if its corrsponding determinant is zero.

For example: $A = \begin{bmatrix} 4 & 8 \\ 2 & 4 \end{bmatrix}$ is a singular matrix as its determint $|A| = 4 \times 4 - 8 \times 2 = 0$

5.2.12. Transpose of a Matrix: When we get a new matrix by intercharging rows and columns of matrix [A], it is called transpose of the matrix and it is written as $[A]'$.

For example: $[A] = \begin{bmatrix} a_{11} & a_{21} \\ a_{12} & a_{22} \end{bmatrix}$ and $[A]' = \begin{bmatrix} a_{11} & a_{21} \\ a_{12} & a_{22} \end{bmatrix}$ so that $[A']' = A$.,

$$[A']' = \begin{bmatrix} a_{11} & a_{12} \\ a_{21} & a_{22} \end{bmatrix} = [A].$$

For given 3×3 matrix

$$[B] = \begin{bmatrix} 1 & 2 & -3 \\ 2 & -5 & -6 \\ -4 & 8 & 7 \end{bmatrix}, \quad [B'] = \begin{bmatrix} 1 & 2 & -4 \\ 2 & -5 & 8 \\ -3 & -6 & 7 \end{bmatrix}.$$

For given $[A] = \begin{bmatrix} 7 \\ 5 \\ 9 \end{bmatrix}$, $[A'] = [7 \quad 5 \quad 9]$.

When $A = 3 \times 2$ matrix, $A' = 2 \times 3$ matrix.

5.2.13. Non-singular Matrix: A square matrix $[A]$ is said to be a non-singular matrix when its corresponding determinant exists or it is not zero, i.e. $| A | \# 0$.

For example: $[A] = \begin{bmatrix} 3 & 2 \\ 5 & 4 \end{bmatrix}$ and its determinant is $| A | = 12 - 10 = 2 \# 0$.

$\therefore$ $[A]$ is a non-singular matrix.

5.3. Order of a Matrix

A matrix with 'p' number of rows and 'q' number of columns has the total number of elements equal to $p \times q$. So this matrix $[A]$ is said to be of the order 'p' by 'q'. This is written as $p \times q$. Similalrly a matrix $[B]$ with 'm' rows and 'n' columns, is said to be of order 'm' by 'n' or $m \times n$.

For example: $[A]=\begin{bmatrix} 3 & 2 & 5 & 6 \\ 2 & 0 & 1 & 8 \end{bmatrix}$ is of order $2 \times 4 = 8$. It has 2 rows and 4 columns and its total number of elements are $2 \times 4 = 8$.

Similarly matrix $[B]=\begin{bmatrix} 3 & 2 & 1 \\ 4 & 5 & 0 \\ 2 & 7 & 6 \end{bmatrix}$ is with 3 rows and 3 columns. It is of order $3 \times 3 = 9$ elements.

A matrix of order 2×3 can also be written as

$$A = [a_{ij}]_{2 \times 3} = \begin{bmatrix} a_{11} & a_{12} & a_{13} \\ a_{21} & a_{22} & a_{23} \end{bmatrix}$$

5.4. Algebra of Matrix Addition and Subtraction

5.4.1. Two matrices $[A]$ and $[B]$ can be added and subtracted if they are of the same order $m \times n$. In matrix addition and subtraction, corresponding elements of two matrices are added and subtracted.

If matrix $A = [a_{ij}]$ and $[B] = [b_{ij}]$, $[A] + [B] = [C]$ is of the order $i \times j$.

Thus when $[a_{ij}]_{m \times n}$, $[b_{ij}]_{m \times n}$ $[A] + [B] = [C] = [c_{ij}]_{m \times n}$

For example if $[A]=\begin{bmatrix} a_{11} & a_{12} \\ a_{21} & a_{22} \end{bmatrix}$ $[B]=\begin{bmatrix} b_{11} & b_{12} \\ b_{21} & b_{22} \end{bmatrix}$

$$[A+B]=\begin{bmatrix} a_{11}+b_{11} & a_{12}+b_{12} \\ a_{21}+b_{21} & a_{22}+b_{22} \end{bmatrix}=[C]$$

For example given, $[A]=\begin{bmatrix} 3 & 2 \\ 5 & -1 \end{bmatrix}$ $[B]=\begin{bmatrix} -1 & 4 \\ 2 & 5 \end{bmatrix}$

$$[A+B]=\begin{bmatrix} 3-1 & 2+4 \\ 5+2 & -1+5 \end{bmatrix}=\begin{bmatrix} 2 & 6 \\ 7 & 4 \end{bmatrix}$$

When $[A]=\begin{bmatrix} 2 & 3 \\ 5 & 1 \\ 6 & 4 \end{bmatrix}$ and $[B]=\begin{bmatrix} 4 & 7 & 3 \\ 2 & 8 & 1 \end{bmatrix}$, we can not find $[A \pm B]$

Addition of $[A + B]$ is not possible because $[A] = [a_{ij}]_{3 \times 2}$ and $[B] = [b_{ij}]_{2 \times 3}$ As $[A]$ and $[B]$ are not of the same dimension, we cannot define

$[A + B]$, $[B + A]$, $[A - B]$ and $[B - A]$.

Properties of matrix addition are the following:

(a) Matrix addition is commutative since $[A + B] = [B + A]$.

(b) Matrix addition is associative since $(A + B) + C = A + (B + C)$ where A, B, C are three matrices of the same order.

(c) $A + 0 = 0 + A = A$ where '0' is a null matrix of the same order as A.

Similarly $A + (-A) = (-A) + A = 0$, $A + A = 2A$, $K(A + B) = KA + KB$ and $(K_1 + K_2) A = K_1A + K_2A$

Following are some illustrations on matrix addition and subtraction.

(i) If $[A]=\begin{bmatrix} 3 & 0 \\ -5 & 4 \end{bmatrix}, [B]=\begin{bmatrix} -3 & 5 \\ 6 & -2 \end{bmatrix}$, find $A+B,\ A-B,\ B+A,\ B-A$

$$[A+B]=\begin{bmatrix} 3-3 & 0+5 \\ -5+6 & 4-2 \end{bmatrix}=\begin{bmatrix} 0 & 5 \\ 1 & 2 \end{bmatrix}$$

$$[A-B]=\begin{bmatrix} 3-(-3) & 0-5 \\ -5-6 & 4-(-2) \end{bmatrix}=\begin{bmatrix} 6 & -5 \\ -11 & 6 \end{bmatrix}$$

$$[B-A]=\begin{bmatrix} -3-3 & 5-0 \\ 6-(-5) & -2-4 \end{bmatrix}=\begin{bmatrix} -6 & 5 \\ 11 & -6 \end{bmatrix}$$

$$[A+B]=[B+A]=\begin{bmatrix} 0 & 5 \\ 1 & 2 \end{bmatrix}$$

But $[A - B] \neq [B - A]$ and $[A - B] = -[B - A]$

(ii) If $[A]=\begin{bmatrix} x & -3 & y \\ 5 & z & -2 \end{bmatrix}\ [B]=\begin{bmatrix} 4 & x & z \\ x & y & 3 \end{bmatrix}$

$$[A+B]=\begin{bmatrix} x+4 & x-3 & y+z \\ x+5 & y+z & 1 \end{bmatrix}$$

$$[A-B]=\begin{bmatrix} (x-4) & -(x+3) & (y-z) \\ (5-x) & (z-y) & -5 \end{bmatrix}$$

(iii) If $[A]=\begin{bmatrix} 1 & 3 & 4 \\ 5 & 2 & 6 \\ 1 & 4 & 0 \end{bmatrix}\ [B]=\begin{bmatrix} 1 & 0 & 0 \\ 0 & 1 & 0 \\ 0 & 0 & 1 \end{bmatrix}$, find $A-2B$

$$2B=2\begin{bmatrix} 1 & 0 & 0 \\ 0 & 1 & 0 \\ 0 & 0 & 1 \end{bmatrix}=\begin{bmatrix} 2 & 0 & 0 \\ 0 & 2 & 0 \\ 0 & 0 & 2 \end{bmatrix}$$

$$A-2B=\begin{bmatrix}1&3&4\\5&2&6\\1&4&0\end{bmatrix}-\begin{bmatrix}2&0&0\\0&2&0\\0&0&2\end{bmatrix}=\begin{bmatrix}-1&3&4\\5&0&6\\1&4&-2\end{bmatrix}$$

(iv) Given the following simultaneous equations represent them in the matrix form.

$x+y=1.\ y-z=0,\ x-z=2$ and $y+w=5$

This can be written as, $\begin{bmatrix}x+y&y-z\\x-z&y+w\end{bmatrix}=\begin{bmatrix}1&0\\2&5\end{bmatrix}$

(v) Given the matrices $[A]=\begin{bmatrix}3&4\\5&6\end{bmatrix}$ and $[B]=\begin{bmatrix}1&2\\3&4\end{bmatrix}$, If $K=2$, $K_1=3$, $K_2=1$

Evaluate $K(A+B)=KA+KB$ and $(K_1+K_2)A=K_1A+K_2B$

$$[A+B]=\begin{bmatrix}3&4\\5&6\end{bmatrix}+\begin{bmatrix}1&2\\3&4\end{bmatrix}=\begin{bmatrix}4&6\\8&10\end{bmatrix}$$

$$K(A+B)=2\begin{bmatrix}4&6\\8&10\end{bmatrix}=\begin{bmatrix}8&12\\16&20\end{bmatrix}=KA+KB=2A+2B$$

$$KA=2\begin{bmatrix}3&4\\5&6\end{bmatrix}=\begin{bmatrix}6&8\\10&12\end{bmatrix},\quad KB=2\begin{bmatrix}1&2\\3&4\end{bmatrix}=\begin{bmatrix}2&4\\6&8\end{bmatrix}$$

$$KA+KB=\begin{bmatrix}6&8\\10&12\end{bmatrix}+\begin{bmatrix}2&4\\6&8\end{bmatrix}=\begin{bmatrix}8&12\\16&20\end{bmatrix}$$

$\therefore K(A+B)=KA+KB$ is Proved for $K=2$

$$(K_1+K_2)A=(3+1)\begin{bmatrix}3&4\\5&6\end{bmatrix}=4\begin{bmatrix}3&4\\5&6\end{bmatrix}=\begin{bmatrix}12&16\\20&24\end{bmatrix}$$

$$K_1A=3\begin{bmatrix}3&4\\5&6\end{bmatrix}=\begin{bmatrix}9&12\\15&18\end{bmatrix},\quad K_2A=1\begin{bmatrix}3&4\\5&6\end{bmatrix}=\begin{bmatrix}3&4\\5&6\end{bmatrix}$$

$$K_1A+K_2A=\begin{bmatrix}9&12\\15&18\end{bmatrix}+\begin{bmatrix}3&4\\5&6\end{bmatrix}=\begin{bmatrix}12&16\\20&24\end{bmatrix}$$

$\therefore (K_1+K_2)A=K_1A+K_2A$, Proved for $K_1=3$ and $K_2=1$.

(vi) Represent the following matrix equations in the form of simultaneous equations.

$$A\begin{bmatrix}5\\3\\2\end{bmatrix}+B\begin{bmatrix}4\\0\\-2\end{bmatrix}+C\begin{bmatrix}1\\2\\0\end{bmatrix}=\begin{bmatrix}12\\15\\18\end{bmatrix}$$

This can be rewritten as

$$\begin{bmatrix}5A\\3A\\2A\end{bmatrix}_{3\times1}+\begin{bmatrix}4B\\0\\-2B\end{bmatrix}_{3\times1}+\begin{bmatrix}C\\2C\\0\end{bmatrix}_{3\times1}=\begin{bmatrix}12\\15\\18\end{bmatrix}_{3\times1}$$

$\therefore$ $5A+4B+C=12$, $3A+2C=15$, $2A-2B=18$ are the required system of equations.

(vii) Represent the following system of equations in matrix form

$5x+3y=12$

$x+2y=10$

$-3x+y=7$

This can be written as

$$\begin{bmatrix}5&3\\1&2\\-3&1\end{bmatrix}\begin{bmatrix}x\\y\end{bmatrix}=\begin{bmatrix}12\\10\\7\end{bmatrix}$$

$$\downarrow \quad \downarrow \quad \downarrow$$

$$3\times2 \quad 2\times1=3\times1$$

If we expand it, we get the above three equations.

(viii) If $A=\begin{bmatrix}2&3\\4&7\end{bmatrix}, B=\begin{bmatrix}1&3\\4&6\end{bmatrix}, C=\begin{bmatrix}1&-1\\0&2\end{bmatrix}$, Find X if $3A-2B+4X=5C$

Rearranging this we get $4X=5C-3A+2B$

$$5C=5\begin{bmatrix}1&-1\\0&2\end{bmatrix}=\begin{bmatrix}5&-5\\0&10\end{bmatrix},\quad 3A=3\begin{bmatrix}2&3\\4&7\end{bmatrix}=\begin{bmatrix}6&9\\12&21\end{bmatrix}$$

$$2B=2\begin{bmatrix}1&3\\4&6\end{bmatrix}=\begin{bmatrix}2&6\\8&12\end{bmatrix},\quad 5C-3A+2B=\begin{bmatrix}5&-5\\0&10\end{bmatrix}-\begin{bmatrix}6&9\\12&21\end{bmatrix}+\begin{bmatrix}2&6\\8&12\end{bmatrix}$$

$$=\begin{bmatrix}5-6+2&-5-9+6\\0-12+8&10-21+12\end{bmatrix}=\begin{bmatrix}1&-8\\-4&1\end{bmatrix}$$

$$4x=\begin{bmatrix}1&-8\\-4&1\end{bmatrix},\quad x=\frac{\begin{bmatrix}1&-8\\-4&1\end{bmatrix}}{4}=\begin{bmatrix}\frac{1}{4}&-2\\-1&\frac{1}{4}\end{bmatrix}$$

(ix) If $[A]=\begin{bmatrix}-2 & 3\\ 0 & 5\\ 3 & 4\end{bmatrix}$, find matrix M, such that $2A - M = 0$

$$[M]=2A=2\begin{bmatrix}1 & 2\\ 3 & 0\\ 6 & 8\end{bmatrix}=\begin{bmatrix}2 & 4\\ 6 & 0\\ 12 & 16\end{bmatrix}$$

5.5. Matrix and Scalar Multiplication

5.5.1 Two matrices A and B can be multiplied only if they are conformable for the multiplication. AB is conformable if the number of columns of A matrix is equal to the number of rows of B matrix. Suppose we have the matrices

$[A] = 1 \times n$ or $A = [a_{ij}]_{1 \times n}$, and $[B]$ is of $n \times 1$ order or $B = [b_{ij}]_{n \times 1}$

AB is conformable for multiplication since j of $[A]$ = i of $[B]$ or the number of columns of $[A]$ = number of rows of $[B]$. Thus AB is conformable. The order of AB matrix is known from

$[A] = 1 \times n$

$[B] = n \times 1$

After cancelling n, we get $AB = 1 \times 1$ matrix

For example:

$$[A]A=\begin{bmatrix}a_{11} & a_{12} & a_{13} & \ldots\ldots & a_{1n}\end{bmatrix} \textit{ and } [B]=\begin{bmatrix}b_{11}\\ b_{21}\\ b_{31}\\ .\\ b_{n1}\end{bmatrix}$$

$[AB] = a_{11}\,b_{11} + a_{12}\,b_{21} + a_{13}\,b_{31} + \ldots\ldots\ldots\ldots + a_{1n}\,b_{n1}$

$[AB] = \sum_{j=1}^{n} a_{ij}b_{ij}$, where $i = 1, 2, 3 \ldots\ldots\ldots n$ and $j = 1, 2, 3 \ldots\ldots\ldots n$

Numerically if $[A]=\begin{bmatrix}2 & 3 & -1 & 6\end{bmatrix}$ and $[B]=\begin{bmatrix}4\\ 5\\ 2\\ 1\end{bmatrix}$

$[A] = 1 \times 4$, $[B] = 4 \times 1$, $[AB] = 1 \times 1$ matrix

$[AB] = [2 \times 4 + 3 \times 5 + (-1)(2) + 6 \times 1] = [24 + 15 - 2 + 6] = [43]$

If $[A]=\begin{bmatrix}2\\3\\-1\\6\end{bmatrix}, [B]=[4 \quad 5 \quad 2 \quad 1]$, $A=4\times 1,\ \ B=1\times 4,\ \ AB=4\times 4$ matrix

$$[AB]=\begin{bmatrix}(2)(4) & (2)(5) & (2)(2) & (2)(1)\\(3)(4) & (3)(5) & (2)(3) & (3)(1)\\(-1)(4) & (-1)(5) & (-1)(2) & (-1)(1)\\(6)(4) & (6)(5) & (6)(2) & (6)(1)\end{bmatrix}=\begin{bmatrix}8 & 10 & 4 & 2\\12 & 15 & 6 & 3\\-4 & -5 & -2 & -1\\24 & 30 & 12 & 6\end{bmatrix}_{4\times 4}$$

To obtain [*AB*], the row vector of [*A*] matrix is multiplied by the column vector of [*B*] matrix. Thus the first row of [*A*] is multiplied by by the first, second and successive columns of [*B*]. Likewise the second row of [*A*] is multiplied by the first, second and successive columns of [*B*] and so on.

5.5.2. Properties of Matrix Multiplication

(a) If [*AB*] and [*BA*] are conformable, matrix multiplication is said to be associative so that $A\ (BC) = (AB)\ C$ provided *A, B, C* are of the order $m \times n$, $n \times p$ and $p \times q$ respectively.

(b) Multiplication of matrices is distributive with respect to addition of matrices like

$A\ (B + C) = AB + AC$ provided A is of order $m \times n$ and *B* and *C* matrices are of order $n \times p$ each.

(c) The matrix multiplication is not always commutative because for most of the time [*AB*] # [*BA*]. If [*AB*] = [*BA*] , then only it is commutative. Given that [*AB*] and [*BA*] are defined and they are of the same order, $m \times n$, then also [*AB*] # [*BA*] in most of the cases.

(d) The product of two matrices can be zero even if neither *A* nor *B* are zero or null matrices.

(e) When $AB = 0$, it is not necessary that $BA = 0$, as *AB* # *BA*.

(f) The pre and post multiplication of a matrix by an identity matrix gives us the original matrix. Thus $AI = IA = A$.

(g) $A^2 = A.\ A$, if *A* is a square matrix;

(i) $(AB)' = B'A'$ where B' and A' are the transpose of *B* and *A* matrices.

5.5.3. Scalar Multiplication

If matrix $[A] = [a_{ij}]$ is of order $m \times n$ and let '*K*' be any scalar, the scalar multiplication of *A* by *K* is *KA*. This *KA* is obtained when each element of *A* matrix is multiplied by *K*.

Thus $KA = [KA]_{m\times n}$ while $A = [a_{ij}]_{m\times n}$

For example for $A=\begin{bmatrix}2 & -3\\0 & 6\\1 & 4\end{bmatrix}_{3\times 2}$ and $K = 2$

$$\therefore\ KA = 2A = 2\begin{bmatrix} 2 & -3 \\ 0 & 6 \\ 1 & 4 \end{bmatrix}_{3\times 2} = \begin{bmatrix} 4 & -6 \\ 0 & 12 \\ 2 & 8 \end{bmatrix}_{3\times 2}$$

$$\text{If } K = \frac{1}{3}\ KA = \frac{1}{3}A = \frac{1}{3}\begin{bmatrix} 2 & -3 \\ 0 & 6 \\ 1 & 4 \end{bmatrix}_{3\times 2} = \begin{bmatrix} \frac{2}{3} & -1 \\ 0 & 2 \\ \frac{1}{3} & \frac{4}{3} \end{bmatrix}_{3\times 2}$$

5.5.4. Following are the properties of Scalar Multiplication

(a) If $[A]$ and $[B]$ are two matrices of the same order and K is any scalar, then $K(A + B) = KA + KB$

(b) When K_1 and K_2 are two scalar and B is a matrix, then $K_1K_2(B) = K_2(K_1B) = K_1(K_2B)$.

(c) Similarly $(K_1 + K_2)B = K_1B + K_2B$.

(d) Any matrix multiplied by zero is zero $\therefore\ 0(A) = 0$ and $K(0) = 0$.

5.6. Properties of transpose of a Matrix

5.6.1. If matrix A is of order $m \times n$ then the transpose of A is A' is of the order $n \times m$.

Thus if $[A] = [a_{ij}]$ then $[A]' = [a_{ji}]$

5.6.2. Transpose of a matrix $[A]'$ is obtained by interchanging rows and columns of matrix $[A]$. Thus $(i, j)^{th}$ elements of $[A]$ become $(j, i)^{th}$ of $[A]'$

5.6.3. If A is any matrix and K is the scalar, then $(KA)' = K'A'$.

5.6.4. The transpose of the sum of two matrices is the sum of their transposes. Thus $(A + B)' = A' + B'$.

5.6.5. The transpose of the transposed matrix is the original matrix itself Thus $(A')' = A$.

5.6.6. The transpose of the product of two matrices is the product taken in the reverse order of their transposes. Therefore $(AB)' = B'A'$.

5.6.7. The transpose of a symmetric matrix is the original matrix itself. Thus if A is a symetric matrix, $A' = A$. If $A' = A$ then A is said to be a symmetric matrix.

For example, $A = \begin{bmatrix} 3 & 2 & 1 \\ 2 & -1 & 4 \\ 1 & 4 & 5 \end{bmatrix}$, $A' = \begin{bmatrix} 3 & 2 & 1 \\ 2 & -1 & 4 \\ 1 & 4 & 5 \end{bmatrix} = A$

Similarly the transpose of a diagonal matrix as such a unit matrix is also the original matrix.

5.7. Determinants

5.7.1. Each square matrix has its corresponding determinant. Determinant is written by enclosing elements of the matrix by vertical bars | |.

If matrix $A = \begin{bmatrix} 2 & 3 \\ 5 & 8 \end{bmatrix}$, Its determinant is $|A| = \begin{vmatrix} 2 & 3 \\ 5 & 8 \end{vmatrix}$

The value of the determinant is expressed as a single number.

For 2×2 matrix, its determinant is evaluated by cross multiplieation of diagonal elements.

$\therefore |A| = (2 \times 8) - (3 \times 5) = 16 - 15 = 1.$

Symbolically if $[A] = \begin{bmatrix} a_{11} & a_{12} \\ a_{21} & a_{22} \end{bmatrix}, |A| = \begin{vmatrix} a_{11} & a_{12} \\ a_{21} & a_{22} \end{vmatrix} = (a_{11})(a_{22}) - (a_{12})(a_{21})$.

However for higher order matrices like 3×3 matrix, the evaluation of determinant is not that of the simple cross multiplication. A 3×3 matrix is given as follows:

$$[A] = \begin{bmatrix} a_{11} & a_{12} & a_{13} \\ a_{21} & a_{22} & a_{23} \\ a_{31} & a_{32} & a_{33} \end{bmatrix}, |A| = \begin{vmatrix} a_{11} & a_{12} & a_{13} \\ a_{21} & a_{22} & a_{23} \\ a_{31} & a_{32} & a_{33} \end{vmatrix} = a_{11} \begin{vmatrix} a_{22} & a_{23} \\ a_{32} & a_{33} \end{vmatrix} - a_{12} \begin{vmatrix} a_{21} & a_{23} \\ a_{31} & a_{33} \end{vmatrix} + a_{13} \begin{vmatrix} a_{21} & a_{22} \\ a_{31} & a_{32} \end{vmatrix}$$

$$= a_{11}(a_{22}a_{33} - a_{23}a_{32}) - a_{12}(a_{21}a_{33} - a_{23}a_{31}) + a_{13}(a_{21}a_{32} - a_{22}a_{31})$$

5.7.2. Given $[A] = \begin{bmatrix} 1 & 2 & 3 \\ 2 & 3 & 3 \\ 4 & 6 & 5 \end{bmatrix}, |A| = \begin{vmatrix} 1 & 2 & 3 \\ 2 & 3 & 3 \\ 4 & 6 & 5 \end{vmatrix} = 1 \begin{vmatrix} 3 & 3 \\ 6 & 5 \end{vmatrix} - 2 \begin{vmatrix} 2 & 3 \\ 4 & 5 \end{vmatrix} + 3 \begin{vmatrix} 2 & 3 \\ 4 & 6 \end{vmatrix}$

$$= 1(15 - 18) - 2(10 - 12) + 3(12 - 12) = (1)(-3) - 2(-2) + 3(0) = 1$$

5.7.3. The process of evaluating a 3×3 determinant can be understood from the examples shown above. For illustratations, we have an additional example below:

$$A = \begin{bmatrix} a_1 & b_1 & c_1 \\ a_2 & b_2 & c_2 \\ a_3 & b_3 & c_3 \end{bmatrix} \text{ and } |A| = \begin{vmatrix} a_1 & b_1 & c_1 \\ a_2 & b_2 & c_2 \\ a_3 & b_3 & c_3 \end{vmatrix}$$

$$= a_1 \begin{vmatrix} b_2 & c_2 \\ b_3 & c_3 \end{vmatrix} - b_1 \begin{vmatrix} a_2 & c_2 \\ a_3 & c_3 \end{vmatrix} + c_1 \begin{vmatrix} a_2 & b_2 \\ a_3 & b_3 \end{vmatrix}$$

$$= a_1(b_2c_3 - b_3c_2) - b_1(a_2c_3 - a_3c_2) + c_1(a_2b_3 - b_2a_3)$$

It is noticed that for evaluating $|A|$ we have multiplied a_1 by $\begin{vmatrix} b_2 & c_2 \\ b_3 & c_3 \end{vmatrix}$ which is obtained by deleting the row and column where a_1 is placed. Similarly $b_1$is multiplied by $\begin{vmatrix} a_2 & c_2 \\ a_3 & c_3 \end{vmatrix}$ which is obtained by deleting the row and column $b_1$contains and the same is applied to c_1.

5.7.4. Example of evaluating 2×2 and 3×3 determinants are cited below:

$$[A]=\begin{bmatrix} 3 & 2 \\ -1 & 5 \end{bmatrix}, \ |A|=\begin{vmatrix} 3 & 2 \\ -1 & 5 \end{vmatrix}=(3)(5)-(-1)(2) = 15+2=17$$

$$A=\begin{bmatrix} 5 & 3 & 4 \\ -1 & 4 & 3 \\ 2 & -3 & 1 \end{bmatrix}, \ |A|=\begin{vmatrix} 5 & 3 & 4 \\ -1 & 4 & 3 \\ 2 & -3 & 1 \end{vmatrix}$$

$$|A|=5\begin{vmatrix} 4 & 3 \\ -3 & 1 \end{vmatrix}-3\begin{vmatrix} -1 & 3 \\ 2 & 1 \end{vmatrix}+4\begin{vmatrix} -1 & 4 \\ 2 & -3 \end{vmatrix}$$

$$= 5\,(4+9) - 3\,(-1-6) + 4\,(3-8) = 5\,(13) - 3\,(-7) + 4\,(-5) = 66$$

5.8. Minors and Cofactors

There are first order, second order and third order determinanants, which are defined on the basis of rows and columns. Since only square matrices have their corresponding determinants, 2×2 and 3×3 determinants are second and third order determinants. 2×2 determinant is evaluated by cross-multiplication of elements. However for evaluating a 3×3 determinant, we need to expand the 2×2 determinants formed after deleting the row and column contains the element. The process of evaluating this 3×3 determinant has been shown below. The sub-matrices formed while evaluaing the determinant are called minor of the element. Thus each element has its minor and cofactor. For example, given

$$|A|=\begin{vmatrix} 5 & 3 & 4 \\ -1 & 4 & 3 \\ 2 & -3 & 1 \end{vmatrix}, \text{ Minor of element 5 is } \begin{vmatrix} 4 & 3 \\ -3 & 1 \end{vmatrix}.$$

This 2×2 determinant is formed by deleting the first row and first column where 5 is placed. By the similarly process minor of each element can be obtained. For example minor of 3 is obtained by deleting first row and second column.

$$\text{Minor of } 3 = \begin{vmatrix} -1 & 3 \\ 2 & 1 \end{vmatrix}, \text{ Minor of } 4 = \begin{vmatrix} -1 & 4 \\ 2 & -3 \end{vmatrix}, \text{ Minor of } -1 = \begin{vmatrix} 3 & 4 \\ -3 & 1 \end{vmatrix}$$

$$\text{Minor of } 4 = \begin{vmatrix} 5 & 4 \\ 2 & 1 \end{vmatrix}, \text{ Minor of } 3 = \begin{vmatrix} 5 & 3 \\ 2 & -3 \end{vmatrix}$$

$$\text{Minor of } 2 = \begin{vmatrix} 3 & 4 \\ 4 & 3 \end{vmatrix}, \text{ Minor of } -3 = \begin{vmatrix} 5 & 4 \\ -1 & 3 \end{vmatrix}, \text{ Minor of } 1 = \begin{vmatrix} 5 & 3 \\ -1 & 4 \end{vmatrix}$$

Cofactor of an element is the minor of that element multiplied by $(-1)^{i+j}$ where 'i' stands for the row and j for the column for the corresponding element.

Form the same example, when minor of 5 is $\begin{vmatrix} 4 & 3 \\ -3 & 1 \end{vmatrix}=13$, its cofactor is

$$(-1)^{i+j}\begin{vmatrix} 4 & 3 \\ -3 & 1 \end{vmatrix} \text{ where } i=1,\ j=1 \text{ and } (-1)^2 = +1$$

$$\therefore \text{ minor of 5 is } \begin{vmatrix} 4 & 3 \\ -3 & 1 \end{vmatrix} = 13 \text{ and its cofactor is } (-1)^2\begin{vmatrix} 4 & 3 \\ -3 & 1 \end{vmatrix} = 13$$

Element 3 is placed in first row ($i = 1$) and second column ($j = 2$),

$$\text{Minor of 3 is } \begin{vmatrix} -1 & 3 \\ 2 & 1 \end{vmatrix} = -7 \text{ and cofactor is } (-1)^{1+2}\begin{vmatrix} -1 & 3 \\ 2 & 1 \end{vmatrix} = (-)\begin{vmatrix} -1 & 3 \\ 2 & 1 \end{vmatrix} = 7$$

In this process minor and cofactors of each element are evaluated.

The minor and cofactor of 4 ($i = 1, j = 3$) are evaluated as

$$\text{Monor is } \begin{vmatrix} -1 & 4 \\ 2 & -3 \end{vmatrix} = -5 \text{ and cofactor is } (-1)^{1+3}\begin{vmatrix} -1 & 4 \\ 2 & -3 \end{vmatrix} = +\begin{vmatrix} -1 & 4 \\ 2 & -3 \end{vmatrix} = -5$$

Finally we can obtain the cofactor matrix containing the cofactors of all elements of the matrix. It can be written as C_A, where

$$C_A = \begin{bmatrix} A_{11} & A_{12} & A_{13} \\ A_{21} & A_{22} & A_{23} \\ A_{31} & A_{32} & A_{33} \end{bmatrix}, \text{ and } A_{11} = +\begin{vmatrix} 4 & 3 \\ -3 & 1 \end{vmatrix} = 4+9 = 13$$

$$A_{12} = (-)\begin{vmatrix} -1 & 3 \\ 2 & 1 \end{vmatrix} = -(-1-6) = -(-7) = 7, \quad A_{13} = (+)\begin{vmatrix} -1 & 4 \\ 2 & -3 \end{vmatrix} = (3-8) = -5$$

$$A_{21} = (-)\begin{vmatrix} 3 & 4 \\ -3 & 1 \end{vmatrix} = -(3+12) = -15, \quad A_{22} = (+)\begin{vmatrix} 5 & 4 \\ 2 & 1 \end{vmatrix} = (5-8) = -3$$

$$A_{23} = (-)\begin{vmatrix} 5 & 3 \\ 2 & -3 \end{vmatrix} = -(-15-6) = 21, \quad A_{31} = +\begin{vmatrix} 3 & 4 \\ 4 & 3 \end{vmatrix} = (9-16) = -7$$

$$A_{32} = -\begin{vmatrix} 5 & 4 \\ -1 & 3 \end{vmatrix} = -(15+4) = -19, \quad A_{33} = +\begin{vmatrix} 5 & 3 \\ -1 & 4 \end{vmatrix} = (20+3) = 23$$

$$C_A = \begin{bmatrix} 13 & 7 & -5 \\ -15 & -3 & 21 \\ -4 & -19 & 23 \end{bmatrix} \text{ and } |A| = 5(A_{11}) + 3(A_{12}) + 4(A_{13}) = 5 \times 13 + 3(7) + 4(-5) = 66$$

5.9. Properties of Determinants

Following are the important properties of determinants:

5.9.1. Determinant of a matrix $[A]$ and determinant of its transpose are the same. Thus $|A| = |A'|$. This implies that by interchanging all the rows or columns of a matrix, the value of its determinant remains unchanged.

For example for 2×2 matrix.

$$A = \begin{bmatrix} 3 & 2 \\ 5 & 7 \end{bmatrix}, \ |A| = \begin{vmatrix} 3 & 2 \\ 5 & 7 \end{vmatrix} = 21 - 10 = 11$$

$$[A'] = \begin{bmatrix} 3 & 5 \\ 2 & 7 \end{bmatrix}, \text{and } |A'| = \begin{vmatrix} 3 & 5 \\ 2 & 7 \end{vmatrix} = 11$$

Similarly for 3×3 matrix

$$[A] = \begin{bmatrix} 1 & 2 & 3 \\ 5 & 0 & 7 \\ 2 & 1 & 6 \end{bmatrix}, \ |A| = \begin{vmatrix} 1 & 2 & 3 \\ 5 & 0 & 7 \\ 2 & 1 & 6 \end{vmatrix} = -24$$

$$[A'] = \begin{bmatrix} 1 & 5 & 2 \\ 2 & 0 & 1 \\ 3 & 7 & 6 \end{bmatrix}, \ |A'| = \begin{vmatrix} 1 & 5 & 2 \\ 2 & 0 & 1 \\ 3 & 7 & 6 \end{vmatrix} = -24$$

5.9.2. If any column on row is shifted over any adjacent column or row, the value of the determinant will remain unchanged but the sign of the determinant changes.

For example:

$$|A| = \begin{vmatrix} 2 & 3 & 5 \\ -1 & 2 & 1 \\ 0 & 5 & 3 \end{vmatrix}$$. If we change column 1 and 2, we get

$$|A| = (-1) \begin{vmatrix} 3 & 2 & 5 \\ 2 & -1 & 1 \\ 5 & 0 & 3 \end{vmatrix},$$ If we again change row 1 and 2, we will get

$$|A| = (-1)^2 \begin{vmatrix} 2 & -1 & 1 \\ 3 & 2 & 5 \\ 5 & 0 & 3 \end{vmatrix}$$ and so on.

5.9.3 When there is any common factor in the elements of a row or column, it can be taken out.

For example $|A| = \begin{vmatrix} 4 & 1 & 3 \\ 8 & 2 & 4 \\ 16 & 3 & 5 \end{vmatrix}$, the common factor in first column is 4

So we can take out 4 and get $|A| = 4\begin{vmatrix} 1 & 1 & 3 \\ 2 & 2 & 4 \\ 4 & 3 & 5 \end{vmatrix}$

The common factor in the second row is 2 so it can also be taken out.

$$|A| = 4\times 2\begin{vmatrix} 1 & 1 & 3 \\ 1 & 1 & 2 \\ 4 & 3 & 5 \end{vmatrix}$$

5.9.4 If all the elements in a row or column is multiplied by a scalar *K*, the value of the determinant is also multiplied by *K*. Similarly if all the elements of a row or column are divided by *K*, the value of the determinant is also divided by *K*.

For example $|A| = \begin{vmatrix} 1 & 2 & 3 \\ 3 & 0 & 5 \\ 2 & 1 & 4 \end{vmatrix}$, Multiplying the first row by 2 we get

$$|A| = \begin{vmatrix} 2 & 4 & 6 \\ 3 & 0 & 5 \\ 2 & 1 & 4 \end{vmatrix} = 2\begin{vmatrix} 1 & 2 & 3 \\ 3 & 0 & 5 \\ 2 & 1 & 4 \end{vmatrix}$$

If $|A| = \begin{vmatrix} 3 & 5 \\ 3 & 8 \end{vmatrix} = 24 - 15 = 9$, Multiplying first column by *K* we get

$|A| = \begin{vmatrix} 3K & 5 \\ 3K & 8 \end{vmatrix} = 24K - 15K = K(9)$, the value of the determinant is therefore multiplied by *K*.

When we divide first column by 3, the value of the determinant is also divided by 3. Thus originally

$|A| = \begin{vmatrix} 3 & 5 \\ 3 & 8 \end{vmatrix} = 24 - 15 = 9$, Applying $K = \frac{1}{3}$ we get,

$$|A| = \begin{vmatrix} 3K & 5 \\ 3K & 8 \end{vmatrix} = \begin{vmatrix} \frac{3}{3} & 5 \\ \frac{3}{3} & 8 \end{vmatrix} = \begin{vmatrix} 1 & 5 \\ 1 & 8 \end{vmatrix} = 3$$

Thus $|A| = \frac{1}{3}\begin{vmatrix} 3 & 5 \\ 3 & 8 \end{vmatrix} = \frac{24-15}{3} = \frac{9}{3} = \frac{9}{K} = \frac{9}{3} = 3$

5.9.5. If any two rows or columns of a determinant are exactly identical, the value of the determinent will be zero. So we need not evaluate the determinant in this case.

For example $A = \begin{vmatrix} 2 & 3 \\ 2 & 3 \end{vmatrix} = 6 - 6 = 0$, and $|A| = \begin{vmatrix} 1 & 2 & 3 \\ 2 & 3 & 0 \\ 1 & 2 & 3 \end{vmatrix} = 0$ as first and third row are identical

If we evaluate the detreminant we get $|A| = 1\begin{vmatrix} 3 & 0 \\ 2 & 3 \end{vmatrix} - 2\begin{vmatrix} 2 & 0 \\ 1 & 3 \end{vmatrix} + 3\begin{vmatrix} 2 & 3 \\ 1 & 2 \end{vmatrix} = 0.$

5.9.6. If any two rows or columns are multiplies of each other, the value of determinant will be zero.

For example $A = \begin{vmatrix} 3 & 5 \\ 6 & 10 \end{vmatrix} = 0$, as R_2 is muliple of R_1, [$R_2 = 2R_1$], $\therefore |A| = 30 - 30 = 0$.

Similarly if $A = \begin{vmatrix} 1 & 3 & 2 \\ 3 & 9 & 1 \\ 4 & 12 & 5 \end{vmatrix}$, $|A| = 0$ because C_2 is multiple of C_1, $\{C_2 = 3\,C_1\} \therefore |A| = 0$.

If we evaluate $|A|$ we will get $|A| = 1\begin{vmatrix} 9 & 1 \\ 12 & 5 \end{vmatrix} - 3\begin{vmatrix} 3 & 1 \\ 4 & 5 \end{vmatrix} + 2\begin{vmatrix} 3 & 9 \\ 4 & 12 \end{vmatrix}$

$= 1\,(45 - 12) - 3\,(15 - 4) + 2\,(36 - 36) = 33 - 33 + 2\,(0) = 33 - 33 = 0.$

5.9.7. If a determinant is of the type $|A| = \begin{vmatrix} x+y & 3 & 2 \\ y+z & 5 & 7 \\ z+x & 4 & 1 \end{vmatrix}$

It can also be written as the sum of two determinants

$$|A| = \begin{vmatrix} x & 3 & 2 \\ y & 5 & 7 \\ z & 4 & 1 \end{vmatrix} + \begin{vmatrix} y & 3 & 2 \\ z & 5 & 7 \\ x & 4 & 1 \end{vmatrix}.$$

Numerically if $|A| = \begin{vmatrix} 5 & 3 & 2 \\ 8 & 4 & 3 \\ 11 & 5 & 4 \end{vmatrix}$

$$= \begin{vmatrix} 3+2 & 3 & 2 \\ 5+3 & 4 & 3 \\ 7+4 & 5 & 4 \end{vmatrix} = \begin{vmatrix} 3 & 3 & 2 \\ 5 & 4 & 3 \\ 7 & 5 & 4 \end{vmatrix} + \begin{vmatrix} 2 & 3 & 2 \\ 3 & 4 & 3 \\ 4 & 5 & 4 \end{vmatrix} = \begin{vmatrix} 3 & 3 & 2 \\ 5 & 4 & 3 \\ 7 & 5 & 4 \end{vmatrix}$$

↓

0 (as $C_1 = C_3$)

$$= \begin{vmatrix} 3 & 3 & 2 \\ 5 & 4 & 3 \\ 7 & 5 & 4 \end{vmatrix} = \begin{vmatrix} 1+2 & 3 & 2 \\ 2+3 & 4 & 3 \\ 3+4 & 5 & 4 \end{vmatrix} = \begin{vmatrix} 1 & 3 & 2 \\ 2 & 4 & 3 \\ 3 & 5 & 4 \end{vmatrix} + \underbrace{\begin{vmatrix} 2 & 3 & 2 \\ 3 & 4 & 3 \\ 4 & 5 & 4 \end{vmatrix}}_{0\ (\text{as } C_1 = C_3)}$$

$$= \begin{vmatrix} 1 & 3 & 2 \\ 2 & 4 & 3 \\ 3 & 5 & 4 \end{vmatrix} = \begin{vmatrix} 1 & 1+2 & 2 \\ 2 & 1+3 & 3 \\ 3 & 1+4 & 4 \end{vmatrix} = \begin{vmatrix} 1 & 1 & 2 \\ 2 & 1 & 3 \\ 3 & 1 & 4 \end{vmatrix} + \underbrace{\begin{vmatrix} 1 & 2 & 2 \\ 2 & 3 & 3 \\ 3 & 4 & 4 \end{vmatrix}}_{0}$$

$$= \begin{vmatrix} 1 & 1 & 2 \\ 2 & 1 & 3 \\ 3 & 1 & 4 \end{vmatrix} = \begin{vmatrix} 1 & 1 & 1+1 \\ 2 & 1 & 1+2 \\ 3 & 1 & 1+3 \end{vmatrix} = \underbrace{\begin{vmatrix} 2 & 1 & 1 \\ 2 & 1 & 1 \\ 3 & 1 & 1 \end{vmatrix}}_{0} + \underbrace{\begin{vmatrix} 1 & 1 & 1 \\ 2 & 1 & 2 \\ 3 & 1 & 3 \end{vmatrix}}_{0} = 0$$

5.9.8. If any column or row or a multiple of any column or row is added to or subtracted from any other column or row, the value of the determinant remains unchanged.

For example $|A| = \begin{vmatrix} 6 & 5 \\ 3 & 4 \end{vmatrix} = 24 - 15 = 9$

Add 2 times the secend column to the 1st column so that $C_1 = C_1 + 2\,C_2$

We get $|A| = \begin{vmatrix} 6+10 & 5 \\ 3+8 & 4 \end{vmatrix} = \begin{vmatrix} 16 & 5 \\ 11 & 4 \end{vmatrix} = 64 - 55 = 9$

Similarly when we subtract C_2 from C_1 also we get $C_1 = C_1 - C_2$ so that

$$|A| = \begin{vmatrix} 6-5 & 5 \\ 3-4 & 4 \end{vmatrix} = \begin{vmatrix} 1 & 5 \\ -1 & 4 \end{vmatrix} = 4 + 5 = 9$$

So the value of the determinant remains unchanged if we add or subtract any row or column or their multiple to any row or column.

For example $|A| = \begin{vmatrix} 2 & 3 & 4 \\ 5 & 6 & 7 \\ 8 & 9 & 10 \end{vmatrix}$

We can change C_3 and C_2 as $C_3 = C_3 - C_2$ and $C_2 = C_2 - C_1$ and we get

$$|A| = \begin{vmatrix} 2 & (3-2) & (4-3) \\ 5 & (6-5) & (7-6) \\ 8 & (9-8) & (10-9) \end{vmatrix} = \begin{vmatrix} 2 & 1 & 1 \\ 5 & 1 & 1 \\ 8 & 1 & 1 \end{vmatrix} = 0$$, [C_2 and C_3 are identical].

5.10. Inverse of Matrix

We can evaluate inverse of a square matrix of 2×2 and 3×3 order. If matrix is $[A]$, its determinant is $|A|$. Its inverse is written as A^{-1}. When we multiply this square matrix by its inverse we will get an identity matrix of the same order.

$\therefore [A]\,[A^{-1}] = I.$

In ordinary algebra when $x \times y = 1$, then $y = \frac{1}{x} = x^{-1}$ and $x = \frac{1}{y} = y^{-1}$.

This is read as y is inverse of x and x is inverse of y. The product of x and its inverse $[(x)(x^{-1})] = I$(identiy metarx), provided inverse of x exists.

Inverse of a matrix serves very useful purpose in economices when it is required to evaluate the simultaneous equations (linear equations only). The inverse of the matrix is also used in solving input-output model when final demand vector changes. The formula used for solving inverse of 2×2 or 3×3 matrices are the same. For finding inverse divide the adjoint of the matrix by its corresponding determinant

$\therefore A^{-1} = \frac{\text{Adjoint}\,[A]}{|A|}$ or $A^{-1} = \frac{\text{Adj.}\,A}{|A|}$, where *Adj.* $[A]$ is transpose of the cofactor matrix of A.

For a 2×2 matrix A, as such $[A] = \begin{bmatrix} 3 & 2 \\ 5 & 7 \end{bmatrix}$, $|A| = 21 - 10 = 11$ and $A^{-1} = \frac{\text{Adj.}\,[A]}{|A|}$,

Where Adj. $A = \begin{bmatrix} A_{11} & A_{21} \\ A_{12} & A_{22} \end{bmatrix}$ and $A_{11} = (+)\,7 = 7,\ A_{12} = (-)\,5 = -5,\ A_{21} = (-)\,2 = -2,\ A_{22} = (+)\,3 = 3$

$$A^{-1} = \frac{\begin{bmatrix} 7 & -2 \\ -5 & 3 \end{bmatrix}}{11} = \begin{bmatrix} \frac{7}{11} & \frac{-2}{11} \\ \frac{-5}{11} & \frac{3}{11} \end{bmatrix}$$

When we evaluate $A \times A^{-1}$ we will always obtain an identity matrix of the same order, 2×2 for this.

$\therefore A^{-1} A = I$. This is also verified below:

$$[A^{-1}][A]=\begin{bmatrix}\frac{7}{11} & \frac{-2}{11}\\ \frac{-5}{11} & \frac{3}{11}\end{bmatrix}\begin{bmatrix}3 & 2\\ 5 & 7\end{bmatrix}=\begin{bmatrix}\left(\frac{7}{11}\times 3\right)+\left(\frac{-2}{11}\times 5\right) & \left(\frac{7}{11}\times 2\right)+\left(\frac{-2}{11}\times 7\right)\\ \left(-\frac{5}{11}\times 3\right)+\left(\frac{3}{11}\times 5\right) & \left(-\frac{5}{11}\times 2\right)+\left(\frac{3}{11}\times 7\right)\end{bmatrix}$$

$$=\begin{bmatrix}\frac{11}{11} & \frac{14-14}{11}\\ \frac{-15+15}{11} & \frac{-10+21}{11}\end{bmatrix}=\begin{bmatrix}1 & 0\\ 0 & 1\end{bmatrix}$$

Matrix inverse in case of a 3×3 matrix is evaluated below:

$$[A]=\begin{bmatrix}2 & -3 & 0\\ 3 & 1 & -2\\ -1 & 0 & -4\end{bmatrix},\quad A^{-1}=\frac{\text{Adj.}[A]}{|A|}$$

$$|A|=2\begin{vmatrix}1 & -2\\ 0 & -4\end{vmatrix}+3\begin{vmatrix}3 & -2\\ -1 & -4\end{vmatrix}+0\begin{vmatrix}3 & 1\\ -1 & 0\end{vmatrix}=-8-42=-50.$$

$$A_{11}=+\begin{vmatrix}1 & -2\\ 0 & -4\end{vmatrix}=-4,\quad A_{12}=-\begin{vmatrix}3 & -2\\ -1 & -4\end{vmatrix}=-(-12-2)=14$$

$$A_{13}=+\begin{vmatrix}3 & 1\\ -1 & 0\end{vmatrix}=+1,\quad A_{21}=-\begin{vmatrix}-3 & 0\\ 0 & -4\end{vmatrix}=-(+12)=-12$$

$$A_{22}=+\begin{vmatrix}2 & 0\\ -1 & -4\end{vmatrix}=(-8)=-8,\quad A_{23}=-\begin{vmatrix}2 & -3\\ -1 & 0\end{vmatrix}=-(-3)=3$$

$$A_{31}=+\begin{vmatrix}-3 & 0\\ 1 & -2\end{vmatrix}=6,\quad A_{32}=-\begin{vmatrix}2 & 0\\ 3 & -2\end{vmatrix}=4,\quad A_{33}=+\begin{vmatrix}2 & -3\\ 3 & 1\end{vmatrix}=2+9=11$$

$$A^{-1}=\frac{1}{|A|}\begin{bmatrix}A_{11} & A_{21} & A_{31}\\ A_{12} & A_{22} & A_{32}\\ A_{13} & A_{23} & A_{33}\end{bmatrix}=\frac{1}{-50}\begin{bmatrix}-4 & -12 & 6\\ 14 & -8 & 4\\ 1 & 3 & 11\end{bmatrix}$$

$$A^{-1} = \begin{bmatrix} \frac{-4}{-50} & \frac{-12}{-50} & \frac{6}{-50} \\ \frac{14}{-50} & \frac{-8}{-50} & \frac{4}{-50} \\ \frac{1}{-50} & \frac{3}{-50} & \frac{11}{-50} \end{bmatrix} = \begin{bmatrix} \frac{4}{50} & \frac{12}{50} & \frac{-6}{50} \\ \frac{-14}{50} & \frac{8}{50} & \frac{-4}{50} \\ \frac{-1}{50} & \frac{-3}{50} & \frac{-11}{50} \end{bmatrix}$$

For verification we can see that $A \times A^{-1}$ is an identity matrix of 3×3 order.

5.11. Simultaneous Linear Equations and Matrix Inverse Method: Illustrations

(1) Solve for x and y if

$2x + 3y = 9$

$4x + 2y = 10$

These equations are written in matrix form as

$$\begin{bmatrix} 2 & 3 \\ 4 & 2 \end{bmatrix} \begin{bmatrix} x \\ y \end{bmatrix} = \begin{bmatrix} 9 \\ 10 \end{bmatrix}, \; \begin{bmatrix} x \\ y \end{bmatrix} = \begin{bmatrix} 2 & 3 \\ 4 & 2 \end{bmatrix}^{-1} \begin{bmatrix} 9 \\ 10 \end{bmatrix}$$

$$\begin{bmatrix} 2 & 3 \\ 4 & 2 \end{bmatrix}^{-1} = \frac{1}{|A|} \begin{bmatrix} A_{11} & A_{21} \\ A_{12} & A_{22} \end{bmatrix}, \text{ where } |A| = \begin{bmatrix} 2 & 3 \\ 4 & 2 \end{bmatrix} = 4 - 12 = -8,$$

$A_{11} = 2,\ A_{12} = -4,\ A_{21} = -3$ and $A_{22} = 2$

$$\begin{bmatrix} x \\ y \end{bmatrix} = \frac{1}{-8} \begin{bmatrix} 2 & -3 \\ -4 & 2 \end{bmatrix} \begin{bmatrix} 9 \\ 10 \end{bmatrix}.$$ Solving these we get

$$x = \frac{(2)(9) + (-3)(10)}{-8} = \frac{18 - 30}{-8} = \frac{-12}{-8} = 1.5$$

$$y = \frac{(-4)(9) + (2)(10)}{-8} = \frac{-36 + 20}{-8} = \frac{-16}{-8} = 2$$

The required solution are $x = 1.5$ and $y = 2$

If we substitute these values obtained in the equations we will get the same answer. For example,

$2x + 3y = 2\,(1.5) + 3\,(2) = 9$ and $4x + 2y = 4\,(1.5) + 2\,(2) = 10$ for $x = 1.5$ and $y = 2$

[This step is taken only for verification purpose. Thus this need not form a part of the answer]

(2) S o A, B and C from the following linear equations by using matrix inverse methed.

$$A - 2B + 3C = 1$$

$$3A - B + 4C = 3$$

$$2A + B - 2C = -1$$

Rewriting these equations in matrix form

$$\begin{bmatrix} 1 & -2 & 3 \\ 3 & -1 & 4 \\ 2 & 1 & -2 \end{bmatrix} \begin{bmatrix} A \\ B \\ C \end{bmatrix} = \begin{bmatrix} 1 \\ 3 \\ -1 \end{bmatrix} \text{ or } \begin{bmatrix} A \\ B \\ C \end{bmatrix} = \begin{bmatrix} 1 & -2 & 3 \\ 3 & -1 & 4 \\ 2 & 1 & -2 \end{bmatrix}^{-1} \begin{bmatrix} 1 \\ 3 \\ -1 \end{bmatrix}$$

$$\begin{bmatrix} 1 & -2 & 3 \\ 3 & -1 & 4 \\ 2 & 1 & -2 \end{bmatrix}^{-1} = \frac{1}{|A|} \begin{bmatrix} A_{11} & A_{21} & A_{31} \\ A_{12} & A_{22} & A_{32} \\ A_{13} & A_{23} & A_{33} \end{bmatrix}$$

$$|A| = 1 \begin{vmatrix} -1 & 4 \\ 1 & -2 \end{vmatrix} + 2 \begin{vmatrix} 3 & 4 \\ 2 & -2 \end{vmatrix} + 3 \begin{vmatrix} 3 & -1 \\ 2 & 1 \end{vmatrix}$$

$$= 1\,(2 - 4) + 2\,(-6 - 8) + 3\,(3 + 2) = -2 - 28 + 15 = -15$$

$$A_{11} = + \begin{vmatrix} -1 & 4 \\ 1 & -2 \end{vmatrix} = 2 - 4 = -2, \quad A_{12} = - \begin{vmatrix} 3 & 4 \\ 2 & -2 \end{vmatrix} = -(-6 - 8) = 14$$

$$A_{13} = + \begin{vmatrix} 3 & -1 \\ 2 & 1 \end{vmatrix} = 3 + 2 = 5, \quad A_{21} = - \begin{vmatrix} -2 & 3 \\ 1 & -2 \end{vmatrix} = -(4 - 3) = -1$$

$$A_{22} = + \begin{vmatrix} 1 & 3 \\ 2 & -2 \end{vmatrix} = (-2 - 6) = -8, \quad A_{23} = - \begin{vmatrix} 1 & -2 \\ 2 & 1 \end{vmatrix} = -(1 + 4) = -5$$

$$A_{31} = + \begin{vmatrix} -2 & 3 \\ -1 & 4 \end{vmatrix} = (-8 + 3) = -5, \quad A_{32} = - \begin{vmatrix} 1 & 3 \\ 3 & 4 \end{vmatrix} = -(4 - 9) = 5$$

$$A_{33} = + \begin{vmatrix} 1 & -2 \\ 3 & -1 \end{vmatrix} = (-1 + 6) = 5,$$

$$\begin{bmatrix} A_{11} & A_{21} & A_{31} \\ A_{12} & A_{22} & A_{32} \\ A_{13} & A_{23} & A_{33} \end{bmatrix} = \begin{bmatrix} -2 & -1 & -5 \\ 14 & -8 & 5 \\ 5 & -5 & 5 \end{bmatrix}$$

$$\begin{bmatrix} A \\ B \\ C \end{bmatrix} = \frac{1}{-15} \begin{bmatrix} -2 & -1 & -5 \\ 14 & -8 & 5 \\ 5 & -5 & 5 \end{bmatrix} \begin{bmatrix} 1 \\ 3 \\ -1 \end{bmatrix}$$

$$A=\frac{(-2)(1)+(-1)(3)+(-5)(-1)}{-15}=\frac{-2-3+5}{-15}=0$$

$$B=\frac{(14)(1)+(-8)(3)+(5)(-1)}{-15}=\frac{14-24-5}{-15}=\frac{-15}{-15}=1$$

$$C=\frac{(5)(1)+(-5)(3)+(5)(-1)}{-15}=\frac{5-15-5}{-15}=\frac{-15}{-15}=1$$

$\therefore A = 0, B = 1, C = 1,$

By substituting these values obtained in any one of these equations, we can verify whether solutions are correct or not. For example, $A-2B+3C=0-2(1)+3(1)=-2+3=1$. It is verified that these values of *A, B, C* satisfies the linear equation $A-2B+3C=1$.

5.12. Solution of Simultaneous Equations Applying Cramer's Rule

Solution of simultaneous linear equations by matrix inverse method is an important process of obtaining numerical values of the variables. However an oversimplified formula of solving simultaneous linear equations has been developed by using determinants. It is called Cramer's rule. By using this method one can evaluate the system of equations without inverting the matrix, but simply by solving the required determinants. Since Cramer's rule is a more convenient way of solving the unknown values in the linear equations than the matrix inverse method. This method can be used to solve equations unless it is specifically mentioned to solve the equations by matrix inverse method.

The operation of Cramer's rule is stated below, for problems involving two unknowns in two linear equations as

$a_{11}x+a_{12}y=h_1$

$a_{21}x+a_{22}y=h_2$

The determinant is $|A|=\begin{vmatrix} a_{11} & a_{12} \\ a_{21} & a_{22} \end{vmatrix}$

Solution for x and y by Cramer's Rule is obtained in the following process:

$$\frac{1}{\begin{vmatrix} a_{11} & a_{12} \\ a_{21} & a_{22} \end{vmatrix}}=\frac{x}{\begin{vmatrix} h_1 & a_{12} \\ h_2 & a_{22} \end{vmatrix}}=\frac{y}{\begin{vmatrix} a_{11} & h_1 \\ a_{21} & h_2 \end{vmatrix}}$$

$$x=\frac{\begin{vmatrix} h_1 & a_{12} \\ h_2 & a_{22} \end{vmatrix}}{\begin{vmatrix} a_{11} & a_{12} \\ a_{21} & a_{22} \end{vmatrix}} \text{ and } y=\frac{\begin{vmatrix} a_{11} & h_1 \\ a_{21} & h_2 \end{vmatrix}}{\begin{vmatrix} a_{11} & a_{12} \\ a_{21} & a_{22} \end{vmatrix}}$$

5.13. Illustrations on Application of Cramer's Rule

(1) Solve the following simultaneous equations using Cramer's rule.

$4x - 6y = -8$ and $5x + 3y = 12$

These equations are first rewritten in matrix form and then solved:

$$|D| = \begin{vmatrix} 4 & -6 \\ 5 & 3 \end{vmatrix} = 12 + 30 = 42, \; |D_x| = \begin{vmatrix} -8 & -6 \\ 12 & 3 \end{vmatrix} = -24 + 72 = 48$$

$$|D_y| = \begin{vmatrix} 4 & -8 \\ 5 & 12 \end{vmatrix} = 48 + 40 = 88$$

$$x = \frac{|D_x|}{|D|} = \frac{48}{42} = \frac{8}{7}, \text{ and } y = \frac{|D_y|}{|D|} = \frac{88}{42} = \frac{44}{21} \text{ or } x = 1.143 \text{ and } y = 2.095 .$$

By substituting these values we can also get

$$4x - 6y = 4\left(\frac{8}{7}\right) - 6\left(\frac{44}{21}\right) = \frac{32}{7} - \frac{88}{7} = -8,$$

$$5x + 3y = 5\left(\frac{8}{7}\right) + 3\left(\frac{44}{21}\right) = \frac{40 + 44}{7} = 12$$

This indicates that the calculated x and y values are correct. (This is only for self verification).

(2) Solve the following simultaneous equations using cramer's rule.

$2x_1 + 4x_2 + x_3 = 10$

$x_1 - 3x_2 - 2x_3 = 5$

$3x_1 + 9x_2 + x_3 = 12$

The solution of x_1, x_2 and x_3 are provided by the formula

$$x_1 = \frac{|D_{x_1}|}{|D|}, \; x_2 = \frac{|D_{x_2}|}{|D|}, \; x_3 = \frac{|D_{x_3}|}{|D|}$$

where $|D_{x_1}| = \begin{vmatrix} 10 & 4 & 1 \\ 5 & -3 & -2 \\ 12 & 9 & 1 \end{vmatrix}, \; |D_{x_2}| = \begin{vmatrix} 2 & 10 & 1 \\ 1 & 5 & -2 \\ 3 & 12 & 1 \end{vmatrix}$ and

$$|D_{x_1}| = \begin{vmatrix} 2 & 4 & 10 \\ 1 & -3 & 5 \\ 3 & 9 & 12 \end{vmatrix} \text{ and } |D| = \begin{vmatrix} 2 & 4 & 1 \\ 1 & -3 & -2 \\ 3 & 9 & 1 \end{vmatrix}$$

$$|D_{x_1}| = 10\begin{vmatrix} -3 & -2 \\ 9 & 1 \end{vmatrix} - 4\begin{vmatrix} 5 & -2 \\ 12 & 1 \end{vmatrix} + 1\begin{vmatrix} 5 & -3 \\ 12 & 9 \end{vmatrix} = 10\,(-3+18) - 4\,(5+24) + 1\,(45+36) = 115$$

$$|D| = \begin{vmatrix} 2 & 4 & 1 \\ 1 & -3 & -2 \\ 3 & 9 & 1 \end{vmatrix} = 2\begin{vmatrix} -3 & -2 \\ 9 & 1 \end{vmatrix} - 4\begin{vmatrix} 1 & -2 \\ 3 & 1 \end{vmatrix} + 1\begin{vmatrix} 1 & -3 \\ 3 & 9 \end{vmatrix}$$

$$= 2\,(-3+18) - 4\,(1+6) + 1(9+9) = 30 - 28 + 18 = 20$$

$$x_1 = \frac{|D_{x_1}|}{|D|} = \frac{115}{20} = 5.75$$

$$|D_{x_2}| = \begin{vmatrix} 2 & 10 & 1 \\ 1 & 5 & -2 \\ 3 & 12 & 1 \end{vmatrix} = 2\begin{vmatrix} 5 & -2 \\ 12 & 1 \end{vmatrix} - 10\begin{vmatrix} 1 & -2 \\ 3 & 1 \end{vmatrix} + 1\begin{vmatrix} 1 & -5 \\ 3 & 12 \end{vmatrix}$$

$$= 2\,(5+24) - 10\,(1+6) + 1\,(12-15) = 58 - 70 - 3 = -15$$

$$x_2 = \frac{|D_{x_2}|}{|D|} = \frac{-15}{20} = -0.75,$$

$$|D_{x_3}| = \begin{vmatrix} 2 & 4 & 10 \\ 1 & -3 & 5 \\ 3 & 9 & 12 \end{vmatrix} = 2\begin{vmatrix} -3 & 5 \\ 9 & 12 \end{vmatrix} - 4\begin{vmatrix} 1 & 5 \\ 3 & 12 \end{vmatrix} + 10\begin{vmatrix} 1 & -3 \\ 3 & 9 \end{vmatrix}$$

$$= 2\,(-36-45) - 4\,(12-15) + 10\,(9+9) = -162 + 12 + 180 = 30$$

$$x_3 = \frac{|D_{x_3}|}{|D|} = \frac{30}{20} = 1.5$$

The required solution is $x_1 = 5.75$, $x_2 = 0.75$ and $x_3 = 1.5$

[For verification, we can substitute these x_1, x_2 and x_3 values in any one of these equations. Let us substitute these in first equation to get $2x_1 + 4x_2 + x_3 = 2\,(5.75) + 4\,(-0.75) + 1.5 = 11.5 - 3 + 1.5 = 10$

Thus the values obtained are found correct. (This is attempted for self-verification only)]

5.14. Matrix Algebra to Solve Input-output Models

Matrix algebra serve a very useful purpose in economics and planning. It has got wide applications. Matrices, determinant and matrix inverse are extensively used for practical purposes. By applying matrix method we can determine the equilibrium quantities of output produced by the nth sectors of an economy so that an internal consistency is reached with neither excess demand nor excess supply of output. This forms the topic of Leontief's open Input-Output model, details of which are cited below.

5.14.1. Leontief's Input-output model and steps to obtain the equilibrium output

Input-output analysis is a technique developed by Prof, W.W. Leontief. This technique is applied to solve the problems like what should be the equilibrium levels of output of different goods to be produced by each industry or sector for given fixed technological coefficents for output of each sector so that the output of goods produced by each industry must be equal to the demand for these output by the consumers and other industries using thm as inputs. This refers to inter-industry consistency model. This can be illustrated by an example of three sectors economy, producing three different products. These outputs are used as inputs by each of the producing sectors including the sector generating this output. The balance of the output is used as final demand by the consumers, who supply the primary input, labour to the industries producing the final output. The economy is said to be in equilibrium when demand for outputs of each industry or sector is exactly matching the quantity supplied of it. This eventually provides equilibrium to the economy as a whole.

The basic fact is that in an economic system, the output of each industry serves as input of that industry and input for all other industries and the rest of the output are consumed by the consumers. There is a mutual relationship among these existing industries which lead to equilibrium between supply and demand. To simplify the analysis, let us illustrate a model with 2 sectors, named agricultural sector (x_1) and industrial sector (x_2) and final demand for output of each of these sectors by the consumers are denoted by d_1 and d_2.

Accordingly the output produced by x_1 and x_2 sectors are divided into:

$x_1 = x_{11} + x_{12} + d_1$ and $x_2 = x_{21} + x_{22} + d_2$

Final output of x_1 sector is retained by this sector itself. This amount is equal to x_{11}. The output of x_1 using sector 2 as input is equal to x_{12}, while the remaining of the output of x_1 are consumed by consumers, which is indicated by d_1. Similarly output x_2 using x_1 secter as input is equal to x_{21}. The output x_2 retained by the sector itself is x_{22}, while the balance of the output of this sector are used by consumers and this is equal to d_2. These are brought together in the following table 5.1.

Table 5.1

Input-output table

Supply	Demand	Total Demand
X_1	$x_{11} + x_{12} + d_1$	X_1
X_2	$x_{21} + x_{22} + d_2$	X_2

Input-output model is used to detremine output in each secter so that total supply of X_1 is equal to total demand for X_1 and so on. It also indicates that the production function of X_1 is such that X_1 output is produced by using x_{11} of X_1 output and x_{21} of X_2 output. Similalry X_2 sector for producing its total output will be using x_{12} of X_1 output and x_{22} of X_2 output as inputs. Moreover these secters also make use of the primary input labour units to produce final output. Therefore in the production function, it is essential to include the total labour requirements. This is denoted by L_1 and L_2 for producing total outputs of X_1 and X_2 sectors respectively. Therefore the production function of X_1 and X_2 can be shown as

$x_1 = f(x_{11}, x_{21}, L_1)$ and $x_2 = f(x_{12}, x_{22}, L_2)$

The total labour supply and labour requirement by these secters are indicated by $L = L_1 + L_2$

5.14.2. Technology coefficient matrix and solution for the equilibrium output

We can derive the technology coefficient matrix to find solution for equlibrium output in different sectors of the economy. For this an exercise of two sector is repeated here. Of course this can be extended to 'n' sectors model as well.

$X_1 = a_{11} x_1 + a_{12} x_2 + d_1$ and $X_2 = a_{21} x_1 + a_{22} x_2 + d_2$

Taking final demand vecter to one side, the equations are rearranged as

$(x_1 - a_{11} x_1) - a_{12} x_2 = d_1$ and $- a_{21} x_1 + (x_2 - a_{22} x_2) = d_2$

Rearranging these equations and rewriting them in matrix form we get

$x_1 (1- a_{11}) + (- a_{12}) x_2 = d_1$ and $x_1 (- a_{21}) + (1- a_{22}) x_2 = d_2$ Finally,

$$\begin{bmatrix} (1-a_{11}) & -a_{12} \\ -a_{21} & (1-a_{22}) \end{bmatrix} \begin{bmatrix} x_1 \\ x_2 \end{bmatrix} = \begin{bmatrix} d_1 \\ d_2 \end{bmatrix} \text{ and}$$

$$\begin{bmatrix} x_1 \\ x_2 \end{bmatrix} = \begin{bmatrix} (1-a_{11}) & -a_{12} \\ -a_{21} & (1-a_{22}) \end{bmatrix}^{-1} \begin{bmatrix} d_1 \\ d_2 \end{bmatrix}$$

In generalised form we can write the same as $X = [I - A]^{-1} [d]$

$$\text{where } I = \begin{bmatrix} 1 & 0 \\ 0 & 1 \end{bmatrix},\ A = \begin{bmatrix} a_{11} & a_{12} \\ a_{21} & a_{22} \end{bmatrix} \text{ and } [I - A] = \begin{bmatrix} (1-a_{11}) & -a_{12} \\ -a_{21} & (1-a_{22}) \end{bmatrix}$$

The technology coefficients are a_{11}, a_{12}, a_{21} and $a_{22.}$ They are to be evaluated from the data or elsewhere given to us in advance along with the final demand vectors,which are exogeneousely determined in the system. With these we would be able to solve for the equilibrium output X_1 and X_2,by finding $[1 - A]^{-1}$ and then multiplying this inverted $[1 - A]$ matrix by the final demand vector. Numerical examples are cited below for illustrations.

5.14.3. Illustrated Problems on input-output models

[1] An economy is consisting of two sectors X_1 and X_2 Total output produced by these sectors, the input-output transactions in these sectors with their final demands and labor requirements are given in the following table 5.2. If final demand changes to 150 and 200, obtain the the new equilibrium levels of output of these sectors and the total labour requirements to produce these new outputs.

Table 5.2
Input-output table

Sectors producing output	Sectors using output as input & labour		Final demand	Total
	X_1	X_2		
X_1	60	160	50	270
X_2	90	150	110	350
Labour	30	80	—	—

We are given $X_1 = x_{11} + x_{12} + d_1$, where $x_{11} = 60$, $x_{12} = 160$ and

$X_2 = x_{21} + x_{22} + d_2$, where, $x_{21} = 90$, $x_{22} = 150$

We need to write this in a different form so as to include the technology coefficients a_{11}, a_{12}, a_{21} and a_{22}. Accordingly the equations are changed to

$X_1 = a_{11}\ x_1 + a_{12}\ x_2 + d_1$ and $X_2 = a_{21}\ x_1 + a_{22}\ x_2 + d_2$ where,

$$a_{11}x_1 = x_{11} \therefore a_{11} = \frac{x_{11}}{x_1}, \quad a_{21}\ x_1 = x_{21} \therefore a_{21} = \frac{x_{21}}{x_1},$$

$$a_{12}\ x_2 = x_{12} \therefore a_{12} = \frac{x_{12}}{x_2} \quad a_{22}\ x_2 = x_{22} \therefore a_{22} = \frac{x_{22}}{x_2}$$

From the information provided in table $X_1 = 270$, $X_2 = 350$ we can obtain

$$a_{11} = \frac{x_{11}}{x_1} = \frac{60}{270} = 0.222, \text{ and } a_{12} = \frac{x_{12}}{x_2} = \frac{160}{350} = 0.457$$

$$a_{21} = \frac{x_{21}}{x_1} = \frac{90}{270} = 0.333, \text{ and } a_{22} = \frac{x_{22}}{x_2} = \frac{160}{350} = 0.429$$. Substituting them we get

$$[A] = \begin{bmatrix} a_{11} & a_{12} \\ a_{21} & a_{22} \end{bmatrix} = \begin{bmatrix} 0.22 & 0.46 \\ 0.33 & 0.43 \end{bmatrix}$$

$$\begin{bmatrix} (1-a_{11})x_1 - a_{12}x_2 = d_1 \\ -a_{21}x_1 + (1-a_{22})x_2 = d_2 \end{bmatrix}$$. This can be written in matrix form as

$$\begin{bmatrix} (1-a_{11}) & -a_{12} \\ -a_{21} & (1-a_{22}) \end{bmatrix} \begin{bmatrix} x_1 \\ x_2 \end{bmatrix} = \begin{bmatrix} d_1 \\ d_2 \end{bmatrix} \text{ and } \begin{bmatrix} x_1 \\ x_2 \end{bmatrix} = \begin{bmatrix} (1-a_{11}) & -a_{12} \\ -a_{21} & (1-a_{22}) \end{bmatrix}^{-1} \begin{bmatrix} d_1 \\ d_2 \end{bmatrix},$$

$$\begin{bmatrix} x_1 \\ x_2 \end{bmatrix} = \begin{bmatrix} (1-0.222) & -0.457 \\ -0.333 & (1-0.429) \end{bmatrix}^{-1} \begin{bmatrix} 50 \\ 110 \end{bmatrix} = \begin{bmatrix} 0.778 & -0.457 \\ -0.333 & 0.571 \end{bmatrix}^{-1} \begin{bmatrix} 50 \\ 110 \end{bmatrix}$$

Or $x = [I - A]^{-1} [d]$, where $x = \begin{bmatrix} x_1 \\ x_2 \end{bmatrix}$ and

$$\begin{bmatrix} x_1 \\ x_2 \end{bmatrix} = \frac{\text{Adjoint}[I - A]}{|I - A|} \begin{bmatrix} 50 \\ 110 \end{bmatrix} \text{ and Adjoint.} [I - A] = \begin{bmatrix} A_{11} & A_{21} \\ A_{12} & A_{22} \end{bmatrix}, \text{ where}$$

$A_{11} = +0.571$, $A_{12} = +0.333$, $A_{21} = +0.457$, $A_{22} = +0.778$ and

$|I - A| = (0.778)(0.571) - (-0.333)(-0.457) = 0.292$. Substituting them we get

$$\begin{bmatrix} x_1 \\ x_2 \end{bmatrix} = \frac{\text{Adjoint}[I - A]}{|I - A|} \begin{bmatrix} d_1 \\ d_2 \end{bmatrix} = \frac{1}{0.292} \begin{bmatrix} 0.571 & 0.457 \\ 0.333 & 0.778 \end{bmatrix} \begin{bmatrix} 50 \\ 110 \end{bmatrix}. \text{ From this we get}$$

$$x_1 = \frac{(0.571)(50) + (0.457)(110)}{0.292} = \frac{78.82}{0.292} = 270.$$

$$x_2 = \frac{(0.333)(50) + (0.778)(110)}{0.292} = \frac{102.23}{0.292} = 350.$$

We are given the problem where final demand are changed to 150 and 200 so that new equilibrium output X_1 and X_2 are to be different. These outputs are obtained by replacing the final demand vector while keeping $[I - A]^{-1}$ as it is. This is because the technology coefficient matrix has remained unchanged. The final new outputs of X_1 and X_2 are worked out as;

$$\begin{bmatrix} x_1 \\ x_2 \end{bmatrix} = \frac{1}{0.292} \begin{bmatrix} 0.571 & 0.457 \\ 0.333 & 0.778 \end{bmatrix} \begin{bmatrix} 150 \\ 200 \end{bmatrix}$$

$$X_1 = \frac{(0.571)(150) + (0.457)(200)}{0.292} = \frac{177.05}{0.292} = 606.34 = 606$$

$$X_2 = \frac{(0.333)(150) + (0.778)(200)}{0.292} = \frac{205.55}{0.292} = 703.94 = 704$$

$X_1 = 606$ and $X_2 = 704$, are the required equilibrium quantities of output of X_1 and X_2. The next question is the total labour requirements to produce these new output X_1 and X_2. For this, it is required to determine the labour coefficient for both X_1 and X_2 output. This can be obtained from information given in the table. We are given that to produce 270 units of output X_1 total labour units required is 30 and for producing a total of output of 350 of X_2, the required labour units is 80. From thiswe can evaluate the the labour requirements or coefficient denoted as l_1 and l_2 to produce one unit of X_1 and X_2 output respectively. For this the simple formula used is

$l_1 = \frac{L_1}{x_1} = \frac{30}{270} = 0.111$. and $l_2 = \frac{L_2}{x_2} = \frac{80}{350} = 0.229$

Now for producing these new quantity of $X_1 = 606$ units, total labour units required will be $l_1 x_1 = (0.111)(606) = 67.33 = \approx 67$ units, while for producing new quantity of $X_2 = 704$ units, total labour units required will be $L_2 = l_2 x_2 = (0.229)(704) = 161.22 \approx 161$.

Thus total labour requirement is $l_1 x_1 + l_2 x_2 = 67.33 + 161.22 = 228.55 \approx 228.5$.

(2) Given the following input-output transaction table and labour requirements, find

(a) The technology coefficient matrix for the two secter input-output model.

(b) If the technology coefficient matrix remains unchanged, find the level of output when final demand changes to 75 and 100 respectively $[d_1 = 75, d_2 = 100]$.

(c) What is the total labour requirement for producing this new equilibrium output.

Table 5.3

Input-output table for 2 sectors

Producing Sectors	**Receiving Sector**		**Final demand**	**Total demand**
	X_1	X_2		
X_1	25	30	45	100
X_2	60	40	50	150
Labour	40	90	—	—

We are given $X_1 = 100$, $X_2 = 150$ and $X_1 = x_{11} + x_{12} + d_1$,

From the table we obtain $x_{11} = 25$, $x_{12} = 30$, $d_1 = 45$ and likewise $X_2 = x_{21} + x_{22} + d_2$, where $x_{21} = 60$, $x_{22} = 40$, $d_2 = 50$.

The technology coefficient matrix is

$$[A] = \begin{bmatrix} a_{11} & a_{12} \\ a_{21} & a_{22} \end{bmatrix} \text{ where } a_{11} x_1 = X_{11} \therefore a_{11} = \frac{x_{11}}{X_1} = \frac{25}{100} = 0.25$$

$a_{12} X_2 = x_{12}$, and $a_{12} = \frac{x_{12}}{X_2} = \frac{30}{150} = 0.2$, From $a_{21} X_1 = x_{21}$, $a_{21} = \frac{x_{21}}{X_1} = \frac{60}{100} = 0.6$

For $a_{22} X_2 = x_{22}$, $a_{22} = \frac{x_{22}}{X2} = \frac{40}{150} = 0.267$, Substituting all these we get the coefficient matrix

$$A = \begin{bmatrix} 0.25 & 0.2 \\ 0.60 & 0.267 \end{bmatrix}$$

The input-output model for two secter in the matrix form is given as $X = [I - A]^{-1}[d]$

or $[I - A][x] = [d]$ $\therefore$ $x = [I - A]^{-1}[d]$

For $A = \begin{bmatrix} 0.25 & 0.2 \\ 0.60 & 0.267 \end{bmatrix}$, $[I - A] = \begin{bmatrix} 1 & 0 \\ 0 & 1 \end{bmatrix} - \begin{bmatrix} 0.25 & 0.20 \\ 0.60 & 0.267 \end{bmatrix} = \begin{bmatrix} 0.75 & -0.20 \\ -0.60 & 0.733 \end{bmatrix}$ and

$$\begin{bmatrix} x_1 \\ x_2 \end{bmatrix} = \frac{\text{Adjoint}[I - A]}{|I - A|}\begin{bmatrix} d_1 \\ d_2 \end{bmatrix} \text{ and Adjoint } [I - A] = \begin{bmatrix} A_{11} & A_{21} \\ A_{12} & A_{22} \end{bmatrix}$$

where $A_{11} = +0.733$, $A_{12} = -(-0.60) = +0.60$, $A_{21} = -(-0.20) = +0.20$, $A_{22} = +(0.75)$

$|I - A| = (0.75)(0.733) - (-0.20)(-0.60) = 0.5498 - 0.12 = 0.43$

$$\begin{bmatrix} x_1 \\ x_2 \end{bmatrix} = \frac{1}{0.43}\begin{bmatrix} 0.733 & 0.20 \\ 0.60 & 0.75 \end{bmatrix}\begin{bmatrix} 45 \\ 50 \end{bmatrix}$$

$$X_1 = \frac{(0.733)(45) + (0.2)(50)}{0.43} = \frac{42\text{-}985}{0.43} = 100$$

$$X_2 = \frac{(0.60)(45) + (0.75)(52)}{0.43} = \frac{64.5}{0.43} = 150$$

Now we need to change the final demand to 75 to 100 respectively. Accordingly the new equilibrium output will be different. To obtain this we need to insert the new final demand in the place of the final demand vector as worked out below:

$$\begin{bmatrix} x_1 \\ x_2 \end{bmatrix} = \frac{1}{0.43}\begin{bmatrix} 0.733 & 0.20 \\ 0.60 & 0.75 \end{bmatrix}\begin{bmatrix} 75 \\ 100 \end{bmatrix}$$

$$X_1 = \frac{(0.733)(75) + (0.20)(100)}{0.43} = \frac{74 - 975}{0.43} = 174.3 = 174$$

$$X_2 = \frac{(0.60)(75) + (0.75)(100)}{0.43} = \frac{120}{0.43} = 279.07 = 279$$

Since we are given the labour requirements to produce $X_1 = 100$ and $X_2 = 150$ units of output in the table, from this information we need to compute the labour coefficients for producing X_1 and X_2. These are denoted as l_1 and l_2. Since $L_1 = 40$ for producing $X_1 = 100$, we obtain

$\therefore\ l_1 = \dfrac{L_1}{x_1} = \dfrac{40}{100} = 0.4$. In a similarl process since $L_2 = 90$ for $X_2 = 152$, $\because l_2 = \dfrac{L_2}{x_2} = \dfrac{90}{150} = 0.6$

Total labour requirements to produce the new equilibriumoutput of $X_1 = 174$ and $X_2 = 279$ is L.

$\therefore L = l_1 X_1 + l_2 X_2 = (0.4)(174) + (0.6)(279) = 69.6 + 167.4 = 237.$

5.15. Solved questions of T.Y.B.A. (Economics) papers of Mumbai University

(1) April, 2004, .

(i) You are given the following input-output data:

Table 5.4

Producing Sectors	**Receiving Sector**		**Final demand**	**Total demand**
	1	2		
1	10	4	16	30
2	16	18	6	40
Labour	4	18	—	—

Find,

(a) Technology matrix and levels of output if final demand are changed to 8 and 3 respectively.

(b) Labour requirements for producing these new levels of output.

Let us denote the output of sector l as X_1 and for sector 2 as X_2.

$\therefore$ we are given, $X_1 = x_{11} + x_{12} + d_1 = 30$, where $x_{11} = 10$, $x_{12} = 4$, $d_1 = 16$ and

$X_2 = x_{21} + x_{22} + d_2 = 40$, where $x_{21} = 16$, $x_{22} = 18$, $d_2 = 6$

Labour used to produce these 30 and 40 units of X_1 and X_2 output are 4 and 18 respectively. This means $L_1 = 4, L_2 = 18$. From these information labour coefficients l_1 and l_2 can be calculated. We need to use the information given in the table to obtain the technology coefficient matrix as computed below:

Technology coefficient matrix is $A = \begin{bmatrix} a_{11} & a_{12} \\ a_{21} & a_{22} \end{bmatrix}$

The input-output model in matrix form is $X = AX + d$ or $X[I - A] = d$ and

$X = [I - A]^{-1}\ [d]$

The coefficients a_{11}, a_{12}, a_{21} and a_{22} are computed as

$$x_{11} = a_{11}\ x_1 \therefore a_{11} = \frac{x_{11}}{x_1} = \frac{10}{30} = 0.333\ ,\ x_{12} = a_{12}\ x_2 \therefore a_{12} = \frac{x_{12}}{x_2} = \frac{4}{40} = 0.1$$

$$x_{21} = a_{21}\ x_1 \therefore a_{21} = \frac{x_{21}}{x_1} = \frac{16}{30} = 0.533\ ,\ x_{22} = a_{22}\ x_2 \therefore a_{22} = \frac{x_{22}}{x_2} = \frac{18}{40} = 0.45$$

$$A = \begin{bmatrix} 0.333 & 0.1 \\ 0.533 & 0.45 \end{bmatrix},\ [I - A] = \begin{bmatrix} 1 & 0 \\ 0 & 1 \end{bmatrix} - \begin{bmatrix} 0.333 & 0.1 \\ 0.533 & 0.45 \end{bmatrix} = \begin{bmatrix} 0.667 & -0.1 \\ -0.533 & 0.55 \end{bmatrix}$$

$$[I-A]^{-1} = \frac{\text{Adjoint}[I-A]}{|I-A|} = \frac{\begin{bmatrix} A_{11} & A_{21} \\ A_{12} & A_{22} \end{bmatrix}}{|I-A|}$$

Where $A_{11} = +(0.55) = 0.55$, $A_{12} = (-0.533) = 0.533$, $A_{21} = -(-0.1) = 0.1$, $A_{22} = +(0.667) = 0.667$

$X = [I-A]^{-1}[d]$, and $|I-A| = (0.667)(0.55) - (-0.1)(-0.533) = 0.3136$

$$\therefore \begin{bmatrix} x_1 \\ x_2 \end{bmatrix} = \frac{1}{0.314}\begin{bmatrix} 0.55 & 0.1 \\ 0.533 & 0.667 \end{bmatrix}\begin{bmatrix} 16 \\ 6 \end{bmatrix}$$

$$X_1 = \frac{(0.55)(16)+(0.1)(6)}{0.314} = \frac{9.4}{0.314} = 30$$

$$X_2 = \frac{(0.55)(16)+(0.667)(6)}{0.314} = \frac{12.53}{0.314} = 40$$

We are required to find final output for changes in the final demand, which are 8 and 3 for X_1 and X_2 respectively. For this we have to insert these figures in to the final demand vector to get the new equilibrium output as shown below:

$$\begin{bmatrix} x_1 \\ x_2 \end{bmatrix} = \frac{1}{0.314}\begin{bmatrix} 0.55 & 0.1 \\ 0.533 & 0.667 \end{bmatrix}\begin{bmatrix} 8 \\ 3 \end{bmatrix}$$

$$X_1 = \frac{(0.55)(8)+(0.1)(3)}{0.314} = \frac{4.7}{0.314} = 14.97 = 15$$

$$X_2 = \frac{(0.533)(8)+(0.667)(3)}{0.314} = \frac{6.265}{0.314} = 19.95 = 20$$

$\therefore$ $x_1 = 15$ and $x_2 = 20$ are the required levels of output.

The labour coefficients for X_1 and X_2 are l_1 and l_2 where

$$l_1 = \frac{L_1}{x_1} = \frac{4}{30} = 0.133 \text{ and } l_2 = \frac{L_2}{x_2} = \frac{18}{40} = 0.45$$

Total labour requirements to produce the new levels of output are

$L = L_1 + L_2$. or $L = l_1 x_1 + l_2 x_2 = (0.133)(15) + (0.45)(20) = 10.995 = 11$

(ii) Evaluate the following determinants: (5)

$$(a) \begin{vmatrix} 4 & 11 & 10 \\ 7 & 2 & 6 \\ 1 & 5 & 4 \end{vmatrix} \qquad (b) \begin{vmatrix} 8 & 7 & 6 \\ 6 & 9 & 7 \\ 9 & 7 & 8 \end{vmatrix}$$

$$(a) \begin{vmatrix} 4 & 11 & 10 \\ 7 & 2 & 6 \\ 1 & 5 & 4 \end{vmatrix} = 4\begin{vmatrix} 2 & 6 \\ 5 & 4 \end{vmatrix} - 11\begin{vmatrix} 7 & 6 \\ 1 & 4 \end{vmatrix} + 10\begin{vmatrix} 7 & 2 \\ 1 & 5 \end{vmatrix}$$

$$= 4(8-30) - 11(28-6) + 10(35-2) = -88 - 242 + 330 = 0.$$

(b) $\begin{vmatrix} 8 & 7 & 6 \\ 6 & 9 & 7 \\ 9 & 7 & 8 \end{vmatrix} = 8\begin{vmatrix} 9 & 7 \\ 7 & 8 \end{vmatrix} - 7\begin{vmatrix} 6 & 7 \\ 9 & 8 \end{vmatrix} + 6\begin{vmatrix} 6 & 7 \\ 9 & 7 \end{vmatrix}$

$= 8\,(72 - 49) - 7\,(48 - 63) + 6\,(42 - 81) = 184 + 105 - 234 = 55.$

(2) October, 2003

(i) Solve the system of equations by cramer's rule (4)

$3x_1 + 4x_2 + 5x_3 = 18$

$2x_1 - x_2 + 8x_3 = 13$

$5x_1 - 2x_2 + 7x_3 = 20$

In Cramer's rule the solution for x_1 x_2 and x_3 are given by

$$x_1 = \frac{|Dx_1|}{|D|},\ x_2 = \frac{|Dx_2|}{|D|},\ x_3 = \frac{|Dx_3|}{|D|}$$

Where $|D| = \begin{vmatrix} 3 & 4 & 5 \\ 2 & -1 & 8 \\ 5 & -2 & 7 \end{vmatrix}$, $|Dx_1| = \begin{vmatrix} 18 & 4 & 5 \\ 13 & -1 & 8 \\ 20 & -2 & 7 \end{vmatrix}$, $|Dx_2| = \begin{vmatrix} 3 & 18 & 5 \\ 2 & 13 & 8 \\ 5 & 20 & 7 \end{vmatrix}$, $|Dx_3| = \begin{vmatrix} 3 & 4 & 18 \\ 2 & -1 & 13 \\ 5 & -2 & 20 \end{vmatrix}$

Solving these determinants we get

$$|D| = \begin{vmatrix} 3 & 4 & 5 \\ 2 & -1 & 8 \\ 5 & -2 & 7 \end{vmatrix} = 3\begin{vmatrix} -1 & 8 \\ -2 & 7 \end{vmatrix} - 4\begin{vmatrix} 2 & 8 \\ 5 & 7 \end{vmatrix} + 5\begin{vmatrix} 2 & -1 \\ 5 & -2 \end{vmatrix}$$

$= 3\,(-7 + 16) - 4\,(14 - 40) + 5\,(-4 + 5) = 27 + 104 + 5 = 136.$

$$|Dx_1| = \begin{vmatrix} 18 & 4 & 5 \\ 13 & -1 & 8 \\ 20 & -2 & 7 \end{vmatrix} = 18\begin{vmatrix} -1 & 8 \\ -2 & 7 \end{vmatrix} - 4\begin{vmatrix} 13 & 8 \\ 20 & 7 \end{vmatrix} + 5\begin{vmatrix} 13 & -1 \\ 20 & -2 \end{vmatrix}$$

$= 18\,(-7 + 16) - 4\,(91 - 160) + 5\,(-26 + 20) = 162 + 276 - 30 = 408.$

$$|Dx_2| = \begin{vmatrix} 3 & 18 & 5 \\ 2 & 13 & 8 \\ 5 & 20 & 7 \end{vmatrix} = 3\begin{vmatrix} 13 & 8 \\ 20 & 7 \end{vmatrix} - 18\begin{vmatrix} 2 & 8 \\ 5 & 7 \end{vmatrix} + 5\begin{vmatrix} 2 & 13 \\ 5 & 20 \end{vmatrix}$$

$= 3\,(-91 - 160) - 18\,(14 - 40) + 5\,(40 - 65) = 207 + 468 - 125 = 136.$

$$|Dx_3| = \begin{vmatrix} 3 & 4 & 18 \\ 2 & -1 & 13 \\ 5 & -2 & 20 \end{vmatrix} = 3\begin{vmatrix} -1 & 13 \\ -2 & 20 \end{vmatrix} - 4\begin{vmatrix} 2 & 13 \\ 5 & 20 \end{vmatrix} + 18\begin{vmatrix} 2 & -1 \\ 5 & -2 \end{vmatrix}$$

$= 3\,(-20 + 26) - 4\,(40 - 65) + 18\,(-4 + 5) = 18 + 100 + 18 = 136.$

$$x_1 = \frac{|Dx_1|}{|D|} = \frac{408}{136} = 3, \; x_2 = \frac{|Dx_2|}{|D|} = \frac{136}{136} = 1, \; x_3 = \frac{|Dx_3|}{|D|} = \frac{136}{136} = 1$$

$\therefore$ The required solution are $x_1 = 3$, $x_2 = 1$ and $x_3 = 1$

To verify our answer we can substitute these values in any of these simultaneous equations, $3x_1 + 4x_2 + 5x_3 = 9 + 4 + 5 = 18$ or $2x_1 - x_2 + 8x_3 = 6 - 1 + 8 = 13$ and so on.

(ii) You are given the following input-output data: (6)

Table 5.5

Producing Sectors	**Receiving Sector**		**Final demand**	**Total demand**
	1	2		
1	5	2	3	10
2	8	9	3	20
Labour	7	9	—	—

Find,

(a) Technology matrix and levels of output if final demand is doubled for both the sectors 1 and 2.

(b) Labour coefficients and total labour requirements to produce these new outputs.

We are given two sectors, which are X_1 and X_2. This reprsents output produced in these sectors.

$X_1 = x_{11} + x_{12} + d_1$ and $X_2 = x_{21} + x_{22} + d_2$.

We are given $X_1 = 10$, $X_2 = 20$ and $x_{11} = 5$, $x_{12} = 2$, $x_{21} = 8$, $x_{22} = 9$, $d_1 = 3$, $d_2 = 3$

The technology coefficient matrix is $A = \begin{bmatrix} a_{11} & a_{12} \\ a_{21} & a_{22} \end{bmatrix}$, need to be evaluated as

$$a_{11}\, x_1 = x_{11} \;\therefore\; a_{11} = \frac{x_{11}}{x_1} = \frac{5}{10} = 0.5$$

$$a_{12}\, x_2 = x_{12} \;\therefore\; a_{12} = \frac{x_{12}}{x_2} = \frac{2}{20} = 0.1$$

$$a_{21}\, x_1 = x_{21} \;\therefore\; a_{21} = \frac{x_{21}}{x_1} = \frac{8}{10} = 0.8$$

The technology coefficient matrix is $A = \begin{bmatrix} 0.5 & 0.1 \\ 0.8 & 0.45 \end{bmatrix}$

The solution for output is given by $X = AX + d$. From this we get

$X - AX = [d]$, $X[I - A] = [d]$ and $X = [I - A]^{-1}[d]$, where $X = \begin{bmatrix} x_1 \\ x_2 \end{bmatrix}$ and

$$\begin{bmatrix} x_1 \\ x_2 \end{bmatrix} = \frac{1}{|I-A|}\begin{bmatrix} A_{11} & A_{21} \\ A_{12} & A_{22} \end{bmatrix}\begin{bmatrix} d_1 \\ d_2 \end{bmatrix}$$

$$A = \begin{bmatrix} 0.5 & 0.1 \\ 0.8 & 0.45 \end{bmatrix} \quad I = \begin{bmatrix} 1 & 0 \\ 0 & 1 \end{bmatrix}$$

$$[I-A] = \begin{bmatrix} 1 & 0 \\ 0 & 1 \end{bmatrix}\begin{bmatrix} 0.5 & 0.1 \\ 0.8 & 0.45 \end{bmatrix} = \begin{bmatrix} 0.5 & -0.1 \\ -0.8 & 0.55 \end{bmatrix}$$

$|I-A| = (0.5)(0.55) - (-0.1)(-0.8) = 0.275 - 0.08$

$|I-A| = 0.195$, $A_{11} = +(0.55) = 0.55$, $A_{12} = -(-0.8) = 0.8$

$A_{21} = -(-0.1) = 0.1$, $A_{22} = +(0.5) = 0.5$

$$\begin{bmatrix} x_1 \\ x_2 \end{bmatrix} = \frac{1}{0.195}\begin{bmatrix} 0.55 & 0.1 \\ 0.8 & 0.5 \end{bmatrix}\begin{bmatrix} 3 \\ 3 \end{bmatrix}$$

$$X_1 = \frac{(0.55)(3)+(0.1)(3)}{0.195} = \frac{1.95}{0.195} = 10 \text{ and } X_2 = \frac{(0.8)(3)+(0.5)(3)}{0.195} = \frac{3.9}{0.195} = 20$$

Now we have to replace the final demands d_1 and d_2, which got doubled. Thus $d_1 = 3 \times 2 = 6$ and $d_2 = 3 \times 2 = 6$.

The solution for new output corresponding to these demand will be

$$\begin{bmatrix} x_1 \\ x_2 \end{bmatrix} = \frac{1}{0.195}\begin{bmatrix} 0.55 & 0.1 \\ 0.8 & 0.5 \end{bmatrix}\begin{bmatrix} 6 \\ 6 \end{bmatrix}$$

$$X_1 = \frac{(0.55)(6)+(0.1)(6)}{0.195} = \frac{3.9}{0.195} = 20 \text{ and } X_2 = \frac{(0.8)(6)+(0.5)(6)}{0.195} = \frac{7.8}{0.195} = 40$$

New levels of output are $X_1 = 20$ and $X_2 = 40$.

The labour coefficients are l_1 and l_2 where $l_1 = \frac{L_1}{x_1} = \frac{7}{10} = 0.7$ and $l_2 = \frac{L_2}{x_2} = \frac{9}{20} = 0.45$

The total labour requirement to produce new levels of output will be

$L = l_1 x_1 + l_2 x_2$, For $x_1 = 20$, $x_2 = 40$, $L = (0.7)(20) + (0.45)(40) = 14 + 18 = 32$

EXERCISE – 5

(1) *(A)* Write the following simultaneous equations in matrix form.

$3x_1 - 2x_2 + x_3 = 8$

$x_1 - 2x_2 + 3x_3 - 12 = 0$

$2x_1 + 2x_2 + 4x_3 + 15 = 0$

(B) If $A = \begin{bmatrix} 2 & 3 \\ 5 & 1 \end{bmatrix}$, $B = \begin{bmatrix} 1 & -2 \\ 4 & 8 \end{bmatrix}$.

Find 'D' matrix where $2A - B - D = 0$.

(C) If $A = \begin{bmatrix} 2 & -1 \\ 3 & 4 \end{bmatrix}$, $B = \begin{bmatrix} -4 & 2 \\ 1 & 7 \end{bmatrix}$, Find $A^2 - B^2$.

(D) Multiply the following matrices

(A) $[A] = [3 \quad 5 \quad -1 \quad 0]$, $[B] = \begin{bmatrix} 2 \\ 3 \\ 0 \\ -5 \end{bmatrix}$

(B) $\begin{bmatrix} 3 & 2 & 6 \\ 4 & 5 & 1 \\ 0 & 2 & -1 \end{bmatrix} \begin{bmatrix} 2 & 1 \\ 6 & 4 \\ 4 & -2 \end{bmatrix}$

(C) $\begin{bmatrix} 1 \\ 2 \\ 3 \end{bmatrix} [1 \quad 8 \quad -1 \quad 3]$

(2) (a) Find the cofactor matrix of A if $A = \begin{bmatrix} 3 & 2 & 1 \\ 5 & 2 & 0 \\ -1 & 1 & 4 \end{bmatrix}$

(b) Find inverse of the following: *(A)* $\begin{bmatrix} 2 & 1 \\ 3 & 5 \end{bmatrix}$ *(B)* $\begin{bmatrix} 1 & 1 & -2 \\ 2 & 3 & 4 \\ 0 & 7 & 6 \end{bmatrix}$ *(C)* $\begin{bmatrix} 7 & 0 \\ 2 & 1 \end{bmatrix}$

(3) Evaluate the following determinants

(A) $\begin{bmatrix} 6 & 1 & 4 \\ 9 & 2 & 7 \\ -1 & 2 & 1 \end{bmatrix}$ *(B)* $\begin{bmatrix} 1 & 3 & 7 \\ 3 & 9 & 2 \\ 5 & 15 & 6 \end{bmatrix}$ *(C)* $\begin{bmatrix} 8 & 2 & 4 \\ 7 & 1 & 3 \\ 3 & 4 & 1 \end{bmatrix}$

(4) Solve the following equations using matrix inversion method.

(A) $x + 3y + 5Z = 15$
$2x + y + 3Z = 13$
$x + 2y + Z = 10$

(B) $2A - B + 3C = 9$
$A + B + C = 6$
$A - B + C = 8$

(C) $9x + 2y = 13$
$7x + 3y = 15$

(D) $2x - 5y + 3Z = 20$
$x + 2y + Z = 10$
$6x + 5y + 2Z = 15$

(5) Solve the following simultaneous equations applying Cramer's rule.

(A) $2x + 3y = 12$
$x - 5y = 20$

(B) $x + y + Z = 8$
$3x - y - Z = 6$
$2x + 5y - 2Z = 4$

(C) $9A + B = 13$
$8A + 2B = 16$

(6) From the following input-output transaction table, find equilibrium levels of output when final demands are changed to 175 and 300 for two sectors. Also find the labour requirement to produce these new quantities of output.

Producing Sectors	**Receiving Sector**		**Final demand**
	1	2	
1	150	200	50
2	175	250	275
Labour	75	250	—

(7) Given the following transaction matrix for 3 sectors, final demand and labour coefficients as

$$A = \begin{bmatrix} 0.2 & 0.2 & 0.3 \\ 0.4 & 0.1 & 0.3 \\ 0.1 & 0.3 & 0.2 \end{bmatrix} \quad d = \begin{bmatrix} 80 \\ 30 \\ 55 \end{bmatrix}, l = \begin{bmatrix} 0.3 & 0.4 & 0.2 \end{bmatrix}, \text{Find}$$

(i) Equilibrium level of output for all these 3 sectors.

(ii) Labour requirements to produce equilibrium levels of output.

(8) If there are 4 sectors, state the balance of equations and derive the input-output model in the matrix form: $X = [I - A]^{-1} [d]$.

❑❑❑

6 Techniques of Partial Derivatives : Functions of Two or More Variables

6.1. Differentiation : More Than One Variable Case

Differentiation of a function in case of one variable is given by $Y = f(X)$, where the dependent variable Y is influenced by one independent variable X. Very often it is found that there are two or more variables influence the dependent variable. This refers to the functions of two or more variables. This is a common situation in the realistic world. In economics we come accross many such functions involving two or more independent variables that influence the dependent variable. Numerous examples can be taken from micro and macroeconomics for illustrations.

In economic theory demand for a commodity say X is defined D_x. Demand for this is functionally related with its own price (P_x), income of the consumer (Y) and price of its related commodity Z (P_z). This can be expreesed mathematically in a functional form : $D_x = f(P_x, P_z, Y)$. This relationship exhibits that there are three independent variables Y, P_x and P_z, that affect the quantity demanded for X, the dependent variable. To illustrate another example, let us have the productioin function for a good say wheat (Q_w). It can be shown to be influenced by the rainall (r), amount of fertilizer (Z), land (L), labour units (l) and technology (T). Their functional relationship can be traced mathematically as $Q_w = f(r, z, k, l, T)$. This signifies that there are five independent variables that are influencing the dependent variable, output of wheat.

To cite another example we have a consumer who wants to purchase two goods X and Y. Total utility is shown to be functionally related with the quantity purchases of these goods. The utility fucntion is defined as $U = f(x, y)$.

All the above illustrations have one common feature that the dependent variable will undergo a change when any of these independent variable changes. From a simple production function $Q = f(k, l)$ where Q is output, k stands for capital and l is labour, the dependent variable Q is said to be functionally related with these two inputs. An incerase or decrease in the independent variables k or l or both, will bring a corresponding change in output. The changes in Q corresponding to a small change in any one of the independnet variable say l, while keeping k constant forms the topic of partial derivatives. This is derived in the following process:

Given $Q = f(l, k)$,

$$Q + \Delta Q = f(l + \Delta l, k),\ \Delta Q = f(l + \Delta l, k) - f(k, l)$$

$$\frac{\Delta Q}{\Delta l} = \frac{f(l + \Delta l, k) - f(k, l)}{\Delta l}$$

Applying limit to the function $\frac{\Delta Q}{\Delta l}$ when Δl approaches zero, we obtain partial derivative of Q with respect to labour (l), when capital (k) is held constant. So we get

$$\lim_{\Delta l \to 0} \frac{\Delta Q}{\Delta l} = \lim_{\Delta l \to 0} \frac{f(l + \Delta l, k) - f(k, l)}{\Delta l} = \frac{\partial Q}{\partial l}$$

This expression is the partial derivative of output Q, *w.r.t.* labour (l).

In s similar process $\frac{\partial Q}{\partial k}$ can be derived. This is the partial derivative of Q, *w.r.t.* capital (k) while keeping labour as parameter.

$$Q + \Delta Q = f(k + \Delta k, l), \Delta Q = f(k + \Delta k, l) - f(k, l)$$

$$\lim_{\Delta k \to 0} \frac{\Delta Q}{\Delta k} = \lim_{\Delta k \to 0} \frac{f(k + \Delta k, l) - f(k, l)}{\Delta k} = \frac{\partial Q}{\partial k}$$

Partial derivatives for demand functions can also be obtained. For example if the demand function for *good X* is given $D_x = f(p_x, y, p_z)$, the partial derivatives of D_x *w.r.t.* its own price (p_x) can be derived as

$$\frac{\partial D_x}{\partial P_x} = \lim_{\Delta P_x \to 0} \frac{f(P_x + \Delta P_x, y, P_z) - f(P_x, y, P_z)}{\Delta P_x}$$

Likewise the Partial derivative of D_x *w.r.t.* income (Y) is

$$\frac{\partial D_x}{\partial y} = \lim_{\Delta y \to 0} \frac{f(y + \Delta y, p_x, p_z) - f(p_x, y, p_z)}{\Delta y}$$

Partial derivative of D, *w.r.t.* price of z (p_z) is obatined by

$$\frac{\partial D_x}{\partial z} = \lim_{\Delta z \to 0} \frac{f(p_z + \Delta p_z, p_x, y) - f(p_x, y, p_z)}{\Delta p_z}$$

Now suppose the utility function is $U = f(x_1, x_2, x_3)$ where x_1, x_2, and x_3 are quantities of three commodities, their partial derivatives will be

$$\frac{\partial U}{\partial x_1} = f_{x1}, \frac{\partial U}{\partial x_2} = f_{x2}, \frac{\partial U}{\partial x_3} = f_{x3}.$$

Partial derivative is denoted by a different symbol (∂) and not 'd'.

Thus the partial derivative of U with respect to X_1 while keeping X_2 and X_3 constant is written as

$$\left(\frac{\partial U}{\partial x_1}\right), \quad \lim_{\Delta x_1 \to 0} \frac{\Delta U}{\Delta x_1} = \frac{\partial U}{\partial x_1} = fx_1$$

In a similar process we get $\lim_{\Delta x_2 \to 0} \frac{\Delta U}{\Delta x_2} = \frac{\partial U}{\partial x_2} = fx_2$ and so on.

6.2. First and Second Order derivatives and Cross Partial Derivatives

Partial derivative of first order is obtained when we take differentiation of U with respect to X_1 in the utility function $U = f(x_1, x_2)$. This is $\frac{\partial U}{\partial x_1}$. Similarly by differentiating U *w.r.t.* X_2 we can obtain $\frac{\partial U}{\partial x_2}$. These partial derivetives are also written as f_{x_1} and f_{x_2} or simply f_1 and f_2. When *'U'* is differentiated partially with respect to x_1 for the second time,we arrive at the second order partial derivative.This is

$$\frac{\partial}{\partial x_1}\left(\frac{\partial U}{\partial x_1}\right) = \frac{\partial^2 U}{\partial x_1^2} = f_{x1x1}$$

In the same process the second order partial derivative of *'U'* *w.r.t.* X_2 can be obtained as

$$\frac{\partial}{\partial x_2}\left(\frac{\partial U}{\partial x_2}\right) = \frac{\partial^2 U}{\partial x_2^2} = fx_2x_2 .$$

These second order pertial derivatives are written as f_{11}, f_{22} or fx_1x_1 and fx_2x_2 and so on. Suppose the given function is $Z = f(x, y)$, the first order and the second order partial derivatives are

$$\frac{\partial Z}{\partial x} = f_x \text{ and } \frac{\partial^2 Z}{\partial x^2} = f_{xx} \text{ and}$$

$$\frac{\partial Z}{\partial y} = f_y \text{ and } \frac{\partial^2 Z}{\partial y^2} = f_{yy}$$

Cross partial derivatives are $f_{xy} = f_{yx}$ or $\frac{\partial^2 Z}{\partial x \partial y} = \frac{\partial^2 Z}{\partial y \partial x}$

The cross partial derivatives for $Z = f(x, y)$ are computed when $Z = f(x, y)$ is first differentiated with respect to X and then differentiated with respect to Y. From this we get $\frac{\partial^2 Z}{\partial x\, \partial y} = \frac{\partial}{\partial y}\left(\frac{\partial Z}{\partial x}\right) = fxy$.

Likewise when $Z = f(x, y)$ is first differentiated *w.r.t.* Y and then *w.r.t.* X, we get

$$\frac{\partial^2 Z}{\partial x\, \partial y} = \frac{\partial}{\partial x}\left(\frac{\partial Z}{\partial y}\right) = fyx$$

However the cross partial derivatives are equal in their value. Therefore it does not matter in whichever way we differentiate. $\therefore \dfrac{\partial^2 Z}{\partial y\,\partial x} = \dfrac{\partial^2 Z}{\partial x\,\partial y}$ or $f_{xy} = f_{yx}$

6.3. Techniques of Partial Differentiation

(1) If the utility function is $U = f(x, y) = 3x^2y + xy^2$, find partial derivatives of *'U'* *w.r.t.* X and Y.

You are given $U = 3x^2y + xy^2$, Partial derivative of U, *w.r.t.* *'x'* is

$$\frac{\partial U}{\partial x} = \frac{\partial}{\partial x}(3x^2y + xy^2) = 3y\frac{\partial}{\partial x}(x^2) + y^2\frac{\partial}{\partial x}(x) = 6xy + y^2 = f_x$$

The Partial derivative of U, *w.r.t.* *'y'* is obtained as

$$\frac{\partial U}{\partial y} = \frac{\partial}{\partial y}(3x^2y + xy^2) = 3x^2\frac{\partial}{\partial y}(y) + x\frac{\partial}{\partial y}(y^2) = 3x^2 + 2 = f_y$$

(2) Find partial derivatives for $Z = 4x^2 + 3xy + y^2$

The process of differentiation is the same as shown in the previous example.

$$fx = \frac{\partial Z}{\partial x} = 8x + 3y,\ fy = \frac{\partial Z}{\partial y} = 3x + 2y$$

(3) The production function is given as $Q = 8L^{0.3}K^{0.7}$, find partial derivatives of Q *w.r.t.* L and K, where L = labour and K = capital.

For $Q = 8L^{0.3}K^{0.7}$

$$\frac{\partial Q}{\partial L} = f_L = \frac{\partial}{\partial L}\left[8L^{0.3}K^{0.7}\right] = 8(0.3)\,L^{0.3-1}K^{0.7} = 2.4L^{-0.7}K^{0.7} = 2.4\left(\frac{K}{L}\right)^{0.7}$$

$$\frac{\partial Q}{\partial K} = f_K = \frac{\partial}{\partial K}\left[8L^{0.3}K^{0.7}\right] = 8(0.7)\,L^{0.3}K^{0.7-1} = 5.6\left(\frac{L}{K}\right)^{0.3}$$

$\dfrac{\partial Q}{\partial L}$ and $\dfrac{\partial Q}{\partial K}$ are also called marginal productivity of labour and capital respectively.

(4) Find f_x and f_y for $Z = 6x^2 + 3xy + y^3$

$$fx = \frac{\partial Z}{\partial x} = \frac{\partial}{\partial x}(6x^2 + 3xy + y^3) = 12x + 3y$$

$$fy = \frac{\partial Z}{\partial y} = \frac{\partial}{\partial y}(6x^2 + 3xy + y^3) = 3(x + y^2)$$

6.4. Rules for Evaluating Partial Derivatives

All the rules of differentiation of a function with one independent variable are also be applied to partial derivatives and cross partial derivatives. However at one time one must consider the changes in one variable only, with respect to which partial derivative is evaluated, thereby keeping the other variables constant. The following rules of differentiation are used for partial derivative:

(i) Product and quotient rule

(ii) Logarithmic and exponential rule

(iii) Substitution rule.

Following illustrations depict the process of computation of partial derivatives by applying these rules.

(1) Given $Z = (3x + 2y)(x + y^2)$, Find f_x and f_y

$$f_x = \frac{\partial Z}{\partial x} = (3x+2y)\frac{\partial}{\partial x}(x+y^2)+(x+y^2)\frac{\partial}{\partial x}(3x+2y)$$

$$= (3x+2y)(1)+(x+y^2)(3) = 6x+2y+3y^2$$

$$f_y = \frac{\partial Z}{\partial y} = (3x+2y)\frac{\partial}{\partial y}(x+y^2)+(x+y^2)\frac{\partial}{\partial y}(3x+2y)$$

$$= (3x + 2y)(2y) + (x + y^2)(2) = 6xy + 6y^2 + 2x$$

(2) If $U = f(x_1\ x_2) = (x_1^2 - 2x_2)^3(x_2+3)^2$, find $\frac{\partial U}{\partial x_1}$ and $\frac{\partial U}{\partial x_2}$ *at* $x_1 = 2$, $x_2 = 3$.

Given $U = (x_1^2 - 2x_2)^3(x_2+3)^2$

$$\frac{\partial U}{\partial x_1} = (x_1^2-2x_2)^3\frac{\partial}{\partial x_1}(x_2+3)^2 + (x_2+3)^2\frac{\partial}{\partial x_1}(x_1^2-2x_2)^3$$

$$= (x_1^2-2x_2)^3\ 2\,(x_2+3)(0) + (x_2+3)^2\ 3\,(x_1^2-2x_2)^2\,(2x_1)$$

$$= 6x_1\,(x_2+3)^2\,(x_1^2-2x_2)^2 = 6\times 2\,(3+3)^2(2^2-2\times 3)^2 = 1728$$

$$\frac{\partial U}{\partial x_2} = (x_1^2-2x_2)^3\frac{\partial}{\partial x_2}(x_2+3)^2 + (x_2+3)^2\frac{\partial}{\partial x_2}(x_1^2-2x_2)^3$$

$$= (x_1^2-2x_2)^3\ 2\,(x_2+3)(1) + (x_2+3)^2\ 3\,(x_1^2-2x_2)^2\,(-2)$$

$$= 2\,(x_1^2-2x_2)^3\,(x_2+3) - 6\,(x_2+3)^2(x_1^2-2x_2)^2$$

$$= 2\,(4-2\times 3)^3\,(3+3) - 6\,(3+3)^2\,(4-2\times 3)^2 = -96-864 = -960$$

(3) For $Z = \frac{(3x^2+2y)}{(x+y^2)}$ find f_x and f_y at $x = 1$ and $y = 2$

$$\frac{\partial Z}{\partial x} = f_x = \frac{\partial}{\partial x}\left[\frac{(3x^2+2y)}{(x+y^2)}\right]$$

$$= \frac{(x+y^2)\frac{\partial}{\partial x}(3x^2+2y)-(3x^2+2y)\frac{\partial}{\partial x}(x+y^2)}{(x+y^2)^2} = \frac{(x+y^2)(6x)-(3x^2+2y)(1)}{(x+y^2)^2}$$

$$= \frac{6x^2+6xy^2-3x^2-2y}{(x+y^2)^2} = \frac{3x^2+6xy^2-2y}{(x+y^2)^2}$$

$$= \frac{3(1)^2 + 6(1)(2)^2 - 2(2)}{[1+(2)^2]^2} = \frac{23}{25} = 0.92, \; f_x(1, 2) = 0.92$$

$$\frac{\partial Z}{\partial y} = \frac{\partial}{\partial x}\left[\frac{(3x^2+2y)}{(x+y^2)}\right]$$

$$= \frac{(x+y^2)\frac{\partial}{\partial y}(3x^2+2y) - (3x^2+2y)\frac{\partial}{\partial y}(x+y^2)}{[x+y^2]^2} = \frac{(x+y^2)(2) - (3x^2+2y)(2y)}{(x+y^2)^2}$$

$$= \frac{2x+2y^2-6x^2y-4y^2}{(x+y^2)^2} = \frac{2x-2y^2-6x^2y}{(x+y^2)^2}$$

$$= \frac{2(1)-2(2)^2-6(1)^2(2)}{25} = \frac{-18}{25}, \quad f_y(1, 2) = \frac{-18}{25} = -0.72$$

(4) Find $\frac{\partial Z}{\partial x}$ and $\frac{\partial Z}{\partial y}$ for $Z = log\,(3x + y)$

$$\frac{\partial Z}{\partial x} = fx = \frac{\partial}{\partial x}[log\,(3x+y)] = \frac{3}{3x+y}$$

$$\frac{\partial Z}{\partial y} = f_y = \frac{\partial}{\partial y}[log\,(3x+y)] = \frac{1}{3x+y}$$

(5) If $Z = e^{x^2y+xy^2}$, find f_x and f_y

$$f_x = \frac{\partial Z}{\partial x} = \frac{\partial}{\partial x}\left(e^{x^2y+xy^2}\right) = e^{x^2y+xy^2}\,\frac{\partial}{\partial x}\left(x^2y+xy^2\right) = (2xy+y^2)\,e^{x^2y+xy^2}$$

$$f_y = \frac{\partial Z}{\partial y} = \frac{\partial}{\partial y}\left(e^{x^2y+xy^2}\right) = e^{x^2y+xy^2}\,\frac{\partial}{\partial y}(x^2y+xy^2) = (x^2+2xy)\,e^{x^2y+xy^2}$$

(6) For $Z = x^2 \log_e y + ye^{x^2}$, find $\frac{\partial Z}{\partial x}$ and $\frac{\partial Z}{\partial y}$

$$\frac{\partial Z}{\partial x} = x^2\,\frac{\partial}{\partial x}(\log_e y) + \log_e y\,\frac{\partial}{\partial x}(x^2) + y\,\frac{\partial}{\partial x}\left(e^{x^2}\right) + e^{x^2}\,\frac{\partial}{\partial x}(y)$$

$$= x^2(0) + \log_e y\,(2x) + y\,(2x)\,e^{x^2} + e^{x^2}(0) = 2x\log_e y + 2xy\,e^{x^2}$$

$$\frac{\partial Z}{\partial y} = x^2\,\frac{\partial}{\partial y}(\log_e y) + \log_e y\,\frac{\partial}{\partial y}(x^2) + y\,\frac{\partial}{\partial y}\left(e^{x^2}\right) + e^{x^2}\,\frac{\partial}{\partial y}(y)$$

$$= \frac{x^2}{y} + \log_e y\,(0) + y\,(0) + e^{x^2}, \quad f_y = \frac{x^2}{y} + e^{x^2}$$

6.5. Higher Order Partial Derivatives and Cross Partial Derivatives

For $Z = f(x, y)$, we have evaluated the first order partial derivatives as f_x and f_y. Higher order partial derivatives can be computed when we differentiate f_x, *w.r.t.* 'x' by keeping 'y' as constant. The result so obtained is $f_{xx} = \frac{\partial^2 Z}{\partial x^2} = \frac{\partial}{\partial x}\left(\frac{\partial Z}{\partial x}\right)$. Similarly when we differentiate f_y *w.r.t.* 'y', we get $= \frac{\partial^2 Z}{\partial y^2} = \frac{\partial}{\partial y}\left(\frac{\partial Z}{\partial y}\right) = f_{yy}$.

The cross partial derivatives are written as f_{xy} and f_{yx} where

$$f_{xy} = \frac{\partial^2 Z}{\partial x\, \partial y} = \frac{\partial}{\partial x}\left(\frac{\partial Z}{\partial y}\right), \text{ and } f_{yx} = \frac{\partial^2 Z}{\partial y\, \partial x} = \frac{\partial}{\partial y}\left(\frac{\partial Z}{\partial x}\right) \text{ and } f_{xy} = f_{yx}$$

The process of computing these partial derivatives are shown below:

(1) Given $z = 2x^2 + 5x^2y + xy^2 + y^2$

Find (a) f_x, f_y *(b)* f_{xx}, f_{yy} (c) Show that $f_{xy} = f_{yx}$

For $Z = 2x^2 + 5x^2y + xy^2 + y^2$

$$f_x = \frac{\partial Z}{\partial x} = 4x + 10xy + y^2, \; f_{xx} = \frac{\partial^2 Z}{\partial x^2} = 4 + 10y$$

$$f_y = \frac{\partial Z}{\partial y} = 5x^2 + 2xy + 2y, \; f_{yy} = \frac{\partial^2 Z}{\partial y^2} = 2x + 2$$

$$f_{xy} = \frac{\partial}{\partial x}\left(\frac{\partial Z}{\partial y}\right) = \frac{\partial}{\partial x}(f_y) = \frac{\partial}{\partial x}(5x^2 + 2xy + 2y) = 10x + 2y$$

$$f_{yx} = \frac{\partial}{\partial y}\left(\frac{\partial Z}{\partial x}\right) = \frac{\partial}{\partial y}(f_x) = \frac{\partial}{\partial y}(4x + 10xy + y^2) = 10x + 2y$$

$f_{xy} = f_{yx} = 10x + 2y$ proved

(2) For the given function $Z = \log_e(3x + y)$, find *(a)* the partial derivatives of the second order, . f_{xx} and f_{yy} *(b)* Show that $f_{xy} = f_{yx}$.

$$(a)\; f_x = \frac{\partial Z}{\partial x} = \frac{\partial}{\partial x}[\log_e(3x + y)] = \frac{3}{3x + y}$$

$$f_{xx} = \frac{\partial}{\partial x}\left[\frac{3}{3x + y}\right] = \frac{(3x + y)\frac{\partial}{\partial x}(3) - 3\frac{\partial}{\partial x}(3x + y)}{(3x + y)^2} = \frac{-9}{(3x + y)^2}$$

$$f_y = \frac{\partial Z}{\partial y} = \frac{\partial}{\partial y}[\log_e(3x + y)] = \frac{1}{3x + y}$$

$$f_{yy} = \frac{\partial}{\partial y}\left[\frac{1}{3x+y}\right] = \frac{(3x+y)\frac{\partial}{\partial y}(1) - 1\frac{\partial}{\partial y}(3x+y)}{(3x+y)^2} = \frac{-1}{(3x+y)^2}$$

(b) It can proved that $f_{xy} = f_{yx}$

$$f_{xy} = \frac{\partial}{\partial x}\left(\frac{\partial Z}{\partial y}\right) = \frac{\partial}{\partial x}\left[\frac{1}{3x+y}\right] = \frac{(3x+y)\frac{\partial}{\partial x}(1) - (1)\frac{\partial}{\partial x}(3x+y)}{(3x+y)^2} = \frac{3}{(3x+y)^2}$$

$$f_{yx} = \frac{\partial}{\partial y}\left(\frac{\partial Z}{\partial x}\right) = \frac{\partial}{\partial y}\left[\frac{3}{3x+y}\right] = \frac{(3x+y)\frac{\partial}{\partial y}(3) - 3\frac{\partial}{\partial y}(3x+y)}{(3x+y)^2} = -\frac{3}{(3x+y)^2}$$

$$\therefore\ f_{xy} = f_{yx} = -\frac{3}{(3x+y)^2} \text{ proved}$$

(3) If $Z = x^2 - xy^3$ Find f_x, f_{xx}, f_y, f_{yy}, and verify that $f_{xy} = f_{yx}$

For $Z = x^2 - xy^3$, $\frac{\partial Z}{\partial x} = fx = 2x - y^3$ and $fxx = \frac{\partial}{\partial x}(fx) = 2$

$$\frac{\partial Z}{\partial y} = f_y = \frac{\partial}{\partial y}(x^2 - xy^3) = -3xy^2 \text{ and } fyy = \frac{\partial}{\partial y}(fy) = -6xy$$

$$fxy = \frac{\partial}{\partial x}(fy) = \frac{\partial}{\partial x}(-3xy^2) = -3y^2$$

$$fyx = \frac{\partial}{\partial y}(fx) = \frac{\partial}{\partial y}(2x - y^3) = -3y^2,$$

$$fxy = fyx = -3y^2$$

(4) Given $Z = x\,log_e\,y + y\,e^{x^2}$ find f_x, f_y, f_{xx}, f_{yy} and show that $f_{xy} = f_{yx}$.

For given $Z = x\,log_e\,y + y\,e^{x^2}$

$$\frac{\partial Z}{\partial x} = f_x = x\frac{\partial}{\partial x}(log_e\,y) + log_e\,y\frac{\partial}{\partial x}(x) + y\frac{\partial}{\partial x}\left(e^{x^2}\right) + e^{x^2}\frac{\partial}{\partial x}(y)$$

$$= x\,(0) + log_e\,y + y\,(2x)\,e^{x^2} + e^{x^2}\,(0) = log_e\,y + 2xy\,e^{x^2}$$

$$fxx = \frac{\partial}{\partial x}(fx) = 2xy\frac{\partial}{\partial x}e^{x^2} + 2y\,e^{x^2}\frac{\partial}{\partial x}(x)$$

$$= 2xy\,(2x)\,e^{x^2} + 2y\,e^{x^2} = 4x^2y\,e^{x^2} + 2y\,e^{x^2} = 2y\,e^{x^2}\,(2x^2+1)$$

$$fy = \frac{\partial Z}{\partial y} = x\frac{\partial}{\partial y}(\log_e y) + \log_e y\frac{\partial}{\partial y}(x) + y\frac{\partial}{\partial y}\left(e^{x^2}\right) + e^{x^2}\frac{\partial}{\partial y}(y)$$

$$= \frac{x}{y} + \log_e y\,(0) + y\,(0) + e^{x^2} = \frac{x}{y} + e^{x^2}$$

$$fyy = \frac{\partial}{\partial y}(fy) = \frac{y\frac{\partial x}{\partial y} - x\frac{\partial y}{\partial y}}{y^2} + \frac{\partial}{\partial y}\left(e^{x^2}\right) = \frac{y(0)-x}{y^2} + 0 = \frac{-x}{y^2}$$

$$fxy = \frac{\partial}{\partial x}(fy) = \frac{\partial}{\partial x}\left(\frac{x}{y} + e^{x^2}\right) = \frac{yx' - xy'}{y^2} + 2x\,e^{x^2} = \frac{y}{y^2} + 2x\,e^{x^2} = \frac{1}{y} + 2x\,e^{x^2}$$

$$fyx = \frac{\partial}{\partial y}(fx) = \frac{\partial}{\partial y}\left(\log_e y + 2xy\,e^{x^2}\right) = \frac{1}{y} + 2x\,e^{x^2}$$

So it is proved that $fxy = fyx = \frac{1}{y} + 2x\,e^{x^2}$

6.6. Partial Derivative of functions with more than two Independent Variables

While evaluating partial derivatives it has been taken a simple case of the functions involving only two independent variables. For example we have $Z = f(x, y)$ or $U = f(x, y)$. However there are functions that incorporate more than two independent variables also. For example we can have utility function as $U = f(x, y, z)$, where U stands for total utility and x, y and z are three different commodities consumed. For this utility function partial derivatives of first order, second order and cross partial derivatives can be obtained.

For given the utility function $U = f(x, y, z)$ partial derivatives are

(i) $\frac{\partial U}{\partial x} = fx$, where $\frac{\partial U}{\partial x} = fx$ is the partial derivative of *'U' w.r.t. 'x'*, when *'y'* and *'z'* are held constants.

(ii) $\frac{\partial U}{\partial y} = fy$ represents partial derivative of *'U' w.r.t. 'y'* when x and z are taken constants and

(iii) $\frac{\partial U}{\partial z} = fz$ is partial derivative of *'U' w.r.t. 'z'*, for *'x'* and *'y'* are considered unchnaged parameters.

For this fucntion, the first order partial derivatives are f_x, f_y, f_z and the second order partial derivatives are f_{xx}, f_{yy}, and f_{zz}. These are obtained as

$$fxx = \frac{\partial^2 U}{\partial x^2},\quad fyy = \frac{\partial^2 U}{\partial y^2},\quad fzz = \frac{\partial^2 U}{\partial z^2},$$

The cross partial derivatives are $fxy = \frac{\partial}{\partial x}\left(\frac{\partial U}{\partial y}\right) = \frac{\partial^2 U}{\partial x\, \partial y}$, $fyx = \frac{\partial}{\partial y}\left(\frac{\partial U}{\partial x}\right) = \frac{\partial^2 U}{\partial y\, \partial x}$

It ia always found that $f_{xy} = f_{yx}$

Similarly $fxz = \frac{\partial}{\partial x}\left(\frac{\partial U}{\partial z}\right) = \frac{\partial^2 U}{\partial x\, \partial z}$ and $f_{zx} = \frac{\partial}{\partial z}\left(\frac{\partial U}{\partial x}\right) = \frac{\partial^2 U}{\partial z\, \partial x}$ and $f_{xz} = f_{zx}$

From $fyz = \frac{\partial}{\partial y}\left(\frac{\partial U}{\partial z}\right) = \frac{\partial^2 U}{\partial y\, \partial z}$, $f_{zy} = \frac{\partial}{\partial z}\left(\frac{\partial U}{\partial y}\right) = \frac{\partial^2 U}{\partial z\, \partial y}$, we can see that $f_{yz} = f_{zy}$.

Following illustrations exhibit the process of evaluating partial derivatives involving three independent variables.

(1) If the utility function is $U = 3x^2y + 4xz + 3z^2y$

(a) Find partial derivatives of *'U' w.r.t. X, Y* and *Z.*

$$fx = \frac{\partial U}{\partial x} = \frac{\partial}{\partial x}(3x^2y + 4xz + 3z^2y) = 6xy + 4z$$

$$f_y = \frac{\partial U}{\partial y} = \frac{\partial}{\partial y}(3x^2y + 4xz + 3z^2y) = 3x^2 + 3z^2$$

$$f_z = \frac{\partial U}{\partial z} = \frac{\partial}{\partial z}(3x^2y + 4xz + 3z^2y) = 4x + 6zy$$

(b) Find the second order derivative of *'U' w.r.t. X, Y* and *Z.*
These derivatives are f_{xx}, f_{yy}, f_{zz}

$$fxx = \frac{\partial}{\partial x}(fx) = \frac{\partial}{\partial x}(6xy + 4z) = 6y$$

$$fyy = \frac{\partial}{\partial y}\left(\frac{\partial U}{\partial y}\right) = \frac{\partial}{\partial y}(fy) = \frac{\partial}{\partial y}(3x^2 + 3z^2) = 0$$

$$fzz = \frac{\partial}{\partial z}(fz) = \frac{\partial}{\partial z}\left(\frac{\partial U}{\partial z}\right) = \frac{\partial}{\partial z}(4x + 6zy) = 6y$$

(c) Find the cross partial derivatives and show that

$fxy = fyx,\ fxz = fzx,\ fyz = fzy$

$$fxy = \frac{\partial}{\partial x}(fy) = \frac{\partial}{\partial x}(3x^2 + 3z^2) = 6x$$

$$fyx = \frac{\partial}{\partial y}(fx) = \frac{\partial}{\partial y}(6xy + 4z) = 6x \quad \therefore\ fxy = fyx = 6x$$

Similarly $fxz = \frac{\partial}{\partial x}\left(\frac{\partial U}{\partial z}\right) = \frac{\partial}{\partial x}(4x + 6zy) = 4$

$$f_{zx} = \frac{\partial}{\partial z}(f_x) = \frac{\partial}{\partial z}(6xy + 4z) = 4 \;\therefore\; f_{xz} = f_{zx} = 4$$

Similarly $f_{yz} = \frac{\partial}{\partial y}(f_z) = \frac{\partial}{\partial y}(4x + 6zy) = 6z$

$$f_{zy} = \frac{\partial}{\partial z}\left(\frac{\partial U}{\partial y}\right)\frac{\partial}{\partial z}(f_y) = \frac{\partial}{\partial z}(3x^2 + 3z^2) = 6z \;\therefore\; f_{zy} = f_{yz} = 6z$$

This shows that the cross partial derivatives are identical.

6.7. Technique of Evaluating Total Differentials

When we apply the technique of partial derivative to $U = f(x, y)$, U is differentiated *w.r.t.* 'x' we get $\frac{\partial U}{\partial x}$, while keeping '$y$' as constant. Similarly by partivally differenting U, *w.r.t.* 'y', to obtain $\frac{\partial U}{\partial y}$, keeping '$x$' as constant. But when it is assumed that both 'x' and 'y' are changing in the given function $U = f(x, y)$, the corresponding total changes in 'U' is shown by finding total differential.

Take for example in demand analysis we study that an indifference curve represents various alternative combinations of two goods say 'q_1' and 'q_2'. When a consumer moves along this indifference curve the amount of satisfaction derived remains unchanged. The movement from say a combination 'A' to another combination 'B' sliding along the curve will result into an increase in the amount of q_1 and decrease in the amount of q_2. This brings no changes in total utility. In mathematical economics we define utility function of the consumer as $U = f(q_1, q_2)$. Moving along the utility curve yields same amount of utility, which means $\partial U = 0$ or $\Delta U = 0$.

If we put MU to mean marginal utility of these goods we can write this as

$\Delta U = (MU_{q1})(\Delta q_1) + (MU_{q2})(\Delta q_2)$ while $MU_{q1} = \frac{\partial U}{\partial q_1}$ and $MU_{q2} = \frac{\partial U}{\partial q_2}$.

Changes in utility from a movemnet along the indifference curve is taken to be zero so that

$\partial U = \frac{\partial U}{\partial q_1}\partial q_1 + \frac{\partial U}{\partial q_2}\partial d_2 = 0.$, where dU gives us total differential of U, *w.r.t.* both q_1 and q_2.

By substituting $\frac{\partial U}{\partial q_1} = f_1$ and $\frac{\partial U}{\partial q_2} = f_2$, we can rewrite it

$\partial U = f_1\,\partial q_1 + f_2\,\partial q_2 = 0$ or $f_1\,\partial q_1 = -f_2\,\partial q_2$ or $\frac{\partial q_2}{\partial q_1} = -\frac{f_1}{f_2}$ or $-\frac{\partial q_2}{\partial q_1} = \frac{f_1}{f_2}$, where

f_1 and f_2 are MU of q_1 and MU of q_2 and $-\frac{\partial q_2}{\partial d_1} = RCS$ [Marginal Rate of Commodity Substitution].

We can also use some other examples from theory of production for finding total differential.

Let us take a farmer producing wheat usng inputs land (k) and labour (l). This is represented by a simple production function, defined $Q = f(k, l)$, (Q = Output). By evlauating partial derivative of Q, *w.r.t.* 'k' and 'l' we obtain marginal products of capital and labor. This is shown as $\frac{\partial Q}{\partial k}$ and $\frac{\partial Q}{\partial l}$ respectively.

$\frac{\partial Q}{\partial k}$ shows that Q is partially diffentiated *w.r.t.* land (k) when labour (l) is kept unchanged., while by evaluating $\frac{\partial Q}{\partial l}$, we partially differentiate Q, *w.r.t.* labour (l) by keeping land (k) constant. But when small changes are made by both the inputs land (k) and labour (l), the resultant change in output will be shown by finding total differential of Q. This is

$$\Delta Q = \frac{\Delta Q}{\Delta k}.\Delta k + \frac{\Delta Q}{\Delta l}\Delta l \text{ or } \partial Q = \frac{\partial Q}{\partial k}.\partial k + \frac{\partial Q}{\partial l}\partial l \text{ or } \partial Q = f_1\,\partial k + f_2\,\partial l \text{, where}$$

$$f_1 = \frac{\partial Q}{\partial k} \text{ and } f_2 = \frac{\partial Q}{\partial l}$$

If there are 'r' number of independent variables with mathematical expression given by

$Z = f(x_1, x_2, \cdots\cdots, x_r)$, where $x_1, x_2, ...x_r$ are independent variables and Z is the dependent variable,

Total diffential of Z is $\partial Z = f_1\,\partial x_1 + f_2\,\partial x_2 + \cdots\cdots + f_r\,\partial x_r$ where,

$$f_1 = \frac{\partial Z}{\partial x_1},\ f_2 = \frac{\partial Z}{\partial x_2},\ \ldots\ f_r = \frac{\partial Z}{\partial x_r}.$$

∂Z brings out the changes in the variable Z resulting from a small change in the use of all the independent variables $x_1, x_2, ..., x_r$.

To simplify the evaluation of total differential further we can have another simple function represented as $Z = f(a, b)$. Its total diffential is $\partial Z = f_a\,\partial a + f_b\,\partial b$. Given the utility function $U = f(x, y, z)$, total differntial of Z is evaluated as

$$\partial Z = f_1\,\partial x + f_2\,\partial y + f_3\,\partial z \text{, where } f_1 = \frac{\partial U}{\partial x},\ f_2 = \frac{\partial U}{\partial y},\ f_3 = \frac{\partial U}{\partial z}$$

6.8. Rules for evaluating total differential

(1) Total differential of the sum or difference of terms.

(i) Find total differential of $U = 3x^2y + xy^2 - xy$

Given $U = 3x^2y + xy^2 - xy$,

$$\partial U = 3y\frac{\partial}{\partial x}(x^2)\partial x + 3x^2\frac{\partial}{\partial y}(y)\partial y + y^2\frac{\partial}{\partial x}(x)\partial x + x\frac{\partial}{\partial y}(y^2)\,\partial y$$

$$-y\frac{\partial}{\partial x}(x)\partial x - x\frac{\partial}{\partial y}(y)\,\partial y$$

$= 3y\,(2x)\,\partial x. + 3x^2\,(1)\,\partial y + y^2\,1.\,\partial x. + x\,(2y)\,\partial y - y.1.\,\partial x - x.1.\,\partial y$

$\partial U = 6xy\,\partial x + 3x^2\partial y + y^2\partial x + 2xy\partial y - y\partial x - x\partial y$

(ii) Find total differential of $Z = 5x^2 + xy - 3y^3$

$\partial Z = 10x\partial x + y\partial x + x\partial y - 9y^2\partial y = \partial x\,(10x + y) + \partial y\,(x - 9y^2)$

(iii) $U = x^3y^4$, find total differential

$\partial U = 3x^2y^4\partial x + 4x^3y^3\partial y$

(iv) $U = f(x, y, z) = 3x^2y + xy^3 - xz^2 + y^2z$

$\partial U = 3x^2\partial y + 6xy\,\partial x + y^3\,\partial x + 3xy^2\partial y - z^2\partial x - 2xz\partial z + 2yz\partial y + y^2\partial z$

(2) Illustrations on application of the product rule:

If $U = xy, \quad \partial U = y\dfrac{\partial}{\partial x}(x)\partial x + x\dfrac{\partial}{\partial y}(y)\partial y = y\partial x + x\partial y$

(i) $U = (x + y^2)(3x - y^2)$

For given $U = (x + y^2)(3x - y^2)$

$$\partial U = (x + y^2)\partial\left(3x - y^2\right) + (3x - y^2)\,\partial(x + y^2)$$

$\partial U = (x + y^2)(3\partial x - 2y\,\partial y) + (3x - y^2)(\partial x + 2y\,\partial y)$

$= 3x\,\partial x - 2xy\,\partial y + 3y^2\partial x - 2y^3\partial y + 3x\,\partial x + 6xy\,\partial y - y^2\partial x - 2y^3\partial y$

$= 6x\,\partial x + 4xy\,\partial y + 2y^2\partial x - 4y^3\partial y$

$\partial U = \partial x\,(6x + 2y^2) + \partial y\,(4xy - 4y^3)$

(ii) Given $U = (x^2 + y)(2x - y^2)$, find ∂U

$\partial U = (x^2 + y)(2\partial x - 2y\partial y) + (2x - y^2)(2x\,\partial x + \partial y)$

$= 2x^2\,\partial x - 2x^2y\,\partial y + 2y\,\partial x - 2y^2\partial y + 4x^2\,\partial x + 2x\,\partial y - 2xy^2\,\partial x - y^2\,\partial y$

$= 6x^2\,\partial x + 2y\,\partial x - 2xy^2\,\partial x - 3y^2\,\partial y - 2x^2y\,\partial y + 2x\,\partial y$

$= \partial x\,(6x^2 + 2y - 2xy^2) + \partial y\,(2x - 2x^2y - 3y^2)$

(iii) *Given* $Z = (x^2 + y^2)(2x^2 - y)$, find ∂Z

$\partial Z = (x^2 + y^2)\,\partial\,(2x^2 - y) + (2x^2 - y)\,\partial\,(x^2 + y^2)$

$= (x^2 + y^2)(4x\,\partial x - \partial y) + (2x^2 - y)(2x\,\partial x + 2y\,\partial y)$

$= 4x^3\,\partial x - x^2\,\partial y + 4xy^2\,\partial x - y^2\,\partial y + 4x^3\,\partial x + 4x^2y\,\partial y - 2xy\,\partial x - 2y^2\,\partial y$

$= \partial x\,(8x^3 + 4xy^2 - 2xy) + \partial y\,(4x^2y - x^2 - 3y^2)$

(3) Total differential in case of quotient.

(i) Given $U = \dfrac{x^2}{x + y}$, find total differential ∂U.

$$\partial U = \frac{(x + y)\partial\left(x^2\right) - x^2\,\partial\left(x + y\right)}{(x + y)^2}$$

$$= \frac{(x + y)(2x\,\partial x) - x^2\,(\partial x + \partial y)}{(x + y)^2} = \frac{2x^2\,\partial x + 2xy\,\partial x - x^2\,\partial x - x^2\,\partial y}{(x + y)^2}$$

$$\partial U = \frac{x^2\,\partial x + 2xy - x^2\,\partial y}{(x + y)^2} = \frac{\partial x\,(x^2 + 2xy) - x^2\,\partial y}{(x + y)^2}$$

(ii) Given $U = \dfrac{x}{x+y}$, find ∂U

$$\partial U = \frac{(x+y)\partial(x) - x\partial(x+y)}{(x+y)^2} = \frac{(x+y)(\partial x) - x(\partial x + \partial y)}{(x+y)^2}$$

$$= \frac{x\partial x + y\partial x - x\partial x - x\partial y}{(x+y)^2} = \frac{y\partial x - x\partial y}{(x+y)^2}$$

(iii) If $U = \dfrac{x^2+y^2}{x+y}$, find ∂U.

Given $U = \dfrac{x^2+y^2}{x+y}$, $\partial U = \dfrac{(x+y)\partial(x^2+y^2) - (x^2+y^2)\partial(x+y)}{(x+y)^2}$

$$= \frac{(x+y)(2x\,\partial x + 2y\,\partial y) - (x^2+y^2)(\partial x + \partial y)}{(x+y)^2}$$

$$= \frac{2x^2\,\partial x + 2xy\,\partial y + 2xy\,\partial x + 2y^2\,\partial y - x^2\,\partial x - x^2\,\partial y - y^2\,\partial x - y^2\,\partial y}{(x+y)^2}$$

$$= \frac{x^2\,\partial x + 2xy\,\partial x - y^2\,\partial x + y^2\,\partial y + 2xy\,\partial y - x^2\,\partial y}{(x+y)^2}$$

$$\partial U = \frac{\partial x\,(x^2 + 2xy - y^2) + \partial y\,(y^2 + 2xy - x^2)}{(x+y)^2}$$

(iv) Given $Z = \dfrac{xy}{x^2+y^2}$, find ∂Z.

$$\partial Z = \frac{(x^2+y^2)\partial(xy) - xy\,\partial(x^2+y^2)}{(x^2+y^2)^2}$$

$$= \frac{(x^2+y^2)(y\,\partial x + x\,\partial y) - xy\,(2x\,\partial x + 2y\,\partial y)}{(x^2+y^2)^2}$$

$$= \frac{x^2 y\,\partial x + x^3\,\partial y + y^3\,\partial x + xy^2\,\partial y - 2x^2 y\,\partial x - 2xy^2\,\partial y}{(x^2+y^2)^2}$$

$$\partial Z = \frac{-x^2 y\,\partial x + y^3\,\partial x - xy^2\,\partial y + x^3\,\partial y}{(x^2+y^2)^2} = \frac{\partial x\,(y^3 - x^2 y) + \partial y\,(x^3 - xy^2)}{(x^2+y^2)^2}$$

(4) Application of Chain rule for finding total differential.

(i) Given $U = \sqrt{x+y}$, find ∂U.

Substituting $x + y = t$, $U = \sqrt{t} = t^{\frac{1}{2}}$,

$$\partial U = \partial\left(t^{\frac{1}{2}}\right) = \frac{1}{2}t^{\frac{1}{2}-1}\,\partial t \text{, where } x + y = t\text{, } \therefore\ \partial x + \partial y = \partial t$$

$$\partial U = \frac{1}{2}t^{-\frac{1}{2}}\,\partial t = \frac{1}{2\sqrt{t}}\partial t = \frac{1}{2\sqrt{x+y}}(\partial x + \partial y) = \frac{\partial x + \partial y}{2\sqrt{x+y}}$$

(ii) Given $Z = \sqrt{5x^2 + 2y^2}$, find ∂Z.

Substitute $5x^2 + 2y^2 = U$, $\therefore$ $10x\,\partial x + 4y\,\partial y = \partial U$.

$$\partial Z = \partial\left(\sqrt{U}\right) = \frac{1}{2}U^{-\frac{1}{2}}\,\partial U = \frac{1}{2\sqrt{u}}\partial u = \frac{(10x\,\partial x + 4y\,\partial y)}{2\sqrt{5x^2+2y^2}}$$

(iii) Given $Z = (8x^2 + 3y^3)^5$

Substitute $8x^2 + 3y^3 = U$, $\therefore$ $\partial U = 16x\,\partial x + 9y^2\,\partial y$

$\partial Z = \partial\,(8x^2 + 3y^3)^5 = \partial\,(u)^5 = 5(u)^4\,\partial u = 5\,(8x^2 + 3y^3)^4\,(16x\partial x + 9y^2\partial y)$

(5) Total differential when logarithmic and exponential rules are applied.

(i) For $U = 3x\,log_e\,(1 + y)$, find ∂U

$$\partial U = 3\,log_e\,(1+y)\,\partial x + \frac{3x}{1+y}\partial y$$

(ii) For $U = 5x^2\,log_e\,(3 + 2y^2)$, find ∂U

$$\partial U = 5\,log_e\,(3+2y^2)\,2x\,\partial x + \frac{5x^2\,(4y\,\partial y)}{3+2y^2}$$

$$\partial U = 10x\,log_e\,(3+2y^2)\,\partial x + \frac{20x^2 y\,\partial y}{(3+2y^2)}$$

(iii) For $Z = e^{x^2}e^{-y}$ find ∂Z

$$\partial Z = e^{x^2}e^{-y}\partial(x^2) + e^{x^2}e^{-y}\partial(-y) = 2xe^{x^2}e^{-y}\partial x - e^{x^2}e^{-y}\partial y$$

(iv) Given $Z = a^x e^y$ find ∂Z

$$\partial Z = e^y\frac{\partial}{\partial x}\left(a^x\right)\partial x + a^x\frac{\partial}{\partial y}\left(e^y\right)\partial y = e^y a^x\,log\,a\,\partial x + a^x e^y\,\partial y$$

(v) Given $Z = 3.5^x e^{y^2}$, find ∂Z

$$\partial Z = 3.\,e^{y^2}\,\partial(5^x) + 3.5^x\,\partial(e^{y^2}) = 3.(5^x)\,e^{y^2}\,log\,5\,\partial x + 3.(5^x)e^{y^2}\,(2y\,\partial y)$$

$$= 3.5^x e^{y^2}\,log_e 5\,\partial x + 6y5^x\,e^{y^2}\,\partial y$$

(vi) Given $Z = log_e \sqrt{x^2 + y^2}$, find ∂Z

$$Z = log_e \sqrt{u}\ , \text{ if } x^2 + y^2 = u$$

$$\partial Z = \frac{1}{\sqrt{u}} \partial\left(\sqrt{u}\right) = \frac{1}{\sqrt{x^2 + y^2}} \partial (x^2 + y^2)^{\frac{1}{2}}$$

$$\partial Z = \frac{\frac{1}{2}\left(x^2 + y^2\right)^{-\frac{1}{2}} (2x\,\partial x + 2y\,\partial y)}{\left(x^2 + y^2\right)^{\frac{1}{2}}} = \frac{(2x\,\partial x + 2y\,\partial y)}{2\left(x^2 + y^2\right)}$$

(vii) Given $U = f(x, y)$ where U is utility and x, y are commodities find ∂U.

$$\partial U = \frac{\partial U}{\partial x}\partial x + \frac{\partial u}{\partial y}\partial y = f_1 \partial x + f_2 \partial y$$

(viii) If $Q = f(x_1 x_2)$ where Q is output and x_1 and x_2 ae quantition of inputs, find ∂Q.

$$\partial Q = \frac{\partial Q}{\partial x_1}\partial x_1 + \frac{\partial Q}{\partial x_2}\partial x_2 = f_1 \partial x_1 + f_2 \partial x_2$$

where $f_1 = MPx_1 = \left(\frac{\partial Q}{\partial x_1}\right)$, $f_2 = MPx_2 = \left(\frac{\partial Q}{\partial x_2}\right)$

(ix) If the Cobb-Douglas production function is given as $Q = AL^{\alpha}\ K^{\beta}$ where Q = output, L = labour, k = capital, A, α, β are parameters. Find ∂Q.

$$\partial Q = \frac{\partial Q}{\partial L}\partial L + \frac{\partial Q}{\partial k}\partial K = \alpha\, A\, L^{\alpha-1}\, K^{\beta} \partial L + \beta\, A\, L^{\alpha}\, K^{\beta-1} \partial K$$

$$= \frac{\alpha\, A\, L^{\alpha}\, k^{\beta}}{L}\partial L + \frac{\beta\, A\, L^{\alpha}\, K^{\beta}}{K}\partial K = \alpha\left(\frac{Q}{L}\right)\partial L + \beta\left(\frac{Q}{K}\right)\partial K$$

$$\partial Q = \alpha(AP_L)\partial L + \beta(AP_k)\partial K$$

6.9. Maxima and Minima of functions involving two variables: $Z = f(x, y)$

The explicit function in case of one independent variable is given by $y = f(x)$.
The given function is said to have a minimum when

$$y' = f'(x) = \frac{\partial}{\partial x} f(x) = 0\,,\ y'' = f''(x) = \frac{\partial^2}{\partial x^2} f(x) = \frac{\partial}{\partial x} f'(x) > 0\,.$$

Thus $\frac{\partial y}{\partial x} = 0$ and $\frac{\partial^2 y}{\partial x^2} > 0$

The given function is said to be a maximum when

$$y' = f'(x) = \frac{\partial}{\partial x} f(x) = 0\,,\ y'' = f''(x) = \frac{\partial^2}{\partial x^2} f(x) = \frac{\partial}{\partial x} f'(x) < 0\,.$$

Thus $\frac{\partial y}{\partial x} = 0$ and $\frac{\partial^2 y}{\partial x^2} < 0$

However when $\frac{\partial y}{\partial x} = 0$ and also $\frac{\partial^2 y}{\partial x^2} = 0$. The given function is said to have a point of inflexion.

The conditions for maximum and minimum in case of two independent variables can also be defined. For this we will take a function shown in $Z = f(x, y)$. The conditions for maxima and minima in case of two variables is given in table-6.1 and for three varaiables it is shown in table 6.2

Table 6.1. Necessary and sufficient conditions for maxima and minima in case of two variables

$y = f(x)$

Given function is $y = f(x)$	Necessary Condition	Sufficient Condition
Maximum	$\frac{\partial y}{\partial x} = f'(x) = 0$	$\frac{\partial^2 y}{\partial x^2} = f''(x) < 0$
Minimum	$\frac{\partial y}{\partial x} = f'(x) = 0$	$\frac{\partial^2 y}{\partial x^2} = f''(x) > 0$

Table 2. Necessary and sufficient conditions for maxima and minima in case of three variables

$Z = f(x, y)$

Given function $Z = f(x, y)$	Necessary Condition	Sufficient Condition
Maximum	$\frac{\partial z}{\partial x} = f_x = 0$	$\frac{\partial^2 z}{\partial x^2} = f_{xx} < 0$
	$\frac{\partial z}{\partial y} = f_y = 0$	$\frac{\partial^2 z}{\partial y^2} = f_{yy} < 0$ $(f_{xx})(f_{yy}) > (f_{xy})^2$
Minimum	$\frac{\partial z}{\partial x} = f_x = 0$ $\frac{\partial z}{\partial y} = f_y = 0$	$\frac{\partial^2 z}{\partial x^2} = f_{xx} > 0$ $\frac{\partial^2 z}{\partial y^2} = f_{yy} > 0$ $(f_{xx})(f_{yy}) > (f_{xy})^2$

6.10. Illustrations on Maxima and Minima of Functions with Two Independent Variables

(1) Find the maxima or minima for the given function $Z = x^2 + y^3 + y^2 - xy + 5$

The given function is $Z = f(x, y) = x^2 + y^2 + y^3 - xy + 5$

For maxima or minima we need to evaluate f_x, f_y, f_{xx}, f_{xy} and f_{yy}.

$$f_x = \frac{\partial z}{\partial x} = 2x - y = 0\,,\ f_{xx} = \frac{\partial^2 z}{\partial x^2} = \frac{\partial}{\partial x}\left(\frac{\partial z}{\partial x}\right) = 2 > 0$$

$$f_y = \frac{\partial z}{\partial y} = 2y + 3y^2 - x = 0\,,\ f_{yy} = \frac{\partial^2 z}{\partial y^2} = \frac{\partial}{\partial y}\left(\frac{\partial z}{\partial y}\right) = 2 + 6y$$

and $f_{xy} = \frac{\partial}{\partial x}(f_y) = \frac{\partial}{\partial x}\left(2y - 3y^2 - x\right) = -1$

$$f_{yx} = \frac{\partial}{\partial y}(f_x) = \frac{\partial}{\partial y}(2x - y) = -1\,, \quad f_{xy} = f_{yx} = -1$$

To find x and y values we need to solve the equations $f_x = f_y = 0$.

From $f_x = 2x - y = 0,\ \ 2x = y,\ x = \frac{y}{2}$

$2y + 3y^2 - x = 0 \ \therefore 2y + 3y^2 - \frac{y}{2} = 0$ or $\frac{4y + 6y^2 - y}{2} = 0$

or $4y + 6y^2 - y = 0,\ 6y^2 + 3y = 0$ or $3y\,(2y + 1) = 0$.

If $3y \neq 0$, $\ 2y + 1 = 0$ or $y = -\frac{1}{2}$ and $x = \frac{y}{2} = -\frac{1}{4}$

The pair of x and y values are $y = -\frac{1}{2}$ and $x = -\frac{1}{4}$

If $3y = 0$, $\therefore$ The pair of x and y values are $x = 0$, and $y = 0$

If we take $x = y = 0$, $f_{xx} = 2 > 0$, $f_{yy} = 2 > 0$ $f_{xy} = -1$

$\therefore (f_{xx})(f_{yy}) - (f_{xy})^2 > 0$ as $4 > 1$

$\therefore$ The function has a minimum at $x = 0$ and $y = 0$.
This gives us one of the solutions.

Now we will be taking $x = \frac{-1}{4}$ and $y = \frac{-1}{2}$

From these we get $f_{xx} = 2 > 0$, $\ f_{yy} = 2 + 6y = 2 + 6\left(-\frac{1}{2}\right) = 2 - 3 = -1$

Since $f_{xx} = 2 > 0$ and $f_{yy} = -1 < 0$, the given function has no solution for either maxima or minima since f_{xx} and f_{yy} have opposite signs and thereby the second order condition is not satisfied. If f_{xx} and f_{yy} have opposite sign, the given function has a saddle point, neither a maximum nor a minimum.

(2) Given $U = 4x^2 - xy + y^2 - x^2$, find maxima or minima or saddle point as the case may be.

Given $U = 4x^2 - xy + y^2 - x^2$,

$$f_x = \frac{\partial U}{\partial x} = 8x - y - 2x = 0 \quad \text{or} \quad 6x - y = 0$$

$$f_y = \frac{\partial U}{\partial y} = -x + 2y = 0 \quad \text{or} \quad 2y - x = 0$$

$$f_{xx} = \frac{\partial^2 U}{\partial x^2} = \frac{\partial}{\partial x}(f_x) = \frac{\partial}{\partial x}(6x - y) = 6 > 0$$

$$f_{yy} = \frac{\partial^2 U}{\partial y^2} = \frac{\partial}{\partial y}(f_y) = \frac{\partial}{\partial y}(2y - x) = 2 > 0$$

$$f_{xy} = \frac{\partial}{\partial x}\left(\frac{\partial U}{\partial y}\right) = \frac{\partial^2 U}{\partial x\,\partial y} = \frac{\partial}{\partial x}(-x + 2y) = -1$$

$$f_{yx} = \frac{\partial}{\partial x}\left(\frac{\partial U}{\partial y}\right) = -1, \ (f_{xy})^2 = (-1)^2 = 1$$

The given function has a minimum since both necessary and sufficient conditions for minimum are fulfilled.

$f_x = f_y = 0$, $f_{xx} > 0, f_{yy} > 0$ and $(f_{xx})(f_{yy}) > (f_{xy})^2 \cdot (6)(2) > 1$

6.11. Solved Questions of T.Y.B.A (Economics) Papers of Mumbai University

April, 2002, T.Y.B.A./ECO/ M.U.

(1) Find the first and second order partial derivatries of the function: $Z = (5x^2 + 3y^2)(3x - 4y)$:

$$f_x = \frac{\partial Z}{\partial x} = (5x^2 + 3y^2)\frac{\partial}{\partial x}(3x - 4y) + (3x - 4y)\frac{\partial}{\partial x}(5x^2 + 3y^2)$$

$= (5x^2 + 3y^2)\,3 + (3x - 4y)(10x) = 15x^2 + 9y^2 + 30x^2 - 40xy = 45x^2 - 40xy + 9y^2$

$$f_{xx} = \frac{\partial^2 Z}{\partial x^2} = \frac{\partial}{\partial x}(45x^2 - 40xy + 9y^2) = 90x - 40y$$

$$f_y = \frac{\partial Z}{\partial y} = \frac{\partial}{\partial y}(5x^2 + 3y^2)(3x - 4y)$$

$= (5x^2 + 3y^2)(-4) + (3x - 4y)(6y) = -20x^2 - 12y^2 + 18xy - 24y^2 = -20x^2 - 36y^2 + 18xy$

$$f_{yy} = \frac{\partial^2 Z}{\partial y^2} = -72y + 18x$$

$$f_{yx} = \frac{\partial}{\partial y}\left(\frac{\partial Z}{\partial x}\right) = \frac{\partial}{\partial y}(45x^2 - 40xy + 9y^2) = -40x + 18y$$

$$f_{xy} = \frac{\partial}{\partial x}\left(\frac{\partial Z}{\partial y}\right) = \frac{\partial}{\partial x}(-20x^2 - 36y^2 + 18xy) = -40x + 18y$$

$f_{xy} = f_{yx} = -40x + 18y$

Oct., 2001, T.Y.B.A./ECO/ M.U.

(2) Find the extreme values of the function: $Z = x^2 + 2x + y + y^2$:

To determine maxima or minima of the function, called extreme values of the function, we need to evaluate and set $f_x = f_y = 0$. This is the necessary condition for either maxima or minima. Then the second order conditions are to be applied to the given function to determine maxima or minima.

Given $Z = x^2 + 2x + y + y^2$

$f_x = 2x + 2 = 0,\ f_y = 1 + 2y = 0\ \therefore\ 2x = -2,\ \ x = -1$

$2y = -1$ and $y = -\frac{1}{2}$

$$f_{xx} = \frac{\partial}{\partial x}(f_x) = 2 > 0,\ f_{yy} = \frac{\partial}{\partial y}(f_y) = 2 > 0,\ f_{xy} = f_{yx} = 0$$

$(f_{xx})(f_{yy}) - (f_{xy})^2 > 0$. Thus the given function has a minimum since

$f_{xx} > 0, f_{yy} > 0$ and $(f_{xx})(f_{yy}) - (f_{xy})^2 > 0$ at $x = -1$ and $y = \frac{-1}{2}$.

$(f_{xx})(f_{yy}) > (f_{xy})^2$, $(2)(2) > 0$

The function Z has a minimum at $x = -1,\ y = \frac{-1}{2}$.

This minimum value of Z is Z for $x = -1,\ y = \frac{-1}{2}$. This is equal to

$$Z = x^2 + 2x + y + y^2 = (-1)^2 + 2(-1) + \left(\frac{-1}{2}\right) + \left(\frac{-1}{2}\right)^2 = -\frac{5}{4}$$

(3) **Oct., 2002, T.Y.B.A./ECO/ M.U.**

(i) Find all the partial derivatives of : $Z = x^3 + y^3 + 4xy^2 + 3x^2y + 10$.

Given $Z = x^3 + y^3 + 4xy^2 + 3x^2y + 10$

$$f_x = \frac{\partial Z}{\partial x} = 3x^2 + 4y^2 + 6xy,\ f_y = \frac{\partial Z}{\partial y} = 3y^2 + 8xy + 3x^2$$

$$f_{xx} = \frac{\partial^2 Z}{\partial x^2} = \frac{\partial}{\partial x}\left(\frac{\partial Z}{\partial x}\right) = 6x + 6y,\ f_{yy} = \frac{\partial^2 Z}{\partial y^2} = \frac{\partial}{\partial y}\left(\frac{\partial Z}{\partial y}\right) = 6y + 8x$$

$$f_{xy} = \frac{\partial}{\partial x}\left(\frac{\partial Z}{\partial y}\right) = 8y + 6x,\ f_{yx} = \frac{\partial}{\partial y}\left(\frac{\partial Z}{\partial x}\right) = 8y + 6x$$

$$f_{xy} = f_{yx} = 8y + 6x$$

(ii) Examine the function : $U = 3x + 2y - 2x^2 + xy - y^2$ for maxima or minima

Given $U = 3x + 2y - 2x^2 + xy - y^2$

For finding maxima or minim we need to evaluate x and y values by setting $f_x = f_y = 0$. This is the necessary or first order condition for either maxima and minima. The second order condition for maxima is

$fxx < 0$, $fyy < 0$ and $(fxx)(fyy) > (fxy)^2$ while for minima, the conditions are $fyy > 0$, $fxx > 0$ and $(fxx)(fyy) > (fxy)^2$

If f_{xx} and f_{yy} have apposite signs, it has a saddle point and for this $(f_{xx})(f_{yy}) < (f_{xy})^2$

Given $U = 3x + 2y - 2x^2 + xy - y^2$

$$fx = \frac{\partial U}{\partial x} = 3 - 2x + y = 0,\ fy = \frac{\partial U}{\partial y} = 2 + x - 2y = 0$$

Solving these equations we get x and y values

$$-2x + y = -3 \cdots\cdots (1)$$
$$x - 2y = -2 \cdots\cdots (2)$$

Multiply equation (2) by 2 and adding this to other equation we get

$$-2x + y = -3$$
$$\underline{2x - 4y = -4}$$
$$-3y = -7$$

or $y = \frac{7}{3}$. Substituting y in equation $x - 2y = -2$ we get

$$x = -2 + 2y = -2 + 2\left(\frac{7}{3}\right) = \frac{-6+14}{3} = \frac{8}{3},\ \therefore\ x = \frac{8}{3},\ y = \frac{7}{3}$$

For sufficient condition, $fxx = \frac{\partial}{\partial x}(fx) = -2 < 0$ and

$$fyy = \frac{\partial}{\partial y}(fy) = -2 < 0 \text{ and } fxy = \frac{\partial}{\partial x}(fy) = 1,\ fyx = \frac{\partial}{\partial y}(fx) = 1$$

$(f_{xx})(f_{yy}) > (f_{xy})^2$ or $(-2)(-2) > 1, 4 > 1$

Thus the given function 'U' has a maximum at $x = \frac{8}{3}$ and $y = \frac{7}{3}$.

This maximum value is U at $x = \frac{8}{3}$ and $y = \frac{7}{3}$. This is equal to $U = 3x + 2y - x^2 + xy - y^2$

$$= 3\left(\frac{8}{3}\right) + 2\left(\frac{7}{3}\right) - \left(\frac{8}{3}\right)^2 + \left(\frac{8}{3}\right)\left(\frac{7}{3}\right) + \left(\frac{7}{3}\right)^2 = 6.333$$

(4) **April, 2002, T.Y.B.A./ECO/ M.U.**

(i) Find the second order partial derivatives of the following function :

$Z = x^3 y + 2xy^2$

Given $Z = x^3 y + 2xy^2$. $fx = \frac{\partial Z}{\partial x} = 3x^2 y + y^2$, $fxx = \frac{\partial^2 Z}{\partial x^2} = 6xy$

$$fy=\frac{\partial Z}{\partial y}=x^3+2xy\ ,\ fyy=\frac{\partial^2 Z}{\partial y^2}=2x$$

$$fxy=\frac{\partial}{\partial x}(fy)=\frac{\partial}{\partial x}\left(x^3+2xy\right)=3x^2+2y$$

$$fyx=\frac{\partial}{\partial x}(fx)=\frac{\partial}{\partial y}=\left(3x^2y+y^2\right)=3x^2+2y\ ,\ fxy=fyx=3x^2+2y$$

(ii) Determine the extreme value of the function: $Z = x^3 + xy - y^2 + 2x + y$

Given $Z = x^3 + xy - y^2 + 2x + y$

For extreme values of the function $f_x = f_y = 0$. This is the first order condition for both maxima and minima.

$$fx=\frac{\partial Z}{\partial x}=-2x+y+2=0 \quad fy=\frac{\partial Z}{\partial y}=x-2y+1=0$$

Solving these equations we get x and y values

$$x-2y=-1\cdots\cdots(1)$$

$$-2x+y=-2\cdots\cdots(2)$$

Multiplying (1) by (2) and solving the equations we obtain

$$2x-4y=-2$$

$$-2x+y=-2$$

$$-3y=-4\ ,\ y=\frac{4}{3}$$

$$x=-1+2y=-1+2\left(\frac{4}{3}\right)=\frac{-3+8}{3}=\frac{5}{3}$$

$\therefore\ x=\frac{5}{3}$ and $y=\frac{4}{3}$. These x and y values can give either maximum or minimum of Z, which can be varified from second order derivatives

f_{xx} and f_{yy}, $fxx=\frac{\partial}{\partial x}(fx)=-2\ ,\ fyy=\frac{\partial}{\partial y}(fy)=-2\ ,$

$$fxy=\frac{\partial}{\partial x}(fy)=1\ ,\ f_{yx}=\frac{\partial}{\partial y}(f_x)=1$$

$(f_{xx})(f_{yy}) > (f_{xy})^2 \quad (-2)(-2) > (1)^2$

Thus the given function z has a maximum at $x=\frac{5}{3}$ and $y=\frac{4}{3}$ and this maximum value of Z is

$Z=-x^2+xy-y^2+2x+y$ at $x=\frac{5}{3}$ and $y=\frac{4}{3}$.

$$Z=-\left(\frac{5}{3}\right)^2+\left(\frac{5}{3}\right)\left(\frac{4}{3}\right)-\left(\frac{4}{3}\right)^2+2\left(\frac{5}{3}\right)+\left(\frac{4}{3}\right)=2.333$$

(iii) Compute the marginal productivities of labour and capital at $L = 2$ and $K = 3$ for the production function: $Q = 2L^2 k + 3L k^3 + 6L + 9k$ (5)

$$MP \text{ of capital } (k) = \frac{\partial Q}{\partial k}, \quad MP \text{ of capital } (L) = \frac{\partial Q}{\partial L}$$

$$\frac{\partial Q}{\partial k} = \frac{\partial}{\partial k}\left(2L^2k + 3Lk^3 + 6L + 9k\right) = 2L^2 + 9Lk^2 + 9$$

$$\frac{\partial Q}{\partial L} = \frac{\partial}{\partial L}\left(2L^2 k + 3Lk^3 + 6L + 9k\right) = 4Lk + 3k^3 + 6$$

Now given $L = 2$, $k = 3$

$$MP_k = \frac{\partial Q}{\partial k} = 2L^2 + 9Lk^2 + 9 = 2(2)^2 + 9(2)(3)^2 + 9 = 8 + 162 + 9 = 179$$

$$MP_L = \frac{\partial Q}{\partial L} = 4Lk + 3k^3 + 6 = 4(2)(3) + 3(3)^3 + 6 = 24 + 27 + 6 = 57$$

$MP_k = 179$, $MP_L = 57$ at $L = 2$, $k = 3$

EXERCISE – 6

(A) Find the first and second order partial derivatives of the following functions and verify that $f_{xy} = f_{yx}$

(i) $u = (3x + 5y)\, e^{y^2}$

(ii) $z = 5\sqrt{xy^2}$

(iii) $u = \dfrac{5x^2}{3x - 2y + 6}$

(iv) $z = \dfrac{x^2}{y^3} + \dfrac{y^2}{x^3}$

(v) $z = 8x^2 + \dfrac{x}{y} + 6y^2$

(vi) $u = \dfrac{x^3 + y^3}{x^2 + y^2}$

(vii) $u = \log(5 + y^2) + x^2$

(B) *(i)* If the production function is $q = f(x, y) = xy + 0.3x^2 - 0.5y^2 + 8$, where q = output, x and y are inputs, find

(a) AP and MP of x and y *(b)* Evaluate them at $x = 1$, $y = 2$

(ii) If the production function is $q = f(x, y, z)$ where q = output and x, y, z are inputs, Find MP of x, y, z for $q = 7x^{0.5}\, y^{0.3}\, z^{0.2}$

(iii) If the production function is given as $Q = 0.2\, L^{0.5}\, k^{0.5}$

(a) Determine the MP of labour and capital.

(b) Evaluate them at $L = k = 2$.

(C) Find the total differential of the following functions:

(i) $U = x^3 y^4 - x^4 y^3$

(ii) $U = (x^2 + y^2)(x - 2y)$

(iii) $Z = \dfrac{xy}{x^2 + y^2}$

(iv) $Z = x^3 e^{2y}$

(v) $U = \sqrt{x^3 + 2y + 5}$

(vi) $V = \dfrac{x^2 + y^2}{x + y}$

(vii) $Z = 3y^3 e^{x^2}$

(D) Examine the following functions for maxima or minima or saddle point as the case may be

(i) $U = \dfrac{4}{3}x^3 + 2y^2 - 4x + 8y$

(ii) $Z = x^3 - xy + x^2 + y^2 + 8$

(iii) $U = 4xy - x^2 - 3y^2$

(iv) $U = 5x^2 + 2y^2 - 3xy$

(v) $U = x^2 + y^2 + xy$

(E) (i) If $Z = e^{3x^2} + 6y^3$, find ∂Z.

(ii) If $Z = \sqrt{xy^2 + yx^2}$, find ∂Z.

(iii) Examine the following function for maxima or minima and find this value for
$Z = 2x^2 + 2y^2 + 8 - 6x - 3y + 5xy$

(iv) State the necessary and sufficient conditions for minimum, maximum and saddle point for the function with two independent variables of type $U = f(x, y)$.

❑ ❑ ❑

7 APPLICATIONS OF PARTIAL DERIVATIVES IN ECONOMICS

7.1. Introduction

Partial derivatives are extensively used in economics and commerce. In the demand analysis a consumer while purchasing 'n' number of goods can measure the partial elasticities of demand for a commodity say q_1, with respect to it's own price (p_1) and prices of other related goods $p_2, p_3, ...p_n$. These goods are assumed to be related with one another. Partial derivative is applied to obtain consumer's equilibrium with regard to more than two goods where the graphical solution breaks down.

In theory of production, for given the production function, we can evaluate marginal products of factor inputs employed at various levels of their employment by a firm. Partial derivatives are useful to explain firm's behaviour.

As we will see in this chapter partial derivatives are employed to provide a mathematical analysis of the economic concepts relating theory of demand and utility analysis, production functions, market analysis, price discrimination and many more aspects covered by micro and macroeconomics. It enables a consumer to find optimum purchases of goods from given the budget constraint. The firm uses partial derivatives to find solutions to the problems relating maximizing profit or net revenue.

7.2. Partial Elasticities of Demand

The demand function for x_1 and x_2 goods are shown to be

$x_1 = f_1 (p_1, p_2)$, $x_2 = f_2 (p_1, p_2)$

The rate of change in quantity demanded for $x_1$due to change in it's own price p_1, while keeping the price of other good p_2 constant can be obtained from the derivative $\frac{\partial x_1}{\partial p_1}$. Likewise $\frac{\partial x_1}{\partial p_2}$ provides the rate of change in x_1, *w.r.t.* p_2, when p_1 is remained unchanged. In a similar process partial derivatives $\frac{\partial x_2}{\partial p_2}$ and $\frac{\partial x_2}{\partial p_1}$ are obtained to represent the rate of change in x_2 *w.r.t.* its own price p_2 and x_1 *w.r.t.*, p_1 respectively. If these goods x_1 and x_2 are assumed normal or luxury goods, the sign of the derivatives $\frac{\partial x_1}{\partial p_1}$ and $\frac{\partial x_2}{\partial p_2}$ are to become negative. The price-demand relationship for these goods is found inverse for which demand curves for these goods are downward sloping.

In the real world situation, when there is any increase or decrease in p_1, it not only results in a fall or rise in its quantity demanded respectively, but at the same time it also affects quantity demanded for its related commodity say, x_2 even if its own price, p_2 remains unchanged. In the situation where a rise in p_1 leads to an increase in demand for x_2 and a fall in p_1 results in a decrease in demand for x_2, the partial derivative of x_2 *w.r.t.* p_1 will be positive, $\frac{\partial x_2}{\partial p_1} > 0$. Likewise when p_2 rises, demand for x_1 also rises or when p_2 falls demand for x_1 decreases , the partial derivative of x_1, *w.r.t.* p_2 will also be positive $\frac{\partial x_1}{\partial p_2} > 0$.

The nature of relationship between two goods x_1 and x_2 is such that the increase or decrease in price of one commodity is accompanied by an increase or decrease in the quantity demanded for the other commodity. In this case these two goods in question are said to be competitive or substitute goods. The relationship between two goods is said to be complementary with each other when the rise or fall in the price of one commodity not only reduces or raises the quantity demanded for it's own but also lowers or raises the quantity demanded of its related commodity. Under this circumstance the partial derivatives of x_1 *w.r.t.* the price of the other good $p_2, \left(\frac{\partial x_1}{\partial p_2} < 0\right)$ is negative. Similarly demand for x_2 *w.r.t.* the price of the other good p_1 is also negative, $p_1, \left(\frac{\partial x_2}{\partial p_1} < 0\right)$

Thus it can be stated that x_1 and x_2 are said to be competitive goods if

$$(a)\ \frac{\partial x_1}{\partial p_1} < 0 \text{ and } \frac{\partial x_1}{\partial p_2} > 0. \quad (b)\ \frac{\partial x_2}{\partial p_2} < 0 \text{ and } \frac{\partial x_2}{\partial p_1} > 0$$

Two commodities are said to be complementary with each other when

$$(a)\ \frac{\partial x_1}{\partial p_1} < 0 \text{ and } \frac{\partial x_1}{\partial p_2} < 0. \quad (b)\ \frac{\partial x_1}{\partial p_1} < 0 \text{ and } \frac{\partial x_1}{\partial p_2} < 0.$$

Partial derivatives useful information regarding the nature of the relationship of the commodities. The relationship we have established for two goods x_1 and x_2 can be extended to generalise it to '*n*' number of goods.

Thus if $x_1 = f_1(p_1, p_2 \ ..., p_n)$, $x_2 = f_2(p_1, p_2 \ ..., p_n)$, ..., and $x_n = f_n(p_1, p_2 \ ..., p_n)$

When partial derivatives of x_1 *w.r.t.* p_2, p_3........,p_n are positive i.e., $\frac{\partial x_1}{\partial p_2}, \frac{\partial x_1}{\partial p_3}, ..., \frac{\partial x_1}{\partial p_n} > 0$ and $\frac{\partial x_1}{\partial p_1} < 0$,

In this case x_1 is said to be related with other goods as a substitute or competitive commodity.

On the contrary when these partial derivatives $\frac{\partial x_1}{\partial p_2}, \frac{\partial x_1}{\partial p_3}, \ldots, \frac{\partial x_1}{\partial p_n}$ are negative, the relationship between x_1 and other goods $x_2, x_3, \ldots, x_n$ is said to be complementay to each other. We can also find out the partial elasticities of demand for these goods.

For convenience we need to restrict our demand analysis to three related goods namely, x_1, x_2 and x_3. Their corresponding prices are p_1, p_2 and p_3. The point elasticity of demand for any of these goods with respect to their own prices and prices of other goods can be computed..

For illustrations the demand functions for these three goods are shown to be

$x_1 = f_1\ (p_1, p_2, p_3),\ x_2 = f_2\ (p_1, p_2, p_3),\ x_3 = f_3\ (p_1, p_2, p_3).$

Partial elasticity of demand for x_1 with respect to it's own price is denoted by e_{11}, where,

$$e_{11} = \frac{\partial x_1}{\partial p_1} \times \frac{p_1}{x_1} = \frac{\partial}{\partial p_1} f_1\ (f_1, p_2, p_3) \times \frac{p_1}{x_1}$$

Like wise partial elasticity of demand for x_2 and x_3 with respect to their own prices are denoted by e_{22} and e_{33} respectively and are shown as

$$e_{22} = \frac{\partial x_2}{\partial p_2} \times \frac{p_2}{x_2} = \frac{\partial}{\partial p_2} f_2\ (p_1, p_2, p_3) \times \frac{p_2}{x_2}$$

$$e_{33} = \frac{\partial x_3}{\partial p_3} \times \frac{p_3}{x_3} = \frac{\partial}{\partial p_3} f_3\ (p_1, p_2, p_3) \times \frac{p_3}{x_3}$$

The cross elasticity of demand for x_1 *w.r.t.* price of x_2 and price x_3 are evaluated and these are denoted by e_{12} and e_{13} where,

$$e_{12} = \frac{\partial x_1}{\partial p_2} \times \frac{p_2}{x_1} = \frac{\partial}{\partial p_2}\{f_1 (p_1, p_2, p_3)\} \times \frac{p_2}{x_1}$$

$$e_{13} = \frac{\partial x_1}{\partial p_3} \times \frac{p_3}{x_1} = \frac{\partial}{\partial p_3}\{f_1\ (p_1, p_2, p_3)\} \times \frac{p_3}{x_1}$$

The cross elasticity of demand for x_2, *w.r.t.* the prices of x_1 and x_3 are symbolically expressed as e_{21} and e_{23} as shwon below:

$$e_{21} = \frac{\partial x_2}{\partial p_1} \times \frac{p_1}{x_2},\quad e_{23} = \frac{\partial x_2}{\partial p_3} \times \frac{p_3}{x_2}$$

The cross elasticity of demand for x_3 *w.r.t* prices of x_1 and x_2 are given as e_{31} and e_{32} and these are

$$e_{31} = \frac{\partial x_3}{\partial p_1} \times \frac{p_1}{x_3},\quad e_{32} = \frac{\partial x_3}{\partial p_2} \times \frac{p_2}{x_3}$$

Illustrations:

Following illustrations are provided to study the process of estimatiing the price elasticity and cross elasticity or partial elasticities of demand.

(1) For given the demand functions for q_1 and q_2 goods as

$q_1 = f\ (p_1\ p_2) = 3 - 2\,p_1 + p_2$

$q_2 = g\ (p_1\ p_2) = 7 + p_1^2 - 3\,p_2$

Determine price elasticity and cross partial elasticity of demand at $p_1 = 2$ and $p_2 = 3$ and state the nature of the relationship between these two goods.

Given $q_1 = 3 - 2p_1 + p_2$

Partial elasticities of demand of q_1 *w.r.t.* p_1 is e_{11} while partial elasticity of demand for q_1 *w.r.t.* p_2 is e_{12} . These are evaluated as

$$e_{11} = \frac{\partial q_1}{\partial p_1} \times \frac{p_1}{q_1} = \frac{\partial}{\partial p_1}(3 - 2p_1 + p_2) \times \frac{p_1}{q_1}$$

$$= (-2)\left(\frac{p_1}{q_1}\right) = -2\left\{\frac{p_1}{3-2p_1+p_2}\right\}. \text{ For } p_1 = 2,\ p_2 = 3$$

$$e_{11} = -2\left\{\frac{(2)}{3-2(2)+3}\right\} = -2,\ e_{11} = -2 < 0.$$

$$e_{12} = \frac{\partial q_1}{\partial p_2} \times \frac{p_2}{q_1} = \frac{\partial}{\partial p_2}(3-2p_1+p_2) \times \frac{p_2}{q_1}$$

$$e_{12} = \frac{p_2}{3-2p_1+p_2} = \frac{3}{3-2(2)+3} = 1.5,\ e_{12} = 1.5 > 0.$$

Partial elasticities of demand for q_2 *w.r.t.* both p_1 and p_2, are evaluated below. These are denoted by e_{21} and e_{22}

$$e_{21} = \frac{\partial q_2}{\partial p_1} \times \frac{p_1}{q_2} \text{ and } e_{22} = \frac{\partial q_2}{\partial p_2} \times \frac{p_2}{q_2}$$

For given $q_2 = 7 + p_1^2 - 3p_2$. From this we can obatin

$$e_{21} = \frac{\partial q_2}{\partial p_1} \times \frac{p_1}{q_2} = \frac{\partial}{\partial p_1}(7 + p_1^2 - 3p_2) \times \frac{p_1}{q_2} = \frac{p_1(2p_1)}{q_2} = \frac{2p_1^2}{7 + p_1^2 - 3p_2}$$

At $p_1 = 2,\ p_3 = 3,\ e_{21} = \frac{2(2)^2}{7 + (2)^2 - 3(3)} = \frac{8}{2} = 4 > 0$

$$e_{22} = \frac{\partial q_2}{\partial p_2} \times \frac{p_2}{q_2} = \frac{\partial}{\partial p_2}(7 + p_1^2 - 3p_2) \times \frac{p_2}{q_2} = \frac{-3(p_2)}{7 + p_1^2 - 3p_2} = \frac{-3(2)}{2} = -3 < 0$$

Since e_{11} and e_{22} are negative while e_{12} and e_{21} are positive, it means the cross elasticities of demand are positive for both q_1 and q_2 . So these goods are called competitive goods or substitutes of each other. Price elasticity of demand for these goods is negative as usual.

(2) If the demand functions for two goods x_1 and x_2 are given by $x_1 = p_1^{-1.5} p_2^{0.7}$ and $x_2 = p_1^{0.8} p_2^{-0.3}$, find

(a) Partial elasticities of demand. *(b)* Do you agree that the demand curve for these goods will slope negative ? Why? *(c)* Determine whether x_1 and x_2 are substitutes or complentary goods.

Given $x_1 = p_1^{-1.5} p_2^{0.7}$

Elasticity of demand for x_1, *w.r.t* its own price p_1 is e_{11} while *w.r.t.* price of x_2 is e_{12}, where

$$e_{11} = \frac{\partial x_1}{\partial p_1} \times \frac{p_1}{x_1} = \frac{\partial}{\partial p_1}(p_1^{-1.5} p_2^{0.7}) \times \frac{p_1}{x_1} = \frac{(-1.5)\, p_1^{-2.5}\, p_2^{0.7}\, p_1}{p_1^{-1.5}\, p_2^{0.7}} = -1.5 < 0$$

$$e_{12} = \frac{\partial x_1}{\partial p_2} \times \frac{p_2}{x_1} = \frac{\partial}{\partial p_2}(p_1^{-1.5} p_2^{0.7}) \times \frac{p_2}{x_1}$$

$$= \frac{p_2}{p_1^{-1.5}\, p_2^{0.7}} \times (0.7)\, p_1^{-1.5}\, p_2^{-0.3} = \frac{(0.7)\, p_1^{-1.5}\, p_2^{0.7}}{p_1^{-1.5}\, p_2^{0.7}} = 0.7 > 0$$

The partial elasticity of demand for x_2, *w.r.t.* p_2 and p_1 are given by e_{22} and e_{21}. These elasticities are evaluated as follows;

$$e_{21} = \frac{\partial x_2}{\partial p_1} \times \frac{p_1}{x_2} = \frac{\partial}{\partial p_1}(x_2) \times \frac{p_1}{x_2}, \text{ Where } x_2 = p_1^{0.8}\, p_2^{-0.3}$$

$$e_{21} = \frac{0.8\, p_1^{-0.2}\, p_2^{-0.3}\, p_1}{p_1^{0.8}\, p_2^{-0.3}} = \frac{(0.8)\, p_1^{0.8}\, p_2^{-0.3}}{p_1^{0.8}\, p_2^{-0.3}} = 0.8 > 0$$

$$e_{22} = \frac{\partial x_2}{\partial p_2} \times \frac{p_2}{x_2} = \frac{\partial}{\partial p_2}(p_1^{0.8}\, p_2^{-0.3}) \times \frac{p_2}{x_2}$$

$$= \frac{(-0.3)\, p_1^{0.8}\, p_2^{-1.3}\, p_2}{p_1^{0.8}\, p_2^{-0.3}} = \frac{-0.3\, p_1^{0.8}\, p_2^{-0.3}}{p_1^{0.8}\, p_2^{-0.3}} = -0.3 < 0$$

Since e_{11} and e_{22} are negative, $e_{11} < 0$, $e_{22} < 0$, and cross elasticities are positive, $e_{12} > 0$, $e_{21} > 0$, these two goods x_1 and x_2 are related by the way of substitutes. The demand curves for these goods will slope downward from left to the right as their price elatsicities of demand are negative.

(3) From the demand function for commodity *A* is given: $X_A = 62.7 - 1.8\, P_A + 0.2\, P_B + 0.7\, P_C$, find

(*a*) Partial elasticities of demand for *A*, *w.r.t.* the prices of *B* and *C*.

(*b*) Evaluate these elasticities at $P_A = 8$, $P_B = 6$, and $P_C = 10$,

(*a*) Price elasticity of demand for *A* ,

$$e_{11} = \frac{\partial X_A}{\partial P_A} \times \frac{P_A}{X_A}, \text{ where } \frac{\partial X_A}{\partial P_A} = \frac{\partial}{\partial P_A}[62.7 - 1.8\, P_A + 0.2\, P_B + 0.7\, P_C] = -1.8$$

$$e_{11} = \frac{(-1.8) P_A}{X_A} = \frac{(-1.8)\ (8)}{62.7 - 1.8 (8) + 0.2\ (6) + 0.7\ (10)} = \frac{-14.4}{56.5} = -0.25 < 0$$

Partial elasticity of demand for *A*, w.r.t. price of commodity *B* is e_{12} ,

$$e_{12} = \frac{\partial X_A}{\partial P_B} \times \frac{P_B}{X_A} = \frac{\partial}{\partial P_B}[62.7 - 1.8\, P_A + 0.2\, P_B + 0.7\, P_C] \times \frac{P_B}{X_A}$$

$$= \frac{0.2\ (P_B)}{X_A} = \frac{(0.2)\ (6)}{56.5} = \frac{1.2}{56.5} = 0.021 > 0$$

(b) Partial elasticity of demand for A, *w.r.t.* price of commodity 'C' is e_{13},

$$e_{13} = \frac{\partial X_A}{\partial P_C} \times \frac{P_C}{X_A} = \frac{\partial}{\partial P_C}\left[62.7 - 1.8P_A + 0.2P_B + 0.7P_C\right] \times \frac{P_C}{X_A}$$

$$= \frac{(0.7)\,(P_C)}{X_A} = \frac{(0.7)\,(10)}{56.5} = \frac{7}{56.5} = 0.124 > 0.$$

It is estimated that, $e_{11} = -0.25$, $e_{12} = 0.021$, $e_{13} = 0.124$ at $P_A = 8$, $P_B = 6$, and $P_C = 10$.

(4) We are given with three commodities X_1, X_2 and X_3. Their corresponding prices are P_1, P_2 and P_3. The demand function for X_3 is given by $X_3 = 7.3 + 0.2\,P_1 + 0.5\,P_2 - 0.4\,P_3$. (a) Find the partial elasticities of demand for X_3, *w.r.t.* P_1, P_2 and P_3 at $P_1 = 8$, $P_2 = 7$ and $P_3 = 4$. (b) State whether X_3 commodity is a competitive or complementay with the commodities X_1 and X_2.

This requires to evaluate e_{31}, e_{32}, e_{33}. These elasticities are evaluated as follows:

$$e_{31} = \frac{\partial X_3}{\partial P_1} \times \frac{P_1}{X_3} = \frac{\partial}{\partial P_1}\left[7.3 + 0.2P_1 + 0.5P_2 - 0.4P_3\right] \times \frac{P_1}{X_3}$$

$$e_{31} = \frac{0.2\,(P_1)}{X_3} = \frac{0.2\,P_1}{7.3 + 2\,P_1 + 0.5\,P_2 - 0.4\,P_3}$$

For $P_1 = 8$, $P_2 = 7$, $P_3 = 4$,

$$e_{31} = \frac{(0.2)\,(8)}{7.3 + 0.2\,(8) + 0.5\,(7) - 0.4\,(4)} = \frac{1.6}{10.8} = 0.148 > 0$$

$$e_{32} = \frac{\partial X_3}{\partial P_2} \times \frac{P_2}{X_3} = \frac{\partial}{\partial P_2}(-7.3 + 0.2\,P_1 + 0.5\,P_2 - 0.4\,P_3) \times \frac{P_2}{X_3}$$

$$e_{32} = \frac{P_2}{X_3} \times (0.5) = \frac{0.5 \times 7}{10.8} = \frac{3.5}{10.8} = 0.324 > 0$$

$$e_{33} = \frac{\partial X_3}{\partial P_3} \times \frac{P_3}{X_3} = (-0.4) \times \frac{P_3}{X_3} = \frac{(-0.4)\,(4)}{10.8} = \frac{-1.6}{10.8} = -0.148 < 0$$

Since cross partial derivatives e_{31} and e_{32} are positive, and X_1 and X_2 are substitutes for commodity X_3

The demand curve for X_3 is negatively sloped for $e_{33} < 0$ because $\frac{\partial X_3}{\partial P_3} < 0$,

(5) The demand function for two goods q_1 and q_2 are given as

$$q_1 = \frac{50}{P_1\sqrt{P_2}} \text{ and } q_2 = \frac{200}{P_2\sqrt[3]{P_1}}$$ where P_1 and P_2 are per unit prices of q_1 and q_2 goods.

Find whether q_1 and q_2 are two competitive or complementary goods. Find the elasticties of demand for q_1 and q_2 with respect to their own prices.

Given $q_1 = \dfrac{50}{P_1\sqrt{P_2}} = \dfrac{50}{P_1 P_2^{\frac{1}{2}}} = 50\, P_1^{-1}\, P_2^{-\frac{1}{2}}$

The cross partial elasticity of demand for q_1 *w.r.t* p_2 is given as e_{12} where

$$e_{12} = \frac{\partial q_1}{\partial P_2} \times \frac{P_2}{q_1} \text{ and } \frac{\partial q_1}{\partial P_2} = (50)\left(-\frac{1}{2}\right) P_1^{-1}\, P_2^{-\frac{1}{2}-1} = -25\, P_1^{-1} P_2^{-\frac{3}{2}}$$

$$e_{12} = (-25\, P_1^{-1}\, P_2^{-\frac{3}{2}}) \times \frac{P_2}{q_1} = \frac{-25\, P_1^{-1}\, P_2^{-\frac{3}{2}}\, P_2}{\dfrac{50}{P_1\sqrt{P_2}}}$$

$$= \frac{-25\, P_1^{-1}\, P_2^{-\frac{3}{2}}\, P_1^{1}\, P_2\, P_2^{\frac{1}{2}}}{50} = \frac{-25\, P_1^{0}\, P_2^{0}}{50} = -\frac{1}{2} = -0.5 < 0$$

The cross partial elasticity of demand for q_2 *w.r.t.* P_1 is given as e_{21} where

$$e_{21} = \frac{\partial q_2}{\partial P_1} \times \frac{P_1}{q_2},\ \frac{\partial q_2}{\partial P_1} = \frac{\partial}{\partial P_1}\left[\frac{200}{P_2\, P_1^{\frac{1}{3}}}\right] = \frac{\partial}{\partial P_1}\left[200\, P_2^{-1}\, P_1^{-\frac{1}{3}}\right]$$

$$= \frac{-200}{3} P_2^{-1}\, P_1^{-\frac{1}{3}-1} = \frac{-200}{3}\, P_2^{-1}\, P_1^{-\frac{4}{3}}$$

$$e_{21} = \frac{-200\, P_2^{-1}\, P_1^{-\frac{4}{3}}}{3} \times \frac{P_1}{q_2} = \frac{-200\, P_2^{-1}\, P_1^{-\frac{4}{3}} P_1}{\dfrac{3(200)}{P_2\, P_1^{\frac{1}{3}}}}$$

$$= -\frac{(200)\, P_2^{-1}\, P_1^{-\frac{4}{3}}\, P_1\, P_2\, P_1^{\frac{1}{3}}}{3\,(200)} = -\frac{P_2^{0}\, P_1^{0}}{3} = -\frac{1}{3} = -0.333 < 0$$

Since cross partial derivatives are negative, it implies that q_1 and q_2 are two complementary goods. The elasticity of demand q_1 *w.r.t.* its own price P_1 is e_{11} and elasticity of demand for q_2 *w.r.t.* P_2 is e_{22}. These elasticities are evaluated and found negative.

$$e_{11} = \frac{\partial q_1}{\partial P_1} \times \frac{P_1}{q_1} = \frac{\partial}{\partial P_1}\left[50\, P_1^{-1}\, P_2^{-\frac{1}{2}}\right] \times \frac{P_1}{q_1}$$

$$= \frac{-50\, P_1^{-2}\, P_2^{-\frac{1}{2}}\, P_1}{\dfrac{50}{P_1\, P_2^{\frac{1}{2}}}} = \frac{-50\, P_1^{-2}\, P_2^{-\frac{1}{2}}\, P_1\, P_1\, P_2^{\frac{1}{2}}}{50} = -1 < 0$$

$$e_{22} = \frac{\partial q_2}{\partial P_2} \times \frac{P_2}{q_2} = \frac{\partial}{\partial P_2}\left[200\, P_2^{-1}\, P_1^{-\frac{1}{3}}\right] \times \frac{P_2}{q_2} = \frac{-200\, P_2^{-2}\, P_1^{-\frac{1}{3}}\, P_2\, P_2\, P_1^{\frac{1}{3}}}{200} = -1 < 0$$

(6) The estimated demand function for commodity q_1 is $q_1 = 175.3\, y^{0.82} p_1^{-0.76} p_2^{0.8}$, where y = income, p_1 = Price of q_1 and p_2 is price of q_2 commodity.

(a) Find the income elasticity of demand for q_1.

(b) If income increases by 1000 rupees, how much of this increased income will be spent in q_1? State the reason for that.

(c) Find the cross partial elasticities of demand.

(d) What happens to the quantity demanded for q_1 if price of q_2 decreases but price of q_1 or P_1 remaining the same and why?

G $q_1 = 175.3\, y^{0.82} p_1^{-0.76} p_2^{0.8}$, Income elasticity of demand for q_1 is (e_y)

$$e_y = \frac{\partial q_1}{\partial y} \times \frac{y}{q_1},\ \frac{\partial q_1}{\partial y} = \frac{\partial}{\partial y}\left[175.3 y^{0.82} p_1^{-0.76} p_2^{0.8}\right] = 143.75 y^{-0.18} p_1^{-0.76} p_2^{0.8}$$

$$e_y = \frac{143.75\, y^{-0.18} p_1^{-0.76} p_2^{0.8}\, y}{175.3\, y^{0.82}\, p_1^{-0.76}\, p_2^{0.8}} = \frac{143.75}{175.3} = 0.82 > 0$$

(b) Since income elasticity of demand is positive, the commodity q_1 is a superior good. When income increases by Rs. 1000, the consumer will spend (0.82) (1000) = Rs. 820 out of Rs.1000 on commodity q_1. This is shown by

$$\Delta E = e_y(\Delta y) = 0.82 \times 1000 = \text{Rs. } 820.\ \therefore \Delta E = \text{Rs. } 820$$

(c) Cross partial elasticity of demand is given by e_{12} where.

$$e_{12} = \frac{\partial q_1}{\partial P_2} \times \frac{P_2}{q_1} = \frac{\partial}{\partial P_2}\left[175.3\, y^{0.82} p_1^{-0.76} p_2^{0.8}\right] \times \frac{P_2}{q_1}$$

$$= \frac{(175.3)(0.8)\, y^{0.82} p_1^{-0.76} p_2^{-0.2} p_2}{175.3 y^{0.82}\, p_1^{-0.76}\, p_2^{0.8}} = 0.8 > 0$$

Since $e_{12} = 0.8 > 0$, any rise in price of q_2 will lead to a rise in quantity demanded for q_1 as $\frac{\partial q_1}{\partial P_2} > 0$. q_1 and q_2 are two competitive goods.

7.3. Applications of Partial Derivatives in Utility Analysis

(1) If the utility function is given as $U = f(q_1\ q_2) = 3q_1^2 + 2q_1 q_2 + q_2^2$

Find MU of q_1 and q_2 at $q_1 = 1$ and $q_2 = 2$ for given $U = 3q_1^2 + 2q_1q_2 + q_2^2$

$$MU_{q_1} = \frac{\partial U}{\partial q_1} = 6q_1 + 2q_2,\ MU_{q_2} = \frac{\partial U}{\partial q_2} = 2q_1 + 2q_2$$

For $q_1 = 1, q_2 = 2$, $MU_{q1} = 6(1) + 2(2) = 10$, $MU_{q_2} = 2(1) + 2(2) = 6$.

(2) If $U = f(x, y) = a\,x + b\,y + c\sqrt{x\,y}$, Determine the marginal rate of commodity substitution of two goods $'x'$ and $'y'$ ($MRCS$)

For given $U = f(x, y)$, the indifference curve representing various alternative combinations of x and y goods will yield the same level of satisfaction to the consumer.

In terms of partial derivative it means the total differential of U *w.r.t.* $'x'$ and $'y'$ is zero. $\therefore\ \partial u = 0$.

$$\partial U = \frac{\partial}{\partial x} f(x, y)\,\partial x + \frac{\partial}{\partial y} f(x, y)\,\partial y = 0.$$

or $f_1(x, y)\partial x + f_2(x, y)\,\partial y = f_1\,\partial x + f_2\,\partial y = 0$. Rearranging this we get,

$$-\frac{\partial y}{\partial x} = \frac{f_1}{f_2},\ \text{where } f_1 = MU_x \text{ and } f_2 = MU_y, \text{ and } -\frac{\partial y}{\partial x} = MRCS$$

For we are given $U = a\,x + b\,y + c\sqrt{x\,y}$

$$\frac{\partial U}{\partial x} = a + \frac{1}{2} c\,(x\,y)^{\frac{1}{2}}(y) = a + \frac{c\,y}{2\sqrt{x\,y}} = \frac{2\,a\sqrt{x\,y} + c\,y}{2\sqrt{x\,y}}$$

$$\frac{\partial U}{\partial x} = b + \frac{1}{2} c\,(x, y)^{\frac{1}{2}}(x) = b + \frac{c\,x}{2\sqrt{x\,y}} = \frac{2b\sqrt{x\,y} + c\,x}{2\sqrt{x\,y}}$$

$$-\frac{\partial y}{\partial x} = MRCS = \frac{\partial U/\partial x}{\partial U/\partial y} = \frac{2a\sqrt{x\,y} + cy}{2b\sqrt{x\,y} + cx}$$

7.4. Partial Derivatives and the Production Functions

(1) The production function of a commodity is given $q = f(K,L)$, where K = capital, L = labour and q is output. If the production function is $q = 10L + 5K - 2L^2 + 5K^2 + 7KL$, find MP of labour and capital. Evaluate them at $L = 2$ and K = 3 units.

For $q = 10L + 5K - 2L^2 + 5K^2 + 7KL$

$$MP_k = \frac{\partial q}{\partial k} = 5 + 10K + 7L \text{ and } MP_L = \frac{\partial q}{\partial L} = 10 - 4L + 7K$$

For given K = 3 and $L = 2$, $MP_k = \frac{\partial q}{\partial k} = 5 + 10K + 7L = 5 + 10\,(3) + 7\,(2) = 49$ and

$$MP_L = \frac{\partial q}{\partial L} = 10 - 4L + 7K = 10 - 8 + 21 = 23$$

(2) When the production function of a commodity x is $X = f(a, b, c)$ where $a, b, c,$ are some quantities of inputs A, B and C and output is X, determine the marginal products of these inputs and evaluate them if $a = b = c = 2$

$X = 12a + 20b + 5c - 2a^2 + 2b^2 + ab^2c^2$

$$MP_a = \frac{\partial X}{\partial a} = 12 - 4a + b^2c^2,\ MP_b = \frac{\partial X}{\partial b} = 20 + 4b + 2abc^2 \text{ and } MP_c = \frac{\partial X}{\partial c} = 5 + 2ab^2c$$

For given $a = b = c = 2$,

$MP_a = 12 - 4(2) + (2)^2\ (2)^2 = 20$, $MP_b = 20 + 4(2) + 2(2)\ (2)\ (2)^2 = 60$ and

$MP_c = 5 + 2\ (2)\ (2)^2\ (2) = 37.$

(3) If the production function is given by $Q = f(K,L,N,)$ where N =Land, K= Capital, L= Labour, find marginal products of these inputs for $N = 1$, $K = 2$, $L = 2$

$$Q = f(K,L,N) = 75N + 50K - N^2 - 4K^2 - 5NL + 3LK$$

$\frac{\partial Q}{\partial N} = MP_N = 75 - 2N - 5L$. At N = 1, K = 2 and L = 2,

Marginal product of land = $\frac{\partial Q}{\partial N} = MP_N = 75 - 2N - 5L = 63$

$$\frac{\partial Q}{\partial K} = MP_K = 50 - 8K + 3L = 40,\ \frac{\partial Q}{\partial L} = MP_L = -5N + 3K = 1$$

Marginal productivities of land, capital and labour are 63, 40 and 1 respectively.

(4) If the production function is $Q = f(K,L) = AL^{\alpha}K^{\beta}$, Find marginal and average proiducts of labour and capital.

We are given $Q = f(K,L) = AL^{\alpha}K^{\beta}$, their marginal products are

$$MP_L = \frac{\partial Q}{\partial L} = \frac{\partial}{\partial L}\left[AL^{\alpha}K^{\beta}\right] = \alpha AL^{\alpha-1}K^{\beta} = \alpha\left(\frac{Q}{L}\right) = \alpha(AP_L)$$

$$MP_K = \frac{\partial Q}{\partial K} = \frac{\partial}{\partial K}\left[AL^{\alpha}K^{\beta}\right] = \beta AL^{\alpha}K^{\beta-1} = \beta\left(\frac{Q}{K}\right) = \beta(AP_K)$$

$$AP_L = \frac{Q}{L} = \frac{AL^{\alpha}K^{\beta}}{L} = AL^{\alpha-1}K^{\beta},\quad AP_K = \frac{Q}{K} = \frac{AL^{\alpha}K^{\beta}}{K} = AL^{\alpha}K^{\beta-1}$$

(5) The production function for commodity q is given as

$q = f(x\,y) = 2.03x^{0.58}y^{0.42}$, Find MP and AP of inputs x and y

$$MP_x = \frac{\partial q}{\partial x} = (2.03)\ (0.58)\ x^{-0.42}y^{0.42} = 1.177\left(\frac{y}{x}\right)^{0.42}$$

$$AP_x = \frac{q}{x} = \frac{2.03^{0.58}\,y^{0.42}}{x} = 2.03\ x^{-0.42}y^{0.42} = 2.03\left(\frac{y}{x}\right)^{0.42}$$

$$MP_y = \frac{\partial q}{\partial y} = (2.03)(0.42)x^{0.58}y^{-0.58} = 0.853\left(\frac{x}{y}\right)^{0.58}$$

$$AP_y = \frac{q}{y} = \frac{2.03^{0.58}y^{0.42}}{y} = 2.03\ x^{0.58}y^{-0.58} = 2.03\left(\frac{x}{y}\right)^{0.58}$$

7.5. Homogeneous Production Functions

Homogeneous production functions and constant elasticity of substitution (CES) production functions are relevant to study in economics as they are very often used in theory of firm. The Cobb-Douglas production function is an empirically established one for the firm. These functions have got some special characteristics that make them amenable to algebraic treatment. From economic theory we have learnt that output increases in some proportion to the increase in inputs. There are increasing, constant and decreasing returns to scale the frim can experience in the long run. Returns to scale can be increasing when a given increase in all inputs in certain porpotion results in to a greater increase in the propotion of output. In case of constnat returns, inputs and output increase in the same propotion. When returns to scale is decreasing output will increase in a propotion less than the propotionate increase in inputs.

For given a typical production function $q = f(a, b)$, where *'a'* and *'b'* are units of inputs A and B used to produce output q. When both these inputs are increased by a constant *'t'*, the output *'q'* will increase by the amount *'t'* raises to the power *'k'*. Thus production function becomes $f = (ta, tb) = t^k f(a, b) = t^k q$. The production function exhibits an increase in output by t^k times the original output q, when both the inputs are increased by constant *'t'*. The above production function is said to be homogeneous of degree k.

Returns to scale is said to be increasing if $k > 1$, decreasing if $k < 1$ and constant when $k = 1$. The production function is homogenous of degree one is a common type of prodction function. It is the empirically found production function. This type of production function is also named linear homogeneous production function

7.5.1. Illustrations Exhibiting Homogenous Production Functions

(1) For $q = f(x, y)$, the independent variables (inputs) are x and y while the dependent variable is *'q'*, the final product. When these independent variables are increased by a fixed proportion *'t'*, the original function q changes to t^k times q by $t^k q$.

Suppose the original function given is , $q = f(x,y) = \frac{x^2}{y^2} + \frac{y^2}{x^2}$.

$$f(tx, ty) = \frac{(tx)^2}{(ty)^2} + \frac{(ty)^2}{(tx)^2} = \frac{t^2x^2}{t^2y^2} + \frac{t^2y^2}{t^2x^2} = t^0\left[\frac{x^2}{y^2} + \frac{y^2}{x^2}\right] = t^0 q = q.$$

The above function $q = \frac{x^2}{y^2} + \frac{y^2}{x^2}$ is said to be homogeneous of degree zero since there is no change in the original function consequent upon the variables increased by *'t'* times. The function raises to the power of 't' which is equal to zero. This gets multiplied by the original function. Thus the function is said to be homogeneous of degree zero.

(2) Given $Z = f(x,y) = x^2 - y^2$, find whether it is homogeneous or not when inputs, x and y are increased by *'t'*.

The given function changes to

$f(tx, ty) = (xt)^2 - (yt)^2 = t^2(x^2 - y^2) = t^2 Z$. The function Z is homogeneous of degree 2.

(3) Given $Z = f(x, y) = \sqrt{3x^2 + 2xy - 5y^2}$, Establish its homogeneity if possible.

Given $Z = f(x, y) = \sqrt{3x^2 + 2xy - 5y^2}$, if the 'x' and 'y' increase by 't',

$tZ = ft(x, y) = f(tx, ty) = \sqrt{3(tx)^2 + 2(tx)(ty) - 5(ty)^2}$

$= \sqrt{3t^2x^2 + 2t^2xy - 5t^2y^2} = t\sqrt{3x^2 + 2xy - 5y^2} = tZ$

This exhibits that when 'x' and 'y' are increased by a constant 't', the original function is increased by 't' times Z. This function is said to be homogeneous of degree one.

(4) If the function is $Z = f(a, b) = a^3 + 3a^2b + 3ab^2 + b^3$, test the homogeneity of the function.

To test the homogeneity of the above function we need to change the original function to 't' times Z so that the function becomes $f(ta, tb) = (ta)^3 + 3(ta)^2(tb) + 3(ta)(tb)^2 + (tb)^3$

$= t^3a^3 + 3a^2bt^3 + 3t^3ab^2 + t^3b^3 = t^3[a^3 + 3a^2b + 3ab^2 + b^3] = t^3 Z$

Thus as independent variables a and b are increased by constant 't', the original function Z is increased by t^3 times Z. The function therefore is homogeneous of degree 3.

7.5.2. Non-Homogeneous Functions

It can be verified that all functions are not homogeneous. Thus when independent variables are increased by a fixed proportion, the function does not increase always by t^k times the original function. This case refers to the functions which are called non-homogeneous functions.

Following illustrations are extended to establish this.

(1) $Z = 3x^2 + x^2y + xy^2 + y^3 = f(x, y)$, Establish the degree of homogeneity of this function.

For establishing degree of homogeneity we need to find whether or not the given function is homogeneous. This requires us to multiply the indepedent variables by some constant say 't' so that the given function changes to, $Zt = 3x^2t^2 + x^2yt^3 + y^3t^3 = t^2[3x^2 + x^2yt + xy^2t + y^3t] \# t^2Z$

Since $3x^2x^2yt + xy^2t + y^3t \# Z$, it is a non-honogeneous function.

(2) $Z = f(x_1 x_2) = x_1^3 + x_1 x_2 + x_2^2$, Establish its degree of homogeneity.

To determine the degree of homogeneity we can find first whether or not the given function is homogeneous. This requires to multiply the indepedent variables by constant 't' so that

$Zt = (tx_1, tx_2) = (x_1t)^3 + (x_1t)(x_2t) + (x_2t)^2$

$= x_1^3t^3 + x_1x_2t^2 + x_2^2t^2 = t^2[x_1^3t + x_1x_2 + x_2^2] \neq t^2 f(x_1 x_2) \neq t^2 Z.$

Thus the given function is not a homogeneous one.

7.5.3. Establish the Degree of Homogeneity for the Following Functions

(1) $Q = f(x_1 x_2) = x_1^{0.64} x_2^{0.36}$, Multiplying a constant 't' we get

$(t x_1, t x_2) = (x_1 t)^{0.64} (x_2 t)^{0.36} = x_1^{0.64} x_2^{0.36} t^{0.64+0.36} = t x_1^{0.64} x_2^{0.36} = tQ$

The function its homogeneous of degree one as the original function changes to $t^1 Q$.

(2) $Q = f(L, K) = 0.78\ L^{0.68}\ K^{0.24}$. Given this function we need to multiplying it by a constant 't'

$f_1(tk, tl) = 0.78(tL)^{0.68}(Kt)^{0.24} = t^{0.92}[0.78 L^{0.68} K^{0.24}] = t^{0.92} f(K, L) = t^{0.92} Z$,

Since Z changes to Z $t^{0.92,}$ the function its homogeneous of degree $0.92 < 1$.

(3) $Q = f(K, L) = K^{\alpha} L^{1-\alpha} + AL + BK$, Changing it by tQ, we get

$f(tK, tL) = (Kt)^{\alpha}(Lt)^{1-\alpha} + A(Lt) + B(Kt) = K^{\alpha}\ L^{1-\alpha}\ t^{\alpha+1-\alpha} + ALt + BKt$

$= t[K^{\alpha} L^{1-\alpha} + AL + Bk] = t f(K.L) = tQ.$

This function is homogeneous of degree one as 't' raises to the power 1.

(4) $Z = f(a, b, c, d) = \sqrt[3]{3a - b + 7c - 5d}$, multiplying by 't' we get

$f(ta, tb, tc, td) = \sqrt[3]{3(at) - (bt) + 7(ct) - 5(dt)}$

$= \sqrt[3]{t[3a - b + 7c - 5d]} = \sqrt[3]{t}.\sqrt[3]{3a - b + 7c - 5d} = t^{\frac{1}{3}} f(a, b, c, d) = t^{\frac{1}{3}} Z.$

The function is thus homogenous of degree $\frac{1}{3}$ for 't' raises to $\frac{1}{3}$

(5) $f(x, y) = \dfrac{3Hxy - \alpha x^2 + \beta y^2}{K_1 x + K_1 y}$, where $H, \alpha, \beta, K_1, K_2$ are constants.

To test homogeneity we change the function by multiplying it by constant 't' so that we get

$$f(tx, ty) = \frac{3H(tx)(ty) - \alpha(tx)^2 + \beta(ty)^2}{K_1(tx) + K_2(ty)}$$

$$= \frac{t^2[3Hxy - \alpha x^2 + \beta y^2]}{t[K_1 x + K_2 y]} = t f(x, y) = tZ.$$

The function is homogenous of degree one.

7.6. The Cobb-Douglas Production Function

The Cobb-Douglas production function is used for attempting an empirical verification of the marginal productivity theory of distribution. This production function has fulfilled the postulates of Euler's theorem, which states that total product gets exhausted when factors are rewarded according to their marginal physical productivity. The economists C. W. Cobb and P. H.Douglas have given a generalised type of production function for manufacturing sector. This is given by $q = A K^{\alpha} L^{\beta}$, where '$q$' is total output, K = Capital,

L = Labour, A, α and β are positive constants. This production function $q = A K^{\alpha} L^{\beta}$ is homogeneous of degree α + β. When α + β = 1, it becomes a linearly homogeneous production function

For $q = A k^{\alpha} L^{1-\alpha}, if\ (\alpha+\beta)=1,\ \beta = 1-\alpha$. This production function posseses the following features :

(a) It satisfies Euler's theorem. It states that for $q = A k^{\alpha} L^{1-\alpha}$, it can be established that

$K(MP_K) + L(MP_L) = q$. We need to prove that $K\dfrac{\partial q}{\partial K} + L\dfrac{\partial q}{\partial L} = q$. This is shown below:

$$K\,[\alpha A K^{\alpha-1} L^{1-\alpha}] + L\,[(1-\alpha) A K^{\alpha} L^{-\alpha}] = \alpha A K^{\alpha} L^{1-\alpha} + (1-\alpha) A K^{\alpha} L^{1-\alpha}$$

$$= A K^{\alpha} L^{1-\alpha}\,[\alpha + (1-\alpha)] = A K^{\alpha} L^{1-\alpha} = q.$$

This production function exhibits that the total output *'q'* is distributed between the inputs Labour and Capital in the respective proportion of (1− α) and α. Prof. Douglas has estimated α from the time series data and found that it represents the share of capital while (1− α) shows share of labour in the total output.

(b) α and (1− α) also represent the elasticity of output (Q), *w.r.t.* Capital and labour respectively.

Accordingly Labour elasticity of output is given by:

$$L_e = \frac{MP_L}{AP_L} = \frac{\partial q/\partial L}{q/L} = \frac{(1-\alpha) A K^{\alpha} L^{-\alpha}}{A K^{\alpha} L^{1-\alpha}/L} = \frac{(1-\alpha) A K^{\alpha} L^{1-\alpha}}{A K^{\alpha} L^{1-\alpha}} = (1-\alpha)$$

Similarly Capital elasticity of output is evaluated as

$$K_e = \frac{MP_K}{AP_K} = \frac{\partial q/\partial K}{q/K} = \frac{\alpha A K^{\alpha-1} L^{1-\alpha}}{A K^{\alpha} L^{1-\alpha}/K} = \frac{\alpha A K^{\alpha} L^{1-\alpha}}{A K^{\alpha} L^{1-\alpha}} = \alpha$$

$$\therefore \alpha = \frac{MP_K}{AP_K},\ MP_K = \alpha\frac{q}{K} = \alpha AP_k \text{ and } (1-\alpha) = \frac{MP_L}{AP_L},\ MP_L = (1-\alpha)\frac{q}{L} = (1-\alpha) AP_L$$

The firm is in equilibrium at the point where the prevailing wage rate (W) is equal to the Value of Marginal Product (VMP), where VMP = Price × MP of the factor input labour.

$\therefore W = (MP_L)(P)$, where P = price of the product. From $W = (1-\alpha)\dfrac{q}{L}P$, we get $(1-\alpha) = \dfrac{WL}{Pq}$.

This represent the percentage share of labour in total output. WL is the total wage bill and *'pq'* is the total revenue of the firm. In a similar process, we can obtain the percentage share of capital in total revenue of the firm, which is obtained as

$$\alpha = \frac{MP_K}{AP_K}, \text{ or } MP_K = \frac{\alpha q}{K} = \frac{i}{P},\ \therefore \frac{\alpha q}{K} = \frac{i}{P},\ \alpha = \frac{iK}{pq}$$

Thus *'iK'* is the total payment to Capital. $\dfrac{iK}{pq}$ is the share of Capital in total output or total revenue *(pq)*. The exponents α and (1 − α) thus represent the share of capital and labour in total output. They stand for the elasticity of output with respect to the respective inputs, capital and labour.

7.7. Elasticity of Substitution for Cobb-Douglas Production Function

The general form of Cobb-Douglas production function is given as $Q = A\,K^{\alpha}\,L^{\beta}$. If Prices of inputs capital and labour are denoted as r_1 and r_2, the elasticity of substitution is given by the following formula:

$$\sigma = \frac{\left(\frac{L}{K}\right)\partial\left(\frac{K}{L}\right)}{\left(\frac{r_2}{r_1}\right)\partial\left(\frac{r_1}{r_2}\right)},$$ where 'σ' stands for the elasticity of substitution.

Firm is in equilibrium when, $\frac{r_1}{r_2} = \frac{f_L}{f_K}$ from this we can define

$$\frac{r_1}{r_2} = \frac{f_L}{f_K} = \frac{\beta A K^{\alpha} L^{\beta-1}}{\alpha A\,K^{\alpha-1}\,L^{\beta}} = \frac{\beta A K^{\alpha}\,K^{\beta}\,.\,K}{\alpha\,AK^{\alpha}\,L^{\beta}\,L} = \left(\frac{\beta}{\alpha}\right)\left(\frac{K}{L}\right)$$

$$\therefore \frac{r_1}{r_2} = \frac{\beta}{\alpha}\frac{K}{L} \text{ or } \frac{r_2}{r_1} = \frac{\alpha}{\beta}\frac{L}{K}.$$

$$\sigma = \frac{\left(\frac{L}{K}\right)\partial\left(\frac{K}{L}\right)}{\left(\frac{r_2}{r_1}\right)\partial\left(\frac{r_1}{r_2}\right)} = \frac{\left(\frac{L}{K}\right)\partial\left(\frac{K}{L}\right)}{\left(\frac{\alpha}{\beta}.\frac{L}{K}\right)\partial\left(\frac{\beta}{\alpha}.\frac{K}{L}\right)} = \frac{\left(\frac{L}{K}\right)\partial\left(\frac{K}{L}\right)}{\left(\frac{\alpha}{\beta}.\frac{\beta}{\alpha}\right)\frac{L}{K}\partial\left(\frac{K}{L}\right)} = 1$$

$\therefore$ σ = 1, for α + β = 1.

However it can also be verified that σ = 1, even if Cobb-Douglas production function is homogeneous of degree α + β, which is not a linear in itself. It is only when α + β = 1 so that β = 1 – α, the production function is a linear homogeneous one.

The value of σ is significant as it shows the degree of substitution between inputs, capital and labour. Thus σ lies between 0 and infinity (∞). When σ = 0, two given inputs can not be substituted. Wwhen σ = ∞, the two factors are said to be perfect substitutes. If σ approaches ∞, the iso-quant tends to be flatter and for σ approaches zero, iso-quant tends to be vertical parallel to *Y*– axis.

For linearly homogenous production functions, σ = 1. Therefore for Cobb-Douglas productions function of type $Q = AK^{\alpha}\,L^{1-\alpha}$ we will always get σ = 1.

But all linear homoencoes production functions do not have unitary elasticity of substitution, σ = 1. It can be exhibited that the production function which is a linear homogeneous one, but it does not possess unitary elasticity of substitution. It depicts a constant elasticity of substitution i.e., σ ≠ 1, but it is constant.

7.8. Joint Products

A producer normally produces only one product (q_1) and sells it in the market at price (P_1) for maximizing profit. His profit unction is defined by $\pi = R - C$, where *R* is the revenue while *C* stands for total cost. The firm maximizes π, *w.r.t.* output (q_1), The conditions laid down for profit maximization are $\frac{\partial \pi}{\partial q} = 0$ and $\frac{\partial^2 \pi}{\partial q^2} < 0$.

This will determine the equilibrium output the firm produces. However these conditions of profit maximization are slightly modified when there is imposition of tax or granting of subsidy by the government. Accordingly equilibrium price, quantity and levels of profit also changes

But how does a firm recahes equlibrium when there is a case of multiple production is important to study. The conditions for profit maximization under the situation of multiple products porduced by the entrepreneur need to be detremined. For simplicity let us assume that the firm who is producing two products q_1 and q_2. These are to be sold at unit prices P_1 and P_2 respectively in the market. The firm will maximize profit under this situation when demand functions for q_1 and q_2 and the joint cost function are given to him. Following illustrations are expalined to examine this situation.

For given $R = f(q_1 q_2) = R_1 (q_1) + R_2 (q_2)$ and $C = C(q_1 q_2)$, where *'C'* represents the joint cost function of the firm. R stands for revenue. The revenue and profit function are given as

$R_1 (q_1) = p_1 q_1$ and $R_2 (q_2) = p_2 q_2$ so that $\pi = R - C = P_1 q_1 + P_2 q_2 - C$

Following necessary and sufficient conditions are to be fulfilled for profit maximization.

The necessary condition requires

$\frac{\partial \pi}{\partial q_1} = 0$ and $\frac{\partial \pi}{\partial q_2} = 0.$, while the second-order or sufficient conditon requires

$$\frac{\partial^2 \pi}{\partial q_1^2} < 0, \quad \frac{\partial^2 \pi}{\partial q_2^2} < 0, \text{ and } \left(\frac{\partial^2 \pi}{\partial q_1^2}\right)\left(\frac{\partial^2 \pi}{\partial q_2^2}\right) > \left(\frac{\partial^2 \pi}{\partial q_1 \partial q_2}\right)^2$$

Illustrations:

(1) The joint cost function of the firm is given $C = x^2 + xy + 3y^2$, where *'x'* and *'y'* are two different products the firm produces. The per unit market prices are Rs. 7 and Rs. 20 respectively for *x* and *y*.

Find profit maximizing outputs of '*x*' and '*y*' the firm wll produce .

Firm's profit function is defined as $\pi = R - C$, where $R = R_1 (x) + R_2 (y)$

Since we are given $p_1 = 7$ and $p_2 = 20$, $\therefore = R = 7x + 20y$ and $C = x^2 + xy + 3y^2$

Accordingly $\pi = R - C = 7x + 20y - x^2 - xy - 3y^2$.

Maximizing π, *w.r.t* the output '*x*' and '*y*' we get

$$\frac{\partial \pi}{\partial x} = 7 - 2x - y = 0 \text{ or } 2x + y = 7 \quad \text{..........(1)}$$

$$\frac{\partial \pi}{\partial y} = 20 - x - 6y = 0 \text{ or } x + 6y = 20 \quad \text{..........(2)}$$

Solving (1) and (2) are get,

$2x + y = 7$ and

$-(2x + 12y = 40)$

This gives $-11y = -33$ and $y = 3$.

Substituting the value of *'y'* in equation (1) we get, $2x + y = 7$ and $x = 2$. We need to examine the second-order conditions whic are given by

$$\frac{\partial^2 \pi}{\partial x^2} = -2 < 0, \quad \frac{\partial^2 \pi}{\partial y^2} = -6 < 0, \quad \frac{\partial^2 \pi}{\partial x \partial y} = -1, \quad \frac{\partial^2 \pi}{\partial y \partial x} = -1 \text{ and}$$

$$\left(\frac{\partial^2\pi}{\partial x^2}\right)\left(\frac{\partial^2\pi}{\partial y^2}\right)>\left(\frac{\partial^2\pi}{\partial y\partial x}\right)^2 \text{ as } (-2)(-6) > (-1)^2 \text{ or } 12 > 1$$

So the sufficient condition for π maximization are also fulfilled.

From this we get firm's profit maximizing quantities of output x and y as . $x = 2$ and $y = 3$.

Maximum profit at these levels of output produced are given by

$\pi = 7x + 20y - x^2 - xy - 3y^2 = 7(2) + 20(3) - (2)^2 - (2)(3) - 3(3)^2 = 37$

(2) If the demand functions for two commodities x_1 and x_2 are given as

$x_1 = 42 - 2P_1 - P_2$ and $x_2 = 48 - P_1 - 2P_2$ and the average cost of production for x_1 and x_2 are *Rs*. 3 and *Rs*. 2 respectively, determine the prices and quantities of x_1 and x_2 that will maximize profit of the firm.

For average costs we get total cost function is $C = AC_{x_1} \times x_1 + AC x_2 \times x_2 = 3x_1 + 2x_2$ and $\pi = R - C = R_1(x_1) + R_2(x_2) - C$.

From $x_1 = 42 - 2P_1 - P_2$ and $x_2 = 48 - P_1 - 2P_2$, one can obtain

$R_1(x_1) = P_1 x_1 = P_1(42 - 2P_1 - P_2) = 42P_1 - 2P_1^2 - P_1 P_2$

$R_2(x_2) = P_2 x_2 = P_2(48 - P_1 - 2P_2) = 48P_2 - P_1 P_2 - 2P_2^2$

$C = 3x_1 + 2x_2 = 3(42 - 2P_1 - P_2) + 2(48 - P_1 - 2P_2)$

$= 126 - 6P_1 - 3P_2 + 96 - 2P_1 - 4P_2 = 222 - 8P_1 - 7P_2$

$\pi = R - C = 42P_1 - 2P_1^2 - P_1 P_2 + 48P_2 - P_1 P_2 - 2P_2^2 - 222 + 8P_1 + 7P_2$

$\pi = 50P_1 - 2P_1^2 - 2P_1 P_2 + 55P_2 - 2P_2^2 - 222$. For profit maximum apply the derivatives,

$$\frac{\partial\pi}{\partial P_1} = 50 - 4P_1 - 2P_2 = 0. \text{ or } 4P_1 + 2P_2 = 50 \quad \ldots\ldots\ldots\ldots\ldots (1)$$

$$\frac{\partial\pi}{\partial P_2} = -2P_1 + 55 - 4P_2 = 0. \text{ or } 2P_1 + 4P_2 = 55 \ldots\ldots\ldots\ldots\ldots\ldots (2)$$

The second order conditions are also verified to:

$$\left(\frac{\partial^2\pi}{\partial P_1^2}\right)\left(\frac{\partial^2\pi}{\partial P_2^2}\right)>\left(\frac{\partial^2\pi}{\partial P_1\partial P_2}\right)^2,$$

$$\frac{\partial^2\pi}{\partial P_1^2} = -4 < 0, \quad \frac{\partial^2\pi}{\partial P_2^2} = -4 < 0$$

$$\frac{\partial^2 \pi}{\partial P_1 \partial P_2} = \frac{\partial^2 \pi}{\partial P_2 \partial P_1} = -2, \text{ and } \left(\frac{\partial^2 \pi}{\partial P_1^2}\right)\left(\frac{\partial^2 \pi}{\partial P_2^2}\right) > \left(\frac{\partial^2 \pi}{\partial P_1 \partial P_2}\right)^2 \text{ as } (-4)(-4) > (-2)^2 \text{ or } 16 > 4.$$

Profit maximizing prices are obtained by solving equations 1 and 2. These are

$4P_1 + 2P_2 = 50$ (1) and $2P_1 + 4P_2 = 55$. (2)

Multiplying equation 2 by 2 and subtracting it from 1 we get,

$4P_1 + 2P_2 = 50$, and $-(4P_1 + 8P_2 = 110)$ so that $-6P_2 = -60$, and $\therefore P_2 = 10$.

Substituing this we can obtain P_1. This is obatined as $2P_1 = 55 - 4P_2 = 55 - 4(10) = 15$, $P_1 = 7.5$

Substituing P_1 and P_2 we can obtain $x_1 = 42 - 2P_1 - P_2 = 42 - 15 - 10 = 17$ and

$x_2 = 48 - P_1 - 2P_2 = 48 - 7.5 - 20 = 20.5$.

The required solution are

$\boxed{x_1 = 17}$ and $\boxed{x_2 = 20.5}$, $\boxed{P_1 = \text{Rs. } 7.5}$ and $\boxed{P_2 = \text{Rs. } 10}$

$\pi = 50P_1 - 2P_1^2 - 2P_1P_2 + 55P_2 - 2P_2^2 - 222$

$= 50(7.5) - 2(7.5)^2 - 2(7.5)(10) + 55(10) - 2(10)^2 - 222 = \boxed{\text{Rs. } 240.5}$

7.9. Equilibrium Conditions for a Multi-plant Monopolist

The theory of monopoly is modified to cover a wide variety of situations. There are the situations under which the monopolist is selling its output (q) in different markets at different prices. This refers to the practice of price discrimination by the monopolist. The equilibrium conditions stating profit maximization of the monopolist under price discrimination are different form the conditions for profit maximization by a simple monopolist.

Consider another situation, where the monopolist is selling its products in a single market although he produces his output in two separate plants. This case refers to the situation of multi-plant monopolist. The conditions for profit maximaization under this situation are different and thus needs to be studied. Under this situation profit of the monopolist is the difference between his total revenue and total production costs incurred in both the plants.

Suppose the monopolist's total output is X, which is the sum total of x_1 and x_2. The firm produces in two plants for which we sum up $X = x_1 + x_2$, where x_1 is the quantity of the output produced in plant I while x_2 is the output produced in plant 2. His total revenue will be, $R = R(x_1 + x_2) = R(x_1) + R(x_2)$ and total cost is $C = C_1(x_1) + C_2(x_2)$. Profit function is $\pi = R(x_1 + x_2) - C_1(x_1) - C_2(x_2)$

For profit maximization, the necessary condition is to obtain the partial derivatives of profit π, *w.r.t.*, x_1 and x_2, and then setting them to zero. This is derived as

$$\frac{\partial \pi}{\partial x_1} = 0, \frac{\partial \pi}{\partial x_2} = 0, \therefore \frac{\partial \pi}{\partial x_1} = \frac{\partial}{\partial x_1}[R(x_1 + x_2) - C_1(x_1) - C_2(x_2)] = 0$$

$$= R'(x_1 + x_2) - C_1'(x_1) = 0 \text{ or } R'(x_1 + x_2) = C_1'(x_1) \text{ .... } (1)$$

$$\therefore \frac{\partial \pi}{\partial x_2} = \frac{\partial}{\partial x_2}\left[R(x_1+x_2) - C_1(x_1) - C_2(x_2)\right] = 0 \quad \text{or} \quad R'(x_1+x_2) = C_2'(x_2) \text{.........(2)}$$

This requires $= R'(x_1+x_2) = C_1'(x_1) = C_2'(x_2)$

The necessary condition requires the monopolist to equalise the MC of producing output in each plant with the MR of whole output produced.

The second order conditions for profit maximization requires that the Hassian determinant is to be positive. This implies that the marginal cost curve in each plant must be rising more rapidly than the MR of the output as a whole.

$$H = \begin{vmatrix} R'' - C_1'' & R'' \\ R'' & R'' - C_2'' \end{vmatrix} > 0 \text{. This is fulfilled if } \frac{\partial^2 \pi}{\partial x_1^2} < 0, \ \frac{\partial^2 \pi}{\partial x_2^2} < 0.$$

$$\frac{\partial^2 \pi}{\partial x_1^2} = \frac{\partial}{\partial x_1}\left(\frac{\partial \pi}{\partial x_1}\right) = \frac{\partial}{\partial x_1}\left[R'(x_1+x_2) - C_1'(x_1)\right]$$

$$= R''(x_1+x_2) - C_1''(x_1) < 0 \text{ or } R''(x_1+x_2) < C_1''(x_1)$$

Similarly, $\frac{\partial^2 \pi}{\partial x_2^2} = R''(x_1+x_2) - C_2''(x_2) < 0$ or $R''(x_1+x_2) < C_2''(x_2)$

This equilibrium condition can also be shown diagramatically below where $\Sigma MR = MR_1 + MR_2$,

$\Sigma MC = MC_1 + MC_2$

The monopolist is in equilibrium when $\Sigma MC = \Sigma MR$

At equlibrium point, $MC_1 = MC_2 = \Sigma MR = \Sigma MC$

The monopolist equates MR of whole output with MC, MC_1 and MC_2

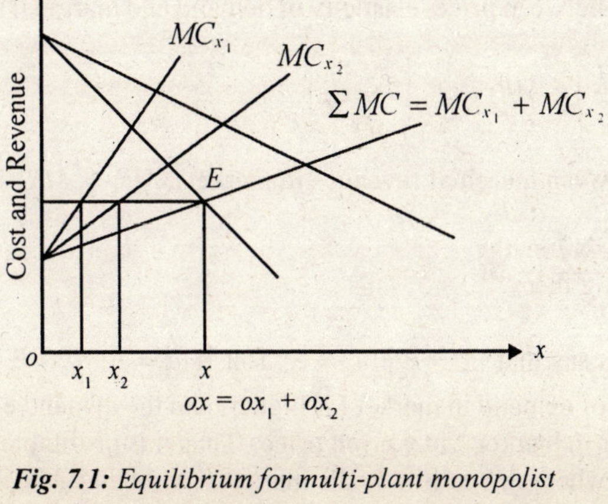

Fig. 7.1: Equilibrium for multi-plant monopolist

7.10. Equilibrium of the Monopolist Under Price Discrimination

The monopolist need not sell the entire output in a single market at uniform price. Under certain circumstance, the monopolist resorts to price discrimination when it is profitable to him. The technique of price discrimination refers to the situation under which the monopolist is selling its products in different markets at different prices to maximize profit. The price he will fix in these sub-markets would depend on the relative price elasticity of demand prevailing in these sub-markets.

There are two different cases of price discrimination, which are referred to

(a) Market discrimination and *(b)* Perfect price discrimination.

7.10.1. Market Discrimination

Under the situation of market pı ice discrimination, the monopolist will be selling its product in two or more but distinct markets by charging a different price in each sub-market. However price descrimination is conceivable only if the buyers in the dearer market can not find it convenient physically or economically to buy the monopolist's product from the cheaper market. This precondition can limit the possibilities of price discrimination.

Moreover despite the fact that price discrimination is possible, the monopolist may not go for it since it gives no guarantee for increasing profits from this practice of price discrimination all the time. Thus it is practical only if price discrimination is profitable to him.

The discriminating monopolist is said to be in equilibrium under price discrimination when he equalizes the marginal revenue from both the markets with the marginal cost of producing his total output.

The discriminating monopolist's profit function under this situation is defined

$$\pi = R_1(x_1) + R_2(x_2) - C(x_1 + x_2)$$

Maximizing π, *w.r.t.* x_1 and x_2 and setting them to zero we get,

$$R_1'(x_1) - C'(x_1 + x_2) = 0, \text{ or } R_1'(x_1) = C'(x_1 + x_2)$$

$$R_2'(x_2) - C'(x_1 + x_2) = 0 \text{ or } R_2'(x_2) = C'(x_1 + x_2)$$

$\therefore R_1'(x_1) = R_2'(x_2) = C'(x_1 + x_2)$ or At equilibrium point, $MR_1 = MR_2 = MC$

The relationship between price, elasticity of demand and marginal revenue are given in each market as

$$MR_1 = P_1\left(\frac{e_1 - 1}{e_1}\right), \quad MR_2 = P_2\left(\frac{e_2 - 1}{e_2}\right)$$

The equality between marginal revenues in markets, $MR_1 = MR_2 = \text{MC}$ implies that

$$P_1\left(\frac{e_1 - 1}{e_1}\right) = P_2\left(\frac{e_2 - 1}{e_2}\right) = MC.$$

From this we can say that $P_1 = P_2$ if $e_1 = e_2$, But if $e_1 \neq e_2$, $P_1 \neq P_2$

When elasticity of demand in market I is higher than the demand elasticity in market 2, *MR* in market I will be higher than *MR* in market 2 at a given price. Thus it is profitable to the monopolist to transfer some goods from the market where *MR* is low to the market with higher *MR*. This makes him to charge a higher price in the market with low demand elasticity and a lower price in the market having a high elasticity of demand.

Therefore when $e_1 > e_2$, $P_1 < P_2$ or $P_2 > P_1$ or when $e_2 > e_1$, $P_1 > P_2$ or $P_2 < P_1$

The monopolist in his attempt to equalize *MR* in each of the sub markets with the *MC* of the whole output can increase total revenue without affecting total cost by transferring some units of the product form the low *MR* market to the high *MR* market. In this process he will be charging a higher price in market with low demand elasticity and a lower price in the market with high demand elasticity. This transfer of goods will continue until marginal revenues in both the markets are made equal with the marginal cost.

How the monopolist will fixe price and output in different markets under market discrimination can be illustrated with the help of following illustrations

Let us suppose demand elatsicity in two markets are the same,

$e_1 = e_2 = 4$. The equilibrium under price discrimination implies that $MR_1 = MR_2 = MC$.

or $P_1\left(\dfrac{e_1 - 1}{e_1}\right) = P_2\left(\dfrac{e_2 - 1}{e_2}\right) = MC.$

Let us suppose $MC = 30$. With $e_1 = e_2 = 4$, the equilibrium under price discrimination requires the monopolist to set marginal revenues equal with the marginal cost:

$\therefore\ P_1\left(\dfrac{4-1}{4}\right) = P_2\left(\dfrac{4-1}{4}\right) = 30$ or $P_1\,(0.75) = P_2\,(0.75) = 30$. From this we get

$\therefore\ P_1\,(0.75) = 30$ or $P_1 = 40$ and $P_2\,(0.75) = 30$ or $P_2 = 40$

Thus it is verified that the profit maximizing monopolist under price discrimination will charge the same price from both the markets since the price elasticity of demand in these two markets are the same. From this we can find that when demand elasticity in two distinct markets are equal $(e_1 = e_2)$, for a given marginal cost, *MC*, the monopolist will fix a single price in both these markets. This will maximize his profits. Under this situation he does not discriminate prices as otherwise it will render him to reduce total profit from sale of goods in sub-markets. However when $e_1 \neq e_2$, he can maximize net revenue by resorting to the method of price discrimination. For example suppose, $e_1 = 4$ and $e_2 = 2$ and $MC = 30$,

The equilibrium condition in this case requires him to equalize marginal revenues with MC as shown:

$P_1\left(\dfrac{4-1}{4}\right) = P_2\left(\dfrac{2-1}{2}\right) = 30.$ or $P_1\,(0.75) = P_2\,(0.5) = 30$

$\therefore\ P_1\,(0.75) = 30$ $\therefore\ P_1 =$ Rs. 40. and $P_2\,(0.5) = 30$ $\therefore\ P_2 =$ Rs. 60.

It is evident that the monopolist is fixing a higher price in market 2 where demand elasticity is low and a lower price in market 1 where demand elasticity is high, for we have obtained $P_1 =$ Rs. 40 while $e_1 = 4$ and $P_2 =$ Rs. 60 for $e_2 = 2$, for given the $MC = 30$.

Algebraically this condition is realized when $MR_1 = MR_2 = MC$

If $e_1 = e_2$, For $MR_1 = MR_2$, $P_1\left(\frac{e_1-1}{e_1}\right) = P_2\left(\frac{e_2-1}{e_2}\right)$ or $\frac{P_1}{P_2}\frac{\left(\frac{e_2-1}{e_2}\right)}{\left(\frac{e_1-1}{e_1}\right)} = 1$,

Therefore $p_1 = p_2$ when $e_1 = e_2$

When $e_1 > e_2$, $\frac{P_1}{P_2}\frac{\left(\frac{e_2-1}{e_2}\right)}{\left(\frac{e_1-1}{e_1}\right)} < 1$ or $\frac{P_1}{P_2} < 1$ or $P_1 < P_2$,

Therefore $p_1 < p_2$ when $e_1 > e_2$

When $e_2 > e_1$, $\frac{P_1}{P_2}\frac{\left(\frac{e_2-1}{e_2}\right)}{\left(\frac{e_1-1}{e_1}\right)} > 1$ or $\frac{P_1}{P_2} > 1$ or $P_1 > P_2$,

The necessary and sufficient conditions for equilibrium under price discrimination aredefined as:

The profit function is defined as, $\pi = R_1(x_1) + R_1(x_2) - C(x_1 + x_2)$, where X = total output, x_1 = output the monopolist is selling in market 1 and x_2 = output sold in market 2.

$X = x_1 + x_2$ and $C(x_1 + x_2) = C(x)$, the total cost of producing the whole output X.

The necessary condition for equilibrium under price discrimination is given by

$$\frac{\partial \pi}{\partial x_1} = 0, \ \frac{\partial \pi}{\partial x_2} = 0.$$

From this we will get $R_1'(x_1) = MC = C'(x_1 + x_2)$ and $R_2'(x_2) = MC = C'(x_1 + x_2)$

Thus at equilibrium $R_1'(x_1) = R_2'(x_2) = C'(x_1 + x_2)$

The second order condition is that the relevant Hessian Determinant $|\bar{H}|$ is to be positive, where

$$|\bar{H}| = \begin{vmatrix} R''-C'' & C'' \\ C'' & R_2''-C'' \end{vmatrix} > 0. \text{ or } (R_1''-C'')(R_2''-C'')-(C'')^2 > 0$$

$R_1''-C'' < 0$ or $R_1'' < C''$, and $R_2''-C'' < 0$ or $R_2'' < C''$

This implies that *MR* in each market must be increasing less rapidly than the *MC* for the entire output.

$R_1''(x_1) < C''(x_1 + x_2)$ and $R_2''(x_2) < C''(x_1 + x_2)$

Illustration:

(1) If the monopolist faces the cost function $C = 20 + 10x$, where C = total cost and x = output. He intends to sell his X output produced in two distinct markets, 1 and 2. The demand functions for his product in these markets are given as P_1 and P_2 respectively, where, $P_1 = 40 - 2.5x_1$, $P_2 = 90 - 10x_2$ and $(x_1 + x_2 = X)$.

(a) Can the monopolist resort to price discrimination? If so, determine the prices, output and profit under his action as a discriminating monopolist.

(b) determine the demand elasticity in these two markets.

We are given $P_1 = 40 - 2.5x_1$, $P_2 = 90 - 10x_2$ and $C = 20 + 10\,(x_1 + x_2)$

The equilibrium for discriminating monopolist requires to equate $MR_1 = MR_2 = MC$.

$$MR_1 = \frac{\partial R_1}{\partial x_1},\ MR_2 = \frac{\partial R_2}{\partial x_2},\ MC = \frac{\partial C}{\partial x}$$

Given $C = 20 + 10x$, $MC = \dfrac{\partial C}{\partial x} = 10.$

From $P_1 = 40 - 2.5x_1$, $P_2 = 90 - 10x_2$ we get

$R_1 = P_1\,x_1 = (40 - 2.5x_1)\,x_1 = 40x_1 - 2.5x_1^2$ and $MR_1 = \dfrac{\partial R_1}{\partial x_1} = 40 - 5x_1$,

Likewise $R_2 = P_2\,x_2 = 90\,x_2 - 10\,x_2^2$ and $MR_2 = \dfrac{\partial R_2}{\partial x_2} = \dfrac{\partial}{\partial x_2}(90\,x_2 - 10\,x_2^2) = 90 - 20\,x_2$

For equilibrium $MR_1 = MC$ and $MR_2 = MC$. Equalizing $MR_1 = MC$ we get

$\therefore\ 40 - 5x_1 = 10,\ 5x_1 = 30,\ \therefore\ x_1 = 6$

Likewise from $MR_2 = MC$ we get, $\therefore\ 90 - 20x_2 = 10,\ 20x_2 = 80,\ \therefore x_2 = 4.$

Thus $x_1 = 6$ and $x_2 = 4$ are required equilibrium output. From these we get the prices as

$P_1 = 40 - 2.5x_1 = 40 - 2.5\,(6) = 25$ and $P_2 = 90 - 10x_2 = 90 - 10\,(4) = 50$.

The profit function is $\pi = R_1\,(x_1) + R_2\,(x_2) - C\,(x_1 + x_2)$

$= 40\,x_1 - 2.5\,x_1^2 + 90\,x_2 - 10\,x_2^2 - 20 - 10\,(x_1 + x_2)$

$= 40\,(6) - 2.5\,(6)^2 + 40\,(4) - 10\,(4)^2 - 20 - 10(6 + 4) = 230$, $\pi = 230$.

Since $MR_1 = P_1\left(\dfrac{e_1 - 1}{e_1}\right) = 10\,(MC)$, $P_1\left(\dfrac{e_1 - 1}{e_1}\right) = 10$

or $P_1\left(1 - \dfrac{1}{e_1}\right) = 10$ or $P_1 - \dfrac{P_1}{e_1} = 10$. Since $P_1 = 25$, $25 - 10 = \dfrac{P_1}{e_1}$

or $15 = \frac{P_1}{e_1}$ or $e_1 = \frac{25}{15} = 1.67, e_1 = 1.67$

Likewise $MR_2 = P_2\left(\frac{e_2 - 1}{e_2}\right) = 10$ or $P_2\left(1 - \frac{1}{e_2}\right) = 10$

$P_2 - \frac{P_2}{e_2} = 10$ and $P_2 = 50$, or $50-10=\frac{P_2}{e_2}$ or $e_2 = \frac{P_2}{40} = \frac{50}{40} = 1.25$

In this way we have derived $e_1 = 1.67$, $P_1 = 25$ and $e_2 = 1.25$, $P_2 = 50$

Since $e_1 > e_2$, $P_1 < P_2$

As evident the equilibrium profit π under price discrimination is larger than the amount of profit under the situation of the equilibrium in simple monoply.

(2) The monopolist is facing the following demand functions in two distinct market.

$P_1 = 14 - 2q_1$ and $P_2 = 26 - 3q_2$ $[q = q_1 + q_2]$, Monopolist's total cost function is given

$C = 8 + 2(q_1 + q_2)$, determine the prices he will be charging from different markets so as to maxim ze profit under price discrimination. Find the elasticities of demand in these markets. What is the amount of profit of the dscriminating monopolist?

We are given $P_1 = 14 - 2q_1$. From this we get $R_1 = P_1 q_1 = 14q_1 - 2q_1^2$

From $P_2 = 26 - 3q_2$, we can obtain $R_2 = P_2 q_2 = 26q_2 - 2q_2^2$

Equilibrium under price discrimination requires $\frac{\partial R_1}{\partial q_1} = \frac{\partial R_2}{\partial q_2} = \frac{\partial C}{\partial q}$,

From total cost function $C = 8 + 2(q_1 + q_2) = 8 + 2q$, we get $MC = \frac{\partial C}{\partial q} = 2$

$\frac{\partial R_1}{\partial q_1} = \frac{\partial}{\partial q_1}(14q_1 - 2q_1^2) = 14 - 4q_1$ and $\frac{\partial R_2}{\partial q_2} = \frac{\partial}{\partial q_2}(26q_2 - 3q_2^2) = 26 - 6q_2$

Equating MR_1 with MC we can solve for q_1 as $14 - 4q_1 = 2$, $\therefore q_1 = 3$.

Similarly we can solve for q_2 by equating MR_2 with MC. This provides $26 - 6q_2 = 2$, $\therefore q_2 = 4$.

For $q_1 = 3$, $q_2 = 4$, $P_1 = 14 - 2q_1 = 14 - 6 = 8$,

Likewise we can get $P_2 = 26 - 3q_2 = 26 - 12 = 14$,

The relationship between *MR*, Price, marginal cost and elasticity of demand are given by

$MR_1 = P_1\left(1 - \frac{1}{e_1}\right) = 2$, $MR_2 = P_2\left(1 - \frac{1}{e_2}\right) = 2$

We can determine elasticities of demand in these two markets from their relationship.

Since $P_1 = 8, \therefore P_1\left(1-\frac{1}{e_1}\right) = 2$ or $8\left(1-\frac{1}{e_1}\right) = 2$

$$1-\frac{1}{e_1} = \frac{2}{8}, 1-\frac{2}{8} = \frac{1}{e_1} \text{ or } \frac{1}{e_1} = \frac{6}{8} \qquad \therefore e_1 = \frac{8}{6} = 1.3336$$

Likewise $MR_2 = P_2\left(1-\frac{1}{e_2}\right)=2$ and $P_2 = 14$,

$$\therefore 14\left(1-\frac{1}{e_2}\right) = 2 \text{ or } 1-\frac{1}{e_2} = \frac{2}{14} \text{ and } 1-\frac{2}{14} = \frac{1}{e_2} \text{ or } \frac{1}{e_2} = \frac{12}{14} \text{ or } e_2 = \frac{14}{12} = 1.167.$$

$e_1 = 1.333$ and $P_1 = 8$. $e_2 = 1.167$ and $P_2 = 14$

Since $e_1 > e_2$, $P_1 < P_2$ and $\pi = P_1 q_1 + P_2 q_2 - C(q_2 + q_2)$. Monopoly profit is given by

$\pi = (8)(3) + (14)(4) - 8 - 2(q_1 + q_2) = 24 + 56 - 8 - 2(7) = 58$

7.11. Effect of Profit Tax and Sales Tax on Price and Output of Monopoly Product

The equilibrium of the monopolist is given by the condition that $\frac{\partial \pi}{\partial q} = 0. \frac{\partial^2 \pi}{\partial q^2} < 0$.

When these conditions are fulfilled the firm will obtain price-quantity combination that maximizes monopoly profit. However these equilibrium conditions are modified after imposition of tax on monopoly output or profits. The profit tax is also called a lump-sum tax, imposed on the monopolist. The nature of this tax is such that this leaves the optimum price-quantity combination set by the monopolist unaltered to the pre-tax situation, although monopoly profit shrinks. However when a sales tax or excise duty is imposed on monopoly product, it will reduce his profit by raising price and reducing level of output produced. The extent to which price wil rise will depend on demand elastciity of the monopoly product. We will first examine equilibrium conditions of the monopolist when profit tax is imposed.

Monopoly equilibrium when a lump-sum tax is imposed

A lump-sum tax is to be paid by the monopolist regardless of the physical quantity of output or value of sales of the output. The profit function becomes $\pi = R(q) - C(q)$, where 't' is the amount of tax collects the Government from the monopolist. When we maximize π function *w.r.t.* output q by differenting it with respect to output, the constant term 't' varnishes and equilibrium quantity remains the same, as derived below:

$$\pi = R(q) - C(q) - t$$

$$\frac{\partial \pi}{\partial q} = R'(q) - C'(q) = 0, \text{ or } R'(q) - C'(q) = 0 \text{ or } R'(q) = C'(q) \text{ or } MR = MC.$$

This is the same condition as the one derived under simple monopoly equilibrium without imposition of tax. The second order condition can also be shown to be the same like that of pre-tax situation. This is

$$\frac{d^2 \pi}{d q^2} = R''(q) - C''(q) < 0 \text{ or } R''(q) < C''(q)$$

Thus the equilibrium price-quantity combination are remained unchanged. A profit tax requires the monopolist to pay a specified proportion of the profit as tax without bringing any alteration to the existing equilibrium price and quantity.

Therefore Tax $(t) = t\,[R(q) - C(q)]$ and $\pi = [\,R(q) - C\,(q)] - t\,[\,R(q) - C\,(q)]$ where $0 < t < 1$

By rearranging this we get $\pi = [\,R(q) - C\,(q)]\,[1 - t]$ and differentiating π, w.r.t. q we get,

$$\frac{\partial \pi}{\partial q} = (1 - t)\,\frac{\partial}{\partial q}\{R(q) - C(q)\} = 0$$

$$\frac{\partial \pi}{d\,q} = (1-t)[\,R'(q) - C'(q)] = 0$$

$R'(q) - C'(q) = 0$ or $R'(q) = C'(q)$. Since $(1-t) \neq 0$ as $t \neq 1$. For $(1-t) > 0$, $0 < t < 1$.

The equality between *MR* and *MC* is the required condition. Therefore the price and output levels are still unaffected when lumpsum tax or profit tax is imposed on the monopolist.

7.11.1 Monopoly Price, Output and Profit with the Imposition of a Specific Tax on Monopoly Product

When a specific tax of Rs '*t*' per unit of the monopoly output is imposed, it is added to the total cost. This will affcet the monopolist's price, output and profit in the post-tax situation. In this case 'C' changes to

$C = C\,(q) + t\,q$, where '*t*' is the tax per unit of q.

The π function becomes $\pi = R\,(q) - C\,(q) - t\,q$.

Maximizing π, *w.r.t.* q we get,

$$\frac{\partial \pi}{d\,q} = \frac{\partial}{d\,q}[\,R(q) - C(q) - tq] = 0.$$

$$\frac{\partial \pi}{\partial q} = [R'(q) - C'(q) - t] = 0, \text{ or } R'(q) = C'(q) + t$$

The monopolist will maximizes profit after a specific tax is imposed by equalizing marginal revenue with marginal cost plus the tax per unit of output. The second-order condition to be fulfilled is given as:

$\dfrac{\partial^2 \pi}{\partial q^2} = R''(q) - C''(q) < 0$ or $R''(q) < C''(q)$. This condition is the same as before.

The imposition of a specific tax which is the same as before will reduce equilibrium out-put and raises price of the monopoly product. Therefore it is always advised to collect an equivalent amount of tax revenue by levying profit tax rather than a specific tax since it distorts the price-quantity combination of monopoly product.

7.12. Solved Questions of TYBA (Economics) Papers of Mumbai University

(1) April 2004,

Establish the degree of homogeneity of the following function:

$f(x, y, z) = x^2 - 5xy + z^2$

Multiprinting $f(x, y, z)$ *by 'k'*,

$f(xk, yk, zk) = (xk)^2 - 5\,(xk)\,(yk) + (zk)^2 = x^2k^2 - 5xyk^2 + z^2k^2$

$= k^2\,(x^2 - 5\,xy + z^2) = k^2\,(x, y, z)$

The above function is homogeneous of degree 2 since when the input variables are multiplied a constant 'k' the function changes to K^2 times the original function.

(2) Oct' 2003,

Determine if the following function is homogeneous and apply Euler's theorem to test the homogeneity.

$$Z = \frac{x^3 + y^3 + w^2}{xyw}$$

Given $Z = f(x,y,w)$, it is said to be homogeneous when the variables $x,y,w,$ are multiplied by some constant say 'k', the function changes to k' times Z, so that it is homogenous of degree 't', where 't' can take any value like –1, 0, 1, 2. For this functions the Euler's theorem can be applied. This is shown below:

$$x\frac{\partial Z}{\partial x} + y\frac{\partial Z}{\partial y} + \frac{\partial Z}{\partial w} = k'\,Z.$$

The above function Z is homogeneous or not can be proved as follows:

$$tZ = \frac{(xt)^3 + (yt)^3 + (wt)^2}{(xt)(yt)(wt)} = \frac{x^3t^3 + y^3t^3 + w^2t^2}{xywt^3}$$

$$= \frac{t^2\,[x^3t + y^3t + w^2]}{t^3\,[xyw]} = \frac{1}{t}\left[\frac{x^3t + y^3t + tw^2}{xyw}\right] \neq t^{-1}Z$$

The above function is found not homogeneous. Therefore Euler's theorem can not be applied to this function. .

(3) Oct' 2002,

Establish the degree of homogeneity for

$$f\,(x, y, z) = \frac{2\,x - 3\,y}{5\,z.}$$

Multiplying x, y, z by a constant 't', if we get the function changes to $t^k f(x, y, z)$ then it is said to be homogeneous of degree k. This can be verified as

$$f\,(xt, yt, zt) = \frac{2xt - 3yt}{5zt} = \frac{t}{t}\left[\frac{2x - 3y}{5z}\right] t^0 Z, \text{where } Z = \frac{2x - 3y}{5z}.$$

The above function is found homogenous of degree zero.

(4) April 2002,

(a) Determine whether the following function is homogenous and apply Euler's theorem if they are homogenous.

$Z = x^3 + z\,x^2 y + y^2$

Since $z = f(x, y)$, multiplying x, y by a constant 't', we get

$(xt)^3 + 2(xt)^2\,(yt) + (yt)^2 = x^3\,t^3 + 2x^2\,yt^3 + y^2t^2$

$= t^2\,[x^3\,t + 2x^2\,yt + y^2] \neq t^2\,z.$

The above function is not homogeneous and for this reason the Euler's theorem is inapplicable. This theorem is given by

$$x\frac{\partial z}{\partial x} + y\frac{\partial z}{\partial y} = t\,z$$

(3) Consider four commodities A, B, C and D. Their prices are given as P_A, P_B, P_C and P_D respectively. The estimated demand for commodity B is given by

$$D_B = 49.07 + 0.02\,P_A - 0.36\,P_B + 0.03\,P_C + 0.03\,P_D$$

Find *(a)* the partial elasticity of demand for B, *w.r.t* the prices of P_A, P_B, P_C and P_D *(b)* Evaluate these elasticties when $P_A = 1$, $P_B = 2$, $P_C = 3$, $P_D = 1$.

Given $D_B = 49.07 + 0.02\,P_A - 0.36\,P_B + 0.03\,P_C + 0.03\,P_D$

The partial elasticties of demand , D_B *w.r.t.* P_A, P_B, P_C *and* P_D, can be written as e_{21}, e_{22}, e_{23}, e_{24}, which are evaluated as

$$e_{21} = \frac{\partial D_B}{\partial P_A} \times \frac{P_A}{D_B},\quad e_{22} = \frac{\partial D_B}{\partial P_B} \times \frac{P_B}{D_B}$$

$$e_{23} = \frac{\partial D_B}{\partial P_C} \times \frac{P_C}{D_B} \text{ and } e_{24} = \frac{\partial D_B}{\partial P_D} \times \frac{P_D}{D_B}$$

$$e_{21} = \frac{\partial}{\partial P_A}(49.07 + 0.02\,P_A - 0.36\,P_B + 0.03\,P_C + 0.03\,P_D)\frac{P_A}{D_B}$$

$$e_{21} = \frac{(0.02)\,P_A}{49.07 + 0.02\,P_A - 0.36\,P_B + 0.03\,P_C + 0.03\,P_D.} = \frac{0.02P_A}{D_B}$$

Similarly,

$$e_{22} = \frac{-0.36\,(P_B)}{D_B},\quad e_{23} = \frac{0.03(P_C)}{D_B} \text{ and } e_{24} = \frac{0.03(P_D)}{D_B}$$

Given $P_A = 1$, $P_B = 2$, $P_C = 3$, $P_D = 1$.

$$D_B = 49.07 + 0.02\,P_A - 0.36\,P_B + 0.03\,P_C + 0.03\,P_D$$

$$= 49.07 + 0.02\,(1) - 0.36\,(2) + 0.03\,(3) + 0.03\,(1) = 48.49$$

$$e_{21} = \frac{(0.02)\ (P_A)}{D_B} = \frac{(0.02)\ (1)}{48.49} = 0.00041$$

$$e_{22} = \frac{(0.36)\ (P_B)}{D_B} = \frac{0.72}{48.49} = -0.015$$

$$e_{23} = \frac{(0.03)(P_C)}{D_B} = \frac{(0.03)(4)}{48.49} = 0.0025$$

$$e_{24} = \frac{(0.03)(P_D)}{D_B} = \frac{0.03(1)}{48.49} = 0.00062.$$

(5) May 2000,

The demand function for two goods x_1 and x_2 are given as

$$x_1 = P_1^{-1.7}\ P_2^{0.8},\quad x_2 = P_1^{0.5}\ P_2^{-0.2}$$

Determine whether the commodities are complementary or competitive.

To determine this we are required to find the cross elasticities of demand for these goods. Demand elasticity of x_1 *w.r.t.* price of x_2 and x_2 *w.r.t.* price of x_1 are to be computed. These are given by e_{12} and e_{21}, where

$$e_{12} = \frac{\partial\, x_1}{\partial\, P_2} \times \frac{P_2}{x_1} \text{ and } e_{21} = \frac{\partial\, x_2}{\partial\, P_1} \times \frac{P_1}{x_2}$$

$$e_{12} = \frac{\partial}{\partial\, P_2}\,(P_1^{-1.7}\ P_2^{0.8})\,\frac{P_2}{x_1}$$

$$= \frac{(0.8\ P_1^{-1.7}\ P_2^{-0.2})\ (P_2)}{P_1^{-1.7}\ P_2^{0.8}} = \frac{(0.8)\ P_1^{-1.7}\ P_2^{0.8}}{P_1^{-1.7}\ P_2^{0.8}} = 0.8,\ e_{12} = 0.8 > 0.$$

$$e_{21} = \frac{\partial}{\partial\, P_1}\,\frac{(P_1^{0.5}\ P_2^{-0.2})\ P_1}{x_1} = \frac{(0.5)\ P_1^{-0.5}\ P_2^{0.2}\ P_1}{P_1^{0.5}\ P_2^{-0.3}} = \frac{(0.5)\ p_1^{0.5}\ P_2^{-0.2}}{P_1^{0.5}\ P_2^{-0.5}} = 0.5 > 0$$

Since e_{12} and e_{21} are positive, the goods x_1 and x_2 are said to be substitutes of each other. In other words they are compertive goods.

(6) October 1999,

Apply Euler's theorem to determine whether the following functions are homogeneous or not.

(a) $Z = 2x^4 - 4y^4$

To test the above function $Z = 2x^4 - 4y^4$ is homogeneous, we need to multiply the function by *(t)*. From this we get $(2xt)^4 - 4(yt)^4 = t^4\ [2x^4 - 4y^4] = t^4 Z$.

Thus the function is homogeneous of degree 4, ($k = 4$).

Applying Euler's theorem we get $x\,\dfrac{\partial z}{\partial x} - y\,\dfrac{\partial z}{\partial y} = k\ z$,

$$x\ [8x^3] - y\ [16y^3] = 8x^4 - 16y^4 = 4\ [2x^4 - 4y^4] = 4z = 4z.$$

(b) $Z = \dfrac{x^3 + y^3 + w^3}{x y w}$, Multiplying *x, y, w,* by *t* we get,

$$\frac{(xt)^3 + (yt)^3 + (wt)^3}{(xt)\,(yt)\,(wt)} = \frac{t^3}{t^3}\left[\frac{x^3 + y^3 + w^3}{x y w}\right] = t^0\ [z],$$

It is homogenous of degree zero

Applying Euler's theorem we will get , $x\dfrac{\partial z}{\partial x} + y\dfrac{\partial z}{\partial y} + z\dfrac{\partial z}{\partial w} = z$,

EXERCISE – 7

(1) Find the *MP* and *AP* of inputs at $x = 2$ and $y = 3$ for the following production function. $Q = f(x, y) = 8x^2 + 10xy + 3y^2$.

(2) Find the MP_L and MP_K for the production function $Q = 1.08\,L^{0.72}\,L^{0.28}$ and show that $L\dfrac{\partial Q}{\partial L} + K\dfrac{\partial Q}{\partial k} = Q$.

(3) Given the estimated demand function for commodity *x*, find partial elasticises of demand for *x* with respect to price of *y*, and price of *z*. $P_x = 2, P_y = 3, P_z = 5$ and $D_x = 38.72 - 0.03,\ P_X + 0.32,\ P_y + 0.39\ P_z$.

(4) If the demand for two goods X_1 and X_2 are given as $X_1 = P_1^{-1.7}\ P_2^{0.6}$ and $X_2 = P_2^{-1.3}\ P_1^{0.8}$

Determine whether X_1 and X_2 are competitive or complementary goods,

(5) Determine the partial elasticities of X_1 *w.r.t.* price of X_2 and X_2 *w.r.t.* price of X_1, where,

$$X_1 = \frac{1}{P_1^2\,P_2^2} \text{ and } X_2 = \frac{1}{P_1^3\,P_2^3}$$

(6) Determine whether the following Utility function has a maximum or minimum; $U = f(xyz) = -2x^3 + 3xz - 2y - y^2 - 5z^2$

(7) Are the following functions homogeneous? Verify.

(a) $Z = f(x, y) = 3x^2y + 3xy^2 + y^2 - 8$

(b) $Q = Ax_1^{\alpha}\,x_2^{\beta}$

(c) $P = 1.32\ L^{0.68}\ k^{0.32}$

(d) $f(x,y) = \dfrac{x^2}{y^3}$

(e) $P = [BK^{-e} + \alpha L^{-e}]^{-1/e}$

(8) State the properties of linearly homogeneous functions.

(9) State Euler's theorem, can you apply it to following

(a) $Q = AK^{\alpha}\,L^{\beta}$

(b) $f(x,y) = 3x^2y + 2xy^2 + y^3$

(c) $Z = f(x,y) = x_1^3 + 4x_1^2\,x_2 + 4x_2^3$

(10) If production function, $Q = f(x, y, z)$ is given as $Q = Ax^{\frac{1}{3}}y^{\frac{1}{5}}z^{\frac{1}{2}}$, find MP of x, y and z.

(11) If $P_1 = 12 - x_1$, $P_2 = 8 - 2x_2$ and joint cost function is $C = 12 + 6x_1 + 3x_2$. Determine prices and quantities of x_1 and x_2 that maximize profit of the monopolist.

(12) The demand functions and joint cost functions facing a monopolist are given as $X = P_1 - 14$ and $Y = P_2 - 18$ and $C = 6X - 5Y$, where X and Y are two products and C is the Cost. Dtermine equilibrium quantities of X, Y and the prices that maximize the monopoly profit.

(13) A discriminating monopolist faces demand function in two markets as $P_1 = 18 - 5x_1$ and $P_2 = 180 - 20x_2$ and $C = 50 + 30(x_1 + x_2)$. Find the price and output he will fix in these markets. Also find demand elasticities.

(14) The demand and cost function of the monopolist are $P = 30 - 2x$ and $C = 20 + 5x$, find equilibrium prices, output and profit. What happens to these values when the government imposes a specific tax of Rs. 3 per unit of output.

(15) Find the elasticity of substitution and show that it is one for $Q = AK^{\alpha}L^{\beta}$.

❑ ❑ ❑

8 LINEAR PROGRAMMING

8.1. Concept of Programming and Linear Programming

Many problems arise in the decision-making process. The problem of optimization is a common feature in all economic activities. The economic agents like a firm, a consumer and an industry confront with the problems of optimizing a given function, say maximization of profits or sales and minimization of costs.

Programming is a technique in planning applied to achieve an optimum solution to the given problem. For example, the firm's objective of the maximization of net revenue from the sale of various units of a product mix it decides to produce. The firm here confronts with certain resource constraints. Usually in the production process various types of inputs are used in some fixed proportions. The decision problems accordingly are formulated, analyzed and solved mathematically with the help of a mathematical programming called Linear programming.

Linear programming as a technique provides solution to the problem of optimizng behavior of a firm, who confronts with an objective function of either maximizing revenue or minimizing cost subject to some side conditions called restrictions. These are expressed in the form of inequalities.

The problems relating to maximization or minimization of a function can also be solved with the help of the derivatives. However application of derivative is confined to the equations like $Y = 3x^2 + 2x$. Therefore in the presence of the constraints and not the equations and when these constarints limit the decision-making authority for finding optimal solution to the decision variables, the application of derivative is ruled out. The objective function is to be optimized subject to these constraints in the frøm of inequalties. This necesiates the application of linear programming technique for optimal solutions.

Linear programming is applied to obtain optimum solution when a linear objective function is to be satisfied subject to some restrictions, called structural constraints. These are either of $\geq$ or $\leq$ types. It is a mathematical programming, which is practical in nature, in almost all fields of economics including planning, this programming technique is employed to achieve the desired objective of optimum allocation of resources.

We can state the concept of linear programming *as a technique involving the problems of optimization of a linear objective function of certain decision variables subject to the structural constraints or side conditions which are inequalities and not equations.*

The application of such programming technique can be illustrated by citing an example. Suppose we have a production manager who is confronted with the problem of decision-making regarding an appropriate production mix of two products X and Y. Production of each unit of X and Y requires the use of three types of inputs, labour, capital and raw material in some quantities before they are turned in to the final shape. Per unit market prices of these two products are known to the manager. He has an objective function of maximization of net revenue from an optimum product mix. He has a maximum amount of these inputs for utilization. These are given and known to the manager.

The problem he confronts with is to determine the optimal quanties of X an Y products that will maximize his profits, represented by the objective function. This problem can be formulated as a Linear programming problem of maximization type, as stated below.

8.2. Formulation of a Linear Programming Problem

8.2.1 Formulate a linear programming problem of maximization type

Illustration 1:

Use the following information to formulate a linear programming problem:

Let us suppose that the production of each unit of X requires 8 units of labour and 2 units of capital, while each unit of product Y requires use of 1 unit of labour and 4 units of capital inputs. The firm has a maximum quantity of 30 and 20 units of labour and capital respectively for use. Per unit market price of X and Y are Rs. 3/- and Rs. 5/- respectively. The firm's objective is to maximize his profit function by making an optimal use of these available resources. For this the optimal combination of X and Y products are to be determined. The above problem is presented in table- 8.1.

Table 8.1

Resources	Resource combination for producing one unit of X	Resource combination for producing one unit of X	Available capacity of inputs
Labour	8	1	30
Capital	2	4	20
Price per unit	Rs. 3/-	Rs. 5/-	———

The objective function is stated as:

Maximize: $f = 3x + 5Y$

Subject to:

$8X + Y \leq 30$ Labour Constraint

$X + 4Y \leq 20$ Capital Constraint

$X \geq 0,\ Y \geq 0$ Non-negative restrictions

The first part of the Linear Programming Problem is the objective function, which is given by $f = 3x + 5Y$. The second part of the Linear Programming Problem refers to the structural constraints. For the above problem we have two constraints shown in the form of inequalities of $\leq$ type. The third part of the Linear Programming Problem is the non-negativity restrictions. This demands the decision variables X and Y are to be positive or zero at the most. These variables cannot take a negative value.

The structural constraints are formulated from the information given in the table regarding the resource to be used for production. The constraint $8X + Y \leq 30$, implies that one unit of X and Y products can be produced by using 8 and 1 units of labour inputs respectively while the firm can not use more than 30 units of labour input. However he has freedom to use less than or equal to 30 units of this available input. Similar explanation can be extended for the second structural constraint $X + 4Y \leq 20$. Its implication is that one unit of X and Y products require use of 1 and 4 units of capital inputs respectively when the firm can use at the most 20 units of capital input at his disposal. Of course the firm can use less than or equal to 20 units of this input. The firm confronts the problem of determining an optimal quantities of X and Y he will produce so as to maximize the above stated objective function: $f = 3x + 5Y$.

Illustration 2:

From the following information formulate a Linear Programming Problem:

Let us suppose a production manager intends to produce two types of toys, A and B. Their production require use of three types of inputs labour, capital and raw materials in some fixed quantities before these products are put in to their final shape. The firm intends to maximize profit from sale of the toys in the market. Per unit market prices of the toys are known to the firm and are fixed. One unit of '*A*' type toy fetches Rs. 20/- while one unit of '*B*' type toy fetches Rs. 30/-. The use of these three different types of resources go into the production of these toys are provided in the following table- 8.2.

Table 8.2

Resources	**Resource combination for producing one of *A* type Toy**	**Resource combination for producing one of *B* type Toy**	**Available capacity of the inputs**
Labour	1	3	12
Capital	3	1	9
Raw material	1	1	5
Price per unit	Rs. 20/-	Rs. 30/-	—

From the information given in the table we can formulate a linear programming problem of maximization type. The objective function for the above problem is to maximize profit. It is given as maximize: $f = 20A + 30B$. This function is formulated from the data given on per unit prices of these two types of toys as Rs.20 and Rs.30 for 'A' and 'B' respectively. The informtaion regarding resource use for porducing these two types of toys enable us to formulate the required structural constraints. These are as follows:

$A + 3B \leq 12$ Labour Constraint

$3A + B \leq 9$ Capital Constraint

$A + B \leq 5$ Raw Material Constraint

The non-negativity restriction states that the decison variables are to be non-negative, $A \geq 0$, $B \geq 0$. We can rewrite this linear programming problem of maximization type in a complete form as

Maximize: $f = 20A + 30B$

Subject to:

$$A + 3B \leq 12$$
$$A + B \leq 9$$
$$A + B \leq 5$$
$$A \geq 0, B \geq 0.$$

8.2.2 Formulating a linear programming problem of minimization type:

Linear Programming Problem enables one to deal with the problems when the objective functions are either of maximization type or of minimization types. We have already demonstrated how programming of maximization type can be formulated with two or more structural constraints.

The following illustrations relate to the Linear Programming Problems of minimization types.

Illustration 3:

With the help of the following information formulate a Linear programming problem:

Suppose we have a farmer who uses three different types of fertilizers to produce wheat from land. He is required to use at least 40, 30 and 12 kg's of three types of fertilizers named 1, 2 and 3. These fertilizers are available in two different bags leveled '*A*' and '*B*'. Each Bag '*A*' costs Rs. 50 while each Bag '*B*' costs Rs. 60 to the farmer. Each of the Bag '*A*' contains 5, 3 and 4 kg's of these three types of fertilizers, while in each of the Bag '*B*', 4, 5 and 1 kg's of these fertilizers are contained. The problem the farmer confronts is that how many bags of '*A*' and '*B*' he shall purchase so that he can fulfill the required minimum quantities of these fertilizers and at the same time he can minimise the total cost.

We need to formulate this as a linear programming problem. The above information is compiled and reproduced in a tabular form, shown in table 8.3. The objective function and structural constraints are also derived from these information.

Table 8.3

Fertilizers	**Each bag *A* contains kg's of three types of fertilizers**	**Each bag *B* contains three types of fertilizers in kg's**	**Minimum requirements of fertilizer in kg's**
Type 1	5	4	40
Type 2	3	5	30
Type 3	4	1	12
Cost per Bag	Rs. 50/-	Rs. 60/-	—

The objective function of the farmer is to minimize total cost. This is to be shown in a linear objective function formulated from the information regarding cost of each of the '*A*' and '*B*' bags. These are Rs. 50 and Rs. 60 per bag of '*A*' and '*B*' respectively as given in data. From this the objective function can be framed as Minimize: $Z = 50A + 60B$. This objective function is to be minimized subject to the structural constraints, which are formulated from information contained in the table 8.3. Thus we have three structural constraints and these are

$5A + 4B \geq 40$ Fertilizer 1 constraint

$3A + 5B \geq 30$ Fertilizer 2 constraint

$4A + B \geq 12$ Fertilizer 3 constraint

$A \geq 0, B \geq 0$ Non-negativity restriction

We can rewrite them in a complete form and symbolically as:

Minimize: $Z = 50A + 60B$

Subject to:

$$5A + 4B \geq 40$$
$$3A + 5B \geq 30$$
$$4A + B \geq 12$$
$$A \geq 0, B \geq 0$$

8.3. Conditions for Application of Linear Programming

A Linear Programming technique is applied by a decision maker for selecting the best from a set of feasible alternative actions. In the technique the objective function and structural constraints limiting the decision variables are expressed in linear forms. The application of LPP requires some conditions to be fulfilled. In other words Linear Programming can be applied only when the following conditions are satisfied:

(a) The decision-making authority has a well identified objective function, measurable in quantitative terms. This objective function need to be optimized subject to certain constraints. The objective function is in the form of either maximization or minimization types. For example maximization of sales or profit by a firm or minimization of a cost function etc.

(b) The activities shown in the programming are quantifiable and identifiable. For example a firm is engaged in the production of three types of products X_1, X_2 and X_3 in some quantities. The objective function is profit maximization to be achieved from purchasing and using inputs in certain quantities as these are to be given and fixed.

(c) The resource inputs to be allocated into the production of final products are identifiable, measurable and quantifiable. These are also known to the decision-maker or user in advance. The supply of these inputs are also given and fixed.

(d) The variables represented by the objective function and shown in structural constraints are linear in nature. This means the relationships involved in the problem are only of first degree.

When these conditions are fulfilled the problem can be formulated and solved as a linear programming problem. Its solution involves optimizing the linear objective function which is defined already before applying the programming. After formulating the Linear Programming problem of either maximization or minimization types, various methods are applied for detrmining solution. The usual procedure is to apply either graphical method or simplex method for obtaining optimal solution to the given Linear Programming Problem..

8.4. Generalization of a Linear Programming Problem

A Linear Programming Problem.of maximization and minimization types can also be generalized and presented as indicated below:

8.4.1 Generalization of linear programming problem in case of maximization:

Let us suppose a firm intends to produce '*n*' number of commodities named $Y_1, Y_2, Y_3 \ldots. Y_n$. For producing them he uses '*m*' number of resource inputs. These are available in the maximum quantities shown by $B_1, B_2, B_3 \ldots. B_m$. The market price per unit of these products are given by $P_1, P_2, P_3 \ldots. P_n$. From these information we can define the firm's objective function, which is the maximization of profit. This linear objective function is given as

Maximize; $Z = P_1Y_1 + P_2Y_2 + P_3Y_3 + \ldots\ldots + P_nY_n$.

The use of resource inputs in some given quantities are shown in linear relationship. This is provided below in a tabular form. The production of each unit of Y_1 requires a_{11} of resource input 1, a_{21} of resource input 2 and so on. Similarly each unit of product Y_2 requires use of a_{12} of resource input 1, a_{22} of resource input 2 and so on. Likewise each unit of Y_n requires a_{1n} of resource input 1, a_{2n} of resource input 2 and finally a_{nm} of resource input '*m*'.

Table 8.4

Resource Inputs	**Resource inputs used to produce each unit of these '*n*' number of products**						**Maximum available capacity of the resource inputs**
—	Y_1	Y_2	Y_3	Y_4	....	Y_n	—
1	a_{11}	a_{12}	a_{13}	a_{14}	....	a_{1n}	B_1
2	a_{21}	a_{22}	a_{23}	a_{24}	....	a_{2n}	B_2
3	a_{31}	a_{32}	a_{33}	a_{34}	....	a_{3n}	B_3
•	•	•	•	•	•	•	•
•	•	•	•	•	•	•	• • •
•	•	•	•	•	•	•	•
M	a_{m1}	a_{m2}	a_{m3}	a_{m4}	....	a_{mn}	B_m

The three parts of the above LPP of maximization can be written in the following expressions:

The first part refers to the objective function. In above example it is the maximization of profit function of the firm. This is given as: Maximize; $Z = P_1Y_1 + P_2Y_2 + P_3Y_3 + \ldots\ldots + P_nY_n$.

This objective function is to be optimized subject to the following structural constraints, which are formulated from the information contained in the table.

$a_{11}Y_1 + a_{12}Y_2 + a_{13}Y_3 + a_{14}Y_4 + \ldots\ldots + a_{1n}Y_n \leq B_1$.

$a_{21}Y_1 + a_{22}Y_2 + a_{23}Y_3 + a_{24}Y_4 + \ldots\ldots + a_{2n}Y_n \leq B_2$.

$a_{31}Y_1 + a_{32}Y_2 + a_{33}Y_3 + a_{34}Y_4 + \ldots\ldots + a_{3n}Y_n \leq B_3$.

• • • .... • • • • •

• • • .... • • • • •

• • • .... • • • • •

• • • .... • • • • •

$a_{m1}Y_1 + a_{m2}Y_2 + a_{m3}Y_3 + a_{m4}Y_4 + \ldots\ldots + a_{mn}Y_n \leq B_m.$

$Y_1 \geq 0,\ Y_2 \geq 0,\ Y_3 \geq 0,\ \ldots\ldots,\ Y_n \geq 0,$

We can rewrite the above general Linear Programming Problem of maximization type in an abbreviated form by using the summation sign (Σ) and matrix formulation, as shown below:

Max $Z = \sum_{j=1}^{n} P_j Y_j$, where $j = 1, 2, 3, 4, \ldots\ldots, n$

Subject to

$\sum_{j=1}^{n} a_{ij} Y_j \leq Bi$, where $i = 1, 2, 3, 4, \ldots\ldots$, m and $j = 1,2,3, \ldots\ldots, n$.

and $Y_j \geq 0$, where $j = 1, 2, 3, \ldots\ldots, n$.

8.4.2 Generalization of linear programming problem of minimization type:

We can generalize the previous example of the farmer who is supposed to be using '*m*' different types of fertilizers available in 'n' different bags leveled as $X_1, X_2, X_3 \ldots . X_n$. The minimum requirements of these fertilizers are given by the constraint such as $B_1, B_2, B_3 \ldots . B_m$. The market price per bag of '*m*' different levels are shown by $P_1, P_2, P_3 \ldots . P_n$.

From these information firm's objective function can be defined to be the minimization of cost. This is represented by the linear objective function:

Minimize; $f = P_1X_1 + P_2X_2 + P_3X_3 + \ldots\ldots + P_nX_n$.

The quantities of the fertilizers each bag contains are given in a tabular form. in the equations they depict linear relationship. Each bag leveled X_1 contains a_{11} of fertilizer input 1, a_{21} of fertilizer input 2 and so on. Similarly each bag leveled X_2 contains a_{12} of fertilizer input 1, a_{22} of fertilizer input 2 and so on. Finally each bag leveled X_n contains a_{1n} of fertilizer input 1, a_{2n} of fertilizer input 2 and finally a_{nm} of fertilizer input '*m*'.

Table 8.5

Fertilizer inputs	**'n' different leveled Bags containing quantities of 'm' different types of fertilizers**						**Minimum requirement of fertilizers**
—	X_1	X_2	X_3	X_4	....	X_n	—
1	a_{11}	a_{12}	a_{13}	a_{14}	....	a_{1n}	B_1
2	a_{21}	a_{22}	a_{23}	a_{24}	....	a_{2n}	B_2
3	a_{31}	a_{32}	a_{33}	a_{34}	....	a_{3n}	B_3
•	•	•	•	•	•	•	•
•	•	•	•	•	•	•	•
•	•	•	•	•	•	•	•
M	a_{m1}	a_{m2}	a_{m3}	a_{m4}	....	a_{mn}	B_m

The three parts of the above linear programming problem of minimization is written in a different form. The first is to state the objective function. This is the maximization of costs by the firm given by

Minimize; $f = P_1X_1 + P_2X_2 + P_3X_3 + \ldots\ldots + P_nX_n$.

This objective function is to be realized subject to the following structural constraints derived from the information projected in table 8.5 and shown as

$$a_{11}X_1 + a_{12}X_2 + a_{13}X_3 + a_{14}X_4 + \ldots\ldots + a_{1n}X_n \geq B_1.$$
$$a_{21}X_1 + a_{22}X_2 + a_{23}X_3 + a_{24}X_4 + \ldots\ldots + a_{2n}X_n \geq B_2.$$
$$a_{31}X_1 + a_{32}X_2 + a_{33}X_3 + a_{34}X_4 + \ldots\ldots + a_{3n}X_n \geq B_3.$$
$$\cdot\cdot \quad \cdot \quad \ldots\ldots\ldots \cdot \quad \cdot \quad \cdot \quad \cdot\cdot$$
$$\cdot\cdot \quad \cdot \quad \ldots\ldots\ldots \cdot \quad \cdot \quad \cdot \quad \cdot\cdot$$
$$\cdot\cdot \quad \cdot \quad \ldots\ldots\ldots \cdot \quad \cdot \quad \cdot \quad \cdot\cdot$$
$$\cdot\cdot \quad \cdot \quad \ldots\ldots\ldots \cdot \quad \cdot \quad \cdot \quad \cdot\cdot$$
$$a_{m1}X_1 + a_{m2}X_2 + a_{m3}X_3 + a_{m4}X_4 + \ldots\ldots + a_{mn}X_n \geq B_m.$$
$$X_1 \geq 0, X_2 \geq 0, X_3 \geq 0, \ldots\ldots, X_n \geq 0,$$

We can rewrite this as a generalized form of linear programming problem of minimization type in an abbreviated form by using the summation sign (Σ). These are shown in matrix form as:

Minimize: $f = \sum_{j=1}^{n} P_j X_j$, where $j = 1, 2, 3, 4, \ldots\ldots, n$

Subject to

$\sum_{j=1}^{n} a_{ij} X_j \geq Bi$, where $i = 1, 2, 3, 4, \ldots\ldots, m$ and $j = 1,2,3, \ldots\ldots, n$.

and $X_j \geq 0$, where $j = 1, 2, 3, \ldots\ldots, n$.

The above generalized linear programming problems of both maximization and minimization types are written in matrix form as shown below:

linear programming problem (Maximization)	linear programming problem (Minimization)
Max: $f = PY$	Min; $Z = CX$
Subject to	Subject to
$aY \leq B$	$aX \geq B$
$Y \geq 0$	$X \geq 0$

'P' in the matrix refers to the row matrix containing the coefficient of the objective function of the maximization problem. Its logical corollary is C, which stands for the row matrix containing the coefficients of the objective function of the minimization problem. 'Y' is the column matrix containing the decision variables in the maximization problem, while 'X' is the column matrix containing the decision variables in the minimization problem.

'a' matrix contains the coefficients of the constraints in both these cases of maxmization and minimization, although these coefficients are different in their values in both the cases. The reader must note that it is expressed only in the form of symbols. Matrix 'B' is the column matrix that contains resource constraints. The constraints in case of the maximization problem are of $\leq$ types while for the problem of minimization they are of $\geq$ type.

However a given problem of programming may contain the mixed constraints so that some constraints are of $\leq$ types and others are of $\geq$ types and there may be still other constraints which are of = types. For this type of problems the constraints are to be converted in to the required signs before application of any method is made to obtain solutions to the given problem.

This type of situations will be discussed later on. The most important point readers can notice is that the decision variables are non-negative quantities and at the most it can be zero. This is denoted the non-negativity restrictions of the programming. This is applied to the problem of maximization and minimization types.

8.5. Assumptions of Linear Programming

This mathematical programming technique can be applied only when certain assumptions are fulfilled. Therefore application of linear programming problem rests on the following assumptions:

(1) *Proportionality is a fundamental assumption of linear programming:* There is an existence of proportionality in both the objective function and the structural constraints. It is for this reason that when the objective function is to maximize: f = 20X + 30Y, its implication is that one unit of product X is earning Rs. 20 while a unit of 'Y' product is fetching Rs. 30. The total revenue generated by the firm is equal to the total quantities of X multiplied by 20 plus total quantity of Y multiplied by 30 This explanation is also applicable to the structural constraints. It is because of this assumption, returns to scale is constant. Thus it is neither increasing nor decreasing returns to scale operate in the production process.

(2) *Constant prices:* The prices of inputs and output are also assumed to be constant and known to the user of this programming technique while finding optimal solution to the problem.

(3) *The linear programming model is based on the assumption of certainty:* The assumptions underlying the programming model is that various parameters like the coefficients of objective function and structural constraints and resource values are known to the user and are c[illegible]

(4) *Assumption of divisibility:* The decision variables are continuous and t[illegible] be obtained in fractional values also. The firm may produce 2/3rd units of a product alth[illegible] many situations we may get integer values for the decision variables. Therefore the activit[illegible] made finite and divisible.

(5) *Linear relationships:* The programming is stated in linear relations. This is applied to both the objective function and the structural constraints. This means all variables are raised to their power one.

(6) *Presence of constraints in the activities:* Linear programming is applied to the problems involving the constraints which are in the form of inequalities. This is owing to the technological limitations. In case of the problems involving maximization, use of a given resource can not exceed the maximum capacity which are given and known to its user.. For minimization problems the resource to be used can not be less than certain specified quantity. This is indicated by constraints of more than types.

(7) *Non-negativity restrictions:* This programming technique assumes that decision variables are non-negativequantities or at the most it can be zero. Therefore solution to a linear programming problem is achieved only when the decision variables obtained are non-negative. A firm for example producing output obviousely can not reach a solution with negative output as this is rendered impossible.

8.6. Graphical Solution to Linear Programming Problems

After the problem is stated and formulated in the form of a linear programming problem of either maximization or minimization type, the next step is to obtain its optimal solution. The solution can be achieved by applying either the graphical method or the simplex method, called the algebraic method. The algebraic method is widely used. this can also be the the only method useful when linear programming problem exceeds two decision variables.

First we will explain how graphical solutions to the linear programming problems are obtained and then we will make use of the simplex method for finding optimal solutions to the linear programming problems. Readers can make a note that the application of graphical method prerequisites the decision variables to be restricted to only two since a graph can represent only two variables on its two axes.

The graphical solution to a linear programming problem of maximization type are demonstrated first and then the same for the minimization problems are dealt with.

Following steps are useful for graphical solution to both the maximization and minimization problems:

The first step is the identification of the objective function and structural constraints. It is required to plot each of the constraints on graph and shade the region satisfying these constraints. While shading the feasible region on the graph the negative values for the decision variables are not considered due to the assumption of non-negativity restriction. The region of basic feasible solution satisfying all the constraints which are of ≥ types or ≤ types are to be located on the graph. The next step is to determine the extreme points or corner points of the area of feasible region since at least any one of the extreme points will provide solution to the given linear programming problem.

An alternative solution to the linear programming problem is to plot the linear objective function on the graph by assigning some arbitrary values to it so as to determine slope the linear objective function. The lines parallel to this linear line are drawn so as to get one of these lines becoming tangent to at least one of the extreme points. This will determine optimal solution in the area of feasible region. In case of the problems involving maximization the line farthest from the origin and tangent to the extreme point in the basic feasible solution is the required solution. For minimization type of problems the objective linear line close to the origin and tangent to one of the extreme points of feasible region will provide the required optimal solution. Some illustrations are used in the following texts for analytical purpose.

8.6.1 Graphical Solution to linear programming problems of maximization: Graphical solution to the linear programming problems involving maximization are illustrated below:

Illustration 1:

Let us suppose a typical firm who is producing two products X_1 and X_2 which he sales in the market for maximizing profit. The per unit market prices of X_1 and X_2 are given and known to him as Rs. 4 and Rs. 5 respectively. The firm's objective function is defined accordingly, This refers to the maximization of profit function : Maximize : $Z = 4X_1 + 5X_2$.

To produce these products the firm makes use of two inputs, capital and labour. The production of one unit of X_1 requires use of 2 units of capital and 4 units of labour while one unit of X_2 requires 3 units of capital and 2 units of labour. The firm can use at the most 18 units of capital and 20 units of labour inputs. However he can use less than these available quantities of inputs if he so desires.

The problem confronts the firm is how he will alloacte these available resouce inputs labour and capital optimally so that the product mix he selects will yield maximum profit to him. The above information can be used to obtain two structural constraints in regard to these two inputs are formulated and shown below. These are expressed in linear form.

$2X_1 + 3X_2 \leq 18$ Capital constraint

$4X_1 + 2X_2 \leq 20$ Labour constraint

The non-negativity restriction requires $X_1 \geq 0, X_2 \geq 0$

This linear programming problem is expressed in a complete form as:

Maximize: $Z = 4X_1 + 5X_2$

Subject to

$$2X_1 + 3X_2 \leq 18$$
$$4X_1 + 2X_2 \leq 20$$
$$X_1 \geq 0, X_2 \geq 0$$

We need to plot these structural constraints on a graph. The constraint capital input is given by $2X_1 + 3X_2 \leq 18$. This constraint implies that the alternative combinations of outputs that can be produced will not exceed 18 units of capital. To plot this constraint on graph we need to convert the constraint in to an equation, $2X_1 + 3X_2 = 18$. Plotting of this equation on graph is made easy since it requires to obtain two points, one on Y-axis and another on X-axis. By joining them a straight line is obtained. To locate a point on Y-axis it is required to set $X_1= 0$, which gives $X_2 = 6$. For X-intercept it is required to assign $X_2 = 0$, so that $X_1= 9$. Joining points (0,6) and (9,0) a linear line AB is obtained. This is shown on fig-8.1. However since this constraint is an inequality not an equation, to satisfy this it is required to locate the area satisfying the constraint $2X_1 + 3X_2 \leq 18$. This is the shaded area lying below and on the line *AB* in fig-8.1. The area is restricted to the triangle *OAB* due to the fact that decision variables are to fulfill the non- negative restriction.

The same explanation is extended to plot the labour constraint given by $4X_1 + 2X_2 \leq 20$ on the same graph. Thus the equation $4X_1 + 2X_2 = 20$ is to be plotted. Accordingly two points (0,10) and (5,0) are obtained. They are obtained by setting first $X_1 = 0$ so that $X_2=10$ and then $X_1 = 5$ for $X_2= 0$. The process of obatining these *X* and *Y*-intercepts are similar to the one we got while plotting the capital constraint. The line CD is drawn satisfying this constraint. The required area satisfying this constraint is the area in the triangle OCD.

To determine optimal solution it is required to define the region for acceptable values of X_1 and X_2 variables in relation to both these constraints and the non-negative restriction. This region is called the area of feasible region satisfying both the constraints. This region is area OAED in fig. 8.1.

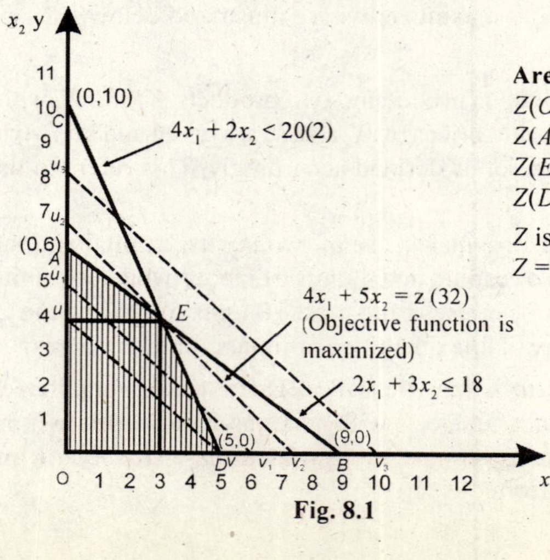

Fig. 8.1

Area of Feasible region is *OAED*

$Z(O) = 4x_1 + 5x_2 = 0$ for $x_1 = x_2 = 0$

$Z(A) = 4x_1 + 5x_2 = 30$ for $x_1 = 0\ x_2 = 6$

$Z(E) = 4x_1 + 5x_2 = 32$ for $x_1 = 3\ x_2 = 4$

$Z(D) = 4x_1 + 5x_2 = 20$ for $x_1 = 5\ x_2 = 0$

Z is maximum at '*E*' where

$Z = 32, x_1 = 3, x_2 = 4$

From this area of basic feasible region four extreme points *O, A, E* and *D* are determined. An infinite alternative combinations of X_1 and X_2 are found in this area.that fulfill both the constraints plotted on the graph. Accordingly any point lying out side the region *OAED* provides infeasible solution and thus are to be rejected. For example a point in the region *ACE* does not fulfill the constraint $2X_1 + 3X_2 \leq 18$ while a point in the region *BED* fails to satisfy the constraint $4X_1 + 2X_2 = 20$.

The extreme points of *OAED* are both basic and feasible.Therefore any one of these extreme points can provide an optimal solution to this problem. It requires us to determine the pair of X_1 and X_2 values from these extreme points or corner points. Point '*E*' is lying on the intersection of two straight lines and the pair of X_1 and X_2 values corresponding to this point can be obtained either by solving two simultaneous equations or by drawing ordinates to both the axes from this intersecting point.

Thus by multiplying capital constraint by 2 and subtracting the equation from the other one we will get $X_1 = 3$ and $X_2 = 4$. These pair of values are substituted in objective function $Z = 4X_1 + 5X_2$ Similar way the pair of values corresponding to othr extreme points are to be substituted in the objective function. These points acordingly will provide *Z* values, which are listed in table 8.6.

Table 8.6

Extreme points	Pair of X_1 and X_2 values	Value of $Z = 4X_1 + 5X_2$
0	$X_1 = 0,\ X_2 = 0$	$4X_1 + 5X_2 = 4\,(0) + 5\,(0) = 0$
A	$X_1 = 0,\ X_2 = 6$	$4X_1 + 5X_2 = 4\,(0) + 5\,(6) = 30$
E	$X_1 = 3,\ X_2 = 4$	$4X_1 + 5X_2 = 4\,(3) + 5\,(4) = 32$ (Maximum)
D	$X_1 = 5,\ X_2 = 0$	$4X_1 + 5X_2 = 4\,(5) + 5\,(0) = 20$

The optimal solution is obtained at 3 units of X_1 and 4 units of X_2 which the firm should porduce to maximize profit. This maximum profit is Rs. 32 for this product mix. Any other product mix in the area of feasible region and at the extreme points will yield profit less than 32. Thus the required solution is X_1=3 and X_2=4 and *Z*= 32.

An alternative way of finding the optimal solution is to plot the objective function on the same graph which wll be passings through the region of basic feasible solution. To determine the line and its slope we can arbitrarily assign some values to *Z*. Let us take $Z = 4X_1 + 5X_2 = 20$. This gives us two points on two axes (0,4) and (5,0). By joining these two points we get linear line UV This is called iso-profit line. This line provides us pair of X_1 and X_2 values that yield profit of Rs. 20. We need to draw the iso-profit lines parallel to *UV* and lying to the right of *UV* so that it is farthest from the origin and tangent to at least one of the extreme points. It is attained by the line U_2V_2. Although the line U_3V_3 will give a larger amount of profit to the firm, this line lies outside the area of feasible region and is unattainable. Accordingly our solution lies at '*E*' which is also obtained from the objective function. This provides the same solution as the one we have obtained from the earlier method.

Illustration 2:

An illustratation of linear programming problem involving three structural constraints are porvided. Let us suppose a farmer is producing two types of products *X* and *Y*. He is required to use three different types of resources, cutting, packaging and grinding operations which are available in hours. The farmer can use 12, 9 and 5 hours at the most from these three resources.

One unit of X requires 1, 3 and 1 hours from cutting, packaging and grinding operations while one unit of product Y requires use of 3, 1 and 1 hours from these three reources. Farmer wants to maximize profit by producing an optimal combination of these two products by selling them in the market at per unit prices Rs. 2 and Rs. 3 for X and Y respectively.

The above information canbe formulated as a linear programming problem of maximization type. This problem in a complete form is shown as follows;

Maximize: $Z = 2X + 3Y$

Subject to

$$X + 3Y \leq 12$$

$$3X + Y \leq 9$$

$$X + Y \leq 5$$

$$X \geq 0,\ Y \geq 0$$

To find an optimal solution to this problem by graphical method it is required to plot these constraints on a graph, shown in fig.8.2. The first constraint is $X + 3Y \leq 12$. This constarint is converted in to equation $X + 3Y = 12$. From this two points (0, 4) and (12, 0) as Y-intercept and X-intercept are obtained. Joining these points the linear line AB is obtained. However since the constraint is an inequality and not the equation, the area satisfying the constraint will be all the points lying on AB and below this line. The required area is the triangle OAB. In the similar way we can plot the other constrints on the same graph fig-8.2. The required line is CD satisfying equation $3X + Y = 9$. The straight line EF is obtained that satisfies the equation of third constraint $X + Y \leq 5$.

The area of the acceptable region satisfying all three constraints called the area of the basic feasible solution is to be determined. This required area is $OAGHD$, shaded in fig-8.2. This region provides all the pairs of X and Y values which satisfy all three constraints and also the non-negativity restriction. Any point outside this region will not fulfill any one or more of the constraints. The pair of X and Y values at the points of intersection G and H can also be obtained by solving two equations intersecting the point or directly by drawing ordinates from the point to both the axes. Thus by solving equations 1 and 2 intersecting at G we get the pair of X and Y values as $X = 1.5$ and $Y = 3.5$. Similarly by solving equations 2 and 3 we obtain $X = 2$ and $Y = 4$ at point H.

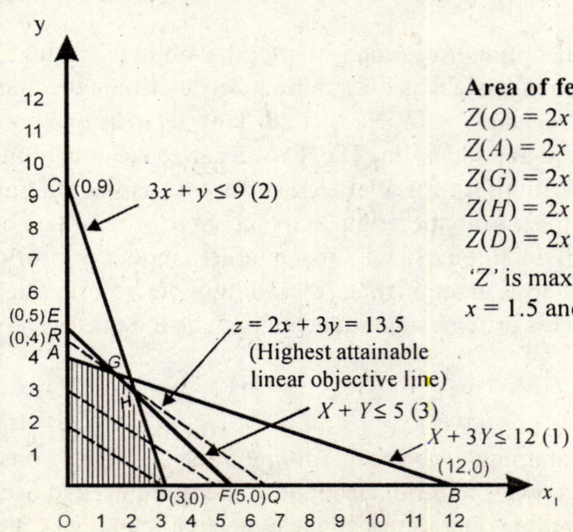

Area of feasible region is *OAGHD*

$Z(O) = 2x + 3y = 0$, at $x = 0$ and $y = 0$

$Z(A) = 2x + 3y = 12$, at $x = 0$ and $y = 4$

$Z(G) = 2x + 3y = 13.5$, at $x = 1.5$ and $y = 3.5$

$Z(H) = 2x + 3y = 13$, at $x = 2$ and $y = 3$

$Z(D) = 2x + 3y = 6$, at $x = 3$ and $y = 0$

'Z' is maximum at 'G' where

$x = 1.5$ and $y = 3.5$ and $z = 13.5$

Fig. 8.2

The next step is to substitute the pairs of X and Y values obtained in the objective function Z for finding Z at these extreme points. These Z values are listed below in table-8.7.

Table 8.7

Extreme points	Pair of X and Y values	Value of $Z = 2X + 3Y$
0	$X = 0,\ Y = 0$	$2X + 3Y = 2(0) + 3(0) = 0$
A	$X = 0,\ Y = 4$	$2X + 3Y = 2(0) + 3(4) = 12$
G	$X = 1.5,\ Y = 3.5$	$2X + 3Y = 2(1.5) + 3(3.5) = 13.5$ (Maximum)
H	$X = 2,\ Y = 3$	$2X + 3Y = 2(2) + 3(3) = 13$
D	$X = 3,\ Y = 0$	$2X + 3Y = 2(3) + 3(0) = 6$

The same solution can be obtained by plotting the linear objective function on the graph. By assigning an arbitrary value to $Z = 2X + 3Y$ we can determine its slope. For $Z = 6$ we get pair of points (0, 2) and (3.0) joining which the straight line KL is obtained. It passes through the area of feasible region. This iso-profit line is clearly attainable. The farmer need to move to the right by drawing the iso-profit lines parallel to KL and also tangent to at least one of the extreme points on the graph. The required line is RQ, tangent to the area of feasible region at point G. Other iso-profit lines will yield porfit less than RQ line at G. Therefore solution lies at G. Profit is maximimum when farmer produces 1.5 of X and 3.5 of Y and total profit is Rs. 13.5, the highest profit.

8.6.2 Graphical Solution to Linear programming problem of minimization: We can demonstrate now the graphical solution to linear programming problems involving minimization types, when the objective function is to minimize the given function. Following illustrations are used for anlaysis.

Illustration 3:

Let us have a hypothetical example of an individual who has an option to purchase two types of food items X_1 and X_2, available in market at prices of Rs. 4 and Rs. 2 respectively. The person wants to buy these food items in some combinations to fulfill his daily minimum vitamin requirements of A_1 and A_2. The daily vitamin requirements to maintain his health is 20 units of A_1 and 15 units of A_2. These two vitamins are available in these two food items in some quantities. Food item X_1 contains 10 and 2 units of vitamins A_1 and A_2 while food item X_2 contains 5 and 3 units of these vitamins respectively.

We need to find the optimum combination of the food items he should buy so as to minimize the cost on food items and at the same time fulfill the minimum vitamin requirements.

This problem can be formulated as a linear programming problem of minimization, where an optimal combination of two food items minimizing cost on food items is to be obtained. These information are tabulated below:

Table 8.8

Vitamins	Food item X_1 containing Vitamins A_1 and A_2	Food item X_2 containing Vitamins A_1 and A_2	Minimum Vitamin requirements to maintain health
A_1	10	2	18
A_2	5	3	15
Price of food items	Rs. 4	Rs. 2	—

The liner programming problem in its complete form has been given as follows:

Minimize: $f = 4X_1 + 2X_2$

Subject to

$$10X_1 + 2X_2 \geq 20$$
$$5X_1 + 3X_2 \geq 15$$
$$X_1 \geq 0, X_2 \geq 0$$

The structural constraints are plotted on a graph shown in fig. 8.3.

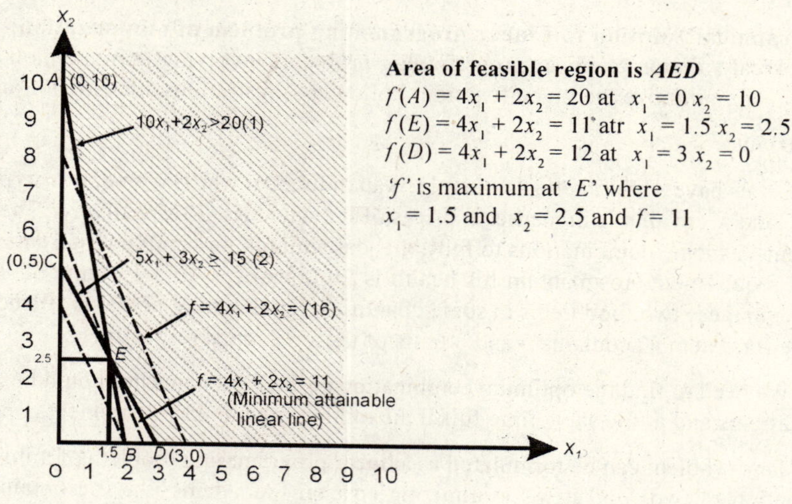

Fig. 8.3

The first constraint is $10X_1 + 2X_2 \geq 20$. We are to convert this in to an equation as $10X_1 + 2X_2 = 20$. Two points on two axes are determined by setting first $X_1 = 0$ so that $X_2 = 10$ and for $X_2 = 0$, $X_1 = 2$. Joining (0, 10) and (2, 0), we obtain straight line *AB*.

The second constraint is $5X_1 + 3X_2 \geq 15$. After converting this in to equation two points on the two axes are obtained by setting first $X_1 = 0$ so that $X_2 = 5$ and for $X_2 = 0$, $X_1 = 3$. By joining (0, 5) and (3, 0) the required straight line *CD* is attained.

Since the constraints are of ≥ type and not equations, the area satisfying the constraint are the points lying on the line *AB* and the area above to the right of line *AB*. For the second constraint the area satisfying it will be all the points on the line *CD* and area above this line. The area of basic feasible solution lies in the area satisfying both the constraints. This area is *AED*. Required solution lies at any one of these extreme points. This corresponds to the pair of X_1 and X_2 values that will provide minimum value to *Z*. The value of *Z* corresponding to these corner points are listed below in table-8.9.

Table 8.9

Extreme points	Pair of *X* and *Y* values	Value of $Z = 4X_1 + 2X_2$
A	$X_1 = 0, X_2 = 10$	$4X_1 + 2X_2 = 4(0) + 2(10) = 20$
E	$X_1 = 1.5, X_2 = 2.5$	$4X_1 + 2X_2 = 4(1.5) + 2(2.5) = 11$ (Minimum Cost)
D	$X_1 = 3, X_2 = 0$	$4X_1 + 2X_2 = 4(3) + 2(0) = 12$

Minimum *Z* value is obtained at point '*E*'. The pair of X_1 and X_2 values at this point provide the minimmum *Z* value, 11. Thus the solution is that the person concerned will purchase 1.5 of X_1 and 2.5 of X_2 food items to minimize total cost. These quantities of X_1 and X_2 will also fulfill the minimum vitamin requirements for the person.

Illustration 4:

Let us suppose we have a farmer who uses three different types of fertilizers, urea, phosphates, nitrogen for cultivation of grain. These fertilizers are used in some minimum quantities measured in KG. These minimum requiremnets are given as 8, 10 and 16 KG's respectively. These fertilizers are available in two different packets leveled as *A* and *B*. The market prices per packet of *A* is Rs. 30 and of *B* is Rs.20.

Each bag of A contains 2, 1 and 1 kg's while each bag of *B* contains 1, 2, and 8 kg's of these three types of fertilizers respectively. The farmer wants to minimize the cost while buying the packets *A* and *B* so that the minimum requirements of fertilizers is also satisfied simultaneously. Formulate this as a linear programming problem and solve it graphically detremining the optimumal combinations of bags *A* and *B* the farmer would buy to minimize total cost. The above information are restructured in following table- 8.10:

Table 8.10

Fertilizers	Each bag *A* containing the fertilizers in kg's	Each bag *B* containing the fertilizers in kg's	Minimum Fertilizer requirement by the farmer
Urea (F_1)	2	1	8
Phosphate (F_2)	1	2	10
Nitrogen (F_3)	1	8	16
Price per bag	Rs. 30	Rs. 20	——

The information depicted in the above table are represented in a complete form of a linear programming problem of minimization as shown below:

Minimize: $Z = 30A + 20B$

Subject to

$$2A + B \geq 8$$
$$A + 2B \geq 10$$
$$A + 8B \geq 16$$
$$A \geq 0,\ B \geq 0$$

The structural constraints plotted on the graph, fig.8.4.

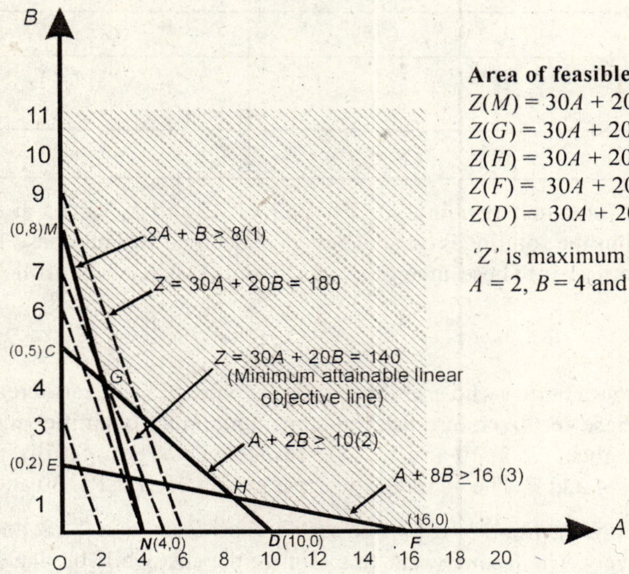

Area of feasible region is *MGHF*

$Z(M) = 30A + 20B = 160$, at $A = 0,\ B = 8$

$Z(G) = 30A + 20B = 140$, at $A = 2,\ B = 4$

$Z(H) = 30A + 20B = 260$, at $A = 8,\ B = 1$

$Z(F) = 30A + 20B = 480$, at $A = 16,\ B = 0$

$Z(D) = 30A + 20B = 160$, at $A = 0,\ B = 8$

'Z' is maximum at 'G' where $A = 2$, $B = 4$ and $Z = 140$

Fig. 8.4

The first constraint is $2A + B \geq 8$. This is converted in to equation $2A + B = 8$. By setting first $A = 0$, we get $B = 8$ and for $B = 0$, $A = 4$. By joining (0, 8) and (4, 0) we get the straight line MN.

The second constraint is $A + 2B \geq 10$. By plotting the equation $A + 2B = 10$ we can find for $A = 0$, $B = 5$, while for $B = 0$, $A = 10$. By joining two points (0, 5) and (10, 0) therequired line obtained is CD. In the same process the third constraint $A + 8B \geq 16$ is plotted on the graph.

The equation $A + 8B = 16$ will give $B = 2$ for $A = 0$ and for $B = 0$, $A = 16$. By joining two points (0, 2) and (16, 0) the straight line EF is drawn.

All these three constraints are of $\geq$ types. Therefore area of the feasible region identified will be all the points on the line and the area above to the right of these lines. Accordingly the basic feasible solution repreesnts the area $MGHF$. The extreme points of the region where our optimal solution can be determined are M, G, H and F. Optimal solution lies at any one of these corner points. This corresponds to one that minimizes the objective function $f = 30A + 20B$. Different values to the objecctive function $f = 30A + 20B$ are obtained at these extreme points.

Point 'M' provides the pair of A and B values as $A = 0$ and $B = 8$. Point 'G' is another extreme point. The pair of A and B values at this point can be determined from the graph directly or by solving the first and the second equations simultaneously intersecting at this point. To find A and B values we need to solve these equations by multipliplying first equation by 2 and subtracting it from the second equation. From this we get $A = 2$ and $B = 4$, as shown below:

$2\,(2A + B = 8) = 4A + 2A = 16$ so that

$$
\begin{array}{l}
4A + 2B = 16 \\
-A - 2B = -10 \\
\hline
3A = 6, \text{ and } A = 2.
\end{array}
$$

Substituting $A = 2$ in $2A + B = 8$, we get $B = 4$ at point G

Point 'H' is another extreme point in the area of feasible region. The pair of A and B values at this point can be determined from the graph directly or by solving the second and third equations simultaneously. By subtracting the third from the second equation, we get

$A + 2B = 10$

$-A - 8B = -16$

$-6B = -6$, and $B = 1$.

Substituting $B = 1$ in $A + 2B = 10$, we get $A = 8$.

At 'F', The pair of A and B values are 16 and 0.

Table 8.11

Extreme points	**Pair of A and B values**	**Value of $Z = 30A + 20B$**
M	$A = 0,\ B = 8$	$30A + 20B = (30)(0) + (20)(8) = 160$
G	$A = 2,\ B = 4$	$30A + 20B = (30)(2) + (20)(4) = 140$ (Minimum)
H	$A = 8,\ B = 1$	$30A + 20B = (30)(8) + (20)(1) = 260$
F	$A = 16,\ B = 0$	$30A + 20B = (30)(16) + (20)(0) = 480$

The same solution can be obtained in an alternative way. This requires us to plot the linear objective function on the same graph. It is called iso-cost line. The objective function, $Z = 30A + 20B$ can be plotted by arbitrarily assigning some values to Z. For example if $Z = 120$, we can get two points (0, 6) and (4, 0) on two axes, joining which the linear iso-cost line UV is obtained. This line is much below the feasible region for which it is required to draw lines parallel to UV. The lowest iso-cost line which is tangent to one of the extreme points of the feasible region is the line U_1V_1. This iso-cost line is tangent to the area of feasible region at point 'G', which gives us the required optimal solution. The minimum cost is Rs. 140 corresponding to this point.. The combination of bags satisfying the constarints and also minimizing total cost will be 2 bags of A and 4 bags of B.

8.7. Graphical Solution to LPP in case of Mixed Constraints

We have got the required solution to the linear programming propblems when the objective function is either of maximization or minimization. For this the structural constrints are to be in the rquired direction. We will now examine the situations under which optimal solution is to be determined to the linear programming problems when the constraints are of mixed types. This refers to the cases involving mixed constraints. For example in case of minimization problems all the structural constraints are to be of $\geq$ type while the problems involving maximization requires the constraints to be of $\leq$ types. However there are possibilities that in a linear programming problem of either maximization or minimization cases all the constraints are not in the required direction, i.e., some constraints are of ≤ types, some are of ≥ types while some other constraints can be in the form of equations. In this case graphical solution to the given problem can be obtained in a slightly different way..

Following illustrations are used to depict this situation. It is required to find optimal solutions for these special cases. We habe the following illustrations for this.

Illustration 5:

Solve graphically the following linear programming problem:

Minimize: $f = 3X + 7Y$

Subject to:

$$4X + 2Y \geq 40$$
$$6X + 14Y \leq 168$$
$$X + 2Y \geq 16$$
$$X \geq 0, \; Y \geq 0$$

These structural constraints are plotted in in figure 8. 5, where the area of the feasible solution has been shaded. Since the constraints are of mixed types the area satisfying these constraints are not in the same direction. First constraint is $4X + 2Y \geq 40$. This constraint is plotted by converting it in to equation $4X + 2Y = 40$. We obtain two points (0, 20) and (10,0) that gives us straight line 'AB'. The area satisfying this constraint are all the points on it and the area above to the right of AB line becuase the constraint is of ≥ type. The second constraint $6X + 14Y \leq 168$ is converted into equation $6X + 14Y = 168$. This gives us two points (0, 12) and (28, 0) and joining them 'CD' straight line is obtained. The area satisfying this constraint is all the points lying on the line 'CD' and area below towards origin of this line. The third constraint is to be plotted on the graph in a similar way. From this we get a straight line 'EF', obtained by joining two points (0, 8) and (16, 0).

The area of basic feasible solution that will be satisfying all these three constraints need to be located. This area is GDFH, shaded in fig- 8.5. As usual the optimal solution lies at any one of these extreme points of the region. To determine optimal solution, we need to obtain the pair of X and Y values corresponding to all of the extreme points. The values obtained are to be substituted in the equation of the objective function. These are listed below in table 8.12.

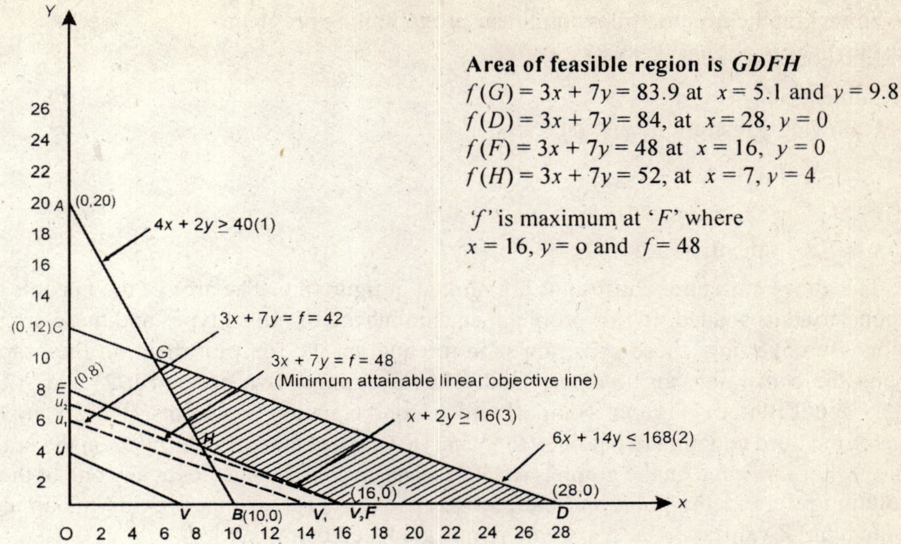

Fig. 8.5

Table 8.12

Extreme points	Pair of *X* and *Y* values	Value of $f = 3X + 7Y$
G	$X = 5.1$, $Y = 9.8$	$3X + 7Y = 3(5.1) + 7(9.8) = 83.9$
D	$X = 28$, $Y = 0$	$3X + 7Y = 3(28) + 7(0) = 84$
F	$X = 16$, $Y = 0$	$3X + 7Y = 3(16) + 7(0) = 48$ (Minimum)
H	$X = 8$, $Y = 4$	$3X + 7Y = 3(8) + 7(4) = 52$

We get the optimal solution at point '*F*', where $X = 16$, $Y = 0$, and $f = 48$, the minimum. Other extreme points like *G*, *D* and *H*, represent thepairs of *X* and *Y* values that yield value of '*F*', exceeding 48, therefore rejected. The same solution is also obtained by plotting the linear objective function on the same graph. To do this an arbitrary value can be assigned to it. Thus $f = 3X + 7Y = 21$. This provides two points (0, 3) and (7, 0) on two axes. Joining these points we get the straight line *UV*. However this line is not falling in the area of feasible region, for which it is required to draw the lines parallel to UV. One such line is tangent to the feasible region. This corresponds the line U_2V_2 (U_2F). The required solution corresponds to this extreme point *F*, to which U_2V_2 is tangent. Any other line passing through this feasible region will contain pair of *X* and Y values that yield '*F*' value larger than 48 and thus indicate non-optimal. The lowest of the iso-cost lines is therefore U_2V_2.

Illustration 6 :

Solve graphically the following linear programming problem

Maximize: $Z = 5X_1 + 7X_2$

Subject to:

$$2X_1 + 3X_2 \geq 6$$
$$X_1 - 2X_2 \leq 4$$
$$3X_1 + 2X_2 \leq 18$$
$$X_1 \geq 0, X_2 \geq 0$$

The above structural constraints are plotted in figure 8.6. The area of the feasible solution satisfying these constarints is shaded. In this problem constraints are of mixed types and these are not in the required direction. By coverting these constraints in to equation we can plot them on the graph so that the area satisfying the constraint can be determined. Thus by joining two points (0, 2) and (3, 0) first equation $2X_1 + 3X_2 = 6$ is ploted on graph. Similarly for second equation two points (0, –2) and (4, 0) are obtained together from third equation two points (0, 9) and (6, 0) are obatined and plotted on the graph. The area of the feasible region is located on the graph is ABDGE. The optimum value lies at any one of these extreme points. The solution refers to the point and the pair of X_1 and X_2 values that provide maximum value to Z. The corresponding Z values at these extreme points are listed below:

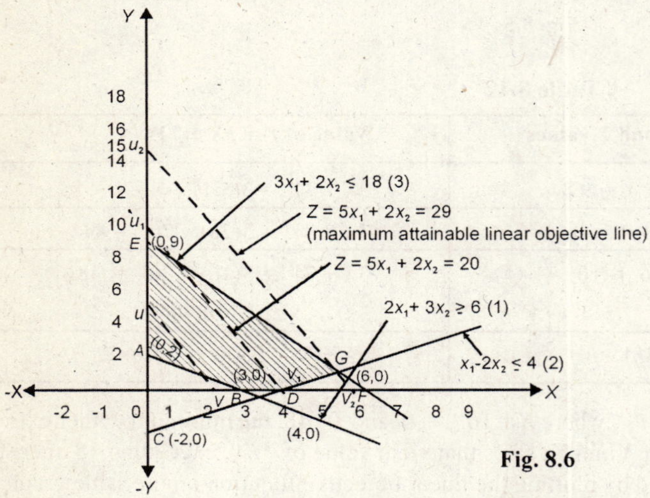

Fig. 8.6

Area of feasible region is *ABDGE*

$Z(A) = 5x_1 + 2x_2 = 4$ at $x_1 = 0, x_2 = 2$

$Z(B) = 5x_1 + 2x_2 = 15$ at $x_1 = 3, x_2 = 0$

$Z(D) = 5x_1 + 2x_2 = 20$ at $x_1 = 4, x_2 = 0$

$Z(G) = 5x_1 + 2x_2 = 29$ at $x_1 = 5.5, x_2 = 0.75$

$Z(E) = 5x_1 + 2x_2 = 18$ at $x_1 = 0, x_2 = 9$

'Z' is maximum at 'G' where $x_1 = 5.5$, $x_2 = 0.75$ and $Z = 29$

Table 8.13

Extreme points	**Pair of X_1 and X_2 values**	**Value of $Z = 5X_1 + 2X_2$**
A	$X_1 = 0, X_2 = 2$	$5X_1 + 2X_2 = 5(0) + 2(2) = 4$
B	$X_1 = 3, X_2 = 0$	$5X_1 + 2X_2 = 5(3) + 2(0) = 15$
D	$X_1 = 4, X_2 = 0$	$5X_1 + 2X_2 = 5(4) + 2(0) = 20$
G	$X_1 = 5.5, X_2 = 0.75$	$5X_1 + 2X_2 = 5(5.5) + 2(0.75) = 29$ (Maximum)
E	$X_1 = 0, X_2 = 9$	$5X_1 + 2X_2 = 5(0) + 2(9) = 18$

The objective function Z is maximized at 'G', where $X_1 = 5.5$ and $X_2 = 0.75$ and $Z = 29$. The same solution can be obtained by plotting the objective function on the graph. This is repreesnted by the linear lines UV and U_1V_1 The highest attainable iso-revenue line is U_3V_3 which is tangent to the extreme point 'G' on the graph. This point provides the required solution.

8.8. Some Special Cases: LPP Without Unique Solution

In linear programming problems of either maximization or minimization an unique optimal solution is achieved. The solution is attained corresponding to any one of the extreme points of the feasible region bounded by the constraints. This also means no other solution to the given problem will provide an alternative that can satisfy the objective function and the constraints.

However there are some special cases where we are not able to obtain an unique solution to the linear programming problem. This case is referred to multiple optimum solution.

8.8.1 Multiple Optimum Solution

It is possible that a given linear programming problem provides more than one optimum solution. This is called multiple optimum solution. This is possible when slope of the objective function coincides with slope of one of the structural constraint plotted on the graph while finding graphical solution to the given problem. This constraint line forms the boundary line in the feasible region. Following LPP depicts this situation:

Solve graphically the following LPP

Maximize: $Z = 4X_1 + 8X_2$

Subject to:

$$X_1 + X_2 \leq 150$$
$$X_2 \leq 80$$
$$2X_1 + 4X_2 \leq 400$$
$$X_1 \leq 100$$
$$X_1 \geq 0, X_2 \geq 0$$

These constraints are plotted on the graph 8.7 below. The line AB repreesnts the first constraint $X_1 + X_2 \leq 150$. The horizontal line 'GH' represents the second constraint $X_2 \leq 80$, while 'EF' depicts teh equation $X_1 \leq 100$ and constraint $2X_1 + 4X_2 \leq 400$ is shown by the CD linear line. By assigning an arbitrary value to $Z = 560$, the objective function $4X_1 + 8X_2$ is plotted on the graph. This enables to locate two points on two axes so as to obtain the iso-profit line 'UV'. This line falls in the feasible region. But we need to draw the parallel iso-profit lines which are farther from the origin and tangent to one of the extreme points. The area of the feasible region satisfying all these constraints is located $OGKQE$.

But the UV line representing the objective function is found parallel to one of the constraint, $2X_1 + 4X_2 = 400$. The line CD represents this. Thus the linear objective function coincides with CD line. Accordingly the same solution is obtained at both the extreme points K and Q on the graph. This also provides an infinite number of optimal solutions represented by all the points lying on the segment KQ of the CD line including extreme points K and Q. Therefore this problem is referred to the case of multiple solutions. The extreme points of the feasible region are evaluated and presnted in table 8.14:

Table 8.14

Extreme points	Pair of X_1 and X_2 values	Value of $Z = 4X_1 + 8X_2$
0	$X_1 = 0, X_2 = 0$	$4X_1 + 8X_2 = 4(0) + 8(0) = 0$
G	$X_1 = 0, X_2 = 80$	$4X_1 + 8X_2 = 4(0) + 8(80) = 640$
K	$X_1 = 40, X_2 = 80$	$4X_1 + 8X_2 = 4(40) + 8(80) = 800$
Q	$X_1 = 100, X_2 = 50$	$4X_1 + 8X_2 = 4(100) + 8(50) = 800$
E	$X_1 = 100, X_2 = 0$	$4X_1 + 8X_2 = 4(100) + 8(0) = 400$

Area of feasible region is *OGKQE*

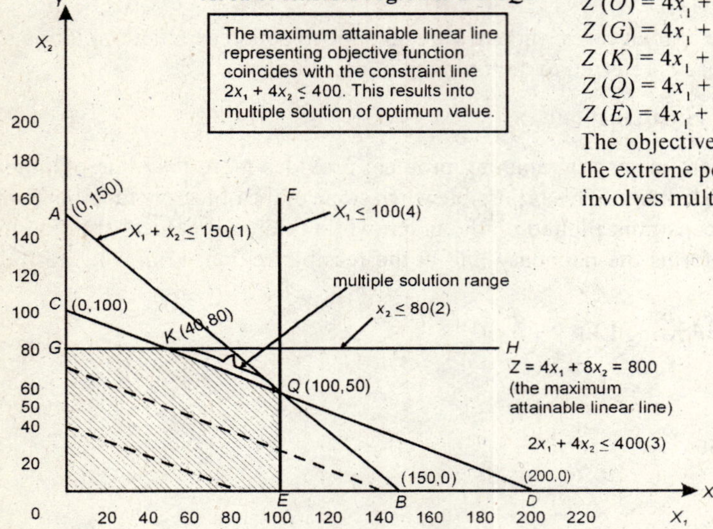

$Z(O) = 4x_1 + 8x_2 = 0$ at $x_1 = x_2 = 0$
$Z(G) = 4x_1 + 8x_2 = 640$ at $x_1 = 0, x_2 = 80$
$Z(K) = 4x_1 + 8x_2 = 800$ at $x_1 = 40, x_2 = 80$
$Z(Q) = 4x_1 + 8x_2 = 800$ at $x_1 = 100, x_2 = 50$
$Z(E) = 4x_1 + 8x_2 = 400$ at $x_1 = 100, x_2 = 0$

The objective function is maximized at both the extreme points K and Q. Thus the problem involves multiple optimal solution case.

Fig. 8.7

8.8.2 Linear programming problem with no unique solution

Another possibility that exists in the linear programming problem is that the problem provides no unique soluton to it. This is due to the fact that we are unable to determine any common feasible region that are found satisfying all the constraints and the non-negative restrictions. For this type of problem it can be said that the constraints are inconsistent. Therefore common feasible area can not be located on a graph when the constraints are plotted. The linear programming problem involving this type of situation is illustrated below:

Maximize: $f = 2X + 3Y$

Subject to:

$$2X + Y \leq 4$$
$$3X - Y \leq 3$$
$$X + Y \geq 5$$
$$X \geq 0, Y \geq 0$$

The structural constraints of the above problem are plotted on graph 8.8. The feasible region corresponding to these constraints are shaded. The first two constraints are of $\le$ types and these are located on the graph. The area satisfying these constraints is shaded *OAEK*. The third constraint is of $\ge$type, which is also plotted on thesame graph. The area satisfying this constraint is shaded. It gives all the points on the line *EF* and above to the right of *EF*. The shaded area formed is not sharing any common area with *OAEK* for which optimal solution can be determined. For this reason it can be stated that this problem has no solution. This is a linear programming problem with no unique solution.

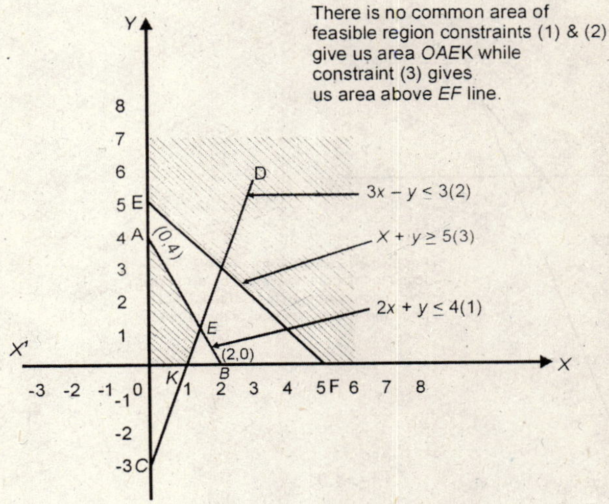

Fig. 8.8

8.8.3 The linear programming problem with unboundedness optimal solution

Another situation that can arise in linear programming problem is referred to the unbounded optimal solution. This is so as we can not determine the solution to the problem. For this type of linear programming problems, we plot the constraints on a graph to obtain the area of feasible region. But the feasible region is found unbounded. Therefore no unique solution can exist for this problem. Under this situation one or more of the decision variables can be increased infinitely without violating the restrictions, the constraint provides

Following illustration is exhibits the case of unbounded solution.

Maximize: $f = 2X + Y$

Subject to:

$$X - Y \le 3$$

$$2X - Y \le 8$$

$$X \ge 0, Y \ge 0$$

By plotting the above two constraints on a graph shown in fig- 8.9, the area of feasible solution obtained and shaded is unbounded. The objective function $f = 2X + Y$ has been plotted on the graph. The linear objective line UV is determined corresponding to $f = 2X + Y = 8$. The lines parallel to UV are drawn to the right since it is a problem of maximization. However as evident from the graph the iso-profit lines attainable can be increased infinitely towards the right. The area of feasible region to the right is seen to be unbounded. This practically means the problem is not correctly formulated since it has no unique solution.

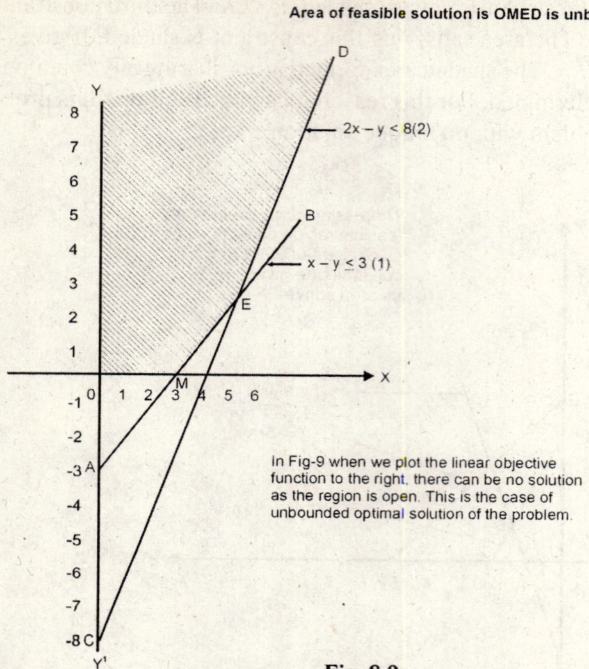

Fig. 8.9

8.8.4 Linear programming problem with redundant constraints

An optimal solution to the Linear programming problem is attained by plotting all the constraints on the graph. From this the area of feasible region is determined. One of the corner points of this region called extreme points provide solution to the problem. However it may happen that one or more of the constraints plotted on the graph fail to form a part of the boundary marking area of feasible region of the problem. The constraint is therefore said to be redundant as it is not required for determining the optimal solution. The inclusion or exclusion of this redundant constraint does not affect solution or the LPP. Following illustration depicts this situation in linear programming problems:

Maximize: $f = 3A + 5B$

Subject to:

$$2A + 3B \leq 60$$
$$5A + 4B \leq 100$$
$$2A \leq 30$$
$$4.5B \leq 45$$
$$A \geq 0,\ B \geq 0$$

This problem is graphically solved in the text of aditional problems and it is provided at the end of the chapter in fig-8.15. It incorporates one of the constraint $2A + 3B \leq 60$, to which the linear line AB represents and this does not form a part of the area of feasible region *OGRTC*. Therefore this constraint is said to be a redundant constraint as it does not affect the optimal solution. Thus even if we exclude this constraint from the problem the solution remains unaltered.

8.8.5 The concept of degeneracy in Linear programming problem

It is important to note the concept of degeneracy in Linear programming problems. In such problems of degenerate optimal solution, we obtain solution without satisfying the condition that the number of variables including the slack variables getting non-zero value are equal to the number of constraints. The solution is said to be basic when the number of non-zero variables must be equal to the number of constraints. But when the solution contains a smaller number of non-zero variables than the number of constraints as illustrated in the follwoing example it refers to the case of degeneracy.

Maximize: $Z = 2X + 3Y$

Subject to:

$$6X + 3Y \leq 18$$

$$X + Y \leq 6$$

$$X \geq 0,\ Y \geq 0$$

The aboveproblem is graphed in fig-8.10. The area of feasible region shaded is *OAB*. Accordingly optimal solution is obtained at one of the extreme point. This corresponds to point '*A*' where $X = 0$, $Y = 6$ and $Z = 18$. At point '0', X and Y values are zero and $Z = 0$, while at point '*B*', $X = 3$ and $Y = 0$ and Z value is 6.

It can be noticed that at the point '*A*' where solution does exist, both the constraints are satisfied and one of the decision variable is zero ($X = 0$). This also means at this point the slack variables $S_1 = S_2 = 0$. The solution exists with only one non-zero variable and this is Y (as $X = S_1 = S_2 = 0$), while the number of constraints are two. This shows that the number of non-zero variables is less than the number of constraints. Therefore the solution is called degenerate.

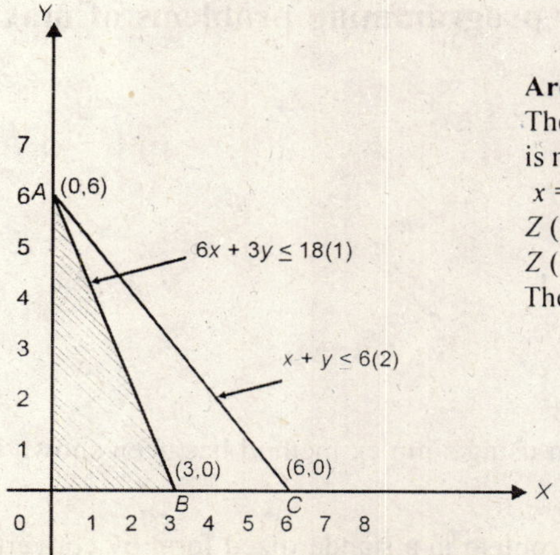

Area of feasible region is *OAB*
The objective function $Z = 2x + 3y$ is maximized at point '*A*' where
$x = 0$, $y = 6$ and $z = 18$
$Z(O) = 0$ for $x = y = 0$
$Z(B) = 6$ for $x = 3$, $y = 0$
The solution at '*A*' is degenerate one

Fig. 8.10

We plot the linear objective function $2X + 3Y$, on a graph by assigning some arbitrarry values to Z. For example take, $Z = 12$. This will give us the linear objective line with two points generated from the objective function equation, (0, 4) and (6, 0), joining which the iso-profit line 'MC' is obtained. The iso-profit line parallel to this line and tangent to the extreme point of feasible region is to be drawn and it is 'AN'. This gives us the solution that corresponds to point 'A' where $Z = 18$.

8.9. Simplex Method

The solution obtained from the graphical method seems to be very efficient for finding optimal solution to Linear programming problems of either maximization or minimization types. But this method suffers from an important drawback that under this method we can handle the problems involving only two decision variables, does not matter how many constraints the problem incorporates.

However in the real-world situation, we come across the cases where decision variables are more than two. Therefore we need to look forward a suitable alternative method to handle this type of situation. The answer to this has been given by the simplex method. This method can be used to solve the Linear programming problems of any magnitude involving two or more decision variables.

Through the simplex algorithm we can obtain optimal solution to linear programming. In graphical solution to the Linear programming problems we have seen that the optimal solution is located at any one of the extreme points of the feasible region bounded by the constraints. The simplex method is found to be relatively efficient. It also considers these extreme pints while determining solution to the problem. The method provides the merit of identifying whether solution to a given problem is optimal or not.

Simplex method is applied when a given Linear programming problems has the constraints with 'bi' being non-negative in nature. Therefore when a constraint $3X - 2Y \geq -8$, it has to be changed in to $-3X + 2Y \leq 8$, obtained by multiplying both sides by -1. The decision variables for a given problem are also to be non-negative.

While using the simplex method in the following texts the problems relating maximization are considered first and then the Linear programming problems involvoing minimization are dealt with.

8.9.1 Solution to the Linear programming problems of maximization types through the simplex method

Example 1:

Maximize; $Z = 8X_1 + 7X_2$

Subject to:

$$2X_1 + 3X_2 \leq 36$$
$$4X_1 + 3X_2 \leq 48$$
$$X_1 \geq 0, X_2 \geq 0$$

The solution to this problem using simplex method has been shown below through some important steps:

The first step is to put the problem in a standardized form by converting the above constraints in to equations. Since the constraints are of $\leq$ type, the conversion is made by introducing slack variables S's in to these constraints. The first constraints is $2X_1 + 3X_2 \leq 36$. To this the slack variable S_1 can be added to the left hand side so that the constraint is rewritten as $2X_1 + 3X_2 + S_1 = 36$. It indicates that when $2X_1 + 3X_2 = 36$,

$S_1 = 0$. For $2X_1 + 3X_2 < 36$, $S_1 > 0$. Likewise If $2X_1 + 3X_2 = 0$, $(X_1 = 0, X_2 = 0)$ $S_1 = 36$. Therefore the limiting values that S_1 can take is '0' and '36'. Thus $0 \le S_1 \le 36$. The value of the slack variable S_1 can take will depend on the values of $2X_1 + 3X_2$. The value of slack variable indicates the amount of unused resource shown by the first constraint.

The second slack variable S_2 is introduced to the second constraint in a similar way . The constraint $4X_1 + 3X_2 \le 48$ is transformed into equation so that $4X_1 + 3X_2 + S_2 = 48$. If $4X_1 + 3X_2 = 48$, $S_2 = 0$. For $4X_1 + 3X_2 < 48$, $S_2 > 0$, and for $4X_1 + 3X_2 = 0$ $(X_1 = 0, X_2 = 0)$, $S_2 = 48$. Thus The limiting values of S_2 is '0' and '48' or $0 \le S_2 \le 48$. The slack variable S_2 assumes a particular value depending on the value $4X_1 + 3X_2$ takes. This slack variable is the indication of the amount of unused resource depicts the second constraint.

After introducing the slack variables, we need to modify the objective function to contain the slack variables also. Their coefficients are taken zero owing to the fact that the cost of unused available resource types is zero. Accordingly the modified objective function becomes:

Maximize: $Z = 8X_1 + 7X_2 + 0S_1 + 0S_2$

Subject to,

$$2X_1 + 3X_2 + S_1 = 36$$

$$4X_1 + 3X_2 + S_2 = 48$$

$$X_1 \ge 0,\ X_2 \ge 0,\ S_1 \ge 0,\ S_2 \ge 0$$

The second step is to present the information of the above problem in a simplex tableau. The initial simplex tableau is simplex tableau 8.1.1.

Simplex Tableau 8.1.1

	$C_i \rightarrow$ ↓	8	7	0	0	—	— →
Basic Variables		X_1	X_2	S_1	S_2	b_i	Replacement ratio
S_1	0	2	3	1	0	36	$\frac{36}{2} = 18$
S_2	0	4	3	0	1	48	$\frac{48}{4} = 12$ →
Z_i	→	0	0	0	0	0	—
$\Delta_j = C_j - Z_i$	→	8 ↑	7	0	0	—	—

Solution is given by $X_1 = 0$, $X_2 = 0$ and $S_1 = 36$, $S_2 = 48$ and

$$Z = 8X_1 + 7X_2 + 0\,S_1 + 0\,S_2 = 8(0) + 7(0) + 0\,(36) + 0\,(48) = 0$$

In the initial tableau, the first row C_j indicates the coefficient values from the objectives function and slack varaibles. In the second row all the basics, non-basic variables (decision variables)and solution are written. Next, the coefficients in the constraint equations are written listing vertically the coefficients of all the variables. The slack variables S_1 appears only in the first equation for which its coefficient is taken zero in the other equations. The same is applicable to S_2. The coefficients of the first constraint are 2, 3, 1, 0 shown in a row. This corresponds to the constraint $2X_1 + 3X_2 + S_1 + 0S_2$.

Similarly the coefficients of $4X_1 + 3X_2 + 0S_1 + S_2$ are 4, 3, 0, 1 shown in another row. The constraint values 36 and 48 are shown in the last column against 'b_i', S_1 and S_2 are the basic variables while X_1 and X_2 are non- basic variables for this problem.

In the initial tableau the basic variables are taken. *Zj* row is formed by multiplying each element of the columns shown by the corresponding coefficient of the variable appearing in the basis and then the products are summed up. For example, for the column headed X_1, we get its corresponding value of Z,

$Z_1 = (0 \times 2) + (0 \times 4) = 0$ and similarly $Z_2 = (0 \times 3) + (0 \times 3) = 0$,

$Z_3 = (0 \times 1) + (0 \times 0) = 0$ and $Z_4 = (0 \times 0) + (0 \times 1) = 0$. The solution is 0.

The last row $\Delta j = Cj - Zj$, is formed as (8–0), (7–0), (0–0), (0 – 0). These values obtained are accordingly 8, 7, 0, 0. The solution is obtained with $X_1 = X_2 = 0$, $S_1 = 36$ and $S_2 = 48$ and $Z = 0$.

The next step is to test whether the solution obtained in simplex tableau 8.1.1 is optimal or not. This can be known from Δj values. If all the values of Δj are either zero or negative ($\Delta j \le 0$), an optimal solution is attained to the problem of maximization. In case of the Linear programming problems involving minimization the entries of Δj row are to be zero or positive ($\Delta j \ge 0$).

From Δj row of the simplex tableau 8.1.1, we can see that all entries are not zero or negative. The positive Δj values are 8 and 7 against the column headed X_1 and X_2 respectively. The highest positive value is 8 corresponds to X_1 non-basic variable. Each of the values in the Δj row indicates the amount of increase in the objective function when one unit of the variable representing the column head are introduced into the solution. The variable corresponding to the largest Δj value is to be selected for entering it in the forthcoming tableau. Therefore this is X_1 variable. The entering variable is thus X_1. The column corresponding to this variable is called *key column*. To decide the basic variable to be departed, we need to divide the '*bi*' values by the corresponding values of *key column*. From this formula we get the replacement ratios (b_i / a_{ij}) for each row. The row with the least positive replacement ratio is to be selected for replacement. This is called the *key row*. In tableau 8.1.1, the row with least ratio is S_2. Therefore the departing or out going variable is S_2 and incoming variable is X_1. The element lying at the intersection of the *key row* and *key column* is '4'. It is termed as the *key element*.

The *key row* is reproduced in tableau 8.1.2 shown below. The elements of this row are obtained by dividing all the elements of key row by key element so that we get '1' in the X_1 row of tableau 8.1.2 in the place of the value 4 of the key row. Accordingly the elements of X_1 row are 4/4, ¾, 0/4, ¼ and 48/4 in tableau 8.1.2.

The row elements of S_1 in tableau 8.1.2 are obtained by applying the following formula:

(Old row element) – (Row element of key column)(corresponding element of the replacement row)

Accordingly we get elements of the S_1 row as

$2 - 2\ (1) = 0$, $3 - 2\ (3/4) = 3/2$, $1 - 2\ (0) = 1$, $0 - 2\ (1/4) = -1/2$, and $36 - 2\ (12) = 12$

Simplex Tableau 8.1.2

	C_i → ↓	8	7	0	0	—	—
Basic Variables		X_1	X_2	S_1	S_2	b_i	Replacement ratio
S_1	0	0	$\frac{3}{2}$	1	$\frac{-1}{2}$	12	$\frac{12}{\frac{3}{2}}=\frac{24}{3}=8$ →
X_1	8	$\frac{4}{4}=1$	$\frac{3}{4}$	$\frac{0}{4}$	$\frac{1}{4}$	$\frac{48}{4}=12$	$\frac{12}{\frac{3}{4}}=\frac{48}{3}=16$
Z_j	→	8	6	0	2	96	—
$\Delta_j = C_j - Z_j$	→	0	1↑	0	−2	—	—

Just like simplex tableau 8.1.1, from tableau 8.1.2 also we find the departing and entering variables. Accordingly the departing variable is decided to be S_1 and entering variable is X_2. The Key row is S_1 and key element is 3/2. The key column is the column headed X_2.

From Simplex tableau 8.1.2, we obtain $X_1 = 12$ and $S_1=12$ and accordingly $X_2 = S_2 = 0$ and $Z = 96$. However since all entries of Δj are not ≤ 0, solution can be improved by introducing and reproducing simplex tableau 8.1.3 in the similar way as we did proceed forformulating simplex tableau 8.1.2.

The elements of key row are reproduced as elements of X_2 in tableau 8.1.3. The elements of this row X_2 are obtained by dividing the elements of key row by key element 3/2 so as to get 1 in its place 3/2 in X_2 row of tableau 8.1.3.

The row elements of X_2 row are obtained in the similar way as earlier.

$$\frac{0}{3/2}=0,\ \frac{3/2}{3/2}=1,\ \frac{1}{3/2}=\frac{2}{3},\ \frac{-1/2}{3/2}=\frac{-1}{3},\ \frac{12}{3/2}=8$$

The entries of the new X_1 row in tableau 8.1.3 has been obtained as

$$1-\frac{3}{4}(0)=1,\ \ \frac{3}{4}-\frac{3}{4}(1)=0,\ \ 0-\frac{3}{4}\left\{\frac{2}{3}\right\}=-\frac{1}{2},\ \ \frac{1}{4}-\frac{3}{4}\left\{-\frac{1}{3}\right\}=\frac{1}{2},$$

$$12-\frac{3}{4}(8)=6$$

Simplex Tableau 8.1.3

	C_i → ↓	8	7	0	0	—	—
Basic Variables		X_1	X_2	S_1	S_2	b_i	Replacement ratio
X_2	7	0	1	$\frac{2}{3}$	$\frac{-1}{3}$	8	
X_1	8	1	0	$\frac{-1}{2}$	$\frac{1}{2}$	6	
Z_j	→	8	7	2/3	5/3	104	—
$\Delta_j = C_j - Z_j$	→	0	0	– 2 / 3	– 5/ 3	—	—

SIMPLEX TABLE: 1

	C_i → ↓	8	7	0	0	—	—
Basic Variables		X_1	X_2	S_1	S_2	b_i	Replacement ratio
S_1	0	2	3	1	0	36	$\frac{36}{2} = 18$
S_2	0	4	3	0	1	48	$\frac{48}{4} = 12$
Z_j	→	0	0	0	0	0	
$\Delta_j = C_j - Z_j$	→	8	7	0	0	—	
S_1	0	0	$\frac{3}{2}$	1	$\frac{-1}{2}$	12	$\frac{12}{3/2} = 8$
X_1	8	$\frac{4}{4} = 1$	$\frac{3}{4}$	$\frac{0}{4}$	$\frac{1}{4}$	$\frac{48}{4} = 12$	$\frac{12}{3/4} = 16$
Z_j	→	8	6	0	2	96	—
$\Delta_j = C_j - Z_j$	→	0	1	0	–2	—	—
X_2	7	0	1	$\frac{2}{3}$	$\frac{-1}{3}$	8	
X_1	8	1	0	$\frac{-1}{2}$	$\frac{1}{2}$	6	
Z_j	→	8	7	2/3	5/3	104	—
$\Delta_j = C_j - Z_j$	→	0	0	–2 /3	–5/3	—	—

In Simplex tableau 8.1.3 we have obtained solution since all entries of Δj are seen to be either zero or negative. The required solution is $X_1 = 6$ and $X_2 = 8$, $S_1 = S_2 = 0$, and $Z = 104$. This solution is also the same as what we obtain from the graphical method applied to the same problem. This was corresponding to extreme point '*E*' (shown in fig-8.16).

The earlier simplex tableau 8.1.1, 8.1.2 and 8.1.3 are shown together in one table. This is simplex table:1. Solution is given by

$X_1 = 6$, $X_2 = 8$ and $Z = 8X_1 + 7X_2 + 0\,S_1 + 0\,S_2 = 8(6) + 7(8) + 0\,(0) + 0(0) = 104$

Example 2:

Solve the following Linear Programming Problem by simplex method.

(TYBA/Econometrics/ Mumbai Univ., 2004)

Maximize: $Z = X_1 + 4X_2 + 5X_3$.

Subject to,

$$2X_1 + X_2 + 3X_3 \leq 36$$
$$X_1 + 2X_2 + X_3 \leq 42$$
$$X_1 \geq 0, X_2 \geq 0, X_3 \geq 0$$

The first step is to get the standardized form of the above Linear Programming problem by converting the constraints in to equations. This is done by introducing slack variables to them when they are of ≤ types. The first constraint is $2X_1 + X_2 + 3X_3 \leq 36$. Introducing slack variable S_1, the constraint becomes $2X_1 + X_2 + 3X_3 + S_1 = 36$. It indicates that for $2X_1 + X_2 + 3X_3 = 36$, $S_1 = 0$ and if $2X_1 + X_2 + 3X_3 < 36$, $S_1 > 0$.

The second slack variable S_2 is introduced to the second constraint $X_1 + 2X_2 + X_3 \leq 42$. This becomes $X_1 + 2X_2 + X_3 + S_2 = 42$, so that $X_1 + 2X_2 + X_3 = 42$ when $S_2 = 0$ and if $X_1 + 2X_2 + X_3 < 42$, $S_2 > 0$.

After introducing the slack variables, it is required to modify the objective function to contain the slack variables also with their coefficients zero. This because of the fact that the cost of unused available resource types is zero. Accordingly the modified objective function becomes:

Maximize: $Z = X_1 + 4X_2 + 5X_3 + 0S_1 + 0S_2$

Subject to,

$$2X_1 + X_2 + 3X_3 + S_1 = 36$$
$$X_1 + 2X_2 + X_3 + S_2 = 42$$
$$X_1 \geq 0, X_2 \geq 0, X_3 \geq 0, S_1 \geq 0, S_2 \geq 0$$

The next step is to present the information of the above problem in a simplex tableau. The initial simplex tableau is given in table 8.2.1 below:

Simplex Tableau 8.2.1

	$C_j \rightarrow$ $\downarrow$	1	4	5	0	0	—	—
Basic Variables		X_1	X_2	X_3	S_1	S_2	b_i	Replacement ratio
S_1	0	2	1	3	1	0	36	$\frac{36}{3} = 12$
S_2	0	1	2	1	0	1	42	$\frac{42}{1} = 42$
Z_j	$\rightarrow$	0	0	0	0	0	0	
$\Delta_j = C_j - Z_j$	$\rightarrow$	1	4	5	0	0	—	

Solution is given by $X_1 = 0$ $X_2 = 0$, $X_3 = 0$ and $S_1 = 36$, $S_2 = 42$ and

$Z = X_1 + 4X_2 + 5X_3 + 0S_1 + 0S_2 = (0) + 4(0) + 0(36) + 0(42) = 0$

In the initial tableau, the C_j, first row indicates the coefficient values from the objectives function. The second row shows all the basics and non-basic variables (decision variables). The coefficients in the constraint equations are written listing vertically the coefficients of all the variables. The slack variable S_1 appears only in the first equation for which its coefficient is taken zero in the other equations. The same is applicable with respect to S_2. The coefficients of the first constraint are 2, 1, 3, 1, 0, and the coefficients of the second constraint are 1. 2, 1, 0, 1. The constraint values 36 and 42 are shown in the last column against 'b_i' the solution vector, S_1 and S_2 are the basic variables while X_1, X_2 and X_3 are non-basic variables for this problem. In the initial tableau the basic variables are taken. Z_j row is formed by multiplying each element of the columns shown by the corresponding coefficient of the variable appearing in the basis and then the products are summed up. The process is similar to the previous example.

For the column headed X_1, we get its corresponding value of Z as:

$Z_1 = (0 \times 2) + (0 \times 1) = 0$ and similarly $Z_2 = (0 \times 1) + (0 \times 2) = 0$,

$Z_3 = (0 \times 3) + (0 \times 1) = 0$, $Z_4 = (0 \times 1) + (0 \times 0) = 0$ and $Z_5 = (0 \times 0) + (0 \times 1) = 0$

The last row $\Delta j = Cj - Zj$, is formed as (1–0), (4–0), (5–0), (0–0), (0–0). This yields the values 1, 4, 5, 0, 0 . The solution is given by $X_1 = X_2 = X_3 = 0$ while $S_1 = 36$ and $S_2 = 42$. The objective function is $Z = 0$.

To test whether the solution obtained in simplex tableau 8.2.1 is optimal or not, we need to see that all entries of $\Delta j = Cj - Zj$ are zero or negative for the problem of maximization. But the entries of $\Delta j = Cj - Zj$ are found positive: 1, 4 and 5 against the column headed X_1, X_2 and X_3. The highest positive value is 5 which corresponds to X_3 non-basic variable. The variable corresponding to this is selected for entering it in the forthcoming tableau. This entering variable is X_3 . The column corresponding to this variable is called *key column*.. To decide the basic variable to be departed we need to divide the '*bi*' values by the corresponding values of *key column*.From this formula we obtained the replacement ratios (b_i / a_{ij}) for each row. The row with the least positive replacement ratio is to be selected for replacement. This is called the *key row* . In tableau 8.2.1, the row with least ratio is S_1. Therefore the departing or out going variable is S_1 and incoming variable is X_3. The element lying at the intersection of the *key row* and *key column* is '*3*'. It is *key element*.

The *key row* is reproduced in tableau 8.2.2 shown below. The elements of this row are obtained by dividing all the elements of key row by key element so as to get '1' in the X_3 row of tableau 8.2.2 in the place of the value 3 of the key row . Other elements of X_3 row are 2/3, 1/3, 3/3, 1/3 and 0/3.

For obtaining the row elements corresponding to S_2 in tableau 8.2.2, following formula is used:

(Old row element) –(Row element of key column)(corresponding element of the replacement row)

From this we get the row element of the S_2 row as

1 –1 (2/3) = 1/3, 2 –1 (1/3) = 5/3 , 1 –1(1) = 0, 0 –1(1/3) = –1 /3,

1–1(0) = 1 and 42 – 1(12) = 30

Simplex Tableau 8.2.2

	$C_j \rightarrow$	1	4	5	0	0	—	—
Basic Variables	$\downarrow$	X_1	X_2	X_3	S_1	S_2	b_i	Replacement ratio
X_3	5	$\frac{2}{3}$	$\frac{1}{3}$	$\frac{3}{3}=1$	$\frac{1}{3}$	$\frac{0}{3}=0$	$\frac{36}{3}=12$	$\frac{12}{1/3}=36$
S_2	0	$\frac{1}{3}$	$\frac{5}{3}$	0	$-\frac{1}{3}$	1	30	$\frac{30}{5/3}=18 \rightarrow$
Z_i	$\rightarrow$	$\frac{10}{3}$	$\frac{5}{3}$	5	$\frac{5}{3}$	0	60	
$\Delta_i = C_i - Z_i$	$\rightarrow$	$1-\frac{10}{3} = -\frac{7}{3}$	$4-\frac{5}{3} = \frac{7}{3}$	$5-5 = 0$	$0-\frac{5}{3} = -\frac{5}{3}$	0	—	—

Just like simplex tableau 8.2.1, here also the departing and entering variables are determined. Accordingly the departing variable is decided to be S_2 while the entering variable is X_2. The Key row is S_2 and key element is 5/3. The key column is the column headed X_2. From Simplex tableau 8.2.2, we obtain $X_3 = 12$ and $S_2=30$ and thus $X_1 = X_2 = S_1 = 0$ and $Z = 60$.

However since all entries of Δj are not ≤ 0 solution can be improved by introducing and reproducing simplex tableau 8.2.3 in the similar way as we did proceed for simplex tableau 8.2.2.The elements of key row are reproduced in tableau 8.2.3. The elements of the row are obtained by dividing the elements of key row by key element 5/3 so as to get 1 in its place in X_2 row of tableau 8.2.3. The row elements of X_2 row are obtained as

$$\frac{1/3}{5/3}=\frac{1}{5},\ \frac{5/3}{5/3}=1,\ 0,\ \frac{-1/3}{5/3}=-\frac{1}{5},\ \frac{30}{5/3}=18$$

The entries of the new X_3 row in tableau 8.2.3 are obtained as

$$\frac{1}{3}-\frac{1}{3}(1)=0,\ 1-\frac{1}{3}(0)=1,\ \frac{1}{3}-\frac{1}{3}\left\{-\frac{1}{5}\right\}=\frac{6}{15},\ 0-\frac{1}{3}\left\{\frac{3}{5}\right\}=-\frac{1}{5},\ 12-\frac{1}{3}(18)=6$$

Simplex Tableau 8.2.3

	C_j ↓	→ 1	4	5	0	0	—	—
Basic Variables		X_1	X_2	X_3	S_1	S_2	b_i	Replacement ratio
X_3	5	$\frac{9}{15}$	0	1	$\frac{6}{15}$	$-\frac{1}{5}$	6	
X_2	4	$\frac{1}{5}$	1	0	$-\frac{1}{5}$	$\frac{3}{5}$	18	
Z_j	→	$\frac{19}{5}$	4	5	$\frac{6}{5}$	$\frac{7}{5}$	102	
$\Delta_j = C_j - Z_j$	→	$1-\frac{19}{5}=-\frac{14}{5}$	0	0	$-\frac{6}{5}$	$-\frac{7}{5}$	—	

In Simplex tableau 8.2.3 we got solution since all entries of Δj are found either zero or negative. The required solution is obtained with X_2=18, X_3 = 6 and $X_1 = S_1 = S_2 = 0$, and the objective function is Z = 102.

The simplex tableau 8.2.1, 8.2.2 and 8.2.3 are reproduced together in one table named Simplex Table: 2

SIMPLEX TABLE : 2

	$C_i \rightarrow$	1	4	5	0	0	—	—
Basic Variables	$\downarrow$	X_1	X_2	X_3	S_1	S_2	b_i	Replacement ratio
S_1	0	2	1	3	1	0	36	$\frac{36}{3} = 12$
S_2	0	1	2	1	0	1	42	$\frac{42}{1} = 42$
Z_j	$\rightarrow$	0	0	0	0	0	0	
$\Delta_j = C_j - Z_j$	$\rightarrow$	1	4	5	0	0	—	
X_3	5	$\frac{2}{3}$	$\frac{1}{3}$	$\frac{3}{3} = 1$	$\frac{1}{3}$	$\frac{0}{3} = 0$	$\frac{36}{3} = 12$	$\frac{12}{1/3} = 36$
S_2	0	$\frac{1}{3}$	$\frac{5}{3}$	0	$-\frac{1}{3}$	1	30	$\frac{30}{5/3} = 18$
Z_j	$\rightarrow$	$\frac{10}{3}$	$\frac{5}{3}$	5	$\frac{5}{3}$	0	60	
$\Delta_j = C_j - Z_j$	$\rightarrow$	$1 - \frac{10}{3} = -\frac{7}{3}$	$4 - \frac{5}{3} = \frac{7}{3}$	$5 - 5 = 0$	$0 - \frac{5}{3} = -\frac{5}{3}$	0	—	—
X_3	5	$\frac{9}{15}$	0	1	$\frac{6}{15}$	$-\frac{1}{5}$	6	
X_2	4	$\frac{1}{5}$	1	0	$-\frac{1}{5}$	$\frac{3}{5}$	18	
Z_j	$\rightarrow$	$\frac{19}{5}$	4	5	$\frac{6}{5}$	$\frac{7}{5}$	102	
$\Delta_j = C_j - Z_j$	$\rightarrow$	$1 - \frac{19}{5} = -\frac{14}{5}$	0	0	$-\frac{6}{5}$	$-\frac{7}{5}$	—	

Solution is given by $X_2 = 18$, $X_3 = 6$ and $Z = X_1 + 4X_2 + 5X_3 + 0\,S_1 + 0\,S_2$

$= (0) + 4(18) + 5(6) + 0(0) + 0(0) = 102$

Example 3 :

Find the values of g_1 and g_2 which will maximize the following objective function by using the simplex method.

(TYBA/Econometrics/ Mumbai Univ., 2002)

Maximize: $P = 5g_1 + 3g_2$.

Subject to,

$$6g_1 + 2g_2 \leq 36$$
$$5g_1 + 5g_2 \leq 40$$
$$2g_1 + 4g_2 \leq 28$$
$$g_1 \geq 0, g_2 \geq 0$$

The above linear programming problem is obatined in its standardized form by converting the above constraints in to equations and by introducing slack variables to the constraints, which are of ≤ types.

The objective function and the structural constraints are now chamged into a different form as shown herewith:

Maximize: $P = 5g_1 + 3g_2 + 0S_1 + 0S_2 + 0S_3$.

Subject to,

$$6g_1 + 2g_2 + S_1 = 36$$
$$5g_1 + 5g_2 + S_2 = 40$$
$$2g_1 + 4g_2 + S_3 = 28$$
$$6g_1 + 2g_2 + S_1 = 36$$
$$g_1 \geq 0, g_2 \geq 0, S_1 \geq 0, S_2 \geq 0, S_3 \geq 0$$

Representing these equations in a simplex tableau, tableau 8.3.1 we get:

Simplex Tableau 8.3.1

	$C_i \rightarrow$	5	3	0	0	0	—	—
Basic Variables	↓	g_1	g_2	S_1	S_2	S_3	b_i	Replacement ratio
S_1	0	6	2	1	0	0	36	$\frac{36}{6} = 6$
S_2	0	5	5	0	1	0	40	$\frac{40}{5} = 8$
S_3	0	2	4	0	0	1	28	$\frac{28}{2} = 14$
Z_j	→	0	0	0	0	0	0	
$\Delta_j = C_j - Z_j$	→	5	3	0	0	0	——	

This tableau provides solution with $g_1 = 0$, $g_2 = 0$, $S_1 = 36$, $S_2 = 40$ and $S_3 = 28$ so that objective function is $P = 5g_1 + 3g_2 + 0S_1 + 0S_2 + 0S_3 = 0$

From Δj row of the simplex tableau 8.3.1 , we can see that all the entries are not zero or negative. We find positive Δj values, 5, 3 against the column headed g_1 and g_2 But the highest positive value is 5, which corresponds to g_1 non-basic variable. Therefore g_1 is selected as the entering or incoming variable in the forthcoming tableau. The column corresponding to this variable is called *key column.*. To decide the basic variable to be departed , we need to divide the '*bi*' values by the corresponding values of *key column*. From this formula we have got the replacement ratios (b_i / a_{ij}) for each row. The row with the least positive replacement ratio is to be selected for replacement. This is called the *key row*. In tableau 8.3.1, the row with least ratio is S_1. Therefore the departing or out going variable is S_1 while the incoming variable is g_1.The element lying at the intersection of the *key row* and *key column* is '*6*'. It is *key element*.

The *key row* is reproduced in tableau 8.3.2 shown below. The elements of this row are obtained by dividing all the elements of key row by key element 6, so that we get '1' in the g_1 row of tableau 8. 3.2 in the place of 6. Accordingly the elements of g_1 row are obtaind as

1, 2/6, 1/6, 0, 0, 6 in tableau 8.3.2.

Simplex Tableau 8.3.2

	$C_j \rightarrow$	5	3	0	0	0	—	—
Basic Variables	$\downarrow$	g_1	g_2	S_1	S_2	S_3	b_i	Replacement ratio
g_1	5	1	$\frac{2}{6}$	$\frac{1}{6}$	0	0	6	$\frac{6}{2/6} = 18$
S_2	0	0	$\frac{10}{3}$	$-\frac{5}{6}$	1	0	10	$\frac{10}{10/3} = 3 \rightarrow$
S_3	0	0	$\frac{10}{3}$	$-\frac{1}{3}$	0	1	16	$\frac{16}{10/3} = 4.8$
Z_j	$\rightarrow$	5	$\frac{10}{6}$	$\frac{5}{6}$	0	0	30	
$\Delta_j = C_j - Z_j$	$\rightarrow$	0	$\frac{8}{6} \uparrow$	$-\frac{5}{6}$	0	0	—	

To obtain the row elements of S_2 and S_3 in tableau 8.3.2, we can apply the following formula:

(Old row element) – (Row element of key column) (corresponding element of the replacement row).

Accordingly we get the row elements of the S_2 row as

5 –5 (1) = 0, 5 –5 (2/6) = 10/3 , 0 –5(1/6) = –5/6. 1 – 5(0) = 1, 0 –5(0) = 0, 40 – 5(6) =10

Similarly the row elements of the S_3 are obtained as

2 –2 (1) = 0, 4 –2 (2/6) = 10/3 , 0 –2(1/6) = –1/3,. 0 –2(0) = 0, 1 –2(0) = 1, 28 – 2(6) = 16

In Simplex Tableau 8.3.2, from Δj row we can see that all of its entries are not zero or negative. The element having positive Δj values is 8/6 against the column headed g_2. Therefore g_2 is selected as the entering or incoming variable in forthcoming tableau 8.3.3. The column corresponding to this variable is called *key column.*. We need to divide the '*bi*' values by the corresponding values of *key column.* From this formula we get the row with the least positive replacement ratio, which is S_2 This is called the *key row*. In tableau 8.3.3, the row with least ratio is S_2. Therefore the out going variable is S_2 while incoming variable is g_2. The element lying at the intersection of the *key row* and *key column* is '10/3'. It is called the *key element*. Simplex tableau 8.3.3 is formulated in the similar process. The row elements of g_2 in tableau 8.3.3 are obtained by dividing all elements of the row by 10/3. Other elements are obtained as

$$0,\ 1,\ \frac{-5/6}{10/3} = -\frac{1}{4},\ \frac{3}{10},\ 0,\ \frac{10}{10/3} = 3$$

The row elements of g_1 and S_3 rows are formed in the similar process as we did while formulating tableau 8.3.2. Accordingly row elements of g_1 are

$$1-\frac{2}{6}(0) = 1,\quad \frac{2}{6}-\frac{2}{6}(1) = 0,\quad \frac{1}{6}-\frac{2}{6}\left\{-\frac{1}{4}\right\} = \frac{1}{4},$$

$$0-\frac{2}{6}\left\{\frac{3}{10}\right\} = -\frac{1}{10},\quad 0-\frac{2}{6}(0) = 0,\quad 6-\frac{2}{6}(3) = 5$$

The row elements of S_3 are

$$-\frac{10}{3}(0) = 0,\quad \frac{10}{3}-\frac{10}{3}(1) = 0,\quad -\frac{1}{3}-\frac{10}{3}\left\{-\frac{1}{4}\right\} = \frac{1}{2},$$

$$0-\frac{10}{3}\left\{\frac{3}{10}\right\} = -1,\quad 1-\frac{10}{3}(0) = 1,\quad 16-\frac{10}{3}(3) = 6$$

Simplex Tableau 8.3.3

	$C_i \rightarrow$ ↓	5	3	0	0	0	—	—
Basic Variables		g_1	g_2	S_1	S_2	S_3	b_i	Replacement ratio
g_1	5	1	0	$\frac{1}{4}$	$-\frac{1}{10}$	0	5	
g_2	3	0	1	$-\frac{1}{4}$	$\frac{3}{10}$	0	3	
S_3	0	0	0	$\frac{1}{2}$	−1	1	6	
Z_i	$\rightarrow$	5	3	$\frac{2}{4}$	$\frac{4}{10}$	0	34	
$\Delta_i = C_i - Z_i$	$\rightarrow$	0	0	$-\frac{2}{4}$	$-\frac{4}{10}$	0	—	

In simplex tableau 8.3.3 we have got the solution for all elements of Δj row are now found zero or negative. The optimal solution is given by $g_1 = 5$ and $g_2 = 3$ and $S_3 = 6$. Substituting these values in the objective function we get the solution as

$$P = 5g_1 + 3g_2 + 0S_1 + 0S_2 + 0S_3 = 5(5) + 3(3) + 0(0) + 0(0) + 0(6) = 34$$

The same solution is obtained by applying the graphical method, attempted in fig-8.17.

Example 4:

Find the optimal values of X_1 and X_2 that will maximize the following objective function by using the simplex method.

(TYBA/Econometrics/ Mumbai University)

Maximize: $Z = 30X_1 + 40X_2$.

Subject to,

$$X_1 + X_2 \leq 200$$
$$8X_1 + 5X_2 \leq 600$$
$$3X_1 + 4X_2 \leq 500$$
$$X_1 \geq 0, X_2 \geq 0$$

First we need to transform the above linear programming problem in to a standardized form. For this the structural constraints are converted in to equations by introducing slack variables.

The objective function and the structural constraints are changed to

Maximize: $Z = 30X_1 + 40X_2 + 0S_1 + 0S_2 + 0S_3$.

Subject to,

$$X_1 + X_2 + S_1 = 200$$
$$8X_1 + 5X_2 + S_2 = 600$$
$$3X_1 + 4X_2 + S_3 = 500$$
$$X_1 \geq 0, X_2 \geq 0, S_1 \geq 0, S_2 \geq 0, S_3 \geq 0$$

Simplex tableau 8.4.1 is formulated by reproducing the information conatined in the constraints.

Simplex Tableau 8.4.1

	$C_j \rightarrow$	30	40	0	0	0	—	—
Basic Variables	$\downarrow$	X_1	X_2	S_1	S_2	S_3	b_i	Replacement ratio
S_1	0	1	1	1	0	0	200	$\frac{200}{1} = 200$
S_2	0	8	5	0	1	0	600	$\frac{600}{5} = 120$
S_3	0	3	4	0	0	1	500	$\frac{500}{4} = 125$
Z_j	$\rightarrow$	0	0	0	0	0	0	
$\Delta_j = C_j - Z_j$	$\rightarrow$	30	40	0	0	0	—	

Solution is given by $X_1 = 0$ $X_2 = 0$, $S_1 = 200$, $S_2 = 600$ and $S_3 = 500$. Substituting these values we get $Z = 30X_1 + 40X_2 + 0S_1 + 0S_2 + 0S_3 = 0$

From the last Δj row of the simplex tableau 8.4.1, we can see that all of its entries are not zero or negative. The positive Δj values are 30 and 40 against the column headed X_1 and X_2 The highest positive value is 40. This decides the incoming non-basic variable, which is X_2. Thus X_2 is selected as the entering or incoming variable for Simplex tableau 8.4.2. The column corresponding to this variable is called *key column*.. To decide the basic variable to be departed , we need to divide the '*bi*' values by the corresponding values of *key column* The replacement ratios (b_i / a_{ij}) for each row is computed. The row with the least positive replacement ratio is selected for departing variable. This row corresponds to the *key row*. In tableau 8.4.1, the row with least replacement ratio is S_2. Therefore departing or out going variable is S_2 and the incoming variable is X_2 The element lying at the intersection of the *key row* and *key column* is '5', called the *key element* .

The *key row* is reproduced in tableau 8.4.2. The elements of this row are obtained by dividing all the elements of key row by key element 5, so that we get '1' in the X_2row in the tableau 8.4.2 in the place of 5. The elements of X_2 row are obtained as 8/5, 1, 0, 1/5, 0 and 120 in tableau 8.4.2.

The row elements of S_1 and S_3 in tableau 8.4.2, are obtained by applying the following formula:

(Old row element) – (Row element of key column) (corresponding element of the replacement row)

Accordingly we get the row elements of the S_1 as

1 –1(8/5) = –3/5, 0, 1, –1/5, 0, 80

Similarly the row elements of the S_3 are also obtained as

3 –4 (8/5) = –17/5, 4 – 4 [(1) = 0, 0–4 (0) = 0,

0 – 4 (1/5) = –4/5, 1 – 4 (0)=1, 500 – 4 (120) = 20

Simplex Tableau 8.4.2

	$C_j \rightarrow$ $\downarrow$	30	40	0	0	0	—	—
Basic Variables		X_1	X_2	S_1	S_2	S_3	b_i	Replacement ratio
S_1	0	$-\frac{3}{5}$	0	1	$-\frac{1}{5}$	0	80	$\frac{200}{1} = 200$
X_2	40	$\frac{8}{5}$	1	0	$\frac{1}{5}$	0	120	$\frac{600}{5} = 120$
S_3	0	$-\frac{17}{5}$	0	0	$-\frac{4}{5}$	1	20	$\frac{500}{4} = 125$
Z_j	$\rightarrow$	64	40	0	8	0	4800	
$\Delta_j = C_j - Z_j$	$\rightarrow$	– 34	0	0	– 8	0	—	

In Simplex tableau 8.4.2, it can be seen that all entries of Δj row are either zero or negative. Therefore solution is obtained with $X_1 = 0$, $X_2 = 120$, $S_1 = 80$ and $S_3 = 20$. Substituting these values in the objective function we get the solution.

$$Z = 30X_1 + 40X_2 + 0S_1 + 0S_2 + 0S_3 = 30(0) + 40(120) + 0(80) + 0(0) + 0(20) = 4800$$

We can reproduce both the simplex tableau in one consolidated table, simplex table -4 shown below:

Simplex Table: 4

	$C_j \rightarrow$ $\downarrow$	30	40	0	0	0	—	—
Basic Variables		X_1	X_2	S_1	S_2	S_3	b_i	Replacement ratio
S_1	0	1	1	1	0	0	200	$\frac{200}{1} = 200$
S_2	0	8	5	0	1	0	600	$\frac{600}{5} = 120$
S_3	0	3	4	0	0	1	500	$\frac{500}{4} = 125$
Z_i	$\rightarrow$	0	0	0	0	0	0	
$\Delta_i = C_i - Z_i$	$\rightarrow$	30	40	0	0	0	—	
S_1	0	$-\frac{3}{5}$	0	1	$-\frac{1}{5}$	0	80	$\frac{200}{1} = 200$
X_2	40	$\frac{8}{5}$	1	0	$\frac{1}{5}$	0	120	$\frac{600}{5} = 120$
S_3	0	$-\frac{17}{5}$	0	0	$-\frac{4}{5}$	1	20	$\frac{500}{4} = 125$
Z_i	$\rightarrow$	64	40	0	8	0	4800	
$\Delta_i = C_i - Z_i$	$\rightarrow$	-34	0	0	-8	0	—	

8.9.2 Basic, basic feasible and basic feasible optimum solution of a linear programming problem

In a linear programming problem it is important for a reader to understand clearly the terms like basic solution, feasible solution, basic feasible solution and basic feasible optimum solution.

The linear programming problem has a system with 'm' number of constraints and 'n' number of variables, both basic and slack variables. As we have already witnessed for application of simplex method we need to convert the constraint of $\leq$ type in to equation by adding a slack variable to it. For example $3X + Y \leq 18$ is converted in to $3X + Y + S_1 = 18$, where the slack variable S_1 is added to the constraint to get it in the form of an equation. When the equation is plotted on the graph we get a straight line by taking $3X + Y = 18$, so that by setting X= 0, we get a point on Y-axis.This is (0, 18). Setting Y = 0, we get point on X-axis, (6,0). Joining these two points (0,18) and (6,0) get the line 'AB' in fig-8.1. Any point on this 'AB' line will represent all the pairs of X and Y values that yield 18 so that the S_1 value at any point on this line will be zero. However all the points lying below the line AB represent pair of X and Y values for which $S_1 > 0$. At the point of origin '0', $X = Y = 0$ and therefore $S_1 = 18$.

In linear programming problem since negative values for X and Y are discarded due to non-negative restrictions, $3X + Y \leq 18$ is to be located by the area OAB in the fig- 8.11. This means $0 \leq S_1 \leq 18$. Positive value of the slack variable means the unutilized capacity of the first resource, represented by the constraint $3X + Y \leq 18$.

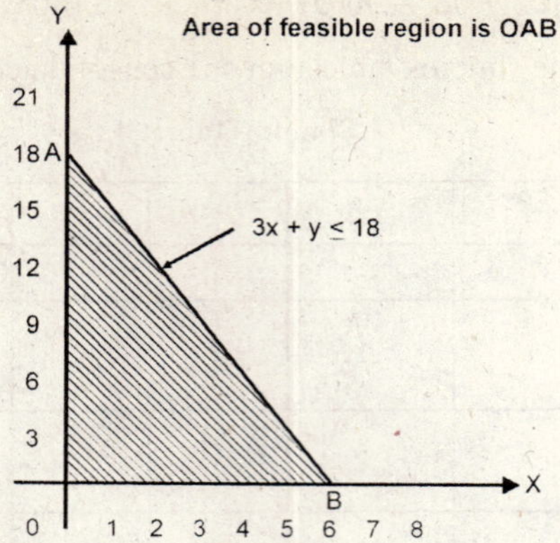

Fig. 8.11

Thus the area OAB specifies the values of X, Y and S_1 and this also satisfies the non-negative restrictions. The linear programming problem having 'n' variables and 'm' number of constraints will have ^nC_m basic solutions.

The concepts relating basic, basic feasible and basic feasible optimum solution can be explained by illustrating the following example:

Example 1:

Maximize: $Z = 4X_1 + 5X_2$.

Subject to,

$$3X_1 + 2X_2 \leq 18$$

$$2X_1 + 5X_2 \leq 20$$

$$X_1 \geq 0,\ X_2 \geq 0$$

Explain the concepts relating basic, basic feasible and basic feasible optimal solution for the given linear programming problem.

Introducing slack variables S_1 and S_2 these constraints are to be converted into equations first and then we can proceed further. The process is done systematically below:

Maximize: $Z = 4X_1 + 5X_2 + 0S_1 + 0S_2$

Subject to,

$$3X_1 + 2X_2 + S_1 = 18$$

$$2X_1 + 5X_2 + S_2 = 20$$

$$X_1 \geq 0,\ X_2 \geq 0,\ S_1 \geq 0,\ S_2 \geq 0$$

The problem has four variables X_1, X_2, S_1 and S_2 and two equations. These are shown in matrix form

$$\begin{bmatrix} 3 \\ 2 \end{bmatrix} X_1 + \begin{bmatrix} 2 \\ 5 \end{bmatrix} X_2 + \begin{bmatrix} 1 \\ 0 \end{bmatrix} S_1 + \begin{bmatrix} 0 \\ 1 \end{bmatrix} S_2 = \begin{bmatrix} 18 \\ 20 \end{bmatrix}$$

For this problem we will have ${}^{n}C_{m}$ basic solutions.

$${}^{n}C_{m} = {}^{4}C_{2} = \frac{4!}{2!2!} = \frac{4 \times 3 \times 2}{2 \times 2} = 6 \text{ basic solutions.}$$

All these basic solutions are not feasible. When we plot the variables and equations on a graph we will see that some of the basic solutions give negative values which are not feasible due to our assumption of non-negative restrictions in linear programming. Therefore all basic solutions are not feasible. Therefore it can be stated that a solution which is basic may or may not be feasible. This is obvious that a basic solution may or may not fall in the feasible region located on the graph. All the basic solutions for the above stated linear programming problem are listed in a table 8.15 below. The table indicates that two of these basic solutions are not feasible. They lie outside the feasible region on the graph, fig. 8.12.

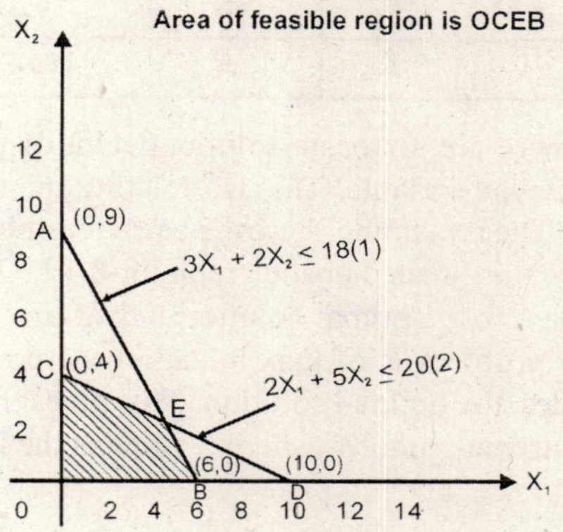

Fig. 8.12

Likewise a solution which is feasible may or may not be basic. The solution is basic only when the number of variables including slack variables getting non-zero is equal to the number of constraints of the problem. Let us take a point showing the pair of X_1 and X_2 values in the area of feasible region *OCEB*. This point is (4, 0). Corresponding to this pair of values we get $X_1 = 4$, $X_2 = 0$, $S_1 = 6$ and $S_2 = 12$. This point (4, 0) lies in the feasible region although this is not basic as for this pair of values we have three non-zero values when there are only two constraints. This has proved that a solution may be feasible and not basic just as a solution can be basic but not feasible. However for linear programming problems we need to search for the solutions which are not only basic but also feasible. This constitutes basic feasible solutions.

The violation of non-negative restrictions make a solution unfeasible although basic. We can also see that the feasible solutions are to be basic for optimal solution. In this eventuality the solution will correspond to only the extreme points of the feasible region OCEB, which are both basic and feasible. Only the extreme points represent or identify the basic feasible solutions. From these basic feasible solutions we need to search for the optimal basic feasible solution, which lies at least at any one of the extreme points, need to be determined or identified. All these alternative solutions are tabulated in table- 8.15

Table 8.15

Solution at various points	X_1	X_2	S_1	S_2	Basic Solution	Feasible Solution	Basic Feasible Solution	$Z = 4X_1 + 5X_2$
Point '0'	0	0	18	20	Yes	Yes	Yes	$4X_1 + 5X_2 = 0$
Point 'C'	0	4	10	0	Yes	Yes	Yes	$4X_1 + 5X_2 = 20$
Point 'A'	0	9	0	– 25	Yes	No	No	————
Point 'E'	$\frac{150}{33}$	$\frac{24}{11}$	0	0	Yes	Yes	Yes	$4X_1 + 5X_2 = 29.1$
Point 'D'	10	0	– 12	0	Yes	No	No	————
Point 'B'	6	0	0	8	Yes	Yes	Yes	$4X_1 + 5X_2 = 24$

The above table shows that there are six basic solutions. Out of them two are not feasible as they involve negative values for any particular variable. This is violating the non-negative restriction of linear programming problem, thus rejected. The remaining 4 are the basic feasible solution (BFS). They correspond to the extreme points of the feasible region shaded on the graph fig-8.12. Only the extreme points 0, C, E and B are both basic and feasible and therefore optimal solution lies at any one these corner points for this problem of maximization. Since the problem is of maximization the corner point yielding the maximum value to the objective function provides the optimal solution. This gives the optimal values of the pair of X_1 and X_2 values. This corresponds to extreme point '*E*' where *Z* value is the highest 29.1. Accordingly optimal values are $X_1 = 150/33$ and $X_2 = 24/11$.

Example 2:

For the following linear programming problem of maximization obtain the basic feasible solution and verify that a solution can be basic but may not be feasible and a solution may be feasible but not basic. Prove that the basic feasible solution lies only at the extreme points of the area of feasible region.

Maximize: $Z = 2X + 3Y$.

Subject to,

$$X + 3Y \leq 12$$
$$3X + Y \leq 9$$
$$X + Y \leq 5$$
$$X \geq 0,\ Y \geq 0$$

Introducing slack variables S_1, S_2 and S_3, these constraints are transformed into equations and the objective function beomes: Maximize: $Z = 4X_1 + 5X_2 + 0S_1 + 0S_2 + 0S_3$

Subject to,

$$X + 3Y + S_1 = 12$$
$$3X + Y + S_2 = 9$$
$$X + Y + S_3 = 5$$
$$X \geq 0,\ Y \geq 0,\ S_1 \geq 0,\ S_2 \geq 0,\ S_3 \geq 0$$

There are five variables in the problem. These are X_1, X_2, S_1 and S_2 and S_3. These three equations in matrix form are

$$\begin{bmatrix}1\\3\\1\end{bmatrix}X+\begin{bmatrix}3\\1\\1\end{bmatrix}Y+\begin{bmatrix}1\\0\\0\end{bmatrix}S_1+\begin{bmatrix}0\\1\\0\end{bmatrix}S_2=\begin{bmatrix}0\\0\\1\end{bmatrix}S_3=\begin{bmatrix}12\\9\\5\end{bmatrix}$$

For this problem we will have ${}^nC_m$ basic solutions.

$${}^nC_m={}^5C_3=\frac{5!}{3!2!}=\frac{5\times4\times3\times2}{3\times2\times2}=10 \text{ basic solutions.}$$

These are presented in table 8.16. The feasible region has been shaded in the graph fig-8.13. As already stated all the basic solutions are not feasible. Some of the basic solutions give negative values which are not feasible due to the non-negative restrictions of the linear programming. Therefore all basic solutions are not feasible. A solution which is basic may or may not be feasible. The basic solutions are not feasible when they lie outside the feasible region on the graph.

Likewise a solution that is feasible may or may not be basic. The solution is basic only when the number of variables including slack variables getting non-zero is equal to the number of constraints of the problem. It can be easily established as we did in the previous example. For linear programming problems we need to search for the solutions which are not only basic but also feasible, called basic feasible solutions.

Since the violation of non-negative restrictions makes a solution unfeasible while the feasible solution has to be basic. In this eventuality the solution will correspond to only the extreme points of the feasible region OAGHD in fig. 8.13. This provides all relevant information regarding 10 basic solutions out of which only 5 are Basic feasible Solutions (BFS) lying at the extreme points of the graph. This will include the point of origin.

One of these 5 solutions will provide optimum basic feasible solution. It corresponds to the one that yields maximum Z value as shown in table-8.16.

Table 8.16

Solution at various points	X_1	X_2	S_1	S_2	S_3	Basic Solution	Feasible Solution	Basic Feasible Solution	$Z = 4X_1 + 5X_2$
Point '0'	0	0	12	9	5	Yes	Yes	Yes	$2X + 3Y = 0$
Point 'A'	0	4	0	5	1	Yes	Yes	Yes	$2X + 3Y = 12$
Point 'E'	0	5	– 3	4	0	Yes	No	No	————
Point 'C'	0	9	–15	0	–4	Yes	No	NO	————
Point 'G'	1.5	3.5	0	1	0	Yes	Yes	Yes	$2X + 3Y = 13.5$ (Maximum)
Point 'H'	2	3	4	0	0	Yes	Yes	Yes	$2X + 3Y = 13$
Point 'T'	1.875	3.375	0	0	–0.25	Yes	No	No	————
Point 'B'	12	0	0	–27	–7	Yes	No	No	————
Point 'F'	5	0	7	–6	0	Yes	No	No	————
Point 'D'	3	0	9	0	2	Yes	Yes	Yes	2X+3Y= 6

Optimum value is achieved at point G where two equations are intersecting and this provide the optimum values of X = 1.5, Y = 3.5and Z = 13.5, the maximum. Other four extreme points of BFS have corresponding Z values less than the one obtained at G. There are five other basic solutions shown at points, E, C, T , B and F which are unfeasible since they do not fulfill the non-negativity restriction of the linear programming.

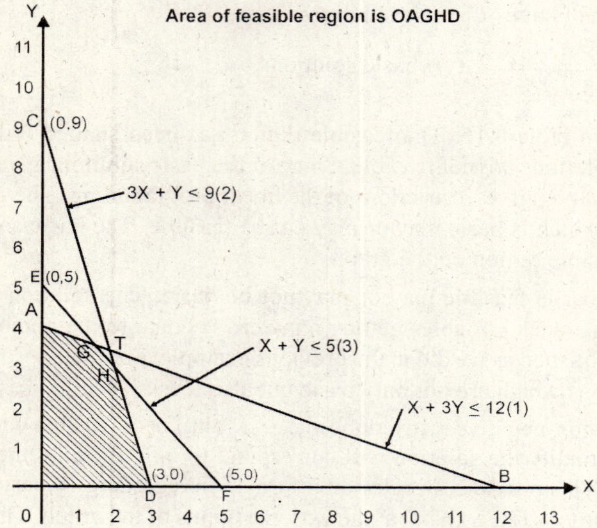

Fig. 8.13

8.9.3 Simplex method to solve Linear programming problems of minimization types: application of big 'M' method

The solution of the Linear programming problems concerning minimization is similar to that of the problem of maximization types, except that there are some points of difference exist between them. The simplex method used to solve the minimization problem involving the use of Big 'M' method is little cumbersome. This has been illustrated below:

Example : 3

Minimize : $f = 7X_1 + 8X_2$.

Subject to,

$$10X_1 + 15X_2 \geq 150$$

$$20X_1 + 15X_2 \geq 240$$

$$X_1 \geq 0, X_2 \geq 0$$

For converting the inequalities shown by the constraints in to equations we have to subtract slack variables in this case because the constraints are of ≥ types. To this we need to add the artificial variables in the left hand side of the equations. The addition of artificial variables is important since the slack variables becomes negative when the decision variables are becoming zero. This violates the non-negative restriction of the programming technique. After these adjustments the above constraints and objective function are to be rewritten as

Minimize : $f = 7X_1 + 8X_2 + 0S_1 + 0S_2 + MA_1 + MA_2$

Subject to,

$$10X_1 + 15X_2 - S_1 + A_1 = 150$$

$$20X_1 + 15X_2 - S_2 + A_2 = 240$$

$$X_1 \geq 0,\ X_2 \geq 0,\ S_1 \geq 0,\ S_2 \geq 0,\ A_1 \geq 0,\ A_2 \geq 0$$

The coefficient of the artificial variable is M, representing a number, larger than any finite number. It is for this reason that it is called Big-M method. When the problem is of minimization type, in the objective function the coefficient of artificial variables will be positive M values.

Simplex tableau 8.5.1 is formed that provides us with initial solution to the problem of minimization. In the initial solution we need to take the artificial variables as the basics. The solution to the problem however will not include any artificial variable.

For the minimization problem, like that of maximization problem we have to compute the Zj and Δj rows similar to the simplex of maximization type problem. The difference however is that for minimization problem the optimal solution is said to be achieved when all the entices of Δj row are either zero or positive. It implies that the presence of any negative entry of this row is an indication that the solution can improve.

Simplex Tableau 8.5.1

	C_i → ↓	7	8	0	0	M	M	—	—
Basic Variables		X_1	X_2	S_1	S_2	A_1	A_2	b_i	Replacement ratio
A_1	M	10	15	– 1	0	1	0	150	$\frac{150}{10} = 15$
A_2	M	20	15	0	– 1	0	1	240	$\frac{240}{20} = 12$ →
Z_j	→	30M	30M	– M	– M	M	M	—	
$\Delta_j = C_j - Z_j$	→	7 – 30M↑	8 – 30M	M	M	0	0	—	

For getting revised simplex tableau 8.5.2, we need to see that all the entries of the Δj row are zero or positive. However from tableau 8.5.1, we can notice that some of the entries are negative and the highest negative is (7–30M) and this corresponds the column heading X_1. This is an indication that the incoming variable is X_1. Accordingly the key column is the column headed by X_1. The outgoing variable will be decided on the basis of the lowest replacement ratio and the process is similar to that of the maximization problem. This minimum ratio is 12. Therefore the departing variable is A_2. This is the key row. The entering variable is X_1. Entries of the row in tableau 8.5.2 is obtained by dividing the elements of key row by key element 20, so that we get 1 in place of 20 in the new row formed in forthcoming tableau 8.5.2.

The entries of key row X_1 are obtained as

20/20 = 1, 15/20 = ¾, 0, –1/20, 0, 1/20, 240/20 = 12.

The entries of the new A_1 row in tableau 8.5.2 is made by applying the following formula

New row element = Old row element - (element of key column of the row) (element of the new replacement row)

Accordingly we get the row entries as

10 – 10 (1) = 0, 15 – 10 (3/4) = 15/2, –1 – 10 (0) = – 1 ,

0 – 10 (–1/20) = ½ , 1– 10 (0) =1, 0–10 (1/20) = –1/2 and 150 – 10 (12) = 30

By entering these elements we formulate the new simplex tableau, 8.5.2

Simplex Tableau 8.5.2

	$C_j \rightarrow$ ↓	7	8	0	0	M	M	—	—
Basic Variables		X_1	X_2	S_1	S_2	A_1	A_2	b_i	Replacement ratio
A_1	M	0	$\frac{15}{2}$	– 1	$\frac{1}{2}$	1	$-\frac{1}{2}$	30	$\frac{30}{15/2}=4$
X_1	7	1	$\frac{3}{4}$	0	$-\frac{1}{20}$	0	$\frac{1}{20}$	12	$\frac{12}{3/4}=16$
Z_j	→	7	$\frac{30M+21}{4}$	–M	$\frac{10M-7}{20}$	M	$\frac{(-10M+7)}{20}$	—	
$\Delta_j = C_j - Z_j$	→	0	$8-\left(\frac{30M+21}{4}\right) = \frac{11}{4}-\frac{30M}{4}$	M	$\frac{-(10M-7)}{20}$	0	$\frac{(30M-7)}{20}$	—	

The highest negative element of Δ*j* row is the column heading X_2. Therefore the incoming variable is X_2 and the key row is A_1. The key element is 15/2. Simplex tableau 8.5.3 is formed in the similar way as tableau 8.5.2. This tableau has been produced below.

The entries of X_2 are shown as

1–3/4(0)=1, 3/4 – 3/4(1) = 0, 0 – 3/3 (–2/15) = 1/10, –1/20 – 3/4(1/15) = –1/10, 0 – 3/4(2/15) = –1/10,
1/20 – 3/4(–1/15) = 1/10, 12 – 3/4(4) = 9.

Simplex Tableau 8.5.3

	C_i ↓	→ 7	8	0	0	M	M	—	—
Basic Variables		X_1	X_2	S_1	S_2	A_1	A_2	b_i	Replacement ratio
X_2	8	0	1	$-\frac{2}{15}$	$\frac{1}{15}$	$\frac{2}{15}$	$-\frac{1}{15}$	4	
X_1	7	1	0	$\frac{1}{10}$	$-\frac{1}{10}$	$-\frac{1}{10}$	$\frac{1}{10}$	9	
Z_j	→	7	8	–0.367	–0.167	0.367	0.167	95	
$\Delta_j = C_j - Z_j$	→	0	0	0.367	0.167	M–0.367	M –0.167	—	

Since all entries of Δj row are zero or positive [$\Delta j \geq 0$], optimal solution is obtained and this is given by $X_1 = 9$ and $X_2 = 4$ and $S_1 = S_2 = A_1 = A_2 = 0$

Thus $f = 7X_1 + 8X_2 + 0S_1 + 0S_2 + MA_1 + MA_2 = 7(9) + 8\,(4) = 95$, the minimum.

The graphical solution to the same problem can give us the same solution. Plot the equation $10X_1 + 15X_2 \geq 150$ and get 'AB' line. Plotting other equation we will get the linear line CD. The intersectrion point of these lines is 'E'. The fesible region is CEB and the 'f' values corresponding to these points are given as

$f(E) = 95$ for $X_1 = 9$ and $X_2 = 4$,

$f(C) = 128$ and $f(B) = 105$,

Thus minimization is achieved at 'E' where $f = 95$. [Readers themselves can atempt this exercise]

Example 6:

Solve the following linear programming problem by using Big-M method

Minimize : $Z = 36Y_1 + 40Y_2 + 28Y_3$

Subject to

$$6Y_1 + 5Y_2 + 2Y_3 \geq 5$$
$$2Y_1 + 5Y_2 + 4Y_3 \geq 3$$
$$Y_1 \geq 0,\ Y_2 \geq 0,\ Y_3 \geq 0$$

The application of Big-M method by introducing slack variables and artificial variables as we did in example 1 has been illustrated below.

We need to first convert the inequalities in to equations. Accordingly the objective function and structural constraints are changed to

Minimize: $Z = 36Y_1 + 40Y_2 + 28Y_3 + 0S_1 + 0S_2 + A_1 M + A_2 M$

Subject to

$$6Y_1 + 5Y_2 + 2Y_3 - S_1 + A_1 = 5$$
$$2Y_1 + 5Y_2 + 4Y_3 - S_2 + A_2 = 3$$

Simplex tableau 6.1 has been given below where artificial variables are taken as the basic variables. The initial solution is shown in tableau 8.6.1

Simplex Tableau 8.6.1

	C_j ↓ →	36	40	28	0	0	M	M	—	—
Basic Variables		Y_1	Y_2	Y_3	S_1	S_2	A_1	A_2	b_i	Replacement ratio
A_1	M	6	5	2	– 1	0	1	0	5	5/5 =1
A_2	M	2	5	4	0	– 1	0	1	3	3/5 = 0.6
Z_j	→	8M	10M	6M	– M	– M	M	M	—	
$\Delta_j = C_j - Z_j$	→	36–8M	40–10M	28 – 6 M	M	M	0	0	—	

The solution is said to be optimal when all the entries of Δj row are zero or positive. This is not attained in the initial solution because M constitute a positive value larger than any number. Therefore readers can notice that the second column will yield the highest negative. Thus Y_2 is selcted as the incoming variable. The column headed this variable is the key column. From replacement row we will decide the outgoing variable corresponding to the lowest replacement ratio. This is A_2 variable. Thus in tableau 8.6.2 the incoming or entering variable is Y_2 while departing variable is A_2. Accordingly tableau 8.6.2 is formed and for this the procedure followed is the same as we did earlier..

The entries of key row Y_2 is obtained as follows: 2/5, 1, 4/5, 0, –1/5, 0, 1/5 and 3/5.

The entries of the new A_1 row is made similar to the previous example The formula applies is New row element = Old row element-(element of key column of the row) (element of the new replacement row)

Accordingly we get the row entries

6 – 5 (2/5) = 4, 5 – 5 (1) = 0, 2 – 5 (4/5) =– 2 , –1 –5(0) =–1, 1, 1, – 1, 2,

The column of Δj row having the highest negative is 20–4M. Accordingly the incoming variable is Y_1 and the out going variable is decided to be A_1 Thus in tableau 8.6.3 we will get the row elements of Y_1 and Y_2 as shown below:

The row elements of Y_1 are obtained as follows:

4/4 =1, 0, –2/4, –1/4, ¼, ¼, –1/4, and 2/4

The entries of the new Y_2 row is made similar to the one shown earlier.

Accordingly we get the entries of the row as

2/5 – 2/5 (1)= 0, 1– 2/5(0)) = 1, 4/5 – (2/5)(–1/2) = 1,

0- 2/5(–1/4) = 1/10, –1/5 – 2/5(1/4) = –3/10,

0– 2/5(1/4) =–1/10, 1/5– 2/5(–1/4) = 3/10, 3/5 – 2/5 (2/4) = 2/5

Simplex Tableau 8.6.2

	$C_j \rightarrow$ ↓	36	40	28	0	0	M	M	—	—
Basic Variables		Y_1	Y_2	Y_3	S_1	S_2	A_1	A_2	b_i	Replacement ratio
A_1	M	4	0	-2	-1	1	1	-1	2	2/4 = 0.5
Y_2	40	$\frac{2}{5}$	1	$\frac{4}{5}$	0	$-\frac{1}{5}$	0	$\frac{1}{5}$	$\frac{3}{5}$	(3/5)(5/2)=1.5
Z_j	→	16 + 4M	40	32 – 2M	– M	M – 8	M	8 – M	—	
$\Delta_j = C_j - Z_j$	→	20 – 4M	0	2M – 4	M	8 – M	0	– 8	—	

Simplex Tableau 8.6.3

	$C_j \rightarrow$ ↓	36	40	28	0	0	M	M	—	—
Basic Variables		Y_1	Y_2	Y_3	S_1	S_2	A_1	A_2	b_i	Replacement ratio
Y_1	36	1	0	$-\frac{1}{2}$	$-\frac{1}{4}$	$\frac{1}{4}$	$\frac{1}{4}$	$-\frac{1}{4}$	$\frac{2}{4}$	
Y_2	40	0	1	1	$\frac{1}{10}$	$-\frac{3}{10}$	$-\frac{1}{10}$	$\frac{3}{10}$	$\frac{2}{5}$	
Z_j	→	36	40	22	– 5	– 3	5	3	34	
$\Delta_j = C_j - Z_j$	→	0	0	6	5	3	M – 5	M – 3	—	

Since all the entries of Δj are positive or zero, we have arrived at the optimal solution with $Y_1 = 2/4$ and $Y_2 = 2/5$ and $A_1 = A_2 = S_1 = S_2 = 0$. From these we get Z value $= 36Y_1 + 40Y_2 = 36(2/4) + 40(2/5) = 34$.

The solution obtained for this problem of minimization resembles some symmetry with its dual, the problem of maximization. This problem we have already solved in the maximization case in the example 3. The problem solved here is the dual of the example-3, the problem of maximization. We can compare the solution tableau 8.6.3 and tableau 8.3.3. This has been examined in the topics concerning primal and dual.

8.10. Duality of the Linear Programming Problem

The concept of duality implies that linear programming problems exist in pairs for which there is a dual for every linear programming problem. We have explained the Linear programming problems relating both maximization and minimization. In fact corresponding to every minimization problem there exists its counterpart, a maximization problem and for every maximization problem there is an existence of its counterpart a minimization problem. The original linear programming problem is called primal while its counterpart is its dual. The optimal values of the objective function in the primal and its dual are identical. Therefore one needs to solve the easier of the two for a given problem.

It can be examined how dual of a linear programming problem can be obtained from its primal. Before application of dual of a linear programming problem it is important to express the programming in a standard form. It implies that the variables are to be non-negative and the structural constraints are to be in the desired direction. Therefore in case of the minimization problem the constarints are to be of ≤ types while for minimization problem these are to be of ≥ type. When the constraints are not in right direction they are to be changed by multiplying the constraint by – 1 on both sides of it. The derivation of the dual from primal has been projected in the following illustrations:

Example 1:

Find dual of the following linear programming problem:

Primal

Maximize: $f = 5X_1 + 2X_2 + 3X_3$

Subject to

$$X_1 + 2X_2 + 3X_3 \le 18$$
$$2X_1 + X_2 + 5X_3 \le 12$$
$$X_1 \ge 0, X_2 \ge 0, X_3 \ge 0$$

The constraints in matrix form can be rewritten as

$$\begin{bmatrix} 1 & 2 & 3 \\ 2 & 1 & 5 \end{bmatrix} \begin{bmatrix} X_1 \\ X_2 \\ X_3 \end{bmatrix} \le \begin{bmatrix} 18 \\ 12 \end{bmatrix}$$

$$X_1 \ge 0, X_2 \ge 0, X_3 \ge 0$$

Dual

Minimize: $Z = 18Y_1 + 12Y_2$

Subject to

$$\begin{bmatrix} 1 & 2 & 3 \\ 2 & 1 & 5 \end{bmatrix}^T \begin{bmatrix} Y_1 \\ Y_2 \end{bmatrix} \ge \begin{bmatrix} 5 \\ 2 \\ 3 \end{bmatrix} = \begin{bmatrix} 1 & 2 \\ 2 & 1 \\ 3 & 5 \end{bmatrix} \begin{bmatrix} Y_1 \\ Y_2 \end{bmatrix} \ge \begin{bmatrix} 5 \\ 3 \\ 2 \end{bmatrix}$$

These structural constraints are shown differently as

$$Y_1 + 2Y_2 \ge 5$$
$$2Y_1 + Y_2 \ge 2$$
$$3Y_1 + 5Y_2 \ge 3$$
$$Y_1, Y_2 \ge 0$$

Basically the rules for the transformation from Primal to Dual are as follows::

(a) When the primal problem is of maximization type its corresponding dual will have an objective function of minimization type.

(b) The constraint values of the maximization problem, forms the coefficient values of the new variables in the objective function of the dual.

(c) The inequality sign in the constraints of the primal is reversed in the dual constraints. However the sign of the deecsion variables are non-negative and they are shown by $\geq$ sign in both primal and dual.

(d) The coefficient matrix for the dual constraints is nothing but the transpose of the coefficient matrix of the primal constraints.

(e) It is because of this relationship between the primal and the dual it can be observed that the dual of the dual is the primal, the original problem.

We can generalize the primal and dual in a matrix form as given:

Primal	*Dual*
Maximize : $P = P' X$	Minimize : $f = B' Y$
Subject to,	Subject to,
$AX \leq B$	$A' Y \geq P$
$X \geq 0$	$Y \geq 0$

Example

Primal

$$\text{Max} : \Pi = 3X_1 + 5X_2$$

Subject to,

$$\begin{bmatrix} 1 & 2 \\ 3 & 1 \end{bmatrix} \begin{bmatrix} X_1 \\ X_2 \end{bmatrix}, \leq \begin{bmatrix} 12 \\ 9 \end{bmatrix}$$

This give us structural constraints

$$X_1 + 2X_2 \leq 12$$

$$3X_1 + X_2 \leq 9$$

$$X_1, X_2 \geq 0$$

Dual

$$\text{Min: } C = \begin{bmatrix} 12 \\ 9 \end{bmatrix}^T \begin{bmatrix} Y_1 \\ Y_2 \end{bmatrix}, \text{ or } C = 12Y_1 + 9Y_2$$

Subject to,

$$\begin{bmatrix} 1 & 3 \\ 2 & 1 \end{bmatrix} \begin{bmatrix} Y_1 \\ Y_2 \end{bmatrix}, \geq [3 \quad 5]^T = \begin{bmatrix} 3 \\ 5 \end{bmatrix}$$

Rewriting these structural constraints

$$Y_1 + 3Y_2 \geq 3$$

$$2Y_1 + Y_2 \geq 5$$

$$Y_1, Y_2 \geq 0$$

8.10.1 Duality of the linear programming problem in case of mixed constraints

When a linear programming problem has mixed constraints all structural constraints are not in the required direction. Therefore it is required to convert them in to the right direction before applying any solution. This is also necessary to find its dual.

Following illustrations are cited as examples:

Illustration 1:

Maximize: $f = 10X_1 + 25X_2$

Subject to.

$$3X_1 + 5X_2 \leq 18$$
$$X_1 + 3X_2 \leq 12$$
$$2X_1 - X_2 \geq -5$$
$$X_1, X_2 \geq 0$$

The first two constraints are in right direction although the third constraint is of $\geq$ type, in opposite direction. This constraint has to be converted in to $\leq$type by multiplying both sides of the constraint by -1 so that it becomes $-2X_1 + X_2 \leq 5$.

The above problem can be rewritten in a compete form as

Maximize: $f = 10X_1 + 25X_2$

Subject to,

$$3X_1 + 5X_2 \leq 18$$
$$X_1 + 3X_2 \leq 12$$
$$-2X_1 + X_2 \leq 5$$
$$X_1, X_2 \geq 0$$

It is now possible to find its dual since all the constraints are in proper direction. Accordingly its dual is given by:

Minimize : $Z = 18Y_1 + 12Y_2$

Subject to,

$$3Y_1 + Y_2 - 2Y_3 \geq 10$$
$$5Y_1 + 3Y_2 + Y_3 \geq 25$$
$$Y_1, Y_2, Y_3 \geq 0$$

Illustration 2:

Maximize: $Z = 8X_1 + 10X_2 + 3X_3$

Subject to,

$$2X_1 - 3X_3 \leq 4$$
$$X_1 + 5X_2 \leq 12$$
$$X_1 + 2X_2 - X_3 \geq -5$$
$$3X_1 + X_2 - 2X_3 = 7$$
$$X_1, X_2, X_3 \geq 0$$

The first two constraints are in right direction although the last two constraints are in different direction. The third one is of $\geq$ type and the fourth constraint is an equation. These are to be converted in to right direction before finding its dual and also for applying the simplex method. To convert the third constraint in to $\leq$ type we need to multipy both sides of the constraint by -1, so that it becomes $-X_1 - 2X_2 + X_3 \leq 5$.

The last constraint is an equation. It can be represented by a pair of inequalities of $\leq$ type and $\geq$ type. Accordingly we get $3X_1 + X_2 - 2X_3 \leq 7$ and $3X_1 + X_2 - 2X_3 \geq 7$. The $\geq$ type constraint is required to be chnaged in to $\leq$ type by multiplying both sides of it by -1. Accordingly we get these constraints as

$3X_1 + X_2 - 2X_3 \leq 7$ and $-3X_1 - X_2 + 2X_3 \leq -7$

Now we would be able to rewrite the primal problem of maximization in a standard form as

Maximize: $Z = 8X_1 + 10X_2 + 3X_3$

Subject to,

$$2X_1 - 3X_3 \leq 4$$
$$X_1 + 5X_2 \leq 12$$
$$-X_1 - 2X_2 + X_3 \leq 5$$
$$3X_1 + X_2 - 2X_3 \leq 7$$
$$-3X_1 - X_2 + 2X_3 \leq -7$$
$$X_1, X_2, X_3 \geq 0$$

Thedual of this primal problem can be obtained as

Minimize : $f = 4Y_1 + 12Y_2 + 5Y_3 + 7Y_4 - 7Y_5$

Subject to,

$$2Y_1 + Y_2 - Y_3 + 3Y_4 - 3Y_5 \geq 8$$
$$5Y_2 - 2Y_3 + Y_4 - Y_5 \geq 10$$
$$-3Y_1 + Y_3 - 2Y_4 + 2Y_5 \geq 3$$
$$Y_1, Y_2, Y_3, Y_4, Y_5 \geq 0$$

8.10.2 Comparing the optimal solution of primal with its dual

There is a relationship between the optimal solution we get from solving the primal problem and its dual. This can be elucidated by using the following linear programming problem. We have already solved this problem above.

Primal

Maximize: $P = 5g_1 + 3g_2$.

Subject to,

$$6g_1 + 2g_2 \leq 36$$
$$5g_1 + 5g_2 \leq 40$$
$$2g_1 + 4g_2 \leq 28$$
$$g_1 \geq 0, g_2 \geq 0$$

Dual

Minimize: $f = 36Y_1 + 40Y_2 + 28Y_3$

Subject to,

$$6Y_1 + 5Y_2 + 2Y_3 \geq 5$$
$$2Y_1 + 5Y_2 + 4Y_3 \geq 3$$
$$Y_1, \geq 0, Y_2 \geq 0, Y_3 \geq 0$$

The optimal solution of the primal problem is given in tableau 8.3.3

Simplex Tableau 8.3.3

	$C_i \rightarrow$ ↓	5	3	0	0	0	—	—
Basic Variables		g_1	g_2	S_1	S_2	S_3	b_i	Replacement ratio
g_1	5	1	0	$\frac{1}{4}$	$-\frac{1}{10}$	0	5	
g_2	3	0	1	$-\frac{1}{4}$	$\frac{3}{10}$	0	3	
S_3	0	0	0	$\frac{1}{2}$	–1	1	6	
Z_j	→	5	3	$\frac{2}{4}$	$\frac{4}{10}$	0	34	
$\Delta_j = C_j - Z_j$	→	0	0	$-\frac{2}{4}$	$-\frac{4}{10}$	0	—	

The optimal solution of its dual, the minimization problem has also been solved above and the final tableau is reproduced here below:

By comparing the simplex tableau 8.3.3 and 8. 6.3, we can find that they are related in many ways. The structural variable g_1 in the primal corresponds to the surplus variable S_1 in its dual and g_2 corresponds to S_2 of the dual. Similarly the structural variables Y_1, Y_2 and Y_3 in the dual corresponds to the slack variables S_1, S_2 and S_3 of the primal.

In Δj row of the primal we get S_1 as 2/4, S_2 as 4/10 and S_3 =0. These values form the numerical values of the variables in the optimal solution of dual Y_1 = 2/4, Y_2 = 4/10 Or 2/5 and Y_3 = 0.

Simplex Tableau 8.6.3

	$C_i \rightarrow$ ↓	36	40	28	0	0	M	M	—	—
Basic Variables		Y_1	Y_2	Y_3	S_1	S_2	A_1	A_2	b_i	Replacement ratio
Y_1	36	1	0	$-\frac{1}{2}$	$-\frac{1}{4}$	$\frac{1}{4}$	$\frac{1}{4}$	$-\frac{1}{4}$	$\frac{2}{4}$	
Y_2	40	0	1	1	$\frac{1}{10}$	$-\frac{3}{10}$	$-\frac{1}{10}$	$\frac{3}{10}$	$\frac{2}{5}$	
Z_1	→	36	40	22	– 5	– 3	5	3	34	
$\Delta_j = C_j - Z_j$	→	0	0	6	5	3	M – 5	M – 3	—	

Similarly from the Δj row of the dual we get S_1= 5 and S_2 = 3, which becomes the numerical values of the variables in the optimal solution of the primal, g_1 = 5 and g_2 = 3.

The artificial variables are not considered since they do not correspond to the variables in the primal problem of maximization type.

Thus it has been found that the optimal solution of the dual can be known from the optimal solution of the primal problem while the optimal solution of the primal can also be known from the optimal solution of its dual. It is for this reason that we need not solve both the primal and its dual, but only the easier of the two can be solved for finding optimal solution to the given problem. When the primal problem is of minimization type with 3 variables and 5 constraints, its solution will be tedious. Therefore we can solve the problem by finding its dual and solving the dual only. The dual will contain 5 variables and only 3 constraints so that it is required to add to this three slack variables for applying simplex method to get optimal solution, which is of maximization type. This solution will be easier than the primal problem of minimization type which requires us to apply Big-M method. This will be cumbersome to solve.

This is the benefit of applying duality in linear programming problems for finding optimal values to the problems of linear programming.

8.11. Additional solved problems on Linear programming

Exercise:1: A firm is engaged in the production of two products X_1 and X_2. The production of one unit of X_1 requires 5 units of labour and 1 unit of capital inputs while one unit of X_2 requires use of 5 units of labour and 3 units of capital,. The firm has a total availability of 20 units of labour and 6 units of capital at his disposal for use. The firm intends to maximize net revenue from the sale of these products in the market at unit price of Rs. 2 and Rs, 3 for X_1 and X_2 respectively.

Formulate the above as a linear programming problem and solve it graphically to find the optimum product mix that maximizes firm's profit and at the same time fulfills the above restrictions. The firm's objective function is the maximization of profit.

This can be stated as Maximize $Z = 2X_1 + 3X_2$. The constraints are formulated from the above information called structural constraints. These are

$5X_1 + 5X_2 \leq 20$ labour constraint

$X_1 + 3X_2 \leq 6$ capital Constraint

$X_1 \geq 0, X_2 \geq 0,$ Non-negativity constraint

For finding solution we need to plot these constraints on a graph by first converting them in to equations and then shading the required feasible region. This has been depicted in fig-8.14.

For the first constraint $5X_1 + 5X_2 \leq 20$, we can set $X_1 = 0$ so that $X_2 = 4$, for $X_2 = 0$ we get $X_1 = 4$. In this process we get two points (0,4) and (4,0), plotting them on the graph we obtain AB linear line. The area satisfying the labour constraint will be all the points on this line and area below the line. This forms the area OAB. Similarly the second constraint can be plotted on the graph. This will give two points (0,2) and (6,0), joining which we will get CD straight line and area satisfying this constraint will be the triangle OCD. The area of the feasible region satisfying both the constraints is to be shaded. This area located on the graph is OCEB. Optimal solution lies at any one of the extreme points of this region. For this it is required to obtain the pair of X_1 and X_2 values corresponding to these extreme points. These values are to be substituted in the objective function to determine Z value for these extreme points. This has been listed below:

Table 8.17

Extreme points	Pair of X_1 and X_2 values	Value of $Z = 2X_1 + 3X_2$
0	$X_1 = 0, X_2 = 0$	$2X_1 + 3X_2 = 2(0) + 3(0) = 0$
C	$X_1 = 0, X_2 = 2$	$2X_1 + 3X_2 = 2(0) + 3(2) = 6$
E	$X_1 = 3, X_2 = 1$	$2X_1 + 3X_2 = 2(3) + 3(1) = 9$ Maximum
B	$X_1 = 4, X_2 = 0$	$2X_1 + 3X_2 = 2(4) + 3(0) = 8$

Z is maximum at point '*E*'. This is the required optimal solution. It gives the optimal values $X_1 = 3$ and $X_2 = 1$ obtained from '*E*'. These values maximize daily profit of the firm and this is equal to Rs. 9.

One can also draw linear lines to the objective function and plot them on the same graph to get the same solution. This is done by assigning some arbitrary value, say, 6 to Z so that we get two points (0,2) and (3,0). Plotting them on the graph the iso-profit line *CN* is obtained. The lines parallel to this are drawn to get an iso-profit line *PQ* tangent to the feasible region at one of the extreme point and this is point '*E*'. This is the highest iso-profit line attainable. It is farthest from the origin and also tangent to the feasible region. Required solution is obtained at point '*E*'. Optimal values are $X_1 = 3$ and $X_1 = 1$ and $Z = 9$.

Area of feasible region is OCEB

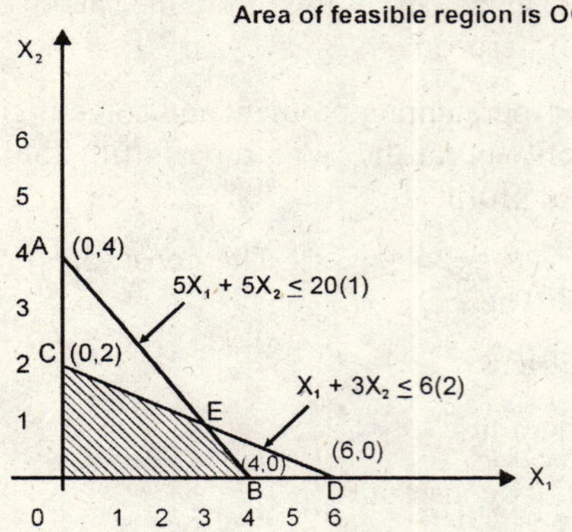

Fig. 8.14

Exercise: 2 A manufacturer of toys producing two varieties of toys A and B, fetching market price of Rs.3 and Rs.5 per unit of A and B respectively. He uses two different types of machines M and N and two types of resources cutting and packaging for manufacturing these toys..

These machines and resources are available to the manufacturer for limited hours. Production of one of A type toy requires use of 2 and 5 hours from cutting and packaging resources and 2 hours use of machine M. Manufacturing of one unit of toy B requires use of 3 and 4 hours from cutting and packaging and 4 ½ hours use of machine N. The resources cutting, packaging, machine M and N are available to him for a maximum of 60, 100, 30 and 45 hours respectively.

The manufacturer wants to produce an optimum mix of two types of toys so as to maximize profit from the sale of these toys in the market. Formulate the above as a linear programming problem and solve it graphically to find the optimum product mix that maximizes profit and at the same time fulfills the above restrictions.

The objective function of the problem is the maximization of profit. Accordingly,

Maximize : $f = 3A + 5B$

The structural constraints are formulated from the above information as

$2A + 3B \leq 60$	Cutting constraint
$5A + 4B \leq 100$	Packaging constraint
$2A \leq 30$	Machine M constraint
$4.5B \leq 45$	Machine M constraint
$A \geq 0, B \geq 0,$	Non-negativity restrictions

For finding solution we need to plot these constraints on a graph by first converting them in to equations and then shading the required feasible region. This has been depicted in fig-8.15

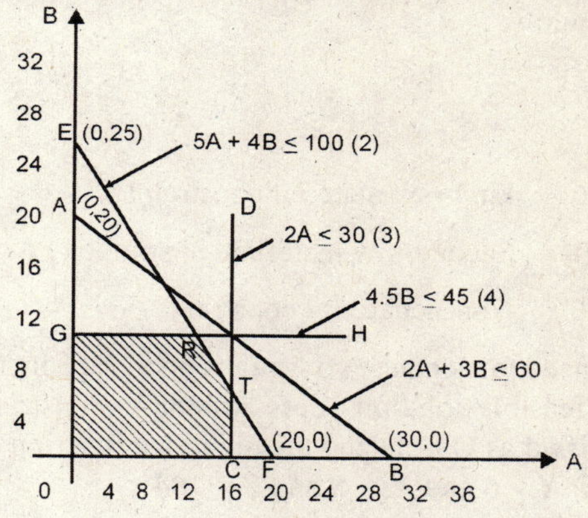

Fig. 8.15

The first constraint is $2A + 3B \leq 60$. By setting $A = 0$ we can get B and A for $B = 0$. From this exercise two points (0, 20) and (30, 0) are obtained, joining which we get the linear line *KL*. The area satisfying this constraint is *OKL*. In a similar process other constraints are plotted on the graph. Constraint $5A + 4B \leq 100$ is plotted and this satisfies the area *OPQ*. The third constraint $2A \leq 30$ is plotted on the graph. It provides the vertical straight line *CD* while from the last constraint we get the horizontal straint line *GH*. The required area of feasible region satisfying all these constraints is OGRTC. For finding optimal solution we can proceed in the similar way as we did earlier. *Z* values corresponding to these extreme points are listed in the following table:

Table 8.18

Extreme points	**Pair of *A* and *B*, Toys**	**Value of *Z* = 3*A* + 5*B***
0	$A = 0, B = 0$	$3A + 5B = 3(0) + 5(0) = 0$
G	$A = 0, B = 10$	$3A + 5B = 3(0) + 5(10) = 50$
R	$A = 12, B = 10$	$3A + 5B = 3(12) + 5(10) = 86$ Maximum
T	$A = 15, B = 6.25$	$3A + 5B = 3(15) + 5(6.25) = 76.25$
C	$A = 15, B = 0$	$3A + 5B = 3(15) + 5(0) = 45$

The objective function f is seen maximum at point R and the required optimal solution is given by A= 12 and B =10. The maximimum profit is equal to Rs. 86. We can obtain the same solution through plotting of the linear objective function on the same graph to get this solution.

Exercise: 3

Consider a problem when a firm is using two types of raw material to produce two different types of products, X_1 and X_2. The market prices are Rs. 8 and Rs. 7 per unit of X_1 and X_2 respectively. The production of one unit of X_1 requires 2 and 4 units of the first and second type of raw material respectively while production of one unit of X_2, requires 3 units use of each of these two types of raw material. The firm has a maximum of 36 and 48 units of these two type of raw materials respectively at his disposal.

Formulate the above problem as a linear programming problem and solve it graphically.

The problem is shown below:

Maximize : $Z = 8X_1 + 7X_2$

Subject to,

$2X_1 + 3X_2 \leq 36$ First raw material constraint

$4X_1 + 3X_2 \leq 48$ Second raw material constraint

$X_1 \geq 0, X_2 \geq 0,$ Non-negativity constraint

For finding solution we need to plot these constraints on a graph by first converting them in to equations and then shading the required feasible solution.These structural constraints are plotted on graph 3 and the area of feasible region is identified as OAED and the objective function is maximized at point E. this point gives us the optimum values of $X_1 = 6$ and $X_2 = 8$ and $Z = 104$.

The extreme points are shown in the following table also

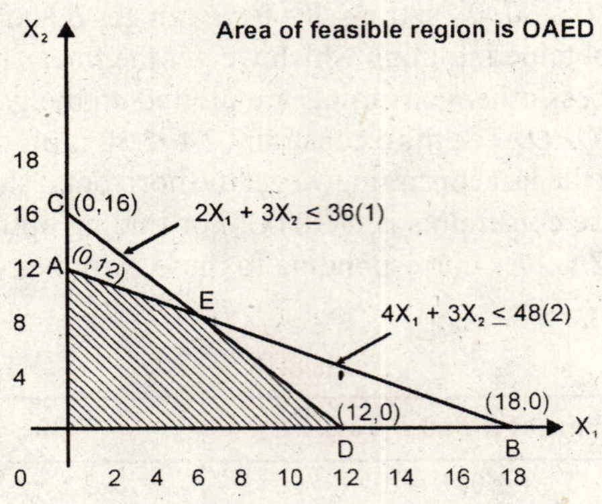

Fig. 8.16

Table 8.19

Extreme points	Pair of X_1 and X_2 values	Value of $Z = 8X_1 + 7X_2$
0	$X_1 = 0, X_2 = 0$	$8X_1 + 7X_2 = 8(0) + 7(0) = 0$
A	$X_1 = 0, X_2 = 12$	$8X_1 + 7X_2 = 8(0) + 7(12) = 84$
E	$X_1 = 6, X_2 = 8$	$8X_1 + 7X_2 = 8(6) + 7(8) = 104$ Maximum
D	$X_1 = 12, X_2 = 0$	$8X_1 + 7X_2 = 8(12) + 7(0) = 96$

One can also draw linear lines to plot the objective function on the same graph to get the required solution.

EXERCISE – 8

(1) Find the values of g_1 and g_2 which will maximize the following objective function by using the graphical solution to LPP.

Maximize : P (Profit) = $5g_1 + 3g_2$.

Subject to,

$$6g_1 + 2g_2 \leq 36$$
$$5g_1 + 5g_2 \leq 40$$
$$2g_1 + 4g_2 \leq 28$$
$$g_1 \geq 0, g_2 \geq 0$$

The graphical solution has been given in fig-8.17 below. The optimal values are $g_1 = 5$ and $g_2 = 3$ and $Z = 34$. The solution to this exercise are similar to the one shown above.

(2) Solve the following linear programming problem both by simplex method and graphically to find optimal values

Area of feasible region is OEGHB

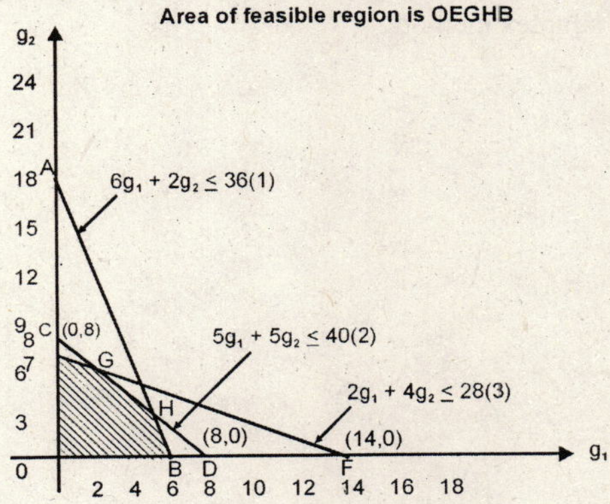

Optimal solution is at 'H' where $g_1 = 5$, $g_2 = 3$

Fig. 8.17

that minimize the objective function:

Minimize: $Z = 2X + 3Y$.

Subject to,

$X + Y \geq 6$
$2X + Y \geq 7$
$X + 4Y \geq 8$
$X \geq 0, Y \geq 0$

(3) Minimize by applying Simplex Method, : $Z = A + 2B$

Subject to,

$A + 8B \geq 2$
$-8A - 3B \leq -5$
$A \geq 0, B \geq 0$

(4) Solve graphically the following LPP

Minimize : $Z = \frac{8X}{100} + \frac{1Y}{10}$

Subject to,

$X + Y \leq 30{,}000$
$X \geq 5{,}000$
$Y \leq 10{,}000$
$X \geq 0, Y \geq 0$

(5) Rewrite the following LPP in standard form so that simplex method can be applied to it for obtaining optimal values of the decision variables.

Maximize : $f = 5X_1 + 2X_2 + 3X_3 + X_4$

Subject to,

$3X_1 + X_2 + 6X_3 + X_4 \leq 42$
$-X_1 + 2X_2 - 3X_3 - X_4 \geq -6$
$8X_1 - 5X_2 + 6X_3 - 2X_4 \geq 60$
$4X_1 + 3X_3 + 4X_4 = 30$
$X_1, X_2, X_3, X_4 \geq 0$

(6) Solve the following LPP using simplex method

Maximize: $f = 21X + 15Y$

Subject to,

$-X - 2Y \geq -6$
$4X + 3Y \leq 12$
$X \geq 0, Y \geq 0$

(7) Solve by simplex method

Minimize: $Z = 20g_1 + 30g_2 + 5g_3$

Subject to,

$4g_1 + 3g_2 + g_3 \leq 40$
$2g_1 + 5g_2 \leq 28$
$8g_1 + 2g_3 \leq 36$
$g_1, g_2, g_3 \geq 0$

(8) What is the relation between primal and dual of a linear programming problem?

(9) State the assumptions of a linear programming problem.

(10) State the advantages of simplex method over graphical solution to a linear programming problem.

❑ ❑ ❑

9 CONSTRAINED OPTIMIZATION: USE OF LAGRANGE MULTIPLIER METHOD

9.1 Constrained Optimization Problems: An introduction

Different types of functions are studied in mathematics and mathematical economics. In the application of mathematics to economic analysis we have studied that there can be one independent variable influencing the dependent variable. This is given by $y = f(x)$.

The maximization of the given function requires

$\frac{dy}{dx}$ to be zero and to be negative

The minimization of a function requires $\frac{dy}{dx} = 0$ and $\frac{d^2y}{dx^2}$ to be positive.

When two independent variables are influencing the dependent variable in the given function $Z = f(x, y)$, there is use of partial derivatives and total differntials. The maxima and minima of these functions are defined accondingly.

$Z = f(x, y)$ has a maxima when $f_x = f_y = 0$ and $f_{xx} < 0, f_{yy} < 0$ and $(f_{xx})(f_{yy}) > (f_{xy})^2$

For minima the required conditions are $f_x = f_y = 0$ and $f_{xx} > 0$, $f_{yy} > 0$ and $(f_{xx})(f_{yy}) > (f_{xy})^2$.

The variables x and y are said to be independent of each other.

We will study now a different type of problem. The variables involving certain problems are found interrelated and interdependent Take for example the utility function a consumer faces is $U = f(q, q_2)$, where q_1 and q_2 are some quantities of two goods detremining total utility (U). The consumer has a given amount of money to spend on these goods q_1, and q_2. If he purchases a larger quantity of one good he cannot afford to have more quantity of the other good due to limited money at his disposal. This problem is referred to constrained optimization behaviour of consumer. He is required to maximize his utility function subject to the buget constraint. The buget constraint is formulated on the basis of the data on the market prices of two goods he wants to buy and his money expenditure on them.

Suppose consumer's given amount of money expenditure is *'y'* which he wants to spend on two goods, whose per unit market prices are P_1 and P_2.The budget constraint formulated is $p_1 q_1 + p_2 q_2 \leq y°$. This inequality implies that his total expenditure on these two goods is $(p_1 q_1 + p_2 q_2)$, which can not exceed money $(y°)$ at his disposal. The constrained utility maximization enables him to obtain optimal quantities of two goods thta maximizes his utility function $U = f(q_1 q_2)$, subject to the budget constraint $p_1 q_1 + p_2 q_2 = y°$.

This type of situation arises in economics. It relates to the economic units like a consumer or a profit maximizing firm .The firms confront the similar situations like constrained output maximization subject to a cost cosntraint while buying inputs in the production process. Firms also face a similar situation like constrained cost minimization subject to the production of a given amount of output. There are also the situations of constrained profit maximization and constrained sales revenue maximization by a firm subject to the minimum profit and so on. All these problems are solved with the help the method of lagrange multiplier method. This method is widely used in economics.

9.2. Lagrange Multiplier Method

Lagrange multiplier method can be analyzed by using some illustrations. We can examine this method by taking a consumer or a producer aiming at the maximization of an objective functions subject to some constraints. Maximizing utility function of a consumer subject to the budget constraint is shown below:

For given the utility function $U = 8xy - 2y^2$ and the budget constraint of the consumer is $2x + y = 12$, we need to obtain the optimum qunatity purchases of these two goods by applying Lagrange multiplier method. For applying this method we need to combinethe utility function with the budget constraint by introducing a new variable λ [lambda] called lagrange multiplier.

The new function becomes $Z = f(x, y) + \lambda\,(12 - 2x - y)$.

The first order condition for maximization is to set

$$f_x = \frac{\partial Z}{\partial x} = 0\,,\quad f_y = \frac{\partial Z}{\partial y} = 0\,,\ \text{and}\ f_\lambda = \frac{\partial Z}{\partial \lambda} = 0$$

By setting these partial derivatives to zero we can solve the equations so obtained and determine values of the variables that maximize utiity function.

The reqired solution is obtained from $Z = 8xy - 2y^2 + \lambda\ (12 - 2x - y)$ and

$$f_x = \frac{\partial Z}{\partial x} = 8y - 2\lambda = 0 \cdots\cdots (1)$$

$$f_y = \frac{\partial Z}{\partial y} = 8x - 4y - \lambda = 0 \cdots\cdots (2)$$

$$f_\lambda = \frac{\partial Z}{\partial \lambda} = 12 - 2x - y = 0 \cdots\cdots (3) \text{ or } 2x + y = 12$$

Since $8y = 2\lambda$, $\lambda = \frac{8y}{2} = 4y$

Substitute the value of 'λ' in equation (2) $8x - 4y - \lambda = 0$ and get

$8x - 4y - 4y = 0$, or $8x - 8y = 0$ or $x = y$,

Substituting $x = y$ in equation 3, we get $3x = 12$ or $x = 4$. Thus required solution are $y = 4$ and $x = 4$.

Maximum utility is obtained by substituting these 'x' and 'y' values in utility function.

This gives us, $U = 8xy - 2y^2 = 8(4)(4) - 2(4)^2 = 96$

9.3. Constrained Utility Maximization by a Consumer

Given the utility function $U = f(x_1, x_2)$ and the budget constraint $y^\circ = p_1 x_1 + p_2 x_2$, where x_1 and x_2 are quantities of two different goods, the problem lies in maximizing the utiity function subject to the budget constraint. The corresponding market prices of two goods are p_1 and p_2. Consumer can maximize her utility function by applying the lagrange multiplier method.

Since the problem confronting the consumer is the maximization of utility $U = f(x_1, x_2)$ subject to the budget constraint $y^\circ = p_1 x_1 + p_2 x_2$ where y° is the fixed money expenditure of the consumer on x_1 and x_2 goods. We can apply the rules relating constarined optimization. For this the first order condition is to set the first order partial derivativatives of a new function V with respect to different qunatities and lagrange multiplier λ. This new function V is defined as $V = f(x_1, x_2) + \lambda(y^\circ - p_1 x_1 - p_2 x_2)$

Setting $\frac{\partial V}{\partial x_1} = 0$, $\frac{\partial V}{\partial x_2} = 0$, $\frac{\partial V}{\partial \lambda} = 0$ we obtain

$$\frac{\partial V}{\partial x_1} = f_{x_1} = f_1 - \lambda p_1 = 0 \cdots\cdots (1)$$

$$\frac{\partial V}{\partial x_2} = f_{x2} = f_2 - \lambda p_2 = 0 \cdots\cdots (2)$$

$$\frac{\partial V}{\partial \lambda} = f_\lambda = y^\circ - p_1 x_1 - p_2 x_2 = 0 \cdots\cdots (3)$$

From equation (1) we get

$$f_1 - \lambda p_1 = 0 \quad \text{or} \quad f_1 = \lambda p_1, \quad \text{or} \quad \lambda = \frac{f_2}{p_2}$$

From equation (2) we get,

$$f_2 - \lambda p_2 = 0 \quad \text{or} \quad f_2 = \lambda p_2, \quad \text{or} \quad \lambda = \frac{f_2}{p_2}$$

$$\lambda = \frac{f_1}{p_1} = \frac{f_2}{p_2} \quad \text{or} \quad \frac{f_1}{p_1} = \frac{f_2}{p_2}$$

The ratio of marginal utilites of two goods $\left(\frac{f_1}{f_2}\right)$ must be equal to the ratio of prices of two goods $\left(\frac{p_1}{p_2}\right)$, where $\frac{f_1}{f_2}$ is the marginal rate of commodity substitution between x_1 and x_2 (*MRCS*).

This implies that the first-order condition for utility maxisation requires equality between the *MRCS* and the ratio of prices of two goods, $\left(\frac{f_1}{f_2} = \frac{p_1}{p_2}\right)$. This requires that the slope of the indifference curve and slope of the price line are to be equal at the point of equilibrium.

$MRCS = \frac{f_1}{f_2}$ depicts the slope of indifference curve while $\frac{p_1}{p_2}$, the ratio of prices of two goods, repreesnts the slope of the budget line. It implies that the first-order condition is fulfilled only at the point of tangency between the given indifference curve and price line. This is the necessary or first-order condition of utility maximization, which requires the price line to be tangent to the indifference curve.

$\frac{f_1}{f_2} = \frac{p_1}{p_2} = \lambda$ also indicates that MU and price ratios of two goods are to be equal and these are made equal to the λ, which can be interpreted as the marginal utility of money for the consumer.

The *MRCS* is $-\frac{dx_2}{dx_1}$. It shows a decrease in the quanty of x_2 due to a given increase in quantity of x_1. It can be derived that $RCS = -\frac{dx_2}{dx_1} = \frac{f_1}{f_2}$.

It is equal to the ratio of MUx_1 to MUx_2 or $\frac{f_1}{f_2} = \frac{\partial U/\partial x_1}{\partial U/\partial x_2}$.

This can be derived from utility function, $U = f(x_1, x_2)$. We know from economic theory that the level of satisfaction derived by a consumer when he slides along the indifference curve remains unchanged, which also means the change in utility (*du*) is zero. This requires to evaluate the total diffential of *U*, as shown below:

$$\therefore\ du = f_1\, dx_1 + f_2\, dx_2 = 0. \text{ or } f_2\, dx_2 = -f_1\, dx_1$$

$$\text{or} \quad -\frac{dx_2}{dx_1} = \frac{f_1}{f_2}, \quad MRCS = \frac{f_1}{f_2} \text{ as } -\frac{dx_2}{dx_1} = MRCS$$

The second-order or sufficient condition for consumer's equilibrium requires that the indifference curve at the tangeney point must be convex to the origin. The tangency point is shown when , $\left(\frac{f_1}{f_2} = \frac{p_1}{p_2}\right)$.

The convexity of the indifference curve at this tangency point requires that the sign of $\frac{\partial^2 x_2}{\partial x_1^2}$ to be positive. Follwoing illustrations are cited for further analysis on consumer's equilibrium.

Illustrations:

(1) Given the utility function $U = f(q_1\, q_2) = q_1\, q_2$, and the budget constraint is $4q_1 + 6q_2 = 96$, find the equilibrium quantities of q_1 and q_2 that will maximize consumer's utility function.

To derive the optimum quantity combination of two goods we need to define a new function called *V*, the lagrange function. It combines the utility function and the budget constraint together. In this new function obtained below λ (lambda) is used and it is called lagrange multiplier.

$V = q_1\, q_2 + \lambda\, [96 - 4q_1 - 6q_2]$.

Partially differntiating V with respect to $.q_1$ and q_2 and setting them to zero we get the equations. Solving these equations obtained we get optimum quantities of two goods.

$$\frac{\partial V}{\partial q_1} = q_2 - 4\lambda = 0, \quad q_2 = 4\lambda$$

$$\frac{\partial V}{\partial q_2} = q_1 - 6\lambda = 0, \quad q_1 = 6\lambda$$

$\frac{\partial V}{\partial x} = 96 - 4q_1 - 6q_2 = 0$ or $4q_1 + 6q_2 = 96$. Substituting q_1 *and* q_2 in the equation we get

$4(6\lambda) + 6(4\lambda) = 96$, or $48\lambda = 96$ $\therefore$ $\lambda = 2$. From this we get $q_1 = 6\lambda = 12$ and $q_2 = 4\lambda = 8$

Thus the optimum quantities of these two goods that will maximize consumers utility function are $q_1 = 12$, $q_2 = 8$. This maximum utility is $U = q_1\, q_2 = 12 \times 8 = 96$.

(2) Find the optimum quantity combination of two goods q_1 and q_2 the consumer purchases when the utility function and the budget constraint are given as $U = q_1^{1.5} q_2$ and $3q_1 + 4q_2 = 90$ respeatively.

Given $U = q_1^{1.5} q_2$ and the budget constraint $3q_1 + 4q_2 = 90$, it is required to obtain equilibrium quantities of two goods by applying the lagrange multiplier method. The lagrangian function is defined W which combines both utility function and budget coonstraint as shown below:

$$W = q_1^{1.5} q_2 + \lambda\left[90 - 3q_1 - 4q_2\right],$$

Taking the partial derivatives of W, *w.r.t.*, q_1, q_2 and λ, and setting them to zero,

$$\frac{\partial W}{\partial q_1} = 1.5q_1^{0.5} q_2 - 3\lambda = 0 \cdots\cdots (1),$$

$$\frac{\partial W}{\partial q_2} = q_1^{1.5} - 4\lambda = 0 \cdots\cdots (2)$$

$$\frac{\partial W}{\partial \lambda} = 90 - 3q_1 - 4q_2 = 0 \cdots\cdots (3)$$

From equation 1 and 2 we get $\lambda = \frac{1.5q_1^{0.5} q_2}{3}$ and $\lambda = \frac{q_1^{1.5}}{4}$,

Dividing the λ 's we obtain $\frac{1.5q_1^{0.5} q_2}{3} \div \frac{q_1^{1.5}}{4} = 1$ or $\frac{1.5q_1^{0.5} q_2}{3} \times \frac{4}{q_1^{1.5}} = 1$

or $2q_1^{0.5} q_2 = q_1^{1.5}$ or $\frac{2q_1^{0.5} q_2}{q_1^{1.5}} = 1$ or $\frac{2q_2}{q_1} = 1$ or $2q_2 = q_1$

Substituting this in equation (3) we get $3q_1 + 4q_1 = 90$ or $3(2q_2) + 4q_2 = 90$

$\therefore$ $q_2 = 9$ and from this we get $q_1 = 2q_2 = 18$.

Thus the optimum quantities of q_1 and q_2 are 9 and 18 respectively. These quantities will maximize utility function These quantities also satisfy the order conditions for utiltiy maximization as provided below:

The first-order condition of utility maximization is

$$MRCS = \frac{dq_2}{dq_1} = -\frac{f_1}{f_2} = -\frac{p_1}{p_2} \text{ or } \frac{f_1}{f_2} = \frac{p_1}{p_2}.$$

This is nothing but the equality between slope of indifference curve and slope of price line.

$$\frac{f_1}{f_2} = \frac{\partial U/\partial q_1}{\partial U/\partial q_2} = \frac{1.5q_1^{0.5}q_2}{q_1^{1.5}} = \frac{1.5q_2}{q_1} = \frac{1.5(9)}{18} = \frac{13.5}{18} = 0.75$$

and $\frac{p_1}{p_2} = \frac{3}{4} = 0.75 \quad \therefore \frac{f_1}{f_2} = \frac{p_1}{p_2} = 0.75$

The second-order condition demands indifference curve to slope convex at the tangency point so that

$\frac{d^2q_2}{dq_1^2} > 0$, We have derived $\frac{dq_2}{dq_1} = -\frac{f_1}{f_2} = -1.5q_2\, q_1^{-1}$ so that $\frac{d^2q_2}{dq_1^2}$ is

$$\frac{\partial}{\partial q_1}\left(\frac{\partial q_2}{\partial q_1}\right) = \frac{\partial}{\partial q_1}\left[-1.5q_2q_1^{-1}\right] = \frac{1.5q_2}{q_1^2} > 0 \text{ as } q_2 = 9, \quad q_1 = 18$$

Thus equilibrium quantities of two goods $q_1 = 18$, $q_2 = 9$ satisfy both the order conditions for utility maximization. The convexity of indifference curve is given by the derivatives

$\frac{dq_2}{dq_1} < 0$ and $\frac{d^2q_2}{dq_1^2} > 0$. These conditions are fulfilled.

9.4. Constrained Optimization Problem Facing a Firm

Technically a firm is a roducing agent, porduces goods and services for sale in the market. Entrepreneurs and managers take decision regarding what goods are to be produced and in what quantity so as to gain maximum profits. The job facing the entrepreneur is the transformation of inputs into output. For this purpose they are provided with the production functions by the technical experts. The job of an economist is confined to the firm's behaviour in regard to applying the conditions that can materialize the firm to attain constrained output maximization or constrained cost minimization and constrained revenue maximization as it is required.

Profit of the firm is the difference between revenue from the sale of output in the market and cost incured from hiring various factors of production in some quantities. Profit can be positive or regative or zero.

The production function can be a single continuous function where one output is to be produced (q_1) by using two inputs (x_1) and (x_2). In its simple form this is given as $Q = f(x_1\ x_2) = x_1^{\alpha}\ x_2^{\beta}$ where α, β are the positive constants. There are different types of production functions of interest to the managers.

An enterpreneur can use different inputs to produce her output. Some of the outputs of one firm can also be used as inputs by other firms. Inputs are classified into fixed and variable inputs. This classification is made for a specific period of time. Therefore there is a short-run during which firm can alter its output by altering quantities of variable inputs only while employing a fixed quantity of fixed inputs. Accordingly, firm's total cost in the short-run is comprised of total variable cost and total fixed cost.

Mathematically if $q = f(x_1, x_2)$ and per unit prices of these inputs are r_1 and r_2 respecvtively while fixed cost is given by the parameter 'b'. With these data firm's total cost function can be formulated and shown to be $C = r_1 x_1 + r_2 x_2 + b$.

This analysis of the firm is analogous to that of a consumer. When a consumer purchases commodities to maximize utility function subject to her budget constnaint, the firm's problem is to combine inputs in an optimum proportion so as to maximize the output subject to a cost constraint.

While the consumer has got an utility function to be maximized, the firm on the other hand has got a production function to face. However there are some differences that exist between these two. For example while the utility function is subjective, the production function is said to be objective in nature. Moreover a single firm may produce more than one output as well. The rational consumer maximizes utility for a given income. The analogons action of the firm is to maximize output for a given cost. He may go for minimizing cost for producing a given level of output as well. We will study these problems as constained output maximization and constrained cost minimization.

Constrained Output Maximization:

The firm's typical simple production function is $q = f(x_1\ x_2)$ and the total cost constraint is $C° = r_1 x_1 + r_2 x_2 + b$, where '$b$' is the fixed cost. The firm's objective is to maximize output *(q)* subject to the cost constraint.

To find solution we need to define a new function (lagrange). It is formulated by combining production and cost functions, called 'V' where $V = f(x_1\ x_2) + \mu\ (C° - r_1 x_1 - r_2 x_2 - b)$, μ = Lagrange multiplier. It is a non-zero quantity, $\mu \neq 0$. Setting the partial derivative of V, *w.r.t.*, x_1, x_2 and μ to zero we get,

$$\frac{\partial V}{\partial x_1} = f_1 - r_1\ \mu = 0 \cdots\cdots(1) \quad \text{or} \quad \mu = \frac{f_1}{r_1}$$

$$\frac{\partial V}{\partial x_2} = f_2 - r_2\ \mu = 0 \cdots\cdots(2) \quad \text{or} \quad \mu = \frac{f_2}{r_2}$$

$$\frac{\partial V}{\partial \mu} = C° - r_1 x_1 - r_2 x_2 - b = 0 \cdots\cdots(3) \quad \text{or } C° = r_1\ x_1 + r_2\ x_2 + b.$$

Solving equations (1) and (2) we get.

$$\mu = \frac{f_1}{r_1} = \frac{f_2}{r_2} \quad \text{or} \quad \frac{f_1}{f_2} = \frac{r_1}{r_2},$$ where f_1 and f_2 are marginal products of inputs.

$$f_1 = MPx_1 = \frac{\partial f(x_1 x_2)}{\partial x_1},\quad f_2 = MPx_2 = \frac{\partial f(x_1 x_2)}{\partial x_2}$$

The first-order condition for output maximization is the equality between the ratio of marginal products*(MP)* of two inputs and the ratio of the prices of two inputs *i.e.* $\frac{f_1}{f_2} = \frac{r_1}{r_2}$. The Second-order condition requires the isoquant to slope convex at the equilibrium point.

From economic theory we know that for the production function given as $q = f(x_1\ x_2)$, the movement along the iso-quant results into no change in the output. This means $dq = 0$. We can derive this as

$$\partial q = f_1\ \partial x_1 + f_2\ \partial x_2 = 0. \text{ or } \quad -\frac{\partial x_2}{\partial x_1} = \frac{f_1}{f_2}$$

The slope of the iso-quant is shown by the Mariginal Rate of Technical substitution (*MRTS*) of x_1 for x_2 inputs so that the same level of output is maintained on an iso-qaunt. Slope is negative as $MRTS = -\frac{\partial x_2}{\partial x_1} = \frac{f_1}{f_2}$. The first order condition derived so far is $\frac{f_1}{f_2} = \frac{r_1}{r_2}$, This implies that the slope of the iso-quant is equal to the slope of the iso-cost line.

$\frac{f_1}{f_2} = \frac{r_1}{r_2}$ depicts the tangency point , where $MRTS = \frac{f_1}{f_2}$ and slope of iso-cost line is $= \frac{r_1}{r_2}$.

The geometric interpretation of this is that the optimum input combination of x_1 and x_2 is provided at the point of tangency between the iso-quant and the given iso-cost line. Thus for a given iso-cost line C(1) the maximum attainable output is q_{200}, while for iso-cost line C (2), the corresponding maximum attainable output is is q_{300} and so on.

The second-order condition, called the sufficient condition is also to be fulfilled at the point of equilibrium. This condition requires that the relevant bordered Hessian determinant must be positive.

Thus $|\overline{H}| > 0$ where, $|\overline{H}| = \begin{vmatrix} f_{11} & f_{12} & -r_1 \\ f_{21} & f_{22} & -r_2 \\ -r_1 & -r_2 & 0 \end{vmatrix} > 0$

This condition is fulfilled only if the iso-quant is convex to the origin. This condition requires that not only $\frac{dx_2}{dx_1} = \frac{-f_1}{f_2} < 0$, the sioquant slopes negative. However it must be convex downward or $\frac{d^2x_2}{dx_1^2} > 0$. This implies that iso-quant is to take negative slope and at the same time it is convex to the origin at the point of tangeney between the price line and the given indifference curve. this provides producer's equilibrium point.

$$\frac{d^2x_2}{dx_1^2} = \frac{d}{dx_1}\left(\frac{dx_2}{dx_1}\right) = \frac{d}{dx_1}\left[\frac{-f_1}{f_2}\right] = -\frac{d}{dx_1}\left[\frac{f_1}{f_2}\right]$$

$$\frac{d^2x_2}{dx_1^2} = \frac{f_3}{f_2}\left[2f_{21}f_1f_2 - f_{11}f_2^2 - f_{22}f_1^2\right] \cdots\cdots (3)$$

$$|\overline{H}| = f_{11}\left(-r_2^2\right) - f_{12}\left(-r_1\, r_2\right) - r_1\left(-f_{21}r_2 + f_{22}\, r_1\right)$$

$$= -f_{11}\, r_2^2 + f_{12}\, r_1\, r_2 + f_{21}\, r_1\, r_2 - f_{22}\, r_1^2$$

$$= \left(2f_{12}\, r_1\, r_2 - f_{11}\, r_2^2 - f_{22}\, r_1^2\right) > 0 \cdots (4)$$

The bracket in $\frac{d^2x_2}{dx_1^2}$ is same as $|\overline{H}|$ because $\frac{f_1}{r_1} = \mu$ and $\frac{f_2}{r_2} = \mu$

Therefore $r_1 = \frac{f_1}{\mu}$ and $r_2 = \frac{f_2}{\mu}$.

By substituting these in $|\overline{H}|$ we get $2f_{12}\, r_1\, r_2 - f_{11}\, r_2^2 - f_{22}\, r_1^2$

$$= 2f_{12}\left(\frac{f_1}{\mu}\right)\left(\frac{f_2}{\mu}\right) - f_{11}\left(\frac{f_1}{\mu}\right)^2 - f_{22}\left(\frac{f_1}{\mu}\right)^2 = \left[\frac{2f_{12}\, f_1\, f_2 - f_{11}\, f_2^2 - f_{22}\, f_1^2}{\mu^2}\right] > 0$$

or $\left(2f_{12}\,f_1\,f_2 - f_{11}\,f_2^2 - f_{22}\,f_1^2\right) > 0$

Therefore second order condition is satisfined only if $\dfrac{d^2x_2}{dx_1^2} > 0$ so that

$\dfrac{d^2x_2}{dx_1^2} = \dfrac{1}{f_2^3}\left(2f_{12}\,f_{12} - f_{11}\,f_2^2 - f_{22}\,f_1^2\right) > 0$ *as* $f_2^3 > 0$. Thus $\dfrac{d^2x_2}{dx_1^2} > 0$

This states that the iso-quant at the tangency point is conex downward.

9.5. Illustrations on Constrained Output Maximization

(1) The production function is $q = f(k, l) = \sqrt{KL}$. Per unit prices of capital and labour are Rs. 8 and Rs. 4 respectively. Find

(a) The maximum output the entreprenuer can produce from a total outlay of Rs. 120, which he wants to spend on these inputs.

(b) Verify that corresponding to the optimum input combination the slope of the iso-quant and slope of the iso-cost line are equal.

Solution: Given $q = \sqrt{KL} = k^{\frac{1}{2}}L^{\frac{1}{2}}$, the cost constraint can be formulated from the information given on prices of inputs and outlay. Accordingly we can get the the iso-cost line
$C° = 8K + 4L = 120$.

The enterpreneur is required to maximize $q = \sqrt{KL} = K^{\frac{1}{2}}\,L^{\frac{1}{2}}$, subject to the cost constraint $8K + 4L = 120$. The solution is obtained by combining these two functions by defining a lagrangian function Z. Then setting its partial derivative *w.r.t.* *K*, *L* and μ as zero we can get the required solution . Accordingly the lagrangian function Z is defined

$Z = K^{\frac{1}{2}}\,L^{\frac{1}{2}} + \mu\left[120 - 8K - 4L\right]$ and

$\dfrac{\partial Z}{\partial K} = \dfrac{1}{2}K^{-\frac{1}{2}}\,L^{\frac{1}{2}} - 8\mu = 0 \cdots\cdots (1)$ or $\dfrac{\sqrt{L}}{16\sqrt{K}} = \mu$

$\dfrac{\partial Z}{\partial L} = \dfrac{1}{2}K^{\frac{1}{2}}\,L^{-\frac{1}{2}} - 4\mu = 0 \cdots\cdots (2)$ or $\dfrac{\sqrt{K}}{8\sqrt{L}} = \mu$

$\dfrac{\partial Z}{\partial \mu} = 120 - 8K - 4L = 0 \cdots\cdots (3)$ or $8K + 4L = 120$

Solving for μ we get, $\dfrac{\sqrt{L}}{16\sqrt{K}} = \dfrac{\sqrt{K}}{8\sqrt{L}}$

or $8L = 16K$ or $L = 2K$

Substituting this in equation (3) we get, $8K + 4\,(2K) = 120$

or $16K = 120$ $\therefore$ $K = 7.5$ and $L = 2K = 15$

These input quantities are also satisfying the cost constraint, $8K + 4L = 8\ (7.5) + 4\ (15) = 120$.

Thus the entrepreneur will use 7.5 units of capital and 15 units of labour for maximizing total output $q = \sqrt{K\,L}$. The maximum output produced is $q = \sqrt{(7.5)\,(15)} = \sqrt{112.5} = 10.6$ units

(b) It can be verified that these input combinations satisfy the order conditions for producer's equilibrium. This is also referred to the problem of the least-cost combination of inputs. The slope of the iso-quant is equal to slope of the iso-cost line when firm uses these quantities of capital and labour we have determined. This can also be verified that

Slope of the iso-quant is $-\dfrac{dK}{dL} = \dfrac{f_L}{f_K}$ and slope of the iso-cost line is $\dfrac{r_1}{r_2} = \dfrac{4}{8} = 0.5$, [r_1 = price of labour per unit (4) and r_2 = price of capital per unit (8)].

It can be verified that slope of iso-quant is also 0.5

$$\therefore \frac{f_L}{f_K} = \frac{4}{8} = \frac{1}{2} = 0.5, \text{ where } f_L = \frac{\partial}{\partial L}\left[K^{\frac{1}{2}}\, L^{\frac{1}{2}}\right] = \frac{\sqrt{K}}{2\sqrt{L}} \text{ and } f_K = \frac{\partial}{\partial K}\left[K^{\frac{1}{2}}\, L^{\frac{1}{2}}\right] = \frac{\sqrt{L}}{2\sqrt{K}} \text{ and}$$

$$\frac{f_L}{f_K} = \frac{\sqrt{K}}{2\sqrt{L}}\,\frac{2\sqrt{K}}{\sqrt{L}} = \frac{2K}{2L} = \frac{K}{L} = \frac{7.5}{15} = \frac{1}{2} = 0.5, \quad \therefore \frac{f_L}{f_K} = \frac{r_1}{r_2}$$

Thus it is proved that the slope of the iso-quant and slope of the iso-cost line are equal for these equlibrium qunatities of inputs.

9.6. Illustrations on Constrained Cost Minimization

(1) The production function of a firm is given by $Q = 5\sqrt{K\,L}$ The price of labour per unit is Rs. 2 and price of capital per unit is Rs. 4. Find the optimum combination of capital and labour that will minimize total outlay of the firm , when he has decided to produce 30 units of output. The fixed cost is given Rs. 15.

Solution:

Given the production function is $Q = 5\sqrt{K\,L} = 5K^{\frac{1}{2}}L^{\frac{1}{2}}$, we can formulate the total cost constraint from the information given to us on prices of inputs. Thus total cost is C, where $C = 2L + 4K + 15$. The entrepreneur is required to minimise total cost for having decided to produce a given level of output, 30 units.

For production function is given $q = 5L^{0.5}\ K^{0.5} = 30$, firm is required to minimize total cost for producing 30 units of output. This problem is referred to constrained cost minimization subject to the output given fixed.

we need to define the lagrangian function Z for this problem which requires combining both output and cost functions as $Z = 2L + 4K + 15 + \mu\left[30 - 5L^{0.5}K^{0.5}\right]$

Setting the partial derivatives of *Z, w.r.t.*, L , K and μ equal to zero we get,

$$\frac{\partial Z}{\partial L} = 2 - \mu\, 5\, (0.5)\, L^{-0.5}K^{0.5} = 0 \cdots\cdots (1) \quad \text{or} \quad \mu = \frac{2\sqrt{L}}{2.5\,\sqrt{K}}$$

$$\frac{\partial Z}{\partial K} = 4 - \mu 5\,(0.5)\, L^{0.5} K^{-0.5} = 0 \cdots\cdots (2) \text{ or } \mu = \frac{4\sqrt{K}}{2.5\sqrt{L}}$$

$$\frac{\partial Z}{\partial \mu} = 30 - 5\, L^{0.5} K^{0.5} = 0 \cdots\cdots (3) \quad \text{or } 5\, L^{0.5} K^{0.5} = 30$$

By dividing μ obtained above we get,

$$\frac{2\sqrt{L}}{2.5\sqrt{K}} \times \frac{2.5\sqrt{L}}{4\sqrt{K}} = 1 \; or \; \frac{L}{2K} = 1 \; or \; L = 2K$$

Substituting this in equation (3) we get $5\, L^{0.5}\, K^{0.5} = 30$ or $5\,(2K)^{0.5}\, K^{0.5} = 30$

or $\sqrt{2}\,K = 6$ and $K = \dfrac{6}{\sqrt{2}} = 4.243$ and $L = 2K = 8.486$.

The input combinations that minimise total cost for producing $q = 30$ units are thus $K = 4.243$ and $L = 8.486$ units. It can be verified that these input combinations yield output $q = 30$

$$q = 5\sqrt{L\,K} = 5\sqrt{(4.243)\,(8.486)} = 5 \times 6 = 30$$

The minimum cost is $C = 2L + 4K + 15 = 2\,(8.486) + 4\,(4.243) + 15 = 48.94$

It can be also be verified that these input combinations fulfil the order conditions laid down for constrained cost minimization. The first-order condition to be satisfierd is the same, i.e., slope of iso-quant is equal to slope of the iso-cost line. Mathematically we got,

$\dfrac{f_L}{f_K} = \dfrac{r_1}{r_2} = \dfrac{2}{4} = 0.5$. Since r_1 and r_2 stand for the price of labour and capital per unit, thier ratio is 0.5, the ratio of marginal porducts are alos to be 0.5. This has been derived,

$$\frac{f_L}{f_K} = \frac{\partial Q/\partial L}{\partial Q/\partial K} = \frac{2.5L^{-0.5}K^{0.5}}{2.5K^{-0.5}L^{0.5}} = \frac{2.5K}{2.5L} = \frac{K}{L} = \frac{4.243}{8.486} = \frac{2}{4} = 0.5$$

9.7. Solved Questions of TYBA (Economics) Papers of Mumbai University:

April' 2004

(1) M aZ = $2x^3 + 3y^3$, subject to $5x + 6y = 10$, by using Lagrange multiplier method for finding the optimal values:

For given $Z = 2x^3 + 3y^3$, we need to maximize Z, subject to the constraint $5x + 6y = 10$. This requires us to combine these two functions defined as Lagrangian function 'V' so that

$V = 2x^3 + 3y^3 + \lambda\,[10 - 5x - 6y]$, where λ = Lagrange multiplier.

Setting partial derivative of V, *w.r.t.*, variables x, y and λ and equating them to zero we get,

$$\frac{\partial V}{\partial x} = 6x^2 - 5\lambda = 0 \cdots\cdots (1), \quad \frac{\partial V}{\partial y} = 9y^2 - 6\lambda = 0 \cdots\cdots (2)$$

$$\frac{\partial V}{\partial \lambda} = 10 - 5x - 6y = 0 \cdots\cdots (3)$$

Solving (1) and (2) we get $6x^2 = 5\lambda$

or $\lambda = \frac{6x^2}{5}$ and $9y^2 = 6\lambda$ or $\lambda = \frac{9y^2}{6}$. Solving these we get λ,

$$\therefore \frac{6x^2}{5} = \frac{9y^2}{6} \quad \text{or} \quad 36x^2 = 45y^2, x^2 = \frac{45}{36}y^2 \quad \text{or} \quad x = \sqrt{\frac{45}{36}y^2} = \frac{\sqrt{45}}{6}y$$

Since $x = \frac{\sqrt{45}}{6}y$, substituting this value in equation (3) we get $5x + 6y = 10$.

or $\frac{5\sqrt{45}}{6}y + 6y = 10$ or $5\sqrt{45}\, y + 36y = 60$ *or* $y[33.54 + 36] = 60$ and

$$y = \frac{60}{69.541} = 0.863 \text{ and } x = \frac{\sqrt{45}}{6}y = \frac{6.7082(0.863)}{6} = 0.965$$

$\therefore$ The required solution are $x = 0.965$, $y = 0.863$ and $Z = 2x^3 + 3y^3 = 1.797 + 1.928 = 3.78$

(2) Using Lagrange multiplier (λ) method, find the optimum value Z for the following function:
Max: $Z = 20x + 20y - x^2 - y^2$, s. t. $2x + 5y = 10$. (Oct. 2003)

For using the Lagrangian multiplier method we define a new function V as $V = 20x + 20y - x^2 - y^2 + \lambda[10 - 2x - 5y]$ and setting the partial derivatives of V *w.r.t* the x, y and λ to zero we obtain

$$\frac{\partial V}{\partial x} = 20 - 2x - 2\lambda = 0 \cdots\cdots (1), \quad \frac{\partial V}{\partial y} = 20 - 2y - 5\lambda = 0 \cdots\cdots (2)$$

$$\frac{\partial V}{\partial \lambda} = 10 - 2x - 5y = 0 \cdots\cdots (3) \text{ or } 2x + 5y = 10 \ldots\ldots (4)$$

Rearranging equation (1) we get, $20 = 2x + 2\lambda$

or $2\lambda = 20 - 2x \; \therefore \; \lambda = 10 - x$.

From equation (2), $5\lambda = 20 - 2y$, *or* $\lambda = 4 - \frac{2}{5}y$

Solving λ, we get, $10 - x = 4 - \frac{2}{5}y$ or $10 - 4 = x - \frac{2}{5}y$ or $6 = \frac{5x - 2y}{5}$ or $5x - 2y = 30$-----(5)

Solving these two simultaneous equations $5x - 2y = 30$ (5) and $2x + 2y = 10$ (4) , we can obtain the required solution for x and y, For this multiply equation 4 by 5 and equaion 5 by 2 and eliminate x to get $10x - 4y = 60$ and $10x + 25y = 50$. From this we get

$y = \frac{-10}{29}$ and substituting this value of y in equation $2x + 5y = 10$, we obtain

$$2x = 10 - 5y = 10 - 5\left(\frac{-10}{29}\right) = 10 + \frac{50}{29} = \frac{340}{9} \cdot \text{ or } x = 5.862$$

Thus required solution are $x = 5.862$ and $y = -0.345$, $2x + 5y = 2\,(5.862) + 5\,(-0.345) = 10$

and $Z = 20x + 20y - x^2 - y^2 = 20\,(5.862) + 20\,(-0.345) - (5.862)^2 - (-0.345)^2 = 75.858$

The required solutions: $x = 5.862$, $y = -0.345$ and $Z = 75.858$

(3) Maximize : $Z = x^2 + 3xy - 6y$, s. t. $x + y = 50$. (April, 2003)

It is required to maximize $Z = x^2 + 3xy - 6y$, *s.t.*, $x + y = 50$

Combining these two functions and using lagrangian method defined

V, where $V = x^2 + 3xy - 6y + \lambda\,[50 - x - y]$.

Setting derivative of V, *w.r.t.*, variables x, y and λ to zero, we obtain,

$$\frac{\partial V}{\partial x} = 2x + 3y - \lambda = 0 \cdots\cdots (1) \text{ or } \lambda = 2x + 3y$$

$$\frac{\partial V}{\partial y} = 3x - 6 - \lambda = 0 \cdots\cdots (2) \text{ or } \lambda = 3x - 6$$

$$\frac{\partial V}{\partial \lambda} = 50 - x - y = 0 \cdots\cdots (3) \text{ or } x + y = 50$$

Solving equations (1) and (2), we get

$2x + 3y = 3x - 6$ or $3x - 2x - 3y = 6$ or $x - 3y = 6$ ....(4)

Solving $x + y = 50$ and $x - 3y = 6$, the required values so obtained are

$y = 11$ and $x = 39$ and $Z = x^2 + 3xy - 6y = (39)^2 + 3\,(39)\,(11) - 6(11) = 2742$.

EXERCISE – 9

(1) If the utility function of a consumer is given as $U = q_1^2 q_2 - 15q_1$, where q_1 and q_2 are quantities of two goods, find the optimum quantities that will maximize the utility function. For this the budget constraint is given as $2q_1 + 8q_2 = 156$.

(2) Find the least cost combination of inputs x_1 and x_2 if the production function is $Q = 20x_1^{0.75} x_2^{0.25}$ and cost constraint is $3x_1 - x_2 = 120$.

(3) Find the maxima or minima as the case may be for the function

$Z = 5x_1^2 + 6x_2^2 - x_1 x_2$, s.t. $x_1 + 2x_2 = 48$ Find the maximum or minimum value.

(4) Maximize $q = x_1 x_2$, s.t., $x_1 + 2x_2 = 8$.

(5) If the utility function is given as $U = xy$ and the budget constraint is $5x + 10y = 200$. Maximize 'U' subject to the budget constraint.

(6) If the demand function for a commodity is given as $q_x = f(P_x, P_z, y)$ where P_x and P_z are the prices of X and Z commodities and 'Y' is income, find income and cross elasticity of demand at y = Rs. 800 and P_z = Rs. 50. The demand function is $q_x = 450 - 4P_x + 2.5P_z + 0.3y$.

(7) Given $U = x^2 y$ and the budget constraint $2x + 4y = 16$, find optimum combination of x and y that maximizes 'U'.

(8) Find the optimum commodity purchases for a consumer when utlity function is $U = q_1^{1.5} q_2$, and prices are $P_1 = 5$ and $P_2 = 3$ whie income is Rs. 150.

(9) State the first-order and second order conditions for profit maximization subject to the given production function.

(10) If the production function is $q = 10x_1 + 20x_2 - 3x_1^2 - 5x_2^2$ and prices of x_1 and x_2 inputs are Rs. 5 and Rs. 6 respectively, determine equilibrium output, profits and the least cost input combinations. Price per unit of output is given Rs. 4.

(11) Maximize $U = 4\sqrt{x_1 x_2}$ subject to the budget constraint $180 = 5x_1 + 6x_2$.

❑❑❑

10 TECHNIQUES OF INTEGRATION

10.1. The Process of Integration

Integration is an important concept in calculus. It is related to differentiation. Differentiation is the process of finding the rates of changes in '*y*' *w.r.t.* '*x*' is $\frac{dy}{dx} = f'(x)$. When total utility (U) is the function of units of a good (x) consumed and if it is given as $U = 3x^2$, $\frac{dU}{dx} = 6x$. This is the marginal utility. Similarly when total output (Q) is functionally related to labour units (l), and this is given as $Q = 5l^3$, the marginal product of labour is $\frac{dQ}{dl} = 15l^2$.

In mathematical operations we can obtain their reverse functions. Thus for given the marginal utility we can find to the total utility function. Similarly from marginal product we will get total product function. This reverse process of differentiation is called integration.

For $Y = f(x) = x^2$, $\frac{dy}{dx} = f'(x) = 2x$

The integration of $f'(x)\,dx$ or $2\,xdx$ is shown as $\int 2xdx$ where "$\int$" is the symbol used to denote the process of integration. '*dx*' is written by the side of $2x$ or $f'(x)$ to mean that the function is integrated *w.r.t* '*x*'.

It implies that when derivative is evaluated with respect to '*x*', integration is also taken with respect to '*x*' i.e. $\frac{dy}{dx} = f'(x)$ and $\int f'(x)\,dx = f(x) + C$.

In the example:

$\int 2x\,dx = x^2 + C$ and $\frac{d}{dx}(x^2 + C) = 2x$.

'C' is a constant that appears in integration. This may assume any value for which the integral is called "infinite integral". However when differentiation is taken *w.r.t* 'x', this constant term 'C' or 'k' vanishes and we get the original function.

By definition when differentiation of $F(x)$ is $f'(x)$ then integration

$\int f'(x)\,dx = F(x) + C$ is the original function.

While taking integration of a function, the power of the function integrated increases by one and divide it by the new exponent formed and then add a constant 'C' to it.

For example, $\int x^2\,dx = \frac{x^{2+1}}{2+1} + C = \frac{x^3}{3} + C$

Similarly $\int x^n\,dx = \frac{x^{n+1}}{n+1} + C$.

The exponent (n) changes to $(n + 1)$ and then it is divided by $(n + 1)$

We can not evaluate integration of x^{-1} as $\int x^{-1}\,dx$, gives us $-1 + 1 = 0$ when formula is applied to it.

Therefore for this function the standard formula is given and this will be used all the time.

It is given as $\int x^{-1}\,dx = \int \frac{1}{x}\,dx = \log x + C$, also we can obtain $\frac{d}{dx}[\log x + C] = x^{-1}$

10.2. Rules of Integration

Following important rules used for finding indefinite integrals;

10.2.1. Power of the Function Rule

(1) $\int x^5\,dx = \frac{x^6}{6} + C$

(2) $\int \frac{1}{x^3}\,dx = \int x^{-3}\,dx = \frac{x^{-3+1}}{-3+1} + C = \frac{x^{-2}}{-2} + C = -\frac{1}{2x^2} + C$

(3) $\int dx = \int x^0\,dx = x + C$ as $[x^0 = 1]$.

(4) $\int x^{\frac{2}{3}}\,dx = \frac{x^{\frac{2}{3}+1}}{\frac{2}{3}+1} + C = \frac{3}{5}x^{\frac{5}{3}} + C = \frac{3}{5}\sqrt[3]{x^5} + C$

(5) $\int \sqrt{x}\,dx = \int x^{\frac{1}{2}}\,dx = \frac{x^{\frac{1}{2}+1}}{\frac{1}{2}+1} + C = \frac{2}{3}\sqrt{x^3} + C$

10.2.2. Integration of Sum or Difference

(1) $\int (x^2 - x + 3)\, dx = \int x^2\, dx - \int x\, dx + \int 3\, dx = \frac{x^3}{3} - \frac{x^2}{2} + 3x + C$

(2) $\int (x^2 - \frac{1}{x})\, dx = \int x^2\, dx - \int \frac{1}{x} dx = \frac{x^3}{3} - \log x + C$

(3) $\int (e^x - \frac{1}{x^2})\, dx = \int e^x\, dx - \int x^{-2}\, dx = e^x + \frac{1}{x} + C$

10.2.3. Integration of Logarithmic and Exponential Functions

(1) $\int e^x\, dx = e^x + C,$ for we obtain $\frac{d}{dx}\left[e^x + C\right] = e^x$

(2) $\int a^x\, dx = \frac{a^x}{\log_e a} + C$ for er get $\frac{d}{dx}\left[\frac{a^x}{\log_e a} + C\right] = \frac{a^x \log_e a}{\log_e a} + 0 = a^x$

(3) $\int 7^x\, dx = \frac{7^x}{\log_e 7} + C$

(4) $\int (e^x + \frac{1}{x^5})\, dx = \int e^x\, dx + \int x^{-5}\, dx = e^x - \frac{1}{4x^4} + C$

(5) $\int \left(\frac{1}{x^3} + \frac{3}{x\sqrt{x}} + 5\right) dx$

$= \int x^{-3}\, dx + 3\int \frac{1}{x\sqrt{x}}\, dx + \int 5\, dx = \frac{x^{-2}}{-2} + \frac{3x^{-\frac{3}{2}+1}}{-\frac{3}{2}+1} + 5x + C$

$= -\frac{1}{2x^2} + (3)(-2)\, x^{-\frac{1}{2}} + 5x + C = -\frac{1}{2x^2} - \frac{6}{\sqrt{x}} + 5x + C$

(6) $\int \frac{\sqrt[3]{5x}}{7}\, dx = \int \frac{(5x)^{\frac{1}{3}}}{7}\, dx = \int \frac{(5)^{\frac{1}{3}}}{7} \int x^{\frac{1}{3}}\, dx$

$= \frac{5^{\frac{1}{3}} \times 3}{7 \times 4} x^{\frac{4}{3}} + C = \frac{3 \times 5^{\frac{1}{3}}}{28} x^{\frac{4}{3}} + C.$

(7) $\int \frac{x+2}{x-2}\, dx = \int \frac{x-1+3}{x-1}\, dx = \int \frac{x-1}{x-1}\, dx + 3\int \frac{1}{x-1}\, dx$

$= x + 3\log_e (x-1) + C$

(8) $\int \frac{\sqrt[5]{4x}}{8}\, dx$

$= \int \frac{(4x)^{\frac{1}{5}}}{8}\, dx = \frac{(4)^{\frac{1}{5}}}{8} \int x^{\frac{1}{5}}\, dx = \frac{5 \times 4^{\frac{1}{5}}\, x^{\frac{6}{5}}}{8 \times 6} + C = \frac{5 \times 4^{\frac{1}{5}}\, x^{\frac{6}{5}}}{48} + C.$

(9) $\int \frac{1}{x\sqrt{x}}\, dx$

$= \int \frac{1}{x^{\frac{3}{2}}}\, dx = -\frac{2}{\sqrt{x}} + C$

(10) $\int (3\sqrt{x} + \frac{t}{\sqrt{x}} - \frac{6}{x})\, dx$

$= 2\sqrt{x^3} + 2t\sqrt{x} - 6 \log_e x + C.$

(11) $\int \frac{x^3 - 5}{x}\, dx$

$= \int x^2\, dx - 5 \int \frac{1}{x}\, dx = \frac{x^3}{3} - 5 \log_e x + C$

(12) $\int \frac{5\sqrt[3]{3x}}{7}\, dx$

$= \frac{5}{7} \int (3x)^{\frac{1}{3}}\, dx = \frac{5 \times 3^{\frac{1}{3}}}{7} \int x^{\frac{1}{3}}\, dx = \frac{15}{28} \times 3^{\frac{1}{3}}\, x^{\frac{4}{3}} + C$

(13) $\int \frac{x^{\frac{5}{2}} + x^{\frac{3}{2}} - x^{\frac{1}{2}} + 3x}{x}\, dx$

$= \int x^{\frac{3}{2}}\, dx + \int x^{\frac{1}{2}}\, dx - \int x^{-\frac{1}{2}}\, dx + 3 \int dx$

$= \frac{2}{5} x^{\frac{5}{2}} + \frac{2}{3} x^{\frac{3}{2}} - 2\sqrt{x} + 3x + C.$

(14) $\int \frac{x + 3}{x - 2}\, dx$

$= \int \frac{x - 2 + 5}{x - 2}\, dx = \int dx + 5 \int \frac{1}{x - 2}\, dx$

$= x + 5 \log_e (x - 2) + C.$

(15) $\int \frac{5x^2 + 8 - \sqrt{x}}{x^2}\, dx$

$= 5\int dx + 8 \int x^{-2}\, dx - \int x^{-\frac{3}{2}}\, dx$

$= 5x - \frac{8}{x} + \frac{2}{\sqrt{x}} + C.$

(16) $\int(e^{8x} + 5e^{3x} + x^7)\, dx$

$= \int(e^{8x}\, dx + 5\int(e^{3x}\, dx + \int x^7\, dx$

$= \frac{1}{8} e^{8x} + \frac{5}{3} e^{3x} + \frac{x^8}{8} + C$

(17) $\int \frac{1}{e^x}\, dx$

$= \int e^{-x}\, dx = -e^{-x} + C = -\frac{1}{e^x} + C$ {Note that $\frac{d}{dx}\left(\frac{-1}{e^x} + C\right) = \frac{1}{e^x}$.}

(18) $\int \frac{e^{\sqrt{x}}}{\sqrt{x}}\, dx = \int \frac{e^{x^{\frac{1}{2}}}}{x^{\frac{1}{2}}}\, dx = 2\, e^{\sqrt{x}} + C$.

[Note that $\frac{d}{dx}[2\, e^{\sqrt{x}} + C] = \frac{d}{dx}[2\, e^{\sqrt{x}}] = 2\, e^{\sqrt{x}}\, \frac{d}{dx}\sqrt{x} = 2\, e^{\sqrt{x}}\, \frac{1}{2\sqrt{x}} = \frac{e^{\sqrt{x}}}{\sqrt{x}}$]

(19) $\int\sqrt{e^x\, dx} = \int(e^x)^{\frac{1}{2}}\, dx = 2\sqrt{e^x} + C$

so that $\frac{d}{dx}[2\sqrt{e^x} + C] = \frac{d}{dx}[2\sqrt{e^x}] = \frac{2}{2}(e^x)^{-\frac{1}{2}}\, \frac{d}{dx} e^x = \frac{2e^x}{2\sqrt{e^x}} = \frac{e^x}{\sqrt{e^x}} = \frac{e^x\sqrt{e^x}}{e^x} = \sqrt{e^x}$

(20) $\int(8e^{2x} - \frac{5}{x^3})\, dx = 8\int e^{2x}\, dx - 5\int x^{-3}\, dx$

so that $= 4\, e^{2x} + \frac{5}{2x^2} + C$.

10.2.4 Some Standard Results of given Functions

(1) $\int x^n\, dx = \frac{x^{n+1}}{n+1} + C$

so that $\frac{d}{dx}\left[\frac{x^{n+1}}{n+1} + C\right] = x^n$

(2) $\int\frac{1}{x}\, dx = \log_e x + C$ so that $\frac{d}{dx}[\log_e x + C] = \frac{1}{x}$.

(3) $\int e^x\, dx = e^x + C$

and $\int e^{3x}\, dx = \frac{e^{3x}}{3} + C$ so that $\frac{d}{dx}\left[\frac{e^{3x}}{3} + C\right] = \frac{d}{dx}\left(\frac{e^{3x}}{3}\right) = \frac{1}{3}\cdot 3e^{3x} = e^{3x}$

(4) $\int a^x \, dx = \dfrac{a^x}{\log_e a} + C$

so that $\dfrac{d}{dx}\left[\dfrac{a^x}{\log_e a} + C\right] = \dfrac{d}{dx}\left(\dfrac{a^x}{\log_e a}\right) = \dfrac{a^x \log_e a}{\log_e a} = a^x.$

(5) $\int \dfrac{1}{\sqrt{1-x^2}} = dx = Sin^{-1}\, x$

as $\dfrac{d}{dx}[\sin^{-1} x] = \dfrac{1}{\sqrt{1-x^2}}$

(6) $\int \dfrac{1}{\sqrt{a^2 - x^2}}\, dx = \sin^{-1} \dfrac{x}{a}$ as $\dfrac{d}{dx}\left(\sin^{-1} \dfrac{x}{a}\right) = \dfrac{1}{\sqrt{a^2 - x^2}}$

10.2.5 Integration by the Method of Substitution

Integration is not so simple as in case of differentiation. Therefore for integrating a given function, there is a need to transform the function to some standard form. This requires substitution.

Following illustrations are used to simplify this process.

(1) $\int (3\,dx + 5)^6 \, dx$

Take $(3x + 5)$ as U and take total differential on both sides

$$\frac{d}{dx}(3x + 5)\, dx = \frac{d}{du}(u)\, du$$

$$3dx = du, \therefore dx = \frac{du}{3}$$

$$\int (3x + 5)^6 \, dx = \int u^6 \frac{du}{3} = \frac{1}{3}\int u^6 \, du$$

$$= \frac{1}{3}\frac{u^7}{7} + C = \frac{1}{21}(3x + 5)^7 + C.$$

(2) $\int x\sqrt{(x^2 + 3)}\, dx.$

Take $x^2 + 3 = u$

$$2x\, dx = du \text{ and } dx = \frac{du}{2x}$$

$$\int x\sqrt{x^2 + 3}\, dx = \int x\sqrt{x}\, \frac{dy}{2x} = \frac{1}{2}\int \sqrt{x}\, dx$$

$$= \frac{1}{2}\frac{u^{\frac{3}{2}}}{\frac{3}{2}} + C = \frac{2}{6}(x^2+3)^{\frac{3}{2}} + C = \frac{1}{3}\sqrt{(x^2+3)^3} + C.$$

(3) $\int \frac{x}{3x^2+5}\,dx$

Take $3x^2 + 5 = u$ and then finding total differntial we get

$6x\,dx = du$ and $dx = \frac{du}{6x}$

$$\therefore \int \frac{x}{3x^2+5}\,dx = \int \frac{x}{u}\cdot\frac{du}{6x} = \frac{1}{6}\int \frac{1}{u}\cdot du$$

$$= \frac{1}{6}\log_e u + C = \frac{1}{6}\log_e (3x^2+5) + C.$$

(4) $\int e^{kx}\,dx = \frac{1}{k}e^{kx} + C$

so that $\frac{d}{dx}\left[\frac{1}{k}e^{kx} + C\right] = \frac{d}{dx}\left[\frac{1}{k}e^{kx}\right] = e^{kx}$

(5) $\int 5a^{3x}\,dx = 5\int a^{3x}\,dx$

Take $3x = u$ so that $3\,dx = du$ and $dx = \frac{du}{3}$

$$5\int a^u \frac{du}{3} = \frac{5}{3}\int a^u\,du = \frac{5}{3}\frac{a^u}{\log_e a} + C = \frac{5}{3}\frac{a^{3x}}{\log_e x} + C$$

(6) $\int \frac{x}{x-5}\,dx = \int \frac{x-5+5}{x-5}\,dx$

$$= \int dx + 5 = \int \frac{1}{x-5}\,dx = x + 5\log(x-5) + C.$$

(7) $\int (x^3+2)^3 = 3x^2\,dx$

Take $x^3 + 2 = u$ so that $= 3x^2\,dx = du$ and $dx = \frac{du}{3x^2}$

$$\int u^3 \cdot 3x^2 \cdot \frac{du}{3x^2} = \int u^3 du = \frac{u^4}{4} + C = \frac{(x^2+2)^4}{4} + C$$

(8) $\int = \frac{x^2}{x^6 + 1} dx$

Take $x^3 = u$ so that $x^6 = u^2 \cdot$ Finding total differential we get

$3x^2\, dx = du$ and $dx \frac{du}{3x^2}$

$$\int \frac{x^2}{u^2 + 1} \frac{du}{3x^2} = \frac{1}{3} \int \frac{1}{u^2 + 1} du$$

$$= \frac{1}{3} \tan^{-1} u + C = \frac{1}{3} \tan^{-1} x^3 + C$$

(9) $\int \frac{1}{\sqrt{x} + 3} dx,$

Take $\sqrt{x} = u$, so that $\frac{1}{2\sqrt{x}} dx = du$ and $dx = 2\sqrt{x}\, du = 2u\, du$

$$\int \frac{1}{\sqrt{x} + 3} dx = \int \frac{1}{u + 3} 2u\, du = 2 \int \frac{u}{u + 3} du$$

$$2 \int \frac{u + 3 - 3}{u + 3} du = 2 \int du - 6 \int \frac{1}{u + 3} du$$

$$= 2u - 6 \log_e (u + 3) + C$$

$$= 2(\sqrt{x}) - 6 \log_e (\sqrt{x} + 3) + C$$

(10) $\int \frac{\log_e x}{x} dx$

Take $\log_e x = u$, so that $\frac{1}{x} dx = du$ and $du = x\, du$

$$\int \frac{u}{x} x\, du = \int u\, du = \frac{u^2}{2} + C = \frac{(\log_e x)^2}{2} + C$$

(11) $\int \frac{(\log_e x)^5}{x} dx$

If $\log_e x = \text{u}$, $dx = x\, du$

$$\int \frac{u^5}{x} \cdot x\, du = \int u^5 dx = \frac{u^6}{6} + C = \int \frac{(\log_e x)^6}{6} + C$$

(12) $\int \frac{1}{x \log_e x} dx$

If $\log x = u$, $dx = x\, du$

$$\int \frac{1}{xu} x\, du = \int \frac{1}{u} du = \log_e u + C = \log_e (\log_e x) + C$$

(13) $\int \frac{3x}{(3x+2)^2} dx = \int \frac{3x+2-2}{(3x+2)^2} dx$

$$= \int \frac{1}{3x+2} dx - 2 \int \frac{1}{(3x+2)^2} dx$$

Take $3x + 2 = u$ so that $3dx = du$, $dx = \frac{du}{3}$. Substituting these we get

$$= \int \frac{1}{3x+2} dx - 2 \int \frac{1}{(3x+2)^2} dx = \int \frac{1}{u} \frac{du}{3} - 2 \int \frac{1}{u^2} \frac{du}{3}$$

$$= \frac{1}{3} \int \frac{1}{u} du - 2 \int u^{-2} \frac{du}{3} = \frac{1}{3} \log_e u - \frac{2}{3} \left\{ \frac{u^{-1}}{-1} \right\} + C$$

$$= \frac{1}{3} \log_e (3x+2) + \frac{2}{3(3x+2)} + C$$

(14) $\int \frac{e^{3x}}{1+e^{3x}} dx$

If $1 + e^{3x} = u$, $3e^{3x}\, dx = du$, $dx = \frac{du}{3e^{3x}}$. Substituting these we get

$$\int \frac{e^{3x}}{1+e^{3x}} dx = \int \frac{e^{3x}}{u} \cdot \frac{du}{3e^{3x}} = \frac{1}{3} \int \frac{1}{u} du$$

$$= \frac{1}{3} \log_e (1 + e^{3x}) + C$$

(15) $\int \frac{1}{16x^2 + 4} dx = \int \frac{1}{(4x)^2 + (2)^2} dx$

$$= \frac{1}{2} \tan^{-1} \left(\frac{4x}{2} \right)$$

(16) $\int\sqrt{8x+3}\,dx$

If $8x + 3 = u$, $8dx = du$ and $dx = \frac{du}{8}$. Substituting these we get

$\int\sqrt{8x+3}\,dx =$

$$\int\sqrt{u}\,\frac{du}{8} = \frac{1}{8}\int\sqrt{u}\,du = \frac{1}{8}\frac{u^{\frac{3}{2}}}{\frac{3}{2}} + C$$

$$= \frac{2}{24}\sqrt{(8x+3)^3} + C$$

(18) $\int\frac{1}{(9x+5)^3}\,dx$

If, $9x+5 = u$, $9dx = du$, $dx = \frac{du}{9}$ so that,

$$\int\frac{1}{(9x+5)^3}\,dx = \int\frac{1}{u^3}\cdot\frac{du}{9} = \frac{1}{9}\int u^{-3}\,du = -\frac{1}{18\,(9x+5)^2} + C$$

(19) $\int x^2\,e - x^3\,dx$

If, $e^{-x^3} = u$, $-3x^2 e^{-x^3}\,dx = du$ and $dx = \frac{du}{-3x^2\,e^{-x^3}}$ so that

$$\int x^2\,e^{-x^3}\,dx = \int\frac{x^2\,e^{-x^3}\,du}{-3x^2\,e^{-x^3}} = -\frac{1}{3}\int du$$

$$= \frac{1}{3}u + C = -\frac{1}{3}e^{-x^3} + C$$

(20) $\int\frac{x^2}{5x^3+2}\,dx = \frac{1}{15}\log_e(5x^3+2) + C$

(21) $\int\frac{3x^2}{x^3+8}\,dx = \log_e(x^3+8) + C$

(22) $\int\frac{2x^3+1}{x^4+2x}\,dx$

if $x^4 + 2x = u$, $(4\,x^3 + 2)\,dx = du$ and

$dx = \frac{du}{(4x^3+2)}$. Substituting this we get

$$\int \frac{2x^3+1}{x^4+2x}\,dx = \int \frac{(2x^3+1)}{u}\,\frac{du}{(4x^3+2)}$$

We can also write $(2x^3+1) = \frac{1}{2}(4x^3+2)$ and get

$$\therefore \int \frac{\frac{1}{2}(4x^3+2)}{u} \cdot \frac{du}{(4x^3+2)} = \frac{1}{2}\int \frac{1}{u} \cdot du$$

$$= \frac{1}{2}\log(4x^3+2) + C$$

(23) $\int 6x\sqrt{x^2+5}\,dx$

Take $\sqrt{x^2+5} = u$ and $x^2+5 = u^2$ so that $2x\,dx = 2\,udu$ and $dx = \frac{2u\,du}{2x}$

$$\int 6x\sqrt{x^2+5}\,dx = \int 6x\,u \cdot \frac{2u\,du}{2x}$$

$$= 6\int u^2\,du = \frac{6}{3}u^3 + C = \frac{6}{3}(x^2+5)^{\frac{3}{2}} + C$$

$$= 2\sqrt{(x^2+5)^3} + C$$

(24) $\int \sqrt{\frac{3+\log x}{x}}\,dx$

if $3+\log x = u$, $\left(\frac{1}{x}\right)dx = du$ and $dx = x\,du$. Substituting these we get

$$\int \sqrt{\frac{3+\log x}{x}}\,dx = \int \frac{\sqrt{u}}{x}\,x\,du = \int \sqrt{u}\,du$$

$$= \frac{2}{3}\sqrt{(3+\log x)^3} + C$$

10.2.6 Solved Questions of TYBA Economics Papers of Mumbai University on Integration:

(1) $\int x(x^2+1)^2\,dx$ **(May 2000)**

By taking $x^2+1 = u$, so that $2xdx = du$ and $dx = \frac{du}{2x}$ and

$$\int x\,(x^2+1)^2\,dx = \int x\,u^2\,\frac{du}{2x} = \frac{1}{2}\int u^2\,du = \frac{1}{2}\,\frac{u^3}{3} + C$$

$$= \frac{1}{6}\,(x^2+1)^3 + C$$

(2) $\displaystyle\int \frac{(x^4+3x^2+4x+5)}{4}\,dx$ **(May 2000)**

$$= \frac{1}{4}\int x^4\,dx + \frac{3}{4}\int x^2\,dx + \int x\,dx + \frac{5}{4}\int dx$$

$$= \frac{x^5}{20} + \frac{3x^3}{12} + \frac{x^5}{2} + \frac{5x}{4} + C$$

$$= \frac{x^5}{20} + \frac{x^3}{4} + \frac{x^2}{2} + \frac{5}{4}x + C.$$

(3) $\displaystyle\int \frac{12x}{6x^2+12}\,dx$ **(Oct. 2000)**

Take $6x^2 + 12 = u$, so that $12x\,dx = du$, $dx = \dfrac{du}{12x}$

$$\int \frac{12x}{6x^2+12}\,dx = \int \frac{12x}{u}\cdot\frac{du}{12x} = \int \frac{1}{u}\,du = \log\,(6x^2+12) + C$$

(4) $\displaystyle\int (2x+5)^5\,dx$

if $2x + 5 = u$, $2dx = du$ and $dx = \dfrac{du}{2}$ and

$$\int (2x+5)^5\,dx = \int u^5\,\frac{du}{2} = \frac{1}{2}\,\frac{u^6}{6} + C = \frac{1}{12}\,(2x+5)^6 + C$$

(5) $\displaystyle\int (x^2 + x + e^x + 2^x)\,dx$ **(May 2001)**

$$= \int x^2\,dx + \int x\,dx + \int e^x\,dx + \int 2^x\,dx$$

$$= \frac{x^3}{3} + \frac{x^2}{2} + e^x + \frac{2^x}{\log_e 2} + C$$

(6) $\displaystyle\int (3x-2)^5\,dx$ **(May 2001)**

$$= \frac{1}{18}\,(3x-2)^6 + C$$

(7) $\int (4x + 3)(2x + 1)\, dx$ **(May 2001)**

$$= \int (8x^2 + 10x + 3)\, dx = \frac{8x^3}{3} + 5x^2 + 3x + C$$

(8) $\int \frac{2x + 5}{x^2 + 5x - 13}\, dx$

$$= \log(x^2 + 5x - 13) + C$$

(9) $\int (e^x + \frac{1}{x} + x^3)\, dx = e^x + \log_e x + \frac{x^4}{4} + c.$

(10) $\int x(x^2 - 1)^2\, dx$ **(Oct. 2001)**

$(x^2 - 1) = u$ so that $dx = \frac{du}{2x}$, and the function is $= \frac{1}{6}(x^2 - 1)^3 + C$

(11) $\int \frac{x^4 + 1}{x^2}\, dx = \int x^2\, dx + \int x^{-2}\, dx$ **(Oct. 2001)**

$$= \frac{x^3}{3} - \frac{1}{x} + C$$

(12) $\int (2x + \frac{1}{4x} + e^{3x} + 5)\, dx$

$$= 2\int x\, dx + \frac{1}{4}\int \frac{1}{x}\, dx + \int e^{3x}\, dx + 5\int dx$$

$$= x^2 + \frac{1}{4}\log_e x + \frac{1}{3}e^{3x} + 5x + C$$

(13) $\int \frac{x^4 - 2}{x^3}\, dx$ **(April 2003)**

$$\int \frac{x^4}{x^3}\, dx - 2\int x^{-3}\, dx = \frac{x^2}{2} + \frac{1}{x^2} + C$$

(14) $\int \left[\frac{1}{(3-x)^2} + (3-x)^2\right] dx$ **(Oct. 2003)**

$$= \int \frac{1}{(3-x)^2}\, dx + \int (3-x)^2\, dx$$

Take $3 - x = u$, $-dx = du$ and $dx = -du$

$$= \int \frac{1}{u^2}(-du) + \int u^2(-du) = -\int \frac{1}{u^2}\, du - \int u^2 du$$

$$= \frac{1}{(3-x)} - \frac{1}{3}(3-x)^3 + C$$

(15) $\int \left(3 + \frac{x}{5}\right)^3 dx$ **(Oct. 2003)**

Take $3 + \frac{x}{5} = u$ so that $\frac{1}{5}dx = du,\ dx = 5du.$ and

$$\int \left(3 + \frac{x}{5}\right)^3 dx = 5\int u^3\, du = \frac{5}{4}(3 + \frac{x}{5}) + C$$

(16) $\int \left\{\frac{2}{3}x^3 - \frac{1}{2x^{\frac{3}{2}}} + \frac{4}{\sqrt{x}} - 1\right\} dx$ **(April 2004)**

$$= \frac{2}{3}\int x^3 - \frac{1}{2}\int x^{-\frac{3}{2}}\, dx + 4\int x^{-\frac{1}{2}}\, dx - \int dx$$

$$= \frac{2x^4}{12} - \frac{1}{2}(-2)\frac{1}{\sqrt{x}} + 8\sqrt{x} - x + C$$

(17) $\int (3x-2)(x+4)\, dx$ **(April 2004)**

$$= \int (3x^2 + 10x - 8)\, dx$$

$$= x^3 + 5x - 8x + C$$

10.2.7 Integration by Parts (Integration of a product of the function)

The product of two functions are 'u' and 'v' and thus.

$$\int uv dx = u \int v dx - \int \left[\frac{d}{dx}u \int v dx\right] dx$$

Though we can take either of the product terms as u or v, but normally the function be choosen as 'u' should be the one which is easy to differentiate and 'v' should be the function which can be easily integrated.

Following are useful illustrations on this: :

(1) $\int x e^x\, dx$

Tale $x = u$ and $e^x = v$, so that

$$\int xe^x\,dx = x\int e^x\,dx - \int\left[\frac{d}{dx}\cdot x\int e^x\,dx\right]dx$$

$$= xe^x - \int[1.e^x]\,dx = xe^x - e^x + c.$$

(2) $\int x^2 e^x\,dx$

Take $x^2 = u$ and $e^x = u$

$$\int x^2 e^x\,dx = x^2\int e^x\,dx - \int\left[\frac{d}{dx}x^2\int e^x\,dx\right]dx$$

$$= x^2 e^x - \int 2x.e^x\,dx = x^2 e^x - 2\int xe^x\,dx$$

$$= x^2 e^x - 2\left[x\int e^x\,dx - \int\left[\frac{d}{dx}x\int e^x\,dx\right]dx\right]$$

$$= x^2 e^x - 2\left[xe^x - e^x\right] + C$$

$$= x^2 e^x - 2xe^x + 2e^x + C = e^x(x^2 - 2x + 2) + C.$$

(3) $\int(\log x)\,dx = \int 1.(\log x)\,dx$

Take $u = \log x$ and $v = 1$.

$$\int(\log x)\,dx = \log x\int dx - \int\left[\frac{d}{dx}\log x\int dx\right]dx$$

$$= x\log x - \int\left(\frac{1}{x}\cdot x\right)dx = x\log x - x + C$$

$$= x[\log x - 1] + C$$

(4) $\int x^2\log x\,dx$

Taking $\log x = u$, $x^2 = v$.

$$\log x\int x^2\,dx - \int\left[\frac{d}{dx}\log x\int x^2\,dx\right]dx$$

$$= \frac{x^3}{3}\log x - \int\frac{1}{x}\cdot\frac{x^3}{3}\,dx$$

$$= \frac{x^3}{3}\log x - \frac{1}{3}\,\frac{x^3}{3}\,dx = \frac{x^3}{3}\left(\log x - \frac{1}{3}\right) + C$$

(5) $\int x^n\log x\,dx$

$$= \log x\int x^n\,dx - \int\left[\frac{d}{dx}\log x\int x^n\,dx\right]dx$$

$$= \frac{x^{n+1}}{n+1} \log x - \int \frac{1}{x} \cdot \frac{x^{n+1}}{n+1} dx$$

$$= \frac{x^{n+1}}{n+1} \log x - \frac{1}{n+1} \cdot \frac{x^{n+1}}{n+1} + C$$

$$= \frac{x^{n+1}}{n+1} \left(\log x - \frac{1}{n+1} \right) + C$$

(6) $\int \sqrt{x} \log x \, dx$

$$= \log x \int \sqrt{x} \, dx - \int \left[\frac{d}{dx} \log x \int \sqrt{x} \, dx \right] dx$$

$$= \frac{2}{3} x^{\frac{3}{2}} \log x - \frac{2}{3} \int \frac{1}{x} \cdot x^{\frac{3}{2}} dx$$

$$= \frac{2}{3} \sqrt{x^3} \log x - \frac{2}{3} \int x^{\frac{1}{2}} dx$$

$$= \frac{2}{3} \sqrt{x^3} \log x - \frac{4}{9} \sqrt{x^3} + C = \frac{2}{3} \sqrt{x^3} \left[\log x - \frac{2}{3} \right] + C$$

(7) $\int (\log x)^3 \, dx$

If $u = (\log x)^3$ and $v = 1$

$$(\log x)^3 \int dx - \int \left[\frac{d}{dx} (\log x)^3 \int dx \right] dx$$

$$= x (\log x)^3 - \int \frac{3 (\log x)^2}{x} \cdot x \, dx$$

$$= x (\log x)^3 - 3 \int (\log x)^2 dx$$

Now $\int (\log x)^2 dx = (\log x)^2 \int dx - \int \left[\frac{d}{dx} (\log x)^2 \int dx \right] dx$

$$= x (\log x)^2 - \int \frac{2 (\log x)}{x} \cdot x \, dx = x (\log x)^2 - 2 \int (\log x) \, dx$$

$$= x (\log x)^2 - 2 \int \log x \int dx - \int \left[\frac{d}{dx} \log x \int dx \right] dx$$

$$= x\,(\log x)^2 - 2x\,(\log x) + 2\int dx$$

$$= x\,(\log x)^2 - 2x\,(\log x) + 2x + c$$

$$\int(\log x)^3\,dx = x(\log x)^3 - 3\int(\log x)^2\,dx$$

$$= x(\log x)^3 - 3\left[x\,(\log x)^2 - 2x\,(\log x) + 2x\right] + C$$

$$= x(\log x)^3 - 3x\,(\log x)^2 + 6x\,(\log x) - 6x + C$$

(8) $\int(\log x)^2\,dx$

$$= (\log x)^2\int dx - \int\left[\frac{d}{dx}(\log x)^2\int dx\right]dx$$

$$= x\,(\log x)^2 - 2x\,(\log x) + 2x + C$$

(9) $\int x\,e^{2x}\,dx$

Take $u = x,\ v = e^{2x}$

$$x = \int e^{2x}\,dx - \int\left[\frac{d}{dx}x\cdot\int e^{2x}\,dx\right]dx$$

$$= \frac{x}{2}e^{2x} - \int\frac{e^{2x}}{2}\,dx = \frac{x}{2}e^{2x} - \frac{1}{2}\int e^{2x}\,dx$$

$$= \frac{x}{2}e^{2x} - \frac{1}{4}e^{2x} + C = \frac{e^{2x}}{2}\left[x - \frac{1}{2}\right] + C$$

(10) $\int x^3\,e^{3x}\,dx$

$$= x^3\int e^{3x}\,dx - \int\left[\frac{d}{dx}x^3\int e^{3x}\,dx\right]dx$$

$$= \frac{x^3}{3}e^{3x} - \int\frac{3x^2\,e^{3x}}{3}\,dx = \frac{x^3}{3}e^{3x} - \int x^2\,e^{3x}\,dx$$

$$= \frac{x^3}{3}e^{3x} - \left[x^2\int e^{3x} - \int\left[\frac{d}{dx}x^2\int e^{3x}\,dx\right]dx\right]$$

$$= \frac{x^3}{3}e^{3x} - \frac{x^2}{3}e^{3x} + \frac{2}{3}\int x\,e^{3x}\,dx$$

$$= \frac{x^3}{3}e^{3x} - \frac{x^2}{3}e^{3x} + \frac{2}{3}\left[x\int e^{3x}\,dx - \int\left[\frac{d}{dx}x\int e^{3x}\,dx\right]dx\right]$$

$$= \frac{x^3}{3}e^{3x} - \frac{x^2}{3}e^{3x} + \frac{2}{3}\left[\frac{x}{3}e^{3x} - \frac{1}{3}\int e^{3x}\,dx\right]$$

$$= \frac{x^3}{3}e^{3x} - \frac{x^2}{3}e^{3x} + \frac{2}{3}\cdot\frac{x}{3}e^{3x} - \frac{2}{9}\cdot\frac{e^{3x}}{3} + C$$

$$= \frac{e^{3x}}{3}\left[x^3 - x^2 + \frac{2}{3}x - \frac{2}{9}\right] + C$$

10.3. Definite Integral and its Properties

When, $y = f(x)$, $\frac{dy}{dx} = f'(x)$ and $\int f'(x)\,dx = f(x) + C$

This is an indefinite integral since the costant 'C' can take any value. Its value is unknown. However when integral of $f'(x)$ exists for all values of x from 'a' to 'b' with a < b, we can evaluate

$$\int_a^b f'(x)\,dx = [f(x) + C]_a^b = f(b) + C - f(a) - C = f(b) - f(a) = [f(x)]_a^b$$

This is a definite integral of x lies between limits 'a' and 'b' where 'a' is the lower limit and 'b' is the upper limit. For example:

$$\int_a^b x\,dx = \left[\frac{x^2}{2} + C\right]_a^b = \frac{(b)^2}{2} + C - \frac{(a)^2}{2} - C = \frac{b^2}{2} - \frac{a^2}{2}$$

This difference $f(b) - f(a)$ gives us the change in the integral of x when x changes from $x = a$ to $x = b$ and $b > a$. Suppose $a = 1$, and $b = 3$, then

$$\int_1^3 x\,dx = \left[\frac{x^2}{2} + C\right]_1^3 = \frac{(3)^2}{2} + C - \frac{(1)^2}{2} - C = \frac{9}{2} - \frac{1}{2} = \frac{8}{2} = 4$$

For evaluating definite integral we need to find the indefinite integral first as $f(x) + C$, then put the value of $x = b$ and $x = a$ and then $f(b) - f(a)$. The constant 'C' is cancelled out.

Following properties definite integral has:

(1) $\int_a^b m\,f(x)\,dx = m\int_a^b f(x)\,dx$, where 'm' is a constant and $f(x)$ is integrable on the closed interval (a, b),

(2) The additive property of definite integral is that a definite integral can be expressed as a sum of definite integrals. For example.

$$\int_a^b g(x)\,dx = \int_a^c g(x)\,dx + \int_c^d g(x)\,dx + \int_d^b g(x)\,dx \quad \text{where, } a < c < d < b$$

It means that the area under the curve between a, b is the sum of the areas under the curve between a, c and c, d and d, b.

Numerically $\int_1^3 x^2\, dx = \left[\frac{x^3}{3} + c\right]_1^3 = \frac{26}{3}$

$$= \int_1^2 x^2\, dx + \int_2^3 x^2\, dx = \left[\frac{x^3}{3} + c\right] + \left[\frac{x^3}{3} + c\right]_2^3 = \frac{7}{3} + \frac{19}{3} = \frac{26}{3}.$$

(3) If $g(x)$ and $\varphi(x)$ are integrable on a, b then

$$\int_a^b [g(x) + \varphi(x)]\, dx = \int_a^b g(x)\, dx + \int_a^b \varphi(x)\, dx$$

(4) A definite integral is a function of its limits a and b only and not of the variables which may be changed.

$$\therefore \int_a^b g(x)\, dx = \int_a^b f(y)\, dy = \int_a^b f(z)\, dz$$

(5) A definite integral is equal to zero when the limits of integration are the same

$$\int_a^a g(x)\, dx = [f(x)]_a^a \text{ as } f(a) - f(a) = 0$$

(6) When the limits of integration are interchanged, the sign of definite integral changes.

Therefore $\int_a^b g(x)\, dx = -\int_b^a g(x)\, dx$

For example,

$$\int_1^3 x\, dx = \left[\frac{x^2}{2} + c\right]_1^3 = \frac{8}{3}\cdot \text{ and } \int_3^1 x\, dx = \left[\frac{x^2}{2} + c\right]_3^1 = -\frac{8}{3}$$

10.4 Illustrations and Solved University Questions of TYBA/Economics on Definite Integral

(1) $$\int_2^3 (2 + x^2)\, dx = \int_2^3 2\, dx + \int_2^3 x^2\, dx = \left[2x + \frac{x^3}{3} + C\right]_2^3$$

$$= 2(3) + \frac{(3)^3}{3} + C - 2(2) - \frac{(2)^3}{3} - C$$

$$= 6 + 9 - 4 - \frac{8}{3} = 11 - \frac{8}{3} = 8.333$$

(2) $\int_1^2 (2 + x + x^2)\, dx = \int_1^2 2\, dx + \int_1^2 x\, dx + \int_1^2 x^2\, dx$

$= \left[2x + \frac{x^2}{2} + \frac{x^3}{3} + C\right]_1^2 = 5.833$

(3) $\int_1^4 \sqrt{x}\, dx = \int_1^4 x^{\frac{1}{2}}\, dx = \left[\frac{2}{3}x^{\frac{3}{2}} + C\right]_1^4$

$= \left[\frac{2\sqrt{x^3}}{3} + C\right]_1^4 = \frac{2\sqrt{64}}{3} + C - \frac{2\sqrt{1}}{3} - C = \frac{16}{3} - \frac{2}{3} = \frac{14}{3}$

(4) $\int_1^2 x^3\, dx = \left[\frac{x^4}{4} + C\right]_1^2 = \frac{15}{4}$

(5) $\int_1^2 x^3 (1 + x^4)\, dx$

Take $1 + x^4 = u$ and $4x^3\, dx = du$, $dx = \dfrac{du}{4x^3}$

$= \int_1^2 x^3 u \frac{du}{4x^3} = \frac{1}{4}\int_1^2 u\, du = \frac{1}{4}\frac{u^2}{2} + C = \frac{1}{8}\left[\left(u^2 + C\right)\right]_1^2$

$= \frac{1}{8}\left[(1 + x^4)^2 + C\right]_1^2 = \frac{1}{8}\left[1 + 2^4\right]^2 + C - \frac{1}{8}(1 + 1^4)^2 - C$

$= \frac{1}{8}[17]^2 - \frac{1}{8} \times 4 = \frac{289}{8} - \frac{4}{8} = \frac{285}{8} = 35.625$

(6) $\int_4^3 \frac{1}{(2x - 5)}\, dx$

Take $2x - 5 = u$ so that $2dx = du$, $dx = \dfrac{du}{2}$

$= \int_4^3 \frac{1}{u} \cdot \frac{du}{2} = \frac{1}{2}\int_4^3 \frac{1}{u}\, du = \frac{1}{2}\left[\log(2x-5) + C\right]_4^3$

$= \frac{1}{2}\left[\log(6 - 5) - \log(8 - 5)\right]$

$= \frac{1}{2}\left[\log 1 - \log 3\right] = \frac{1}{2}\left[0 - \log 3\right]$

$= -\frac{1}{2}\log 3 = -\frac{0.477}{2} = -0.2389$

(7) $\int_0^2 \frac{x+3}{x+1}\, dx$ **(TYBA/MU/Oct. 2003)**

$$= \int_0^2 \frac{x+1+2}{x+1}\, dx = \int_0^2 dx + 2\int_0^2 \frac{1}{x+1}\, dx$$

$$= \left[x + 2\log(x+1) + C\right]_0^2 = 2 + 2\log(3) = 2 + 2(0.477) = 2.954$$

(8) $\int_0^3 (x^2 - 11x - 2)\, dx$ **(TYBA/MU/April 2003)**

$$\left[\frac{x^3}{3} - \frac{11x^2}{2} - 2x + C\right]_0^3$$

$$= \frac{27}{3} - \frac{11\times 9}{2} - 6 = 9 - 49.5 - 6 = 446.5$$

(9) $\int_4^9 \frac{dx}{x\sqrt{x}}$ **(TYBA/MU/April 2003)**

$$= \int_4^9 x^{-\frac{3}{2}}\, dx = \left[-\frac{2}{\sqrt{x}} + c\right]_4^9 = -\frac{2}{\sqrt{9}} + \frac{2}{\sqrt{4}}$$

$$= -\frac{2}{3} + 1 = \frac{1}{3} = 0.333$$

(10) $\int_1^2 (x^5 + 1)\, dx$ **(TYBA/MU/Oct. 2002)**

$$= \int_1^2 x^5\, dx + \int_{-1}^2 dx = \left[\frac{x^6}{6} + x + C\right]_{-1}^2$$

$$= \frac{64}{6} + 2 - \frac{1}{6} + 1 = \frac{64}{6} - \frac{1}{6} + 3 = \frac{64 - 1 + 18}{6} = \frac{81}{6} = 13.5$$

(11) $\int_1^2 (x^3 - 2x - 3)\, dx$ **(TYBA/MU/Oct. 2001)**

$$= \left[\frac{x^4}{4} - x^2 - 3x + C\right]_1^2 = \frac{(2)^4}{4} - (2)^2 - 3(2) - \frac{1}{4} + 1 + 3 = -2.25$$

(11) $\int_0^3 \frac{dx}{\sqrt{3x+7}}$, **(TYBA/Oct. 99)**

Take $3x + 7$ as u so that $3dx = du$ and

$$\int_0^3 \frac{dx}{\sqrt{3x+7}} = \int_0^3 \frac{1}{\sqrt{u}} \cdot \frac{du}{3} = \frac{1}{3}\int_0^3 u^{-\frac{1}{2}}\, du = \left[\frac{2}{3}\sqrt{u} + C\right]_0^3$$

$$= \left[\frac{2}{3}\sqrt{3x+7} + C\right]_0^3 = \frac{2}{3}\sqrt{16} = \frac{8}{3}.$$

(13) $\int_0^2 \frac{x^2 5^x + 3x^2 + 5x}{x^2}\, dx$

$$= \int_0^2 5^x\, dx + 3\int_0^2 dx + 5\int_0^2 \frac{1}{x}\, dx$$

$$= \left[5^x \log 5 + 3x + 5 \log x + C\right]_0^2$$

$= 25 \log 5 + 6 + 5 \log 2 = 25(0.699) + 6 + 5(0.301) = 24.98$

(14) $\int_{-2}^3 (1 - \frac{3}{x^4})\, dx = \int_{-2}^3 dx - 3\int_{-2}^3 x^{-4}\, dx$

$$\left[x + \frac{1}{x^3} + C\right]_{-2}^3 = 3 + \frac{1}{27} + C - (-2) - \frac{1}{(-2)^3} - C$$

$$= \frac{1}{27} + \frac{1}{8} + 5 = 5.162$$

(15) $\int_{-1}^2 (x^5 + 1)\, dx$ **(TYBA/Oct./2002/M.U.)**

$$\int_{-1}^2 x^5 dx + \int_{-1}^2 dx = \left[\frac{x^6}{6} + x + C\right]_{-1}^2 = \frac{64}{6} + 2 - \frac{1}{6} + 1 = \frac{63}{6} + 3 = 13.5$$

10.5 Definite Integral and the area Under the Curve

Definite integral is useful in finding the area under the curve for a given function $y = f(x)$ when it is a continuous function. We can obtain the area under the curve in the interval (a, b) where $b > a$. We find the curve in the interval of $x = a$ and $x = b$, for $b > a$. This area is given by

$$A = \int_a^b f(x)\, dx$$

(1) For example given the function $y = 3x$, we can obtain the area bounded by the region $y = 3x$ and x-axis between $x = 1$ and $x = 3$.

This area under the curve is $A = \int_1^3 3x\,dx$

$$= \left[\frac{3x^2}{2} + C\right]_1^3 = \frac{3(3)^2}{2} + C - \frac{3(1)^2}{2} - C$$

This is diagrammatically shown in fig - 10.1. For finding the area first we plot $y = 3x$, represented by the linear line. x-axis and y- axis depict x and y vaules measured numerically.

From $y = 3x$, when $x = 0$, $y = 0$:, $x = 1$, $y = 3$ and for $x = 2$, $y = 6$ and so on.

The shaded area is the required solution of the problem.

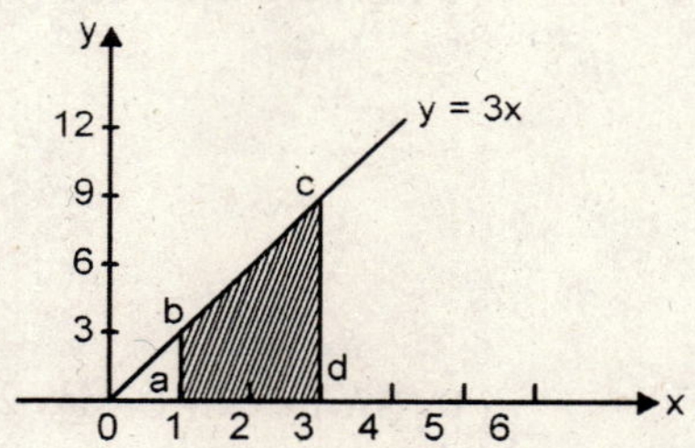

Fig. 10.1: *Area between $1 \leq x \leq 3$*

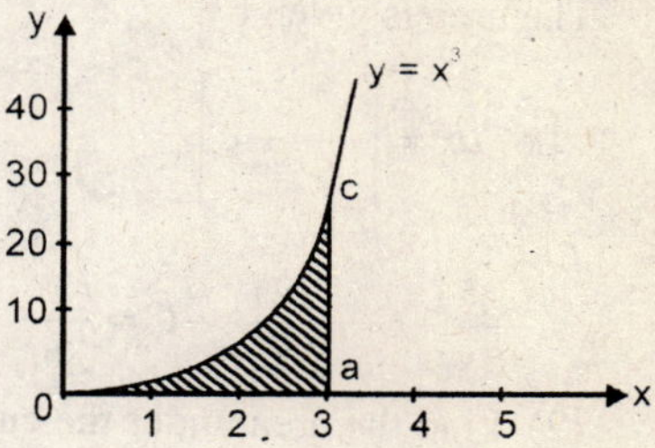

Fig. 10.2: *Area between $0 \leq x \leq 3$*

(2) Find the area bounded by the region $y = x^3$ and x-axis for $0 \leq x \leq 3$

We need to plot the curve $y = x^3$ in the diagram (fig 10.2), when $x = 0$, $y = 0$; for $x = 1$, $y = 1$; for $x = 2$, $y = 8$ and so on. This area is calculated as

$$\int_0^3 x^3\,dx = \left[\frac{x^4}{4} + c\right]_0^3 = \frac{(3)^4}{4} + c - \frac{(0)^4}{4} - c = \frac{3^4}{4} = \frac{84}{4} = 20.25$$

(3) Find the area bounded by the x-axis and the curve $y = \sqrt{x}$ for $1 \leq x \leq 4$.

The area is $\int_1^4 \sqrt{x}\,dx = \left[\frac{x^{\frac{3}{2}}}{\frac{3}{2}} + C\right]_1^4$

$$= \left[\frac{2}{3}\sqrt{x^3} + C\right]_1^4 = \frac{2}{3}\sqrt{4^3} + C - \frac{2}{3}\sqrt{1^3} - C$$

$$= \frac{2}{3}\sqrt{64} - \frac{2}{3}\sqrt{1} = \frac{16}{3} - \frac{2}{3} = 4.67.$$

(4) Find the area under the curve when $y = 8 - x^2$ and $0 \leq x \leq 2$

The area is obtained as

$$\int_0^2 (8 - x^2)\, dx = \left[8x - \frac{x^3}{3} + C\right]_0^2 = 8(2) - \frac{8}{3} = 13.333$$

(5) Find the area under the curve for $y = x^2 + 4x + 5$ and $-2 \leq x \leq 2$

The area is given by

$$\int_{-2}^2 (x^2 + 4x + 5)\, dx = \left[\frac{x^3}{3} + 2x^2 + 5x + C\right]_{-2}^2$$

$$= \frac{(8)}{3} + 8 + 10 + C - \frac{(-2)^3}{3} - 2(-2)^2 - 5(-2) - C = 20 + \frac{16}{3} = 25.33$$

(6) Calculate the area under the curve $y = x^5$ between $x = 2$ and $x = 3$

The area is given by. **(TYBA/ECO/M.U/Oct 2000)**

$$\int_{-2}^3 x^5\, dx = \left[\frac{x^6}{6} + c\right]_2^3$$

$$= \frac{(3)^6}{6} + C - \frac{(2)^6}{6} - C = \frac{(3)^6}{6} - \frac{(2)^6}{6} = 110.833$$

(7) Find the area under the curve (TYBA/ECO/MU/May 2001)

(i) $$\int_2^3 x(x+1)\, dx = \int_2^3 (x^2 + x)\, dx$$

$$= \left[\frac{x^3}{3} + \frac{x^2}{2} + c\right]_2^3 = \frac{(3)^3}{3} + \frac{(3)^2}{2} + C - \frac{(2)^3}{3} - \frac{(2)^3}{2} - C = 8.833$$

(ii) $$\int_0^1 \frac{x^2 - 3x - 4}{\sqrt{x}}\, dx = \int_0^1 \frac{x^2}{\sqrt{x}}\, dx - 3\int_0^1 \frac{x}{\sqrt{x}}\, dx - 4\int_0^1 \frac{1}{\sqrt{x}}\, dx$$

$$= \int_0^1 x^{\frac{3}{2}}\, dx - 3\int_0^1 \sqrt{x}\, dx - 4\int_0^1 x^{-\frac{1}{2}}\, dx$$

$$= \left[\frac{2}{5}\sqrt{x^5} - \frac{6}{3}\sqrt{x^3} - 8\sqrt{x} + C\right]_0^1 = -\frac{48}{5} = -9.6$$

(8) Find the area bounded by the region $y = \sqrt{x}$ and x-axis between $x = 4$ and $x = 9$.

(TYBA/April 2004)

The area is given by

$$\int_4^9 \sqrt{x}\, dx = \left[\frac{2}{3}x^{3/2} + c\right]_4^9 = \left[\frac{2}{3}\sqrt{x^3} + C\right]_4^9 = \frac{2}{3}\sqrt{9^3} + C - \frac{2}{3}\sqrt{4^3} - C$$

$$= \frac{2}{3}\left[\sqrt{9^3} - \sqrt{4^3}\right] = \frac{2}{3}(27 - 8) = \frac{38}{3} = 12.667$$

EXERCISE – 10

(1) Evaluate the following integrals :

(a) $\int x^6 \, dx$ (b) $\int (x^6 + 3) \, dx$

(c) $\int e x^3 \, dx$ (d) $\int \sqrt{x} \, dx.$

(e) $\int e^{3x} \, dx.$ (f) $\int \sqrt{x} \, dx.$

(g) $\int \frac{1}{x+1} \, dx.$ (h) $\int \frac{1}{x \sqrt{x}} \, dx.$

(i) $\int (3\sqrt{x} - \frac{5}{\sqrt{x}}) \, dx.$

(j) $\int (3 - 2x)(2x + 3) \, dx.$

(k) $\int a^x \, dx.$ (l) $\int \frac{a^2}{x^2 - 2} \, dx.$

(m) $\int x e^x \, dx.$ (n) $\int x^2 e^{2x} \, dx.$

(o) $\int \sqrt{5x + 2} \, dx.$ (p) $\int e^{8x} \, dx.$

(q) $\int \frac{1}{(5x + 3)^3} \, dx.$

(2) Find the area bounded by the region $y = f(x)$ and X - axis between the given values of x.

(a) $y + 4x^3$ *for* $1 \leq x \leq 3.$

(b) $y + \frac{x^3}{3}$ *for* $0 \leq x \leq 1.$

(c) $y + 2x^2$ *for* $1 \leq x \leq 2.$

❑ ❑ ❑

11 ECONOMIC APPLICATIONS OF INTEGRATION

11.1. Introduction

Integral caculus has got wider applications in economics. We will study some of these important applications of definite integral in economics. With the help of integration total cost and total revenue functions, consumer's and porducer's surplus are detremined. The inequalities of income and Gini coeffcieint are measured with the help of the techniques of integration. These appliactions are illustrated in this chapter:

11.2. Determining Consumer's and Producer's Surplus using Integration

(a) Consumer's surplus is the difference between the price a consumer is prepared to pay and actual price of the commodity that she pays. It is the difference between the potential price and the actual price.

The demand function for a commodity (q) is given as $p = f(q)$, where p = pice. Consumer's surplus is determined corresponding to the given price and quantity. This is given by p_o and q_o. Consumer's surplus is illsutrated with the help of a diagram in Fig.11.1, where market price is p_0 and the corresponding demand is q_o for the given demand curve dd_1. These are the equilibrium price and quantity. The consumer is willing to pay price higher than p_o for some quantities of the commodity q. Thus the total money she is willing to pay is equal to the area $0DE\, q_0$. This area is shown by

$\int_o^{q_o} f(q)\, dq$. Actual expenditure incurred is $p_0 q_0$. Accordingly Consumer's Surplus is located in the figure shown below. The same is obtained from the folowing formula

$$\text{Consumer's Surplus} = \int_o^{q_o} f(q)\,dq - p_o\, q_o$$

In terms of diagram consumer's surplus is the area of the curve below the demand function from 0 to q_0 minus $0p_0Eq_0$. This area is shaded and it is equal to Dp_0E.

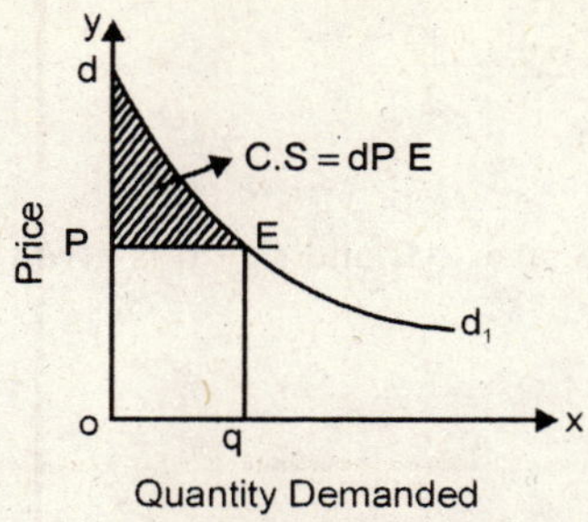

Fig. 11.1 : Consumers surplus.

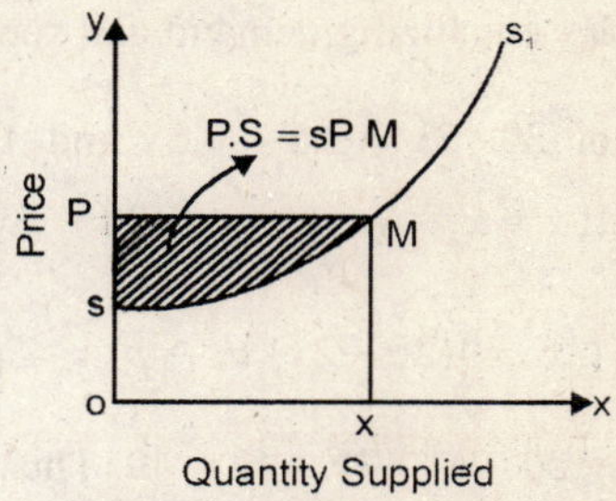

Fig. 11.2 : Producer's surplus

(b) Producer's Surplus:

Producer will supply different quantities of a commodity at different prices, which we can write as q_i quantities supplied at p_i prices. The supply function is given by $p = f(q)$. The supply curve depicting the supply function graphically will slope upward from left to the right as in Fig.11.2.

If equilibrium price and quantities are p_o and x_o respectively, so that the firm or producer will sell all its x_o quantities at p_o price. In this way he gets a surplus for those quantities of x output which he is ready to sale at the price below the equilibrium price. Graphically producer's surplus is the difference between the area $0p_oMx_o$ and the area covered under the supply curve till the equilibrium level of output $0SMx_o$.

By using integral techniques we can obtain producer's surplus. The formula used for determining producer's surplus is given as

Producer's Surplus $= p_o x_o - \int_o^{x_o} f(x)\, dx$, where '$x$' stands for quantity sold of good 'x'.

11.3 Illustrations on Consumer's and Producer's Surplus

(1) If the demand function is given as $P = 25 - 2q - q^2$, Find consumer's surplus at $q = q_o = 3$

If $q_o = 3$, $P_0 = 25 - 2(3) - 3^2 = 10$, Consumer's Surplus (C. S.) is given by

$$C.S. = \int_0^{q_0} (25 - 2q - q^2)\, dq - p_o q_o = \int_o^3 (25 - 2q - q^2)\, dq - p_o q_o = \int_o^3 (25 - 2q - q^2)\, dq - 3 \times 10$$

$$= \left[25q - q^2 - \frac{q^3}{3} + C \right]_0^3 - 30$$

Thus Consumer's Surplus $= \left[25\,(3) - (3)^2 - \frac{27}{3} \right] - 30 = 27$

(2) The demand function is given as $p = 20 - 2x$ where p = price and 'x' is quantity demanded.

The supply function is $p = 2.5 + \frac{x}{2}$. Find consumers' surplus at equilibrium price.

Solution: Equilibrium price is p_o. It corresponds to the price when demand is equal to supply.

By equalizing demand and supply functions,we get $20 - 2x = 2.5 + \frac{x}{2}$

or $20-2x = 2.5 + 0.5x$ and $17.5 = 2.5x$ or $x = 7$

If $x = x_o = 7$, $p = p_o = 20 - 2x = 20-14 = 6$. Accordingly C. S. at $x_o = 7$ and $p_o = 6$ is given by

$$C.S. = \int_0^7 (20-2x)\,dx - p_o x_o = [20x - x^2 + c]^7 - 42$$

$= 20\,(7) - (7)^2 - 42 = 49$. Thus consumer's surplus is 49.

(3) If the demand law is given as $p = 51 - 4q - q^2$ Find consumer surplus at *(a)* $q_o = 3$ and *(b)* $p_o = 46$.

Solution: *(a)* Consumer surplus for $q = q_o = 3$ is given by

$$C.S. = \int_0^{q_o} (51 - 4q - q^2)\,dq - p_o\, x_o$$

If $q_o = 3$, $p = p_o = 51 - 4\,(3) - (3)^2 = 30$. $\therefore q_o = 3$ and $p_o = 30$.

$$C.S. = \int_0^3 (51 - 4q - q^2)\,dq - (3 \times 30)$$

$$= \left[51q - 2q^2 - \frac{q^3}{3} + c\right]_0^3 - 90 = 51(3) - 2\,(3)^2 - \frac{(3)^3}{3} - 90 = 36$$

$\therefore$ Consumer's surplus $= 36$ at $q_o = 3$, $p_o = 30$.

(b) We need to detremine Consumer's surplus for given price $P_o = 46$.

For $P_o = 46$, we can workout for q_o. From $p = 51 - 4q - q^2 = 46$ or $51 - 46 - 4q - q^2 = 0$,

or $q^2 + 4q - 5 = 0$, we get

$q^2 + 5q - q - 5 = 0$ or $(q + 5)\,(q - 1) = 0$> This gives us $q + 5 = 0$ or $q = -5$, which is impossible.

The second solution is $q - 1 = 0$ or $q = 1$. Since q can not be negative $\therefore q = 1$ is the equilibrium quantity. Accordingly we have obtained equilibrium price and quantity as $p_o = 46$, $q_o = 1$, respectively.

We need to evaluate Consumer's surplus corresponding to these price and quantity.

$$C.S. = \int_0^1 (51 - 4q - q^2)\,dq - 46 \times 1 = \left[51q - 2q^2 - \frac{q^3}{3} + c\right]_0^1 - 46$$

$= 51 - 2(1)^2 - \frac{1}{3} - 46 = 2.667$, thus consumer's surplus is 2.667.

11.4 Solved University Questions on Consumer's and Producer's Surplus

(1) If the demand and supply functions are given as $p = 16 - D^2$ and $p = 4 + D$ respectively. Find Consumer's surplus at equilibrium price. **(TYBA/2003)**

Solution: Equilibrium price corresponds to the price when demand and supply are equal.

$\therefore$ $16 - D^2 = 4 + D$ or $16 - D^2 - D - 4 = 0$.

or $12 - D^2 - D = 0$ or $D^2 + D - 12 = 0$.

or $D^2 + 4D - 3D - 12 = 0$ or $(D + 4)(D - 3) = 0$. From this we get two solutions,

$\therefore$ $D = -4$ or $D = 3$. Since quantity demanded can not be negative $D = 3$ is equilibrium quantity.

For $D = 3$, $P = 16 - D^2 = 7$. $\therefore$ Euqilibrium price and quantity are $D_o = 3$, $P_o = 6$.

$$C.S. = \int_0^{D_o} (16 - D^2)\, dD - Po\, Do = \int_0^3 (16 - D^2)\, dD - (3 \times 7)$$

$$= \left[16D - \frac{D^3}{3} + C\right]_0^3 - 21 = 16(3) - 9 - 21 = 18$$

Produces surplus (*P. S)* at equilibrium price and quantity is given by

$$P.S. = Po\, Do - \int_0^3 (4 + D)\, dD = 21 - \left[4D - \frac{D^2}{2} + c\right]_0^3$$

$$= 21 - 4(3) - \frac{9}{2} = 4.5 \therefore C.S. = 18 \text{ and } P.S. = 4.5$$

(2) The demand and supply functions of a commodity are given as $D = 10 - 3p$ and $S = 2p - 1$ respectively, find consumer's surplus and producer's surplus. **(TYBA / ECO/ 2002)**

Solution: The formula for Consumer's Surplus (CS) and Producer's Surplus (PS) are given as

$$C.S. = \int_O^{Do} D\,dD - D_o P_o \text{ and } P.S. = P_o S_o - \int_O^{So} S\,dS.$$

To obtain equilibrium price we need to equate $D = S$.

$\therefore$ $10 - 3p = 2p - 1$ *or* $p = 2.2 = P_o$.

The demand and supply functions can be rearranged for determining Consumer's and Producer's surplus so that $p = f(D)$ and $p = f(S)$

From $D = 10 - 3p$, $p = \frac{10}{3} - \frac{D}{3}$

and from $S = 2p - 1$, $p = \frac{S}{2} + \frac{1}{2}$

$$C.S = \int_0^{D_o} \left\{\frac{10}{3} - \frac{D}{3}\right\} dD - D_o P_o$$

For $P_o = 2.2$. $D_o = 10 - 3p = 3.4$. and $S_o = 2p - 1 = 3.4$. $[D_o = S_o]$

$$C.S = \int_0^{D_o} (\frac{10}{3} - \frac{D}{3}) dD - (3.4)(2.2) = \left[\frac{10}{3} D - \frac{D^2}{3 \times 2} + c\right]_0^{3.4} - 7.48$$

$$= \frac{10}{3}(3.4) - \frac{(3.4)^2}{6} - 7.48 = 1.926, \quad \text{Consumer's surplus} = 1.93$$

$$P.S. = P_0 S_0 - \int_0^{3.4} \left(\frac{5}{2} + \frac{1}{2}\right) ds = (3.4)(2.2) - \left[\frac{S^2}{4} + \frac{1}{2}s + C\right]_0^{3.4}$$

$$= 7.48 - \frac{(3.4)^2}{4} + \frac{3.4}{2} = 2.89$$

Producer's surplus = 2.89

(3) The demand and supply function of a good are given by $D = 100 - 3p$ and $S = 2p - 1$. Find consumer's and producer's surplus at equilibrium price. **(TYBA / ECO / 2001)**

After solving the demand and supply functions by equating them, we get the equilibrium price as $P_0 = 20.2$. For this price, demand = supply or $D_o = S_o = 39.4$

By rearranging demand function we get $p = \frac{5}{2} + \frac{1}{2}$

$$C.S = \int_O^{Do} \left(\frac{100}{3} - \frac{D}{3}\right) dD - P_o D_o. = \int_0^{39.4} \left(\frac{100}{3} - \frac{D}{3}\right) dD - (20.2)(39.4)$$

$$= \left[\frac{100}{3} D - \frac{D^2}{6} + C\right]_0^{39.4} - 795.88 = \frac{100}{3}(39.4) - \frac{(39.4)^2}{6} - 795.88 = 258.\ 726,$$

Thus $C.S = 258.726$.

$$P.S. = P_o S_o - \int_O^{So} \left(\frac{5}{2} + \frac{1}{2}\right) ds = 795.88 - \int_0^{39.4} \left(\frac{5}{2} + \frac{1}{2}\right) ds$$

$$= 795.88 - \left[\frac{5^2}{4} + \frac{5}{2} + c\right]_0^{39.4}$$

$$= 795.88 - \left(\frac{39.4}{4}\right)^2 - \frac{(39.4)}{2} = 388.09,$$

Thus the required solutions are, $C.S = 258.726$ and $P.S. = 388.09$

11.5 Consumer's Surplus Under Perfect Competition and Monopoly

Under pure or perfect competition price is determined by equating demand and supply functions. Thus for given the demand and supply functions equilibrium price P_0 can be determined by equating these two. After that the formula of consumer's surplus can be applied.

$$\text{Consumer's surplus} = \int_{O}^{Do} DdD - P_o D_o$$

Consumer's surplus under monopoly is determined in a different way because the monopolist is in equilibrium when MR is equal to marginal cost ($MR = MC$). The MC function is the supply function for the monopolist Under monopoly, price $> MR = MC$. Here we need to equate MR with MC. After finding equilibrium price and quantities, we can apply the formula of $C.S.$

$$C.S. = \int_{O}^{Do} DdD - P_o D_o$$

Illustrations:

If the demand and supply laws are $P_d = (5 - q)^2$ and $P_s = 14 + 2q$, where p = price and q = quantity demanded or supplied.

(a) Find consumer's surplus when demand and price are determined under pure competition.

Solution: Equilibrium price is determined by equating demand and supply function as shown here,

$\therefore (5 - q)^2 = 14 + 2q$ or $25 - 10q + q^2 = 14 + 2q$

or $q^2 - 12q + 11 = 0.$ or $q(q - 11) - 1(q - 11) = 0$

or $(q - 11)(q - 1) = 0$. This gives us equilibrium quantity, either $q = 11$ or $q = 1$

If $q = 11$, $p = (5 - q)^2 = (-6)^2 = 36$ and for $q = 1$, $p = (5 - 1)^2 = 16$.

Since competitive price is lower, we need to take p = 16, as equilibrium price. For this price we get equilibrium quantity $q = 1$. Thus $P_o = 16$ and $q_o = 1$

Cosnumer's surplus at these price and quantity is given by

$$C.S = \int_{0}^{q_o} (5-q)^2\, dq - p_o q_o . = \int_{o}^{q_o} (25 - 10q + q^2)\, dq - p_o\, q_o.$$

$$= \int_{o}^{1} (25 - 10q + q^2)\, dq - 16 \times 1 = \left[25q - 5q + \frac{q^3}{3} + c \right]_0^1 - 16$$

$$= 25 - 5 + \frac{1}{3} - 16 = 4.33. \therefore C.S = 4.33$$

(b) Find consumers surplus under monopoly.

To find monopoly price and quantity at equilibrium we need to equate marginal revenue and marginal cost, $MR = MC$, where $MC = 14 + 2q$ = Supply function.

$$MR = \frac{d}{dq}(TR), \quad TR = Pq = (25 - 10q + q^2)q$$

For $R = 25q - 10q^2 + q^3$, $MR = \frac{dR}{dq} = 25 - 20q + 3q^2$. Equating MR = Mc we get

$25 - 20q + 3q^2 = 14 + 2q$ or $3q^2 - 22q + 11 = 0$.

Sloving this quadratic equation, we can obtain equilibrium quantity as shown below:

$$q = \frac{-(-22) \pm \sqrt{(-22)^2 - 4\,(3)\,(11)}}{6} = \frac{22 \pm 18.762}{6}$$

This gives $q = 0.54$ or or $q = 6.794$. If $q = 0.54$, $p_d = (5-q)^2 = 19.89$ and if $q = 6.794$, $p_d = (5-q)^2 = 3.22$

Since monopoly prince is normally higher, equilibrium price and quantity are $p = 19.89$ and $q = 0.54$. At these price and quantity consumer's surplus will be

$$C.S = \int_0^{q_0} (25 - 10q + q^2)\,dq - P_0 q_0$$

$$= \left[25q - 5q + \frac{q^3}{3} + C \right]_0^{0.54} - 10.714 = 0.1385$$

Under Monopoly consumer's surplus is less when compared to the same under perfect competition because monopoly price is higher than the competitive price.

(i) Find the consumer's surplus under pure competition if demand and supply functions for a good are $p = 16 - 2\,D$ and $4\,p = 7D + 4$ respectively **(TYBA / MU/ Eco/May, 2001)**

Solution: To find consumer's surplus under pure competition we need to find equilibrium price and quantities by equalising demand and supply functions.

For given demand fucntion $P = 16 - 2D$ and supply function is $4P = 7D + 4$ or $P = 7/4\,D + 1$

From $P_s = P_d$ we get $D = 4$

For $D = 4$, equilibrium price is $P = 16 - 2D = 8 = P_o$

Consumer's surplus corresponding to $P_o = 8$ and $D_o = 4$ is given as

$$C.\,S. = \int_0^4 (16 - 2D)\,dD - P_o D_o$$

$$= \int_0^4 (16 - 2D)\,dD - 32 = \left[16\,D - D^2 + c \right]_0^4 - 32 = 16$$

(ii) If the demand law is given by $p = 38 - x^2$ and $MC = 2 + x^2$, find Consumer's surplus (x = output)

The equilibrium price is determined by equating MR and MC.

From given price we can obtain total revenue, $R = (P)\,(x) = 38x - x^3$

From 'R' we can get , $\text{MR} = \frac{dR}{dx} = 38 - 3x^2$. For equilibrium $MR = MC$.

Thus $38 - 3x^2 = 2 + x^2$ or $x^2 = 9$ and $x = 3$. For $x = x_0 = 3$, $p = P_0 = 38 - x^2 = 29$

Consumer's surplus at $x_o = 3$ and $P_o = 29$ is obtained as

$$C.S. = \int_0^{x_0}(38 - x^2)\,dx - x_0 p_0 = \int_0^{3}(38 - x^2)\,dx - (3)\,(29)$$

$$\left[38x - \frac{x^3}{3} + c\right]_0^3 - 87 = 38\,(3) - 9 - 87 = 18$$

(iii) Given the demand function $P = 8 - 2x$ and the supply function $P = 2 + x$, find consumers and producers surplus. **(TYBA/MU/ECO/2000)**

Solution: Given $P = 8 - 2x$ and $P = 2 + x$, equilibrium price is determined by equating these two so that $8 - 2x = 2 + x$ or $8 - 2 = 3x$ or $x = 2$

From $x_0 = 2$, $p = P_0 = 8 - 2x = 4$ and consumer's surplus is

$$C.S = \int_0^2(8 - 2x)\,dx - P_o\,x_o = \left[8x - x^2 + c\right]_0^2 - 2\times 4 = 4$$

$$\text{Producer's surplus } (P.S) = p_o x_o - \int_0^2(2 + x)dx$$

$$= 8 - \left[2x + \frac{x^2}{2} + C\right]_0^2 = 8 - 4 - 2 = 2$$

11.6 Revenue and Cost Functions and Definite Integral: Solved Questions of TYBA (Eco) University Papers

(a) Total cost function is C where $C = f(a) + b$, $f(a)$ = TVC and b = TFC. From this we get $C = TVCX + TFC$. For Q = 0, $C = b$ ($TVC = 0$, when Q = 0)

Illustrations:

(1) Given MC function $f'(q) = 2 + x^2 + 3x$, find Total Cost fucntion when $TFC = 20$

$$TC = \int f'(q)dx = 2\int dx + \int x^2\,dx + 3\int dx$$

$$= 2x + \frac{x^3}{3} + \frac{3x^2}{2} + C$$

For $x = 0$, $TC = TFC = 20$. From the TC function, TC = 0 + C = 20

∴ C = 20. Finally substituting C =20 we get

$$TC = 2x + \frac{x^3}{3} + \frac{3x^2}{2} + 20.$$

(2) If the marginal cost function is $f'(q) = 8 + 5\sqrt{q} + \frac{8}{\sqrt{q}}$, Find TC if $TFC = 10$.

$$TC = \int f'(q) = \int\left\{8 + 5\sqrt{q} + \frac{8}{\sqrt{q}}\right\}dq = \int(8+5q^{\frac{1}{2}} + 8q^{-\frac{1}{2}})dx$$

$= 8q + \frac{10q^{\frac{3}{2}}}{3} + 16q^{\frac{1}{2}} + C$, For $q = 0$, $TC = 0 + C = 10$.

$\therefore TC = 8q + \frac{10}{3}\sqrt{q^3} + 16\sqrt{q} + 10.$

(3) If the MR function is given by $Y = 10 - bx$, find total revenue and average revenue functions. (TR = 0 for $x = 0$) **(TYBA/ECO/April 2004)**

We are given $MR = \frac{dR}{dX} = 10 - 6x$, where x = Output.

From this marginal revenue we can obtain total revenue function. This is obatined as

$TR = \int(10 - 6x)\,dx = 10x - 3x^2 + C$

When $x = 0$, $TR = 0$. $\therefore$ $TR = 0 + C = 0$, as $x = 0$. $\therefore$ $C = 0$

$\therefore$ $TR = 10x - 3x^2 + 0 = 10x - 3x^2$

$AR = \frac{TR}{x} = 10 - 3x$.

The required solutions are TR = $10x - 3x^2$ and AR = $10 - 3x$

(4) Given the MR function, find the total revenue (R) and AR when $R(0) = 0$.

$MR = 18 - \frac{6}{3}q$,

We are given $MR = 18 - \frac{6}{3}q$. From this we get total revenue as

$TR = \int\left\{8 - \frac{6}{3}q\right\}dq = 8q - q^2 + C$. For $q = 0$, $TR = 0$. $\therefore$ $C = 0$ and

$\therefore$ $TR = 8q - q^2$ and $AR = \frac{TR}{q} = 8 - q$ are required solutions.

(5) If MR function is $MR = \frac{a}{(q+b)^2} - c$, where q = Output, show that the demand law is

$P = \frac{a}{b(q+b)} - c$.

Solution: From marginal revenue we can get total revenue and average revenue functions.

$$TR = \int\left(\frac{a}{(q+b)2} - c\right)dq = a\int\frac{1}{(q+b)^2}dq - c\int dq$$

$$TR = \frac{-a}{(q+b)} - cq + k$$

For $q = 0$, $TR = 0$, or $0 = \frac{-a}{b} + k \therefore k = \frac{a}{b}$. and $TR = \frac{-a}{q+b} - cq + \frac{a}{b}$.

$$= \frac{-ab + aq + ab}{b(q+b)} - cq = \frac{aq}{b(q+b)} - cq$$

The required solutions are $TR = \frac{aq}{b(q+b)} - cq$ and $AR = \frac{TR}{q} = \frac{a}{b(q+b)} - c.$

(6) If the MR function is $MR = \frac{6}{(x+2)^2} - 8$, where x = output, find TR function if $TR = 0$ for $x = 0$ and show that the demand function is $P = \frac{3}{x+2} - 8$.

Solution: We are given $MR = \frac{6}{(x+2)^2} - 8$. From this we can get TR as

$$TR = \int\left[\frac{6}{(x+2)^2} - 8\right]dx = 6\int\frac{1}{(x+2)^2}dx - 8\int dx$$

$TR = \frac{-6}{x+2} - 8x + k.$, When $x = 0$, $0 = \frac{-6}{2} + k \therefore k = \frac{6}{2} = 3$

$$TR = \frac{-6}{x+2} - 8x + 3 = \frac{-6 + 3(x+2)}{x+2} - 8x = \frac{3x}{x+2} - 8x$$

Price is obtained as $P = \frac{TR}{x} = \frac{3}{x+2} - 8$ is the required demand function

(7) If the marginal cost is $MC = 2 + 6x + 12x^2$ and total cost of zero output is 20. Find the total cost and average cost functions. What will be the total cost if output is 20 ? (x = output).

(TYBA/ECO/Oct. 2003)

We are given $MC = 2 + 6x + 12x^2$. From this we can derive total cost 'TC' as

$$TC = \int(2 + 6x + 12x^2)dx = 2x + 3x^2 + 4x^3 + C$$

For $C(0) = 20$, when $x = 0$, $TC = C = 20$.

$\therefore$ $TC = 2x + 3x^2 + 4x^3 + 20$ is the required TC function.

$AC = \frac{TC}{x} = 2 + 3x + 4x^2 + \frac{20}{x}$. is the required *AC* function.

$C\,(20) = TC$ when $x = 20$. This is obatined as, $TC = 2(20) + 3\,(20)^2 + 4\,(20)^3 + 20 = 33{,}260$

$\therefore$ TC = 33,260 when 20 units of output are produced.

11.7 Consumption and Saving Functions: Illustrations and Solved University Questions

In connection with Keynesian theory of employment, national income identity is shown to be the summation of national consumption and national aggregate savings. Income is denoted Y, where it is equal to consumption (C) plus savings (S). Thus symbolically, $Y = C + S$.

Average propensity toconsume and save are, *APC* and *APS*. These rae computed using the formula:

$$APC = \frac{C}{Y} \text{ and } APS = \frac{S}{Y},\ \frac{C}{Y} + \frac{S}{Y} = 1 \text{ or } APC + APS = 1$$

Marginal propensity toconsume and save are derived from $\Delta Y = \Delta C + \Delta S$

Dividing ΔY both sides we get

$$\frac{\Delta Y}{\Delta Y} = \frac{\Delta C}{\Delta Y} + \frac{\Delta S}{\Delta Y} \text{ or } 1 = \text{MPC} + \text{MPS}, \text{ where } MPC = \frac{\Delta C}{\Delta Y} \text{ and } MPS = \frac{\Delta S}{\Delta Y}$$

If *MPC* is known we can determine *MPS* or for *MPS* is known, *MPC* can be easily obtained. By using integral calculus, consumption and saving functions are also determined.

The consumption function is $C = f(\text{Y})$ where C = Consumption and Y = Income.

The saving function is $S = \text{g}\,(\text{Y})$ where S = Savings. These consumption and saving functions are obatined from their corersponding marginal fucntions. In mathematical form we can show that

$$MPC = \frac{dC}{dY} \text{ where } C = f(Y).,\ MPC = b = \frac{d}{dY}(C) = \frac{d}{dy} f(Y) = f'(Y) \text{ and}$$

$$MPS = 1 - MPC = 1 - b = 1 - \frac{dC}{dY} = \frac{dS}{dY}. = \frac{d}{dY}\, g\,(Y) = g'\,(Y)$$

Illustrations:

(1) If *MPC* is given as $0.5 - 0.003Y$, find the consumption function when consumption equals 0.4 at zero level of income.

Solution : For given $MPC = 0.5 - 0.003Y$, the consumption function is $C = f(Y)$.

We can also write MPC as

$$MPC = \frac{dC}{dY} = f'\,(Y) = 0.5 - 0.003Y$$

For finding consumption function we need to use the formula given as

$$C = \int f'(Y)dy = \int (0.5 - 0.003Y)dY = 0.5Y - \frac{0.003\,Y^2}{2} + k.$$

We are given C = 0.4 for $Y = 0$. Substituting thiswe get

$$0.4 = 0.5\,(0) - \frac{0.003(0)}{2} + k \quad \text{or } k = 0.4.$$

Substituting the value of 'k' we get obtain the requied consumption function as

$$C = 0.5y - \frac{-0.003}{2}\,y^2 + 0.4.$$

(2) If $MPS = \frac{1}{5}$, find consumption function (C) when consumption amounts to 180 for income is zero. Also find the saving function if $Y = C + S$.

Solution: We are given $MPS = \frac{dS}{dY} = \frac{1}{5} = 0.2.$ Since $MPC + MPS = 1$,

$$\therefore MPC = 1 - \frac{dS}{dY} = 1 - 0.2 = 0.8 = \frac{dC}{dY} = f'(Y)$$

The required consumption function will be $C = \int f'(Y)dY = \int (0.8)\,dY = 0.8Y + k.$

We are given $C = 180$ for $Y = 0$. $\therefore$ $180 = 0.8\,(0) + k$ or $k = 180$.

The required consumption function is $C = 0.8Y + 180$.

From given $MPS = 0.2$, we can obtain the required saving function.

If $s = MPS = g'(Y) = \frac{dS}{dY} = 0.2$, where S = Saving function, $s = MPS$.

The required saving function is $S = \int g'(Y)\,dY = \int 0.2\;dY = 0.2Y + k_1$

Thus $S = 0.2\,Y + k_1$ and C = 0.8Y + 180.

Since $Y = C + S$, $Y = 0.8Y + 180 + 0.2Y + k_1$ or $Y - Y = 180 + k_1$ and $k_1 = -180$.

Substituting this we can get the required saving function $S = 0.2$ Y + $k_1 =$ 0.2Y – 180.

It can be verified that we will get $C + S = Y$ from the obtained $S = -180 + 0.2Y$ and $C = 180 + 0.8$Y.

(3) Given the $MPS = 0.05 - 0.004y$ Find the savings function when savings are – 0.25 for income is zero.

Solution: We are given $s = MPS = g'(Y) = \frac{dS}{dY} = 0.05 - 0.004Y$. From this we can get

$S = \int g'(Y)\,dY = \int (0.05 - 0.004Y)\,dY$ is the required saving function. Accordingly

$$S = \int (0.05 - 0.004Y)dY = 0.05Y - 0.002Y^2 + k = 0.05Y - 0.002Y^2 + k$$

We are given $S = -0.25$ for $Y = 0$, $\therefore k = -0.25$

Subsituting this we get the required saving function, $S = 0.05Y - 0.002Y^2 - 0.25$

(4) If $MPS = 0.6 + \frac{0.2}{Y^2}$ where Y = income. Find consumption and savings functions if consumption is 90.002 for income is 100.

Solution: For given $MPS = 0.6 + \frac{0.2}{Y^2}$, the saving function is

$$S = \int \left\{0.6 + \frac{0.2}{y^2}\right\} dY = 0.6 \int dY + 0.2 \int Y^{-2} dY = 0.6Y - \frac{0.2}{Y} + k$$

Since $Y = S + C$ and $C = Y - S$, we get $C = Y - \left[0.6Y - \frac{0.2}{Y} + k\right]$ or

$$C = Y - 0.6Y + \frac{0.2}{Y} - k = 0.4Y + \frac{0.2}{Y} - k$$

We are given $C = 90.002$ for $Y = 100$.

$$\therefore 90.002 = 0.4(100) + \frac{0.2}{100} - k \text{ or } k = 0.4\,(100) + \frac{0.2}{100} - 90.002 = -50$$

$$C = 0.4y + \frac{0.2}{y} - k \text{ where } k = -50$$

$\therefore$ The requied consumption function is $C = 0.4Y + \frac{0.2}{Y} + 50$

We have obatined both consumption and savings functions. From the above functions we can get $Y = C + S$ if attempted. This is shown below:

$$C + S = 0.4Y + \frac{0.2}{Y} + 50 - 50 + 0.6Y - \frac{0.2}{Y} = Y$$

(5) Find the consumption function if $MPC = \frac{1}{2} + \frac{1}{4\sqrt{y}}$.

For this it is given that for income is zero, consumption is 500.

Also find the saving function for $Y = C + S$.

Solution: Given $MPC = \frac{1}{2} + \frac{1}{4\sqrt{Y}} = f'(Y)$, the consumption function is

$$C = \int f'(Y)\,dY = \int\left(\frac{1}{2} + \frac{1}{4\sqrt{Y}}\right)dY = 0.5\int dY + 0.25\int Y^{-\frac{1}{2}}\,dY$$

$C = 0.5Y + 0.5\sqrt{Y} + k$. For $Y = 0$, C = 500 given.

$\therefore$ 500 = 0 + k and k = 500.

The required consumption function is $C = 0.5Y + 0.5\sqrt{Y} + 500$.

The savings function can be obtained for $S = Y - C$.

$\therefore S = Y - [0.5Y + 0.5\sqrt{Y} + 500] = Y - 0.5Y - 0.5\sqrt{y} - 500$

$S = 0.5Y - 0.5\sqrt{Y} - 500$. It can be verified that $S + C = Y$.

11.8 Gini Coefficient and Lorenz Curve for Measuring Income Inequalities: Illustrations and Solved University Questions

Gini coefficient is a measure of inequalities of distribution of income. This inequality can be shown diagrammatically as well. In the figure-11.3, X-axis shows the cumulative percentages of income while cumulative percentages of individuals are represented along the Y-axis. When these two percentages are equal we will get all the points lying on the main diagonal line, *OC*, which is a 45^0 line starting from the origin. This line of perfect equality brings about that 25% of individuals get 25% of income and 50% individuals receive 50% income and so on. This is a rare phenomenon to observe anywhere in the world. There is an evidence of inequalities of income distribution every where and this is measured in terms of the Lorenz Curve. This curve measures the extent of inequalities. This curve is *OAC* in fig -11.4. Each point on the curve shows the percentages of income received by a given percentage of individuals. When there is a perfect equality of distribution of income, the inequalities is zero and thus the curve will coincide with the diagonal line *OC* . In this case the Gini coefficient will be zero since the difference between the line *OC* and *OAC* curve measuring the inequalities of income will not exist.

Following formula.is used to measure Gini coefficient

$$Gini\ coefficient = \frac{Area\ between\ OC\ and\ OAC}{Area\ OBC}$$

Larger the numerical value of the Gini coefficient, more is the extent of inequalities. Therfeore when the coefficient is zero, there is no inequalities and when the coefficient is one, which is the maximum there is a perfect inequality of income. Both being rare to happen the value of G will lie between 0 and 1, where G = Gini coefficient. The Gini coefficient is measured by the follwoing formula:

$G = \dfrac{P}{p + q}$, the area p and q are shown in figure-5.

It can be shown that farther the Lorenz curve from the *OC* diagonal, the greater will be the value of gini coefficient as larger will be the extent of inequalities. In the figure-5, '*p*' is the shaded area, covered by the Lorenz curve and '*q*' is the remaining area of *OBC*.

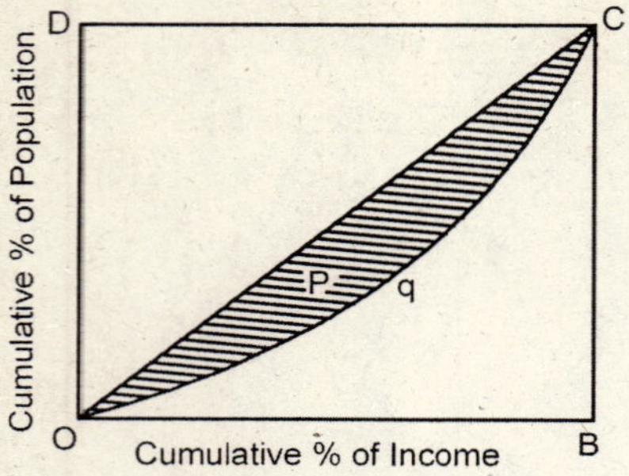

Fig. 11.3 : Measurement of inequality

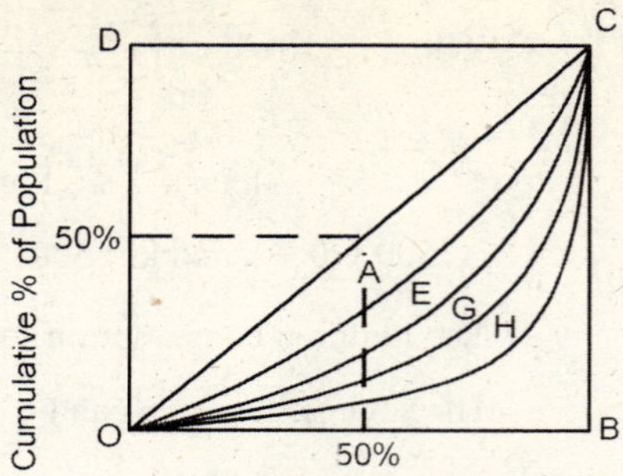

Fig. 11.4 : Lorenz curve and inequalities of Income distrubution

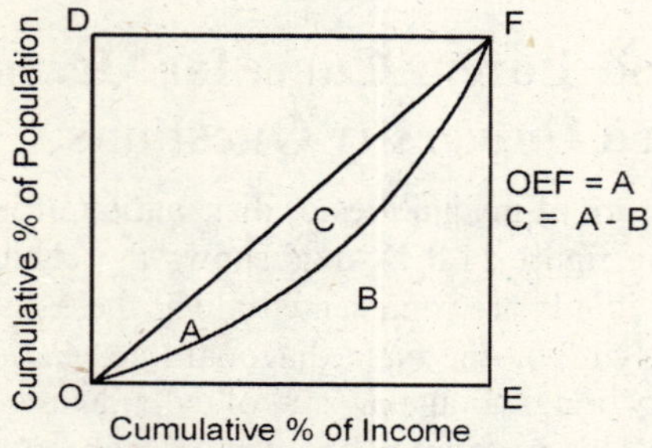

Fig. 11.5 : Measurement of Income inequalities and Lorenz curve.

$OBC = \frac{1}{2} OBCD$ area. If OBCD area = 1. $OBC = \frac{1}{2}$ and $p + q = \frac{1}{2}$.

$$G = \frac{p}{p+q} = \frac{p+q-q}{p+q} = 1 - \frac{q}{p+q}, \text{ for } p + q = \frac{1}{2} \text{ and}$$

$$G = 1 - \frac{q}{\frac{1}{2}} = 1 - 2q$$

If '*x*' stands for the cumulative % of population, the Lorenz function *f(x)* can be used to find the Gini Coefficient by using definite integral. The area of the square is given by $100 \times 100 = 1000$ and thus its half is equal to 5000 and Gini coefficient is.

$$G = \frac{p}{5000} = \frac{p}{p+q}.$$

Illustrations on the calculation of Gini Coefficient

(1) If the Lorenz function is $f(x) = \frac{x^2}{200} + \frac{x}{2}$, find the Gini Coefficient.

To find Gini coefficient 'G' we have to determine the shaded area p (as shown in Fig-5).

To determine this the following formula is used:

$$p = 5000 - \int_0^{100}\left\{\frac{x^2}{200} + \frac{x}{2}\right\}dx = 5000 - \left[\frac{x^3}{600} + \frac{x^2}{4}\right]_0^{100}$$

$$= 5000 - \frac{(100)^3}{600} - \frac{(100)^2}{4} = 5000 - \frac{10{,}000}{6} - \frac{5000}{2} = \frac{2500}{3}.$$

Now $G = \dfrac{p}{p+q} = \dfrac{2500/3}{5000} = \dfrac{2500}{3 \times 5000} = \dfrac{1}{6} = 0.\ 167$

Thus Gini coefficient G = 0.167. The Lorenz function is also used to find the percentage of income held by the highest cumulative 10% or 20% individuals.

This is given by $\dfrac{x^2}{200} + \dfrac{x}{2}$.

For $x = 100\%$, $f\ (x) = f\,(100) = \dfrac{(100)^2}{200} + \dfrac{100}{2} = 50 + 50 = 100.$

If $x = 90\%$, $f\ (90) = \dfrac{(90)^2}{200} + \dfrac{90}{2} = 40.5 + 45 = 85.5$

Thus the percentage of income held by the highest cumulative 10% population will be $f(100) - f(90) = 100 - 85\text{-}5 = 14.5\%$

This means the highest 10% population held 14.5% of income.

Similarly we can find income held by 30% or 50% population. This can be determined by substituting $x = 30$ or 50 as required.

If $x = 50$, $f(50) = \dfrac{(50)^2}{200} + \dfrac{52}{2} = 12 - 5 + 25 = 37.5$

$f(100) - f(50) = 100 - 37.5 = 62.5$

Thus highest 50% people hold 62.5% of income.

Lorenz curve drawn in a unit square.

The equation of the Lorenz curve drawn in a unit square is given by

$Y = ax^2 + Bx$, where $0 \le x \le 1$ and $\alpha \le \beta \le 1$

The whole area is divided in to two equal parts. Thus the area below the diagonal is 0.5.

The area under the Lorenz curve will be between 0 and 1. The area below the Lorenz curve and X-axis is given by.

$$\int_0^1(\alpha x^2 + \beta x)dx = \left.\frac{\alpha x^3}{3} + \frac{\beta x^2}{2}\right]_0^1 = \left[\frac{\alpha}{3} + \frac{\beta}{2}\right]$$

The Area under the diagonal and X-axis is 0.5. The area 'p' which is between the diagonal and the

Lorenz curve is

$$p = \frac{1}{2} - \left[\frac{\alpha}{3} + \frac{\beta}{2}\right]$$

$$\therefore\ p = 0.5 - \left[\frac{\alpha}{3} + \frac{\beta}{2}\right] \text{ and } G = \frac{p}{p+q} = \frac{0.5 - \left(\frac{\alpha}{3} + \frac{\beta}{2}\right)}{0.5}$$

Following steps can be used for obtaining the value of Gini coefficient

(a) First, given the income distribution 'Y', we need to determine the area below the diagonal and X-axis *(b)* Then subtract this from 0.5 and *(c)* divide the residual by 0.5 to obtain Gini Coefficinet of inequality of income distribution.

When the Lorenz curve is drawn in a unit square 'x' varies between 0 and 1. The maximum value of x is 1 and the minimum value of x is 0. The area below the diagonal and X-axis will be equal to

$$\int_0^1 x\,dx = \left[\frac{x^2}{2}\right]_0^1 = \frac{(1)^2}{2} = \frac{1}{2} = 0.5$$

Then the area under the Lorenz curve and X-axis is to be determined and then the Gini coefficient.

Illustrations on Gini coefficient.

(1) Determine the Gini coefficient of inequality of income distribution if Lorenz Curve is given by the equation $y = \frac{1}{10}x + \frac{7}{10}x^2$.

When the Lorenz curve is drawn in a unit square, we get $0 \le x \le 1$.

The area below the diagonal and X-axis as shown in the diagram is 'A' is $OEF = A$.The area below the Lorenz curve and X-axis is 'B' and area between the diagonal and Lorenz curve is C and C = A – B.

We need to find 'A' and 'B' first.

$$A = \int_0^1 x\,dx = \left.\frac{x^2}{2}\right]_0^1 = \frac{1}{2} = 0.5 \text{ and}$$

$$B = \int_0^1 y\,dx = \int_0^1 \left\{\frac{1}{10}x + \frac{7}{10}x^2\right\} dx$$

$$= \left.\frac{1}{10} \times \frac{x^2}{2} + \frac{7}{10} \times \frac{x^3}{3}\right]_0^1 = \frac{1}{20} + \frac{7}{30} = \frac{17}{60},$$

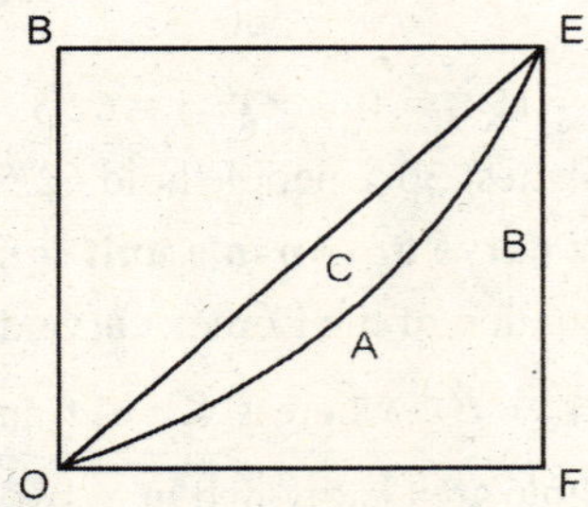

Fig. 11.6 : Measurement of Income inequalities and Lorenz curve.

C = A – B.= 0.5– 0.283 =.0.217.

$$\text{Gini Coefficient} = \frac{A-B}{A} = \frac{C}{A} = \frac{0.217}{0.5} = 0.434.$$

(2) Find the Gini coefficient of inequality of income distribution if the Lorenz curve is given by

$$y = \frac{3}{8}x + \frac{7}{8}x^2$$ **(M.U./Eco//2004)**

The Gini coefficient is given is given by '*G*'. For this we have to find the area below the diagonal and *X*-axis 'A' and then the area between the Lorenz curve and *X*-axis '*B*' and then the area between the diagonal and the Lorenz curve, $C = A - B$.

The equation of the diagonal to the unit square is $y = x$.

$$A = \int_0^1 y\, dx = \int_0^1 x\, dx. = \left.\frac{x^2}{2}\right]_0^1 = \frac{1}{2} = 0.5 \text{ and}$$

$$B = \int_0^1 \left\{\frac{3}{8}x + \frac{7}{8}x^2\right\} dx = \left.\frac{3x^2}{16} + \frac{7x^3}{24}\right]_0^1 = \frac{3}{16} + \frac{7}{24} = \frac{184}{384} = 0.479$$

$$C = A - B = 0.5 - 0.479 = 0.021.$$

$$G = \frac{C}{A} = \frac{0.021}{0.5} = 0.042$$. The Gini coefficnet is 0.042.

(3) Find the Gini coefficient if the Lorenz curve is given by

$11y = 6x^2 + x$

The area between the diagonal and X - axis is

$$A = \int_0^1 x\, dx = \frac{1}{2}.$$

Area between the Lorenz curve and X-axis is B, where $B = \int_0^1 (y)\, dx.$

Since we are given., $11y = 6x^2 + x$ *or* $y = \frac{6x^2}{11} + \frac{x}{11}$ and

$$B = \int_0^1 \left(\frac{6x^2}{11} + \frac{x}{11}\right) dx = \left.\frac{6x^3}{11 \times 3} + \frac{x^2}{11 \times 2}\right]_0^1 = \frac{6}{33} + \frac{1}{22} = \frac{15}{66}$$

Area between the diagonal and the Lorenz curve is

$$C = A - B = \frac{1}{2} - \frac{15}{66} = \frac{18}{66} = 0.273$$ and Gini Coefficient is equal to

$$G = \frac{0.273}{0.5} = 0.546 = 0.55$$

(4) Find the Gini coefficient if the distribution of income is given by the Lorenz curve,

$$y = \frac{4}{15}x + \frac{7}{15}x^2$$ **(M.U./Eco/2000)**

Since A = 0.5 and $B = \int_0^1 \left(\frac{4}{15}x + \frac{7}{15}x^2\right)dx$

$$= \frac{4x^2}{30} + \frac{7x^3}{45}\Big]_0^1 = \frac{4}{30} + \frac{7}{45} = \frac{390}{1350}.$$

$$C = A - B = \frac{1}{2} - \frac{390}{1350} = \frac{570}{2700} \text{ and } G = \frac{\frac{570}{2700}}{0.5} = \frac{570}{(2700)(0.5)} = 0.422.$$

Gini coefficient is 0.422.

11.9. Use of Integrals for Finding Pareto Income Distribution

The distribution of income in a society can be determined with reference to Pareto distribution. This is given by $y = A\,x^{-\mu}$. This shows the number of people earning income more than or equal to 'x'. A and μ are constants. We can find the number of people earning income between x_0 and x_1, when μ is close to 1.5 and A' is constant. $\mu \cong 1.5$ shows the equilibrium distribution of income. By using the definite integral technique, we would be able to determine the number of persons earning income between any two intervals and also earning income above a given amount or level, say x_0. Thus

$$y = \int_{x_0}^{x_1} (Ax^{-\mu})\,dx = A\int_{x_0}^{x_1} x^{-\mu}\,dx = \frac{Ax^{-\mu+1}}{-\mu+1}\Bigg]_{x_0}^{x_1}$$

$$= \frac{A}{-\mu+1}\left[x_1^{-\mu+1} - x_0^{-\mu+1}\right]$$

If the number of individuals 'A' is known and x_0 and x_1 are given, the number of individuals earning income between x_0 and x_1 can be obtained.

Since $\mu = 1.5$, $y = \frac{A}{-1.5+1}\left[x_1^{-1.5+1} - x_0^{-1.5+1}\right]$

$$= \frac{A}{-0.5}\left[x_1^{-0.5} - x_0^{-0.5}\right] = \frac{A}{-0.5}\left[\frac{1}{\sqrt{x_1}} - \frac{1}{\sqrt{x_0}}\right]$$

$$= \frac{A}{0.5}\left[\frac{1}{\sqrt{x_0}} - \frac{1}{\sqrt{x_1}}\right] = 2A\left[\frac{1}{\sqrt{x_0}} - \frac{1}{\sqrt{x_1}}\right].$$

Suppose we are given A = 30,000. we are required to find the number of individuals earning income between 400 and 900, this can be obtained by using the following formula,

$$y = 2\,[30{,}000]\left[\frac{1}{\sqrt{400}} - \frac{1}{\sqrt{900}}\right]$$

$$y = 60{,}000\left[\frac{1}{20} - \frac{1}{30}\right] = \frac{60{,}000 \times 1}{60} = 1000$$

Thus there are 1000 people who earn income between 400 and 900.

The next question is relating to determining how many persons have received income above a given level say Rs. 10,000.

For this our definite integral becomes.

$$y = \int_{10{,}000}^{\infty} A\,x^{-\mu}\,dx = A\left.\frac{x^{-\mu+1}}{-\mu+1}\right]_{10{,}000}^{\infty}$$

$$= \frac{A}{-\mu+1}\left[(\infty)^{-\mu+1} - (10{,}000)^{-\mu+1}\right]$$

$$= \frac{30{,}000}{-0.5}\left[(\infty)^{-0.5} - (10{,}000)^{-0.5}\right] = \frac{30{,}000}{0.5}\left[\frac{1}{\sqrt{10{,}000}} - \frac{1}{\sqrt{\infty}}\right]$$

$$= 60{,}000\left[\frac{1}{100} - \frac{1}{0}\right] = \frac{60{,}000}{100} = 600.$$

There are 600 individuals who earn income above Rs. 10,000.

11.10 Additional Illustrations and Solved University Questions of TYBA (Eco) on Pareto Income Distribution

(1) If $y = 5000\,x^{-\mu}$ where $\mu = 1.5$ find the number of individuals

(a) Earning income between Rs. 2000 to Rs. 5000.

(b) Above Rs. 5000

(c) Above Rs. 10,000.

The Pareto income distribution is given by, $y = \int_{x_0}^{x_1} 5000\,x^{-\mu}\,dx$

$$= 5000\int_{x_0}^{x_1} x^{-\mu}dx = 5000\left.\frac{x^{-\mu+1}}{-\mu+1}\right]_{x_0}^{x_1} = \frac{5000}{-0.5}\left[x_1^{-0.5} - x_0^{-0.5}\right]$$

$$= \frac{5000}{0.5}\left[x_0^{-0.5} - x_1^{-0.5}\right] = 10{,}000\left[\frac{1}{\sqrt{x_0}} - \frac{1}{\sqrt{x_1}}\right]$$

we are given $x_0 = 2000$, $x_1 = 5000$.

$$\therefore\ y = 10{,}000\left[\frac{1}{\sqrt{2000}} - \frac{1}{\sqrt{5000}}\right]$$

$$= 10{,}000\left[\frac{\sqrt{5000} - \sqrt{2000}}{(\sqrt{5000})\,(\sqrt{2000})}\right] = 10{,}000\left[\frac{70.711 - 44.721}{3162.278}\right]$$

$$= \frac{(10{,}000)\,(25.99)}{3162.278} = \frac{259900}{3162.278} = 82.19 = 82$$

Thus there are 82 persons who earn income between Rs. 2000 to Rs.5000

(b) The number of people earning income above Rs. 5000 is given by,

$$y = \int_{5{,}000}^{\infty} 5000\ x^{-\mu}\ dx$$

$$= \frac{5000}{0.5}\left[\frac{1}{\sqrt{5000}} - \frac{1}{\sqrt{\infty}}\right] = 10{,}000\left[\frac{1}{\sqrt{5000}} - 0\right]$$

$$= \frac{10{,}000}{\sqrt{5000}} = 141.42 \cong 141$$

Thus 141 people earn income above Rs. 5000.

(c) The number of people earning income above Rs. 10,000 is given by

$$y = \int_{10{,}000}^{\infty} 5000\ x^{-M}\ dx = \frac{5000}{0.5}\left[\frac{1}{\sqrt{10{,}000}} - \frac{1}{\sqrt{\infty}}\right] = \frac{10{,}000}{\sqrt{10{,}000}} = 100$$

There are 100 people who have income above Rs. 10,000.

(2) When income in a society is distributed by Pareto's law of income distribution and it is given by $y = Ax^{-\mu}$ where $A = 20{,}000$

Find *(a)* the number of individuals having income between Rs. 900 and Rs. 1600.

If *(b)* Above Rs. 16,000.

Solution: (a) The number of individuals earning income between.

Rs. 900 (x_0) and Rs. 1600 (x_1) is given as

$$y = \int_{x_0}^{x^1} Ax^{-\mu}\ dx = \int_{900}^{1600} 20{,}000\ x^{-1.5}\ dx$$

$$= 20,000 \left. \frac{x^{-0.5}}{-0.5} \right]_{900}^{1600} = \frac{20,000}{-0.5}\left[(1600)^{-0.5} - (900)^{-0.5}\right]$$

$$= \frac{20,000}{0.5}\left[(900)^{-0.5} - (1600)^{-0.5}\right]$$

$$= 40,000\left[\frac{1}{30} - \frac{1}{40}\right] = 40,000\left[\frac{4-3}{120}\right] = 333.33 = 333$$

There are 333 people who earn between 900 and 1600.

(B) People earning above 1600 is given by.

$$y = \int_{1600}^{x} A\,x^{-\mu}\,dx = \int_{1600}^{x} 20,000\,x^{-1.5}\,dx$$

$$= \frac{20000}{0.5}\left[\frac{1}{\sqrt{1600}} - \frac{1}{\sqrt{\infty}}\right] = \frac{40000}{400} = 1000$$

1000 people earn above Rs. 1600.

(3) Find the number of individuals with income between Rs. 600 and Rs. 900. If the income of the community is distributed according to Pareto law of income distribution, $y = 10,000x^{-1.5}$ **(M.U./ Eco/2003).**

$$y = \int_{600}^{900} A\,x^{-1.5}\,dx = \int_{600}^{900} 10,000\,x^{-1.5}\,dx$$

$$= \frac{10,000}{-0.5}\left. x^{-0.5}\right]_{600}^{900} = \frac{10,000}{0.5}\left[\frac{1}{\sqrt{600}} - \frac{1}{\sqrt{900}}\right]$$

$$= 20,000\left[\frac{1}{24.495} - \frac{1}{30}\right] = 20,000\,[0.0408 - 0.0333] = 150$$

There are 150 people who earn income between Rs. 600 and Rs. 900.

(4) If the Pareto distribution is given by, $y = 20,000\,x^{-1.5}$.

Find the number of individuals whose income is between Rs. 500 and Rs. 900. **(M.U/Eco/ 2001)**

This is given by,

$$= \frac{20,000}{0.5}\left[\frac{1}{\sqrt{x_0}} - \frac{1}{\sqrt{x_1}}\right] = \frac{20.000}{0.5}\left[\frac{1}{\sqrt{500}} - \frac{1}{\sqrt{900}}\right]$$

$$= 40{,}000\left[\frac{1}{22.36} - \frac{1}{30}\right] = 40{,}000 \times 0.1139 = 456$$

456 individuals earn betwen 500 and 900.

(5) When Pareto distribution is given by $y = 500x^{-1.5}$ find the number of individuals earning income between 500 and 1000 and above 1000. **(M.U/Eco' 2000)**

(a) Individuals earning income between 500 and 1000 is given by.

$$y = 500\int_{500}^{100} x^{-1.5}\,dx = 500\left.\frac{x^{-0.5}}{-0.5}\right]_{500}^{1000} = \frac{500}{0.5}\left[\frac{1}{\sqrt{500}} - \frac{1}{\sqrt{1000}}\right]$$

$= 1000\,[0.04472 - 0.031623] = 13$

13 Persons earn between 500 and 1000.

(b) People earning income above 1000 is given by,

$$y = 500\left.\frac{x^{-0.5}}{-0.5}\right]_{1000}^{\infty} = \frac{500}{0.5}\left[\frac{1}{\sqrt{1000}} - \frac{1}{\sqrt{\infty}}\right] = \frac{500}{0.5}\left(\frac{1}{\sqrt{1000}}\right)$$

$\frac{1000}{\sqrt{1000}} = \frac{1000}{31-623} = 31-62 \approx 32.$ There are 32 peole who earn income above Rs.1000.

EXERCISE – 11

(1) Find total revenue and the demand function for given the following marginal revenue functions :

(*a*) $MR = 12 - 6Q$ Q = Output.

(*b*) $MR = 15 - 4Q$ X = Output.

(2) If the marginal cost is given as $18 - 12Q + 3Q^2$ Find to the cost function (C) if c $(O) = 15$.

(3) If the Pareto income distribution is given by $y = 10{,}000\,x^{-1.5}$ .Find the number of individuals earning between Rs. 900 and Rs. 2500 and above Rs. 5000.

(4) When the equation of the Lorenz curve is $y = \frac{8}{15}x + \frac{7}{15}x^2$. find the Gini-coefficient. Interpret the numerical values of this coefficient.

(5) Find consumers surplus and producers surplus at equilibrium price if the demand and supply functions are $D_x = 12 - 3P$, and $S_x = 2P - 1$ where X is the Commodity and P is the Price.

❑ ❑ ❑